CROQUET
SECRETS

CROQUET SECRETS

The collected writings of John Riches

Edited by Wayne Davies

First printed in Adelaide, South Australia, in January 2008.

Library of Congress Control Number: 2008911892
ISBN: Hardcover   978-1-4363-9766-7
    Softcover   978-1-4363-9765-0

This book was printed in the United States of America.

To order additional copies of this book, contact:
Xlibris Corporation
1-888-795-4274
www.Xlibris.com
Orders@Xlibris.com
46930

CONTENTS

FOREWORD

*H*AVING ONLY RELATIVELY *recently taken up the game, I experienced first hand just how difficult it was to make progress from a novice to any sort of advanced level—and this feeling was intensified as I live on an island way apart from other clubs and players.*

Searching the internet, it became obvious that the name "John Riches" came up again and again. Rather intrigued I intensified my searching and finally found his email address, whereupon I wrote a quick line or two introducing myself and asking a suitable croquet question. Almost immediately I received a answer that went on in so much detail that I could not believe it! Having no local coach, I was eager to improve both my technique and knowledge. How lucky was I to have stumbled upon someone who not only has encyclopedic croquet knowledge combined with great ability, but who also is so eager to share it as well!

Thus were the humble beginnings of a prodigious correspondence between John and myself. In 2 years well over 400 emails have passed back and forth! I have kept up such a constant barrage of questions, films of my technique and situational problems for his analysis that a lesser individual would have given up on me long ago!

Luckily for me John later agreed to visit Nantucket to give 2 weeks of clinics. Whilst he was here we decided to collaborate on a venture to try and publish most of his writings in one book. This was a far bigger task than either of us could have imagined, but one that has also given me immense pleasure.

The following pages reprint most of John's previously published booklets in roughly chronological order. They are a testament to John's deep love of the game, and I hope they are as much help to the reader as they were to me!

Wayne Davies

CROQUET

OPENINGS

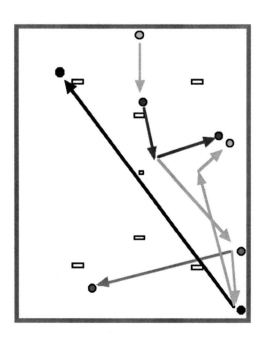

CONTENTS

OPENINGS—INTRODUCTION

IN THE FOLLOWING pages we shall see that there are many different ways of starting a game of croquet. We shall also see that if the players both go about things the right way, they will each have an equal chance of achieving the aim of the opening, which is to be the first player to get a break established.

However things rarely happen this way, as players do not often go about things the right way. This is because they do not know what is the right way FOR THEM.

It will depend on the shots they can play comfortably and with confidence; on their skill; and on their temperament. What is best for one player will not necessarily be best for someone else.

There is a common—in fact, almost universal—tendency for weaker players to simply copy the opening tactics of stronger players, assuming that this must be the right way to do things; but they fail to realise that what will work for a strong player may not work as well for a weaker player because to make it work may require strokes that the weaker player cannot play or control.

It should be realised that if the first four turns are played without any ball being roqueted, the first player is very likely to have the "innings" (i.e. to have his balls together so that he can easily roquet one with the other) at the start of the 5th turn, and this in itself will give him a slightly better than even chance of being the first one to get a break established.

Therefore it is incumbent on the second player to try to avoid such an outcome of the opening, and to do this he will usually need to take one or more calculated risks. He will usually start this process by "setting a tice", which means placing a ball where, if it is left there, he will have about a 50% chance of roqueting it, and thus an equal chance of gaining an advantage from the opening.

This realisation introduces us to the basic principles of tactics that apply at any stage of the game:

1. "Playing safe" by refusing to take risks will result in your opponent having a better than even chance of gaining the advantage. In other words, "To avoid taking risks is too risky".

2. All risks must be carefully assessed by balancing the percentage chance of success against the material gain that success could bring—and the extent to which failure could be disastrous.
3. Be prepared to take a reasonable risk provided if it succeeds you will be able to set up a break. Avoid taking risks that, even if they are successful, will result in you making at best only one or two hoops, without any likelihood of being able to get a break established.

We trust that the following discussion will enable players to better understand and apply these principles in the many and varied opening situations they will discover in this booklet and can expect to meet sooner or later out on the lawn.

STANDARD OPENING

L ET US START by saying that in theory there is no advantage in winning the toss. At the start of a game between two players of similar ability both players should have an equal chance of being the first to get a break established, provided they have a correct assessment of both their own and their opponent's ability.

[Players at international level may disagree with this and consider that the player who hits the first ball into play has a small but definite advantage; but if this true, it is likely to be so only at the very top level.]

Most players who win the toss elect to play first, but this is based more on psychological than purely tactical considerations—a vague notion in the back of the mind that if you put your two balls together and your opponent fails to roquet on the fourth turn, you will have the innings in the fifth turn.

It is indeed true that if that all happens, the player with the innings (i.e. his balls close together to start the turn) at the start of the fifth turn—or any other turn, for that matter—must be conceded a slightly better than even chance of being able to establish a break before his opponent does. But the difference is often small, e.g. 55%-45% or 60%-40%, especially when the opponent's balls are both in places where they will be difficult to use.

However there are many things to be considered and actions to be undertaken before that stage is reached, and the opponent can contrive to ensure that in fact there is a less than even chance of the game reaching such a position at the start of the fifth turn; and in fact he can play the opening in such a way that he is as likely as the first player to get the first established break.

Here it should be pointed out that when both players are capable of setting up and playing all-round breaks if given a reasonable opportunity (here "reasonable" will depend on the ability of the player), the making of one or more hoops without establishing a break is of little consequence, other than that you will still have the innings if your opponent fails to roquet. Until you have made 1-back you will still need at least two turns to finish the game; or three turns if you cannot triple peel. (If you can sextuple peel, you will need to seek advice elsewhere!) In fact, with players who triple peel, making fewer than 6 hoops in the first turn can actually reduce your chance of winning the game, as you will have made it harder for yourself to finish the game in two further turns by triple peeling, and for this reason top players will sometimes "pop" the opponent's ball by peeling it through the first one or two hoops while also making their own first break to 4-back. It must be admitted, however, that with players who are not capable of tripling, there can be an advantage in making just one or two hoops at the start of a game, because it means that your clips are no longer on the same hoop, which makes it easier for you to set up an "ideal leave" to maximise your chance of getting the next break established. (For a full explanation of "ideal leaves" see my booklets "Croquet: Next Break Strategy" and "Croquet: The Teaching of tactics".)

1. FIRST BALL

To a beginner the obvious way to start is by placing the first ball on A-baulk and trying to make hoop 1. It will usually not take him long to realise that this is an unwise move, and he should instead seek to put his first ball in a relatively safe position where he can join up with it in the third turn and hope that his opponent will not roquet in the fourth turn. So he looks for a place on the court which offers his opponent little chance of using his ball, and the best such place is on the east border a yard or two north of level with hoop 4 (see Diag.1).

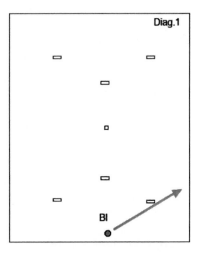

In the second and fourth turns his opponent will have to hit his two balls into play from either A-baulk or B-baulk, and this part of the court is about as far away as you can get from both baulk-lines. There is a similar place on the west border a yard or two south of hoop 2, but the position on the east border is preferred because if the opponent does happen to roquet your ball there it will be further from the hoops (1 and 2) he wants to make.

2. SECOND BALL

The second player has little to gain by shooting at the first ball on the east border (though that is a variant we shall consider later), or could copy the first player's tactic by sending his ball to the corresponding maximum-distance-from-each-baulkline position on the west border. But since few players, if any, can hit roquets of this maximum 17-19 yard distance from baulk 50% of the time, this would involve meekly accepting the likelihood that after all four balls have been played into court the first player will have the innings and a slightly better than even chance of being the first to establish a break.

It is important to be aware that as you (and your opponents) improve, the percentage chance of a break being established in the fifth turn will increase considerably, and this correspondingly makes it less desirable for the second player to adopt purely negative opening tactics.

Therefore the second player wants to "entice" his opponent to NOT join his two balls together on the east border. He does this by placing the second ball somewhat closer to a baulkline, at a distance where he believes he (and also his opponent) has an almost even chance of being able to roquet it from a baulkline. There are various such places which we shall consider later, but the most common one is about 10 yards up the west border from the 1st corner, about level with the rover hoop (see Diag.2).

The exact distance will be determined by the second player's estimation of his (and his opponent's) roqueting percentages at particular distances, and this can be assessed with reasonable accuracy by repeated trials during practice sessions, though it will also depend on the court and weather conditions on any particular day. The judgment of this distance is an important one which can yield the second player either a better than even or less than even chance of establishing a break before his opponent does.

[A "tice" is a ball placed in an enticing position to encourage the opponent to shoot at it; and the length of the tice is its distance from the nearest baulkline.]

In actual fact, it has been worked out statistically that the "correct" length of the "tice" is a distance at which both you and your opponent would be expected to have a 46% chance of roqueting it. The justification for 46% rather than 50% is supposedly that the consequences of roqueting the tice are different depending on which player roquets it (on either the third or fourth turn).

The second player will normally hit his tice in from a position on A-baulk more or less in front of hoop 1, sending it diagonally across the west border at a precisely selected point.

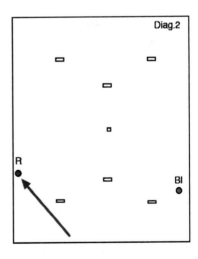

The generally recommended method of determining your tice length is, each time you have a practice session, to place a ball on what you estimate might be a 50% roqueting distance from A-baulk and take 10 shots at it.

If you hit it more than 5 times, next session move it further away; and if you hit it less than 5 times, move it closer.

In a match you can then place it about a yard further away than what you have decided is your 50% roqueting distance, in order to reduce the percentage to about 46%.

If you wish you can also take into account the court and weather conditions, and your estimate of your opponent's roqueting ability.

3.   THIRD BALL

If the second player has correctly judged the length of his tice, the first player, when hitting his other ball into play in the third turn of the game, will be faced with a difficult decision.

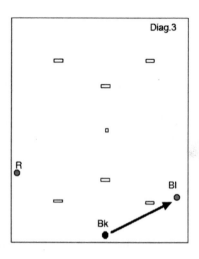

Diag.3

If he follows his original plan of joining up with his first ball on the east border, his opponent will have an almost even chance of roqueting the tice; and if he does so he will have a better chance of setting up an immediate break (by sending the tice ball near hoop 2 with a wide-angle split shot as his own ball goes across the court to roquet one of the opponent's balls and rush the other to hoop 1) than the first player will have if the second player misses the tice.

But if he changes his plan and shoots at the tice, he risks not having his balls together at the start of the fifth turn, and probably allowing the second player to get the innings, together with the slightly better than even chance of being the first to establish a break.

If the first player thinks the tice length is a bit too long to give a 46% chance of roqueting it, then in the third turn he will hit his ball near to the first ball on the east border; but if he thinks he has a better than 46% chance of roqueting the tice, then he should shoot at it. In each case there will be things he needs to consider:

a.   JOINING UP WITH PARTNER

If you shoot at your partner ball (see Diag.3) you take the risk, if you miss, of finishing very close to it on the yard-line and leaving an inviting double target for your opponent in the fourth turn. This, rather than the extra 2-3 yard roqueting distance from A-baulk, is why in the standard opening the first ball is not played to a point on the east border closer to the 4th corner. By placing it further up the border you can retain the option, if the tice is a long one, of shooting at it in the third turn, knowing that (unless your shot is particularly bad) you are unlikely to finish near enough to give the opponent a really inviting double target from A-baulk. He will have a double target from B-baulk, but that shot will be much longer, and is less likely to be hit than if he were to shoot at the tice from A-baulk.

John Riches and Wayne Davies

If he does roquet on the east border, it will also be more difficult to set up a break than if he had roqueted the tice.

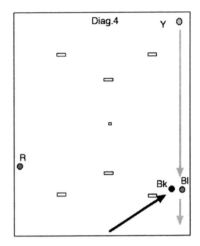

It is also possible to hit the third ball so that it finishes a yard or so short of the first ball and in-lawn, so as to give the first ball a rush to the tice if the opponent fails to roquet from baulk in the fourth turn (see Diag.4). But this requires accuracy of "touch" early in the game, and there is a considerable likelihood that you will either leave a double target from A-baulk, or you will not set yourself a worthwhile rush.

In addition, it leaves the opponent a "safe" shot from B-baulk into the 4ᵗʰ corner where you will now not have a rush to it as you would have had with both of your balls on the east border; and it foregoes the chance of roqueting your partner ball in the third turn. [Perhaps we should point out that at higher levels of play no shot can be considered truly "safe".]

If, in the third turn, you succeed in roqueting your partner ball on the east border, you have at least four choices of continuation:

(1) simply set yourself a rush to the tice, which has the disadvantages explained in the previous paragraph; but may be worthy of consideration in difficult conditions or when the tice is a very long one; or

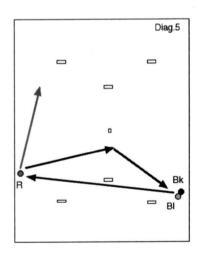

(2) split your partner ball to hoop 2 while going to the tice, and after roqueting the tice, set up a 3-ball break by making hoop 1. This requires great confidence and the ability to play accurate shots at an early stage of the game. The opponent will hit his next ball in from a baulk-line, so if anything goes wrong with your attempt to set up the immediate break you are very likely to leave him with a relatively easy target and all balls out where he can use them; or

(3) take off to the tice, and send it into the court while trying for position to make hoop 1. This is often tried, but is rather pointless because the chance

of continuing the break even if you succeed in making hoop 1 is rather low, and you are taking risks which offer you little gain if they happen to succeed.

(4) Take off to the tice, roquet it, and set up a break for next turn if your opponent fails to roquet.

This can be done in two ways:

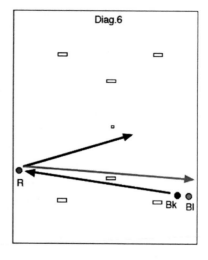

EITHER send the tice ball toward hoop 2, then return near your partner ball on the east border to give yourself a rush to that ball (see Diag.5), OR send the tice ball over near your partner ball on the east border and leave the ball you are playing either near the peg (see Diag.4). This means you are threatening, if the opponent does not roquet with the fourth ball, to roquet his ball, send it to hoop 2, and take your own ball to hoop 1.

Many players find there is a psychological advantage in being able to make hoop 1 from their partner ball. Some fail to consider this possibility because the idea of setting up with one of their balls near an opponent ball does not occur to them. An interesting way of achieving this position is (in the croquet stroke, after roqueting the tice ball) to deliberately send the tice ball out of court a yard north of your own ball on the east border, while running your striker's ball a few yards past the peg.

It can also leave your opponent wondering what you are doing, so you should make sure that he knows you did it deliberately! This may leave a double-target from B-baulk, but it is probably no more likely to be hit than the slightly shorter shot at the ball you have left near the peg, and either shot will be hit less than 50% of the time.

All things considered, if you are capable of setting and playing accurate rushes and would discount the psychological advantage of taking your partner ball to hoop 1, then the first of these alternatives (placing the opponent ball near the maximum-distance point on the west border and setting a rush to it for yourself on the west border) is the better one.

It is also possible in the third turn to shoot from the 3rd corner at your partner ball on the east border, and if you miss, finish in the 4th corner. This seems a rather negative option, based on the assumption that if you join your partner ball on the east border, the opponent is likely to roquet his tice in the fourth turn.

John Riches and Wayne Davies

If the tice is short enough to give the opponent a better than even chance of roqueting it, then assuming that your roqueting ability is the equal of his, you would do better to shoot at it yourself.

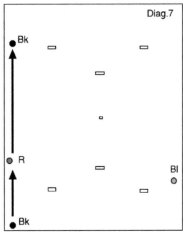

Diag.7

Your object in any opening should be to not only make it as difficult as possible for your opponent to establish a break; it should be to maximise your own chance of establishing a break before he does. You will not achieve this aim by trying to "play safe" and "give him nothing".

An aggressive approach which puts the opponent under immediate pressure is likely to succeed more often, even if it involves a certain amount of risk.

b.   SHOOTING AT THE TICE

The first and main consideration if you choose to shoot at the tice with the third ball is how hard to hit. You should shoot so that, if you fail to roquet, your ball will finish on the border about level with hoop 2 (see Diag.7).

The reason for finishing about level with hoop 2 is so that if the opponent makes a double target from A-baulk with the fourth ball he risks (if he misses and finishes in or near the 2nd corner) you roqueting his ball. You do not actually have to be sure of roqueting a ball in the 2nd corner; you just need to make him think that you might.

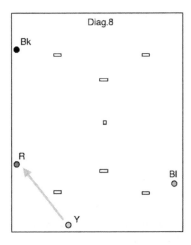

Diag.8

This should cause him to shoot at his tice ball diagonally from a point on A-baulk roughly in front of hoop 1 (see Diag.8), and if he misses this shot you will shoot back down the west yard-line at his two balls, which is why you did not send your ball right into the 2nd corner

This shot at his balls (usually only a single-ball target) is much safer than returning to your partner ball on the east border, even though there is the (rather remote) possibility that you could miss and finish on the 1st corner spot, and he could then contrive to rush a ball into the 1st corner and create a cannon and an easy break.

Creating a cannon by rushing a ball accurately 10 yards along the border into the corner square is by no means as easy at one who has not tried it might imagine.

If, in the third turn, you shoot at the tice and hit it, then your choices are the same as in (3) and (4) above, where you had roqueted your own ball on the east border and taken off to the tice ball.

The best alternative for most players is once again to set up for your next turn by giving yourself a rush to a ball which is either near the peg or near hoop 2

4. FOURTH BALL

In the fourth turn of the game the second player will play his second ball into the court. The general rule is that he should take the shot he is most likely to hit. This will often be a shot from the 1st corner spot at the tice, or else if the first player has shot at the tice and missed, he will shoot at the tice from a position in front of hoop 1 as we have seen above.

Occasionally the opponent's balls will offer him a double target from either A-baulk or B-baulk, but he will only shoot at it (see Diag.9) if he is very confident of hitting it, since if he makes a roquet on an opponent ball he will have more work to do to set up a break than if he shoots at the tice and hits it.

If he hits the tice, then he should be prepared to play a big wide-angle split shot which sends the tice ball somewhere into court near hoop 2 while his own ball goes across the lawn to the two opponent balls on the east border.

This is not a difficult shot, but needs regular practice. It should be played with a flat, roquet-type swing and the swing should be aimed at a point about 3 yards from the centre peg towards hoop 3.

Interestingly, this aiming point remains the same regardless of how far up the west border

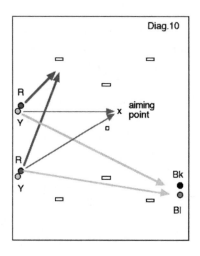

the tice ball has been placed, or how far it was sent when roqueted (see brown arrows in Diag.10).

The strength will depend on the speed of the lawn. There is some risk in playing this shot, but it should be only a slight risk and the pay-off for a successful shot is great—an almost certain all-round break. Do not hold back and risk falling short in order to ensure that your ball does not go out; play it confidently with the intention of getting right over to the opponent's balls.

You must be prepared to write off the one time in 20 or so that your ball may actually go out. It is a small price to pay for the other 19 times when you got (or should have got) the break established.

It is interesting that many players in lower grades use the Standard Opening although if they hit the tice they have no intention of playing this wide-angle split shot to set up a break for themselves. Instead they take off to the opponent's balls.

This greatly reduces their chance of getting the first break from about 80-85% to something like 55-60%, and is poor tactics. If they were never going to make a serious attempt to set up an immediate break, then they should have used a different opening and put the tice somewhere else.

As we have explained previously, "playing safe" by refusing to take a small and justifiable risk in order to establish an immediate break is actually more dangerous than taking the risk. It may avoid giving the opponent a break in his next turn, but it merely postpones the time when he will get his break, and makes it more likely that he will succeed in establishing a break before you do.

5. FIFTH TURN

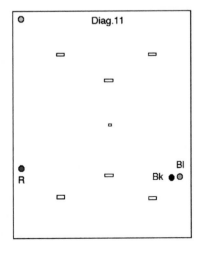

We will now suppose that no roquets have been made in the first four turns. The first player's two balls are within a yard of each other on the east border, and the second player has missed his tice, with the fourth ball finishing in the 2nd corner.

If the conditions are very difficult the first player may now decide to simply set himself a rush to hoop 1 and/or the tice ball (see Diag.11). In doing this he should try to wire the rush from both opponent balls, since if he leaves it open to either of the opponent's balls then that ball should shoot at the rush on the next turn. If he succeeds in wiring the rush, then the opponent must shoot from the 2nd corner back through the tice.

Any of these shots by the opponent will be relatively safe shots for him, in that you have given him a chance to roquet without having a good chance of setting up a break yourself if he misses. Allowing the opponent such "safe" shots is not the way to win most croquet games. That is why you should set the rush only in difficult conditions which make the opponent's chance of roqueting very low.

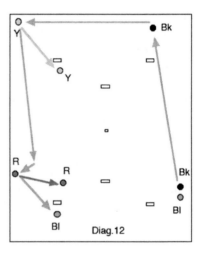

Diag.12

Otherwise, you should play the fifth turn as follows: play the ball nearest to the 4th corner and cut-rush your partner ball to the north boundary in front of hoop 3 (see Diag.12).

Do not (as some misguided people do) leave it in the lawn near hoop 3 to load that hoop. It is a common mistake in many situations to load hoops too far ahead and too early.

Then play a fine take-off to the ball in the 2nd corner, moving the croqueted ball no more than six inches (15 cm) from the yard-line. Roquet the opponent's ball in the corner and pass-roll it out 2-3 yards past hoop 2 as you go to the tice ball. This pass-roll is another shot that should be practised regularly, and should involve little or no risk when played with the correct action.

Some players like to aim the croqueted ball at hoop 2 so that it will hit the hoop if it looks like going too far into court, but this should not be necessary. Nor is it necessary to try to get a rush on the tice to hoop 1.

That would be nice if it happened, but the risk is too great. Some players claim that with plenty of practice they have learnt to get the rush most times, but it seems they would have done better to put the time into practising the approach to hoop 1 from the tice position. Some prefer to take off from the ball in the second corner instead of attempting the long pass-roll, and that option makes a little (but not much) more sense if they have left their partner ball out at hoop 3 instead of on or near the north border; but in any case they are failing to take a very slight risk which has a big pay-off in terms of greatly increasing their chance of getting a break set up in either this turn or their next turn. Such timid tactical play does not win many games at any level.

After playing the pass-roll and roqueting the tice, you play an approach shot to hoop 1. If you can make the hoop you will have an all-round break set up, as we saw in Diag.12.

Load hoop 3 with the ball from hoop 1 as you go to the ball at hoop 2, and after making hoop 2 you can leave that ball anywhere in court and take off to your partner ball on the north border.

If you cannot make hoop 1, or do not want to risk it from the position you have reached, then you have a good alternative: simply hit your ball out of court about a yard to the right (east) of the partner ball you have left near the north border (Diag.13).

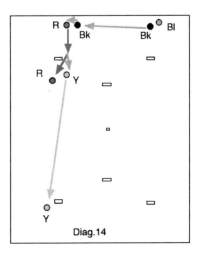

Diag.13

This gives you a very strong "leave" in which you are threatening to play the same ball again, rush your partner ball to the opponent ball at hoop 2, and rush that ball to hoop 1 with at least a 3-ball break established.

The opponent, faced with this leave, is almost compelled to move the ball at hoop 1, even if your balls offer him some sort of double target for his ball at hoop 2; but you should have tried to ensure that he has only a single-ball target by hitting your ball out carefully to a position you had noted after playing the fine take-off from your partner ball earlier in the turn.

Diag.14

If he shoots with his ball from hoop 1 at your balls on the north border, he will give you an immediate rush to hoop 1, with his other ball waiting at hoop 2. If he (foolishly) hits away into (say) the 4th corner, then you should be able to set up at least an immediate 3-ball break by using his other ball. So he will most likely shoot at his partner ball—a 20-yard shot which he knows will give you an easy 4-ball break if it is missed.

After he misses his partner ball and finishes on the north border behind hoop 2, the safest way for you to continue is to (cut-)rush your partner ball along the north yard-line to the ball your opponent has just played, take off behind it and rush that ball out close to his other ball in front of hoop 2, then rush that ball to hoop 1 (see Diag.14).

It is often easy enough to wire the ball you are leaving at hoop 2 from your partner ball, or else leave it about 4 yards in front of hoop 2, so that if you again cannot make hoop 1 you can return to your partner ball on the north yard-line and dare him to either attempt a tice-distance (50%) roquet which would leave you a ball at hoop 1, or a longer roquet which will again give you the fourth ball to use.

This whole method of playing the fifth turn is so strong that it is surprising it has not been more universally written about, adopted and taught. Few players, even at the top level, seem to know about it in sufficient detail to fully maximise their chances of establishing a break before their opponent does.

LONG TICE 'CON'

OTHER OPENINGS

1. THE LONG-TICE "CON"

THIS OPENING IS an attempt to "con" the opponent into depriving himself of his rightful 50% chance in the opening. It works far more often than it should because the opponents often simply fail to think. In actual fact, if he reacts correctly, the opponent's chances could even be slightly better than in the standard opening.

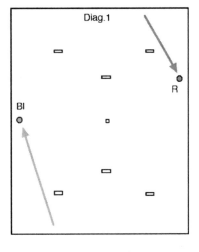

In this opening the first player hits his first ball to the middle of the WEST border, about level with the peg (see blue arrow in Diag.1). It resembles a very long (16-yard) tice, and is designed to lure the opponent into regarding it as just that.

An unwary opponent is very likely to reason, "He has put his ball where I was intending to go, so I will put mine where he should have gone, thereby creating the situation that would have arisen if I had won the toss and hit in first", and in the second turn he will hit his first ball past hoop 4 to the east border.

Now, however, the first player in the third turn does not join his second ball with his first on the west border; instead he shoots at the opponent's ball on the east border, or else hits his ball out a yard to the right (south) of that ball.

This means that in the fourth turn the second player is faced with a situation similar to the one that would have resulted from a standard opening, except that the "tice" is a much longer one than he would have had if he had put it there himself! His chance of roqueting the tice should now be noticeably less than 46%.

Note that the first player no longer has a rush to the north border if the tice is missed, unless he had hit his ball out to the right of the opponent ball instead of attempting to roquet it. Foregoing the chance to roquet, and if successful, set up a stronger position, is something that will not appeal to all players, but perhaps they believe that the satisfaction of having succeeded in tricking the opponent into reducing his chance of roqueting the tice will make up for this.

In any case, if the first player elects to use this opening, he risks the opponent actually doing some thinking before hitting his first ball into play (this is admittedly no great risk with most croquet players), in which case he will not put it in the position we have described on the east border.

Instead, he should hit his ball in from B-baulk to a tice position on the east border about level with the penultimate hoop—just as long or short as he chooses (see red arrow in Diag.15). In fact, this is always where he should put the tice if the first player has neither gone to the east border nor covered the 4th corner (i.e. put the first ball where it could roquet a ball in the 4th corner). The second player would do this in the Standard Opening if he could, but the first player prevents him from "laying a B-baulk tice" by placing the first ball so that a B-baulk tice would give him a double target and allow him to finish near his partner ball if in the third turn he misses the tice—thus he would get an extra chance of roqueting the tice in addition to what he would normally expect to get in the Standard Opening. [In this situation, instead of the B-baulk tice we have described, a good alternative favoured by many top players is the "Duffer" tice which we shall consider later.]

After the second player has laid the B-baulk tice, the first player in the third turn can either shoot at his own long tice on the west border, or from B-baulk at the opponent's tice, but either way he is likely to give the opponent a double-target to shoot at in the fourth turn, or allow the opponent to shoot diagonally from the border in front of hoop 3 at the B-baulk tice, leaving the first player in the fifth turn having to make a fairly long roquet instead of having the innings after no roquets have been hit in the first four turns.

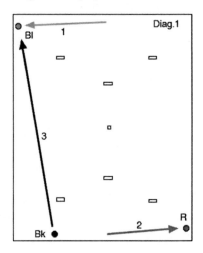

2.   THE 2ND CORNER START

This opening can take two forms:

a.   In the first turn the first player places his ball at the western end of B-baulk and hits it carefully out over the west border about a foot (30 cm) south of the 2nd corner spot (see blue arrow in Diag. 1). The idea is that if the opponent shoots at it from B-baulk he has little to gain if he hits it; and if he misses it he is very likely to leave a double-target for the first player in the third turn.

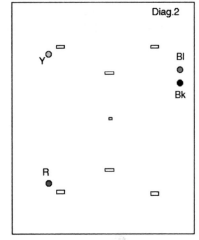

If the second player lays a normal A-baulk tice, then the first player in the third turn can shoot down through it to his own ball in the 2nd corner. If the second player hits his ball near the 4th corner (see red arrow in Diag. 1), the first player can shoot from near the east end of A-baulk at his ball near the 2nd corner (see black arrow in Diag.1).

He is not really expecting to make the 33-yard roquet, but to finish in the corner with his balls a foot apart (too wide to be a really inviting double target) and with a simple cut-rush to either hoop 1 or hoop 2 to set up a break in the 5th turn if in the fourth turn the opponent fails to roquet his own partner ball on the east border.

Or if the opponent shoots at the balls in the 2nd corner and misses, the first player in the fifth turn will be able to make a cannon in the 2nd corner, and if he has practised this cannon he should have a reasonable chance of an immediate break, with the opportunity of setting a fairly strong leave if things go wrong.

If, as is more usual, the opponent ball is on the west border south of your two balls, with all three balls fairly close together, then instead of trying to make a cannon you could play a "bombardment" rush with the corner ball, hitting your partner onto the opponent ball in such a way as to send the opponent ball towards hoop 1.

Once again, the correct answer for the second player was to set either a B-baulk tice or a "Duffer tice", after which it will be apparent that the first player has not gained anything by comparison with his chances in the Standard Opening, and may well have slightly reduced his chances.

If the first player gives himself the rush in the 2nd corner, and the second player in the fourth turn misses his B-baulk tice and finishes in the 4th corner, then the first player has a good chance of making hoop 1, but less chance than in a Standard Opening of establishing a break in the fifth turn. His best procedure (at anything below international level) is probably to try to make hoop 1 with a rush toward the B-baulk tice, and put that ball at hoop 1 while going to the ball in the 4th corner.

Then he can send that opponent ball to hoop 2 while returning to set up a rush parallel to the east border with the ball he has just played (and which is now for hoop 2) having a cut-rush to hoop 3 and his partner ball (for hoop 1) a cut-rush to the south border, so that he is threatening to play at least a 3-ball break in his next turn whichever ball the opponent moves (see Diag.17).

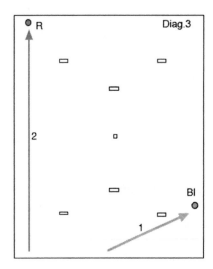

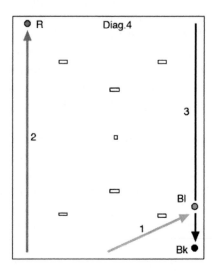

b. There is also a variant of the Standard Opening where the second player, instead of laying a normal A-baulk tice, hits it from A-baulk all the way up the court and over the north border 1-2 yards east of the 2nd corner (see Diag 3). This represents a tice of about 11-12 yards from the west end of B-baulk. The problem here is that if the first player joins up on the east border, the second player is almost forced to shoot at his opponent's balls, since shooting at his own tice gives him less chance

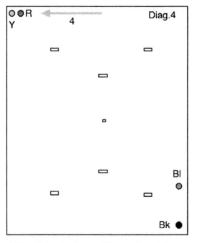

than if it were a normal A-baulk tice: if he hits it, he will not be able to load hoop 2 as he goes to his opponent's balls on the east border, so his own chance of a break in the fourth turn will be less than normal; and if he misses it, the first player has an easier task than normal in setting up a break in the fifth turn.

Another variant worthy of mention is that if the player of the second turn hits his first ball into the 2nd corner as explained in the previous paragraph, then in the third turn his opponent may shoot from the 3rd corner at his own ball on the east border, so that, if he misses, the ball will finish in the 4th corner and his balls will be about 8 yards apart (see Diag.4).

This seems to be a very negative and timid thing for the player of the 3rd turn to do. If the second player in the 4th turn joins his own ball in the 2nd corner (see Diag.5), the player of the fifth turn would need to be almost certain of hitting the 8-yard roquet along the east border; but if that is so, then his chance of hitting either the 12-yard or the 14-yard roquet that he could have attempted in the 3rd turn, instead of the 26-yard one from B-baulk, would presumably have been well over 50%, so he should have taken one of those shots, especially since at that level his opponent could also be presumed to have an excellent chance of roqueting in the fourth turn. Therefore this idea can be justifiable only for players who are very nervous at the start of a game and so concede that the opponent is more likely than not to get the innings before any hoops have been made, and therefore want to make it as difficult as possible for a break to be established.

COME-ON CHALLENGE

3. THE COME-ON CHALLENGE

THIS OPENING IS not to be taken too seriously, although in terms of the percentages it is not so much different from the Standard Opening. It is similar in approach to a boxer dropping his gloves, sticking his chin out, and saying, "Come on, hit me!". It is normally used (in accord with the boxing analogy) only by players who consider themselves much better players (or at least better roqueters) than their opponents.

The first player hits his first ball to a position where it can be fairly easily roqueted by the second player. The usual place, on the rare occasions when this opening is used, is one yard east of the eastern end of A-baulk.

The opponent is then forced to roquet it and has to work out what to do next. His options are similar to those when he succeeds in roqueting the first ball anywhere else on the lawn (more often on the east border in the Standard Opening).

They are—

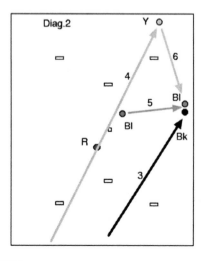

a. roll both balls in near the peg and wire them from each other across the peg, preferably with one ball 3-4 yards from the peg towards hoop 1 and the other a similar distance from the peg towards hoop 3. (See Diag.1) This means that if the opponent joins one of the balls, your shot from baulk in the 4th turn will be not much longer than a tice length.

This forces the first player in the third turn to hit his other ball also near the peg without attempting a roquet, so that he will be able to use it to roquet one of the two balls already there if the opponent does not roquet in the fourth turn.

He is forced to do this if he wants to retain at least an even chance of getting the first break, since he cannot shoot through one of the balls near the peg toward the other baulk because being more than a 'tice' length roquet, his chance of hitting it would be less than 50%; and if he attempts to roquet and stay near one of the balls he risks presenting the opponent with a double target in the fourth turn.

Hitting away somewhere (e.g. to the 2nd or 4th corner) allows his opponent at least two chances to roquet before the first player will be likely to gain control of the situation.

For example, if the first player hits his second ball to a tice position, or to the middle of the east or west border, the second player in the fourth turn can either shoot through it into a corner, or better still, shoot from the other end through one of the balls near the peg at such as angle as to finish on the baulk-line nearest to the tice, about 2-3 yards from the 1st or 3rd corner.

This "covering the double" tactic means that if in the fifth turn the first player plays his ball near the peg and shoots at his partner ball on the border, he risks offering his opponent a very inviting double target in the 6th turn (see Diag.2).

    b.   Send one ball to a short B-baulk tice position (there is no need to have it right on the yard-line) and then hit his own ball out in the 1st corner. (see Diag.3) This amounts to a further "come-on" challenge with roles reversed, in reply to his opponent's effort.

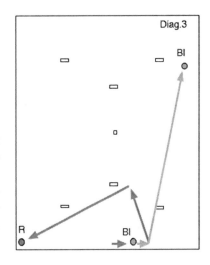

Diag.3

The first player then has to decide between either:

    (1) taking croquet from the ball in the 1st corner and trying to make hoop 1 with little to gain if he is successful and nowhere to safe to go to if he is not; since his opponent will be waiting with a ball to be played from baulk, or

    (2) playing a huge pass-roll to get the ball out of the 1st corner and away from the baulk-line while going to the B-baulk tice ball, again with

little chance of continuing the break (see Diag.4);

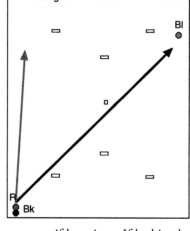

Diag.4

(The second player has in effect said, "OK, I hit you as you challenged me to; now let's see if you can either make hoop 1 or play the big pass-roll under pressure". Unless the lawn is quite fast and he is a very skillful player, his chance of playing this shot successfully and achieving a good leave will be somewhat less than 50%.) or—

(3) shooting from B-baulk at the B-baulk tice while leaving the ball on the 1st corner spot for the opponent to use if he misses. If he hits the tice he will have some chance, though not an easy one, of establishing an immediate break.

If he elects to take the shot at the B-baulk tice he should hit hard, with the idea of rushing it well down the court to a position from which it will be easier for him to send it to hoop 2 while going to the ball in the 1st corner. Staying near the tice ball if he misses would be too risky in this situation.

This option (3) of returning the challenge to the first player is probably the best one for the second player if he roquets with his first ball in any opening situation.

It will be obvious that this "Come-on Challenge" opening is used mainly for psychological reasons, and its best chance of working would be when it is used against an opponent who will be hitting in second and tends to be rather nervous at the start of a game.

 c. Another "safe" and rather conservative option for the second player in answer to the "Come-on Challenge" is to send the first player's ball near the east border and then hit his own ball out to a normal tice position. This converts things back to a Standard Opening. However he needs to consider that if the opponent's ball is not on the yard-line the first player in the third turn may be able to hit out behind it and give himself a useful rush to the tice, though in doing this he would be foregoing a chance to roquet and perhaps risking leaving a double target for the second player in the fourth turn. It may be advisable for the second player to try to put the opponent's ball where it is wired from the east end of A-baulk by hoop 4.

d. Yet another good reply to the "Come-on Challenge" is to leave one ball about a yard west and a foot north of the 4th corner, and the other in a "Duffer" tice position (see Diag.1—the "Duffer tice" will be explained more fully in a later section); but this leave may sometimes be difficult to obtain safely.

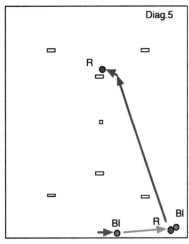

Another opening that can be considered a version of the "Come-on Challenge" is for the first player to hit his first ball 2-3 yards behind hoop 1, intending in his next turn to shoot at his opponent's ball wherever it goes, with the hope of establishing a 3-ball break in the third turn. If the second player roquets this shortish tice ball, he can choose between options a-c—but not option d—explained on the previous two pages.

But besides shooting at the ball behind hoop 1 he also has other options, e.g.—

(1) he can lay a longish B-baulk tice. Then, if in the third turn the first player takes the shorter shot from A-baulk at his own ball, he will have little chance of setting up a break; and if he misses it he will have given the innings away with his balls far apart and it will also be dangerous to join up his balls even in his next turn. If the first player shoots at the longer B-baulk tice and hits it, he will have a good chance of an immediate break (which is why it should be a long tice, to reduce his chance below 50%); but if he misses it the second player can either shoot at the short tice from A-baulk or shoot diagonally at his own longer B-baulk tice so that if he fails to roquet it the first player in the fifth turn will need to move his ball from behind hoop 1 but will have no safe shot available with it.

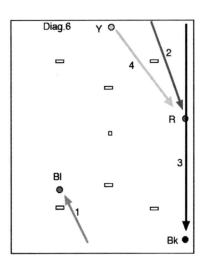

[This is an important reason why in most openings you need to be wary of deliberately putting a ball out into the lawn. Your opponent can often contrive to put his balls together, so that you need to move the ball from the middle of the lawn, but there is nowhere safe to send it.]

(2) he can hit his ball out over the east border about a foot north of the 4th corner spot. This dares the first player to continue with his intention of shooting at it, which would risk leaving an easy double target for the second player in the fourth turn if the roquet is not made, in addition to the option of shooting from A-baulk at the short tice.

(3) he could instead hit his ball out over the west border a foot south of the 2nd corner spot with the same idea, but this also gives the first player a long double target in the third turn and seems to have no advantage over option (2).

(4) A further possibility is to shoot from A-baulk at the opponent's ball so that a miss will finish near the 2nd corner, either a small distance down the west border, or on the north border 2-3 yards from the 2nd corner and a "tice" distance from B-baulk.

In this case setting a "Duffer" tice would be rather dangerous with a ball 4 yards behind hoop 1 for the opponent to use if he roquets the Duffer tice.

4ᵀᴴ CORNER OPENING

4. THE 4ᵀᴴ CORNER OPENING

THIS OPENING CAN take two forms:

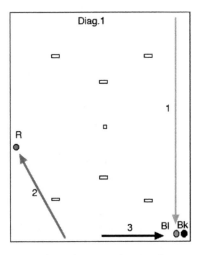

Diag.1

a. We have already seen that it is possible for the first player to hit his first ball to the east border much closer to the 4ᵗʰ corner than in the Standard Opening—e.g. a foot or two from the 4ᵗʰ corner spot. This makes it dangerous for the second player, in his first turn, to shoot at the ball which is already in play. There would in any case be little to gain by hitting it, and a miss would be very likely to leave an easy double target for the first player in the third turn.

It also prevents the second player from laying a B-baulk tice; but of course he can simply lay the usual A-baulk tice at whatever length he chooses, and then the first player in the third turn will be taking a serious risk if he shoots at his own ball, for the same reasons.

Since the second player knows his opponent will have to shoot at his tice, he can make it longer than usual, intending (after his opponent has shot through it toward the 2ⁿᵈ corner) to shoot at the tice ball diagonally from in front of hoop 1, and in order to gain the innings the first player in the fifth turn will have to hit a roquet back down the west yard-line without having a good chance of setting up a break if he succeeds in roqueting.

b. A quite different opening, with new and different challenges, is seen if the first player hits his first ball from B-baulk all the way down the court and out over the south border about 2 feet west of the 4ᵗʰ corner spot (a shot which needs practice). This offers the second player the chance of a 12-yard roquet in his first turn, but he would not have a lot to gain if he hits it.

As we have seen earlier, his safest continuation may be to convert the situation back to a normal Standard Opening. He would also be taking the risk that if he misses on the left (in-lawn) side, he is likely to give an easy double target on his opponent's next turn. Again the B-baulk tice is not a good option for the second player because the 4ᵗʰ corner has been covered, so he will usually lay a normal A-baulk tice, or possibly a "Duffer tice" as examined in the next section. In either case the first player will usually hit his second ball into the 4th corner *without trying to roquet*, thus setting up a cut-rush to hoop 1 and/or the tice ball (see Diag.1) He also had the option of shooting at the tice if it was a short one, with the same chances as in the Standard Opening.

Then, after the first player in the third turn has given himself the rush out of the 4th corner, the second player has two choices:

(1) he can shoot at his tice, and if he roquets it he will probably be no better off than if he had roqueted the tice in the Standard Opening. If he misses the tice the first player has a slightly better than normal chance of using his rush to set up a break in the fifth turn.

(2) he can shoot at the opponent's balls. This involves some risk in that a miss will almost certainly allow the first player in the fifth turn to create a cannon in the 4th corner, and provided he has practised this cannon he should be able to set up an immediate break by sending the roqueted ball to hoop 2 while simultaneously rushing the other ball to hoop 1. There is a chance that if the second player makes the roquet he might also happen to have a cannon, but he is unlikely to have practised this cannon which seldom arises unless you deliberately play for it as in this particular opening.

The second player, in his first turn, can also hit his ball from B-baulk to a point just in from the north border and 2-3 yards short of the 2nd corner, making a short "tice" for himself in the fourth turn if the first player plays into the 4th corner in the third turn; and also a probable double target if the opponent shoots at this short tice from B-baulk.

If the second player shoots with his first ball at the first ball and misses into the corner (so as not to leave a double target), then in the third turn the first player could try to roquet his first ball, but this way there is less chance of creating the cannon and more chance of leaving a double target for the second player in the fourth turn. Therefore he should not shoot, but send his second ball into the court about 5 yards due north of hoop 4 (see Diag.2). Then he threatens in his next turn to (at least) roquet the opponent ball in the 4th corner, and send it to hoop 2 while getting a rush on his partner ball to hoop 1.

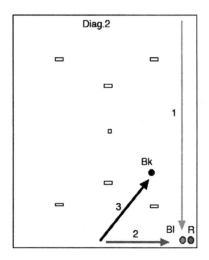

Diag.2

The second player now has three options:

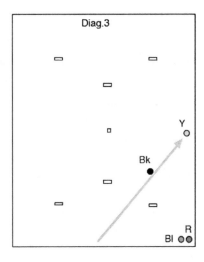

(1) shoot at the 12-yard roquet from A-baulk into the 4th corner. Hitting it will give him a good chance of setting up an immediate break, but missing it will make it even easier for the first player to set up a break by again creating a cannon in the 4th corner, but this time playing it as a "promotion cannon" by lining up the three balls in an almost straight line to hoop 1 and hitting it so as to send the front ball to hoop 1 without having roqueted it, while the striker's ball goes to his partner ball which he had carefully placed about 5 yards in front of hoop 4. Then he can split his partner ball to hoop 2 while going to the unused ball at hoop 1. This "promotion canon" also needs practice because with the full weight of two balls in front of it the striker's ball can tend to fall well short of where you expect it to go, and can also come out at a much wider angle.

(2) shoot at the ball 5 yards in front of hoop 4 (see yellow arrow in Diag.3). This is a slightly longer shot, but not much safer than shooting at the balls in the 4th corner. If he hits it he will need to create a cannon in the 4th corner (and know how to play it) in order to give himself the best chance of setting up an immediate break. If he misses and finishes on the east border about level with the peg, the first player in the fifth turn will roquet the opponent's ball in the 4th corner and send it to hoop 2 while going EITHER to the ball on the east border, which he will send into court while getting a rush on his partner ball to hoop 1; OR to get an immediate rush on his in-lawn partner ball to hoop 1, OR (probably best) to get a rush on his partner ball to the ball on the east border.

Then he will rush that ball to hoop 1, and if unsuccessful he will have a very strong leave with the opponent's balls at hoops 1 and 2. It is important than he should have contrived to leave his partner ball about 2-3 feet from the yard-line so that if necessary he can hit out near it and set up a rush to the ball at hoop 2 (or to the border behind hoop 2 where the opponent's ball from hoop 1 is likely to be) for his next turn.

(3) shoot from B-baulk, possibly making a triple target out of the three balls already in play. This may sound like a good option, but in fact it probably involves a greater risk than either of the other two options, and is seldom taken.

DUFFER TICE

5.a. THE DUFFER TICE

FIRST, THE NAME of this opening requires explanation. It was named after its inventor, a Mr Duff Matthews, an Irish player of about 100 years ago who enjoyed the nickname of "Duffer".

The name is not intended in any way to suggest that there is anything wrong with this quite respectable opening which should give the second player about the same chance of being the first to establish a break as he would have if he set a normal A-baulk tice.

Like the 4th corner opening, it is seen by some people as an aggressive opening and therefore an option to be used mainly by players who have a gambling instinct, but (again like the 4th corner opening) this reputation seems unwarranted as there is no apparent reason why a player who plays second and uses the Duffer tice is conceding his opponent any better chance than if he had instead set a normal A-baulk tice, unless perhaps he is playing against one of the top few players in the world.

After the first player has hit his first ball to the east border, the second player can set a "Duffer tice" by playing his ball from near the west end of B-baulk.

He places it on the baulk-line on an extended line from hoop 1 through hoop 6, and hits it toward hoop 6 so as to stop about one yard short of hoop 6 (i.e. north of, or behind the hoop—see the red arrow in Diag.1).

His idea is that hoop 6 will interfere with any attempt to use the tice ball in setting up a break by rushing it to hoop 1.

He reasons that he himself will not want to rush the tice ball to hoop 1, but the first player probably will if in the next turn he roquets his partner ball on the east border (see the black arrow in Diag.1).

The tice is also placed so that if the first player in the third turn shoots at it, he will need to hit it in order to avoid either finishing near the opposite baulk-line or leaving an inviting double target. If the first player joins his partner ball on the east border without roqueting it, the second player will shoot at the short (9-10 yard)

Duffer tice with probably a better than even chance of roqueting it and setting up an immediate break.

So how can the first player answer this challenge? The obvious way is by "biting the bullet" and shooting at the short Duffer tice, expecting to hit it more often than he will miss it.

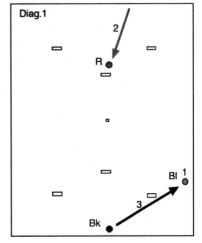

The problem with this is that after roqueting the tice he will have little chance of using his partner ball on the east border to set up a break, so he will have to be satisfied with setting up for his next turn with the opponent ball left near the peg and a rush set to it from the east border.

This is a good leave, but is it worth risking the shot at the Duffer tice for? It depends, of course, on the roqueting percentages of both players, as well as the playing conditions. What alternatives are there for the first player? He has four:

(1) As suggested above, he can shoot at his partner ball from A-baulk and hope that his opponent will not roquet the Duffer tice. With competent players this is likely to involve conceding the opponent a better chance than he gets in the Standard Opening.

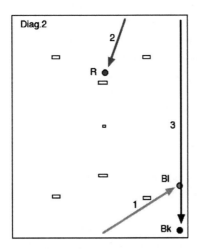

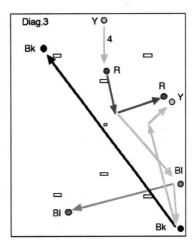

(2) He can shoot from B-baulk at his partner ball, finishing in the 4th corner (see arrow 3 in Diag.2). Then, if the second player roquets the Duffer

tice he will be unlikely to succeed in setting up an immediate break, but should have little difficulty in setting up a very strong leave with his own balls near the east border and the first player's balls at hoops 1 and 2 (see Diag.3 which is rather complicated but illustrates an important setting-up process. On the other hand, the first player's balls are sufficiently close together (8-9 yards) to make it risky for the second player in the fourth turn to shoot gently at his tice and stay near it; while shooting hard at it and missing will hand the advantage to the first player.

(3) He can simply hit his ball to the west border near the 2nd corner. This makes it difficult for the opponent to set up an immediate break if he roquets his own Duffer tice in the fourth turn (although he should be able to set a strong leave for his next turn); and if he misses the tice and goes through to the south border, then the first player in the fifth turn will have a shot through the tice ball to finish near his partner ball. This is generally and correctly regarded as a poor option for the first player in the third turn, as in order to "win" the opening he will need his opponent to miss the Duffer tice in the fourth turn, and then (assuming that the opponent stayed close to the tice) he must hit a 15-yard roquet roquet himself in the fifth turn.

(4) The most common answer is for the first player in the third turn to shoot at the Duffer tice from the 3rd corner spot, so that if he misses he will finish on the west border, roughly in a normal (longish) tice position. This creates a position offering approximately equal chances of being the first to establish a break. The second player in the fourth turn is more or less compelled to shoot gently at the Duffer tice, and if he roquets it he will have to play some accurate shots to set up an immediate break and is unlikely to have a good leave if he does not succeed. If he misses the tice he leaves his two balls out in the lawn, allowing the ball on the west border a "free" shot at them, with the first player having a reasonable chance of setting up an immediate break if he roquets one of the opponent's balls, while if he misses and finishes on the north border the second player will still have only a remote chance of setting up a break before allowing the first player yet another chance to roquet.

Some players have tried using a longer Duffer tice by hitting the ball from the western end of B-baulk to a position just past hoop 6, finishing about 2 yards from hoop 6 in the direction of hoop 1. This makes it a bit harder for the first player if he shoots at it from the 3rd corner spot, and his ball is likely to finish closer to A-baulk if this shot is missed. However it also slightly reduces the chance of the second player roqueting the tice himself in the fourth turn if the first player in the third turn has joined his partner ball on the east border; and if the tice is missed in the fourth turn the ball will finish closer to hoop 1 where the opponent can use it more easily.

b. THE ANTI-DUFFER OPENING

At one stage about 10 years ago some of the world's top players sought to find a way of discouraging the second player from using a Duffer tice. (This in itself was a testimony to the effectiveness of Mr Matthews' idea.)

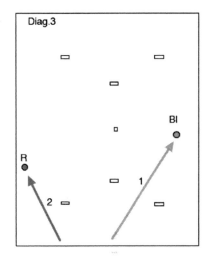

Instead of hitting the first ball of the game to the usual position on the east border, they hit it to a position almost level with the peg and 1-2 yards in-lawn from the east border.

This meant that they were threatening to shoot at a Duffer tice in the third turn with a better chance of setting up an immediate break if they hit it, as there would now be room for them to take off fairly safely and try to get a rush on their partner ball to hoop 1, setting up (perhaps with a bit of luck) an immediate 3-ball break.

The idea was not so much that they would have to do this, but that the opponent would think they MIGHT do it, and so would be deterred from setting a Duffer tice.

However this allowed the second player two other options:

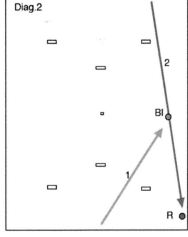

(1) he could, of course, still lay a normal A-baulk tice, which should serve to maintain the balance; or

(2) he could shoot from B-baulk through the first ball so that if he missed he would finish on the east border just north of the 4th corner spot.

Then it would be risky for the first player in the third turn to shoot from A-baulk at his opponent's ball near the 4th corner because of the likelihood of leaving a double target (with a ball far enough in the lawn to be usable); while shooting from B-baulk to stay near his partner ball or at the long double target into the 4th corner will offer little realistic chance of a break if a roquet is made, and will allow the second player in the fourth turn a double or triple target from one of the baulk-lines if it is missed.

In recent years the "Anti-Duffer Opening" seems to have lost some of its former popularity and I assume it is because of this last possible answer.

However it would be wrong to imagine that the Duffer tice has disappeared from top-level play.

It was used by a number of players in the 2008 MacRobertson Shield matches played in Christchurch, New Zealand; and the Anti-Duffer Opening was also used a few times, which suggests that those who used it had sufficient respect for the Duffer tice for them to consider themselves justified in taking steps to discourage their opponents from using it.

6. THE SUPERSHOT OPENING

THIS OPENING HAS been used by some of the world's top players in recent years, and now is being (unfortunately) copied by some of those at lower levels of play.

It has not been in use long enough for all of the percentages to be given thorough trials in competitive play, so the following explanation should be regarded as somewhat tentative.

This opening was developed in response to the realisation that the roqueting ability of a few top players, together with improvements in lawn conditions, mallets and balls, meant that it was becoming difficult to find any place on the court to put a ball where you could be confident that the opponent will have a less than 50% chance of roqueting it.

One might expect this realisation, if true, would result in the winner of the toss electing to hit in second rather than first, so that all the balls would be in play when he hit his second ball into the game with a better than 50% chance of roqueting; but that does not seem to have happened.

Instead, the top players have decided that they need to still play first, but increase their chance of making a break in the third turn.

The reasoning is that if the second player roquets in his first turn he is unlikely to make many hoops with only two balls in play (although on occasion some players have gone right around).

If the first player can roquet his opponent's ball in the third turn, then with his first ball in the middle of the lawn he has a good chance of going to 4-back with a 3-ball break.

Then, when the second player roquets with the fourth ball, he can:

EITHER triple peel your ball and peg it out (an option considered to offer a better than even chance of winning after the tpo has been completed); but you must take into consideration the chance of completing the triple without mishap, and remember that the opponent, who will start his next turn by playing from baulk whatever happens,—which may or may not be an advantage—can take contact if you have made 4-back, with a chance of establishing a 3-ball break with his single ball). Some players believe that if you do the tpo (and so have developed a good 'feel' of the lawn) you should peg out both balls, and if possible have peeled your partner ball through one or two hoops as well;

OR go to 4-back himself and set up, in which case (assuming that you also have at least an even chance of hitting the lift shot) you should get first chance at the triple peel.

As the first player, the way in which you can contrive to increase your chance of making a 3-ball break in the third turn is to hit your first ball into play to a position about 4 yards from the peg in the direction of hoop 1 (see the blue arrow in Diag.1).

Then you are threatening to roquet the opponent's first ball wherever it goes and use the ball near the peg to set up an immediate 3-ball break (which is not without some risk because the second player will be able to play from baulk if at any stage you cannot continue the break).

The concept of the "supershot ball" is different from a "tice", as the player who puts it there is not normally intending to shoot at it himself in his next turn.

The second player then has the following options:

1. He can attempt to roquet the "Supershot tice", but if he hits through to border he will finish rather close to B-baulk.

Sometimes it is possible for him to shoot from the east end of A-baulk and finish near the 2nd corner (see the red arrow in Diag.2).

However if he makes the roquet he has little to gain unless he intends to attempt a 2-ball break.

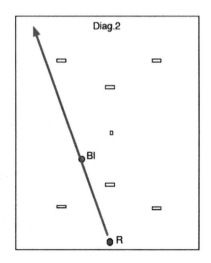

John Riches and Wayne Davies

His best is probably to send the opponent's ball near the west border about level with hoop 6, then hit his own ball out on the east border to a long B-baulk tice position. That at least makes it difficult for the first player to establish a 3-ball break if he should roquet either ball in the third turn.

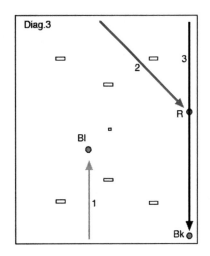

Some players deliberately put the first "Supershot" ball far enough from the peg to encourage the second player to take this shot and finish on the north border about 2-3 feet from the 2nd corner, since they are confident that they will roquet the opponent's ball in the 2nd corner from B-baulk if it misses.

[Note that by ensuring that the second ball will finish near the 2nd corner on the north border rather than the west border, the first player makes it less likely that if his own shot in the 3rd turn at the opponent ball misses, it will leave a double target from B-baulk for the 4th turn.]

Others place the first ball nearer the peg in order to discourage any shot at it.

A gentle shot with the second ball will of course risk leaving a double target (though a risky one) for the first player in the third turn. Those who choose to do this usually shoot from the first corner spot at the first ball, running 3-4 yards past it if they miss it, and are willing to let the first player risk shooting at the (longer) double target, with the risk of finishing near the other baulk or leaving three balls in the middle of the lawn.

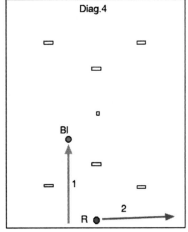

2. The second player can lay a (presumably long) B-baulk tice which is slightly better than an A-baulk tice in this situation (see Diag.3). The first player will then shoot through the B-baulk tice into the 4th corner (see black arrow), having given himself, if his estimate of the percentages is correct, a better than even chance of roqueting the tice and establishing an immediate 3-ball break.

This is probably the best answer to the Supershot Opening for most players, as only a half-dozen or so of the world's top players can actually be relied on to even come near hitting a half-lawn roquet 50% of the time.

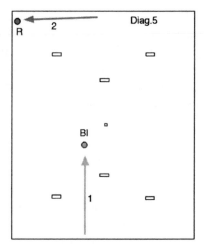

3. He can hit his ball out on the east border near the 4th corner (see the red arrow in Diag.4), where he might think it will be slightly harder for the first player to set up a break in the third turn if he roquets it, and he risks leaving a double target for the fourth turn if he shoots at it and misses. The exact position on the east border should be carefully chosen so that if the first player in the third turn roquets this ball he will find hoop 4 interfering with an attempt to get a rush on the supershot ball to hoop 1.

4. A similar alternative is to hit it out on the west border near the 2nd corner (see the red arrow in Diag.5) and dare the "supershot" opponent to shoot at it. This has become a fairly popular answer to the supershot opening, since if the first player roquets it in the 3rd turn he will need to play a difficult pass-roll to load hoop 2 while going to the supershot ball in order to set up an immediate 3-ball break. The first player should have kept this shot in mind when placing his supershot ball in his first turn.

It is important to realise that, as the first player, you will be virtually forced to take this 13-yard shot at a ball on the west border near the 2nd corner (or on the east border near the 4th corner); and unless you can hit it at least five times out of ten, and can also play the pass-roll, then using the supershot opening will (on averages) give your opponents a better than even chance of establishing the first break.

Hitting your second (3rd turn) ball anywhere else than shooting at the opponent's ball would give him, in the 4th turn, a "free" shot which, if missed, will not allow you much chance of establishing an immediate break.

This probably does not exhaust the possibilities in the "Supershot Opening", and further refinements can be expected, but it is sufficient to say that if you use this opening and leave your first ball near the peg where it can easily be used, you need to be confident of roqueting and using it before your opponent does. Thus it is well named: you do indeed need to be a "supershot".

CONCLUDING REMARKS

Although tactics in the opening provide an interesting field of study, we urge coaches and players to put greater emphasis, and spend more time teaching and learning, the tactics that are important in end-games and middle-games.

When opening tactics are taught, it should be done out on the lawn, not from (say) a white-board, so that the player gets to appreciate the ease or difficulty of each of the options he will need to choose between if the situation arises in one of his games; and he should play both sides in the same opening several times.

CROQUET

ENDGAMES

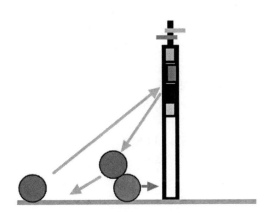

CONTENTS

ENDGAMES AND OPENINGS—INTRODUCTION

THIS BOOKLET is intended mainly for coaches, and for those who are keen to improve their croquet. And to a large extent croquet, at least in its tactical aspect, is like chess. It has long been recognised that if you want to improve rapidly as a chess player, you should study endgames rather than openings—learn just enough about the openings to get by, then spend a lot of time studying endgames.

We believe the same applies to croquet. Tactical mistakes in the opening are far less likely to result in the loss of the game than similar mistakes in the endgame, where you will often not get another chance.

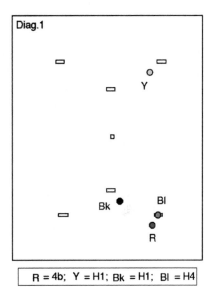

Diag.1

R = 4b; Y = H1; Bk = H1; Bl = H4

So, without denying the importance of knowing how to use sound openings and answer unsound ones used by the opponent, we encourage those who want to improve to first make sure they understand the principles of endgame play.

What is an endgame? It is not possible to give a clear answer to this question. Perhaps the best way to define an endgame is in terms of the tactical considerations that become relevant during a game. In an endgame players should be giving consideration to (among other things) whether or not a break should be taken to the peg; whether or not one or more balls should be pegged out, and the amount of time remaining for the game to be completed if it is a time-limited game.

In Diag 1 the small table under the court diagram indicates the positions of the clips; i.e. red is for 4-back; yellow is for hoop 1; black is also for hoop 1; and blue, which has been playing and has just failed to run hoop 4, is for hoop 4. The player of red and yellow now is to play his turn. He will obviously start the turn by playing red and roqueting blue. Then he will have to decide how to continue the turn, and in particular whether or not he should make 4-back, and possibly also the penultimate and rover hoops, with red.

Since this consideration of whether or not to go to the peg is relevant in this situation, it can be classified from at least one point of view as an "endgame", even though the game may have been in progress for less than half an hour. Some may consider this definition of "endgames" too wide, while others may consider it rather restrictive, since it means we will not be considering standard leaves and strategies unless at least one of the above-mentioned considerations apply.

Another pertinent question is why others seem not to have written specifically on croquet endgames. We are aware that we have undertaken a difficult task, and suspect that may explain why the ground we will cover is not well trodden. Percentages, which provide the only valid basis for all tactical decisions, can change radically when players are aware that they are approaching the end of the game, either because scores are close, or time is running out. The technique needed to play particular strokes, including peeling and pegging out, can also become relevant in an endgame when it was not relevant earlier in the game. We shall make mention of such things, but shall give our attention primarily to tactics. We shall mention many tactical "principles", but again we must stress that correct tactical choices at any stage of the game must be based on a consideration of percentages rather than general principles.

HOW FAR SHOULD I GO?

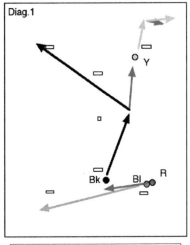

Diag.1

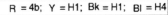

R = 4b; Y = H1; Bk = H1; Bl = H4

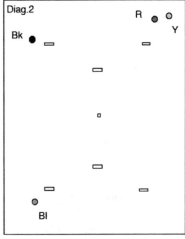

Diag.2

R = 4b; Y = H1; Bl = H1; Bl = H4

RETURNING TO THE situation shown on the previous page, let us try to answer the question of how far the player of red should go. Should he make 4-back and stop on penultimate? Or go to rover? Or go right to the peg?

It is important to realise that even general principles will often apply only to players of a particular range of abilities. For most of our discussions on endgames we shall refer to three types of player: (1) Players at international level, (2) Players at intermediate level, and (3) Players in lower grades.

We shall assume that an international-level player is capable of fairly regularly completing triple peels; an intermediate-level player can often complete an all-round break, and lower-grade players either lack the skills to play breaks, or lack the consistency to complete them with any degree of regularity.

This booklet is primarily aimed at intermediate-level players, though we will sometimes discuss whether the ideas we cover are also applicable to players in lower grades or at international level.

Diag.1 above shows a situation that we might expect to occur shortly after the one diagrammed on the previous page. Red has roqueted blue out of H4 and can continue as illustrated by the arrows which represent the paths of the similarly-coloured balls: The player of red can send blue just past H1, then rush black up the court and send it to H2 while getting a rush on yellow toward the C3, where he will set a rush for yellow to black (see Diag.2). This is not the only way he could set up for yellow, but it is probably the safest. Some may try to wire the opponent's balls at hoop 1, but then taking off to yellow to set a useful rush would be a risky stroke.

Provided blue fails to roquet, the "ideal leave" shown in Diag 2 gives yellow an excellent chance of being able to get a break established in the next turn, by (at least) rushing red to black and black to hoop 1.

We shall see in a later section that stopping on rover makes sense only if you are capable of peeling the rover hoop and pegging out at the end of a break, and your opponent is not.

The continuation we have described follows the general principle: "**Do not make 4-back until your partner has made 1-back**".

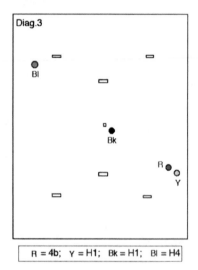

Diag.3

We suggest that intermediate-level players should follow this principle whenever they are in any doubt about whether to make 4-back.

The reasons for setting up for yellow instead of making 4-back with red, and which should always be taken into consideration, are:

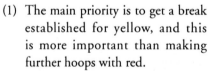

R = 4b; Y = H1; Bk = H1; Bl = H4

(1) The main priority is to get a break established for yellow, and this is more important than making further hoops with red.

(2) You can set a stronger and safer leave for yellow if you have not given a lift.

(3) You may be able to set a leave which will "force" the opponent to play his forward ball, with which he can make fewer hoops. In this case, most opponents will feel compelled to move the blue ball from H1.

(4) If he is capable of doing a tpo, the opponent will find it much harder when he has to play his forward ball.

(5) It avoids the risk of the opponent, if he roquets with either ball, going around and pegging red out—unless he is an international level player and does a tpo.

[We realise that a player below international level may sometimes succeed in triple peeling his opponent and pegging him out, but it would pay to encourage him to attempt it, rather than try to prevent him from doing so, since for such a player it will seldom be his best winning chance.]

A lower-grade player, whose games often go to time and are not pegged out, may also prefer to make the last three hoops with red while he has the chance. If his opponent is of a similar standard, there is little to fear in the possibility of red being pegged out. However in most cases the best advice for such a player would be to set up for his partner ball instead of making 4-back.

International-level players may also decide to go to the peg with red, and set the "diagonal" leave shown in Diag.3. The reasoning here is that you want to give the opponent only one chance to roquet, and if he misses you expect to finish the game in your next turn. If you understand pegged-out games well enough, you may not be concerned about possibly having red pegged out. And if you leave the red clip on 4-back, an international-level opponent may well be capable of tpo-ing your red ball and pegging it out anyway. As against that, it must be considered that the opponent's roquet will be a shorter one than in Diag.2, he will be less constrained to play one particular ball, and if he misses you will not find it quite so easy to establish a break with yellow.

Rough percentage calculations (which a player cannot be expected to undertake during a game) indicate that immediately going to the peg will not represent your best winning chance unless both you and the opponent would expect to establish and complete an all-round break from a situation such as the one in Diag.3 at least 8 times out of 10. A less than 80% chance of completing an all-round break will allow your opponent too many chances to get in with either of his balls, go around and peg out your red ball. However this would by no means guarantee him winning the game, and in fact will not always be a favourable strategy for him to adopt, as we shall see in later sections of this booklet.

It should also be noted that the number of players who are capable of completing 80% of the breaks they begin is much lower than many would think. Players are very likely to over-estimate their chance of not breaking down. It is good to be optimistic, but basing tactical choices on an over-optimistic assessment of your own (and/or the opponent's) ability is not a recommended way to go about winning the maximum number of games.

4-BACK LEAVES

H ERE WE CONSIDER some possible leaves when you have one clip (yellow) on 4-back and take the other ball (red) to the peg.

There are three commonly used leaves:

(1) The vertical leave (see Diag.1).

This leave is usually achieved by leaving blue about 15cm (6 inches) behind penultimate, then making rover from black, with yellow also near rover, and leaving black a similar distance in front of rover so that the blue and black balls are wired from each other by the peg, and neither can easily be roqueted from the nearer baulk-line. Then red is rushed to the east border north of H4 to set a rush for yellow up the court as shown. If necessary, the rush can be achieved by deliberately rolling both balls out over the east boundary from near rover.

An advantage is that the opponent will usually feel that he needs to move the ball at penultimate, which should be his forward ball. Disadvantages are that the opponent will have a long double target from B-baulk (though the rush for yellow should

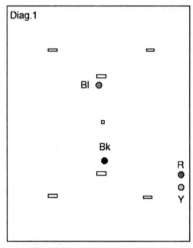

Diag.1

R =peg; Y = 4b; Bk = H1; Bl = 4b

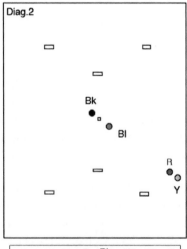

Diag.2

R = peg; Y = 4b; Bk = H1; Bl = 4b

have been set so that H3 is in the way of making an ideal double target, as well as so that H4 interferes with the short shot from A-baulk); and yellow will usually have to make both 4-back and penultimate from the red ball.

(2) Wiring close in at the peg (see Diag.2).

This leave is achieved by leaving red and blue together east of the peg after making penultimate, then making rover from black and rushing black back a yard or two further east of the peg. Then black is sent past the peg to a position wired from blue, blue is roqueted gently and its position adjusted slightly if necessary, and yellow is rushed to the east border and a rush for yellow is set to the two balls at the peg. The wiring should be done so that the peg will not interfere with a rush of either opponent ball to 4-back. Blue must be less than 3 feet from the peg so that the peg will impede the backswing and prevent blue from shooting at red.

An advantage is that if the opponent fails to roquet, yellow can cut-rush red 2-3 yards south of black and used to load penultimate while getting a rush on whichever opponent ball remains near the peg. Another advantage is that the rush for yellow can also be set on the west border, south of H2.

A disadvantage is that there will sometimes be a degree of risk involved when positioning the opponent's balls, as the wiring across the peg needs to be accurate so that the opponent has no part of either of his balls that can be roqueted by playing the other.

A further disadvantage is that there is no pressure on the opponent to play one of his balls rather than the other, so in this case he can take the black ball to B-baulk and shoot at either blue or the opponent's balls. This means that the close-in wired leave is usually used only when the opponent's clips are on the same hoop.

(3) The diagonal 4-back leave (see Diag.4).

This is the leave we would recommend as the standard and best peg-and-4-back leave. It is achieved in the same way as the close-in wired leave: After making penultimate, leave yellow and blue close together a yard east if the peg, then make rover from the black ball. After making rover, try to rush the black ball about 3 yards south-east of blue and yellow (see diag.3) and use a stop-shot to place it approximately where the line through 4-back and penultimate

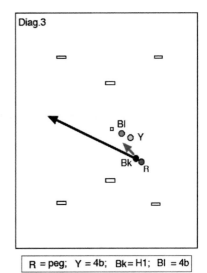

Diag.3

R = peg; Y = 4b; Bk = H1; Bl = 4b

meets the line through hoops 1 and 2, or perhaps slightly closer to the west border if you have a good stop-shot. Then roquet blue, leave it close to the peg and wired from black, and rush yellow to the east border to set the rush. Note that the rush is set higher up the court than in the two previous leaves.

Advantages are that less accuracy is required with the wiring; the opponent is pressured to move blue rather than black; and, if he fails to roquet, you will not need accurate control when rushing red out over the west border (as shown in Diag. 5) from where you can use a stop-shot to send red towards penultimate while getting a rush on black to 4-back.

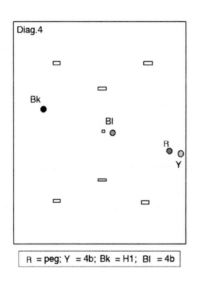
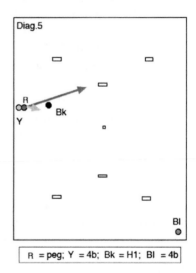

R = peg; Y = 4b; Bk = H1; Bl = 4b   R = peg; Y = 4b; Bk = H1; Bl = 4b

A further advantage is that the stop-shot of red can usually be played with a narrow angle from a point roughly on the rush-line of black to 4-back, thus reducing any likelihood of error.

Disadvantages are that the opponent's shot at your balls from B-baulk is slightly shorter, and the penultimate hoop (and/or the red ball) could possibly interfere with the rushing of black to 4-back.

PENULTIMATE LEAVES

WE SHALL SEE. here and on the next page that it is harder to set a good leave for a centre hoop than for a corner hoop, and that is one reason why you normally should not willingly end a break with your clip on a centre hoop.

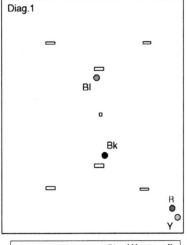

Diag.1

R = peg; Y = pen ; Bk= H1; Bl = 4b

If you have given a lift with red, you will need to set a rush for yellow to penultimate, which is difficult to achieve without leaving a double target for either opponent ball (note that a rush to 4-back here would be of no use).

Both the vertical leave (Diag.1) and the close-in wired leave (Diag.2) are now better than the diagonal 4-back leave (see previous page) where loading rover from the west border would now involve either a wide-angle stop-shot or a stop-shot across the rush-line to penultimate, with less margin for error.

A rush to black near rover is also less good, since even if black can be rushed to penultimate it will be more difficult to peg out if you have to make the rover hoop from your partner ball.

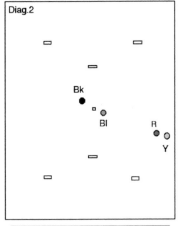

Diag.2

R = peg; Y = pen; Bk = H1; Bl = 4b

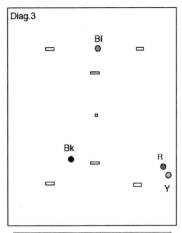

Diag.3

R = peg; Y = pen; Bk = H1; Bl = 4b

The close-in wire is a good leave, but as we have seen, it allows the opponent to play either of his balls without the pressure of thinking that maybe he should be playing the other one.

If there is no lift, things are a little easier, but it is still more difficult to set a good leave than if the yellow clip were on a corner hoop. Diag.3 shows one possibility when you have roqueted with red and want to set up for yellow. With red already having made 4-back you are not likely to have sufficient shots with which to ensure accurate wiring. The idea here is that again the opponent is under pressure to move blue because you are threatening to rush red to the north border and use a stop-shot to load rover while coming in along the rush-line to make penultimate from blue.

ROVER LEAVES

S ETTING A GOOD leave for the rover hoop when your opponent will have a lift is even more difficult than for penultimate, and the only choice seems to be wiring the opponent's balls across the peg. See Diag.1 for one example, where blue is near rover so that the opponent will be under pressure to play his forward ball.

Another possibility is shown in Diag.2, where yellow is threatening to rush red to the peg and take off to get a rush on either opponent ball to rover; but here it is difficult to ensure that the opponent has a longer than 13-yard roquet.

If there is no lift, then wiring the opponent's balls at rover is a good leave (see

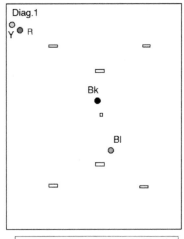

Diag.3), threatening to rush red either to the peg, or a few yards past rover, from where it can be sent back to the peg while going to the remaining opponent ball to make rover.

Care must be taken to ensure that neither of the opponent's balls is wired from both red and yellow, as a wiring lift would allow him to take a shorter shot at his

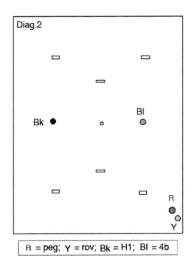

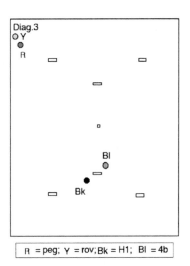

51

partner ball, or else make a double target when shooting at red and yellow from A-baulk. The rush could also be set in the third corner, with the opponent's balls wired so that they are south-west and north-east of rover.

As with all leaves, the most important thing is to plan your leave early enough—well before making the last hoop in your break—so that you will have plenty of time to organise a way of getting all four balls to the desired places using shots that are simple and safe. But there can also be risk involved in positioning balls too early, if it means having to make the final hoops with fewer balls in the break, and therefore fewer options if things start to go wrong.

John Riches and Wayne Davies

THE SINGLE 4-BACK PEEL

DIAG.1 SHOWS A situation where red and yellow are both for 4-back, and red has roqueted yellow in front of 4-back. Red can make the hoop with both balls, then continue the break to the peg.

In Diag.2 red has made 4-back, and can rush yellow back in front of the hoop, and peel yellow through 4-back going to blue, then use blue to load rover, and go back for yellow after making penultimate from black.

Many players like to peel their partner through 4-back in either or these ways "in order to save a lift", but this is a dubious tactic that is probably not worth doing, for several reasons:

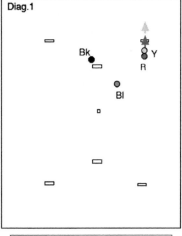

Diag.1

R = 4b; Y = 4b ; Bk = H1; Bl = 4b

(1) As we have seen, with the yellow clip on penultimate, it will be more difficult to set a strong leave for yellow than if the clip were on 4-back.

(2) Even if you will be satisfied with one of the "penultimate leaves" we have seen, it will be harder to achieve it without a useful rush on yellow after making 4-back.

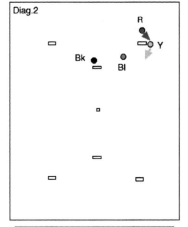

Diag.2

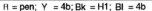

R = pen; Y = 4b; Bk = H1; Bl = 4b

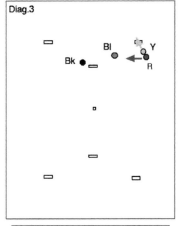

Diag.3

R = pen; Y = 4b;Bk = H1; Bl = 4b

(3) If you forget the peel and set up well for 4-back, and the opponent fails to roquet, you should be able to peg out in your next turn, in which case the opponent will never get to take the lift, and peeling yellow through 4-back would have saved nothing anyway.

(4) There is always some additional risk involved in peeling, and taking even a small risk needs to be justified by some definite gain if you succeed. For example, yellow could stick in the hoop and make it difficult for you to make the hoop with red (Diag 1) or to achieve a good leave (Diag.3). The lesson here is that even when it could "save" a lift, peeling your partner ball through its hoop is often not worth doing unless you intend to peg out in that turn.

PEGGING OUT

MANY PLAYERS HAVE difficulty in pegging out both balls when more than (say) 2 yards from the peg. Diag.1 shows a situation where yellow is pegging out red from about 6 yards east of the peg. If you are close to the peg, a stop-shot action can be used; but at this distance you need a roll stroke to ensure that if yellow misses the peg it will not go too far past it.

First, ensure that the balls are lined up accurately. How you do this will depend on whether you are short-sighted or long-sighted; and whether, if you lie down on the ground (which may be wet), you will be able to get up again.

The ability to play a roll of several yards and keep both balls on line is a very useful one to develop. When pegging out it will not matter if the striker's ball strays slightly from the direct line to the peg, but we shall see later that the same stroke is used in peeling, when both balls will need to stay exactly in the of swing.

The best technique for playing such a stroke is illustrated in Diags 2 and 3. The sighting eye (right eye for most right-handed people) should be vertically above the line of centres of the balls, with the mallet shaft vertical and directly underneath the sighting eye (see Diag.2).

The stroke should be played centre-style, as an equal or three-quarter roll, with a smooth action and long, low follow-through which must also stay in the correct line.

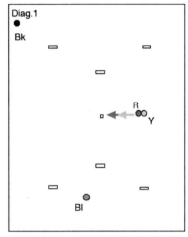

Diag.1

Bk

R
Y

Bl

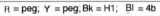

R = peg; Y = peg; Bk = H1; Bl = 4b

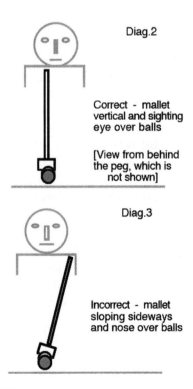

Diag.2

Correct - mallet vertical and sighting eye over balls

[View from behind the peg, which is not shown]

Diag.3

Incorrect - mallet sloping sideways and nose over balls

Many (right-handed) players find it feels more natural for such rolls to have their body centrally behind the balls, i.e. with their nose, instead of their sighting eye, over the line in which they want the balls to travel; and with the mallet shaft sloping sideways to the left shoulder, as illustrated in Diag.3. This may be OK for many of the rolls needed in a game, but many players will experience difficulty if they use it in situations where it is important for both balls to remain in the same line.

The shaft should indeed be sloping—but forwards, not to one side, and with the right hand moved down the shaft sufficiently to achieve the desired equal or three-quarter roll.

Neither a stop-shot action nor a sideways-sloping mallet shaft allow as much accurate control of the direction in which both balls travel.

Foot placement is also important, as is keeping the shoulders still during the swing.

This shot should be practised regularly and over varying distances, as it is an important stroke in various end-game situations (pegging out, peeling and bombardment) where any slight error can well prove to be fatal.

Diag.4 shows yellow about to attempt a "combination pegout" or "bombardment". This type of peg-out is used when yellow, in making rover, accidentally roqueted red. Red is sent as close as possible to the peg, and yellow uses the two opponent balls, first using blue to get a rush on black to a position in line with the peg and red, and further from the peg than red. Then, in the croquet stroke, he sends black onto red, "bombarding" or "cannoning" red onto the peg, before pegging out yellow also. This requires accurate shots, as if red fails to hit the peg, all three remaining balls will be out in the court where the opponent should be able to easily use them.

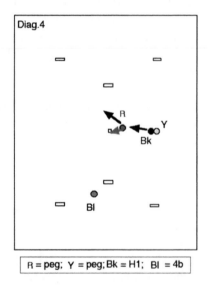

Diag.4

R = peg; Y = peg; Bk = H1; Bl = 4b

Note that red is pegged out if it hits the peg, although it was bombarded onto the peg by the black ball which is not a rover ball. On the other hand, if black had been a rover and yellow had not, then red would not have been pegged out. A rover ball is pegged out if, and only if, it is sent onto the peg in a stroke in which the striker's ball has already made rover and so is a "rover ball".

It is important to know the laws pertaining to pegging out in both level and handicap play, as a mistake at this stage of the game resulting from an incorrect understanding of the laws can be very costly.

Diags 5 and 6 show an interesting situation where red and blue are both rovers, and (as we may suppose in this case) are the only two balls left in the game after yellow and black have both been pegged out. Blue has attempted to peg itself out, but narrowly missed the peg and came to rest between red and the peg.

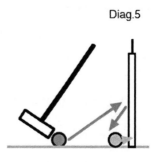

Diag.5

Now red finds that blue is too close to the peg for him to risk trying to hit it away, since if blue should happen to touch the peg it will be pegged out and the opponent will win the game. The only chance for the player of red is to make his red ball jump over the blue ball and hit the peg. If red then falls down and hits blue, sending blue onto the peg, then blue will also be pegged out, but the game will have been won by the player of red and yellow—with the score being recorded as 26-26!

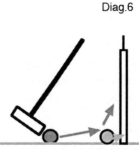

Diag.6

If red fails to jump high enough and hits blue before hitting the peg, and sends blue onto the peg (see Diag.6), then again, provided red also hits the peg, the score will be 26-26 but the game will have been won by the opponent because blue was pegged out before red was. There is no answer to what happens in the extremely unlikely event that red and blue hit the peg simultaneously!

Another interesting refereeing situation occurs when a rover ball hits the peg itself after making a roquet. The ball is not pegged out, although it remained "in play" until it came to rest, and did not become a "ball in hand" when it roqueted the other ball.

WHEN TO PEG OUT ONE BALL

W E SHALL NOW consider whether you should peg out one of your two balls in various situations.

Later we shall consider when you should peg out one of the opponent's balls and leave him with only one ball. The usual advice is that you should not do that if his remaining clip will be on the peg or on one of the last two hoops, as the opponent would then have a better chance of winning than if you had left both his balls in the game.

This might seem to suggest that if you get the chance to do so, you should peg out one of your own balls when your partner ball is for the peg or one of the last two hoops, and you will thereby have a better chance of winning than if you keep both of your balls in the game.

However this does not follow, for two reasons:

(1) At this stage of the game, it makes a big difference to the percentage chances if you, rather than the opponent, have the innings; and

(2) A "better" chance for the opponent can still be less than an even chance, which would usually not be good enough for the player doing the pegging out.

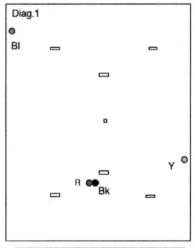

R = peg; Y = peg ; Bk = H1; Bl = 4b

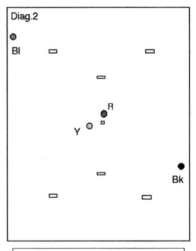

R = peg; Y = peg; Bk = H1; Bl = 4b

In Diag. 1 red had taken off to the opponent's balls in the 2nd corner, rushed black to rover and made the hoop, then roqueted black, but was unable to rush black to yellow.

Should red take off to the peg and peg itself out? The answer is "No!; you should have a better chance of winning if you take off to yellow and either (a) take your balls further up the east border and set yourself a rush to the peg, or (b) roll both your balls to the peg, hoping to peg them both out, but more likely arriving at a situation similar to that shown in Diag.2.

In Diag.2 black has been rushed or split close to the east border, but red failed to get a rush behind yellow and has rolled both balls to the peg, narrowly failing to peg out yellow. Red has one shot remaining, and in this case the red ball should be pegged out.

Why is it right to leave yourself with one ball here, but not in the Diag.1 situation?

In Diag 2, pegging out red will give you about a 60% chance of winning the game in your next turn, since the opponent can be expected to roquet about 4 times out of 10 if he shoots at yellow with either of his balls.

And if he does roquet, you would still have an almost even chance of winning (depending on the ability of your opponent to play a 3-ball break), which means that your chance of winning one way or the other is around 60% + 20% (half of 40%) = 80%. But if in Diag.1 you peg out red, he will go together and you will get only the roughly even (50%) chance, which is less than the chance you could have had by adopting either option (a) or option (b) suggested above.

On the previous page we left a question unanswered: In the situation of Diag.1, which is better—option (a) or option (b)?

For most players, option (b), which involved pegging out at least one of your balls, will be slightly better than rolling up the border and setting the rush as in option (a).

We have seen that option (b) should give about an 80% chance of winning, and if in option (a) the opponent roquets with black (about 3 times out of 10, or more if there is

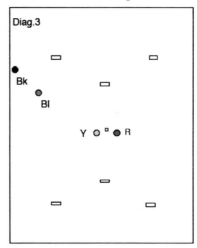

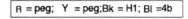

R = peg; Y = peg;Bk = H1; Bl =4b

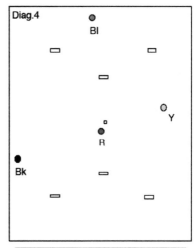

R = peg; Y = peg;Bk = H1; Bl = 4b

a double target), he will have a better chance, with 4 balls in the game, of playing an all-round break.

The positions of the opponent's balls is also important. If red had taken off from the black ball and left it near rover, then he should roll towards the 3rd corner and set a rush to the peg, as black would be likely to roquet a ball left near the peg. That is why, if he planned on using option (b), the player of red should have split black near to the east border as he went to yellow.

Diag.3 shows a different situation where the opponent's two balls are together. We can assume that red had set itself a rush on yellow to the peg, after which black had shot at blue and failed to roquet. Then red rushed yellow close enough to the peg to be confident of pegging out, but in the croquet stroke yellow has missed the peg and now red has one shot remaining.

[Perhaps red should have considered the possibility of using a split pass-roll to peg yellow out while going to the opponent's balls.]

In this case the decision of whether or not to peg out the red ball is a difficult one, and depends on things like the ability of the players, the positions of the opponent's clips, and the amount of time remaining. For most players it may be better not to peg red out, but instead to hit it out of play, e.g. into the 4th corner

The situation shown in Diag.4 is also difficult, as although the opponent's balls are apart, yellow is perhaps not near enough to the peg to be certain of hitting it. If red is pegged out, blue should shoot at black and put pressure on yellow's attempt to peg out, since a failed peg-out attempt will leave yellow where it can fairly easily be used by the opponent.

Here the best option may again be to hit red into the 4th corner.

We do not have space here to consider similar situations with all the different possible positions of the opponent's clips and balls. If the yellow clip is not on the peg, then you also need to consider the likelihood, if you do not peg red out, of the opponent going around and pegging it out anyway, in which case you may be wishing you had pegged it out so that he would have had only three balls with which to play his break.

2 VS 1: 4-BACK TACTICS

A COMMON ENDGAME situation occurs when the opponent has clips on 4-back and the peg, you also have a clip on 4-back, and you take your other ball to the peg. The "obvious" thing to do is peg out the opponent's ball and leave him with one ball against your two. However this does not result in an automatic win, and it can be harder than many players anticipate for the player with 2 balls to finish the game without giving more chances to the opponent than one might wish to give him.

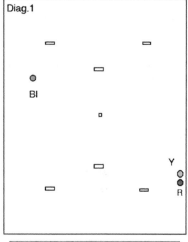

Diag.1 shows a common leave, but it allows the opponent, who will be entitled to lift blue, a double target from B-baulk and/or a shorter shot from A-baulk, and if he roquets he will have some chance of rushing one of your balls to 4-back and making the final three hoops with just two balls. This is not an easy thing to do, of course, and if he misses, you will have the same chance of finishing the game; but it may be a better chance than you would want to give him.

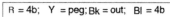
R = 4b;   Y = peg; Bk = out;   Bl = 4b

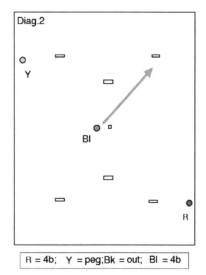

Most players will consider the leave shown in Diag.2 to be safer. Yellow is the peg ball, and red is for 4-back. The balls should be placed as shown rather than the other way around. If the opponent shoots from A-baulk at red and misses, you should have a good rush on his ball to 4-back. Therefore if he wants to shoot, he will shoot at yellow, which can be placed either wired from B-baulk, or about a foot south of level with hoop 2 so that if it is roqueted, hoop 2 will interfere with a roll by the opponent to 4-back.

R = 4b;   Y = peg; Bk = out;   Bl = 4b

This means that he will almost certainly decide not to shoot at either ball, but hit from either B-baulk or where he is (see arrow in Diag.4) to sit in front of his

4-back hoop. (Note: an advantage of the Diag 1 leave was that he did not have this option available to him.)

Then you will shoot with red at yellow, after which the opponent (if he had made good position) can run 4-back and must shoot at your balls on the west border. He may be wired from yellow, and a miss will allow you to rush your partner ball to 4-back, and at worst set a strong trap-line leave. You need to remember that when you make 4-back with red the opponent will be entitled to a lift, but you will not get a lift when he makes 4-back with blue.

Note also that if the red and yellow balls in Diag.2 are interchanged, then the single-ball player may get an extra chance as follows:

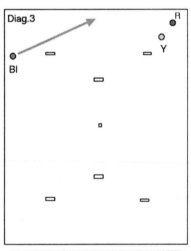

R = 4b; Y = peg; Bk = out; Bl = pen

If he sits in front of 4-back and you shoot with red from the west border to join up with yellow on the east border, then provided the 4-back hoop does not hamper his backswing or stance, he may choose to take the shot at the double target rather than running the hoop; or else he can run the hoop and then shoot at your two balls. The choice between these leaves is sometimes difficult, as there are advantages and disadvantages of either leave.

We have already seen that with four balls in the game, it can be difficult to find a good leave when your clip is on a centre hoop. The same is true when there are three balls left in the game, because there are no effective "trap-lines" for the centre hoops, and setting up close to your hoop would give the opponent relatively safe shots at your balls with balls out in play if he roquets.

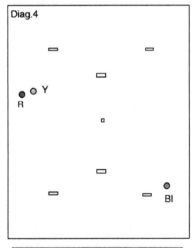

R = pen; Y = peg; Bk = out; Bl = pen

Continuing from the situations discussed on the previous page, we see in Diag.3 a situation that could arise from Diag.2 if red has joined yellow on the west border, then blue has shot at the balls on the west border and missed, after which red has used blue to get a rush on yellow, but did not get as close to 4-back as he wanted, so instead of trying to make 4-back he set up on the trap-line.

If blue now shoots and misses, the player of red should be able to easily finish in his next turn, so since blue cannot take position in front of penultimate, blue instead is hit to the north border with a vague threat of possibly running penultimate from there, and putting some pressure on red as it makes 4-back.

The player of red would now hope to make his last three hoops and peg out using only his partner ball, but if he does not get a rush to penultimate after making 4-back, he could choose to set up as shown in Diag.4. Here blue is entitled to a lift, so red and yellow can be set fairly close to the west border, no more than a yard apart (but without offering blue a useful double target) in order to make sure that red will be able to rush yellow accurately in front of penultimate in the next turn if blue fails to roquet.

Then, after making penultimate, if red does not get a good rush to rover, he will rush yellow to some place on the court where he can wire both balls from blue (which is now likely to be near the 2nd corner), and also give red a rush to rover.

In making this sort of wired leave it is important to remember that the rush is more important than exact wiring, as if blue has no shot he can choose to sit in front of penultimate, making it dangerous for red to try to make rover unless he has a good rush to it.

This would mean that red has to go and move blue from in front of penultimate, after which he cannot set another fully wired leave because he is now responsible for the position of blue.

Players without experience in playing such endings are likely to make tactical errors, due partly to the pressure and their inability to think clearly in tense situations. It is important to have thought through most of the possibilities previously, to get them (and the associated percentages) clear in your mind; and if possible you should practise such endgames by playing small endgames starting (for example) with all four clips on 4-back.

2 VS 1: TACTICS AND LEAVES FOR 2 BALLS

A PART FROM the 4-back situation we have already seen, when should you peg out one of the opponent's balls if the clips are less advanced?

The general rule is that the player with 2 balls can expect to make roughly twice as many hoops as the player with the single ball. Of course, this will depend on many considerations, and mainly on the ability of the players, but it is a reasonable guide to the percentages involved when the two players are of approximately equal ability.

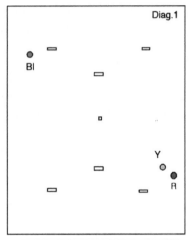

Diag.1 shows a situation where red (for hoop 2) has to make 11 hoops and blue (for 1-back) has to make 6 hoops. With players of equal ability the winning chances should be about equal, but in this case there is also the consideration that the red and blue clips are on the same hoop, though the balls need to make it in different directions.

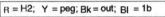

This means that it is dangerous for either player to set up near their hoop, so if yellow has just pegged out black, and blue is entitled to a lift, the player of red will probably choose a leave similar to the one shown.

Blue has two reasonable choices to consider:

(1) shoot at red and yellow from either A-baulk or B-baulk; or

(2) Hit blue into the 2nd corner to "sit over" the hoop.

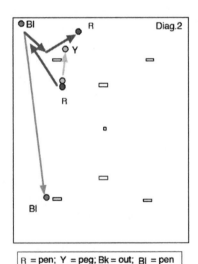

The first option is best when blue has a lift, but if there were no lift, then sitting over the hoop is about as good an option as taking the long shot across the court. However, "sitting over" red's hoop is not likely to be the best option for blue unless blue is for that same hoop, or possibly for the previous hoop (hoop 6), since if blue were for (say) 2-back, then red could rush yellow to 1-back and at least set a trap there with less danger of giving blue an easy break if he roquets.

It is interesting that the two-ball player may actually prefer his opponent to have made one more hoop than he has in this situation

If blue sits in the corner and red does not rush yellow close enough to be certain of making the 1-back hoop, then red should use a pass-roll to place yellow on the trap-line while going to blue, then stop-shot blue to 2-back while trying to make position to run the 1-back hoop. If he cannot make the hoop, he will set up as shown by the arrows in Diag.2. This may seem risky because it allows blue to then shoot with two balls near his hoop.

However the price blue has paid for this possibility is that he has forgone the chance of roqueting in Diag.1, and has given red a reasonable chance of succeeding with the load-and-hold stop-shot to set up an immediate break. Note that if red had made 1-back, then after roqueting yellow he would need to be able to play the big split-shot to load 3-back while going to blue at 2-back. So setting up on the trap-line also had a price; but in this case it was one worth paying!

Having looked at the situations on the previous two pages, we should now be able to understand the following general rules for games where there are two balls against one ball:

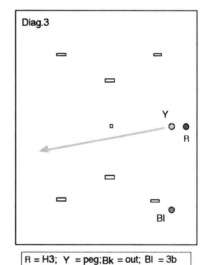

Diag.3

R = H3; Y = peg; Bk = out; Bl = 3b

1. The player with 2 balls should always take a 3-ball break if one is on offer, rather than trying to avoid using the single ball and keep his balls wired from it. The "wiring game" requires very accurate play, and if the opponent will be entitled to lifts he will get chances to shoot anyway.

2. The player with 2 balls should bear in mind the possibility of setting traps by using trap-lines (for a detailed explanation of trap-lines and how to use them, see my other booklets). Diag.3 shows a situation where red (for hoop 3) had set up near the east border and blue (for 3-back) has tried to take position in front of his hoop, but went too far and cannot make the hoop. Now red could rush yellow to the west border (see yellow arrow) and set itself a rush to hoop 3 wired from blue by hoops 4 and 5; but a better option is to use an equal roll to put yellow on the hoop 3 trap-line while trying for

position to run the hoop, and then retire the red ball behind yellow to set the trap if the roll is unsuccessful.

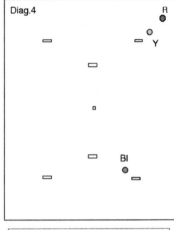

Diag.4

R = H3; Y = peg; Bk= out; Bl = 3b

3. The single-ball player should always shoot if roqueting will give him a 3-ball break. This would apply in Diag 2 (see previous page), but if he is shooting into a trap he will usually need to be on either the same hoop as the opponent, or on the previous hoop. It would also apply in Diag.4, where blue should shoot at red in spite of the fact that red will have a 3-ball break if he misses.

   If the 2-ball player is due to make a lift hoop in the near future, the single-ball player could decide to wait for the lift in the hope of getting a shorter and possibly safer shot, but a thinking opponent will ensure that any roquet he makes from the lift will not give him an easy break.

4. The single-ball player should rarely try to take position to run his hoop. It is usually better and safer to shoot at the opponent's balls. Exceptions can occur when the single (blue) ball has less than half as many hoops to make as the red ball (as in Diag.3), but then only if the single ball's hoop is not one the player with 2 balls will want to make (in either direction) in the immediate future. It should also be noted that sitting in front of a centre hoop will allow the 2-ball player a good chance of setting up a 3-ball break, wherever his clip is.

5. As we saw on the previous page, the single-ball player should consider sitting over the opponent's hoop only if he is also on either that hoop, or on the previous hoop.

All of these rules should be regarded as no more than general guidelines.

We have seen that, in general, it is unwise to peg out an opponent's ball if you have more than twice as many hoops to make with your backward ball as he will need to make with the single ball. The point of this rule is not that the player with the single ball would be more likely to win than the player with two balls. Indeed, even if he has to make more than twice as many hoops, the player with two balls may be the one more likely to win if he is capable of playing an all-round 3-ball break without breaking down; but it is likely that he would have an even better chance of winning by keeping all four balls in the game, at least until he has advanced the clip of his backward ball by several hoops.

Now we consider another tactic for the player with two balls: When will it pay him to peg out his forward ball and enter a game where the players have one ball each?

Again the answer will depend on the abilities of the players, but the general rule often comes as a surprise to people who hear it for the first time— you should peg out your forward ball only when your remaining ball is 5 or more hoops ahead of the opponent's single ball. If you would be less than 5 hoops ahead, your would have a better chance of winning the game than the opponent would if you keep your two balls in the game, at least until you get further ahead.

Commonsense seems to say that even if you are only 2-3 hoops ahead, pegging out your forward ball will deny the opponent the chance of a 3-ball break and should leave you with a better chance of winning than he has. That is true, but it would not be much better than an even chance, and not as good as if you continue with three balls in the game.

In Diag.5 red (for 2-back) is 7 hoops ahead of blue (for hoop 2), so yellow should roquet red, take off to the peg (or better still, split red near to 2-back while going to the peg), and peg itself out. This will give a better winning chance than playing red and rolling both balls across to 2-back. But if red

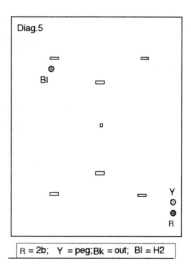

Diag.5

R = 2b; Y = peg;Bk = out; Bl = H2

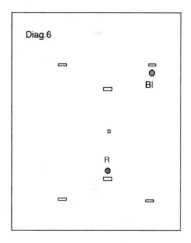

Diag.6

R = rov; Y = out; Bk = out; Bl = H2

is for hoop 5 instead of 2-back, and so is only 3 hoops ahead, it would be wrong to peg yellow out. This is because if both players continue from hoop to hoop, the blue ball, with one or two accurate shots, could catch up until he is only (say) 2 hoops behind. In this he is assisted by the fact that blue will be entitled to lifts, but red will not.

Therefore it could well happen that the situation shown in Diag.6 occurs towards the end of the game. If it is red's turn, he can make rover; but if he then shoots at the peg, or sits near it, blue will have only slightly less than an even chance of winning the game if he can make 4-back and hit the less-than-half-lawn roquet on red. If it is blue's turn in the Diag 6 situation, then he can make 4-back and sit in front of penultimate, again giving himself an approximately even chance of winning.

2 VS 1: TACTICS AND LEAVES FOR THE SINGLE BALL

I T IS OFTEN claimed that "most pegged out games are won by the single ball player". This may or may not be true. Even if statistics were available, it would be necessary to take into account clip positions, time remaining, and other factors which are not normally recorded.

Some factors to be borne in mind are:

1. Players tend to remember games won by the single-ball player as there seems to be some element of surprise about the result, perhaps based on the assumption that most such games result from a player pegging out one of his opponent's balls and thinking that with 2 balls against 1 ball he should be able to win. If the player with two balls wins it is considered less remarkable and therefore less memorable. This problem of "selective memory" affects other tactical situations and choices as well, and causes many difficulties for coaches.

2. When the opponent has pegged out one of your balls, many players feel that they then have nothing to lose when playing with the single ball. Their only chance is to take risks and hope they come off. This leads to a relaxed attitude and aggressive play, both of which are conducive to playing good croquet.

3. In doubles play it is usually the stronger player who will peg out an opponent's ball, leaving his weaker partner to play with two balls against one. The weaker player may feel himself to be under considerable pressure in that he thinks he is expected to win the game from that situation.

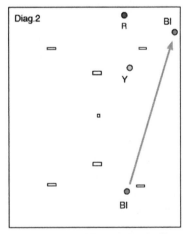

Diag.1

R = H4; Y = peg; Bk = out; Bl = H3

Diag.2

R = H4; Y = peg; Bk = out; Bl = H3

A relatively simple tactic for the single-ball player is illustrated in Diag.1. Blue is for hoop 3, so can estimate his winning chances as very slim. Red has just made hoop 3, but ran too far through the hoop and has missed the roquet back on yellow.

Now blue can shoot at yellow, but a miss would allow red a good chance to continue by roqueting blue and either sending blue to hoop 5 while getting a rush on yellow to hoop 4 to set up a 3-ball break; or simply taking off from blue to get a rush on yellow and continue with his own two balls.

An alternative (though not necessarily better) option for blue would be to put pressure on the 2-ball player by setting a "triangle leave" which involves leaving his blue ball on or near the border and equidistant from the opponent's two balls (see Diag.2).

This dares red to shoot at blue, which is a shot he should roquet (say) 6-7 times out of 10; but in this situation the 20-30% chance of an immediate 3-ball break for blue if red misses may be more than the 2-ball player would want to give him. Red will probably shoot at yellow, but a miss will leave yellow near blue's hoop and red in his forward play, again allowing blue some hope of a 3-ball break. And if yellow is hit away into a corner, blue can shoot at it, and if he roquets, split it to hoop 4 (or somewhere in-court) while going to make hoop 3 from red.

Some important tactical ideas follow from our consideration of Diag.2 on the previous page:

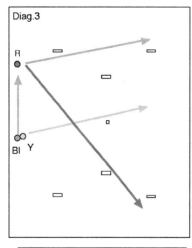

Diag.3

R = 1b; Y = peg; Bk = out; Bl = H3

If the red and yellow balls are well apart, then blue should normally shoot at the yellow (peg) ball. This means that if he misses, the 2-ball player will probably have to use yellow in his next turn and give the single-ball player another chance to roquet. This is especially so when red is near blue's hoop, in which case yellow may not want to risk joining up with red. Therefore, blue would keep shooting a yellow wherever it goes, so it is vital for yellow to wire itself from blue in some distant part of the court where playing red to join up in the following turn will involve less risk. Even then, blue can sit a tice distance away from yellow, if possible on a border, trying to force the 2-ball player to keep playing his peg ball.

An even more important idea is shown in the two diagrams on this page—the "three in line" leave for the single ball.

In Diag.3 blue has roqueted yellow and is for hoop 3. Many players would take off to red, trying for a rush to hoop 3, and hoping to make a few hoops or even set up a break. An alternative to consider is shown by the coloured arrows: While going to red, send yellow about one-third of the way from hoop 3 to hoop 4, then split red to hoop 4, or if possible behind hoop 4, while blue goes to hoop 3. If, as is likely, blue cannot run hoop 3, then blue can sit about 1 yard in front of hoop 3, with a strong leave (for a single ball)—see Diag.4.

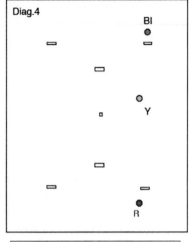

R = 1b; Y = peg; Bk= out; Bl = H3

If blue is not wired from yellow, it is still unlikely that yellow will want to take the shot at blue, provided blue is far enough from the hoop to allow an unimpeded shot at yellow if it should finish on B-baulk. Blue is threatening to run hard through hoop 3, even to the south border,. which (apart from the distance apart of the opponent's balls) is another reason for putting red behind hoop 4 rather than in front of it.

This means that yellow will probably be hit away somewhere, allowing blue a chance to run the hoop, and if he does not get down to red, he can shoot at the yellow (peg) ball with red near his hoop if he makes the roquet.

The whole process involves the single-ball player in taking calculated risks, but as we have seen, that is what he has to do in such situations.
The hoop-running stroke through to the south border needs practice and should be played with a long, smooth, straight and unhurried swing.

This "three-in-line" leave for the single ball is a tactic that few players will think of in a game under pressure unless they have seen it before. The player of blue must decide whether it offers him a better chance in the Diag.3 situation than trying to rush red to hoop 3 and make it, then look for a way to continue the break. It requires one or more reasonably accurate big split-shots, and can be used with red and yellow in different positions, and blue for any odd-numbered corner hoop.

Before leaving the 2 vs 1 situations, we need to consider (here and on the next page) the special case when the single ball is for the peg.

If the two-ball player (red) has many hoops to make, the single-ball player will have a good chance of winning, but with good tactics his opponent can give himself a reasonable chance.

Three key ideas are:

1. The single-ball player will want to avoid giving his opponent a 3-ball break, as he knows it is the only way his opponent can win.
2. The single-ball player should shoot at a ball rather than at the peg, unless the ball is twice as far away as the peg, or a miss would give the 2-ball player a good chance to set up a 3-ball break. It is surprising how often one sees players shooting at the peg when there was a ball only slightly further away that they would have a better chance of roqueting.
3. The 2-ball player cannot afford to roll from hoop to hoop, allowing his opponent to keep shooting at the peg. The chance of the single-ball player missing (say) 8 consecutive shots at the peg is rather remote.

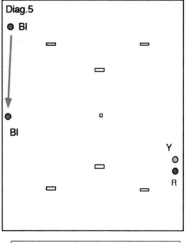

R = H3; Y = peg;Bk = out; Bl = peg

In Diag. 5 blue (for the peg) does not want to shoot at either the peg or the opponent's balls, as if he misses, his opponent may be able to set up a 3-ball break with red, which is for Hoop 3. Therefore he will hit blue to the centre of the west border (see arrow)—where his opponent will not be able to easily use it in a break, and where he will be as close as possible to the peg while remaining on the border out of play.

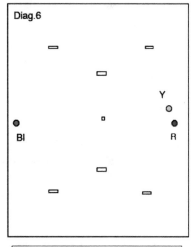

R = H3; Y = peg; Bk = out; Bl = peg

Then the player of red should rush yellow to hoop 3, but he should not approach and make the hoop unless he is reasonably certain of doing so successfully. If the rush ends up too far from the hoop, he should instead roll back and set up as in Diag.6. The idea here is to allow the single-ball player only one shot, either at the peg or at your balls; and make sure that if he misses it you will have a good chance of setting up a 3-ball break. Trying to wire blue from either the peg or from your balls is unnecessary. You take the view that he is "entitled" to one shot—but one only. The player of blue may elect to leave his ball where it is, in which case his opponent will try again to make hoop 3, and again set up on the opposite side of the peg. This process should be practised because the exact positions of red and yellow depend on which hoop you are setting for, and can be important.

These games can be very interesting, but unfortunately, in timed games the amount of time remaining will often become a factor. If he is entitled to lifts, blue can wait until red makes 1-back, since he will then be able to take a safer shot at either the peg or his opponent's balls. The key idea for the 2-ball player is to always set up near the border on the opposite side of the peg from blue; and if possible also on a "trap-line".

Extending the ideas explained on the previous page, and assuming as before that the player of red would have only a remote chance of making many hoops in a break with only his own two balls, we see a situation in Diag.7 where red has progressed around to 1-back and made it, after which blue shot from B-baulk at his opponent's balls and missed into the 4th corner.

Note that if blue had shot from A-baulk at the peg and missed, red would have been able to roquet yellow and roll to a position near the south border, once again ensuring that he will have a 3-ball break if blue shoots at the peg and misses.

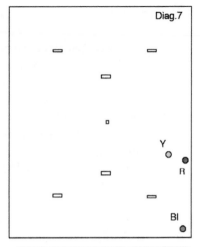

R = 2b; Y = peg; Bk = out; Bl = peg

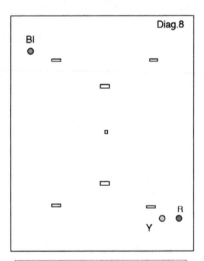

R = 2b; Y = peg; Bk= out; Bl = peg

With blue in the 4th corner, there are two good options for the player of red and yellow:

(1) set up red and yellow in a trap-line position with red about 2 yards and yellow 4 yards from the south border behind 2-back, and send blue between hoop 3 and the 3rd corner; or

(2) set up as illustrated in Diag.8 with a type of "trap" near red's next-but-one hoop (3-back) and blue between hoop 2 and the 2nd corner.

Both of these leaves will require careful shots to set them as accurately as possible, so the player of red and yellow should choose to play the ball with which he is most confident of being able to play the required shots, and check where to send all three balls so that he will have a relatively easy 3-ball break if blue shoots and misses.

Again we stress some important points that are too often overlooked by players in such tense and unfamiliar situations:

1. Be aware of the amount of time remaining at all times. If there is not much time left the player of red may need to take greater risks in attempting to set up a 3-ball break, or else try to make 2-3 hoops with his two balls before again setting up on the opposite side of the peg from blue.
2. Remember who is entitled to lifts, and also "contact" if it applies.

The single-ball player has to assess his chances carefully, taking into account the chance of his opponent being able to continue setting up on the opposite side of the peg and making his next hoop only when there is little or no risk involved.

As soon as he sees that the 2-ball player knows how to use such tactics which are likely to allow the single-ball player only one shot, the single-ball player (if he pegged out his own ball and so is not entitled to lifts) should take the first reasonable shot so that at least his opponent will have to play a longer 3-ball break without breaking down. He could also wait until red is for a centre hoop, when it will be more difficult to set a good leave for red on the opposite side of the peg.

1 VS 1 TACTICS

WHEN EACH SIDE has only one ball, the game will often progress with each player taking position at his next hoop, then running it, and if it is an odd-numbered hoop, trying to run right down and obtain position to run the following hoop in the same turn.

There are many difficult judgments to be made, and the result of the game is likely to depend on which player more accurately assesses the risks involved and consistently plays the percentage shots.

In Diag.1 red (for 2-back) has roqueted blue and faces a long roll to the hoop. The problem is that if he sends blue behind the hoop as in a normal 4-ball game, and cannot make the hoop (or is too far out to risk it), he will not be able to take position in front of 2-back to run it in his next turn, because if he wires red from blue the opponent can claim a wiring lift.

Therefore he will probably prefer to either:

(1) take off to the front of the hoop, hoping to run it and hit across to 3-back, making it dangerous for blue to go in front of 4-back; or

(2) send blue about two-thirds of the way from 2-back to 3-back as shown by the blue arrow. This would mean that if he cannot make 2-back, red can sit in front of the hoop and blue would probably not want to shoot at it; while if red does make 2-back he can shoot at blue knowing that if he misses and finishes on the east border, blue again may consider shooting at red to be too risky.

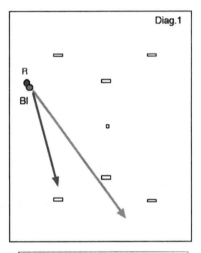

Diag.1

R = 2b; Y = out; Bk = out; Bl = 4b

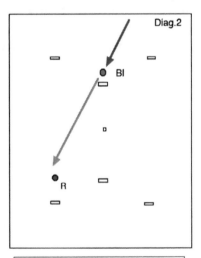

Diag.2

R = 2b; Y = out; Bk= out; Bl = pen

74

Diag.2 shows a situation where red is still for 2-back, but blue has now made 4-back and sat in front of penultimate. If red will now be entitled to a lift, the decision of whether or not the player of blue should have sat in front of penultimate would not have been an easy one.

Now red can play from B-baulk, and hope to rush blue down towards 2-back (see arrows) with a chance of making two or more hoops; or else red can attempt to make the 2-back hoop and sit it front of 3-back, in which case blue can make penultimate but then may decide that he has to retreat towards the west border, since he would probably not want to risk taking position in front of rover where red may well roquet blue after red makes 3-back. Although he would then be 3 hoops behind, red would then still have some winning chances as follows:

If blue makes penultimate and retires towards the west border, red can try to run through 3-back far enough to attempt 4-back also; but even if he can only sit in front of 4-back, blue would be under pressure to take accurate position in front of rover, because if he fails to do so, and red can make 4-back and sit in front of penultimate, blue will not be able to go in front or rover, and it would then be about an even bet as to who will win the game.

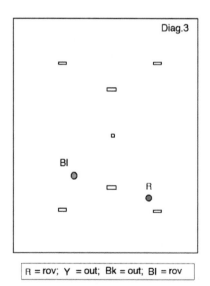

R = rov; Y = out; Bk = out; Bl = rov

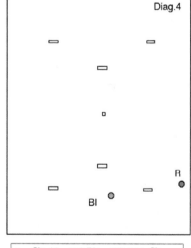

R = 3b; Y = out; Bk = out; Bl = 3b

When both balls are for the same hoop, as shown in Diag.3 which could follow on from the explanation on the previous page, they will usually take up positions on either side of the hoop (rover hoop in this case), wired from each other. It is possible that an impasse could develop, and it is important to ask the referee what he would do to resolve an impasse, so that you can decide whether or not it will be in your

interests to either create or break a
possible impasse.

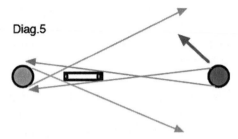

Diag.5

It is more likely that both players
will try to creep around the hoop
until one decides he is in position to
either roquet his opponent's ball, or
attempt to run the hoop. It should
be noted that in Diag.4, where both balls are for a corner (here 3-back) hoop, it
is an advantage to be on the border side of the hoop. Here red has an advantage
because he could afford to risk a shot at blue if it is only partly wired; but if blue
takes a similar shot at red and misses, the balls will be together.

Players will often try to creep in closer to the hoop, not realising that it is a
disadvantage to do so. You should keep your ball about 5-6 yards from the hoop,
depending on your assessment of the roqueting ability of your opponent and
yourself. This keeps the balls at a "tice" (about a 50% roqueting) distance apart.
Each player must decide how much of his ball he can risk giving the opponent to
shoot at, and whether he himself wants to risk shooting past the hoop at a fraction
of the opponent's ball.

In Diag.5 the thin arrows show why is it a disadvantage to be in closer to the hoop.
Blue is too close, which means that red has a large area he can hit into and remain
wired from blue; while blue can move only in a smaller area because red is further
from the hoop. Red can move as indicated by the thicker arrow, forcing blue to
move around toward the rear of the hoop in order to stay wired; and if blue remains
close to the hoop, red can keep wiring from blue and gradually work its way around
to the front of the hoop, then move in close before making it. It should also be
remembered that instead of playing a stroke, you can "pass" or "declare your turn"
if you wish.

A further idea in one-ball endings can be useful at times: In approaching your hoop
you may not be able to put the opponent's ball behind the hoop because if you then
take position in front of your hoop so that you can make it in your next turn, your
opponent could claim a wiring lift. But if you can leave the opponent's ball some
distance in front of your hoop and take position to run the hoop, it will probably
be too risky for him to shoot at your ball because if he misses you will be able to
run the hoop and then use his ball.

In Diag.6 red has roqueted blue near hoop 2. Red is for 4-back. A normal long
roll for the hoop would mean that if red does not gain position to run the hoop
immediately, it will not be able to take position to run it in the next turn either.

Blue here is for penultimate, so if red takes off to 4-back and sits in front. blue will be likely to take the risk of shooting at red.

The best option for red is to send blue near hoop 4—preferably just past it as shown by the blue arrow. Then, if red takes position to run 4-back, blue will be most unlikely to risk shooting at red when a miss would see blue finishing on the north border where red can get a cut-rush on it into the lawn after running through 4-back to the border.

A similar consideration comes into play in Diag.7 where blue was in front of rover and red had taken position to run penultimate. Blue has just run the rover hoop, going well through in order to increase the chance of being able to end the game by shooting at the peg without the rover hoop interfering.

However he now finds that shooting at the peg is very dangerous, because if he misses and finishes on the north border, red will be able to (at least) make penultimate and sit in front of the rover hoop, and another attempt by blue to peg out would then be likely to either finish on the south border where red can run through rover, roquet blue and take off to the peg; or else blue would have to shoot to stay near the peg and risk giving red

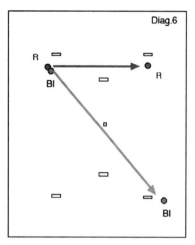

R = 4b; Y = out; Bk = out; Bl = pen

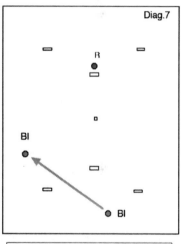

R = pen; Y = out; Bk= out; Bl = peg

a good (possibly double) target to shoot at after making rover.

So again we see a situation where an accurate assessment of the opponent's ability and nervous state (i.e. willingness to take risks) can be of great importance. The player of blue must decide how far from the peg he can afford to send his ball.

He may decide, for example, to place blue as indicated by the blue arrow, trusting that it is far enough away to deter red (after making penultimate) from shooting at blue (since a miss would give the game to blue immediately, and roqueting it would still require him to play a long approach roll to rover), but close enough for blue to have a good chance of either roqueting red (if it sits in front of rover) or hitting the peg in his next turn.

GENERAL ENDGAME TACTICS

IN THE ENDGAME it is easy to forget that some principles that applied earlier in the game may no longer apply.

Diag.1 shows a situation where yellow has set up for red by wiring the blue and black balls at 4-back and setting up as shown towards the 2nd corner with yellow wired from blue by hoop 2.

The opponent elected to shoot with blue (his backward ball) at red, and missed. Then red roqueted blue and used a stop-shot to send blue to rover, while red ran a short distance past yellow and had to rush it back to the north border behind hoop 2. From there he played an angled pass roll to load penultimate while going to black behind 4-back. He succeeded in making the final three hoops and pegging out after some anxious moments, and was surprised when someone suggested later that he had gone about it the wrong way.

After roqueting blue (see Diag.2) he would have been better advised to leave blue (the ball the opponent wants to play) out of play in the 2nd corner, take off to yellow, rush yellow near to the 3rd corner, and send it to load penultimate while coming along the rush-line to get a good rush on black to 4-back. He had no need to bring blue out

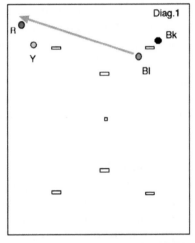

R = 4b; Y = peg; Bk = peg; Bl = pen

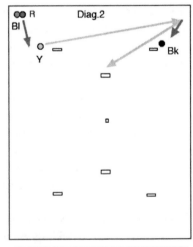

R = 4b; Y = peg; Bk = peg; Bl = pen

into the court, as there would have been no difficult shots needed to finish the game with just three balls by loading rover with black after making 4-back, and leaving yellow near the peg after making penultimate.

Earlier in the game it would have been wrong to deliberately leave an opponent ball out of play and make a break with only three balls. Even if he could see that he would have no problem in making as many hoops as he wanted with the three balls, he would need the fourth ball to ensure that at the end of the break he could set up the best possible leave for his partner ball. But here (Diag.2) the situation is different. After making the last three hoops he will not need to set up for his partner ball, as he will expect to peg out and finish the game, and while making the last three hoops he will not need a pivot ball. In this case it is safer to leave the blue ball out of play so that if something goes wrong the opponent will probably have to play with black, which is already for the peg.

Many games have been lost due to this sort of automatic, routine thinking—or lack of thinking.

After wiring the opponent's balls as in Diag.1, the player of yellow could well have been tempted to set a rush for red to either 4-back or penultimate, but that would have involved a risk of leaving a double target for one of the opponent's balls. If the player of red will be able to play a reasonable pass-roll, he does not need a rush out of the 2nd corner; and if the lack of a rush encourages the opponent to hit blue into (say) the 1st corner, then so much the better.

COMMON ENDGAME MISTAKES

1. Play the ball that can win the game.

IN DIAG.1 THE player of red had been playing his turn when the bell went (i.e. time expired), and he continued the break until he stuck in the 3-back hoop which also happened to be black's hoop. In the last turn of the game the opponent, pleased at his unexpected good fortune, quickly walked out onto the court, played black, roqueted red out of the hoop, made 3-back, sent it to penultimate while getting a rush on yellow to 4-back, made the last three hoops and pegged out his black ball—and lost the game 20-18.

It apparently did not occur to him that if he had played blue and roqueted, then gone around to the peg, he could have won the game 21-20. It is true that his chance of roqueting with blue would not have been good, but it cannot be correct to pass up a chance of winning the game and play a ball that will ensure you lose the game.

There could be an exception if you are playing in a team event and making 5 more points will be sufficient to win the match for your team even if the game is lost; or if it is a round-robin event where "net points" will be used as a tie-break if two players win

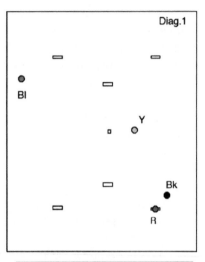

Diag.1

R = 3b; Y = peg; Bk = 3b; Bl = H6

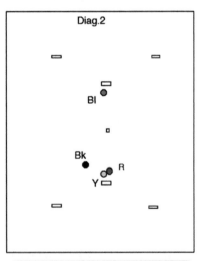

Diag.2

R = H6; Y = 3b; Bk = 4b; Bl = peg

the same number of games; or if blue could be peeled through 2 hoops, but even then most players would want to give themselves a chance of winning the game by playing blue.

2.   Keep track of the score.

In Diag.2 the bell had gone and the player of red was playing the final turn of the game, making a standard 4-ball break. He had just made hoop 5, and now he routinely sent yellow to load 2-back, then rushed black past the peg and used it to load 1-back. His mistake was that he failed to check the current score. Had he done so, he would probably have realised that if he continued his break to the peg and pegged out his red ball, the scores would be level and the opponent, with a lift entitlement, would get to play another turn. In order to ensure that he wins the game, the player of red needs to peel yellow through one hoop (3-back) as well as peg red out in this final turn.

Making the one required peel will be easier if yellow is either the pilot ball at 3-back, or the pivot ball which can also be sent to 3-back; but it will be much harder if he makes 2-back from yellow and then has to find a way to get it to 3-back for peeling as well as load 4-back

An alternative method, if he decides he needs all four ball in the break all the way, is to take red around to rover and peel yellow through 3-back either before or after making rover with red. However he would still need to be sure of pegging red out, and even then he would need to start positioning the balls for the peel at an earlier stage of the break. It is worthwhile to not only look at the clip positions, but double-check that you have added up the scores correctly, especially if you are in a somewhat nervous state and may find it hard to think as clearly as you normally would.

3.   Don't take unnecessary risks.

Diag.3 shows the end of a game where each player had a single ball. Blue was for penultimate and had slightly overhit the shot after making 4-back when he tried to take position to run penultimate. Then red made 2-back and was underhit in trying for position to run 3-back. Now red could not make 3-back, but blue had some chance of making penultimate from a sidey angle.

The player of blue elected to play a jump-shot, but rebounded from the hoop a few yards towards 4-back. Then red took good position for 3-back and the player of

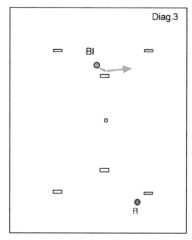

Diag.3

R = 3b; Y = out; Bk = out; Bl = pen

blue found himself in a difficult position, having lost most of the advantage he had enjoyed.

Even if blue had succeeding in making penultimate with the jump-shot, it would have been risky to take position in front of rover with red only 8-9 yards away. He would have given himself a better chance of winning by simply hitting blue gently into the penultimate hoop. Then, after red takes position to run 3-back, he could even consider "passing" (declaring his turn) until red has made 3-back and been hit up to 4-back.

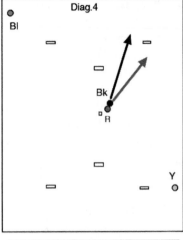

Diag.4

R = 4b; Y = 2b; Bk= peg; Bl = H5

However the player of red could also use shrewd tactics—he could just hit his ball into the 3-back hoop, trying to get it where, in running the hoop, he could do so at an angle and send it close to penultimate, or near enough to be sure of roqueting a ball in front of rover.

[Note that if it is a timed game, red will probably not be able to afford to create an impasse because he could lose on time.]

4. Do only what you need to do.

Diag.4 shows a situation from a timed game where after the extension period (i.e. each player had played a turn after the bell) scores were level, so the game has to be continued until someone scores a point. Red has roqueted yellow and taken off to black, but did not get a rush on it to his 4-back hoop. Then red rolled with black to 4-back as illustrated by the arrows. He finished the roll with red about 2 yards in front of the 4-back hoop, giving himself a rather long shot at the hoop, with an immediate loss of the game if he failed to make the hoop, or tried to sit in front of it so that he could make it in his next turn.

In this situation the player of red could have simply taken off from black and should have been able to obtain good position to run the hoop and end the game.

Note that he does not need a ball to roquet after making the hoop. He may have not wanted to leave black near the peg in case red failed to gain position and run the 4-back hoop; but in that case he should have made sure of sending black close to the north border and almost directly behind the 4-back hoop, so that if necessary he could sit in front of the hoop wired from black.

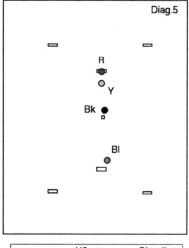

Diag.5

R = pen; Y = H6; Bk = peg; Bl = 4b

5. Don't go too far.

The final situation in our consideration of endgames occurred in a game played by the author (JR) many years ago in the first round of a major tournament. For most of the game I had played poorly, and the situation illustrated in Diag.5 occurred when I had at last established a break with red instead of making odd hoops, and had attempted to make penultimate. The red ball stuck in the hoop as shown, and as I left the lawn, the bell went. I was six points down and would get only one more turn!

My opponent did not have a clear shot at anything with blue from where it was, though he was entitled to a lift if he wanted it. Instead, he decided to simply peg out the black ball. That put me seven points behind, and of course in the final turn I had to play the yellow ball to give myself any chance of winning. I roqueted red, made hoop 6, and somehow managed to set up a 3-ball break and keep it going all the way to the peg, winning the game 23-22. I was extremely lucky to win this game (and the tournament, which I went on to win), but not because I managed to avoid breaking down in the 3-ball break.

My great piece of luck was sticking in the penultimate hoop instead of making it! I had been no more than one foot straight in front of the hoop, and would normally expect to make it without any difficulty. But if I had made the hoop I would have lost the game, as the bell would have gone before i finished the turn and I would not have had another turn in which to catch up and win the game. I had not given any thought to either the game score or the amount of time remaining, but my narrow and very fortunate escape taught me an important lesson.

If I had known the true state of things I should not have tried to make penultimate, but instead stopped the break with red and set up for yellow to play the final turn. It is obvious when you see it, but I wonder how many games have been lost in the way I deserved to lose this one, by the player unthinkingly going too far when his only chance of winning was to stop making hoops in a break he could easily continue, and set up for his partner ball.

CONCLUDING COMMENTS—PEELS

WE HAVE DEALT with peeling to some extent on previous pages, but the reader may wonder why we have not explained how to set for, and play, the various types of triple peel and sextuple peel. The reason is that the booklet is not aimed at world class players who are capable of doing sextuple peels; and triple peels have been dealt with fairly thoroughly in books written by other people, so if we were to explain how to set up and play (for example), straight double peels, standard triple peels, delayed triple peels, very delayed triple peels, straight triple peels, and the many variations of each of these, it would take up many more pages, make the booklet more expensive, and only serve to cover material that the reader could find explained elsewhere by more competent exponents of such things.

Perhaps we should mention that players who are capable of triple peeling often make the mistake of failing to consider percentages. Attempting a triple peel is unlikely to increase your chance of winning a game unless the conditions are conducive to accurate play and you know that once you start a triple peel you can expect to complete it at least 5 times out of 10. After all, it only saves giving your opponent one lift shot, and statistics show that on average even the world's top players miss more lift shots than they hit. Triple peeling an opponent ball is even more dubious unless your completion rate for triples is up around 80%, since if you break down after peeling the opponent's ball through (say) one or two of its last three hoops, the opponent will be likely to save you the trouble of completing the triple by finishing it for you!

CROQUET
CANNONS

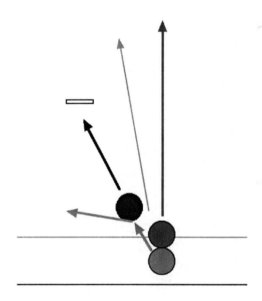

CONTENTS

CANNONS—INTRODUCTORY EXPLANATION

THE NEED FOR these articles on cannons is evidenced by the frequency with which even experienced players miss opportunities to play a cannon that would have enabled them to set up an immediate break. The opportunity to play a particular cannon will occur by accident only occasionally, so some players consider that it is not worth spending a lot of time practising them; but they are missing out on the enjoyment of a fascinating side of croquet. Apart from the fact that they can help you win more games, there is great satisfaction in being able to control three balls simultaneously, and there is scope for the player to use his creative ability, since it is quite possible that he could play a cannon that no-one else has played before from that exact position for that particular hoop.

In all, there are well over 20 different types of cannon, and each one can be played from slightly different positions which will require some minor adjustments to the lining up, line of swing, type of swing, etc. We plan to cover, as thoroughly as space allows, all the different types that a player may ever want to use—and perhaps a few that he would not want to use—and can guarantee the player many hours of on-lawn enjoyment (and some hard work) if he is prepared to study the various possibilities with a view to using them in his games. A big advantage is that it can all be done on your own—you do not even need an opponent to enjoy yourself trying out new ideas for unusual cannons.

When you have learnt a number of new cannons that you had previously not seen or thought of, you will find that opportunities to use them to advantage in your games will start to occur more frequently, especially when you start to use tactics or play shots which are specifically designed to result in the creation of cannon opportunities.

In the articles which follow, we shall try to cover such things as:

1. General theory of cannons—what is, and is not, possible.
2. The different types of cannon—how to line them up and play them.
3. The effect of minor adjustments.
4. The situations where each cannon can be used.
5. Some ways cannons can be deliberately created.

Cannons can be divided into at least ten different types or categories:

1. Standard-type cannons
2. Reverse cannons
3. the BOTT cannon
4. Roll cannons
5. Cannon to a 4th ball

6. Four-ball cannons
7. Cannon with a dead ball
8. Promotion cannons
9. Disjoint cannons
10. In-lawn cannons

Although most cannons will occur in a corner, it is not uncommon for a player, either by accident or by design, to create a cannon anywhere on a border; and from 2008 the last category above (in-lawn cannons) with assume greater importance due to a change in the laws which will provide that in a "3-ball group" (cannon) it will no longer be necessary for at least one of the balls to be a yardline ball before the player can arrange the two balls other than the roqueted ball as he wishes.

For standard cannons, the type of cannon needed in any particular situation will depend on the angle between the directions you want the two balls (the croqueted ball and the rushed ball) to travel in, and the relative distances you want them to go.

Different players may arrange and play their cannons slightly differently due to differences in things such as their strength and stature; the length, weight and flexibility of mallet; the lawn conditions; the type of swing they use; the type of balls; and so on. For each cannon we will make recommendations that we believe will suit the majority of players, but we allow that some players will find it helpful to use other methods at times.

We strongly recommend that the best way to learn to play and use cannons is to not just read about them, but to take this booklet (or pages printed out from the internet if necessary) out on the croquet lawn and try them out. Unless you see them played and get a feel for them, you are unlikely to think of using them when opportunities arise in game situations.

CANNONS—GENERAL THEORY

THIS "GENERAL THEORY" will deal only with standard cannons in which the third (rushed) ball is sent to the hoop the striker wants to make, and the croqueted ball is simultaneously sent to load the following hoop. The striker's ball will roquet the rushed ball during the stroke, so the striker's ball will become a "ball in hand", and where it finishes will therefore be irrelevant. It should be noted that in a cannon the turn will end if the croqueted ball is sent out of court, but it will not matter if the striker's ball goes out.

LAWS
In arranging a cannon, the roqueted ball (which will also be the "croqueted" ball in the cannon) must first be placed in a lawful position, and this must be done without moving any ball that is already in a lawful position. Then the striker must place the other two balls anywhere in contact with the roqueted ball, but not in contact with each other.

ANGLE
The maximum possible angle between the directions in which the two balls can be sent is just under 60 degrees. This will occur in a "wafer" cannon, when the gap between the striker's ball and the rushed ball is as small as possible—usually about 1mm. The minimum angle possible in a normally arranged and played cannon is about 45 degrees. This angle is seen in the most common cannon of all—from the first corner for hoop 1, and is the first one we will deal with separately in the following pages. This means that from many positions on the court it will not be possible to play a standard cannon to rush a ball to your hoop while also loading the next hoop. In some cases there may be a nonstandard cannon that can do the trick, and these will be considered later; but often you just have to accept that although you have created the possibility of playing a cannon, there is no cannon that will be of any use to you in that particular situation.

DISTANCES
The simple rule is that you can send either ball further than the other by hitting more into the ball you want to send further, and less into the other ball. However there are some further considerations:

(1) The size of the gap between the two non-touching balls makes only a slight difference to the distance the striker's ball travels, unless the line of swing or type of swing is also altered. This is contrary to the belief of

many players and the teaching of some coaches, and will be explained further in what follows.

(2) The line of swing (with the same arrangement of the balls), as we have already seen, can make a big difference to the relative distances travelled by the two balls.

(3) The type of swing can also make a difference, with a stop-shot action (usually not recommended) sending the striker's ball the least distance; a normal "drive" swing (usually recommended) sending it a bit further; and a flat, accelerated roll action sending it further still. The accelerated flat roll is a shot that many players find difficult to play, as they are used to swinging the mallet down onto the ball in split-shots and cannot help thinking of the cannon as a type of split-shot.

GAP
The size of the gap can vary from about 1mm, as we have seen, to about 25mm (= one inch). If the gap is wider than 25mm there is a possibility that the striker's ball may not roquet the third ball. There are also cannons we will examine later in which the striker's ball deliberately does not roquet the third ball, but those are non-standard cannons.

LINE OF SWING
The line of swing for the standard corner cannons should be remembered as directly toward a particular point on the court. Some coaches have taught that you can swing through the middle of the striker's ball and the point where the other two balls touch each other, but we shall see that this method of determining the line of swing has disadvantages.

STRENGTH
Almost all cannons need to be hit harder than you think. Most need to be hit hard enough to rush the rushed ball out over the far boundary if the croqueted ball were removed. Players tend to use the force they would need to play a 2-ball split-shot to the two hoops, forgetting that in a cannon there is a third ball that must be moved also, even if it does not matter where it goes.

C1H1 CANNON

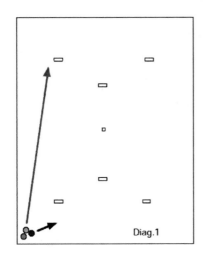

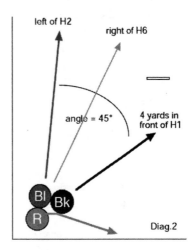

SYMBOLS

IN OUR EXPLANATIONS we will use the following symbols and abbreviations:

LOS = Line of swing
H1, H2, H3 . . . = hoop1, hoop 2, hoop 3, . . . (etc.)
C1, C2, C3, C4 = 1st corner, 2nd corner, 3rd corner, 4th corner.
45°, 60° = 45 degrees, 60 degrees. blue and black arrows = intended paths of same coloured balls. grey arrow = line of swing. red arrow = path of striker's ball (not usually shown).
LUCB = line up croqueted ball (i.e. set line through centres of striker's ball and croqueted ball).
LURB = line up rushed ball (i.e. set line through centres of striker's ball and rushed ball).

C1H1 CANNON
The above diagrams illustrate the cannon played from C1 (the 1st corner) to make H1 (hoop 1) and also load the following hoop (H2).
LUCB to about 1 yard left of (i.e. outside) H2.
LURB to go about 4 yards in front of H1.
LOS = about 1 yard right of H6
Type of swing = normal drive (or rush) stroke with flat mallet (not a stop-shot).

NOTES

The gap should be about 25mm (maximum gap), so that the striker's ball will cut the rushed ball inwards and achieve the minimum 45° angle. When the cannon is correctly arranged, the centres of the 3 balls form a right-angled triangle. These two considerations (gap and right-angle) are not essential to remember, but can be useful checks that the court is correctly shaped and full-size. Many cannon attempts have come to grief because the player was unaware that the court was narrower or shorter than a regulation court, or that the hoops had been moved closer to one of the boundaries. The cannon must be hit noticeably harder than a 2-ball load-and-hold stop-shot from C1 to load H2 and send the striker's ball in front of H1, because there is also the striker's ball that has to be moved.

The croqueted ball will pull slightly inside the LUCB line, and the rushed ball will be cut noticeably inside the LURB line shown on the diagrams.

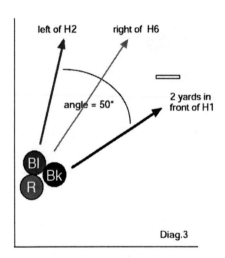

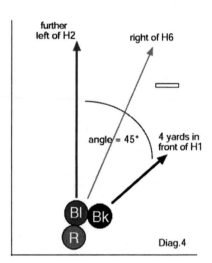

OTHER PLACES

The same cannon can be played, either as shown, or in mirror image: from C2 to make 1-back and load 2-back from C3 to make H3 and load H4
From C4 to make 3-back and load 4-back

ADJUSTMENTS

If the cannon is played from a place near, but not in, the 1st corner, you may need to make some small adjustments as follows:

If playing from 2-3 yards (or more) up the west border as shown in Diag.3, the desired angle will be wider, so you should use a narrower gap and you should be able to send the rushed ball closer to H1.

The LUCB and LOS will probably not need changing until you get almost level with H1, after which the cannon will become impossible.

If playing from 2-3 yards (but no more) east of C1 along A-baulk (see Diag.4), you would theoretically desire a narrower angle of about 40 degrees. But this is impossible, so you will have to compromise by either sending blue further left of H2, or being satisfied to get black more than 3 yards in front of H1—or both, in order to avoid attempting to achieve an angle smaller than the minimum of 45°.

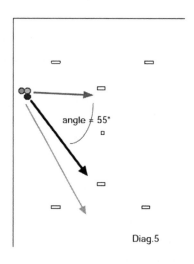

Diag.5

Diagram 5 shows how the same type of cannon can be used from the west border level with H6 to make H5 and load H6. This is also a minimum angle cannon, but in this case the striker's ball must travel further than the croqueted ball, so you have to use a LOS that hits less directly into the croqueted ball. You will probably need a LOS about halfway between hoops 1 and 5 to get maximum ("very fine") cut on the rushed ball, and you may not be able to reliably achieve an angle much smaller than 55°, since you will have to hit quite hard and the elasticity of the balls can cause you to miss the fine cut if you slightly misjudge the LOS.

CANNON MECHANICS

[THIS PAGE CAN be skipped by those not interested in the actual mechanics of cannons.]

EFFECT OF CLOSING THE GAP

More than 20 years ago we were teaching that narrowing the gap in a cannon would result in the striker's ball going further. An old engineer named Lance McLean told me that he had written a computer programme which simulated various croquet strokes, including cannons, and that we were wrong about this. We spent some time experimenting, and finally realised that he was right. After all, what difference does it make in a normal rush if the gap between the two balls is changed from 1mm to 10mm or 25mm? Hardly any! So why would it make a difference when the rush is part of a cannon?

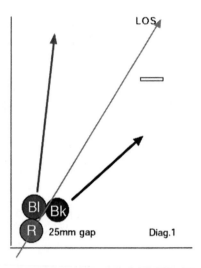

Diag.1

The reason for our misapprehension was that we had also been teaching people to find the LOS by swinging in a line through the centre of the red ball and the point where the blue and black balls touched each other—see Diag.1. When you do this, closing the gap will indeed send the rushed black ball further, but this is due to the fact that you are now swinging in a different direction

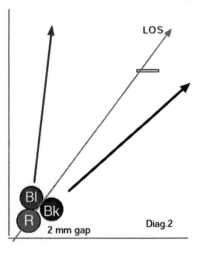

Diag.2

because in closing the gap you have moved the point where the blue and black balls touch—see Diag.2 where the different LOS means you would be hitting less into the blue ball. Closing the gap does not in itself make much difference to the distance travelled by the rushed ball, provided you do not change the line of swing.

With the more elastic balls in common use today, hitting through the "touch point" is no longer a reliable way of choosing the LOS; and in fact the correct LOS for each player will depend to some extent on the type of swing he uses, so you need to go out and try it for yourself to find the exact point on the court at which you should aim for the LOS.

A REMINDER

If you use a point on the court (e.g. one yard right of H6) to establish the line of swing for any type of cannon, always check at the start of the game whether the court is full-size and correctly laid out.

EFFECT OF FOLLOW-THROUGH

The difference between using a stop-shot or a followed-through drive will not affect the distances the balls travel in most cannons. This is also the case with roquets, take-offs and rushes which some people play with a stop-shot action. In these strokes, and also in a cannon, a stop-shot action makes little difference to the distance the ball travels. However a stop-shot action can require accurate timing, and most players find it harder with a stop-shot action to ensure that the mallet is swinging in the correct direction. Following through toward the target or aiming point seems to assist the player to correctly establish and maintain the whole line of the swing—the early part as well as the later part. The swing should be as flat as possible in order to avoid any risk of causing the striker's ball to jump. Contrary to a player's instinctive conviction, he will achieve more power with less effort by using a long, flat swing than by using a higher backswing and high follow-through.

C2H2 CANNON

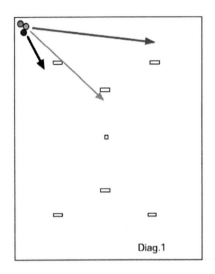

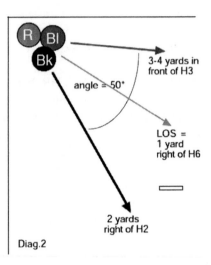

Diag.1

Diag.2

In Diag.2: R, Bl, Bk balls; "3-4 yards in front of H3"; "angle = 50°"; "LOS = 1 yard right of H6"; "2 yards right of H2"

C2H2 CANNON

DIAGS 1&2 ILLUSTRATE the cannon played from C2 (the 2nd corner) to make H2 (hoop 2) and also load the following hoop (H3).

LUCB to about halfway between hoop 3 and the north border.

LURB to go 2 yards right of (i.e. outside) H2.

LOS = about 1 yard right of H6

Type of swing = normal drive (or rush) stroke with follow-through (not a stop-shot).

NOTES

The gap should be about 15mm (a little less than the C1H1 cannon). In this case the angle between the directions of the two balls will be slightly larger—50° rather than 45°. When the balls are arranged they will not quite make a right-angled triangle as for the C1H1 cannon. The LUCB is not directly at H3 in order to allow the wider angle which is easier to control accurately. The croqueted ball can be expected to be pulled slightly inside the LUCB anyway.

The cannon should be hit hard enough to rush a single ball to the far (east) border. If the croqueted ball goes too far, or the rushed ball not far enough, then hit less into the croqueted ball by moving the LOS closer to the peg.

Two similar cannons are shown in Diag 3, but the angle needs to be smaller to avoid sending blue too far behind the hoop you want to load, so you may need to use a 25mm maximum gap as for the C1H1 cannon, and there is no centre hoop to assist in finding the LOS.

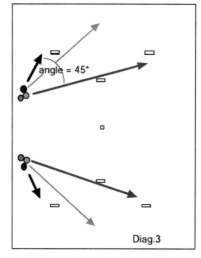

OTHER PLACES

This cannon can also be played—from C1 to make 2-back and load 3-back, but the LOS is then 1 yard left of H5.

It cannot be played from C3 or C4, so is purely a "western side" cannon. However there are places on the west border away from the corners where you could use a similar cannon, as illustrated in Diag 3.

C2H1 CANNON

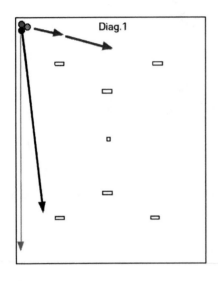

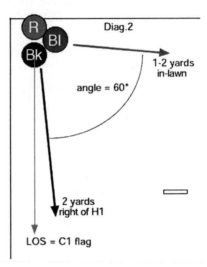

C2H1 CANNON

DIAGS 1&2 ILLUSTRATE the cannon played from C2 to make H1 and load H2. LUCB to about 2 yards in-lawn behind H2
LURB to about 2 yards right of (i.e. outside) H1
LOS = straight down west yard-line, or at the 1st corner flag.
Type of swing = normal drive (or rush) stroke.

NOTES

The gap should be as small as you can make it without the red and black balls actually touching—i.e. 1-2mm. This cannon is often referred to as a "wafer" cannon because it is said to require a "wafer thin" gap.

The angle between the paths of the two (blue and black) balls will be almost exactly 60°, which means that it is impossible to send the blue ball to a good loading position for H2.

With a LOS at the 1st corner flag, the blue ball should finish about 4-5 yards behind H2.

Some players prefer to send the blue ball further in-lawn, which they can achieve by using a LOS aimed slightly in-lawn, i.e. closer to H1;but this means it will also be further from H2; e.g. behind H6 and 4-5 yards in from the north boundary.

These two possible positions are represented in Diag.1 by the two blue arrows.

As with many other cannons, most players do not hit it hard enough. They play it as if they were simply rushing the black ball to H1, forgetting that the blue ball must also be moved.

OTHER PLACES

This cannon can also be played—from C1 to make 1-back and load 2-back, from C3 to make 3-back and load 4-back, from C4 to make H3 and load H4, or from various places on the border for distant hoops as illustrated in Diag.3, where care may need to be taken not to send the blue croqueted ball out over the boundary.

EQUAL DISTANCE CANNON

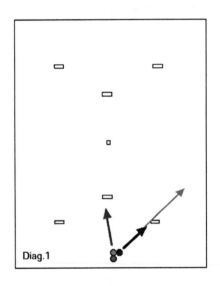

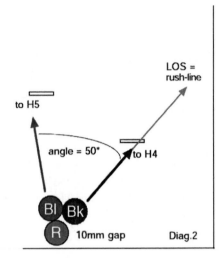

EQUAL DISTANCE CANNON

THIS CANNON OCCURS less often because it is not played from a corner. Instead, it is played from the centre of either the south or north border.

The cannon shown in Diags 1&2 is to make hoop 4 and load H5.

LUCB to H5.

LURB to H4

LOS = same as rush-line; i.e. swing straight through the centres of the red and black balls.

Type of swing = normal drive (or rush) stroke with follow-through (not a stop-shot).

NOTES

The gap should be about 10mm (for many people just wide enough to fit your little finger in there). The angle between the directions of the two balls will be 50° or slightly larger. Most players do not hit hard enough in this cannon, as you need to hit more than twice as hard as you would to play the rush if the croqueted ball were removed.

OTHER PLACES

This cannon can also be played: from the centre of the north border to make 4-back and load penultimate, or from the same place (centre of north border) to make hoop 6 and load 1-back (see Diag.3).

Note that these two versions of the cannon are not mirror-images. You will need to practise lining them up and playing them slightly differently because the distances to the front of the hoops are not quite the same. On the next page we will see yet another way this "equal distance cannon" can be used.

A similar cannon can be played from anywhere near the centre of the east border to make H1 and load H2 (see Diag.3), or to make 1-back and load 2-back; or from the middle of the west border to make H3 and load H4, or to make 3-back and load 4-back.

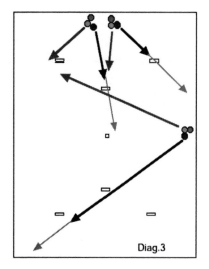

Diag.3

However all these long cannons need to be hit very hard, and some players say they do not have the strength to play them.

REVERSE CANNON

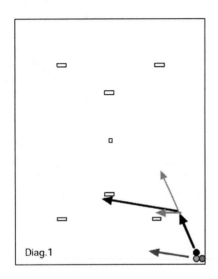

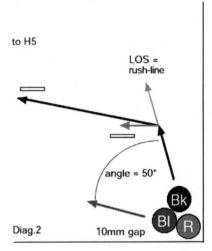

Diag.1

Diag.2

REVERSE CANNON

T HE REVERSE CANNON is actually an equal distance cannon followed by a stop-shot. Its name indicates that the roles of the two balls are reversed.
The cannon shown in Diags 1&2 is to make hoop 4 and load H5.
LUCB to just inside south border.
LURB to 3 yards right of H4
LOS = same as rush-line.
Type of swing = normal drive (or rush) stroke with follow-through (not a stop-shot).

NOTES
Since the angle between hoops 4 and 5 as viewed from C4 is only about 10°, a normal cannon is impossible. The idea here is to put the croqueted ball behind H4 while rushing the black ball to a position east of H4 from which you can send it to load H5 with a stop-shot while making position to run through H4 to the blue ball.

This means that you are using the croqueted ball as the escape ball for H4 and the rushed black ball to load your next hoop—the reverse of their roles in a normal cannon.

As with all equal-distance cannons, this one is usually not hit hard enough. Some players like to send the rushed ball further up the lawn, to follow it up with a split-shot rather than a stop-shot.

This can be achieved by hitting less into the croqueted ball, e.g. swing at H3 or C3 instead of along the rush-line. If the croqueted ball is your partner ball, you would need to think carefully before sending it to H5 in this cannon, in case you cannot make H4.

OTHER PLACES

The "reverse cannon" can also be played from C3 to make 4-back and load penultimate.

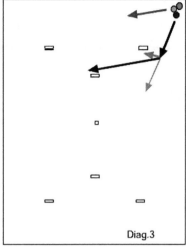

Diag.3

It is possible to use the "reverse roles" idea in other places, but there should be an alternative cannon you could use with more certainty of making your hoop and getting a break established, so these are the only two situations where it is normally used.

C4H1 CANNON

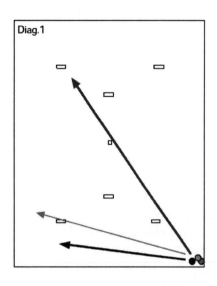

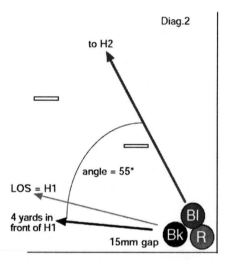

C4H1 ("BIG") CANNON

T HE BALLS TRAVEL further in this cannon than in any other standard cannon, so it requires more power.

Diags 1&2 illustrate this cannon as played from C4 to make H1 and load H2.

LUCB to H2.

LURB to 4 yards left (in front) of H1

LOS = at H1.

Type of swing = normal long drive (or rush) stroke with long follow-through (not a stop-shot).

NOTES

Some players who are less powerfully built than others claim they do not have the strength required to play this cannon, especially on a heavy lawn.

The croqueted (blue) ball will not go directly to H1, but if it is lined up 4 yards in front of hoop 1 it should cut in at least a yard, which most players accept as satisfactory.

Many players and coaches have the idea that the way to achieve more power in long croquet strokes is to use a pendulum-type swing with a higher backswing in order to make greater use of gravity, but this has the disadvantage that it is very difficult to achieve exact timing when you are swinging the mallet as fast as possible in an effort to achieve maximum power.

It is more important to ensure that when the mallet contacts the ball it is travelling exactly in a horizontal line, so that all the force is transferred from the mallet through the centre of the striker's ball and into the rushed ball. The best way to achieve this is to use a long, flat swing, and of course it will help if the player has a heavy mallet, is tall, uses an upright stance and a mallet with a long shaft, has long arms, and is physically strong. However many players without these desirable attributes find that with practice they can manage it unless the lawn is very heavy. Some resort to using a side-style swing, but most players should be capable of playing the shot centre-style, and so achieving greater accuracy, if they go about it the right way.

For this cannon some players use a golf-style swing which easily provides the needed power, but needs a lot of practice and can have disadvantages, one of which is the possibility of damaging the lawn. The C4H1 cannon, however it is played, should always be watched by a referee.

OTHER PLACES

The "C4H1 cannon" can also be played— from C1 to make 3-back and load 4-back, or from C2 to make H3 and load H4, or from C3 to make 1-back and load 2-back.

REFEREEING

Other standard cannons are not normally considered "questionable strokes", so do not need to be watched by a referee provided the player knows how to arrange them correctly.

B.O.T.T. CANNON

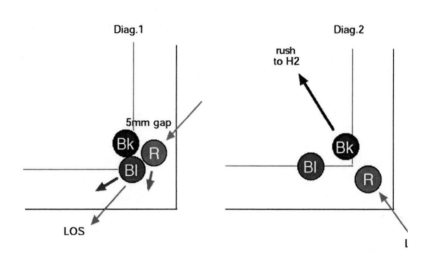

Diag.1

5mm gap

Bk

R

Bl

LOS

Diag.2

rush
to H2

Bk

Bl

R

B.O.T.T. CANNON

T HE AIM OF this cannon is merely to obtain a good rush to your hoop.

Diags 1&2 illustrate the BOTT cannon as played from C4 to make H2.

LUCB to move away from the black ball into the yard-line area.

LURB to remain stationary,

LOS = a little left of centre of croqueted ball

Type of swing = sharp but gentle stop-shot.

NOTES

The B.O.T.T. cannon is used whenever there is no possible cannon that can be used to both rush a ball to the hoop you want to make, and also load the following hoop. This occurs when the hoop you want to make is at the far end of the court.

All you can hope to do is get a good rush to your hoop, leaving the croqueted ball behind.

The best way to achieve an accurate rush is illustrated in the two diagrams at the top of this page.

In the illustrations the cannon is played in C4 to obtain a rush to H2.

The inner lines in the diagrams represent the yard-lines.

The arrangement of the balls can be explained and achieved in the following stages:

(1) leaving the croqueted ball in its correct place on the yard-line, remove the other two balls.

(2) place the striker's (red) ball as if you were going to take off from the roqueted ball to your hoop.

In this case red could also be placed as if to take off from the left side of blue instead of the right side, thus producing a mirror-image of the cannon illustrated above.

(3) pick up the black ball, **reach over the top** of the other two balls, and place it so as to make a fairly tight triangle, with a gap of 5mm or less. [Thus the name: BOTT = Ball Over The Top]

(4) Walk around into the court and play red with a sharp but gentle stop-shot, sending blue away from black into the yard-line area, while red stops on the rush-line of black to H2.

Note that in this cannon black does not move.
Because the third (black) ball remains stationary, you can work out exactly where you want red to finish so that it will have a simple rush on black to H2.
Be careful not to send blue out, but you must hit it far enough (about a foot) so that when it is yard-lined it will not interfere with your intended rush.

OTHER PLACES
The "BOTT cannon" can be played from C4 for H5, H6, 1-back, penultimate or rover.

From C4 it would not normally be played for the other hoops because there are better cannons you could use.
It can similarly be played from any corner, of from any point on a yard-line, when all you need is an accurate rush to your hoop.

The BOTT cannon has replaced the two cannons described on the next page, but it needs careful practice, and players sometimes become confused trying to remember how to arrange it.

BOTT ALTERNATIVES

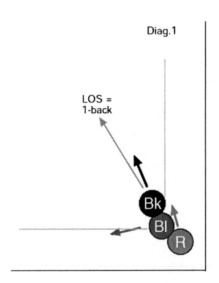

Diag.1

LOS =
1-back

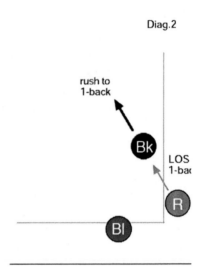

Diag.2

rush to
1-back

Bk

LOS
1-bac

R

Bl

WORM" or "BANANA" CANNON

FOR MANY YEARS this cannon was popular, probably because the BOTT cannon had not been invented until more recently.

The "worm" cannon is illustrated in Diags.1&2. The balls are arranged in an almost straight line, pointing in the direction of the desired rush, with a slight bend in it which will cause the croqueted (blue) ball to be squeezed out to one side when the red ball is hit towards the black ball. It is played as a

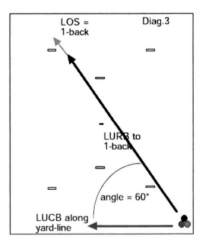

Diag.3

LOS =
1-back

LUR to
1-back

angle = 60°

LUCB along
yard-line

gentle "tap", causing the balls to all move only a short distance. It is usually played with the mallet sloping forward so that the striker's (red) ball will move forward and finish not too far from the black ball.

It is a satisfactory alternative to the BOTT cannon for players who have practised it and can control it confidently, or who have forgotten how to arrange a BOTT cannon; but with all three balls needing to be moved, good control is more difficult than in a BOTT cannon.

The obtaining of a good rush is also more likely to be affected by slight slopes in the lawn near the corner area than the BOTT cannon would be where the black ball does not move.

MINIMAL GAP CANNON

It is also possible in this situation to play a cannon similar to the C2H1 cannon (see p.8), with a 1mm (minimal) gap; but the long rush is harder to control with accuracy, and care is needed to ensure that the croqueted ball does not go out. If the player is wanting to make 1-back instead of H2, there may be some value in having the blue ball near the border behind 2-back; but there is also the possibility that after he makes 1-back it could create a problem of needing to get the ball away from the baulk-line.

ROLL CANNON

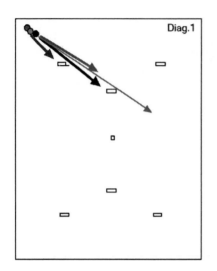

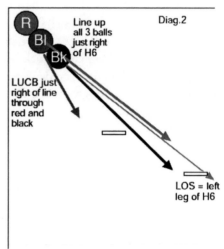

ROLL CANNON

ALL 3 BALLS are placed in line and then rolled forward.

First, place all three balls in a line pointing just outside the right (west) leg of H6.

Then move the blue ball slightly so that its centre is about 1-2mm to the right of this line.

Close any gaps so that the line has a very slight bend in it, but if blue were removed red would have rush on black aiming just right of H6 (see Diags 1&2).

LOS = at left (far) leg of H6; i.e. very slightly to the left of the line of the balls.

Type of swing = exaggerated pass-roll action with long follow-through and mallet sloping forward.

NOTES

The idea here is to roll both red and black near enough to H6 while blue is squeezed out towards 1-back. Normally black is not roqueted in the cannon, though it is possible for red to catch up to black and roquet it, which will not be a problem. After playing the stroke red can proceed to roquet black (if it did not roquet it in the cannon) and make hoop 6, with blue loading 1-back.

This cannon must be played with an exaggerated pass-roll action, and could perhaps better be referred to as a "pass-roll cannon". You should imagine the black ball removed and play it as if you are pass-rolling blue to H6 while red would go almost to the far (west) border.

It requires regular practice, but if arranged and played correctly players can learn to consistently have red and black stop close together near H6, while sending blue reasonably close to 1-back.

If blue does not go far enough, the line was too curved. The displacement of blue from the original straight line needs to be hardly noticeable.

OTHER PLACES

There is no other place where we would recommend attempting this type of cannon. Some have tried it from C2 to make H5 and load H6, but it would require considerable strength and an exceptionally fast lawn to have much chance of being successful.

REFEREEING

The roll cannon can be somewhat controversial. Some referees may want to rule it a fault because the mallet remains in contact with the striker's ball for a considerable time. However the current (2007) laws allow the mallet to remain in contact with the striker's ball as long as (and for a short after) the striker's ball is still in contact with the croqueted ball. Here the 3rd (black) ball tends to prevent blue moving quickly away from red, so the allowable time you can legally maintain contact between mallet and striker's ball is longer than in a normal 2-ball pass-roll.

CANNON TO 4TH BALL

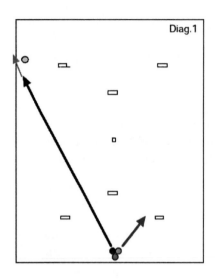

Diag.1

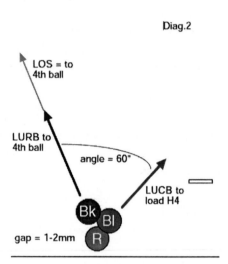

Diag.2

CANNON TO 4TH BALL
LUCB to load next hoop
LURB to 4th ball
LOS = to 4th ball
Type of swing = long, flat, and hard

NOTES

THIS IS THE same as the C2H1 (minimal gap) cannon, but the objective is to rush black to the 4th (yellow) ball, which of course must be alive. Then the yellow ball will be rushed to the hoop you want to make.

Diags.1&2 show such a cannon played from the centre of the south border for H3. Blue is sent to load H4 and yellow will be rushed to H3.

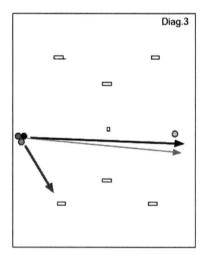

Diag.3

For this cannon to be possible, the 4th ball needs to be so placed that the lines to H4 and the yellow ball make an angle of about 60°

Most players tend not to hit hard enough. You need more force than if you were simply rushing black to yellow, because blue must be moved as well. Black can be rushed right out.

The LOS must be judged according to the distance blue has to move. Hitting straight along the rush-line will normally send blue about a third of the rush distance (e.g. see Diag.3).

OTHER PLACES

There are many other places on the borders from which a cannon can be played to the 4th ball, depending on the positions of the 4th ball and the hoop you want to make. However it is a rare type of cannon because the 4th ball must still be alive and the angle must be right.

This cannon is less likely to be played from a corner, because of the angle required. However it is possible (for example) to play it from C4 for 1-back with the yellow ball near C3. Blue would be sent to load 2-back as black is rushed to yellow; but considerable strength is required, and many players would content themselves with simply playing a BOTT cannon.

CREATING A 4-BALL CANNON

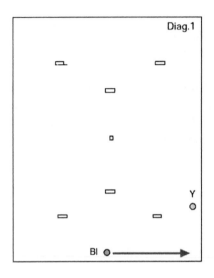

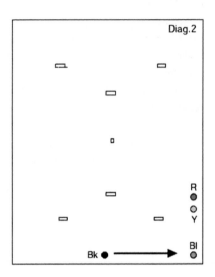

BEFORE EXPLAINING HOW to arrange and play a 4-ball cannon, we will look at how one can occur in a game situation, since they are so rare that some players may doubt that one could ever occur.

Creating a 4-ball cannon is often not the best thing to do, even if you have an easy chance to do so; but here we give one example of a situation where a player might well decide to create one:

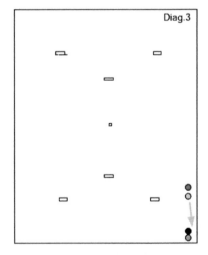

Diag. 1 shows a situation where In a standard opening the first ball (yellow) has been played to the east border, and the player of the second turn (blue), instead of setting a tice on the west border, has chosen to hit blue into the 4th corner.

This is a reasonable move (though a foot north of C4 would probably have been better), since if red now shoots at blue and roquets he is unlikely to be able to establish a break, and he risks leaving a double target for black if he misses.

So red shoots at yellow, after which black takes the shortest shot from A-baulk at blue, as shown in Diag.2.

Some would argue that in the 3rd turn red should have shot from B-baulk at yellow and blue, finishing in C4 if he misses, but others would prefer to shoot at yellow as in the Diags.

Then, in the 5th turn after all shots so far have been missed, red has the opportunity to rush yellow into C4 and create a 4-ball cannon (see Diag.3), and it is probably the correct thing for him to do. (It was also possible for yellow to cut-rush red to H3 and play a take-off or split-shot back to the balls in C4.) In this case the 4-ball cannon would be played with yellow—the partner ball—as the croqueted ball, but there are other ways that 4-ball cannons can occur, and in the following discussion of 4-ball cannons we have retained our practice of the previous sections where we had blue as the croqueted ball and black as the rushed ball, leaving yellow as the 4th ball.

4-BALL CANNONS

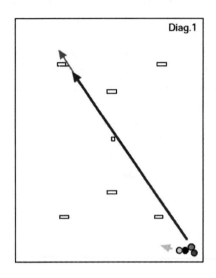

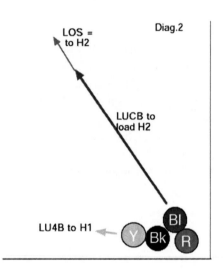

4-BALL CANNON
LUCB to load next hoop (H2)
Line up 3rd and 4th balls to current hoop (H1)
LOS = to next hoop (H2)
Type of swing = normal drive

NOTES

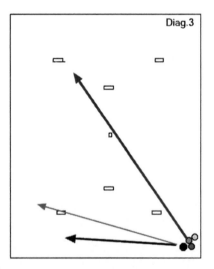

Dᴵᴬᴳˢ 1&2 SHOW a 4-ball cannon from C4 for H1.
The 3rd (black) ball is placed in contact with the croqueted (blue) ball, with a small gap between it and the striker's (red) ball. Then the 4th (yellow) ball is placed in contact with black, so that the centres of black and yellow are in line with H1. The cannon is played to send blue to H2 while red just grazes black, which will hardly move at all. Yellow should be moved no more than a yard or so toward H1. Then red takes croquet from black and gets a simple rush on yellow to H1.

The danger with this cannon is that there is often a tendency to hit too hard and send the croqueted ball too far, or even out of court, which would end the turn. This is because the player knows that most long cannons need to be hit hard, and forgets that in this case only one ball has to be moved the long distance, while the other balls will barely move at all.

A similar arrangement can be used to rush to any other hoop while loading the following hoop, but if there is a suitable 3-ball cannon you can use, then you may prefer to use it. For example, in this case, the "standard" C4H1 cannon could be used by arranging three balls as explained in the section on that cannon (see p.11), and placing the 4th ball so that it touches the blue ball and will not be moved in the 3-ball cannon (see Diag.3).

Players who lack the strength to play the difficult C4H1 cannon will prefer to use the 4-ball cannon followed by a simple rush as described above if they get the chance to do so.

4-BALL CANNON ALTERNATIVES

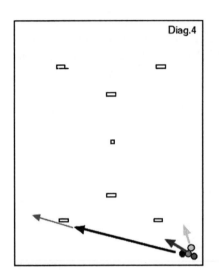

Diag.4

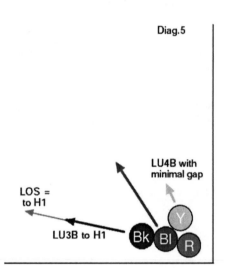

Diag.5

LU4B with minimal gap

LOS = to H1

LU3B to H1

Bk Bl R Y

4-BALL PROMOTION CANNON Diag.6

DIAGS 4&5 SHOW a second way of arranging and playing a 4-ball cannon from C4 for H1. Here the black ball is "promoted" to H1 without being roqueted, and therefore it will remain alive [See a later section for more "promotion" cannons].

The three balls (red, blue and black) are placed in line to H1, then blue is moved slightly to the in-lawn side of the line so that it will be squeezed in-lawn, and will not go out and end the turn.

The 4th (yellow) ball is placed so that red will contact it, but will move it only a yard or two. Once again you need to be careful not to hit too hard and send black too far.

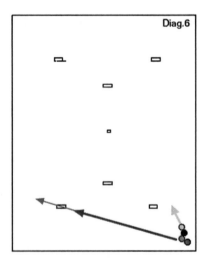

Diag.6

NOTES

This second method places a live (black) ball at the hoop you want to make, but requires a big split-shot with yellow to load H2 and go to black.

For most players we recommend the first method because they will find the rush from C4 to H1 easier than the big split from C4 to H1 and H2.

The first method can also be more easily adapted for other hoops. For 4-ball cannons a stop-shot action can be a good idea.

Diag. 6 shows the first method being used from C4 to make 1-back. The blue ball is sent to load 2-back while black and yellow barely move. Then yellow will be rushed to 1-back. There is no good way of loading 2-back while rushing a ball to 1-back in the cannon, nor of promoting a ball to 1-back while rushing a ball to 2-back.

OTHER PLACES

4-ball cannons are very rare and are almost always played from corners. The rarity is because a player who has an opportunity to create a 4-ball cannon would almost always do better to adopt some other line of play. These 4-ball cannon arrangements need practice and can be used in other corners for various hoops when there is no good 3-ball cannon available. For example, a mirror image of the cannon in Diag.6 can be played from C3 to make H1.

CREATING A DEAD-BALL CANNON

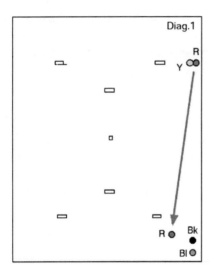

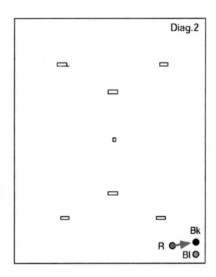

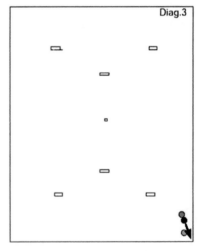

LIKE 4-BALL CANNONS, dead-ball cannons occur very rarely, but in this case it is often because players do not think of them and do not understand how to play them. Some even think incorrectly that the Laws do not allow them.

Diag. 1 shows a situation where blue and black have joined up in C4 and red, which is for 4-back, has shot from near H1 or H2 and roqueted yellow on the east border near H3. With the yellow clip still on H1, red would not want to make any more hoops, but if possible he wants to set up the lawn for yellow by placing the opponent's balls at H1 and H2.

He takes off as shown in Diag.1, and now he could roquet blue and use a "disjoint cannon" (if he knows how to play them—see a later section where they are explained).

He would probably do better to rush black into C4 and create a normal cannon which would allow him to easily put the opponent's balls at H1 and H2 before returning to set a rush for yellow.

If he fails to cut black into the corner, he can either (1) roll both black and red into the corner square (being careful not to send either ball out), or (2) send black into the square with a stop-shot, then yard-line it on the south border in contact with blue, and roquet blue without moving black.

Either of these two methods would create a "dead-ball" cannon in which red will take croquet from blue and can arrange black anywhere in contact with blue, but will not be able to roquet black in the cannon stroke because he has already used black and it is now a "dead ball". The dead-ball cannon must be understood and played quite differently from a normal cannon, but with practice can effectively be used to send the opponent's balls to positions near H1 and H2. However there is a disadvantage as compared with the normal cannon in that red will have to be hit back near yellow from some distance away, making it harder to ensure a good rush for yellow.

DEAD-BALL CANNONS

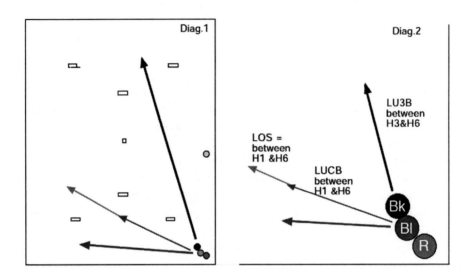

Diag.1

Diag.2

LU3B between H3&H6

LOS = between H1 &H6

LUCB between H1 &H6

DEAD BALL CANNON

DIAGS. 1&2 SHOW a situation where red has taken off from yellow to the opponent's balls near C4, roqueted black, failed to create a normal cannon, and instead created a dead-ball cannon with blue as the croqueted ball (as explained on the previous page). Instead, he could have used a stop-shot to send blue to H1, then turned around, roqueted black and sent it to H2 while returning to yellow. However the roquet under pressure after the stop-shot may be longer than is desirable, and if black is the opponent's backward ball there could be reason to send it to H2 rather than H1 so as to "force" the opponent to move his forward blue ball in the next turn.

The balls should be arranged as shown, and the cannon must be hit fairly hard to send blue 3-4 yards in front of H1 and black between H3 and H6 to a deep position about 5 yards from the north boundary. Note that the blue ball will not go in the direction it was lined up (see blue arrows). Then red is hit back to yellow, giving yellow a rush toward C3.

Why not send black to H2?—because it is difficult to achieve a narrower angle than the one illustrated. If black is lined up and sent towards H2, then blue is likely to go out over the south boundary. This need not happen, but in order to prevent it you will need to line blue up closer to H6 and hit with considerable strength, using a long pass-roll action with one hand down near the head of the mallet. Most players would need to use a side-style or golf-type swing in order to achieve the required force unless the lawn is very fast, and this would make control difficult. The dead-ball cannon as illustrated is also not an easy shot and requires careful practice, as the type and straightness of the player's swing will have an effect on the way the balls need to be lined up, which can vary from one player to another. However it can at times be the best way to set up the lawn, so time spent practising it is likely to bring a reward sooner or later.

REFEREEING

Many players will ask: Why not use the normal C4H1 cannon (see the explanation earlier) to send the opponent's balls to H1 and H2? That cannon also requires considerable strength, but there are two other reasons—

(1) The C4H1 cannon would be a fault if played with a dead ball. Most referees would not realise it, but in the C4H1 cannon there must inevitably be a double-hit on the striker's ball. This does not matter in a normal cannon because it is caused by roqueting the rushed ball; but if the black ball is dead there will be no roquet and the stroke will be a fault.

(2) In the C4H1 cannon the striker's ball will go out over the south boundary. This also does not matter in a normal cannon, but when no roquet is made in the cannon it will end the striker's turn.

PROMOTION CANNONS

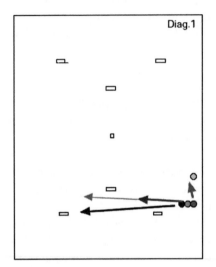

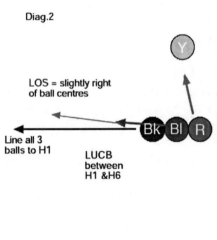

PROMOTION CANNON

THIS IS ANOTHER cannon in which no roquet is made. The aim is to send a live (black) ball to the hoop you want to make while your red ball goes to where it can easily roquet the 4th (yellow) ball. Notice that in this case yellow is not part of the cannon and may be several yards away (but not too far).

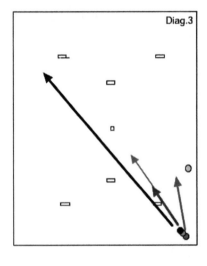

NOTES

Diags 1 & 2 show the promotion cannon being played from where it is sometimes created soon after the start of a game: on the east border, when all four balls have been hit to the east border in the opening turns.

Black will be sent to hoop 1 using a stop-shot action. Blue and red will travel only short distances, with red finishing near the unused yellow ball. Then red can roquet yellow and use a split-shot to send it to H2 while going to H1 where the black ball is still alive, so red can use it to make H1 with a break set up.

In the cannon stroke most players expect red to go further into the lawn, as it would if the black ball were removed and red was playing a normal stop-shot to send blue to H1. But red tends to squirt out sideways at almost a right-angle, staying close to the east border. This is because the full weight of two balls (instead of only one) is squarely in front of red, and therefore the line of swing needs to be only slightly to the right of the line of centres of the three balls.

Diag.3 shows a promotion cannon played from C4 for H2. It needs to be played as a roll stroke rather than a stop-shot. Again the line of swing should be only slightly right of the 3-ball line, and you need to be very careful to avoid red going out over the east border due to the sideways "squirting" effect we have already mentioned.

DISJOINT CANNONS

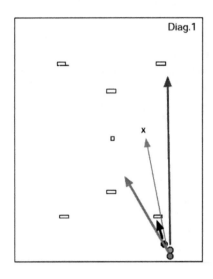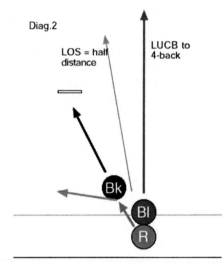

DISJOINT CANNONS

THESE HAVE ALSO been referred to as "delayed", "open", or "pseudo" cannons. They are played as cannons, but are sometimes not considered "true" cannons because they do not involve a "3-ball group", so only the striker's ball can be moved when arranging the balls for the stroke.

Diags 1&2 show a situation where red is for 3-back and has roqueted blue, then measured it onto the yard-line almost in front of the 3-back hoop. The black ball is not a yard-line ball and is about one foot from blue in the direction of the hoop.

The aim here is to play a croquet stroke which will send blue to load 4-back while red runs into black and knocks it close to the 3-back hoop. Few players would think of this in a game situation, and instead would either rush black to the hoop, leaving blue behind; or stop-shot blue to 4-back then turn around, roquet black and roll to the hoop from the yard-line; or send blue just past 3-back, then roquet black and send it to 4-back with a load-and-hold stop-shot.

The disjoint cannon gives a better chance of setting up the immediate break, but is avoided by many players—even by those who think of it—because they do not understand the mechanics of disjoint cannons which are quite different from other cannons and croquet strokes, and need to be specially practised.

The balls are arranged and the stroke played using the as following steps:

1. Place red in contact with blue to send blue to 4-back (see blue arrow in Diag.1).
2. Imagine a line through the centres of red and black, allowing for a slight cut on black if desired, and extend it twice as far as you want to rush black (see red arrow in Diag,1)
3. Find point 'x' on the lawn, halfway between the far ends of these two arrows. This will be the aiming point for the LOS (see grey arrow in Diag.1)
4. Play a croquet stroke (a flat-mallet "roll") which, if the black ball were removed, would send the blue and red balls to the positions indicated by the arrows in Diag.1.

Red will not go where it was aimed, because it will contact black and rush black towards 3-back. The type of swing used needs to be a very flat, and slightly accelerated stroke which will be different from the way most players would normally play a croquet stroke to send the balls those distances. Normally you would probably slope the mallet forward and hit slightly down on the ball, but in the disjoint cannon you must use a stroke that would send the red and blue balls to those places without any forward slope of the mallet-shaft, which should remain vertical.

DISJOINT CANNON MECHANICS

B Y FAR THE most common way that we see players missing opportunities to increase their chances of setting up breaks is in overlooking the possibility of using a disjoint cannon. Every type of cannon we have considered can also be played as a disjoint cannon, often in more than one different way. However they are harder to create than normal cannons and have been seldom taught and therefore are poorly understood.

For these reasons we give the following explanations in the form of questions and answers that we hope will help a player to design and play his own disjoint cannons as opportunities arise.

1. Why should the 3rd ball be no more than a foot away from the croqueted ball?

    Because it is often difficult to control the exact angle at which the striker's ball will come off the croqueted ball when you use the type of flat, accelerated stroke required. In many cases this can cause the striker's ball to miss the 3rd ball you are hoping to rush. Even when they know the correct LOS, many players find it psychologically difficult to avoid such problems by swinging in the required direction. If the angle is narrow (as in the illustrations on the previous page), then a disjoint cannon can be more safely played with the 3rd ball further away—e.g. three feet or even further.—but be wary of trying this with a wide-angle croquet stroke.

2. Why play the stroke as if sending the striker's ball twice as far as the desired rush?

    Because in most cases only about half of the force from the striker's ball will be transferred to the rushed ball, even if the rushed ball is contacted centrally.

3. Why must the swing be flat and the mallet shaft vertical?

    Because in a disjoint cannon any slight tendency for the striker's ball to jump, which would not matter in most croquet strokes, will be likely to result in the striker's ball not making central contact with the rushed ball, and that in turn will cause the rushed ball to fall short of where it is intended to go. This principle also applies, of course, in any type of rush stroke.

COMMON ERRORS IN TECHNIQUE

The following things need to be avoided in disjoint cannons:

(1) Do not swing toward the 3rd (black) ball. If you do, your striker's ball will almost certainly come off at too wide an angle and will miss completely the ball you want to rush.

(2) Do not use a curved swing. Many players, although they are often unaware of it, would use a curved swing in playing the type of croquet stroke needed to send the red and blue balls to the imagined positions if the black ball were removed, with the swing curving toward where they want the striker's ball to go. In a disjoint cannon care must be taken to ensure that the swing and follow-through are straight and remain in the direction of the correctly chosen LOS. Be precise in finding "point x" to determine the LOS. Some players have difficulty accurately judging the position of this aiming point.

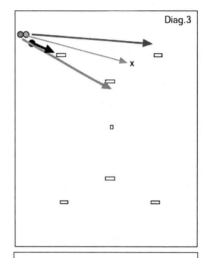

Diag.3

Disjoint cannon from west border for H2-flat three-quarter roll action needed

(3) Do not concentrate on the hoop to which you hope to send the rushed ball. Looking too long at the hoop will tend to make you hit only hard enough to send the croqueted ball that far; but as we have explained, you need to play so as to send it at least twice that distance. Therefore you need to concentrate, not on the hoop, but on the end-point of the imaginary red arrow, and play a stroke that would send the striker's ball to that point while also sending the croqueted ball to load the next hoop.

DISJOINT CANNON EXAMPLES

ERE WE GIVE, with brief notes, some of the many different types of disjoint cannon.

Most disjoint cannons are played for a fairly close hoop. The 3rd (black) ball cannot be moved, so needs to have been in the right place, or else red must rush blue to a suitable place.

Ways of creating disjoint cannons will be further explained in a later section.

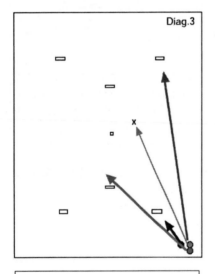

Disjoint cannon from C4 for 3-back-flat accelerated drive action needed.

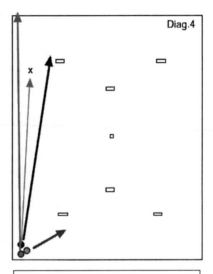

Disjoint cannon from C1 for 1-back-hard, flat drive (take-off) action needed,

In Diag.3 red has rushed blue into C4 and then discovered that when blue was placed on the corner spot it did not quite touch black, which is on the south yard-line. He can play a disjoint cannon similar to the standard C1H1 "right-angle" cannon (in mirror image), but will need some acceleration on the striker's ball.

Diag.4 shows a disjoint "wafer" cannon from C1 for 1-back. Point 'x' is as shown because the imagined red arrow would continue off the lawn and halfway across another lawn. The stroke needs to be hit quite hard.

The disjoint reverse cannon shown in Diag 5 is one of the easier disjoint cannons to play, but must be hit harder than a normal reverse cannon, which we have seen is also often not hit hard enough.

If black is a foot or more from blue (perhaps on the east border, with blue on the C4 spot) then it is possible to use a different disjoint cannon to send blue to H5 while red "cannons" into black and rushes it to H4. However this requires a very pronounced flat pass-roll action which needs practice and is difficult to control.

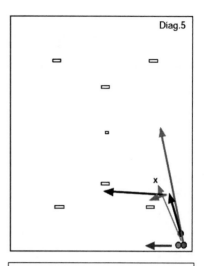

Diag.5

Disjoint cannon from C4 for H4-flat, firm drive action needed,

MORE DISJOINT CANNONS

Please note that in some of the diagrams here and elsewhere in this booklet the exact positions of the balls cannot be accurately represented because of the limits of computer graphics.

It has been necessary to show the balls larger in proportion to the lawn distances than they would be if drawn accurately to scale, and this can sometimes give a distorted impression.

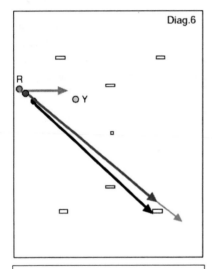

Diag.6

Disjoint cannon to 4th ball from north border for 4-back. Flat drive needed.

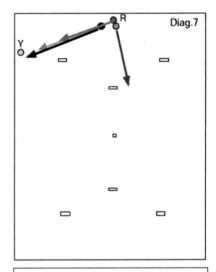

Diag.7

Disjoint promotion cannon to 4th ball from west border for 3-back. Hard drive needed.

In Diag.6 red "promotes" the live black ball to 3-back while going to the unused yellow ball, which will then be used to load 4-back as red goes to make 3-back from black. The stroke needs to be hit hard, and care must be taken that the blue ball does not go out of court and end the turn.

In Diag. 7 red (for 4-back) has roqueted blue on the north border and plays a thick take-off to send blue near penultimate while also rushing black to the unused yellow ball on the west border. Then he will rush yellow to 4-back. The angle between the directions of the blue and black arrows needs to be almost a right-angle, so blue is sent wide, to the east of penultimate, and it is easier if black is not too close to blue when both are on the yard-line.

In Diag. 8 another thick take-off action is used, sending blue to load rover while black is rushed to penultimate. Again the angle is close to a right-angle. A narrower angle is possible, e.g. if the cannon is played from several yards further south, but it would require a pass-roll action, making it very difficult to get enough force into the rush using the necessary flat, accelerated swing.

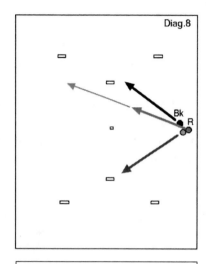

Diag.8

Disjoint cannon from east border for penultimate. Firm, flat drive action needed.Hard drive needed.

CANNON TO DEAD 4TH BALL

THIS TYPE OF cannon is seen by some players as risky. although it is usually not difficult to play.

It involves sending the croqueted ball, rather than the striker's ball, as close as possible to the 4th ball which in this case has already been used.

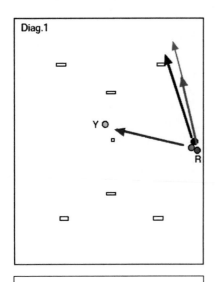

Diag.1	**Diag.2**
Cannon to dead 4th (yellow) ball, played as a 45° equal-distance cannon	Using the two balls after red has made H3, to load H5 and rush blue to H4.

Diags 1&2 illustrate the idea that it is also possible to play a cannon in which the croqueted ball is deliberately sent close to the used 4th ball. Here red is for H3 and has taken off from yellow, leaving it near the peg, and has created a cannon on the east border.

There is no way he can load H4 while rushing a ball to H3, so most players would use a wafer cannon that sends blue a few yards into court. After making H3 they would then need to get a rush on blue to H4.

This is much easier and more certain if blue and yellow are close together, but of course sending blue close to yellow requires the player to be confident of making H3.

In this case it is played as an equal-distance cannon rather like the ones we have seen in previous sections (e.g. the C4H4 cannon).

Diag.3 shows a similar, but longer, cannon. Red is for H5 and has already used yellow. The angle (as seen from C3) between H5 and H6 is too narrow to allow a cannon which rushes black to H5 and also loads H6, so blue is sent close to yellow near 1-back while black is rushed to H5, and after making H5 red does not need a forward rush, but can use the two balls near 1-back to get a rush to H6 and continue the break.

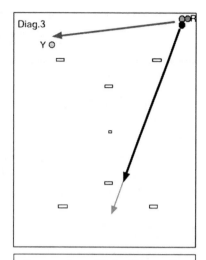

Diag.3

Cannon from C3 for H5, sending blue croqueted ball near dead 4th yellow ball.

IN-LAWN CANNONS

MANY PEOPLE HAVE the idea that cannons can be played only from a corner or the border.

Indeed, such has been the case with all of the cannons we have considered so far. However we often see opportunities missed to play in-lawn (mostly disjoint) cannons, and if proposed changes to the laws go ahead they will be seen more often, though still rarely, in future.

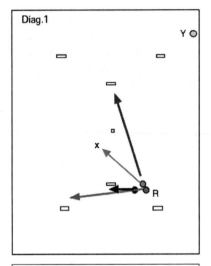

In-lawn disjoint cannon to load H6 and rush to H5. Flat drive needed.

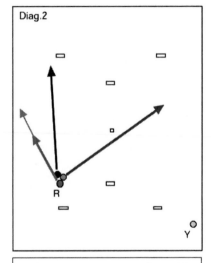

In-lawn cannon to rush to H2 while sending the croqueted ball forward.

Diag.1 shows a type of opportunity that almost every player has missed at least once. Red has roqueted (rushed ?) blue after making H4, and it has come to rest less than a foot east of black. Most players do not realise that they can use a disjoint cannon to quite easily load H6 with blue while knocking black closer to H5.

Diag.2 shows a situation where red has made H1 and roqueted blue, with blue coming to rest in contact with black. Black cannot be moved to arrange the cannon (though it will be able to be moved after the laws are changed in 2008), but it is at least worth checking whether it is placed so as to allow some sort of cannon in which black can be rushed to H2 while blue is more usefully placed than if it were simply left where it is, behind the play.

In Diag.3 red has made H6 and roqueted blue. The player should now use a wide-angle stop-shot to send blue to 2-back while also rushing black closer to 1-back. With some practice this should be safer than using a normal stop-shot to load 2-back, followed by a 5-6 yard roquet back on black which will knock black further from 1-back instead of closer.

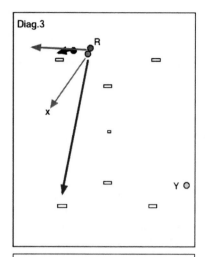

In-lawn disjoint cannon to load 2-back and rush to 1-back. Played as a thick take-off.

BOMBARDMENT

USE OF TERMS.

COACHES ARE SOMETIMES asked about the difference between a "cannon", a "promotion", and a "bombardment". These terms are not clearly defined and are used with varying meanings in different places.

CANNON: This usually refers to a stroke involving a 3-ball or 4-ball "group" of balls as defined in the Laws. However we have used the term in this booklet to include various other strokes such as "disjoint" cannons, "promotion cannons" and "in-lawn" cannons which do not fulfill the definition of a "group of balls" as required under the laws. Some people also say things such as: "Red hit yellow, and yellow cannoned into black, sending it through the hoop". Here they are using the term "cannoned" as it is used in the game of billiards.

PROMOTION: This term is most often (but not always) used with connotations of moving a ball, without actually roqueting it, to a more favourable position—usually loading the hoop you want to make.

Diag.1 shows three balls on the A-baulk yard-line in front of H1, spaced about a foot apart. If red is for H4, the player of red can rush yellow onto black at an angle which will cause black to go to H4, and remain alive. Then the player can measure yellow onto the yard-line and send it to H5 while going to black to make H4, with a break set up.

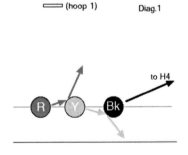

(hoop 1)   Diag.1

to H4

This sort of double-rush is usually referred to as a "promotion" of the black ball, but some would say it is a "bombardment" of black, or that yellow has "cannoned" into black and sent it to H4.

BOMBARDMENT: This term usually has connotations that a ball is moved away from a position where it is in the way or difficult to use. Most shots referred to as

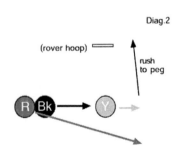

Diag.2

(rover hoop)

rush
to peg

"bombardments" are played over short distances, whereas a cannon or promotion will often involve longer distances.

Diag.2 illustrates a stroke that is often Diag.2 used at the end of a triple peel, after the player of red has peeled yellow through the rover hoop and also made the hoop with red.

He now wants to rush yellow to the peg and peg out both balls, but will have difficulty rushing yellow past the rover hoop to the peg, so he roquets black and uses it as shown to "bombard" yellow away from an awkward position to a more favourable position.

He can use an equal-roll action to send red also into position for the desired rush, or if blue is nearby he can roquet blue and take off to get good position for the rush on the "bombarded" yellow ball to the peg.

MORE BOMBARDMENTS

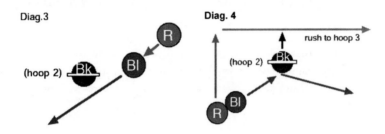

Diag.3

Diag. 4

(hoop 2)

rush to hoop 3

(hoop 2)

IN DIAGS 3&4 black had stuck in H2. Red is for H3 and has taken off to the opponent's balls, hoping to roquet black and get a rush on blue to H3. He finds that he cannot roquet black, so he rushes blue to a position where he can use it to bombard black through the hoop (giving black the hoop), while sending red where he will then be able to rush black to H3.

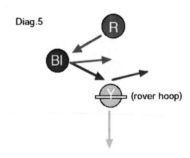

Diag.5

(rover hoop)

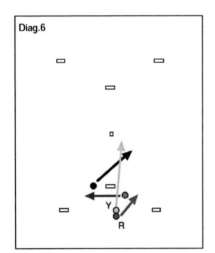

Diag.6

These shots need practice because it is easy to forget that only about half of the force

In Diag.5 the player of red is finishing a triple peel. He has attempted to peel yellow, but it stayed in the rover hoop. He can now either use a half-jump to send yellow through the hoop as he makes it himself; or, if there is an unused ball (blue) nearby, he can roquet it and use it to bombard yellow out of the hoop while making position with red to run the hoop.

Diag.7

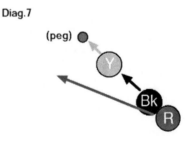

(peg)

from the croqueted ball in transferred in the bombardment, so red often goes too far. A stop-shot action is usually needed.

In Diags 6&7 the player of red has made rover, but in doing so unfortunately roqueted yellow and now finds that the rover hoop prevents him from pegging out yellow in the croquet stroke. So he sends yellow as close to the peg as he can, then rushes blue to black and black to a position where he can use black to bombard yellow onto the peg, after which he will use his last stroke to peg red out and finish the game.

CREATING AND USING CANNONS

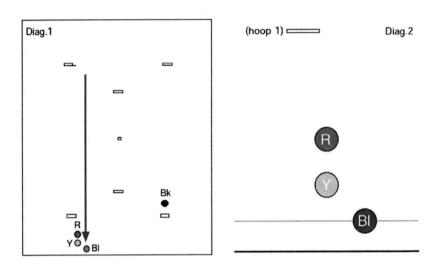

Diag.1

(hoop 1)

Diag.2

Bk

R

Y

Bl

R

Y

Bl

DIAGS 1&2 SHOW a common type of game situation where all clips are still on H1. Your red and yellow balls are set up near A-baulk in front of H1, with a rush in to H1. Black is at H4. Blue was at H2, but has just shot at your balls and missed (see Diag.1). Diag.2 is not drawn to scale, as the balls are shown much larger than they actually would be in relation to the lawn distances. It is intended to show that blue is now on the yard-line, yellow is about one foot in-lawn from blue, and red is a foot further in-lawn.

If you were red and yellow, and it is now your turn, how would you proceed?

Most players would choose between the following four options:

(1) Play yellow, roquet blue, and send it a short distance into the lawn while getting a rush on red to H1. Make H1 with a rush to either blue, black or H2, and gradually try to establish a break.

(2) Play yellow, roquet blue, use a stop-shot to send it to H2, then turn around, roquet red and roll with it for H1 with a break established if you are successful.

(3) Play yellow, rush red to H1, then take off back to blue and send it to H2 using a load-and-hold stop-shot. (Or similarly, roquet blue, put it at H1, and play the load-and-hold stop-shot with red.)

(4) Play yellow, roquet blue, send it to H2 with a split-shot in which yellow goes to black at H4, then (if you fail to get a rush back to red) take off back to red and make H1.

Many players are surprised when a coach suggests that there are these four different ways of continuing that should all be considered before deciding on one of them. They will usually need some prodding before they can think of the four ways.

Some players will consider the possibility of creating a cannon, but even the most experienced and skillful players are likely to be astonished when told that there are at least seven different ways they can create and use a type of cannon in this situation, and almost all of them will give a better chance of establishing an immediate break than any of the four alternatives listed above, though some of the cannons would need to have been practised previously so that you know how to play them and can do so with confidence.

We shall illustrate and describe these seven different cannons, which are all similar to cannons we have seen on previous pages. The important point we are making here is not that you are wrong if you fail to create and use a cannon in this situation, but that if, when confronted with such situations, you do not give consideration to the various cannon possibilities in addition to the continuations that do not involve cannons, then you are very likely missing opportunities to make things easier for yourself and increase your chances of winning games by setting up breaks.

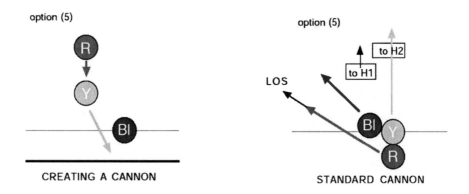

Continuing from the situation illustrated on the previous page, on this page and the next two pages we will examine the cannon possibilities that the player of red and yellow should consider in addition to the four possible options we have already given.

In such a situation the obvious (or maybe not so obvious) way to create a cannon is to play red and rush yellow out (or into the yard-line area) behind blue (see 1st Diag. above).

(5) If yellow, when measured in, touches blue, then you will have created a true cannon and can arrange it by moving the blue ball. However the cannon will be played from the yard-line almost directly in front of H1, so you will not be able to send blue closer than about 5 yards from H1, since we have seen that the minimum angle for a standard cannon is about 45° (see 2nd Diag.) above. In order to achieve the minimum angle and avoid sending the blue ball too far, you will need to change the LOS and play it as a wide-angled stop-shot so that red just clips the edge of the blue ball. If care is not taken there is a possibility that red could fail to roquet blue and will end the turn by going out.

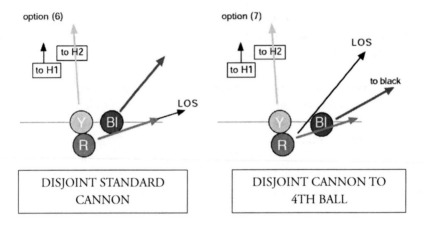

DISJOINT STANDARD
CANNON

DISJOINT CANNON TO
4TH BALL

(6) If yellow is measured onto the yard-line west of blue and very close to it but not touching it, then a disjoint standard cannon similar to option (5) is possible. Again the minimal angle is needed (see Diag.).

(7) If yellow is measured in a little further from blue, then a good cannon possibility is shown in the Diag., where blue is rushed to the black ball which will then be rushed back to make H1. As with all long cannons, this one needs to be hit very hard and with the correct LOS.

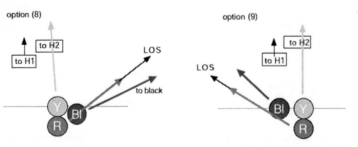

"WAFER" CANNON TO 4TH BALL

DISJOINT "RIGHT-ANGLE"
CANNON

John Riches and Wayne Davies

(8) Rushing blue to the black ball near H4, and then rushing black back to H1, was also possible in a standard "wafer" cannon when yellow was measured in touching blue and you could move the blue ball to arrange the cannon. This is illustrated in the Diag. and is similar to the C2H1 cannon.

If you have to play a disjoint cannon, and so cannot move the blue ball, then this possibility of rushing blue to black and loading H2 with yellow in the same stroke (as in option.6) will depend on the closeness of the yellow ball to the blue ball.

(9) If the yellow ball is yard-lined east of the blue ball, but not touching it, then the only possible useful cannon will again be the disjoint standard ("right-angle") cannon similar to the C1H1 cannon (see Diag.), but played as a wide-angle stop-shot as we saw in options (5) and (6). Here the angle is slightly better than in option (5) because you are playing the cannon from a position which is slightly east of the line of H1 and H2.

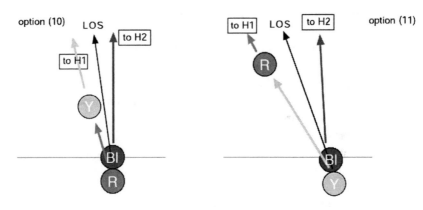

STANDARD DISJOINT CANNON   STANDARD DISJOINT CANNON

(10) A standard disjoint cannon can be created by playing red and gently roqueting blue instead of yellow. Then blue is sent to H2 while red runs into yellow and knocks ("cannons" or "promotes" or "bombards") yellow closer to H1. This is probably the best cannon to use in the situation we have been considering, provided you know how to play it as explained on an earlier page.

(11) A similar cannon could also be created by playing yellow and roqueting blue (see Diag.); but with the 3rd (red) ball a further foot away, it becomes slightly more difficult to control.

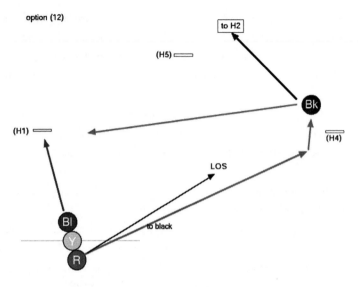

option (12)

(H5)

to H2

(H1)

(H4)

Bk

LOS

Bl

Y

R

to black

PROMOTION CANNON TO 4TH BALL

(12) In the situation we have being considering, if the player of red succeeds in rushing yellow out directly behind blue, so that when yard-lined the yellow ball will be touching the blue ball, there is yet another possibility as illustrated in the above Diag. This is probably the one that many players will find easiest to use because it can be played with (more or less) a normal takeoff action using a flat mallet swing that does not require much more force than a normal take-off.

The three balls are placed in a straight line to H1, and by playing a "thick take-off" to the black ball it is not difficult to "promote" the unused blue ball to H1. Then you can simply roquet black and use a standard split-shot to send black to H2 while red goes back to make H1 from the unused blue ball.

Most players should concentrate on sending the blue ball close to H1 rather than trying to get a rush on black. The angle between the paths of the red and blue balls will be almost a rightangle, and it is not possible to make the angle narrower as could be done in a normal take-off by standing further forward and hitting down on the red ball with the mallet sloping forward.

A "disjoint promotion cannon to the 4th ball" similar to this could be played if either red or yellow had roqueted blue, but there would be a gap between the roqueted blue ball and the 3rd ball.

So we have seen that there were at least 12 reasonable continuations from our starting position of Diag.1. How many of them would you (or other players in your club) have considered before choosing the option to use in a game? In the games of most players there will occur several opportunities to use cannons by deliberately creating them in ways similar to those explained above. And if you fail in an attempt to create a true cannon (group of balls), there will in most cases be options of disjoint cannons that you can use. But remember: you will need to spend time practising most of these cannons before you use them in an important game.

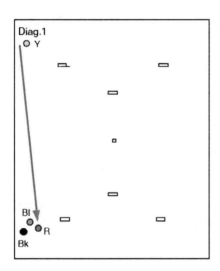

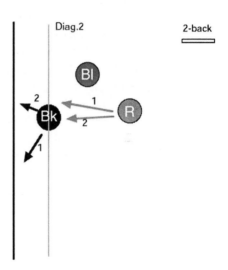

Diag. 1 shows a situation where red is for 2-back and has taken off from yellow to the opponent's balls on the west border north of C1. An enlarged representation of the resulting position is shown in Diag.2, where the player of red must decide how to continue.

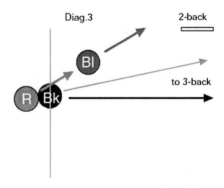

From this position red cannot cut-rush blue to the border behind black so as to create a standard cannon; and even if he could, the angle between the directions of 2-back and 3-back will be too narrow to allow him to load 3-back with black while rushing blue any closer to 2-back than about 5 yards. If he has just made 1-back and given a lift, this would be a dangerous course of action.

So he will do better to roquet black, and in doing so will have two options, as shown in Diag.2:

(1) He can try to cut-rush black as far as he can toward C1 (see arrows numbered '1'), then use a stop-shot to send black a few yards toward 2-back, intending to rush blue to a suitable position from which he can use a "load-and-hold" shot to send blue to 3-back while obtaining position with red to run 2-back. This is not a high percentage option, and would again be considered risky by most players, especially if they have given a lift.

(2) He can roquet black where it is, or, if desired, cut it into the yard-line area a little closer to blue, so as to create the possibility of playing the disjoint cannon shown in Diag.3 (see arrows marked '2'). This is a situation where it pays the player to deliberately create a disjoint cannon rather than a standard (or "true") cannon, as in the disjoint cannon blue can be sent much closer to the 2-back hoop than could be achieved in a standard cannon from this position. Therefore, if he wants to continue the break, the disjoint cannon involves less risk and is the safest option - provided the player knows how to line up and play the disjoint cannon correctly, choosing the correct LOS and using a flat, accelerated action with the bottom hand well down the mallet shaft. It should be remembered that a double-hit in a disjoint cannon caused by making the roquet is not a fault.

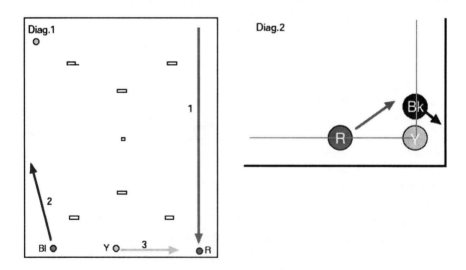

A player who has practised playing cannons can make use of his ability in many ways. For example, he can use an opening strategy designed to create cannon opportunities.

Diag.1 shows the first three turns of a "4th-corner opening" where red is hit from B-baulk to the south border about 2 feet west of C4, then if blue goes to a tice position on the west border, yellow will be hit into C4 without attempting to roquet red, and placed on the corner spot. This dares black to shoot at red, knowing that, if he misses, the player of red will probably find it easy to create a standard C4H1 cannon in C4 in the 5th turn (see Diag.2)

Blue could alternatively have shot at red in the 2nd turn, in which case yellow can shoot at a double target from A-baulk if there is one, or, if blue goes out in the corner, yellow can be hit about 4-5 yards north of H4 (see Diag.3). Then, if black shoots at the balls near C4 and misses, red can again create a "true" cannon, and can play a promotion cannon to the 4th (yellow) ball which has been conveniently placed for that very purpose (see Diag.4).

It can be considered a rather risky opening, but if you are confident in playing these

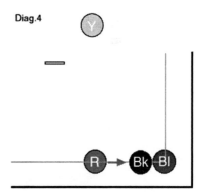

cannons (see earlier explanations), and your opponent has not practised them, then for players below international level it can offer the first player a chance to obtain the first break which is as good as, or better than, he normally gets in a standard opening,

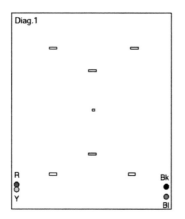

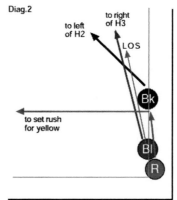

In Diag.1 red (for 4-back) has roqueted yellow (for H2). Red does not want to make 4-back, but wants to set up to give yellow the best possible chance of establishing a break if the opponent fails to roquet. The way to do this is to send one opponent ball left of H2 and the other to the right of H3, with yellow having a rush to either H2 or H3.

If you do not have a good enough stop-shot to send one of the opponent balls to one of these positions, then turn around and roquet the other, then you can instead create a cannon.

Sometimes a "true" cannon can be created by rushing one opponent ball out behind the other, but more often you will need to create a disjoint cannon in which you do not need to send the 3rd (black) ball anywhere in particular, since as long as you roquet it you can send it where you want it in a split-shot as red returns to set the desired rush for yellow. Diags 2&3 show two possible disjoint cannons, and Diag.4 shows the final "ideal leave" set up for yellow.

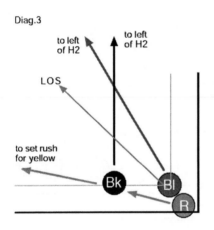

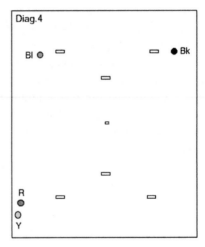

NOTES FOR COACHES

THE COACH NEEDS to realise that there is not a lot of value (unless learning to play cannons is seen as an enjoyable end in itself) in teaching a player how to play cannons unless he also understands how to use them in his games. This is something that many players will need to be taught, as they will not think for themselves of all the ways to use cannons, even after they have been taught to play them confidently.

The coach should choose the right time in the player's development to teach each particular type of cannon, and will need to get the player practising each cannon from as many different court and hoop situations as possible. There are many more situations and variations of cannons than we have been able to cover in this booklet.

It is understandable that some coaches have avoided spending much time teaching cannons, since cannons occur only infrequently in games, and valuable coaching time would often be better spent on other things.

The most useful type of cannon is the disjoint cannon, but as we have seen, there are different varieties of disjoint cannon, of which some require the player to learn a new technique for playing the stroke that takes time to learn and carries with it the possibility of adversely affecting the player's normal swing technique.

The player should start with the simpler disjoint cannons, and keep to ones where he wants to make the nearest hoop and load a distant one, so that he can use a more or less normal flat swing without needing to put his hand down near the mallet head and accelerate the mallet as it contacts the striker's ball. The angle involved between the hoop he wants to make and the hoop he wants to load should be as small as possible until he gains confidence and can attempt wider angles with the 3rd ball further away.

The value of using disjoint cannons to set up "ideal leaves" can be appreciated by the player only after he has the ability to establish and maintain a break once he has set it up, and after he has been taught the various important "ideal leaves" and how to use them. Players and coaches who need such information will find it in other publications by John Riches, e.g. "Croquet: next Break Strategy", "Croquet: Lessons in Tactics", and "Croquet: The Teaching of Tactics". These are (or soon will be) available for downloading from the Oxford Croquet website, or can be found together with other of our writings on our own website at :

"www.croquetprofessionals.com"

Some coaches "teach" cannons only occasionally as an interest-creator, giving a quick demonstration and then moving on to things they consider more important. This use of a new type of cannon as an "attention-grabbing gimmick" is valid in coaching, but of course the player is unlikely afterward to be able to either play the cannon, or understand how to use it in his games. The idea is that if the coach says "Come out an hour early next Saturday morning and I will show you how to play more accurate take-offs", few will be interested enough to come out because they think they already know how to play take-offs; but if he says, "Come out early next Saturday and I will show you some new cannons", they are more likely to be interested. Then he demonstrates an unusual type of cannon, lets them practise it for 10 minutes, and says, "Right! You can practise the cannon further on your own anytime and let me know if you need more help with it. Now, let's look at ways of improving our take-offs".

In conclusion, we say in all sincerity that we hope those who have read this booklet will make the effort and take the time to learn to play the various cannons with confidence, and that they will gain as much enjoyment from implementing the various ideas as we have gained from the researching and documenting of them.

. . . John Riches and Wayne Davies

CROQUET

ERROR CORRECTION

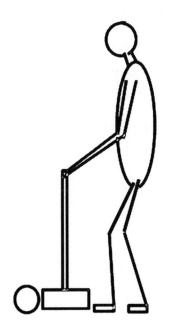

CONTENTS

INTRODUCTION

THESE NOTES ON error correction are intended primarily for use as part of the ACA coach-training courses. Parts of them will be covered in courses at various levels of coach training.

I previously wrote a booklet named "Croquet: Error Correction". These notes represent an updating and (very amateurishly) illustrated version of that booklet, and adopt a quite different approach. Whereas the booklet approached the science of error correction from the viewpoint of the player and what he observes going wrong, these notes approach it from the viewpoint of the coach and the particular error. The player notices that he is missing his roquets consistently on the right-hand side, but has no idea why. The coach notices that the player is swinging across the line and realises that this error will result in roquets being missed consistently to one side.

The coach must be aware that players come in a wide variety of packaging, and they can vary in many ways besides their stature, physical strength and intelligence.

Some players will have the ability to judge spatial relationships and angles, while others will not. Some will be playing croquet as a competitive sport with a burning desire to improve and win as many games as they can as quickly as possible, while others will be playing mainly for social reasons. Some will have a sensitive nature which is easily offended, while others will have a thick skin and will never take offence. Some will have a well-developed sense of humour and be able to laugh at themselves, while others will not appreciate attempts at off-hand humour or put-downs.

An even more important distinction from a coaching viewpoint is the one between "intuitive" or "natural" players and players to whom nothing comes right naturally and have to learn the correct technique one step at a time, making many mistakes along the way. Most top players fall into the first category of "intuitive" players, rather than the latter category of "technicians"; but it may be some comfort to those of us who are somewhat lacking in natural intuitive ability to know that as a general rule it is the technicians who make better coaches. The intuitive player often does not know what he is doing, nor why he is doing it. When he swings his mallet he does not think about how he should be doing it or why he should do it that way; he just does it more or less automatically—and gets it right most of the time. The technician has to work on his game patiently, getting one thing right and then another. He makes many mistakes along the way and learns how to correct them, and this means that he is in a better position to help others—unless perhaps they are intuitive players.

In actual fact, all of us are partly "intuitive" and partly "technical" (I am using "technical" here as to some extent a euphemism for "plodders"), but everyone can improve if they are willing to take advice and work at it.

Some people like to settle into a routine and stay there, needing a lot of convincing before they will attempt anything new; while others are always wanting to experiment, try out new ideas and question the prevailing wisdom. The latter type will not need convincing to try out something different, but they are more likely to need convincing that it is worth persevering with, as they will be less likely to simply accept that it is desirable because the coach says so.

Croquet was apparently never intended to be an easy game, and croquet coaching is not something one can expect to pick up easily either. There will always be more to learn. New and better ways of coaching (and in particular error correction) are constantly being developed—or at least they should be—and a fully trained coach at any level must realise that he can expect to improve as he coaches more different types of player, and he needs to keep up to date with the latest in coaching literature and coaching methods.

We are hoping that coaches will be keen to not only put into practice the ideas explained in the following pages, but also to question them, work out possible improvements, trial new methods of coaching, then document and share the knowledge.

We have referred to croquet coaching as a "science", and like any other science it is not just a matter of learning the current wisdom and applying it; it should involve a dynamic progression in a widely expanding field of knowledge. As we have commented elsewhere on various occasions, there is no doubt that the science of croquet coaching is very much in its infancy.

. . . John Riches.

1. ROQUETS

a. Misalignment

THIS SHOULD BE regarded as an error in technique, as it is almost certain to result in inconsistent roqueting.

If the mallet is not pointing in the direction of the target when it contacts the ball, the ball will usually not travel toward the target as desired.

The coach will be able to detect this error readily if he stands at least 10 yards in front of the player and behind the target[see Diag.1], and the player will have noticed that when he misses roquets it is almost always to the same side. If the player is asked to align his mallet as he would to roquet the target ball, then leave it standing on the ground and walk back several paces to look at its alignment, he too will immediately see that it is not pointing toward the target ball. [Note: it will not help the player to do this each time he wants to line up a roquet, because as soon as he picks up his mallet to swing it, the mallet will no longer be aligned correctly. The correction process, as explained below, is not as easy as that]

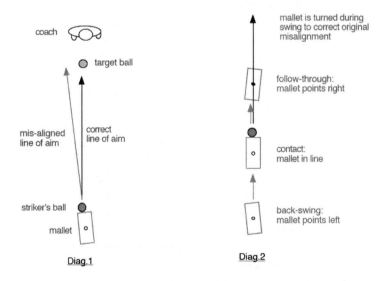

coach

target ball

mis-aligned line of aim

correct line of aim

striker's ball

mallet

Diag.1

mallet is turned during swing to correct original misalignment

follow-through: mallet points right

contact: mallet in line

back-swing: mallet points left

Diag.2

However, many players manage to roquet reasonably well with a misaligned mallet. They achieve this in either of two ways:

(1) They may straighten the alignment as they swing forward and bring the mallet down onto the ball [see Diag.2].

This requires exact timing because the mallet is gradually turning as it swings forward, and will be in the exact required alignment for only a very short period of time, which needs to coincide with the instant it contacts the ball. It is likely that the player will have learnt to coordinate the turning of his mallet so that the alignment is corrected during the swing provided the swing is a normal one of the type he most often uses. This means he is likely to roquet reasonably well at middle distances (say, 10-15 yards), but if he has to swing noticeably faster or slower than usual the timing is less likely to be correct, and the mallet is likely to be still misaligned when it contacts the ball.

Thus he is likely to miss longer roquets and have difficulty controlling the direction of long rushes. Some players who do this also miss short roquets if they try to hit them gently so as not to send the roqueted ball too far. Interestingly, their hoop running may not be noticeably affected unless they try to run the hoop gently, as they will have learnt that for hoop running they need to use the normal swing that they would use for a 10-15 yard roquet. This, of course, means that occasionally they will run the hoop without touching the sides, and go through the hoop much further than intended.

Correction of misalignment:
This can be a difficult error to eliminate, especially if, as is likely, the player is actually committing two errors of technique (misaligning and turning the mallet during the swing) which counteract each other. Correcting only one of the errors is likely to make things worse; and it is usually not worth trying to do anything unless the player is willing to work with the coach for several sessions over (say) at least 2-3 weeks.

Place the balls 8-10 yards apart, stand behind the target ball, then ask the player to stalk the striker's ball and place his mallet on the ground so that it is aligned with the target. (Check that he goes back and stalks in the correct line; some players are unable to do this without help.) While standing over the ball most players find that what looks to be a straight alignment may be a foot or more off to one side of the target. The coach should indicate with his mallet or foot where the mallet is actually pointing, and ask the player to correct the alignment, then go back and stalk again, trying this time to place the mallet with a more correct alignment. He may need to do this many times before he can manage to get it right it consistently. On some occasions, when the mallet is correctly aligned, ask the player to play the shot. If he has been turning the mallet during the swing, he will probably now start missing on the other side of the target ball from the side he was missing on before.

His brain needs to be re-trained to perceive as straight an alignment which previously it has been thinking was off-target; and then the muscles need to be trained to sing the mallet without turning it, because there will no longer be any need to turn the mallet when it starts from a correctly aligned position.

The back-swing needs to be slowed down so that the player can watch it carefully to check that the mallet remains in what has now been established as the correct alignment, and most players find it also helps to use a low and long follow-through. Occasionally a slight alteration in the stance may be needed, as explained under later headings. After watching the straight back-swing, at the start of the forward swing the player should fix his eyes on the back of the ball where the mallet will contact it.

The player can practise between coaching sessions with the help of any willing partner who can indicate whether or not he has the mallet aligned correctly. It can also be useful to practice swinging in front of a long mirror, or along a line marked on the ground, or between two straight lengths of wood, e.g. two broom-handles.

The coach must check later whether the player's roqueting has improved, and may need to work with him for further sessions, or try different approaches, until the player can walk up to the ball, place his mallet down with correct alignment, and then swing the mallet back and forth, keeping it correctly aligned.

b. Swinging across the line

This also not an error in technique and need not concern the coach too much. Contrary to what one would expect, the ball will go where the mallet is pointing, and swinging across does not drag it off-line as one might imagine it would. You can test this by placing a target ball 4-5 yards away, aligning the mallet carefully, and keeping it aligned while swinging across the line at a wide angle—even up to 80 degrees from the correct alignment. Your ball will still hit

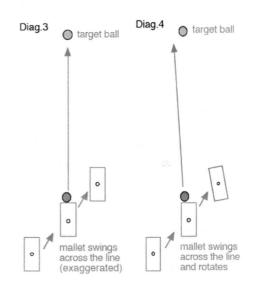

the target, and if you swing across from left to right (see Diag. 3) it may even miss on the left side of the target, not the right as you would expect. This is because the impact is likely to occur toward the left edge of the mallet face rather than in the centre, causing the mallet-head to rotate in an anticlockwise direction (see Diag.4).

Correction of swinging across the line
You could try rotating your bottom hand slightly around the handle, so that the palm of the hand is more directly behind the shaft and your elbow is closer in to

your side (which means you may need your hands further out away from your body). Some players find this helps them to swing the mallet straighter, but it does not suit everyone.

A better method of correcting this error is to take a much slower backswing so that you can watch the mallet go back, checking that it remains in the correct line of swing. If it starts in line, it is more likely to still be in line when it contacts the ball.

When the mallet reaches the top of the backswing, you must transfer your eyes to the point on the ball where you will contact it with the mallet-face, and keep them there during the forward swing.

c. *Twisting the mallet-head prior to impact*

Players sometimes explain a missed roquet by saying: "I twisted the mallet." They say this because they felt the mallet twist in their hands, and/or saw that the head finished up pointing away from the line of swing. The twisting that they notice can occur in various ways and for different reasons, and the coach may need to watch very closely from either behind or in front of the player to see at what stage of the swing the twisting occurs.

If the mallet is twisting out of alignment just before it reaches the ball, it is caused by the player suddenly tightening his grip as the mallet comes onto the ball.

The player will not be aware that he is tightening his grip, nor of its effect, and will usually need to be convinced. One method that usually helps is to ask him to stand up straight and hold his mallet with one hand only, straight out in front of his body, so that the mallet hangs with the head of the mallet not touching the ground. Then ask him to watch for any movement of the mallet head as he tightens the grip on the mallet without moving any other muscles (see Diag.5).

Most players will notice some movement—usually a slight rotation either clockwise or anticlockwise—and will be able to understand what is likely to happen if they align the mallet-head correctly and then suddenly tighten the grip during the swing before it reaches the ball.

It is interesting that many players also find if they repeat this exercise while holding the mallet with the elbow a little higher (more out to the side), the mallet-head may rotate in the opposite direction! The exercise can also be repeated with the other hand, or both hands, on the shaft; and with the player adopting the type of stance he uses when addressing the ball.

Some players will notice very little or no movement in the mallet-head as they tighten the grip, and it is likely that they have found, without realising it, a position for the hands that allows them to tighten the grip without altering the alignment of the mallet-head.

Correction of mallet-twisting before impact
The obvious answer is to refrain from tightening the grip during the swing, but for most people this is not so easy to do.

The player should start by gripping the mallet with the tension he wants to use for the swing. For most shots the grip should be quite firm, but the player should avoid using a "white-knuckle death grip". The idea of this is to have the grip tight enough that it will not be possible to make it much tighter during the swing.

Some players can use a more relaxed grip and manage to resist the temptation to tighten it during the swing, and they do this by keeping the shoulder and upper-arm muscles relaxed also.

Some players like to use a less tight grip for gentle shots, as there is then less psychological pressure to tense the muscles in an effort to get more force into the stroke; but many find it better to keep the tight grip for all strokes except stop-shots.

In long rushes most players find it especially difficult not to tighten the grip, and also for hoop-running in a tense situation. d. *mallet-head twisting on impact*

When the mallet-head twists as it contacts the ball, it is not the player who is ding it. The twisting is caused by an off-centre impact and needs to be handled quite differently.

The further off-centre the impact is on the mallet-face, the more twisting will occur; and of course the more likely it is that the ball will be sent off-line sufficiently to ruin the stroke.

A player needs to train himself to fix his eyes on a particular point (usually the back of the ball) and swing his mallet in such a way that the centre of the mallet-face moves directly toward the point he is looking at. The is the most difficult thing in croquet to do, and for most players it takes a long time to train the muscles to bring about the desired result, especially if they do not use a consistent stance and grip.

Correction of mallet-head twisting on impact
First, the player needs to fix his eyes on the back of the ball where he wants the mallet to contact it.

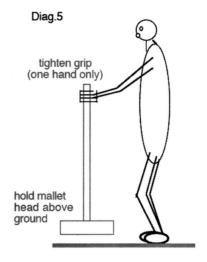

Diag.5

tighten grip (one hand only)

hold mallet head above ground

It is best to practise central contacts using a long, slow backswing; and it does not help much to practise (for example) "roqueting" the peg from the side border of the court, as everything happens too fast to see what is happening.

The player will find it easier if the mallet-shaft is vertical as we have already seen, and he should concentrate on keeping the mallet correctly aligned during the follow-through as well as during the back-swing. Practising a consistent stance and grip may also be necessary.

It is also important to avoid using a loose grip. The importance of this is not that a loose grip makes it harder to achieve a central contact on the mallet-face, but that if the contact is very slightly off-centre, a loose grip will allow the mallet to twist too easily. An over-lapping or interlocking grip can also make it more difficult to prevent even a slight off-centre impact from twisting the mallet.

e.   pushing with the bottom hand

This error in technique is very common, and is almost always combined with other errors such as taking too short a back-swing and hurrying both the back-swing and the forward swing.

It is especially common in players who use a hands-apart grip. The hands-apart grip is not an error in itself, but most players find it very difficult to resist the temptation to push with the bottom hand when their hands are noticeably apart on the mallet shaft.

Pushing with the bottom hand means that the player is using too much wrist action, and this will be easily observed from the side—the wrists will turn as he swings, instead of remaining more or less locked in position (see Diags. 6 and 7).

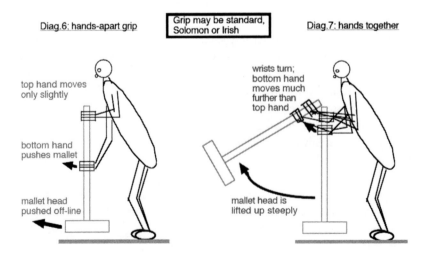

Diag.6: hands-apart grip

Grip may be standard, Solomon or Irish

Diag.7: hands together

top hand moves only slightly

bottom hand pushes mallet

mallet head pushed off-line

wrists turn; bottom hand moves much further than top hand

mallet head is lifted up steeply

Correction of pushing with the bottom hand

The player needs to learn to move both hands forward together horizontally at the same speed, at least during the bottom part of the swing in which the mallet will contact the ball.

Because of the way the human body is constructed, some players find this easier if they use an over-lapping or interlocking grip, and for them this advantage may outweigh the disadvantage of such grips explained in the previous section.

However, unless the grip is obviously one that will not allow a smooth swing, asking a player to change his grip is seldom a wise method of correcting any error.

In this case the coach should place a ball on the yard-line and another ball (the striker's ball) about 3 yards in court. Ask the player to roquet the yard-line ball as follows: He must take a long, slow back-swing and a long, slow follow-through, reaching forward as far as he can to keep the mallet-head travelling parallel to the ground as long as possible before it starts to come up.

He should feel that he is playing the stroke essentially with his top hand, and it may help to make some practice swings with only the top hand on the mallet shaft. He should feel that both hands are moving forward together, in a deliberate action while the wrists are kept firm (see Diag.8).

This low follow-through is easier if the player uses a step-stance rather than a level stance, unless the player is quite tall and/or has a reasonable amount of weight concentrated around his rear section (as is rather common in good croquet players).

The reason for this is that some transfer of weight toward the back is needed to counter-balance the weight of the mallet and arms when they are extended forward, so a lightly built player with a level stance can tend to either step forward during the swing, or achieve a backward shift of weight by bending his knees or bending at the waist.

A player with more weight in his backside can counterbalance the forward movement by making only a very slight and almost imperceptible movement of his rear-end mass.

The player is more likely to push with his bottom hand if he uses a very tight grip, but the coach should be wary about asking the player to loosen his grip too much. As we have already seen, the are some advantages in using a tight grip, as well as possible disadvantages. He may find it easier to avoid pushing with the bottom hand if he uses a step-stance rather than a level stance.

Whatever the stance, the shaft should be held firmly with the fingers rather than tightly in the palms of the hands.

Grip tension can be very important, but unfortunately it is something the coach cannot see.

A grip that is too loose will be likely to lead to him using too much wrist to propel the mallet forward, and a grip that is too tight can result in pushing with the bottom hand. It is important that both hands move forward together, avoiding wrist rotation, more or less as illustrated in Diag.8.

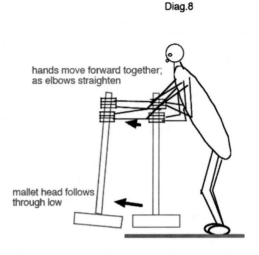

Diag.8

hands move forward together; as elbows straighten

mallet head follows through low

(use weight of mallet)The player must learn to use the weight of the mallet (plus the weight of his arms), assisted by gravity, to swing the mallet with a long, relaxed and slow pendulum-like movement, but staying low in the follow-through rather than coming up.

f.   Hurried back-swing and/or forward swing

Hurrying the swing—or part of it—is one of the most common errors among croquet players at any level. It almost always results in inconsistent roqueting because the player is using many more muscles than he needs to; and the more muscles he uses, the more difficult it will be for him to accurately coordinate them all with exact timing.

Although this problem can occur with any grip it is more likely with players using an Irish grip; quite common with those who use a standard grip; and less common with players using a Solomon grip. Interestingly, it is rare among players who play side-style.

The best timing for the roquet swing resembles the swing of a grand-father clock pendulum, or the way an elephant swings its trunk—very slow and unhurried. There is a natural timing ("period") for a pendulum of any given length, and it is best to use a long pendulum, swinging from the shoulders with the arms acting as an extension of the mallet shaft. It is possible to gain extra power by using a double-pendulum action, with a second pivot at the wrists, but it is hard enough to control accurately a single pendulum, and the second one can introduce problems with direction if the wrists do not hinge (un-cock to turn) at exactly the same rate, as well as problems with timing due to the difficulty of ensuring that the mallet shaft is vertical and the mallet head is travelling horizontally when it contacts the ball. (see Diag.9)

Correction of a hurried swing
To avoid the complications introduced by a pronounced double-pendulum action, the player should use a firm grip and try to keep his wrists more or less locked during the swing.

To overcome the involuntary hurrying of the swing he should use an exercise similar to the one described in the previous section, practising roquets of about 3 yards in length using a long backswing and long, low follow-through. This should be done by roqueting a ball on the yard-line so that neither ball leaves the court (see Dia. 10). At first he will find this difficult using the full swing, as it will require him to perform the whole swing much slower and more deliberately than he has been doing.

When he can do this confidently, place his ball 2-3 feet in front of a hoop and lie a mallet on the ground 2 yards behind the hoop (see Diag.11). Remove the hoop and ask him to hit his ball between the hoop-holes with the same type of full swing so that it stops just short of reaching the mallet. After he has repeated this a number of times, replace the hoop and see if he can do it with the hoop in place and the mallet still in position.

He will then be running the hoop without hurrying the swing, and he will need to practise this many times. In a game, of course, he will not need to use a full swing, but he should use the same timing that he has been practising, with a slow and deliberate back-swing—you can ask him to watch the mallet go back slowly while staying in line—and allowing the mallet to follow through along the ground as an extension of his arms without any attempt to push it forward or use his wrists.

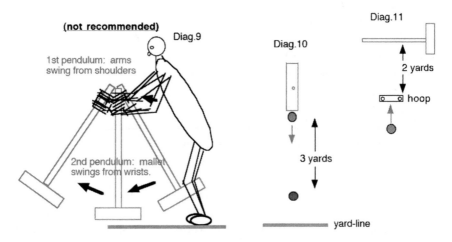

(not recommended)   Diag.9

1st pendulum: arms
swing from shoulders

2nd pendulum: mallet
swings from wrists.

Diag.10

3 yards

yard-line

Diag.11

2 yards

hoop

g. Loose grip

Strictly speaking, it would be incorrect to describe this as an error, and if the player can consistently swing the mallet in a straight line so that the ball is contacted in the centre of the mallet face, it need not cause any difficulties. However few players can do this, and if the ball is not contacted in the centre of the mallet-face the loose grip can allow the impact to result in more twisting than would occur with a tighter grip.

A second consideration is that a loose grip is more likely to allow a double-pendulum action with accompanying difficulties of coordinating wrist rotation and timing, as seen in the previous section.

Correction of a loose grip
If it is decided that a change is needed, the player should not find it difficult to learn to tighten the grip, keep his wrists more rigid (though perhaps not completely locked) and swing from his shoulders rather than his wrists. For many players this will result immediately in more consistent roqueting, though some may need to spend time practising a straight swing until the changed muscle coordination adjusts to their particular stance and swing.

h. Sideways mallet slope

Once again, a sideways mallet slope in itself is not an error, but it can often result in the mallet-face contacting the ball off-centre, which in turn can cause the mallet to twist off-line. In fact, most side-style players play with the mallet shaft leaning quite noticeably sideways, and some manage to roquet quite well.

Players who have a sideways sloping mallet shaft will almost always line up the mallet with the mallet-head resting on the ground, and there is a tendency as soon as they lift the mallet to swing it back for the force of gravity to make the mallet-head swing slightly to the side and hang more vertically underneath the hands, as illustrated in Diag.12.

This will cause the off-centre contact with the ball, and it is common for such players to have learnt over time to turn (twist) the mallet-face slightly so as to counter the twisting effect of the off-centre contact. Thus they are making two "errors", one of which can counteract the other and enable them to hit the roquet; but whenever this sort of thing happens, as it does very frequently with players of all standards, it will mean that the player can roquet consistently only at particular distances.

This is because the amount of twisting needed to correct for the sideways movement due to gravity will vary when the mallet is swung at different speeds to send the ball longer or shorter distances, and the amount of "correction" twisting is likely to remain constant, probably allowing the player to hit middle-distance roquets, but causing

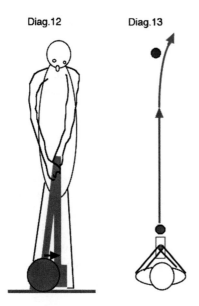

Diag.12   Diag.13

him problems with the longer roquets and also some of his attempted at short roquets.

Another effect of a sideways sloping mallet shaft is subject to debate and disagreement among experts: Some contend that it can impart a spin to the ball which can cause the ball to swerve off-line as it slows down sufficiently for the spin to grip on the lawn surface. For this reason the player will probably have learnt not to play gentle roquets, as by hitting harder he can ensure that the swerving effect due to side-spin on the ball does not start to take effect until after the ball has reached its target.

Other people ridicule this idea and claim that spin on a ball cannot act in this way, as it would have dissipated long before the ball got anywhere near the end of its path, so if a ball curves off its path as it slows down, it will not be due to spin.

It is worth bearing in mind both views, regardless of which is correct.

Correction of Sideways mallet slope

This may not be an easy matter, and first the coach will have to decide whether it is worth trying to correct the mallet slope. It will depend on how much of a problem it is creating for the player.

The reason for the sloping mallet is often connected with the way the player is standing and the eye with which he is sighting. In the illustration on the previous page (Diag. 12) showing a view from the front of the player addressing the ball, if you follow the line of the sloping mallet shaft and extend it upwards, you will see that it will reach the player's left eye, although he is using a right-handed grip with his left hand on top and his right hand underneath. Most right-handed players sight with their right eye, but occasionally you will find a player who is "opposite eyed", or very rarely, one who sights equally with both eyes. (I tell them they are "sighting with their nose"!).

To the player, it appears that his mallet shaft is vertical when in fact it is sloping. If the shaft was vertical it would not be under his dominant (sighting) eye.

You can check which of the player's eyes is dominant by having him point with one finger at a distant object, then close one eye. If the finger still appears to be in line, then the eye that remains open is his dominant eye. If it no longer appears to be in line, he has closed his dominant eye.

Being opposite-eyed can be a disadvantage in croquet for two reasons: (1) it can result in a sloping mallet as shown in the illustrations; and (2) it can mean that if the mallet is swung straight back the mallet shaft will contact the player's thigh (the one under the dominant eye), and to avoid this the player has to swing back around a curve and then find a way of bringing his mallet correctly into line during the forward swing.

This means that for most players whose mallet has a sideways slope, and especially for those who are opposite-eyed, there is a need to change two things—the stance as well as the mallet slope. This can be achieved by asking the player to walk in and take up a stance with the foot under his dominant eye (the left foot for the player in Diag.14) a little further out to the side—about two inches (3 cm) should be sufficient to move the thigh on that side out of the way of a straight backswing. Then he should lean his weight on his other foot (the right foot in the illustration) in order to bring his sighting (left) eye directly over the ball.

Diag.14

Player right-handed but left eye dominant

Player right-handed but left eye dominant

mallet shaft vertical and under dominant eye

left foot moved outward and weight transferred to right foot.

In Diag.14 the blue arrow shows that the player is now standing with his dominant left eye directly over the vertical mallet shaft. The player will need to practise taking up this stance many times, until he can do it almost automatically with thinking about it, in order to ensure that he will get it right in a tense game situation where his mind will probably be on other things.

Then he should watch the mallet swing (slowly) straight back, keeping it in the line of swing, and straight through to contact the ball and follow through low, remaining correctly aligned towards the target ball.

It should be remembered that not all players with sloping mallets will be opposite-eyed, and the problem of having the thigh in the way of a straight back-swing can occur with either step-stance or a level stance.

Whatever the cause of the slope, the coach will need to find a way of helping the player develop a stance and swing that allows the mallet to remain vertical under

John Riches and Wayne Davies

the dominant eye and swing back straight in the desired (extended) line joining the striker's ball and the target.

i.   Cramped swing

Cramping the swing is an error of technique that leads to inconsistent roqueting due to over-use of wrists. If the player addresses the ball with his hands too close to his body, it will not allow his hands to move back and forth freely because they would contact his body. Therefore he has to swing the mallet largely from the wrists instead of from the shoulders.

For most players, depending on their stature, the hands should be about a foot out in front of the body when they address the ball (see Diags 15 and 16), and the trunk should not be too bent over at the waist. It is not good to have your nose almost on the end of the mallet shaft. The elbows should be fairly straight during most of the swing, and the hands should not be clutched in close to the chest.

The hands should move backwards and the forwards quite noticeably with the mallet, and as we have already seen, the arms and mallet should form a single pendulum that swings from the shoulders.

Correction of cramped swing
It sounds easy enough to tell the player that he should stand up straighter and/or keep his hands further out in front of his body, but it is often not so easy to get the player to actually do it in tense game situations. Part of the reason for the cramping is lack of confidence, with the player feeling more secure if he crouches down closer to the ball, especially when he is running a hoop. It is also possible that a short-sighted player may crouch over because when his head is down closer to the ball he can see the outline of the ball more clearly.

The player will be able to stand straighter and move his hands more freely if he can find a way of loosening his shoulder muscles before starting the final swing, and most such players are helped by taking one or two (not too many) loose practice swings, remembering to stand up more, get their hands out in front and keep their wrists firm, before taking the final swing. The practice swings may or may not involve "casting" over the ball, and can be done as a warm-up exercise before the player goes onto the court to start his turn.

Diag.15
cramped stance

elbows too bent

left foot moved outward
and weight transferred
to right foot.

Diag.16
improved stance

elbows straighter

about 1 foot.

j. "Walking"

It is not at all uncommon to see players "walking" or stepping forward as they hit the ball, especially on a long rush, roquet or roll shot. The reason for this is simply that they do it because otherwise they would overbalance and fall forward. The total weight of the forward-moving mallet and arms moves their centre of gravity forward until it is no long directly above their feet, so they become unstable unless some part of the body counterbalances it by moving backwards. The slighter the build of the player, the more difficulty he will have in moving enough weight backward to maintain his equilibrium without it affecting his swing. Some bend their knees, which moves their posterior slightly back, while others achieve the same result, but less effectively, by bending the trunk at the waist. Either of these movements will involve the use of additional muscles that have to be controlled and coordinated. To avoid overbalancing they take a step forward with the forward-swinging mallet, but like bending at the knees or waist, this also results in an unstable platform from which to swing. Some even use the mallet itself as a counter-balance by swinging it right up and backwards over their heads in a highly exaggerated follow-through, but this also is poor technique because the mallet-head needs a long and low follow-through so that the player can see whether or not he is keeping it in line the whole time, and to make the timing of the stroke easier.

Players are more likely to "walk" as they swing if they are slight of build and use a level stance. If you ask a lightly built person with small feet and a level stance to grip the mallet handle with both hands as they would to play a stroke, and then hold the mallet out in front in the position it would reach at the end of their follow-through, they will not be able to do it, and will overbalance forward as illustrated in Diag.17. This should convince them that they need to find a solution to the problem of overbalancing.

Correction of "walking"

The most effective way to solve the problem of overbalancing and walking during the swing is for the player to use a step-stance with one foot well forward of the other. This should immediately enable the player to swing the mallet right through and reach forward with it in the follow-through without overbalancing or needing to step forward (see Diag.18). However it may introduce different difficulties of finding a way to ensure that his hips, and more importantly his shoulders, are consistently taking up a position where they are more or less square to the line of swing.

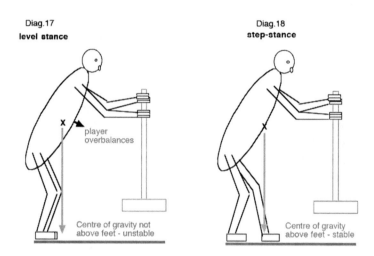

Diag.17
level stance

Diag.18
step-stance

x
player
overbalances

Centre of gravity not
above feet - unstable

Centre of gravity
above feet - stable

k.   Incorrect rear foot placement

Some players take up a stance with one of their feet in the line of swing. They do not realise they are doing this, nor do they realise that the incorrect foot placement causes them (unknowingly) to swing the mallet back around a curve so as to avoid hitting the incorrectly placed foot. This problem is seen surprisingly often, and occurs mainly among players who use a step-stance, although players with a level stance have also been known to do it.

Diag.19 shows how, when the coach views the player from the front and asks him to take up his stance as if addressing a ball, it can be easily seen that if the mallet is swung straight back it will hit the rear foot. This will mean that in order to swing back, the player has to take the mallet around a curve as can be seen in the overhead view illustrated in Diag.20. As the player brings the mallet forward to contact the ball he will need to find a way of bringing it back into the correct line.

[It must be noted that there are world-class players who have used such a curved back-swing, and have managed to roquet extremely well with it, but they do not have their foot placed incorrectly in the line of swing, so there must be a different reason for the curved back-swing.]

Straightening the alignment of the mallet during the forward swing requires accurate and difficult timing, which will vary according to the length of the shot and speed of the mallet, so it is not surprising that most players with such an incorrect foot placement will not be able to roquet consistently.

Correction of incorrect rear foot placement
Because the player does not know he is doing it (and may take some convincing), he will need to learn to consciously walk in and place his rear foot further to the side than he has been doing. It can help to ensure that his foot is pointing parallel to the line of swing, and that his shoulders and hips are reasonably square, since many step-stance players stand with their hips and shoulders slightly rotated as shown in Diag.20, which may not necessarily lead to problems with the swing unless it involves the incorrect foot placement we have described. After taking up his stance the player should check that he can move his mallet straight back without it passing too close to his rear foot. This problem is more likely to be noticed with long shots when he takes a longer back-swing. With hoop running and short roquets his mallet may not swing back far enough to contact his rear foot; but even those shots can be affected by the habit of swinging the mallet back around a curve.

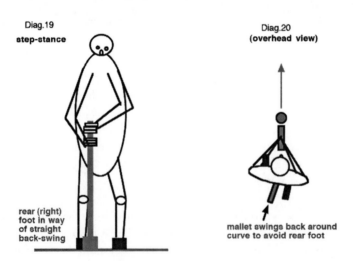

Diag.19
step-stance

rear (right)
foot in way
of straight
back-swing

Diag.20
(overhead view)

mallet swings back around
curve to avoid rear foot

l.   body movement

Like some of the other things we have considered, moving body parts other than the arms may not be an error itself, but it can be a source of error because it will also mean that the shoulders are moving, making it more difficult to control the movement of the arms that are swinging the mallet, and more difficult to coordinate the additional movements with correct timing.

There are two main types of body movement—

(a) *bending the knees*: This is usually done to achieve more power, since it is possible to obtain more power with less effort by using the large muscles in the upper legs. However for most players the difficulty of coordinating and correctly timing the use of the various muscles makes this a dubious method of swinging the mallet.

Players who incorporate a definite and deliberate knees bend into their swing usually have a level (square) stance, use a short mallet (or a short grip), and the back-swing usually starts fairly high, with the knees bending in order to bring the mallet down onto the ball. The follow-through also usually finishes fairly high as the knees start to straighten, and it is likely that during the wing the wrists will rotate to a noticeable extent. So many muscles are brought into action, one set after another, that it must be desirable for most players to find a way of achieving the desired swing by using and coordinating fewer muscles.

(b) *bending at the waist*: This type of body movement is quite different from bending the knees, although both have the effect of causing the player to have to swing his arms from moving shoulders. In fact, this player may not swing his arms much at all. The player will probably have a level stance (unlike the one shown in the diagram), and use a mallet with a long shaft, keeping his nose nearer to the end of the shaft and his hands nearer to his chest than is generally recommended by coaches.

Diag. 20 is an attempt to illustrate this type of swing which is achieved almost entirely with the trunk muscles. The elbows usually remain bent throughout the swing, and the wrists are locked tightly. This means that, in contrast to the knees bender, the player uses very few muscles provided his bending at the waist does not also involve any bending at the knees. The mallet is usually swung back a long way and finishes very high in front. Some players manage to roquet well with this action, and the coach should

Diag.20
bending at the waist

head and shoulders
move up and back

high
follow-through

be wary of trying to change the swing unless there are other problems evident that also need to be corrected.

Correction of body movement
If he wants to change the swing, the coach will need to look for a way that suits the particular player, as what works for one player may not work for another player with the same problem.

The player could be asked to start with a fairly upright step-stance (he can go back to a level stance later if he wishes) and try swinging the mallet back and forth using only the muscles at the top of his shoulders.

He may need to be convinced that if he keeps his wrists firm, swings his arms and mallet as one unit from the shoulders, keeps his arms out in front of his body and takes a long back-swing, he will be able to easily achieve sufficient power for almost any stroke he would wish to play.

He should relax the muscles in his feet, then the muscles in his upper trunk and shoulders; and before swinging he should feel that his shoulders are fixed in space, as if they are locked in position and cannot be moved at all during the swing.

Note that this type of deliberate knees-bend is quite different from the involuntary one seen in players who are very nervous and have an attack of the "yips" or "jitters".

John Riches and Wayne Davies

ROQUETING—
FURTHER COACHING INFORMATION

THE COACH NEEDS to make a careful assessment of the situation before attempting to change the roqueting technique of a player. He should take into account such things as the temperament of the player, his willingness to spend time practising on his own, his propensity to listen and take advice, his future aspirations (aims and goals), etc.

Many players over-rate the importance of roqueting and spend precious practice time working on roquets when the time would have been much more usefully spent in practising croquet strokes such as split-shots, take-offs and hoop approaches, or giving more attention to improving their tactics. As coach I shudder every time I hear someone unthinkingly repeat the old excuse: "Oh, well, if you can't roquet, you can't play croquet!". This is nonsense, as good players will win many games without ever hitting a roquet longer than two yards.

By working for many hours on your roqueting skills you may be able to bring about an improvement in your medium-range roqueting, but for 15-yard roquets it will be only a slight increase in the number of successful roquets from (say) 30% to 33%. This will make only a slight difference to the number of games you win. But by working on croquet strokes, especially big split-shots, you can greatly increase the number of hoops you make in a break from an average of (say) 3 hoops to 6 or more hoops, and can reach the stage where you seldom break down in a break and can also set a leave good enough to give yourself an excellent chance of another all-round break in the next turn. This will enable you to win many more games than the slight increase in your roqueting percentage.

However, players are not easily convinced that they would do far better spending the time practising croquet strokes than practising roqueting and hoop-running; and for this reason the coach must be prepared to assist with roqueting problems even when he knows there are more effective ways he could be helping the player.

As we have noted in the introduction to these coaching notes, players vary considerably from one to another as regards coordination skills, intelligence, determination, willingness to take advice, technical knowledge and understanding, and many other characteristics; and the coach must adapt his approach to the needs of the individual player. This is why individual one-on-one coaching will usually be more effective than group coaching in terms of player improvement.

The coach should be wary of suggesting more than one change at a time. For example, asking an experienced player to adopt a different stance, keep his shoulders still and take a longer backswing would usually be too many changes for the player to attempt at one time. These changes may all be needed before the player's roqueting can noticeably improve, but if possible they should be taken one at a time. The exception to this general rule of coaching occurs when (as we have seen in earlier sections) the player is committing two errors which partly counteract each other. In that case it may be necessary to correct both errors in the one coaching session, but even then the coach should seek a way of correcting one error first without mentioning the other, then work on correcting the second error—and expect to have to repeat the process over several sessions.

It is also often wise to start with small changes rather than radical changes. Sometimes a player's roqueting can be improved markedly by making only a minor change to his technique, e.g. slowing down his back-swing, or relaxing his foot muscles, or keeping his wrists firmer, etc.

Sometimes a player is helped by asking him to or watch his hands (rather than the ball) to see that they are moving back and forth in the line of swing, as it should be immediately obvious that if his hands do not move forward along the desired line of swing, it will be almost impossible for the mallet-head to move in that line.

The coach also needs to be wary of various pieces of well-meaning advice given by players who fancy themselves as coaches and suggest to a player that he should do things such as "pause at the top of the back-swing before starting the forward swing"; or "count one-two-three back and then one-two forward", or "If you are missing on the right, you should aim to the left of the ball you want to roquet", or "try taking a much shorter back-swing, as your back-swing is going crooked and making you miss the roquet", etc. There is no shortage of bad coaching advice available on our croquet lawns, and both players and coaches must learn to discriminate wisely between the rare good advice and the more frequent dubious suggestions made by would-be coaches.

CASTING

IT IS BECOMING more fashionable nowadays for players to "cast" (= take practice swings) over the ball in preparation for a roquet. There are several things a coach should know if he is to advise players about whether and how to engage in this practice.

Aside from annoying the opponent, or merely copying a good player on the dubious assumption that if he does it, casting must be a helpful thing to do, there are at least three more or less valid reasons why a player may choose to cast:

(1) to loosen up the muscles in his arms and shoulders.
(2) to establish the desired line of swing and check that his mallet is aligned to it.
(3) to establish the desired timing of the pendulum-type swing.

There are also various different ways of doing the casting, and the method used will depend on which of the above three things (or possibly a combination of them) the player wishes to achieve as a result of the casting.

After casting above the ball, it will obviously be necessary before the final swing to lower the mallet to a height such that the ball will be contacted in the centre of the mallet face. This can also be accomplished in three different ways:

(a) some players "cast" several times, then place the mallet on the ground behind the ball before taking the final swing. This is OK if the player is using the casting merely to loosen his muscles, but is likely to defeat the purpose if he is using it to check the alignment of the mallet or establish the timing of his swing. Resting the mallet on the ground allows the shaft to move away from the vertical position in which it was (or at least should have been) hanging, so that when it is lifted up to start the final back-swing the alignment is likely to be lost.

(b) others, after casting, lower the mallet deliberately to the desired height, but keep it a few mm off the ground. This can help to retain the correct alignment, so can make sense if the player is using it for either or both of the first two reasons listed above; but it interrupts the timing of the swing, so would not be suitable if he is using the casting to establish the correct timing of the swing.

(c) Perhaps the majority of players who cast seem to continue from the casting so that it leads with a continuous motion into the final swing. This suggests they are using it to establish the timing of the swing (and perhaps for the first two reasons as well) and they want to keep the established rhythm leading into the final swing. The final swing will usually involve a longer back-swing, but the timing will be unchanged, since according to the laws of physics the period (timing) of a pendulum depends only on its length from fulcrum (shoulders) to bottom (mallet head) and is independent of the amplitude (amount of back-swing). The aim is to establish a long, slow, unhurried swing resembling the pendulum of a grandfather clock, or the way an elephant usually swings its trunk, without any pushing of the hands into the mallet shaft.

This third "continuous" method, however, has a further problem: in the final swing the player must find a way of lowering the mallet just enough to bring the mallet head to the required height above ground-level, and must judge the amount of lowering correctly in order to avoid either hitting the ground or "topping" the ball.

Once again, there are three ways of doing it:

(A) by bending at the knees in the final swing.
(B) by bending at the waist in the final swing.
(C) by straightening the elbows in the final swing.

Each of these ways has been used by top players, and as with many other aspects of technique it is usually best to allow the player to adopt the method that seems to him most "natural".

Bending at the knees or waist involves the danger of affecting the previously established alignment. That could also happen, but is less likely to, when the player straightens his elbows.

Straightening the elbows can slightly lengthen the pendulum (which would not happen with bending at the knees or shoulders), which could in theory slightly affect the timing, but this seems to be the method that suits most players who use the casting to establish the timing of the swing.

In this case the knees and shoulders should be kept absolutely still, as the more muscles and body parts you move, the harder it will be to retain the correct alignment and timing.

When all is considered, we suggest that a coach should strongly advise inexperienced players against casting, as they will have more than enough problems to cope with already, without introducing "casting", with its additional possible sources of error.

RUSHES

MANY OF THE errors we have considered in roqueting will apply also to other single-ball strokes such as rushing and hoop-running.

(a) striker's ball jumping

However, with rushes there is often a new problem: The striker can accidentally cause his ball to jump so that it either completely misses the ball he was intending to rush, or rides up over the target ball so that most of the force is lost on impact instead of being transmitted to the ball he wants to rush.

This is usually caused by the player pushing his hands forward too rapidly in the forward swing in a mis-guided effort to get more force into the rushed ball. The mallet head lags behind slightly so that the mallet is sloping slightly forward when it contacts the ball, hitting it down into the ground and causing it to jump (see Diag. 21). The player may also be standing too close to the ball, which can have the same effect.

Coaches sometimes fail to realise, however, that standing too far back can also result in the ball jumping if the mallet is tilted backwards on impact and the ball is contacted above centre with the bottom bevelled edge of the mallet face (see Diag. 22).

In order to ascertain which of these errors is being committed and needs correction, the coach should watch carefully from the side as the player plays a series of rushes. The correction will involve either (in the former case) taking a longer backswing, slowing down the forward swing, swinging from the shoulders and "using the weight of the mallet", or (in the latter case) simply standing closer to the ball and/or with the hands further out from the body. A player who is hurrying the swing may also be helped by using a slight stop-shot action, which involves slowing down the forward movement of the hands before the mallet contacts the ball, so that the mallet head can catch up with them, but there is a danger in that if it is used in other strokes this sort of swing could cause different problems.

A further point of technique that the coach should look for is the tendency to swing from the wrists instead of from the shoulders when rushing. Swinging from the wrists involves using a shorter pendulum with very little "flat" at the bottom of the swing. There will usually be a high follow-through, and although this type of short pendulum is not necessarily an "error" of technique (since a double pendulum can be used to provide more force with less effort), it does make the timing of the swing much more critical.

It is advisable to avoid a double-pendulum action unless the player is exceptionally well coordinated, as the long single pendulum provided by swinging from the shoulders with firm wrists will have a much flatter bottom on it;—i.e. the mallet head will be travelling more or less parallel to the ground for a longer time during which an acceptable contact with the ball can be made without causing the ball to jump or lose force—see illustrations on the next page.

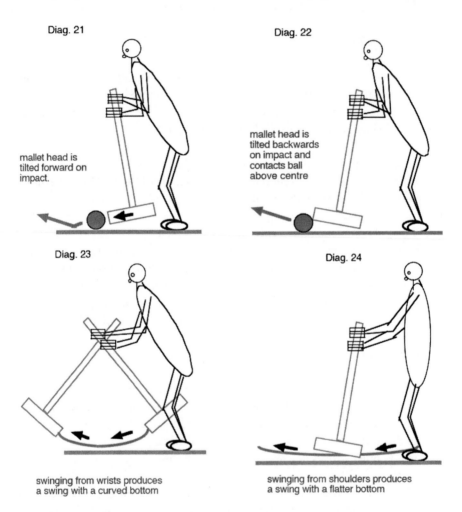

Diag. 21

mallet head is tilted forward on impact.

Diag. 22

mallet head is tilted backwards on impact and contacts ball above centre

Diag. 23

swinging from wrists produces a swing with a curved bottom

Diag. 24

swinging from shoulders produces a swing with a flatter bottom

(b) loss of direction

This is usually caused by the player tightening the grip as the mallet head approaches the ball, and at the same time pushing with the bottom hand. It may be combined with loss of force due to the ball jumping.

To correct this problem the striker must learn (as we have seen previously) to relax the muscles in his feet and shoulders, start with a firmer grip and also keep his wrists fairly firm.

A small deviation from the line of swing can result in a much larger deviation of the rushed ball.

The most effective method of correcting this error is to place the balls close together—about one foot apart—and ask the player to relax, take a long backswing, and let the mallet swing forward smoothly without attempting to "push" it or provide any extra force. He should not try to send the rushed ball any particular distance—just watch and see where it goes. Then the balls can be moved further apart, until he is remaining relaxed while rushing balls up to 2 yards (6 feet) apart.

(c) cut-rushing

Cut-rushes can have their own problems in at least three different ways:

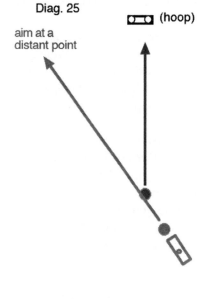

Diag. 25

⬚▭ (hoop)

aim at a
distant point

(1) Even a slight jump can cause the striker's ball to miss the edge of the target ball, so the swing must be flat.

(2) There is a psychological tendency to swing towards the centre of the target ball. This can be best overcome by selecting an aiming point in the distance and focussing on that, rather than on any part of the ball you want to rush.

(3) The great majority of cut-rushes to a hoop that go in the right direction will fall short of the hoop. This is because the player forgets that the finer the cut, the less force is transferred from the striker's ball to the ball he is rushing to the hoop.

One way to overcome this tendency is to select a point well past the hoop and imagine that you are rushing the ball to that point. This is especially important when rushing from behind the hoop, e.g. from hoop 2 to hoop 1

HOOP RUNNING

(a) hurrying the swing

MOST OF THE errors we have seen in relation to roqueting can also occur in hoop-running strokes, but by far the most common error in hoop-running is hurrying the swing. This is often referred to as "jabbing" at the hoop, and involves the player taking very little back-swing, then forcing the mallet rapidly forward with his bottom hand. It is usually accompanied by energetic bending of the knees and other body movement.

Although this error in technique can sometimes be seen in short roquets, it is more likely to occur in hoop-running strokes, and is caused by the psychological effect of the proximity of the hoop. Sometimes a player will use a high follow-through instead of following through low along the ground, due to a subconscious and irrational fear that he may damage his mallet on the hoop.

Correction of hurrying the swing

Here we can use the same method as described in the section on roqueting [see 1(f) "hurrying the swing"]. The coach must find a way of getting the player to take a longer and slower backswing—slow enough for him to watch that the mallet-head remains correctly aligned as he draws it back—and the mallet should be swung forward from the (relaxed) shoulders without any attempt to push the mallet forward with the hands. It is possible to run hoops by swinging only from the wrists, but this usually involves a loose grip and is harder to control. The wrists should be kept firm and both hands should move forward together. A player should be encouraged to keep his hands near the top of the shaft when running hoops, as moving one or both hands down the shaft will increase the tendency to "jab".

(b) hitting the near hoop-leg

This is caused by either mis-alignment of the mallet-head or swinging off-line, usually around a slight curve. The mis-alignment often results from the player trying to hit the ball through the centre of the hoop, when for sharply angled hoops he should be aiming to hit the centre of the ball at the inside edge of the far hoop-leg, as shown in Diag, 26. Well-meaning coaches have been known

Diag. 26

to advise players to make sure in this situation that the edge of the ball misses the near hoop-leg. It is indeed true that in order to run the hoop the ball must miss the near hoop-leg, but this is the wrong advice for a coach to give.

The player will have been training his muscles, probably for years, to coordinate in such a way that he fixes his eyes on a target (the ball he wants to roquet) and swings the mallet so that the mallet swings toward the last thing he has fixed his eyes on. If he fixes his eyes on the nearest hoop-leg, he will be very likely to swing the mallet toward that hoop-leg, instead of swinging it toward the inside edge of the far hoop-leg. He should instead ignore the near hoop-leg, refusing to look at it while aligning the mallet to swing through the centre of the ball and the inside edge of the far hoop-leg as shown in the illustration; then make sure that the back-swing and (low) follow-through remain in this line.

(c) Jumping through hoops

This is not the place to enter into a full consideration of jump shots and the related possible errors, so we will simply say that the player should stand well forward, avoid all body movement other than his arms, and also avoid hitting too sharply down on the ball. A jump shot should normally (unless the stroke is severely hampered with the ball very close to the hoop) be played with a relaxed swing and follow-through, not with a "jab" or stop-shot action.

The recommended grip for jump shots depends on the player's normal grip as follows:

(1) If he uses a Solomon grip he should keep both hands at the top of the shaft.
(2) If he uses a standard grip he could move both hands together a small distance down the shaft. He should not move only one hand down the shaft, and should still swing from the shoulders, not from the wrists. The grip should be firm, not loose.
(3) If he uses an Irish grip he should move both hands well down the shaft. It is important to fix your eyes on the part of the ball you want to contact with the mallet.

HOOP APPROACHES

B Y FAR THE best method of teaching and playing hoop approaches is the "Circle Method" as described in our coach-training courses. We assume here that the player has been taught this method but is handling it incorrectly in one of the following ways:

(a) incorrect slope

With this method the same amount of mallet slope (about 15 degrees, with slight adjustments for greater accuracy as the player improves) can be used for approaches from any direction and length. The player needs to learn to consistently hit the ball with the mallet sloping forward this correct a mount **at the instant the mallet impacts the ball** (see below).

(b) poor judgement of distance

The player needs to learn to look at the distance from the hoop he is approaching, and place his ball so that the croqueted ball is lined up to a point the same distance directly behind the hoop. Players may have difficulty judging this distance accurately until they have practised it for some time. Some may find it helpful to imagine a circle with this radius around the hoop, with the croqueted ball lined up to go to the back of the circle, but most simply judge a distance behind the hoop equal to their distance from the hoop. To find the correct line of swing (aim) they also need to judge one-third of the distance from the hoop to the back of the circle. The judgement of these distances can be a source of error, but its value is that the same method can be used for all hoop approaches, and the player should quickly learn to make the judgements more accurately.

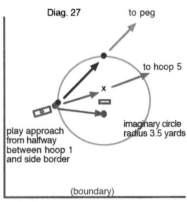

Correction:
Both of the above errors can best be corrected by having the player practise a series of hoop approaches to hoop 1 from a point three and a half yards to the side of the hoop, which will be halfway between the hoop and the side border, and in line with hoops 1 and 4.

From this particular point it so happens that the correct point at the back of the circle where the croqueted ball should be lined up will be directly in line with the peg, and the one-third aiming point for the swing will be directly at hoop 5 (see Diag. 27)

This will not be so when approaching the hoop from some other position, but it is a useful way of checking that the judgement of the distances is correct. Instead of hoop 1, any other corner hoop can be used similarly, approaching the hoop from halfway between the hoop and the side border, and lining up the croqueted ball to the peg and the swing to the nearest centre hoop.

Players who have learnt to play roll strokes before being taught the circle hoop approach (the wrong way around) will often tend to want to use a roll action for hoop approaches. With the balls lined up as described above the striker's ball will go too far, or else the croqueted ball will fall well short of the point at which it is aimed. Both balls should finish on the line of hoops 1 and 2 (more or less) if the correct amount of slope and type of swing are used.

The player must not swing around a curve trying to "shepherd" the striker's ball to the front of the hoop, and should use only the weight of the mallet to play the stroke, without any attempt to accelerate the mallet through the ball in a rolling action. He should allow the weight (inertia) of the two balls to stop most of the mallet's forward movement. This means that to an observer the correctly played hoop approach stroke may appear similar to a stop-shot, but the player should not be consciously using a stop-shot action which would bring timing into the stroke and constitute an extra possible souce of error. The hands are best kept at the top of the shaft in the same position as for roqueting or hoop-running, but it is not incorrect to move one or both hands down the shaft provided the player can resist the temptation to "push" into the ball as in a roll stroke.

(c) inability to adjust

When the player progresses to learning split-shots and has some understanding of "mallet drag" and "ball slip", he will be able to appreciate that the hoop approach is simply one type of split-shot. If he is in front of the hoop and fairly close to it, and wants to ensure a forward rush after making the hoop, he can use a stop-shot to send the croqueted ball further.

There are two other ways in which the player may need to adjust the hoop approach action:

(1) If he is approaching from behind the hoop at an angle, and does not want to simply take off to the front of the hoop (which should be discouraged unless the croqueted ball is where he wants it to be after he has made the hoop), he will probably find that the striker's ball goes too far and the

croqueted ball does not go far enough. This is due to "ball-slip" which refers to the fact that the surfaces of the balls will tend to slip against each other if the angle of split between the directions of the two balls exceeds 60 degrees. This will happen only when approaching from well behind the hoop.

Correction:

When approaching from well behind the hoop at an angle, the player should allow for "ball-slip" by hitting a little more into the croqueted ball (i.e. moving his aiming point for the swing a little more than one-third of the distance from the hoop to the back of the circle—see Diag. 28); and also standing a little further back so that the mallet shaft has less forward slope.

(2) If he is approaching the hoop from more or less directly in front of the hoop and more than three yards from the hoop, he may find that the striker's ball does not finish close enough to the hoop.

Correction:

The player should simply stand further forward to increase the mallet slope and hit down on the ball at a sharper angle. He should not introduce a rolling action into the stroke, as that would again bring timing into it and make it harder to control the striker's ball (see Diag. 29).

This is possible when approaching from the front of the hoop because the exact finishing position ("margin for error") of the striker's ball is less critical when it approaches the hoop from the front than when it approaches from the side.

Diag. 28   Diag. 29

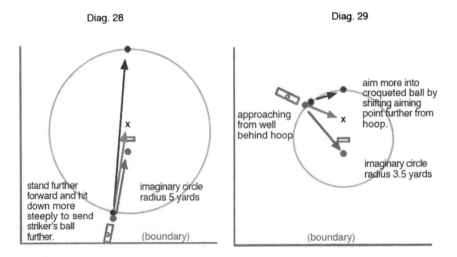

186   John Riches and Wayne Davies

TAKE-OFFS

THE COACH WILL often find it difficult to convince a player that he needs to work on improving his take-offs, as players tend to think they know all there is to know about take-offs. However there are some errors of technique that are commonly seen even when the players have had many years of experience, and that will prevent the player from playing consistently accurate take-offs.

(a) Incorrect lining up

Failure to allow for 'mallet drag' (sometimes called "pull") on the striker's ball by lining up the 'V' between the balls to one side of the target and aiming the swing a similar distance to the other side of the target can either result in a "still ball" fault, or in a left-side take-off it can cause the striker's ball to go off-line to the right of the target. [It must be remembered that the "target" will not always be a ball, as sometimes it will be the position to run a hoop or to get a desired rush.]

Correction of incorrect lining up
The coach should check that the player understands what the 'V' is and how it should be "lined up", as well as how to find the correct line of swing (see Diag. 30). [Players see the 'V' differently. If you place two balls in contact and ask a number of experienced players to tell you where the 'V' is pointing, you can expect to get many different answers.] The player should "stalk" a take-off twice: once to check the lining up of the 'V' which he cannot do while standing over the balls, and a second time to stalk the correct line of swing.

(b) turning the mallet into the croqueted ball

Some players have actually been told by well-meaning coaches to "turn the mallet into the croqueted ball to make sure it moves". This involves swinging across the correct line of swing and makes it very difficult to consistently achieve accuracy of distance.

Correction of mallet turning
The player must learn to ignore the target ball after having lined the balls up correctly. It may help if he imagines instead that he is roqueting an imaginary ball in the correct line of aim (see the grey ball in Diag.31), and must keep the mallet-face square to this line.

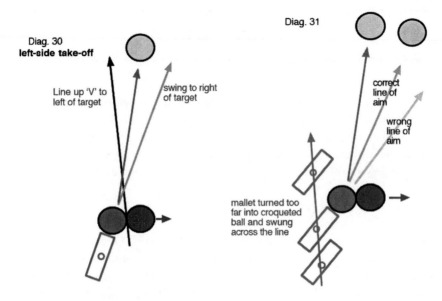

Diag. 30
left-side take-off

Line up 'V' to left of target

swing to right of target

Diag. 31

correct line of aim

wrong line of aim

mallet turned too far into croqueted ball and swung across the line

(c) Incorrect short swing

The tendency with many players is to take approximately the same amount of back-swing for all take-offs (usually no more than one foot), and for a longer take-off they send the striker's ball further by pushing the mallet forward more energetically. This brings more muscles that need coordination into play, and also requires exact timing, so it is not surprising that players who use this method usually have difficulty controlling their take-offs.

Correction of incorrect (short) swing
Since a fine take-off is essentially a single-ball shot, the technique for other single-balls shots applies: the stroke should be played using the weight of the mallet and arms only, without providing additional force from the wrists and forearms. With a take-off this is of even greater importance, since distance is often critical as well as direction. The player should practise controlling the distance the striker's ball goes in a take-off by varying only the height to which he raises his mallet in the back-swing, and using a relaxed, unhurried forward swing.

(d) stop-shot action

Playing take-offs with a stop-shot action is also inadvisable, as once again timing is involved, introducing an additional source of error. Players will often find it difficult to break the habit of using a stop-shot action for take-offs (and usually other single-ball shots as well—a habit which can be developed by playing a lot of Golf Croquet).

Correction of stop-shot take-offs
The player should try to watch the mallet continue in the follow-through, checking that it remains aligned to the aiming point. For take-offs a low follow-through is less necessary than for other single-ball strokes, but it is still a good thing to strive for.

(e)   inconsistent take-offs

Some players fail to achieve consistency in their take-offs because they are content to simply send the ball in the general direction of the target ball (or position). They do not take sufficient care in lining up both the croqueted ball and the line of swing.

Correction of general inconsistency in take-offs
The player must focus on the exact point he wants his ball to go to, and then align things as accurately as possible with respect to that desired finishing point. The player should practise taking off to a ball some distance away and getting a rush on it to a desired hoop. The coach should indicate the desired finishing point and ask him to concentrate on aligning his take-off to go to that point, rather than concentrating too much on the ball he will later be wanting to rush. After lining everything up as illustrated on the previous page, he should take several steps backwards, pause, align his mallet at the selected aiming point, relax his shoulders, then walk in, take up his stance, judge the amount of back-swing he will need, and hit his ball with a smooth, unhurried swing. When taking off across the court to a border ball he should put out of his mind any thought of possibly going out, and play to get right over to the target ball. For most players the danger of falling short is greater than the danger of going out.

(f)   one side only take-offs

It is not uncommon to find players who say they can take-off from one side only of the roqueted ball, or who much prefer one particular side. This will almost always be due to a curved swing, or occasionally they will be turning the mallet out of its correct alignment.

Correction of one-sided take-offs
The player should practise taking off around the court from corner to corner, going both clockwise and anti-clockwise around the court. He must select the point where he wants his ball to finish, and work out exactly how many yards each side of that point he needs to allow when lining up the croqueted ball and finding his aiming point, which will depend on the length of the take-off. This exercise should soon convince him that unless he swings straight at the aiming point few of his take-offs will be successful. Note that players may differ considerably. Some may need to allow more than others on either side of the desired finishing point, and some will need to allow more (or less) for right-side takeoffs than for left-side take-offs. Every player should regularly spend time practising take-offs.

ROLLS

(a) striker's ball falls short

THE MOST COMMON problem that players have with rolls is that the croqueted ball is sent too far and the striker's ball falls short. This will especially apply to long rolls where the striker's ball is intended to go three-quarters (or more) of the distance travelled by the croqueted ball, and in roughly the same direction.

There are at least three different methods the player can use to send the striker's ball further forward than it would go in a normal "drive" croquet stroke in which the mallet is swing through as in a roquet action; and the method of correcting the problem will depend on which method is being used:

(1) If the player is using mallet slope to send the ball forward by "squeezing" it down onto the ground, then he is probably losing the forward slope before the mallet reaches the ball, due to either standing up as he swings, or not moving his top hand forward at the same rate as his bottom hand in order to maintain the mallet slope as the mallet is swung (or pushed) forward.

(2) If the player is placing a hand well down near the head of the mallet and accelerating through the ball(s) then he must learn to hold the acceleration until the mallet gets closer to the ball, and then accelerate the mallet head more rapidly through the ball(s).

If the player is using a side-style rolling action it is likely that both of the above will apply.

Correction of lost forward slope

The coach should stand in front of the player facing him as shown in Diag. 32 and place his hands on the mallet shaft, assisting the player to move the mallet forward while maintaining the forward slope, with a sort of "push-me-pull-you" action, moving the mallet back and forth like a piston. Then the player can try to keep this type of action while hitting a single ball, and then while playing a croquet stroke without trying to achieve any particular distance.

Correction of early acceleration

The coach can ask the player to play a roll from just in front of a hoop, so that the hoop will severely restrict the amount of back-swing the player can use (see Diag.

33); or alternatively, the coach can kneel on the ground and place his hand behind the mallet to prevent it from swinging back more than about six inches (15 cm). In this exercise the player should try to roll the balls as far as possible. Do not worry about "pushing" faults at this stage, as the player must first get the "feel" of using a late acceleration, starting just as the mallet comes onto the ball. This method can also work well with players who are unable to play pass-rolls.

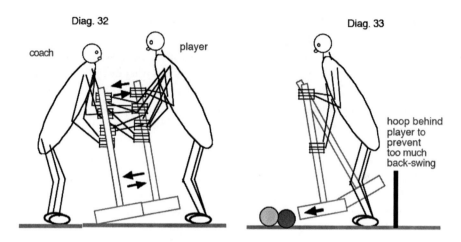

Diag. 32

coach

player

Diag. 33

hoop behind player to prevent too much back-swing

SPLITS

(a) poor control

ONCE AGAIN, THE best method of correcting errors will depend on the method the player is using to play the split-shots. In order to have any chance of playing accurate splits, unless he is a rare "intuitive" player who just "knows" how to play them, it will be important to check that he fully understands the mechanics of split-shots, including the effect of 'pull', 'mallet drag', and 'ball-slip' (as explained in the Coach Training Course material), as well as changes in mallet slope, acceleration and angle of split, and changes in playing conditions.

Provided he uses a reasonable type of swing (hands out in front of his body, top elbow straightening during the swing, and mallet shaft more or less vertical when viewed from the front, rather than on his shoulder) and is swinging straight instead of around a curve, the basic error correction is fairly straightforward.

It is also important that the player is correctly aiming his swing at a point halfway between the two positions where he wants the balls to finish, before allowing as necessary for pull, drag, slip and wideness of angle. If he is "halving the angle" he will be able to achieve accuracy with split-shots only when the balls are required to travel roughly equal distances.

Correction of poor control in splits
If both balls are going too far or falling short of their desired finishing positions, then obviously the player is hitting too hard or not hard enough. For longer splits he should use a higher back-swing and swing the mallet from his shoulders, rather than pushing harder with wrists and forearms.

If the striker's ball is falling short and the croqueted ball going too far, he will need to get more forward slope on his mallet by standing further over the ball or moving one or both hands further down the shaft; or else use more and later acceleration

If the striker's ball is going too far and the croqueted ball is falling short (which is a very rare problem), he should try standing further back, moving his hands higher up the shaft, and/or using less acceleration through the ball(s).

An important exercise to improve accuracy of split-shots is to start with a cannon in the 1ˢᵗ corner for hoop 1, then split from a yard behind hoop 1 to hoops 2 and 3, then from a yard behind hoop 2 to hoops 3 and 4, etc. Do not play any other strokes than splits—do not run any hoops or play any roquets or hoop approaches. When you are practising splits, you should think only about splits, and keep working out why the balls are not going exactly where you intended them to go. In this exercise you need only three balls, and can score yourself a point every time a ball finishes within 2 yards of a hoop. After hoop 6, play the next split from the middle of the north border, and after rover roll both balls from a yard behind rover to within 2 yards of the peg. Try this practice exercise on various occasions and see if you can improve your score out of a possible 26 points.

CONCLUSION

A GOOD COACH OF players at higher levels will need to know far more about error correction than has been covered in these brief notes. For example, he will also need to teach, and correct errors in, strokes such as jump shots, hampered strokes, thick take-offs, peeling, cannons, and so on.

The coach must remember that what works with one player may not work with another, and he should constantly be looking for new and improved methods of correcting errors in technique. Then, of course, there are tactical and psychological errors which the coach also needs to be able to assist players with.

It is important for the coach to follow through with the complete "DRAMA" method of Error Correction, realising that diagnosing the error and telling the player what he is doing wrong is only the beginning of the process which should end with the coach checking that the player is no longer committing the same errors in games when under pressure.

Don't expect too much. Even a slight improvement is an achievement, and most errors in technique are only corrected over several coaching sessions spaced out over several weeks.]

CROQUET
The Teaching of Tactics

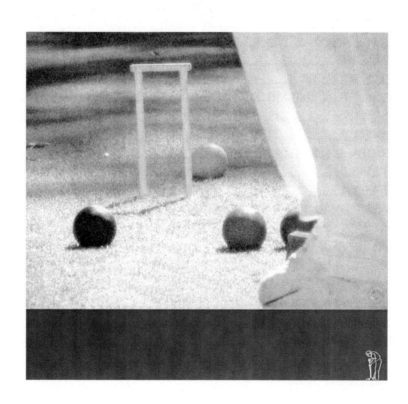

CONTENTS

INTRODUCTION

THIS BOOKLET IS intended primarily for coaches of players who have the ability to play most of the strokes with reasonable consistency, have been shown how to lay out 3-ball and 4-ball breaks, and who, when they get a break well set up, are usually able to maintain it long enough to make several hoops.

There will be much here of benefit to other coaches and players, from beginners to the top level, but some of the ideas presented may prove to be too difficult for relative beginners, and some may turn out to be less relevant to those coaching or playing at the highest (international) level. That is for the coach to judge.

The need for this type of booklet has long been perceived by members of the South Australian Coaching Committee. In the early nineties I wrote a booklet called "Croquet: Lessons in Tactics", and also other booklets which explained some of the topics re-visited in this booklet. Those booklets were aimed at informing players and coaches of tactical ideas they may not have previously considered, but we later realised that although some of our coaches were understanding the ideas well enough, they had not found an effective way of passing them on to the players they were coaching. It also took us a long time to come up with teaching methods with which we were fully satisfied, and which we believed could be used by our coaches most of whom had been given the information, but not been trained in the skills of teaching individuals or groups of players.

An example is that almost every coach, when asked, would insist that he or she teaches players to load hoops ahead. What they mean by this is that they have shown the player how to set up and play a 3-ball or 4-ball break, by making a hoop, then roqueting the escape ball and sending it ahead to load the next-but-one hoop. But the players were frequently missing quite simple opportunities to load hoops, as explained in the section on Hoop Loading, and many players failed to appreciate that it is better to load the next hoop before making the current one, even if it involves some risk and makes it less certain that the current one will be made. Very few players have been taught to think in terms of percentages, yet all tactical decisions should be based on a consideration of percentages.

The "correct" tactical choice in any given situation will be the one that maximises your percentage chance of winning the game; and the choice can usually be reduced to a simpler one: Do whatever maximises your chance of getting a break established before your opponent does. This important perception is explained in detail in my booklet "Next Break Strategy", which many players have found very useful. Some have said it revolutionised their whole approach to the game; but again we found that there are coaches who understand it, but do not know how to teach the players they are coaching to think in terms of percentages and use "Next Break Strategy" in appropriate situations.

Therefore this booklet is written as a set of direct instructions for the coach, explaining how he can go about passing on the tactical ideas we have chosen to cover. The topics have been arranged in approximate order of complexity. There are many other tactical ideas that the coach will need to teach his players. We have not attempted to cover them all, as our intention is merely to help the coach adopt a particular method of instruction, and give sufficient examples of it to enable the coach to develop for himself ways of teaching other tactical ideas by using a similar approach.

The booklet will be printed in a very limited edition, and initially it will be made available only to some State Coaching Directors who agree to trial the methods we recommend, and to a few people who have assisted in the preparation and local trialling of the material we have covered here. It is planned to eventually make it available on the internet, downloadable (together with my other booklets and articles) from: **www.croquetprofessionals.com**

I must express my great appreciation of my co-author Wayne Davies of Nantucket, USA, and my thanks to all members of the SA Coaching Committee for their interest, support, constructive criticism, and patience. Over many years they have been willing to listen to, and spend time discussing and trialling, many of these ideas in order to help sort out the useful from the useless.

John Riches (Australian Croquet Association National Coaching Director, November 2007)

GENERAL COACHING PRINCIPLES

$\mathbf{F}$IRST, WE FEEL there is a need to consider some general principles of coaching and look at how they apply to the teaching of tactics.

1. PLAYERS ARE NOT ALL THE SAME.

    Most coaches will have soon learnt that there is more than one type of player. Some seem to learn and play the game more or less intuitively, and can be referred to as "natural" players. Others have little natural flair or ability and have to learn to do everything the hard way; and it is interesting that these players usually make the best coaches. These differences are noticeable in the way they play the strokes (technique), and also may be seen in the area of tactics. Some people intuitively make good tactical choices, while for others each new tactical idea comes as a revelation that would never have occurred to them if they had been left to their own devices. An intuitive stroke-maker will not necessarily be an intuitive tactician, and in fact it is more than likely that he will not, though there are some notable exceptions for whom the whole game seems to come together naturally and with little effort. The "intuitive" player seems to be able to get away with using what for others would be poor technique (e.g. playing rushes and running hoops with a stop-shot action), while the "technician" will succeed only if he learns to do everything correctly and gives conscious attention to every detail. An experienced coach will distinguish between these two types of player, and other types as well, and will recognise that they need to be coached differently.

    Therefore it is important for the coach to make judgments about which of the ideas presented in this booklet should be taught to any particular player, and at what stage of his development. A truly intuitive tactician (a rare bird indeed) may neither benefit from, nor take much interest in, some of the tactical ideas found in these pages. He will reject any attempt to get him to think in terms of percentages, preferring to rely on his "gut feelings". Unfortunately most of us have the sort of gut that does not "feel" much that can be regarded as reliable, so we need to do derive our tactical choices from some other and higher up body part—in short, we need to think, painful as the experience may be.

2. "IF IT AIN't BROKE, DON't FIX IT".

    Just as with the coaching of technique, if a player is winning consistently by using what appears to be poor tactics, then the coach will almost certainly be wasting his time trying to get the player to change. Wait until he starts losing (you may need to arrange stronger opponents for him) and can see that the tactical approach he is using (e.g. consistently returning wide of partner or hitting balls out of play instead of shooting) is inadequate. Even then it will often not be easy to convince him that the reason for his losses lies in his inferior tactics, rather than the missed roquets and failed hoop attempts which were also apparent in the games of his opponents.

Good and bad tacticians may well miss and hit the same number of roquets, and often the bad tactician will hit more than the good tactician, but the difference is that the good tactician knows how to ensure that every roquet missed by the opponent will give him an easy break; while the poor tactician will usually find that after the opponent misses a roquet he still has little chance of establishing a break.

3.   TELLING AND SHOWING IS NOT COACHING.

Many coaches imagine that coaching involves telling a player what he is doing wrong, or what he should be doing instead, or demonstrating for him how things could and should have been done differently. None of these is real coaching. You are not truly coaching unless you are taking definite steps to ensure that the player not only knows what he has been doing wrongly, and what he needs to do differently, but he actually does do it differently and correctly in games under pressure.

The notes for coaches that follow in this booklet are designed to bring about definite changes in the way the player goes about making tactical choices. It will take time and should not be hurried. The coach will need to return again and again to various ideas in order to check that the player has properly understood how and when to use them, and is in fact thinking of them and using them in important games under real pressure.

4.   TEACH ONE THING AT A TIME.

When you are trying to get a player to think about tactical choices, and to take on board new tactical ideas, avoid asking him at the same time to think about how to play a particular type of shot more accurately, and do not introduce more than one or two new tactical ideas in the same coaching session.

5.   THE COACH DOES NOT OWN THE PLAYER

If you are coaching a player, do not tell other accredited coaches that they must not "interfere" by teaching him their ideas ("because he is my player and I do not want him confused or taught incorrect ideas"). On the contrary, encourage the player to listen to advice from any trained and accredited coach. He will have to learn to distinguish between good and bad advice, even if only from his doubles partners.

6.   RESPECT ACCREDITATION

Advise all players in your club to seek advice from trained and accredited coaches, rather than from good players without any coach training or accreditation; and ask people in the club who are not accredited coaches to refrain from coaching. As with points of technique, often the ideas they pass on with the best of intentions and which are correct for themselves, will not be the most helpful for a player whose stroke-making ability is markedly different from their own and who plays at a different level.

For this same reason, advise the player to watch good players whenever he can, and to note what they do in various situations, but to be wary of assuming that tactical choices which are right and prove successful for the top players must also be correct for those at lower levels. You need to take into account your own percentage chances of succeeding in the line of play you choose, and the percentages of your opponent will also be relevant and could make it suicidal for you to adopt unthinkingly a tactical manouvre which is correct for the top player.

7. TEACHING INVOLVES REVISION AND ASSESSMENT

The coach must understand that even if the player shows that he can recognise the correct tactical ideas and when to use them, that does not mean he will remember and use them tomorrow or next week, or in a different on-court situation. That is why we have tried to suggest more than one court situation in which each of the tactical ideas can be applied. The coach will need to think of other similar situations and return to them in later coaching sessions in order to assess the effectiveness of his teaching.

For most of the topics we have covered, it will probably be best to spread them out over two or more coaching sessions. If there is time left in the coaching session after teaching the new tactical idea, move on to an area of technique or psychology that the player also needs to learn.

8. WATCH THE TIME

Any type of coaching is more effective if presented in 2-3 shorter (say, 45-minute) sessions per week than in one longer session. Beware of overloading the player with new ideas. End the coaching sessions as soon as he shows any sign of weariness.

HOW TO USE THIS BOOKLET

This booklet will be printed in a very limited edition, as it is initially intended for those who train coaches. We suggest that it should not be given to a player to take home and read. In order to lean the new ideas effectively and correctly, the player will need to go through each idea out on the lawn with a good coach in the way we recommend.

In any field of learning, only a small percentage of people can learn effectively from lectures or diagrams or reading books, or even watching demonstrations. They need to try out things for themselves, one thing at a time, and discuss (learn to put into their own words) the new ideas with someone who can keep them on the right track.

WRONG BALL!

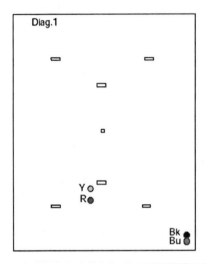

Diag.1

THIS SHOULD PROBABLY be one of the first and most important tactical lessons, yet the point it makes is frequently overlooked, even by experienced players.

The coach should set up the position shown in Diag. 1 and ask the player how he would continue the game as red and yellow, if red is for hoop 5 and yellow is for hoop 4.

Many players will decide to play red, make hoop 5, then take off to the opponent's balls in the 4th corner and rush one of them to hoop 6. Let him play the strokes until his turn ends—most likely with yellow still in the middle of the court. Then point out the disadvantages of what he has done, and ask him if he can think of anything better he could have done.

If he thinks a bit further ahead he may try to rush yellow to 2-back after making hoop 5, hoping to establish a break by making both hoops 6 and 1-back from the one opponent ball. Such forward thinking should be commended, but the player should be encouraged to think again.

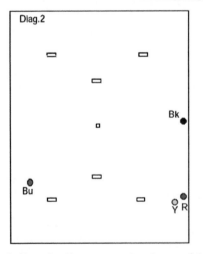

Diag.2

A more advanced thinker may rush yellow to hoop 6, then take off back to the opponent's balls in the 4th corner, and rush one of them to hoop 5 with a 3-ball break set up. Again the student should be permitted to play the strokes and can be commended on his tactical acuity. This would in fact have been the correct thing to do if the yellow clip had been on 4-back (as it will be in another of these topics—see "setting up breaks" on the next page). Then the coach can ask whether the student considered playing yellow instead of red, whereupon the player should be able to both see and explain the advantage of doing so. Again get him to play the strokes and find out how easy it is to set up a break this way-possibly even a 4-ball break by bringing both opponent balls into the court after making hoop 4, or by using a cannon in the 4th corner.

Then set up the position in Diag.2 and ask him how he would continue as the player of red and yellow if red is for hoop 4 and yellow for hoop 1.
He may want to make hoop 4 with red and then try to find a way of continuing the break, and he may even succeed in doing so when asked to demonstrate his idea.

Again the best way is to play yellow. Then use red to load hoop 2 as yellow goes to black, and take off from black to blue, which he should be able to rush closer to hoop 1. Let him try this method and compare it with playing red and making hoop 4. The positions of blue and black can be altered so as to make the choice of which ball to play either easier or more difficult, and of course the choice will also depend on the shots that the player can handle comfortably. He should not try to use a pass-roll to send black near the peg as he goes to blue, since that would involve an unnecessary additional risk. It is good, but not immediately essential, to bring the fourth ball into the break. The principle here is: **A good (though not certain) chance of a break is better than the certainty of making one or two hoops without a break set up.**

SETTING UP BREAKS

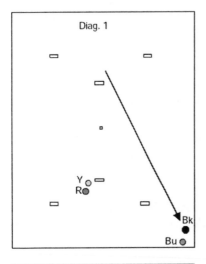

Diag. 1

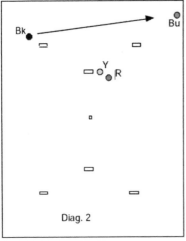

Diag. 2

SET UP THE position shown in Diag.1, where red is for hoop 5 and yellow is for 4-back.

Explain that black was near hoop 6 wired from red and yellow, so he shot at blue in the 4th corner and has missed.

Ask the player to continue by playing either red or yellow, as he would in a game.

Almost every player will play red, make hoop 5 and then find himself needing to get red out of the middle of the lawn, go to the opponent's balls and rush one of them to hoop 6 with no break set up even if everything goes right.

If he is lucky he may get a rush after hoop 5 on yellow to 1-back, leave yellow there, take off to the opponent's balls and rush one of them back to hoop 6—a tall order!

Restore the original position and ask if he can think of a better way of establishing a break.

If he had stopped to think, he would have started by rushing yellow to hoop 6, taking off to the opponent's balls, and rushing one of them to hoop 5—much easier! This is so obvious when you have been shown it; but would you think of it in a game situation under pressure?

The principle is : Always look for a way to load your next hoop before you make the current one.

In the situation shown in Diag.2 red was for hoop 6 and had been set up by his partner near the hoop with a simple rush, wired from black.

Black then shot at blue near the 3rd corner, as shown by the arrow, and missed.

Again ask the player how he would continue as red and yellow in a game.

Most players will play red, roquet yellow gently, make hoop 6, roquet yellow again, and then realise that they will have difficulty continuing the break because they cannot load 2-back before making 1-back.

A better plan would be to try for a rush on yellow to 2-back after making hoop 6 and then take off to the opponent's balls in the 3rd corner. (Ask him to try this method also.)

However, there is still another and better way:

First see if he can find it for himself, then get him to start by rushing yellow to 1-back and taking off from there to the opponent's balls and rushing one of them to hoop 6.

As with the second method, he now has a 3-ball break set up and his only remaining problem is when and how to get the other opponent ball away from B-baulk, which can be discussed with him and will depend on the shots he can play, but is not the subject of this particular exercise.

The principle is: **Instead of starting your turn by asking "How can I make my hoop?", start by asking "How can I load the next hoop before I make my current hoop?"; and if there is any reasonable way to do it, you should always load the next hoop first.**
    Regardless of how many times they have been told this, many players continue to miss such simple opportunities to load hoops ahead and set up easy breaks.

THE THREE-ONE PRINCIPLE

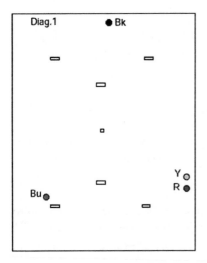

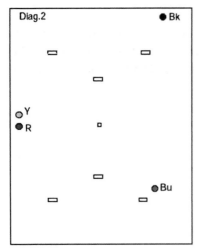

THE HEADING ON this article refers to one of the most important tactical ideas that a player needs to learn as soon as he reaches the stage where he is capable of rushing balls the length of the lawn and playing breaks.

The coach should set up the position in Diag. 1 and ask the player what he would do as black and blue in this situation if all clips are for hoop 1.

Many players will want to automatically shoot with blue at black, so as to return blue near its partner ball, and wait for the opponent to make a mistake.

If the player suggests this, ask him to do it, then get him to play the next turn with red in the way he would expect his opponent to do. If he then roquets yellow and takes off to the black and blue balls, he is not ready to go any further.

He should realise that red has an excellent opportunity to set up a break by rushing yellow toward the 3rd corner, sending it to load hoop 2 with a half-roll as red goes to the opponent balls, and using one of the opponent's balls to get a rush on the other opponent ball to hoop 1.

Then return the balls to the original position and ask him to think of something blue and black could do to avoid giving red such an easy chance to set up a break, and get him to try it by playing the next turn or two for both sides. If he hits blue out on the north border wide of black, red should at least be able to rush yellow up the lawn, send the opponent's balls to hoops 1 and 2, then set himself a rush along the north border toward hoop 2, with an excellent chance of at least a 3-ball break in his next turn.

The player may instead suggest hitting blue to "safety" into (say) the 1ˢᵗ corner, and could also be allowed to play on from there for both sides.

In this case red is given a "free" chance to set up a break, as blue has not even attempted a roquet.

Red can at least rush yellow up the lawn, send black to hoop 2, and either take off from it to blue in an attempt at an immediate break, or (if he thinks that is too hard, or something looks like going wrong) go back to yellow and set himself a rush to blue in the 1ˢᵗ corner. The aim is to help the player realise that the best chance for the player of black and blue is to shoot with blue at red or yellow (or both) in the original position.

He may protest: "But if I miss, that will let him get a rush to hoop 1 and make it!" The point is that it is only one hoop, and winning croquet games now has become for him a matter of setting up breaks, not playing to make just one or two hoops at a time. The "three-one principle" says that if all balls will be on the borders and the opponent's balls are together, the opponent will usually find it much easier to make a break if your balls are also together ("two-two") than if you shoot at his balls and give him a "three-one" set-up.

Diag.2 shows a similar situation where red is for hoop 4; and the coach and player together should be able to find many other situations where the "Three-one Principle" applies.

CONSIDER CONSEQUENCES

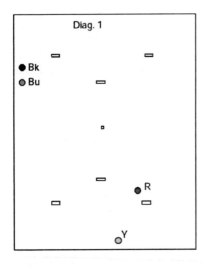

Diag. 1

Bk

Bu

R

Y

THIS EXERCISE IS designed to help the player understand the importance of thinking carefully, and considering possible consequences, before starting a turn.

The coach should set up the position shown in Diag.1 where black is for hoop 2 and the other three balls are all for hoop 1. Ask the player what he would do as red and yellow in this situation.

It should be reasonably clear that it makes little sense to shoot with either red or yellow at the opponent's balls, as it is a long roquet that if missed would give him a good chance of establishing a break with one or other of his balls.

Many players will want to shoot with red at yellow, in order to get red out of the "middle of the lawn" and join up with yellow. This could be a reasonable way of proceeding for a beginner, but if the player and his opponent are capable of making breaks he should give the matter further thought before deciding to undertake what seems to be the obvious course of action.

The key to finding the correct procedure in this type of situation is to consider carefully the consequences of any shot you take, whether you hit it or miss it.

If the player decides to shoot with red at yellow, ask him to do it, then discuss with him:

(1) how easy it will be for the opponent to set up a break if red fails to roquet yellow, and

(2) how easy it will be for him to set up a break himself if red roquets yellow. He should soon be able to realise that by taking the shot with red he is making things easy for his opponent if he misses, and rather difficult for himself if he hits. If necessary, get him to play on for either side until he becomes convinced of this.

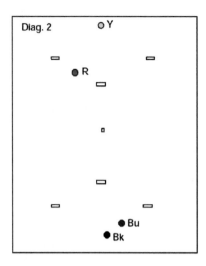

Diag. 2

Then ask him to consider the possible consequences of shooting with yellow at red.

If yellow roquets red, then he will have red in a better position for continuing the break, and if yellow misses red the opponent will find it more difficult to establish a break than if red and yellow were together on the south border.

Therefore, whether he hits or misses the roquet, which of course is the same distance whichever ball he plays, he will be better off if he has done so with yellow rather than with red.

Diag. 2 shows a similar situation where all clips are on hoop 3. Once again he should realise the advantages of playing yellow rather than red.

It can take some time to get a player convinced that he should "hit in" with yellow instead of "hitting out" with red in such situations, and it can be very frustrating when the player who remains unconvinced is your doubles partner who wants you to take the turn and play red!

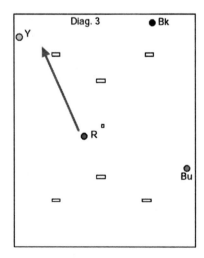

Diag. 3

The coach should set up the position shown in Diag.3 and ask the player what he would do as red and yellow if red and black are for 4-back, yellow is for hoop 2, and blue is for hoop 1.

There seems to be nothing else worth considering than shooting with red at yellow.

Ask him to do it, then ask him what he would do now if he were the opponent, and get him to do that also. Then he can switch back to playing red and/or yellow, and play the following turn.

He should soon realise that after red shoots at yellow and misses, black can shoot at either yellow or blue, and it will not be easy for yellow to make more than one hoop, as attempting to approach H2 from the border with the opponent's balls together would be too risky.

Ask him what he would do if he happened to roquet yellow with red, and he will probably decide that he could not do much better than simply setting a rush for yellow to H2. Then point out that if that is all he wants to do, there was no need to attempt to roquet yellow and risk missing!

Return the balls to the position in Diag.3 and ask the player to try to think of a better plan of action.

By now he should be able to understand why red should not shoot at yellow, but simply hit his ball to a position about halfway between yellow and hoop 2; perhaps a little closer to the hoop than to yellow (see arrow), after which any shot taken by black and missed will give yellow an excellent opportunity to set up a break in the next turn. Ask the player to play on for both sides in order to verify this and fix it in his mind.

Diag. 4 shows a similar situation, but with an important difference. The clips are as for Diag.3 except that yellow is for 1-back; but this time if red were to roquet yellow, the best way to set up for yellow to make 1-back would be to give yellow a rush to 2-back, rather than to 1-back.

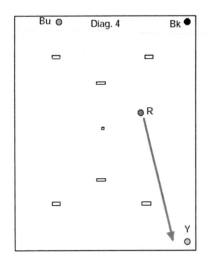

He should therefore not attempt to roquet yellow, but hit red out on the south border about a yard from yellow (see arrow). Then, if the opponent shoots with blue at black and misses, yellow can rush red to 2-back, take off to the opponent's balls, and rush one of them to 1-back. Note that if red had shot at yellow and missed he would have touching balls in the 4th corner and his task of continuing after blue had failed to roquet black would be much harder.

And if blue is hit out to the east border wide of black (e.g. roughly level with hoop 3, then yellow can roquet red gently, leave it on the south border, take off to blue, send blue towards 1-back while going to black in the 3rd corner, and send black to 2-back before returning to set a rush for yellow along the south border to black at 2-back.

This type of possibility is frequently missed by players who fail to think ahead of the consequences of roqueting or failing to roquet.

The next task for the coach is to find a way to ensure that the player will think of this in a game.

HOOP LOADING

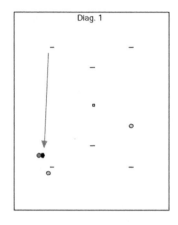

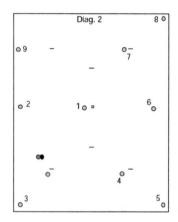

O NE OF THE tactical ideas that few players understand well is the importance of loading hoops ahead, the many ways of doing it, and the best way to do it in particular situations.

Many players would insist that they do make a habit of loading hoops ahead in order to set up breaks, and most coaches would claim that they teach and stress the importance of doing it; but when shown positions such as those given here and asked how they would continue the game, the players would in many cases fail to think of and use the correct method.

It must be admitted that in some of the situations the "correct method" of loading the next hoop before making the current one may involve one or more shots that the player is not comfortable in playing, and so would be unwise to attempt, but most of them will fail to even consider the various possible ways—let alone the best way—in which they could have loaded the next hoop.

In Diag.1 blue has failed to make hoop 1 from his partner (black) ball, and then red has shot from near hoop 2 and roqueted black. Set up the position on the lawn (note where yellow is) and ask the player how he would continue from that position in a game. [With a group of players, ask them to find and try to demonstrate a way that no-one else has yet suggested.]

Many will simply make hoop 1 from blue without even thinking about loading hoop 2. Then suggest that they might have found it easier to make more than one hoop if, before making hoop 1, they had been able to load hoop 2; and ask whether they can find a way of doing it. They will probably be very surprised when you tell them that in fact there are at least 6 ways it can be done, though some of them involve difficult shots that in this position would not be worth using. Hoop 2 can be loaded with any of the three balls (black, blue or yellow) as follows:

(1) with black, by splitting black to hoop 2 while going to yellow, then taking off back to blue.
(2) with black, by stop-shotting black to hoop 2, then turning around to roquet blue.
(3) with blue, by rushing it out to border in front of hoop 1 and using a load-and hold stop-shot.
(4) with yellow, by taking off to it, rushing it to hoop 2, and taking off back to blue to make hoop 1.
(5) with yellow, by taking off to it, and splitting it to hoop 2 while coming back to blue.
(6) with yellow, by taking off to it, and rushing it to the south border, then sending it to hoop 2.

In cases (4), (5)and (6) some players, instead of taking off to yellow, may choose to roll black towards the peg for use as a pivot ball, while going to yellow. Get the player to try each method of loading hoop 2, then select the one he prefers, and ask him why he would not choose the others.

Then move the yellow ball to various other positions as shown in Diag 2, and get him to think about which of the six methods he will use (if any) with yellow in each of the nine positions shown.

In position 8, and possibly also position 5 and 6, he may decide that loading hoop 2 is either impossible or impractical, though a good player may choose to use method (5) with yellow in positions 5 and 6. With yellow in position 7 there is no need to load hoop 2—just make hoop 1 and then get a rush to hoop 2, as hoop 3 is already loaded. In position 9 use a thick takeoff.

The player should also look at similar positions with different hoops in other parts of the court.

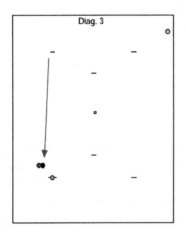

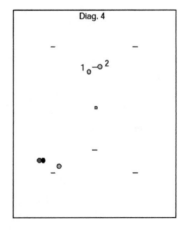

John Riches and Wayne Davies

It can also be helpful to move the black and blue balls to slightly different positions and ask the player whether it changes the method he would use to load hoop 2.

One such position is shown in Diag 3, where blue has stuck in hoop 1, and yellow is not where it can easily be used. This allows a new method called "the old ball-in-the-odd-numbered-hoop trick". The player should take off to blue, roquet it gently leaving it in the hoop, then place red against it and use a stop-shot to send blue to hoop 2 while making the hoop with red, and then roquet black. Blue can then be used to make hoop 2. The idea of using the ball in the hoop to load the next hoop seldom occurs to players in game situations, even after they have been shown, and have practised it, many times. It does need practice, because there are things that can go wrong with it.

The following suggestions may help:

a. Try to place black 3-4 yards behind hoop 1, and out of the way of the coming stop-shot.
b. Try to get red alongside hoop 1 and very close, so that you can roquet blue into a hoop-leg and avoid sending it out of the hoop.
c. Play the stop-shot carefully, have a referee watch it, and be ready for an argument about whether or not you can use the blue ball again to make hoop 2.

This "trick" should also be practised in other odd-numbered hoops. (Why not in even hoops?)

Diag 4 shows two more positions for yellow and a slightly different position for blue. Here the immediate stop-shot of black to hoop 2 (method 2) may be worth considering if the player can play good stop-shots and roquets well, though most players will not find this an attractive method unless black, when roqueted, had been sent further south past hoop 1.

With yellow in position 1, the player may use a long roll in which he sends black to load hoop 2 while going to yellow, then take off back to blue to make hoop 1. However it would also be reasonable here to make hoop 1 first from blue, then roquet either black or blue and get a rush on the other opponent ball to a position from which you can send it to load hoop 3 while getting a rush to hoop 2.

If yellow is in position 2, where it can be rushed neither to hoop 2 nor hoop 3, the only feasible way to give yourself a good chance of an immediate break is to play the roll of black to hoop 2 and red to yellow. This should be recommended only to players who are considered capable of playing the long roll with reasonable control of where the balls will finish. Others will have to content themselves with making only one, or possibly two hoops in the turn, unless they are very lucky.

For an advanced player you could put the yellow ball centrally in hoop 3 and see what he does.

This by no means exhausts the things players should be taught about ways of loading hoops, and we shall later look at using cannons, disjoint cannons, promotion (or bombardment) shots, etc. The coach could choose to teach only a few of these situations in any one session, and use others as revision exercises later.

BALL IN A HOOP

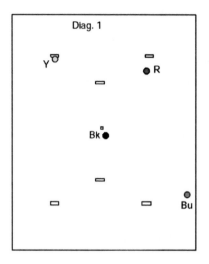

Diag. 1

D IAG.1 SHOWS A situation where the player of blue had made a long roll to hoop 2 with yellow, but unfortunately for him, the yellow ball finished in the hoop and blue was unable to make the hoop, so it was hit back (an attempted "saving shot") through the dead black ball to the east border. Red and black are for 4-back, yellow is for hoop 4, and of course blue is still for hoop 2.

The coach should set up the position on the court, explain what has happened, and ask the player to consider how he would play the next turn in a game as red and yellow.

The first thing the player should notice is that he is entitled to lift the yellow ball and take it to a baulk-line, since it is wired from all other balls and the opponent is responsible for its position. So after checking this with the opponent and the referee, he could take the yellow ball to B-baulk and shoot at red, possibly making a double target with red and blue, or he could shoot at red from the 3rd corner.

The player should be invited to try playing these options, and the results discussed, to help him understand that a disadvantage of these methods of proceeding is that, even if yellow roquets red, the setting up of a break will be likely to require some accurate shots; and, if he fails to roquet, the opponent would have a good chance of regaining the innings.

Another option, which the player should also try, is to shoot from A-baulk, near the 1st corner, at black, so as to finish near red if he misses. This would offer only a small chance of roqueting and is likely to allow black a relatively "safe" shot at his balls if he misses and stays in-court near red. The correct option (for most players) depends on the player realising that he does not need to take the lift immediately, as it can be taken next turn provided his yellow ball has not been moved.

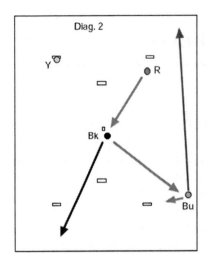

Diag. 2

Diag.2 shows the best way to play the turn.

He should play red, shooting at black. If he misses, red will finish on A-baulk where (unless the opponent roquets) yellow will be able to use it in the next turn. This would make it dangerous for black to shoot at blue and risk leaving two balls near yellow's hoop.

If red roquets black, he should send black near A-baulk while going to blue (see arrows), then roquet blue and send it near B-baulk, after which he should finish by leaving red near hoop 4, possibly trying to wire it from black. This is much better than hitting red back near yellow. Ask the player to do all this in order to see how easy (or difficult) he finds it to play the required strokes, and to show him that in his next turn, unless the opponent roquets, he will be able to lift yellow and start the next turn by roqueting either blue or black from baulk and using it to load hoop 5 while going to make hoop 4 from red.

The coach should also set similar situations in other parts of the lawn, as the most difficult part of coaching is to find a way of ensuring that the player will think of such a tactic in a game situation under pressure.

John Riches and Wayne Davies

RUN HOOP TO CORNER

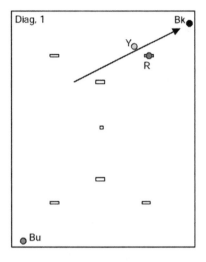

Diag, 1

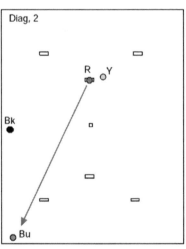

Diag, 2

THIS EXERCISE IS designed to teach the importance of considering all possibilities, rather than looking only at the most obvious. Set up the position shown and explain that Red had failed to make 4-back, such that it can just be touched by a straightedge placed against the playing side of 4-back.

Then black shot from west of penultimate at yellow, and missed, finishing on the east border about 2 yards from the 3rd corner. Yellow is also for 4-back.

Ask the player to think how he would play the next turn if he was red and yellow, and what problem he can see that he would need to solve.

Most players will first think of playing red, making 4-back, and rushing yellow to penultimate, possibly hoping to also make rover. Let them play the turn as they suggest. Then they will realise that they have given a lift and they will have difficulty getting the two opponent balls away from the baulk-lines, let alone obtaining a good leave to enable yellow to finish the game next turn.

Some may then suggest playing yellow, roqueting red gently, and peeling it while going to black. Then black could be sent into the lawn (e.g. to the peg, or past penultimate) while yellow tries to get in position to run the 4-back hoop and use red. That is a useful idea, and there are situations where it would be correct, so the player should be congratulated for thinking of it. Let them try this continuation also.

Then ask them to try to think of any further possibilities. Some will think of it quickly, but others will have great difficulty realising that they should start by hitting red to the 3ʳᵈ corner as it makes the 4-back hoop—or at least close enough to black to be able to roquet it easily.

The stroke needs practice. It must be played very carefully (with a referee watching), and it is important to make it a slow, deliberate stroke without any sort of jabbing or jerking action.

Let the mallet follow through into the hoop-leg.

The secret here is to line it up carefully, then keep your eye on where the centre of the mallet has to go, not on the point where the mallet will strike the ball, as it will probably not be possible to contact the ball with the centre of the mallet face

As a second exercise (possibly used for revision in a later lesson), place red in the penultimate hoop with yellow a yard east of penultimate and black on the west border level with the peg (see Diag. 2).

Explain that red had rushed yellow to penultimate, attempted to make the hoop, and stuck in the hoop, having almost (but not quite) made the hoop. Black then shot at yellow from the east border near C3, and missed. This time red can be hit to blue near the 1ˢᵗ corner as it makes the penultimate hoop. This should enable you to finish with a stronger leave, so is worth doing, even though this time there is no lift involved.

FAILED CANNON ATTEMPT

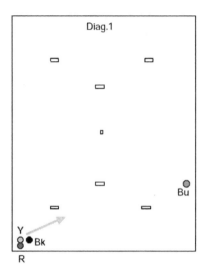

Diag.1

Bu

Y

Bk

R

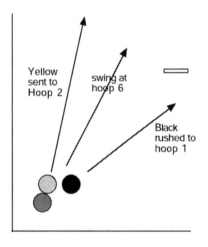

Yellow
sent to
Hoop 2

swing at
hoop 6

Black
rushed to
hoop 1

Set up the position shown in the first diagram, and explain that all clips are still on hoop 1. In the third turn of the game black had missed the tice (yellow), finishing in the 2nd corner; and in the fourth turn red had missed yellow also, but finished near it on the west border. Black then shot back from the 2nd corner at the opponent's balls and missed again, finishing near the first corner.

Then red rushed yellow into the corner, hoping to create a cannon. The rush was successful, but when he got there and measured yellow onto the corner spot, the player of red found it was not quite touching the black ball, since black had not actually gone out in the corner. The yellow and black balls are in fact about an inch (2 cm) apart.

Ask the player how he would continue in a game, having failed to create the hoped-for cannon. (Perhaps you could first get him to play the cannon he would have had if black had been a corner ball.)

When this occurred in a recent game, red (a strong first division player) simply played a gentle take-off, leaving yellow behind and getting a rush on black to hoop 1. He made only the one hoop in that turn.

If this is what the player would do, get him to do it, perhaps trying after hoop 1 to continue by getting a rush to either hoop 2 or to one of the other two balls. Discuss the result, including the leave he finishes with and whether it will give him a good chance of establishing a break in the following turn if the opponent fails to roquet.

Then restore the original position and ask whether he can think of a better way to go about things.

A better option would have been to stop-shot yellow as shown by the arrow, to a position about a yard east and a yard south of hoop 1.

Then he could have roqueted black and used a "load and hold" stop-shot to send black to hoop 2 while holding position to run hoop 1. If he failed to gain position to run the hoop, he would be able to set up a strong "trap-line" leave by hitting red halfway between yellow and the south border. Get him to try this method also, and discuss both its advantages and disadvantages.

If he made the hoop, he could then roquet black and split it to hoop 3 while going to blue, and use a thick take-off to put blue out towards hoop 4 while going to make hoop 2 from yellow with a break fully set up, although he has had to play some difficult shots accurately to achieve it.

However, there is a better option still: The player of red could have played a simple "disjoint cannon" to load hoop 2 with yellow and rush black to hoop 1, with an immediate break set up. The second (enlarged) diagram illustrates the way to play the disjoint cannon. (Make sure you follow through; do not use a stop-shot, as only part of the force will be transferred from red to black.)

This is not a true cannon because the yellow and black balls are not touching, and therefore black cannot be moved; but you can play it in exactly the same way as you would play a normal first-corner cannon. Many players miss opportunities to use disjoint cannons to establish breaks.

PARTNER BALL

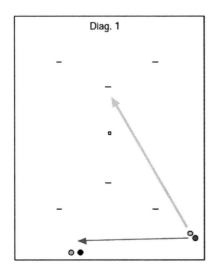

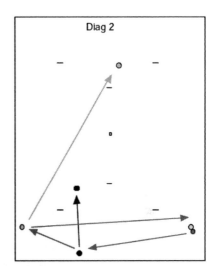

T HIS COULD BE taught to players as soon as they can play split-shots. The coach could teach it to any number of people at the same time, with one or two participating and others watching.

Set up the position in Diag 1 on the lawn and ask the student what he would do if he were playing red which is for hoop 5 and had just started his turn by roqueting yellow which is for 4-back. Ask him to explain why he would do whatever he suggests, then invite him to do it and see how it works out. If he manages to get a break established, congratulate him and tell him you have seen enough.

Then (without further explanation or correction) set up the position in Diag 2 where again red has just roqueted yellow, and the only difference is that the blue ball has been moved to the west border about 8 yards from black. Ask him the same question. Again let him try whatever he suggests he would do.

If he would do different things, ask him to explain his thinking—what would cause him to choose different lines of play in the two situations which may appear somewhat similar?

If he would do the same sort of thing in both positions, you can show him that either:

221

(1) If he took off from yellow to the opponent's balls both times, then in Diag 1 he has passed up a good chance of establishing a break (and get him to try doing it); or

(2) If he sent yellow out into the lawn both times, then in Diag 2 he is taking a big risk of failing to be able to continue the turn and having to choose between returning to his partner ball in mid-lawn, or having to leave yellow in the lawn and hit red away to a corner somewhere, surrendering the innings.

Assuming he is capable of playing the required shots, what should he have done?

In Diag 1 he should split yellow to load hoop 6 while going to the opponent's balls, then roquet one of them and use it to get a rush behind the other ball to hoop 5 (see arrows).

In Diag 2 it would be a mistake to send yellow in-lawn to hoop 6 (or anywhere else in-lawn). He should take off to black, send it to the left of hoop 5 while going to blue, then send blue behind hoop 6 while going back to yellow, and finish by setting a rush for red to blue, threatening in his next turn to load hoop 6 with yellow and get a rush on blue back to make hoop 5. An alternative, if it can be done safely without giving black a double target, would be to set the rush to hoop 5.

The principle illustrated here can perhaps be expressed as **"If you believe you have a better than even chance of setting up an immediate break, do not hesitate to put your partner ball out into the lawn; but if you have only a slight chance, leave it near the border and set up so as to give yourself the maximum chance of a break in your next turn".**

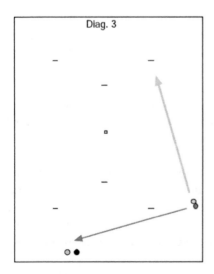

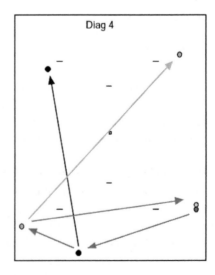

John Riches and Wayne Davies

Now repeat the same two situations, but move the red clip from Hoop 5 to Hoop 2, leaving the yellow clip on 4-back as before. Again ask the player(s) to show how they would play the turn as red, after having roqueted yellow.

In Diag. 3 they could send yellow into the lawn (as in Diag.1) while going to blue and black, but this time they cannot easily load hoop 3 with yellow because (as shown in the diagram) the angle of split would exceed 90 degrees. Instead, they could send yellow to a position near the peg, or near hoop 6, but this noticeably reduces the chance of getting a break fully established as compared with the Diag.1 situation, so involves a greater risk which may no longer be considered worth taking.

Another option is to send yellow only 2-3 yards into the lawn, and hope for a rush to it after making hoop 2.

A third option is to use a normal thin take-off and set up a cannon—either a real cannon or a disjoint cannon—with the opponent's balls, then use them to set the lawn up for yellow in the same positions as achieved (from a slightly different starting situation) in Diag.4

In Diag 4 there is not much justification for sending your partner ball out into the lawn, so setting up a break for red in the next turn is clearly the best option. With the opponent's balls about 8-9 yards apart this is easy to do. [In passing, it may be noted that this is a reason that "returning wide of partner" is seldom a sensible tactic—it simply invites the opponent to set up the lawn by easily sending your balls wherever he wants to.]

There should be little risk in playing the long stop-shots, as no great accuracy is required. Black needs only to be sent close enough to hoop 2 to ensure that the opponent will feel compelled to move it next turn, and blue should be sent about halfway between hoop 3 and the side (east) border. On returning to yellow (which this time should have been left on or very close to the yardline), you can hit red out 2-3 feet south of yellow, giving red a rush up the yard-line to blue.

Then, if the opponent hits away instead of shooting, you can play red, rush yellow to blue, and rush blue to hoop 2.
    If black shoots at your two balls and misses, you can use black to get a rush on yellow to either hoop 2, or to the blue ball.
    If black shoots at blue and misses, you can take off (thickly, for preference) from yellow to black and send black to hoop 3 while getting a rush on blue to hoop 2. Note that this is easier with blue halfway between hoop 3 and the border (using a half-roll) than if blue had been placed closer to the hoop, in which case a full roll would be needed, and would be more difficult to control accurately.

THICK TAKE-OFFS

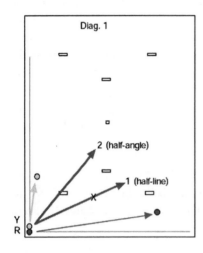

Diag. 1

2 (half-angle)

1 (half-line)

Y
R

ASK THE PLAYER to play a croquet stroke from the 1ˢᵗ corner, with the croqueted ball (yellow) lined up to go up the west yard-line and the 'V' lined up to send the striker's ball (red) along the south yard-line. Ask him to hit the red ball with a flat swing as in a normal take-off, and swing directly at a point (which you will need to mark for him, e.g. by placing your mallet there) halfway between hoops 4 and 5. He should try to keep the mallet head pointing in this direction, and hit hard enough to send the red ball about as far as hoop 4.

The result should be similar to that shown in Diag.1, illustrating two important forces affecting split-shots:

(1) PULL—the croqueted ball will "pull" slightly inside the west yard-line. This pull is noticeably less with the latest (more elastic) Dawson International balls than with the older balls, and if the balls had fallen slightly apart before red was hit, the yellow ball may even sometimes be cut out into the yard-line area.

Explain that pull needs to be taken into account when lining up any split-shot or peel.

(2) DRAG—"mallet-drag" will cause the red ball also to finish in-lawn from the yard-line where the 'V' was lined up. It will also be noticeable that the drag on the striker's ball is greater than the pull on the croqueted ball. Explain that drag must also be allowed for when lining up a split-shot. Ask the player to look at where the red and yellow balls finished, and find the point on the lawn which is halfway between them. This point (point X on the diagram) will turn out to be on, or very close to, the line in which he swung to send the balls to those two positions.

He should also note that the balls were lined up to go along the yard-lines, which make an angle of 90 degrees. If he had instead swung at a line which halved this right-angle, it would have passed through hoop 1, and there would have been no way he could have sent the balls to the places they actually went to.

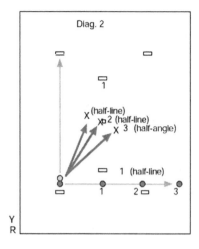

Diag. 2

Get him to play the stroke again (using a flat swing) and swing straight at hoop 1, noting that this time the balls will travel approximately equal distances.

This should convince the player that if he wants the balls to go where they originally went, he will not be able to do it by "halving the angle", but will need to choose his aiming point by "halving the imaginary line" which joins the positions where the two balls are expected to finish.

Diag. 2 shows a similar croquet stroke being played from about a yard behind hoop 1. Ask the player to suggest the correct direction of swing needed to send yellow to hoop 2 and red to each of the three positions shown. The angle is exactly the same (a right-angle) for each of the three strokes, but if he "halves the angle" and sends yellow near to hoop 2, red will go to position 3. To get red to positions 1 and 2 he will have to "halve the line", not "halve the angle".

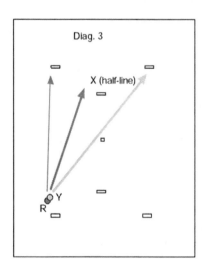

Diag. 3

Now ask the player to line up a stroke from a yard or two behind hoop 1, designed to send yellow to load hoop 3 while red goes to hoop 2.

He should find the line of aim by "halving the line" (see point X on Diag 3), and then moving slightly (about a yard for a split-shot of this length) toward the side where the striker's ball is to go. In this case, he will move from the mid-point about a yard toward hoop 2, as indicated by the dark arrow in the diagram. This is very close to the line he would have obtained if he had "halved the angle", but as we have seen, halving the angle does not work for splits in which one ball will travel much further than the other.

The reason for moving slightly towards the side where the striker's ball will finish is that (as we have also seen) we have to allow for the fact that mallet-drag will be greater than pull. The player will also need to stand forward and hit down on the ball because this split involves a "three-quarter roll".

Another type of split shot is shown in Diag. 4. It is a "thick take-off" where you want to send yellow in front of the rover hoop (to load it, or ready for peeling) while red goes to a ball at penultimate.

Again it must be played with a flat mallet in order to achieve the maximum angle of split.

If we use the above formula we have developed for other splits, we will discover a problem. The aiming point should be more than a yard north (toward penultimate) of the peg, but you will find that either red goes too far or yellow not far enough. This is because there is an additional factor for which allowance must be made, as well as for drag and pull. The third factor is "BALL-SLIP". In a split-shot with a very wide angle, such as a thick take-off, the surface of the red ball, instead of catching on the yellow ball and "dragging" it with it, will tend to slip or slide across the surface of the yellow ball, leaving it behind. This is even more noticeable if the balls are wet.

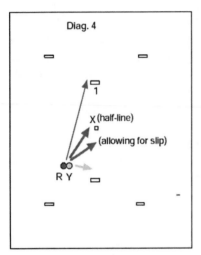

Diag. 4

X (half-line)

(allowing for slip)

R Y

SLIP—In order to counter (or allow for) slip, you need to find the halfway point as previously, then move noticeably towards the side where the croqueted ball will go, rather than the side where the striker's ball will go.

This is because "slip" in this situation will have a greater effect than mallet-drag. In other words, you simply hit more into the croqueted ball.

Ball-slip occurs, and must be allowed for, only when the angle of split (i.e. between the directions of the two balls) exceeds 60 degrees.

The player should practise thick take-offs of varying length from various court positions, finding the point halfway between where he wants the balls to finish and then hitting more into the croqueted ball.

Perhaps the most important thick take-off to practise is from the "tice" position on the west border to load hoop 2 while going to the opponent's balls on the east border level with hoop 5, as it can occur quite often at the start of a game, and it is a big advantage to the player if he can play this stroke confidently.

SETTING UP IN THE MIDDLE

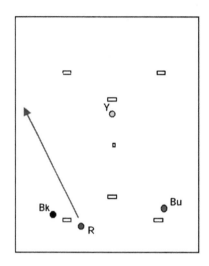

WITH ALL CLIPS on hoop 1, and having used the other two balls, Red rolled to hoop 1 with black, but found that he was unable to make the hoop. He had one remaining shot with red. (In the game, the player decided to hit red to the west border level with yellow, as shown by the arrow.)

Set up this position and ask the player what he would have done as red with his one remaining shot.

The best place for red is near yellow, provided there is no double target offered to black. Players often consider it too risky to leave their two balls out in the lawn in such situations, but the decision to hit red to border is based on poor reasoning.

[It was not possible for red to sit in front of hoop 1 wired from black and be able to run the hoop next turn; and even if it had been possible it would not have been a good option.]

Ask the player to explain the things he would take into consideration in making the decision about where to hit red. Almost all tactical decisions should be based on a consideration of percentages, but few players will mention percentages or probabilities in their explanation.

When asked after the game, the player of red said he would expect his opponent (or himself) to hit a 14-yard roquet about 4 times out of 10, or 40% of the time.

If the player being coached similarly elects to hit the red ball out of play, the coach should similarly ask him to consider how many times out of ten he would expect black (or blue) to roquet, and how many times he himself would expect to roquet in the following turn if the opponent missed.

After hitting red to the west border, he will retain the innings only if the opponent misses and then he himself roquets. The chances of these two things happening would have been about 60% and 40% respectively, regardless of which ball black shoots at. Thus, after he hits red to the border as shown, the chance that the player of red and yellow will retain the innings is 40% of 60%, or 24%.

If the player had hit red to a position near yellow, black would have had one chance to roquet, with a 40% chance of hitting, and red would still have the innings if he missed. Thus the chance of retaining the innings would in this case be 60%.

Which is better: a 24% chance of retaining the innings, or a 60% chance?

In this sort of situation you should not be too concerned about giving black an easy break if he does happen to roquet; as it is more important to ensure that if he misses you will have still have the innings.

In order for hitting away to border to be a reasonable option, the chance of black roqueting would need to be at least 60% in this type of situation. (It is worth noting that international players do not hit 14-yard roquets more than 5 times out of 10 on average.)

After red is hit to border, black can shoot at blue and stay within 3-4 yards of it, then the player of red and yellow will be under considerable pressure to hit the next roquet.

It also makes little sense from a psychological viewpoint to take the pressure off your opponent and put it on yourself.

Of course, one does not plan to set up in the middle of the lawn, and should do so only when things have gone wrong and there is no better option.

TRAP-LINES

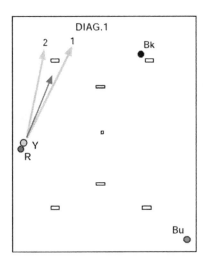

DIAG.1

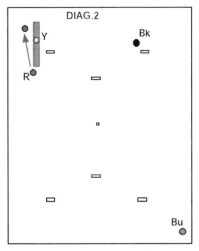

DIAG.2

SET UP THE position in Diag.1 and explain that red had just made hoop 1, but did not get a good forward rush on yellow, so the best he could do was cut it to the position shown on the west border. Invite the player to continue the break with red. Yellow can be for (say) 4-back.

It is fairly clear that there is little point in doing anything other than rolling to hoop 2, since if it can be made there will be a break established with black already loading hoop 3.

Ask the player to play the long roll, and commend him if he is successful in making the hoop. If he does not, ask him to think carefully about where he will place red with his one remaining shot.

Most players will roll yellow to point 1 on the diagram; i.e. to the right (in-lawn) side of hoop 2, reasoning that it will make it easier for them to continue the break if they can make the hoop.

But if they cannot make the hoop, there will be no good place to leave red without either allowing black a "free" shot at yellow, or (if they place red so as to cover the boundary against that shot), allowing black to shoot at blue, and if black fails to roquet, red will have a lot of work to do to set up a break in his next turn.

Then tell the player that you are going to start teaching him about "trap-line" theory, and explain that the "hoop 2 trap-line" is an imaginary line (actually a yard-wide strip of lawn) parallel to the west border and 1-2 yards west of hoop 2.

Show him where this area of lawn is (see the green rectangle in Diag.2), get him to walk along it, and then ask him to play the roll again, trying to send yellow to the left of hoop 2 into the trap-line area (e.g. to point 2 in Diag.1), instead of to the right of hoop 2. If he now cannot attempt to make the hoop, he can place red halfway between yellow and the west border, as shown by the red arrow in Diag.2. Discuss both the advantages and disadvantages of the two rolls. He should note that if he makes hoop 2, then using the trap-line will require him to play a more difficult split-roll to load hoop 4 while going to black at hoop 3, so if he plans to use trap-lines, shots such as this one will need to be part of his practice routine. If he cannot make the hoop, the leave shown in Diag. 2 will give him a much better chance of a break in the following turn, as it will now be very risky for black to shoot at yellow when a miss will allow red to roquet black and stop-shot it back to hoop 3 while holding a rush on yellow to hoop 2.

If black returns to blue, red should be able to rush yellow close to hoop 2, with a

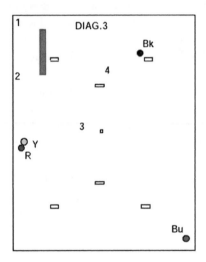

reasonable chance (after making the hoop) of getting a rush on yellow to either hoop 3 or hoop 4 and continuing the break. Try placing yellow in other positions which are not on the trap-line, and consider why it needs to be in the green area shown, as if it is anywhere else it will be either harder for red to cover the border against a shot by black, or less certain that red will be able to make hoop 2 after black shoots at blue and misses.

The player's understanding of "trap-line" theory should be developed over a number of further sessions, rather than trying to cover it all at once.

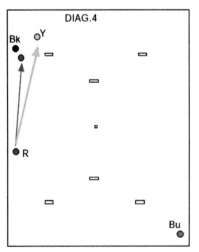

Diag. 3 shows four other places (among many) from which a player playing an approach shot to hoop 2 may consider it wise to send his partner ball to a position on the trap-line. (Note that it must always be the partner ball that is sent to the trap-line, not an opponent ball.)

The exact size of the trap-line area will be determined by the ability of the player to play sharp stop-shots while holing a rush to his hoop, and the decision on whether or not to use the trap-line will depend on how he assesses his chance of making the hoop. If he gives himself a noticeably better than even chance of making the hoop, then he should probably forget about the trap-line and just roll for the hoop normally. The trap-line should be used only when using it will not noticeably reduce your chance of continuing the immediate break

Diag.4 shows a different type of situation where the use of a trap-line should be considered. In another coaching session, set it up on the lawn and ask the player how he would continue the break with red when black is on the west border as shown, instead of loading hoop 3. Many players will want to use a split-roll to send yellow to hoop 3 while going to black (perhaps even trying to get a rush behind black), and roll out to hoop 2 with black. If the player suggests this, get him to do it.

It is good that he is thinking of loading hoop 3 before making hoop 2, but suggest to him that if he also thinks about the possibility of using the hoop 2 trap-line, he may find a better and safer way to continue. Ask him to roll yellow into the trap-line area while going to black (being sure to keep red well in-lawn), then roquet black and send it to hoop 3 while obtaining position with red to run hoop 2. If this is unsuccessful (another shot to practise!) he can retreat red behind yellow (halfway between yellow and the yard-line, not 0on the border) with a rush in to hoop 2 in the following turn if black returns to blue.

The roll to the trap-line can be again played from various positions similar to those shown in Diag.3.

The black ball can also be in different positions on the yard-line, from the middle of the north border, around past the 2nd corner and down to the middle of the west border. In future sessions the player should try if from a number of such positions, e.g. with black in the middle of the west border and the (split-)roll to the trap-line being played from near the peg.

If in Diag.4 the black ball is moved to the 2nd corner spot, the pass-roll needed to send yellow to the trap-line while going to black may be considered risky for some players. This is another shot that needs practice, as in such situations the trap-line play should involve no more risk than sending yellow to hoop 3 while going to black, and is the best way of keeping control of the game.

Diag. 5 shows the trap-line for hoop 4 which is even more useful than the hoop 2 trap-line. This is because using the partner ball to load the next hoop (hoop 5) would leave it out in the lawn if the attempt to gain position to run hoop 4 is unsuccessful.

The shorter distance to the next hoop also means that the trap-line is in this case about halfway between the hoop and the east yard-line, i.e. further from the hoop, since with your partner ball on the trap-line, you will still have enough distance to be able to hold a rush to hoop 4 while using a stop-shot to send a ball from the east yard-line to hoop 5.

Set up the balls as shown in Diag.5 and ask the player to continue playing red, which has just made hoop 3 and not been able to rush yellow any closer to hoop 4. (If the player is a less experienced one, move the red and yellow balls closer to the blue ball so that the long roll he will need to use to put yellow on the trap-line while going to blue is not too difficult for him.)

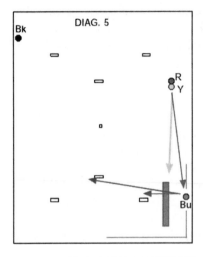

The most likely continuation chosen will be to send yellow to hoop 5 while going to blue, then rolling with blue for position to make hoop 4.

Discuss the result he obtains, and help him understand the danger of putting yellow out near hoop 5 when the making of hoop 4 is far from certain.

Ask him if he can think of a way of using a "trap-line" to retain the option of a good leave while also attempting to continue the break. Discuss where the hoop 4 trap-line is, and why it is further from the hoop than the hoop 2 trap-line he has already seen.

This idea should be considered (depending on where yellow can be rushed to) when blue is anywhere on or near the yard-line within 14 yards of the 4th corner (see the grey line on Diag. 5).

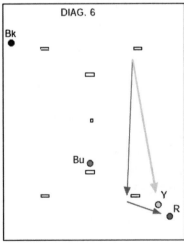

Another way to use the hoop 4 trap-line is shown in Diag. 6, when blue is already at hoop 5. Ask the player to try the "natural" method (having made hoop 3 without a forward rush) of sending yellow to hoop 5 while trying to get a rush on blue, then try it again, using the trap-line method, and discuss the advantages and disadvantages of each method.

In the Diag. 6 situation there is a further option he could try: Send yellow to the trap-line while going to blue, roquet blue (possibly improving the load of hoop 5), and then take off from blue to the front of hoop 4. Many players will find that they have a better chance of making hoop 4 after the 8-yard take-off from hoop 5 than by using the long roll from near hoop 3.

A similar situation would occur if blue were about 6 inches south-east of the peg, so that it could not be rushed to hoop 4 anyway.

It is important that before deciding to use a trap-line in this way, the player assesses the percentages and is convinced that the trap-line play will not noticeably reduce his chance of making hoop 4, and will have the advantage of allowing a safer and stronger leave if he is unable to do so.

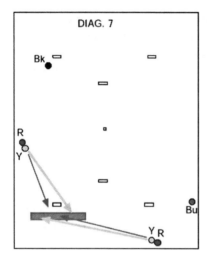

DIAG. 7

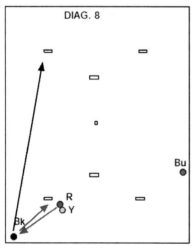

DIAG. 8

The hoop 1 trap-line is also a useful one. As Diag. 7 shows, it is parallel to the south boundary and about one yard south of hoop 1. Two positions from which it is commonly used are shown in Diag. 7—when rolling to hoop 1 soon after the start of the game, from either the tice position on the west border, or from near hoop 4.

Here using the trap-line involves putting your partner ball about a yard in front of hoop 1, instead of behind hoop 1 as in a normal hoop approach. It has the disadvantage of forgoing any chance of obtaining a forward rush after making the hoop, thus making it harder to continue the break. However, when the chance of making the hoop is small, it may be considered safer to retain the option, should you not obtain position to run the hoop, of being able to make a strong leave by placing your red ball halfway between the south border and the yellow ball which is on the trap-line.

This makes it very risky for black to shoot at your balls, as a miss will allow you to set up an immediate break; and if black returns to blue, you should be able to make hoop 1 and then use the opponent's balls to continue the break.

Ask the player to make hoop 1 with red from either or both of the positions shown in Diag 7, as well as from positions near hoop 5 or near the peg.

Discuss with him his options for a leave if the roll is unsuccessful and he fails to get position to run the hoop.

Then explain that hoop 1 also (like hoops 2 and 4) has a trap-line that he can consider using. Help him work out where it is, and how to use it, and get him to try using it from some different positions. Discuss the advantages and disadvantages.

He should understand that if he does succeed in making the hoop he will need to roquet yellow, then play either a very long roll to load hoop 3 with yellow while going to black, or a split-shot in which he sends yellow to hoop 3 while red goes to blue.

Both of these shots need practice if he wants to have the advantage of using the hoop 1 trap-line in such situations. The split-shot to blue needs care, but also allows you to get blue away from the border while taking off to black at hoop 2.

Another use of this trap-line is shown in Diag 8 where red tries to set up a break by taking off to black in the 1st corner and using a load-and-hold stop-shot to load hoop 2 before making hoop 1.

There are similar trap-lines available for use at hoop 3, 1-back, 2-back, 3-back and 4-back; but for most players there are no useful trap-lines for the centre hoops.

Some people refer to this roll of yellow to the trap-line as a "defensive roll", and see it as a rather negative tactic, so they prefer to play the roll with the expectation that they will succeed in making the hoop. We prefer to view it as "setting a trap" for the opponent, and in effect saying to him, "Come on, I dare you to shoot at anything. If you do you'd better not miss, or I will go around."

Seen in this light, it can be viewed as a very aggressive tactic, particularly when the player of red is confident that if he succeeds in making hoop 1 he will be able to continue the break without needing a forward rush.

SETTING UP

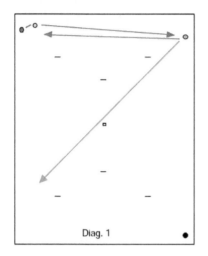

Diag. 1

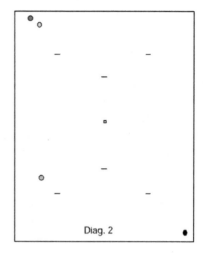

Diag. 2

THIS CAN BE taught to players who have learnt how to play a 4-ball break. It is best taught to one or two students at a time, so that they have to think for themselves and get to practise the strokes involved.

We will look at a way of teaching the student how to go about setting up the lawn from a situation where both opponent balls are out of play. This mainly happens when playing against people who use the very negative "Aunt Emma" tactics of hitting balls out of play without trying to roquet, and waiting for you to make a mistake.

Set up the position shown in Diag 1, with the red clip on hoop 1 and yellow on 4-back, then explain that the opponent has just hit black from near hoop 1 into the 4th corner, and ask the student to work out what he would do if he were playing red and yellow. It should be apparent that trying to roll to the first hoop, and/or set up near it, will achieve little, and he would do better to start working toward establishing a break. It will not matter if he takes 2-3 turns to get the break set up, as long as he does not have to play too many risky shots and the opponent does not get any better chance to roquet than the one he passed up by hitting black from hoop 1 into the 4th corner instead of shooting at one of the other three balls.

It will also not matter which ball you play, and there will sometimes be more than one way to go about it, but here, and in many similar situations, the most straightforward procedure will be to take off to one opponent ball (blue), and put it where the opponent will have to move it in his next turn (i.e. usually near one of your hoops) while returning to your partner ball to set a rush to the other (black) opponent ball. If you can get both opponent balls into court immediately, that will be better still, but often it will not be possible, or the shots involved will be too risky.

It is important that when starting the turn you must think about where you will want your own two balls to be when you set the rush. Here, if the turn is played with red, the yellow ball should be left, if possible, so that red will be able to set up the desired rush to black by hitting red out behind yellow and measuring it onto the yard-line. This may require a slightly thick take-off as red goes to blue. The arrows on the diagram show the shots needed.

The opponent will then be faced with the situation shown in Diag 2. Notice that in this case his rush can be used either to load hoop 2, or to go to black and bring it into play. Any roquet the opponent attempts will involve as much risk as there would have been involved if he had chosen to shoot in his previous turn.

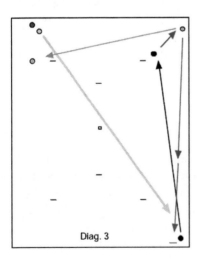

Diag. 3

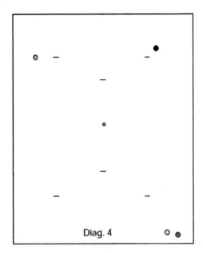

Diag. 4

Ask the student to play the turn as described several times. Make sure he knows the reasoning behind each stroke so that he can use the same thinking in other positions where different strokes may be involved.

In Diag 2, if the opponent shoots with blue at black and misses, red can load hoop 2 with yellow and take off to the balls in the 4th corner to set up a 3-ball break. If the opponent shoots at red and yellow, a miss will give you an extra ball in the 2nd corner. Your rush should have been set far enough from the corner to allow you to use his ball to load hoop 2 while getting a rush to hoop 1.

If he again refuses to shoot and hits blue back into the 3rd corner, Diag 3 shows the shots than can be used to make progress: Rush yellow all the way to the 4th corner, take off behind black, rush it up the lawn, take off to blue, roquet it and put blue also out into the lawn while returning to yellow to set a rush either to hoop 1 (as shown in Diag 4), or to hoop 2, or to one of the opponent's balls.

In this case setting the rush to black, rather than to hoop 1, may serve to once again discourage the opponent from taking any shot, leaving you to rush yellow near black, stop-shot yellow toward hoop 2, and rush black to hoop 1. If blue is where it can be used, so much the better.

Once again the opponent is then faced with a situation (Diag 4) where any roquet he attempts and misses is likely to leave you with a good chance of setting up a break.

Some of the shots you need to play are long ones, but they carry little risk, and if something goes wrong you should be able to return to your partner ball and (provided the opponent fails to roquet) start the process again next turn. Most times the balls will not be as unfavourably placed as they were at the start of this example.

For example, if in Diag 3 your long diagonal rush of yellow to the 4th corner goes astray you could simply roll your two balls toward the 1st corner and set up there for hoop 1. Or alternatively, if the rush goes somewhere near the 4th corner but in the take-off you do not get position to rush black into the lawn, you can use a stop-shot to send black into the lawn somewhere near hoop 2 (there is no point in putting it at hoop 1 as it will be moved anyway), possibly trying to wire it on hoop 4 from your own balls, and give yourself a rush on yellow to either hoop 1, hoop 2 or the blue ball.

This whole procedure of getting the opponent's balls into play needs practice, and you must keep in mind the final position you are aiming for so that you leave your partner ball in a position such that you will not have difficulty returning to it and setting a useful rush for your next turn. The opponent can attempt a roquet, but it will be no less risky than the one he refused to attempt in the beginning.

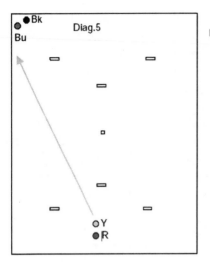

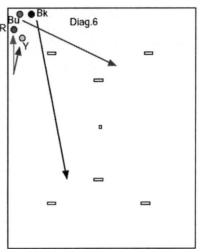

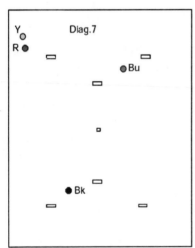

Set up the four balls as shown in Diag. 5 and ask the player how he would continue as red and yellow in a game where his red clip is on 4-back and his yellow clip is on hoop 5.

Most players will choose one of three continuations:

(1) Play red, rush yellow to penultimate, then take off to the opponent's balls and rush one of them to 4-back, setting up a break to take red to the peg. The problem with this is that it is too early to make 4-back when yellow has not yet made 1-back. By making 4-back and giving a lift to the opponent, you make it harder to set a good leave to get a break for yellow, which should be your priority, and you also risk having red pegged out if the opponent gets in with either ball.

(2) Play yellow, roquet red, take off to the opponent's balls, and rush one of them back to hoop 5, with a low percentage chance of getting a break established in this turn and little chance of obtaining a good leave.

(3) Play yellow, roquet red and roll to hoop 5 immediately. For most players this would be too risky, and you would still have work to do after making hoop 5 to set up a break.

Get the player to try these various options so that he can appreciate the advantage of instead setting up the lawn as follows:

Play red (not yellow) and rush yellow near to the opponent's balls. Use a small (pass-) roll if necessary to leave it within 2 yards of the west border as you go to blue. Roquet blue and stop-shot it to a position between hoops 3 and 6, trying to roquet black in the same stroke (a "disjoint cannon"—it needs practice). Send black halfway between hoops 1 and 5 (see Diag.6) and set a rush for yellow to either opponent ball—preferably black in this case (see Diag.7).

Have him play the strokes to obtain this "ideal leave", and discuss with him its advantages. Then imagine that the opponent has shot with either black or blue and missed, and see if he can set up a break for yellow.

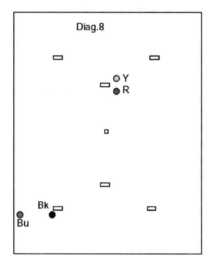

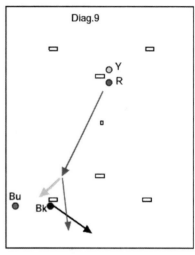

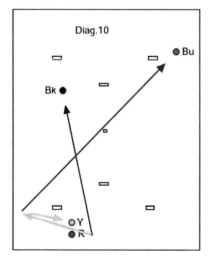

Set up the balls as in Diag. 8, with the red clip on 4-back and yellow clip on the peg. The black ball is close to the western hoop-leg of hoop 1, unable to make the hoop and not rushable up the lawn. It can be imagined that blue has just missed a shot at black from somewhere behind hoop 4.

Ask the player how he would continue as red and yellow in a game.

The likely choices are:

(1) play red, cut-rush yellow part of the way to 4-back, take off to the front of the hoop, run 4-back and then rush yellow to penultimate, hoping to finish the game by using only his own two balls.

Point out that if anything goes wrong with the 2-ball break he will have given a lift, will probably not be able to use the opponent's balls to continue the break, and will not be able to set a good leave.

(2) play red, roquet yellow, take off to black trying to get a rush on it to blue, and rush blue back to 4-back, with a break set up. This option requires some accurate and difficult shots, and with yellow left out in the lawn there will again be little possibility of obtaining a good leave.

Now tell him that you want him to instead play to set up an "ideal leave". Ask him to imagine such a leave—"ideal" places for all four balls (not counting on wiring)—and how he could get them there.

Diags.9 &10 illustrate such a method: Play yellow, rush red towards hoop 1, and send it within 2-3 yards of the south border while getting a rush on black towards the middle of the south boundary.

Send black about 4-5 yards west of penultimate while going to blue on the west border, then send blue east of 4-back and set a rush for red to black. **The important thing is not which option he chooses, but that the choice should be based on a consideration of percentages.** Setting up will give him about a 60% chance of finishing and winning the game in his next turn, since the opponent would roquet no more than 4 times in 10. He would be correct to choose option (1) or(2) if he is convinced it would give him an as good or better chance of winning.

CONSIDER ALL OPTIONS

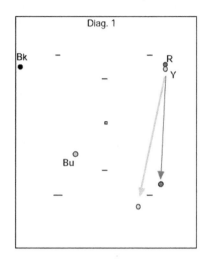

Diag. 1

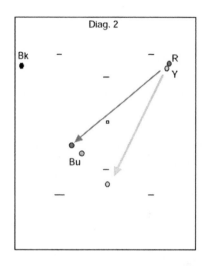

Diag. 2

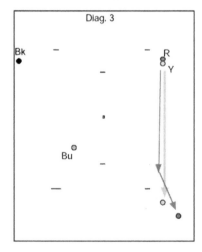

Diag. 3

THE POSITION SHOWN above can be used to teach the importance of considering all tactical options, and to help the player realise that if he does not take the time to think before playing, even in what may appear to be common positions that occur regularly, he is likely to overlook what may have been a better option that would have increased his winning chances.

In Diag.1 red has made hoop 3 and roqueted yellow. Black is on the west border and blue is about half-way between the peg and hoop 1.

Ask the player how he would continue, then get him to do it and discuss the result. Ask him whether he can think of another way (or more than one) in which he could have continued from this position, and discuss which method he prefers, and why.

Players will usually choose between the continuations shown in the first two diagrams:

(1) the immediate long roll of both balls to hoop 4 as in Diag.1, or—
(2) loading hoop 5 with yellow while trying for a rush on blue to hoop 4 (see Diag.2).

He should realise that the immediate roll shown in Diag.1 is for most players a difficult and low percentage shot which is not only unlikely to allow him to continue the break, but will also not give him a good leave when he finds he is unable to run hoop 4, since wherever he places red, blue will probably have either a relatively safe shot at yellow, or (if red tries to cover the boundary against that shot) can return to partner and red will need to play some risky shots to get a break established in the next turn.

As a third option he could improve his leave by rolling yellow to a "trap-line" position as shown in Diag.3, so that if he cannot attempt to make the hoop he can set red with a rush on yellow to hoop 4, covering the border against a shot by blue at yellow.

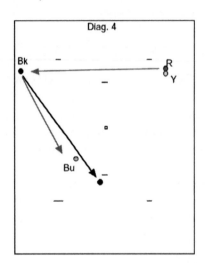

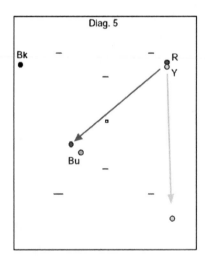

A fourth option is to take off to black and roll it to load hoop 5 while trying for a rush on blue to hoop 4 (see Diag.4). Again get the player to play the shots so that he gains an appreciation of how difficult (or easy) he finds this method. If he fails to get position to run hoop 4, he will have to return to yellow which has been left too far out in the court to allow him to satisfactorily cover the boundary against a shot at it by blue, and also give himself a good chance of a break next turn if blue shoots at black and misses, finishing on the west border.

A better leave would have been possible if instead of taking off from yellow he had played a shot that sent yellow somewhere within 4 yards of the border while going to black. This could be considered as a fifth (and perhaps a sixth) option, which could be achieved by either rolling yellow past hoop 2 with an equal roll as red goes to black, or using a "thick take-off" to send yellow towards the north border in front of hoop 3. Both of these shots introduce a slightly greater element of risk, but allow a safer leave if red cannot make hoop 4, provided you can hit red back to an accurate position near yellow, which will require some skill.

The last option we will look at is one that few players would consider, but is probably the one to be recommended for most players: Use a split shot to send yellow to a "trap-line" position about halfway between hoop 4 and the 4th corner, while red goes to blue (see Diag.5). He will then roquet blue and take off for position to run hoop 4, hopefully having been able to get blue a little better placed near hoop 5. You are not depending on getting a rush on blue, so this shot does not require as much accuracy as some of the other shots we have been considering.

The eight-yard take-off to the front of hoop 4 is probably the option most likely to result in the player being able to make the hoop, and if he cannot make it he can retreat with red to a position half-way between yellow and the corner, making it dangerous for blue to shoot at yellow, and giving himself a rush to hoop 4 if blue returns to black. The rather long take-off for position to run a hoop is a shot that few players would spend much time practising (unless they also play Golf Croquet).

All in all, there is not much to choose between the various options in this situation. In a game the player's choice will depend partly on the shots with which he is most comfortable. The important thing here is not which option he chooses, but that before making a choice he should consider all of the options, rather than just automatically and without thought doing whatever first comes into his head. He should realise that his chance of making hoop 4 is probably less than even, so he should give thought to the situation he will be presenting to the opponent if he cannot continue the break, and should go about trying to establish the break in a way that also retains a good chance of establishing a break in his next turn if he fails to do so in this turn.

Also discuss the effect of changing the position of one of the balls in the original position, e.g. move black out to hoop 2, or place blue near the peg so that it cannot be rushed to hoop 4, or imagine that red has "rushed" yellow to a position somewhere on the east border.

RUSH-LINES

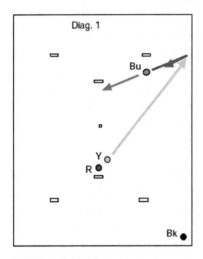

Diag. 1

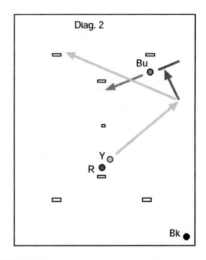

Diag. 2

S ET UP THE position in Diag. 1, where red has just made hoop 5, and ask the player to continue the break. He will have to decide where to rush yellow, and the best place will be to rush it as shown by the yellow arrow in Diag.1. He should rush it to a place on or near the line along which he wants to play the FOLLOWING rush, when he rushes blue to hoop 6. This "rush-line" for blue is shown by a grey arrow. He should rush yellow to a point on the rush-line which is far enough from blue to allow him to send yellow to load 1-back while red

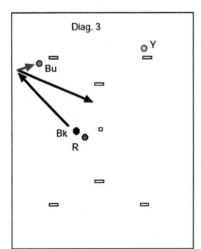

Diag. 3

comes along the rush-line to get the desired rush on blue. Some players will incorrectly rush yellow as shown by the arrows on Diag.2, to a point from which red will need to run across, instead of along, blue's rush-line. The best place to rush yellow to in this instance is a point on or near the east border, and also on or near the intended rush-line. The exact best position will depend on how good a stop-shot or drive the player can comfortably manage, while keeping good control of the red ball.

Having red approach the blue ball along the rush-line means that there is a much smaller margin for error (i.e. a larger "stopping distance") for red in order to finish with a good rush on blue.

[This is illustrated in the diagram on the next page.] Ask the player to try it each way, and show you the area in which he is trying to stop the red ball to get the rush on blue. When the player is convinced of the value of using the rush-line in such a situation, set up the situation shown in Diag.3 where red, in starting a 4-ball break, has made hoop 1 and loaded hoop 3 with yellow while going to the black pivot ball near the peg.

Ask him to play on, and see whether he now understands that he should rush the black ball to the west border so that he can send black back into the centre of the lawn while coming along the rush-line of blue to hoop 2 in order to ensure that he can rush blue even closer to the hoop.

By looking for rush-lines and using them, he will often be able to make his future shots easier, and so increase his chance of continuing the break as long as possible.

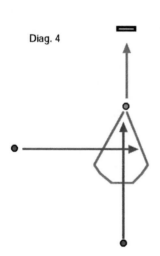

Diag. 4

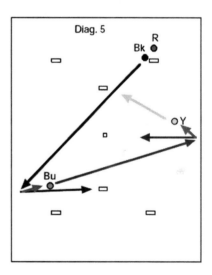

Diag. 5

Diag. 4 is a geometrical illustration of the reasoning behind "rush-line theory". In order to rush blue to the hoop, red will need to finish in the outlined area (or "sector"). The red arrows show that by approaching blue along the rush-line, rather than across it, there will be a longer portion of the red arrow in the desired area, and therefore a longer "acceptable stopping distance" for the red ball. Then set up the position shown in Diag.5, where red has just made 4-back and yellow is for the peg. Ask the player how he would continue. He can either (1) rush black to penultimate and make it without loading rover; or (2) roquet black and send it to rover while trying to get a rush behind yellow; or (3) rush black to rover and then take off to get a rush on either blue or yellow; or (4) he can use rush-line theory. In this situation there are two rush-lines: the rush-line for blue to yellow, and secondly, the rush-line for yellow to penultimate. If he thinks of rush-lines in this way, and can handle the rushes comfortably, he can rush black to the west border (see arrows) and send black to load rover while approaching blue along the first rush-line, then rush blue to the east border and send it towards the centre of the lawn while approaching yellow along the second rush-line.

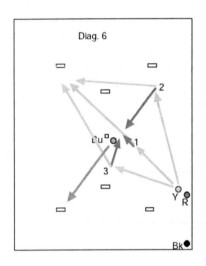

Diag. 6

It is important for the player to realise that there are also situations in which it may be best not to use the rush-line. Diag.6 shows the common situation where, after yellow has gone to 4-back and set a diagonal leave, black has been lifted from hoop 2 and shot from B-baulk at red and yellow, finishing in the 4th corner. Here red can rush yellow to either point 1, followed by a stop-shot with red going across the rush-line of blue to hoop 1; or to point 2, followed by a wide-angle split-shot in which red approaches blue along the rush-line; or to point 3 (a compromise solution), followed by a sharp stop-shot with a fairly narrow angle in which red runs past blue in a direction that could be described as more along the rush-line than across it. Most top players prefer to rush their partner ball to point 1, while some would choose point 3; but very few, if any, would choose in this case to rush yellow to the rush-line and use the wider-angle split-shot which is harder to control.

John Riches and Wayne Davies

IDEAL LEAVES

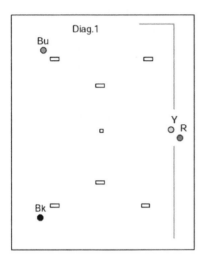

Diag.1

TAKE THE STUDENT out onto the lawn, give him the four balls, and tell him that yellow is for 4-back and red is for hoop 1. Tell him that he is to play a turn with red, and can place the balls wherever he likes.

He is to try to place them in the places that will make it easiest for him to make a break with red if the opponent fails to roquet, and they must be far enough apart that the opponent is not very likely to roquet.

You (the coach) play black or blue from whatever position he sets up, then get him to play red and continue until he either breaks down or has a break fully set up.

The best solution will be to place the opponent's balls so that they are wired from each other at hoop 1, and his own balls with a rush to either hoop 2 or the south boundary near hoop 1.

Almost as good would be to wire the opponent's balls at hoop 2, with his own balls set near the 1ˢᵗ corner so that red has a rush to hoop 1. If he suggests such a leave, commend him on finding the best answer, then ask him to try to find a good set-up if wiring cannot be relied upon.

Unless they have been shown it, few players will suggest the positions shown in Diag.1, which for most players is the "ideal leave" for hoop 1 when the opponent does not have a lift and you have roqueted with your forward (4-back) ball with which you do not want to make any further hoops.

The rush for red is set to the boundary behind hoop 2, or else to blue so that yellow can be cut-rushed to the boundary if desired. It is surprising that many experienced players seem never to have put much thought into finding the best possible leave so as to maximise their chance of getting a break with red in the next turn. They rely on being able to come up with a reasonable leave if one is needed in a game, and often do not realise that they could have increased their winning chances by using a stronger leave. A good player needs to know the BEST places to leave the balls, not only for a partner ball on hoop 1, but for any position of one or both clips. The position that offers maximum winning chances may vary from one player to another according to the shots they can play confidently, but for a player who can comfortably rush a ball the length of the lawn, the illustrated set-up will usually be the one they should aim for.

Show the player this "ideal leave" and discuss its advantages and disadvantages. Ask him what he would expect the opponent to do as black and blue if both his balls are for hoop 1. Get him to do it (or else you, the coach, do it), and then, assuming he does not roquet, have him play red and see if he can establish a break. He should try this also if black has taken and missed some other shot—see the three most likely positions for black in Diag 2 on the next page.

The rush for red can be set anywhere near the east border, or on the north border near the 3rd corner as shown by the grey lines on the diagram. The rush is usually set to blue rather than hoop 1 in order to avoid the risk of leaving black a double target, and also to help dissuade the opponent from shooting with black at your balls. If you set yourself a rush to hoop 1, black will have little hesitation in shooting at your balls; but if you set it as shown, a miss would give you a rush to your hoop that at present you do not have. This is designed to create doubt in the mind of the opponent concerning which shot he should take, and even whether he should shoot at all; since most opponent's will be much less likely to roquet when they are not sure they should be playing the shot. If desired, the red ball can be a yard or more in-lawn from the yard-line so that if black (or blue) does shoot at your balls and miss, you can roquet the opponent's ball and send it into lawn a short distance while getting the rush on yellow, thus making the future of the break a little easier.

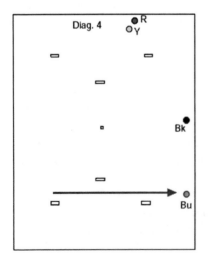

Diag. 4

Explain that sometimes you may be able to get the rush wired (or partly so) from either black or blue (or both), but that should not be seen as a high priority. If you can get it wired from black by hoops 1 and 5, you could consider setting the rush for red to hoop 1, instead of to blue. Get him to try playing on from this situation also.

Diag. 4 shows a situation where the player of blue has just hit his ball out of play, about 10 yards wide of black on the east border. He did this in the hope that the player of red would now try to either:

John Riches and Wayne Davies

(1) rush yellow to hoop 1 and make it; or

(2) cut—rush yellow to hoop 2, take off to black, then try to get a rush behind blue to hoop 1.

Either of these continuations would involve the player of red in taking risks that are difficult to justify. Black or blue would be likely to get further chances to roquet before the player of red can establish a break, and it would be a roughly even bet as to who will be first to establish a break.

The coach should set up the position on the lawn and ask the player he is coaching to demonstrate what he would do if he were red and yellow and was faced with this situation in a game with all clips on hoop 1. Discuss the results and the risks involved, and ask whether he can think of any alternative way of proceeding.

Most players will at first need persuading that there could be a better way to continue than trying to make one or more hoops, and that (unless perhaps they are of international standard or close to it), they should forgo any attempt to make a hoop or set up a break in this turn. Instead, the best chance to get a break established before the opponent does will be to simply set up the lawn, allow the opponent one chance to hit a long roquet, and make sure that if he misses you will have an easy break in your next turn, without the need to play any very accurate or risky strokes.

Diag.5 shows one way in which this can be done: Red can roquet yellow and send it toward the 3rd corner while going to black (this type of wide-angle split-shot may need practice).

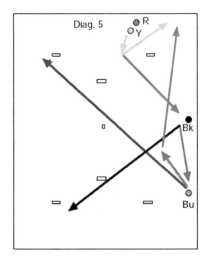

Diag. 5

Then he will send black to hoop 1 (but not directly in front!) while going to blue (without trying to get behind it) and send blue to hoop 2 while going back to set a rush for red on yellow to either hoop 1 or (better still) to hoop 2.

It may look complicated on the diagram, but the shots do not require any great accuracy. The hardest part is to think seven strokes ahead, and work out before you play the first stroke of the turn (roqueting yellow) where you will want the yellow ball to be at the end of the turn when you finally set the "ideal leave".

Get the player to play this turn several times, perhaps starting with the balls in slightly different positions. The rush can be set anywhere along the east border, or on the north border near the 3rd corner as we have seen here.

The final "leave" is shown in Diag, 6, and an alternative version in Diag. 7. It is important that the player knows not only how to set the leave, but how to play the following turn, assuming that the opponent does not roquet.

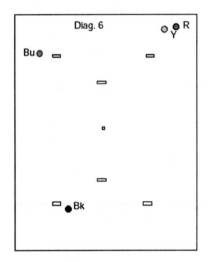

Ask the student to consider the options for the opponent if he is faced with an "ideal leave" such as in Diag.6, and in each case get him to think about how red should play the next turn if the opponent fails to roquet. There are various possibilities, e.g.—

(1)   If black is hit away into the 4th corner, red will rush yellow to blue and then rush blue to hoop 1, with a 3-ball break. He should also consider when and how he will bring the 4th (black) ball into the break, and practise doing it.

(2)   If black shoots at red and yellow and misses, red can use black to get a good rush on yellow to hoop 1. This long rush may also need practice. If hoops or the peg are likely to get in the way of the rush, then yellow can be rushed instead to blue, and blue to hoop 1.

(3) If black shoots at blue and misses, the best way (depending how the rush was set) is to cut-rush yellow to black, take black out to blue, then rush blue to hoop 1. Do not be afraid of leaving yellow only 8-10 yards from black, since if you cannot make hoop 1 the opponent will probably have to move blue from hoop 1.

In Diag 7 the procedure is similar to the above if black is hit into a corner or shoots at red and yellow; but if black shoots at blue and misses the player may need to be convinced that he should rush yellow right to black on the border behind hoop 2, then rush black out to blue, and blue to hoop 1. If he makes hoop 1 but does not get a forward rush, he can either take off to yellow on the border and send it to hoop 3 before making hoop 2 from black, or send blue to hoop 3 with a split-shot while going to black at hoop 2.

Some players will want to start the turn by rushing yellow to hoop 3 and taking off to black on the border behind hoop 2, but loading two hoops ahead is seldom wise.

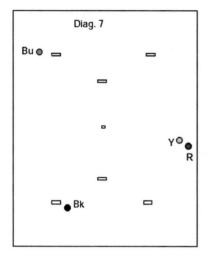

Diag. 7

The player should play through all of these alternative continuations, until he is convinced that by setting an "ideal leave" he is giving himself at least a 70% chance of getting a break established in his next turn—assuming that the opponent is not likely to hit the long roquet more than three times out of ten.

Then re-set the original position of Diag. 5 and ask him whether he can now think of any way of playing that will give him a 70% chance of getting a break established before the opponent does.

Unless he can be convinced that he will be increasing his winning chances by forgoing the chance to start making hoops in his first turn, he will not want to use "ideal leaves" in his games.

The coach can also use this exercise to make the point that using ideal leaves is the best way to defeat negative "Aunt Emma" tactics by an opponent who returns wide of his partner ball instead of shooting; and that returning wide is a poor tactic against an opponent who understands how to set and use ideal leaves.

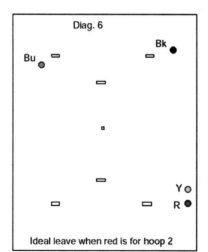

Diag. 6

Ideal leave when red is for hoop 2

The diagrams here and on following page show some further "ideal leaves" for single-clip situations when you have roqueted with your forward (yellow) ball which is for 4-back and you want to set up so as to give red the maximum chance of a break in your next turn, assuming the opponent fails to roquet. In such situations you should not make 4-back with yellow, as your priority should be to get red around, and it will be harder to set so as to ensure a break for red in the following turn if you have given a "lift".

As we have already seen, this can depend on your ability to play the strokes required to set the "ideal leave", and then set up the break after the opponent has missed his one chance to roquet.

Ideal leaves should not be used if you have roqueted with your backward (red) ball unless you assess your chance of establishing an immediate break is very small—e.g. about 20% or less. The "ideal leave" gives a 70% chance of getting a break established before the opponent does, but you should prefer to try for an immediate break even if your chance of establishing an immediate break is only (say) about 40%.

This is because failure to establish an immediate break does not necessarily mean that the opponent will roquet and get a break established before you can, though his chance of doing so will almost always be better than the 30% (or often less) chance he would have after you have set an "ideal leave". In these leaves it is not assumed that either of the opponent's balls will be wired from the other, or from your balls; but you may try to wire them as you set up the leave, and even if he only has to pass close to a hoop, it can make his shot more difficult and decrease his chance of roqueting.

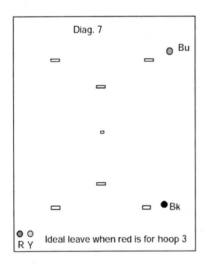

Diag. 7

Ideal leave when red is for hoop 3

In diag. 6 the rush can be set anywhere along the south border, or the southern part of the east or west borders; while in diag.7 it can be set anywhere on the west border, or on the western part of the north or south borders. The rush for red can be set to either of the opponent's balls, or to the position where blue will finish if it shoots at black and misses.

In diag.6 the black ball should be about halfway from hoop 3 to the east border, rather than closer to hoop 3. The reason for this not just to make the opponent's roquet a longer one, but so that if blue shoots at black and misses, and you then need to roll blue out to hoop 3 from the east border while getting a rush on black to hoop 2, it will be easier to make sure of getting a good (though slightly longer) rush to your hoop if the croquet stroke involved is a half-roll rather than an equal roll.

The player should practise setting up these leaves from various positions, working out what shot(s) the opponent is likely to take, and then playing the break with red in the following turn.

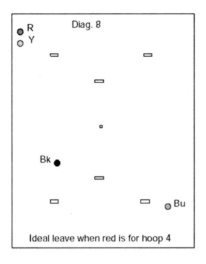

Diag. 8

R
Y

Bk

Bu

Ideal leave when red is for hoop 4

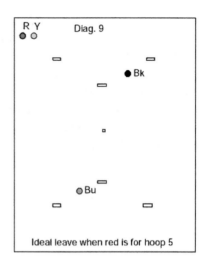

R Y

Diag. 9

Bk

Bu

Ideal leave when red is for hoop 5

In Diag. 8 the rush for red can be set anywhere on the north border, or on the northern part of the east or west borders, but should be set to black, rather than to blue. In Diag. 9 the rush can again be set in various places, but if it is set near the 3rd corner the positions of black and blue should be changed, with blue between hoops 4 and 5, and black between hoops 2 and 6. In Diag. 10 the rush can be set anywhere on the south border, or on the southern part of the east or west borders, and once again it is preferable to set the rush to black, rather than to blue.

The player will need to practise achieving these (or similar) leaves from various positions, supposing that he has roqueted with yellow, or that he has roqueted with red but the opponent's balls are out of play.

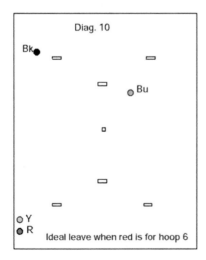

Diag. 10

Bk

Bu

Y
R

Ideal leave when red is for hoop 6

There will in some cases be other alternative leaves that can be used instead of the leaves we have described and illustrated. They may be almost as good as an "ideal leave" for that particular hoop, and may be easier to achieve.

The important thing is not that the player will always use one of these leaves, nor that he will choose to set a leave rather than making an immediate break, but that he will at least give serious consideration to the advantages (and disadvantages) of setting a good leave; and if he does choose to set up, he will know the best positions to aim for.

We are assuming that the player has passed the stage where he will want to set up near his own hoop (which will ensure that he makes the hoop, but will rarely give him a break if the opponent fails to roquet, since the opponent will move the ball at the next hoop). He should note that these leaves are designed to give him a 3-ball break even if the opponent chooses to "finesse" by hitting one of his balls out of play instead of attempting a roquet.

The "ideal leaves" for other hoops (1-back, 2-back, etc.) are similar to the leaves we have illustrated here.

TWO-CLIP IDEAL LEAVES

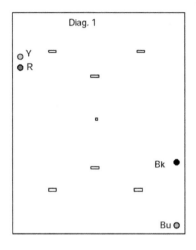

Diag. 1

Bk

Bu

T HE COACH SHOULD set up the position of Diag.1 with the red clip on hoop 1 and yellow clip on hoop 3. The positions of the black and blue clips do not matter. Then ask the player how he would play from this position as red and yellow.

It is likely that he will either:

(1) play red, take off from yellow to black, try from there to get a rush on blue to hoop 1, and end up rolling with blue from near the 4th corner to hoop 1; or

(2) Play yellow, rush red to the south border, take off to blue, then roll blue to hoop 4 while trying to get a rush on black to hoop 3 (or else take off from blue to get the rush).

If he is at or near international class, he should be able to succeed in setting up an immediate break more often than not; but if he is not yet of such exalted rank, he should become convinced that his chance of establishing an immediate break is small, and that by attempting to do so he is likely to lose the innings by trying to make a difficult hoop and failing, or allow the opponent a chance to roquet after which there will still be no easy break set up.

The player should be encouraged to consider whether it would be better, if he could do so, to allow the opponent one long chance to roquet now, since he is likely to get one anyway, but ensure that he will get only the one chance, because a miss will result in the player having an easy break in his next turn. Most players can be convinced of the wisdom of at least giving consideration to such an option, especially in difficult conditions or when they do not feel they are in top form and will need a ball at their hoop in order to have a good chance of making it.

The position shown in Diag. 2 is an "ideal leave" (sometimes referred to as the "diagonal leave") for hoops 1 and 3. It should be apparent to the player that if such a leave can be achieved he will have an easy break in the next turn unless the opponent hits a long roquet. Red and yellow are set diagonally across the corner, close enough to the corner to roquet a corner ball.

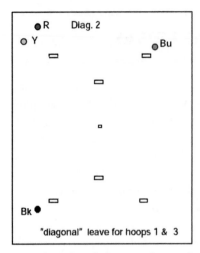

"diagonal" leave for hoops 1 & 3

Perhaps the hardest continuation for the player of red and yellow would be if blue is hit into the 3rd corner, but even then red can roquet yellow and send it out to hoop 2 with a thick take-off to black.

Or if black is hit into a corner, yellow can roquet red and split it to hoop 4 while going to blue.

Any shot the opponent takes and misses will make the break even easier by immediately giving you all four balls to use.

The same leave can be set with red and yellow diagonally across the 4th corner, but it is important to set red and yellow the right way around, with red closer to the east border and yellow closer to the south border.

The same type of leave can be used if your clips are on hoops 2 and 4, with your balls set across the 1st or 3rd corners. Note that you do not need to set a rush for yourself.

The player should be encouraged to practise setting up this leave from various court situations, and before starting to do so he must decide where he wants yellow to end up, as well as whether he will be able to achieve the "diagonal leave" position without taking undue risks.

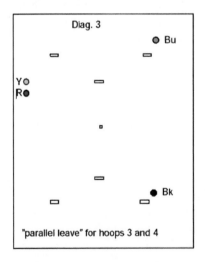

"parallel leave" for hoops 3 and 4

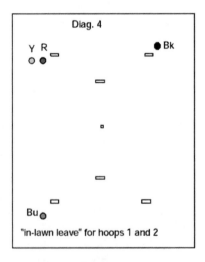

"in-lawn leave" for hoops 1 and 2

Diag. 3 shows the mirror image of a leave mentioned in a previous article for hoops 1 and 2. Red is for hoop 3 and yellow is for hoop 4. Red and yellow should be set out a yard or more from the west yard-line, and if possible in the northern half of the west border, so that yellow can cut-rush red toward hoop 5, or at least to a position from which (if blue is hit into a corner) you can load hoop 5 with red while going to black at hoop 4.

Diag. 4 shows an alternative to the "diagonal leave" for hoops 1 and 2, but it is more dangerous.

Red (for hoop 1) and yellow (for hoop 2) are set out near hoop 2 so that if blue shoots at your balls and misses, you can play yellow and run hoop 2 through to the border in order to roquet blue and immediately bring it into the break.

Diag. 5 is one possible leave for hoops 2 and 5, where red (H2) and yellow (H5) could be in other places on the east or west border, provided hoop 3 or hoop 5 can be loaded as necessary.

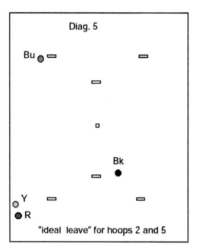

Diag. 5

"ideal leave" for hoops 2 and 5

The player should practise setting up such leaves and playing on from them if the opponent misses various shots. He should also try playing black and blue in order to appreciate the strength of each leave, as some are better than others.

The simple principle in most (but not all) ideal leaves is to set an opponent ball at each of your hoops, and the player should try inventing his own "ideal leaves" for other hoop combinations.

The advantage of using ideal leaves is that you usually know where your clips will be when your opponent finishes a turn he is playing, so you can work out an "ideal leave" to use if you happen to roquet in your next turn.

The most difficult thing is to picture the leave and work out where you will want to set up all four balls if you cannot make a break after you roquet.

This must be done before the start of your turn so that you do not roquet a ball and then realise that you should have rushed it somewhere so as to make it easier to achieve the desired leave.

The aim is that every shot missed by the opponent should give you an easy break.

ROQUET CHECKLIST

1. MUSCLES

   a. warmed up, especially shoulder muscles

2. GRIP

   a. both hands firm
   b. wrists firm (locked?)
   c. grip tension to remain constant

3. STANCE

   a. consistent, well balanced
   b. relaxed (flatten feet onto ground)
   c. sighting eye in line of swing

4. ALIGNMENT

   a. stalk ball to 'square' body
   b. check alignment again before final swing
   c. If you cast, know why and how it should be done

5. PSYCHOLOGY

   a. visualise a successful shot.
   b. smile? open eyes wide? breathe out?

6. CONDITIONS

   a. check for lawn slopes, wind, holes, etc.

7. SWING

   a. long, slow backswing (ready to use weight of mallet)
   b. keep body (knees, shoulders) still
   c. stand tall
   d. keep backswing straight
   e. swing from shoulders, not elbows or wrists

    f.   forward swing slow and deliberate; don't hurry it

    g.   watch mallet hit centre of ball

    h.   follow through low along ground, straightening elbows

8.   RESULT

    a.   note result

    b.   if you fail to roquet, assess likely reason

    c.   decide what you will do different next time

    d.   take steps to ensure you will remember

PRACTICE RECOMMENDATIONS (roquets):

(1) Always make your *first* hit a roquet of about 6 yards—a distance you will not expect to hit unless you get everything right, but will expect to hit if you do get everything right. This is to practise (after sitting out for some time) getting up, walking out onto the lawn, and hitting the first roquet.

(2) Practise success, not failure.

(3) Do not practise the same type of shot, using the same muscles, for too long, as tired muscles cannot be trained to co-ordinate properly.

(4) Practising in short sessions 2-3 times per week is much better than one long practice session.

(5) If things are not going right, seek the help of a coach. It is very difficult to discover your own errors in technique because you cannot watch yourself.

STOP-SHOTS WITH HEAVY MALLETS

RECENTLY THE COACHING Committee has been asked to consider the best way of playing and teaching stop-shots with heavy mallets. During the past 10 years or so there has been a trend toward using mallets weighing well over three and a half pounds, whereas twenty years ago most mallets weighed less than three pounds. It is not certain whether mallets will continue to evolve in this direction, as the increase in weight seems to have been a reaction to the balls that were in use in the early nineties, i.e. Dawson Mk 2 and Barlows, both of which were difficult to rush with a light mallet. Now that we have the more elastic "International" balls it is possible that the fashion could revert to lighter mallets once more. The Pidcock and Fenwick-Elliott mallets may turn out to be a fore-runner in such a trend.

Be that as it may, a number of players who have changed to using the heavier Puckett mallets have found that they can no longer play good stop-shots.

In particular, they can no longer play a stop-shot from the yard-line in front of hoop 1 to load hoop 2 within 2m and hold position to run hoop 1.

This is a shot which can occasionally provide the only good way to establish a break, so it is desirable that a way be found to play it acceptably if at all possible

After gathering information from top players all around the world, and members of our committee spending many hours experimenting out on the lawn, we are ready to pass on to coaches our conclusions regarding the way this shot should be approached.

It must be recognised that this type of stop-shot requires exact timing, especially if the mallet has a flexible handle, and the percentage of desirable results will be lower than with a lighter mallet. This has to be accepted as part of the price you pay for using a heavier mallet which if used properly has advantages in other ways—for rushes, long rolls and long roquets.

METHOD:

1. Stand a little further back from the ball than in (say) a take-off. This should mean that the mallet shaft is tilted very slightly backward as the mallet

contacts the ball, or in other words, the front of the mallet-head is slightly raised.

2. Use a fairly firm grip, but not too tight.

3. Throughout the stroke keep your shoulders still and your eyes fixed on the back of the ball. This is even more important than in other shots, as you need to stop the forward movement immediately after the mallet contacts the ball, so you have to be aware of exactly where in the swing that point will be reached.

4. Draw the mallet back *very slowly*. It may help to picture an archer slowly drawing back the bow-string before letting go to send the arrow on its way.

The action here should be very deliberate, until the mallet has swung back the distance which is necessary for the particular length of stop-shot you are playing. The length of back-swing must be learnt by practising stop-shots of different lengths until you get the "feel" of the amount of backswing needed.

5. The forward swing should be a type of "flick". You could think of it as similar to cracking a whip or flicking someone with a wet towel. You should feel as if you are "flicking" the striker's ball with the mallet-head. This is the most vital thing to get right in order to achieve a maximum-ratio stop-shot when you are using a heavy mallet.

6. The flicking action needs to be almost parallel with the ground, moving the hands deliberately forward and then rapidly backwards so that the mallet head just reaches the balls without any noticeable follow-through. Do not "swing" the mallet down to the ball as in most other strokes; move it more or less horizontally toward the ball.

7. Immediately as it contacts the ball, the mallet's forward motion must be stopped. This can be achieved either by withdrawing the mallet (as with the wet towel), and/or by grounding the mallet which is assisted by the slight backward tilt of the shaft.

8. For an angled stop-shot, e.g. from the 1st corner to load hoop 2 and hold position in front of hoop 1, you will need to establish the direction of swing by finding an aiming point halfway between the points where you expect the two balls to finish. Do not "halve the angle", and do not swing toward hoop 1 where you want the striker's ball to go, as both of these actions would reduce the ratio of the stop-shot.

9. For an angled stop-shot such as this some players find it helpful to deliberately hit the ball off-centre, making contact near the right side of the mallet face.

CONCLUSIONS

The key points are: "very slow backswing" and "flick it".

Players with heavy mallets need to learn the ratios they are capable of achieving for long or short, straight or angled stop-shots. They will also learn to avoid, where possible, using high-ratio stop-shots as they set up and play breaks. In particular, avoid using a sharp stop-shot to load the next-but-one hoop when you need to get a rush on a ball to your current hoop, as the difficulty of timing the stop-shot exactly will mean that you have less chance of achieving exact control over the finishing position of the striker's ball than in most other croquet strokes such as flat-mallet drives or stab-rolls or half-rolls. It may take some time to teach a player to achieve the timing needed for the "flick" as described above.

HOOP APPROACHES (CIRCLE METHOD)

1. GRIP does not matter much. It is recommended to have both hands at the top of the handle, but it is also OK (though no advantage) to move one or both hands down the handle.

2. SLOPE: What matters most is the slope of the mallet at the instant of impact, and that you hit downward on the ball instead of attempting to "roll" it. [Reason: rolls involve an acceleration of the mallet through the ball, and so require accurate timing. The circle method is designed to remove timing as a factor needing to be controlled and coordinated.

3. PRACTICE: Place croqueted ball halfway between hoop 1 and side boundary. Line balls up with peg. Swing at hoop 5. Stand forward so that your mallet slopes forward at about 15 degrees from vertical. Let the weight of the mallet (+ your arms) "fall" through the ball. In other words, allow the weight of the two balls to (almost) stop the forward movement of the mallet. Do not try deliberately to "roll" or follow through; and do not use a "stab" or stop-shot action.

4. Control the strength of the stroke by changing the height of the backswing—i.e. "drop the mallet onto the ball" from a greater or lesser height.

5. CORRECTION: If the shot is played correctly and accurately, both balls should stop in line with hoops 1 and 2, the striker's ball about 2-3 feet in front of hoop 1, and the croqueted ball about 3-3 ½ yards behind it.

   a. Don't be satisfied unless you get BOTH balls travelling the right distance.
   b. If both balls go too far or fall short, change the height of the backswing.
   c. If the striker's ball goes further across the court than the croqueted ball, stand back slightly to reduce the forward slope.
   d. If the croqueted ball goes further across the court than the striker's ball, stand further forward to increase the forward slope.

6. MINOR ADJUSTMENTS: If you are approaching the hoop from some other position, line up the croqueted ball to go as far behind the hoop as your approach position is from the hoop. Small adjustments can be made as follows—

   a. When approaching from fairly close and more directly in front of the hoop, you could use a stop-shot action (not too sharp) to send the croqueted ball further forward. (This introduces timing, but it should be less critical here.)
   b. When approaching from behind, stand further back, swing flatter, and hit more into the croqueted ball in order to counter-act "ball-slip". A take-off is also OK from some positions, by lining up the 'V' carefully outside the hoop.

c. When approaching from further out you could decide to stand further forward to decrease the distance between the finishing positions of the balls.

7. TURNING A CORNER: If you want to "turn a corner" after making the hoop, or get a rush to one side instead of straight ahead, then the easiest way is to imagine the hoop in a slightly different position, usually about 10-15 cm (4-6") to the right or left of the actual hoop, and play an approach to the imaginary hoop.

8. AVOID, where possible, sending the croqueted ball "across the face of the hoop" in a hoop approach.

9. Use this method from anywhere within 4 yards of a hoop. If you are comfortable with it, extend this up to 6-7 yards in any direction. With practice, it will improve consistency by removing timing from the stroke. The only variable is the lawn speed.

10. The practice exercise in point 3 above is useful for checking lawn speed, and can be used for this purpose during the 5-minute hit-up on an unfamiliar lawn.

CIRCLE HOOP APPROACH

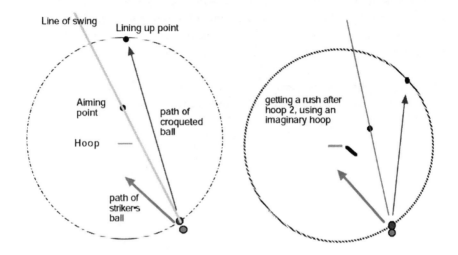

Line of swing

Lining up point

Aiming point

path of croqueted ball

Hoop

path of striker's ball

getting a rush after hoop 2, using an imaginary hoop

THE VALUE OF this method (first expounded, we believe, by the great NZ player Arthur Ross) is that it can be taught to a relative beginner before he has learnt to play the more difficult croquet shots such as pass-rolls, half-rolls, stop-shots, etc.

The traditional way of teaching hoop approaches was to decide where you want the balls to go (e.g. striker's ball 2 feet in front of hoop and croqueted ball 3 yards behind hoop), and then work out which type of croquet stroke will be needed to get them there.

The problem with this method is that each hoop approach can require a different grip, different stance, and a different type of swing; and some of the strokes will require accurate timing of a stop-shot or roll. as well as the judgement of angles in order to allow for "pull", "mallet drag", and/or "ball slip".

The Circle method eliminates all variables other than the pace of the lawn, provided the player can judge two equal distances (or imagine a circle) and can estimate one-third of the distance (i.e. the circle radius). The same type of stroke and method of lining it up can be used for approaches from anywhere around the hoop—in front, alongside, or behind the hoop.

The croqueted ball is lined up to go to a point directly behind the hoop and as far from the hoop as it is when you are lining up the stroke. The mallet is swung toward a point behind the hoop and one-third of the way from the hoop to the lining up point, and the mallet is tilted forward at about 15 degrees and allowed to "fall" onto and through the balls. The angle will vary slightly for different players.

Approaches from behind the hoop with a wide angle of split can be adjusted to allow for "ball-slip" by hitting a little more into the croqueted ball and with slightly less forward slope, while for approaches from further out the player could use more forward slope in order to help the striker's ball finish closer to the hoop.

Players can also learn to use a stop-shot action and hit more into the croqueted ball if they want to send the croqueted ball further forward in order to obtain a forward rush after making the hoop.

John Riches and Wayne Davies

SETTING UP FOR PARTNER

A IM: TO MAXIMISE the chance of establishing at least a 3-ball break for your partner (or partner ball) in your next turn if the opponent fails to roquet or does not attempt to roquet

NOTE: Here we will consider only leaves in which you set up for one ball (your partner ball), assuming that your other ball is already around. It is also important to know the "ideal leaves" for either of your balls when your two clips are on different early hoops, e.g. hoop 1 and hoop 3.

WHERE TO LEAVE THE BALLS
This will depend to some extent on the shots you (or your partner) are capable of playing. Leaves which require long rushes or wide-angled splits are pointless if you cannot play such shots with reasonable accuracy.

Another important consideration, of course, is whether you have given a lift.

Less important considerations are—

(1) the roqueting ability of your opponent(s).
(2) which opponent ball will want to (or be forced to) play.
(3) the positions of the opponent's clips.

OPPONENT'S BALLS
The strongest possible leave is with two opponent balls wired close in across your partner's hoop and a rush set for your partner in the most remote part of the lawn to either that hoop or the following hoop.

However this sort of leave is much less common that the others we will consider, because if you do not make hoops yourself before setting up you will usually not have sufficient shots to enable you to get all the balls and place them accurately; and if you make hoops yourself you will usually have given a lift.

Instead of wiring them at your partner's current hoop the opponent's balls could also be wired at the following hoop, with the rush set to either or these two hoops.

Wherever you leave the opponent's balls, remember to look where his clips are, and if it is also his hoop, you will need to ensure that he will not be able to run the hoop.

Assuming that wiring is impractical, try to leave one opponent ball at your partner's hoop and the other opponent ball at the following hoop. This is usually done with split-shots rather than rushes, and needs to be planned early.

It is more important to make things easy for your partner if the opponent fails to roquet, than to try to reduce his chance of roqueting by giving him the longest possible shot. The attitude should be "I will give you one chance to roquet, but only one. There will not be a second chance, so you'd better hit it!" It is also good to set so that there will be doubt in the opponent's mind concerning which shot he should play. Most players are much less likely to roquet when they are unsure whether or not they should be playing that particular shot.

YOUR BALLS
You should set up your own balls well away from the ball the opponent will need to move. It is not always an advantage to be well away from his other ball, and in fact it can be a disadvantage.

You should set up near a border with a useful rush for your partner, and preferably without offering a double target to either opponent ball.

Before you start your turn you will often need to work out exactly where to leave your balls. In fact this can usually be done while the opponent is playing the previous turn, as you know where your clips will be when you start your turn.

It is best to avoid having to hit back to your partner from a long way away to achieve the desired rush, and where possible you should leave the partner ball 2-3 feet in-lawn from the yard-line so that you will be able to obtain the desired set-up by hitting your ball out over the boundary at the end of your turn.

CROQUET
HAMPERED SHOTS

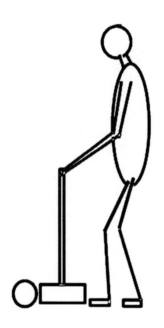

CONTENTS

INTRODUCTION

THIS SECTION WAS written with the intention of including it as part of the ACA's Level 3 "Croquet Specific" Coach-training course. While the "Notes on Error Correction" were written specifically for the purpose of training the coach to recognise and correct errors of technique, the following notes on "Hampered Shots" are written with the primary aim of enabling the coach to teach the player how to play the strokes. However there will be many points explained that the coach can use to correct errors of technique if a player he is coaching is not achieving satisfactory outcomes due to playing the stroke incorrectly.

In the later part (pages 7-9) we have included a consideration of the strokes also from a refereeing viewpoint, since a coach will need to know whether or not the player is committing a fault when he plays the stroke.

In most cases it will be beneficial if the coach himself is able to play and demonstrate the shot correctly, but it is quite possible for a coach to teach most of these strokes even if he cannot play them himself.

It is not recommended that time should be spent teaching hampered strokes to beginners or players at low standard of play. This may seem a strange thing to say because they are the ones who will most often get themselves into such difficult situations. However at a lower standard of play the inability to play a hampered shot is not likely to result in the loss of a game, whereas at higher levels it will often mean that the player is unable to continue a break that he could have continued if he had known how to make the hampered roquet or play the hampered hoop-running stroke; and thereby he may well lose his only chance to win the game.

Players at a standard noticeably below state level would usually be well advised to spend their coaching and practice time improving their technique in other strokes—particularly split-shots—and improving their tactical knowledge of things such as trap-lines, standard leaves, ideal leaves, different ways of loading hoops, endgame tactics, openings, cannons, etc.

The hampered strokes explained here are not the only types of hampered stroke that can be played, and we can expect new shots, together with new ways to play the old shots, will continue to be discovered and developed.

In some cases the playing of hampered strokes will be limited by the player's physical limitations (inability to kneel down comfortably; eyesight; muscular coordination; stature; etc., and it should be remembered that most hampered shots cannot be leant effectively in only one coaching session.

The coach should normally teach only one hampered shot at a time, leaving the others for a future coaching session, as with each shot there are many things the player will need to understand, learn to use, and remember. The coach should also avoid asking (or allowing) the player to play the same hampered stroke too many times, using the same muscles that he is not used to using, as this can entail a risk of repetitive strain injury; and in any case, tired muscles usually cannot be taught to coordinate in any useful way.

The biggest reward for the coach comes when a player he has been coaching tells him, "I used the shot you showed me in a match the other day, and it worked perfectly, so I was able to continue the break. If you hadn't shown it to me, I would not have had any idea what to do!"

I wish to thank again members of the South Australian Coaching Committee who over the years have assisted in trial-ling, criticising and improving many of the following methods and explanations.

I apologise for the (very) amateurish illustrations which unfortunately represent the full extent of my artistic abilities, but perhaps some readers will even derive amusement from them; and if so, they may turn out to be a useful aid in remembering some of the important points we are hoping to get across.

Even when they can be demonstrated in person, some of the hampered shots are far from easy to teach; and it is even more difficult when limited to the use of the written word and sketchy illustrations. Perhaps someone will one day make a video demonstrating these shots viewed from different angles, thus enabling another step forward to be made.

. . . John Riches

HAMPERED SHOTS—THE SLIDE SHOT

I N THIS TYPE of croquet stroke the ball is close to a hoop which prevents the player from taking a normal backswing in order to hit the ball in the centre of his mallet-face.

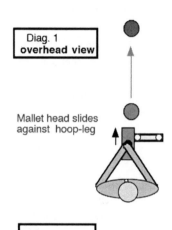

Diag. 1
overhead view

Mallet head slides against hoop-leg

In this type of croquet stroke the ball is close to a hoop which prevents the player from taking a normal backswing in order to hit the ball in the centre of his mallet-face.

There are several errors which the player is likely to commit unless he understands and follows the following important ideas:

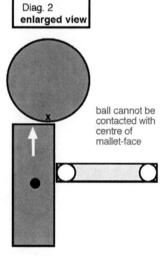

Diag. 2
enlarged view

ball cannot be contacted with centre of mallet-face

(1) The ball will have to be contacted close to one side of the mallet-face, rather than in the centre of the mallet-face (compare point 'x' and the white arrow in Diag. 2).

This will tend to cause the mallet-head to twist (rotate clockwise in these illustrations) on impact with the ball.

To prevent—or at least minimise—this twisting the player must hold the mallet very firmly and move his bottom hand well down the mallet (but be careful not to crush his fingers on the hoop!)

(2) The harder he hits the ball, the more twisting effect will result from the off-centre hit, so he should hit the ball only hard enough to send it just past the target ball.

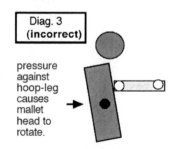

Diag. 3
(incorrect)

pressure against hoop-leg causes mallet head to rotate.

(3) Although the side of the mallet-head will slide along the hoop-leg as a means of keeping the mallet-head correctly aligned, any actual pressure against the hoop-leg will cause the mallet to rotate and lose its alignment as illustrated in Diag. 3.

(4) The mallet must remain in contact with the hoop-leg the whole time. If he moves the mallet back so that it is clear of the hoop-leg, which some players will find it difficult to avoid doing, he is very likely to hit the hoop-leg instead of the ball when he swings it forward. He should draw the mallet back slowly until the front corner of the mallet-head is touching the hoop-leg, then start from there and without any further back-swing, move the mallet straight forward. This shot is easiest when the ball is about 6 inches (15 cm) from the hoop-leg.

(5) The mallet should be moved forward with a flat swing—or rather, a flat forward push—sliding the side of the mallet-head very lightly against the hoop-leg.

The mallet-head should follow through as far as possible towards the target ball, with the player reaching forward and doing his best to keep the mallet-head correctly aligned.

(6) The hitting action should be a deliberate, controlled stroke rather than a hurried jab.

Slide shots are well worth practising regularly, with the balls in various positions, until the player becomes familiar with the distances and extent of hampering that he is comfortable with.

HAMPERED SHOTS—THE SWEEP SHOT

THIS IS NOT a difficult shot when you know the right way to play it, but many players choose to hit their ball away when they could have roqueted with a well-played sweep shot and continued the break.

Diag.1 illustrates a situation where the red ball is about 3 inches (7 cm or just under a ball-diameter) from the left hoop-leg, and the blue ball is a yard away, with the centres of both balls directly in line with the centre of the hoop-leg. Many people imagine it is impossible to play red and roquet blue in this situation, but in fact it is quite possible even when red is only 2 inches (5 cm) from the hoop-leg and blue is two or more yards away.

Although, as we have said, the shot is not difficult when played correctly, there are many things the player needs to know which will constitute errors in technique if he gets them wrong. The diagrams (such as they are) should help illustrate the recommended way of playing this shot.

The main things to note are:

(1) As with the "slide shot", the mallet-head must remain in contact with the hoop-leg the whole time, thus severely restricting the back-swing (see Diags.1 and 2).

(2) The mallet-head is tilted downwards as shown in Diag.3. This allows a longer distance in contact with the hoop-leg and also helps to "hold" the ball against the ground for an instant after the mallet contacts it, increasing the friction between mallet and ball so that the mallet can get more 'purchase' on the ball to keep it in line.

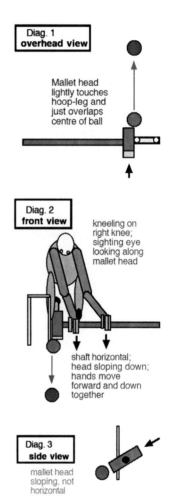

Diag. 1
overhead view

Mallet head lightly touches hoop-leg and just overlaps centre of ball

Diag. 2
front view

kneeling on right knee; sighting eye looking along mallet head

shaft horizontal; head sloping down; hands move forward and down together

Diag. 3
side view

mallet head sloping, not horizontal

Diag. 4
overhead view

INCORRECT - player sideways; cannot line up correctly

(3) The player should kneel (usually on one knee) in front of the hoop with the ball behind the hoop, so that his sighting eye can look straight along the mallet-head to ensure that the direction is correct and the mallet-face (not counting any bevel) will fractionally overlap the centre of the ball (see Diag.1). This places the arms and elbows in a rather awkward position, but it makes the shot more accurate if you can manage it. Some players kneel or stand sideways as show in Diag.4, but this makes it harder, even if they can get their head further forward and more or less in the line of the balls.

(4) The fingers can be either underneath or on top of the shaft. Most player like to have them underneath.

(5) The hands should move forward and downwards together at about the same rate. It is not necessary to pivot with the (left) hand nearer the end of the shaft while pushing with the (right) hand near the mallet-head to move the mallet-head in a circular motion as viewed from above (see curved arrow in Diag.4 where the player may be kneeling on one or both knees, or standing and bending down). A curved swing as illustrated here makes the timing more difficult and tends to lose control of the direction in which the ball is hit.

(6) The ball should be hit with a sudden downward-jabbing action so as not to commit a double hit or a "pushing" fault.

HAMPERED SHOTS—OFF-CENTRE ROQUET

I N THESE SITUATIONS the ball must be contacted off-centre in order to make the roquet, but it will not be possible to use a hoop-leg as a guide by sliding the mallet against it as in the slide shot or sweep shot. Diag. 1 shows a situation where the ball is almost touching the hoop-leg, but it is possible to roquet a ball up to 5 yards away with confidence if you know the correct technique.

The shot is played standing up with the mallet shaft vertical, and the important points to remember are:

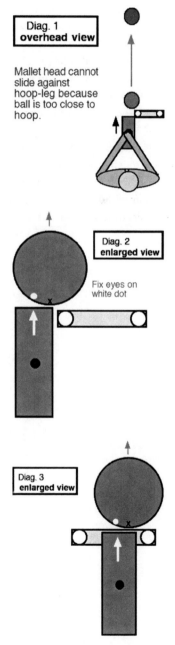

Diag. 1 overhead view

Mallet head cannot slide against hoop-leg because ball is too close to hoop.

Diag. 2 enlarged view

Fix eyes on white dot

Diag. 3 enlarged view

(1) As with the slide shot, the ball will be contacted well off-centre, so to avoid the mallet twisting on impact the player must use a tight grip, with his bottom hand moved well down the shaft.

(2) Once again, he should hit the ball no harder than is needed to just reach the target ball.

(3) The mallet must be lined up without it touching the hoop-leg, allowing a gap of about 2 mm between the mallet and the hoop-leg.

(4) MOST IMPORTANTLY, although the mallet will contact the ball at point 'x' as shown on Diag. 2, the player must fix his eyes on the white spot shown on the red ball in diagram. This is necessary, because over years the player has trained himself to swing his mallet so that the centre of the mallet-face goes toward the point on which he has fixed his eyes. This would result in the mallet hitting the hoop-leg instead of the ball, and that is what

happens almost every time with players who do not know this "secret". Instead of fixing his eyes on the point where the mallet will actually contact the ball, the player must concentrate on the point where he wants the middle of his mallet to go.

(5) The player should use a short, very slow backswing and a slow, deliberate, flat forward movement of the mallet, reaching well forward in the follow-through and trying to keep the mallet moving in the right line.

This idea can also be used when the mallet has to be swung through the hoop as show in Diag.3, and some players also find it useful in "slide shots" to fix the eyes on the point of the ball toward which the middle of the mallet has to go; though when the hoop-leg can be used as a guide it is not as essential as it is here.

Most players, when shown this method of playing off-centre roquets, are surprised at how much easier they find it to confidently make a roquet that they previously would probably not have attempted in a serious game. The slow, smooth and deliberate action without any jabbing or hurrying of the mallet is the hardest part for most players to learn, and as with other hampered shots, regular practice is important.

HAMPERED SHOTS—MALLET IN HOOP

D IAG.1 SHOWS A situation where the mallet, when placed in the hoop, does not quite reach the ball. In this case players may well conclude that a normal roquet is impossible, but provided the target ball is not too far away, the shot may be playable with the mallet tilted backwards as shown in Diag.2, making use of the fact that most hoops will have a bit of "give" in them, especially if the ground is fairly soft.

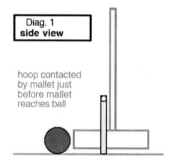

Diag. 1
side view

hoop contacted
by mallet just
before mallet
reaches ball

Care must be taken to use just the right amount of tilt in order to avoid hitting the ball with the bottom edge of the mallet face.

This way, it is often possible to hit a ball when the mallet, placed as in Diag. 1, appears to come as much as 10 mm short of the ball. Players may be understandably nervous about the possibility of break their mallets by playing this shot, but if the shot is played firmly and deliberately, and just hard enough to reach the target ball, rather than attacking the hoop wildly, most mallets will not suffer any noticeable damage.

THE PISTON SHOT

If the ball is further from the hoop, the best option will usually be a "piston shot", as illustrated in Diag.3. For this shot the mallet is inserted into the hoop from the back. A right-handed player will probably find it best to kneel on his right knee, insert his right forearm into the hoop from the front, and grasp the mallet shaft firmly with his right hand down near the mallet head, being careful not to actually touch the mallet head. The

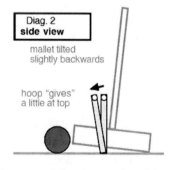

Diag. 2
side view

mallet tilted
slightly backwards

hoop "gives"
a little at top

left hand will hold the shaft above the top of the hoop, and the shot is played by moving the whole mallet forward horizontally with a flat pushing action.

As with most hampered shots, the forward movement should be controlled and deliberate, rather than a "jabbing" action. It is important for the player to keep his eye on the ball, which he may find difficult to do if he is worried about his arm contacting the hoop. Again, the shot should be practised before it is used in a serious game. Roquets of at least 3 yards are quite feasible using a "piston shot".

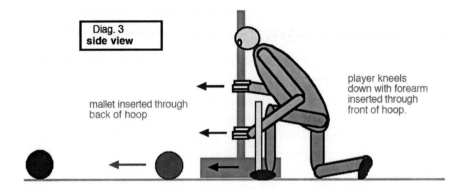

Diag. 3
side view

mallet inserted through
back of hoop

player kneels
down with forearm
inserted through
front of hoop.

The diagrams on this page illustrate three more severely hampered shots in situations where which many players would imagine a roquet to be impossible; but with practice a player can learn to play the shots with confidence that most times the roquet will be made.

In Diag.1 the mallet is inserted into the hoop from the front, and the mallet head must be sloping down at quite a sharp angle. The shot is played with a downward jabbing action (one of the few cases where a "jab" is acceptable) as if trying to make the ball jump. Accuracy is difficult and unless the player has had a lot of practice with this shot he should be advised not to attempt a roquet longer than one yard.

Diag. 2 shows a similar shot, but here the mallet is inserted into the hoop from the back. Again the shot should be played with the mallet sloping steeply forward and down, and with a sharp jabbing action. These two shots are best played with the mallet shaft horizontal and the player's sighting eye looking down along the mallet head in the direction he wants the ball to go (see the "sweep shot" illustration of this rather awkward kneeling position on a previous page). As with other sweep shots the player will need to practise them using both left-handed

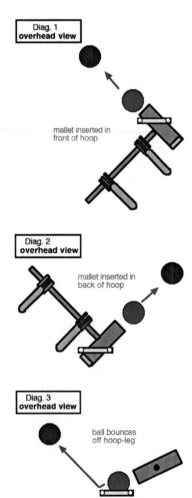

Diag. 1
overhead view

mallet inserted in
front of hoop

Diag. 2
overhead view

mallet inserted in
back of hoop

Diag. 3
overhead view

ball bounces
off hoop-leg

John Riches and Wayne Davies

and right-handed grips. Diags 1 and 2 show the position of the mallet, hands and arms when the stroke is played with a right-handed grip.

Diag. 3 shows another possibility that few players would think of. The blue ball has just made the hoop, but only by a few mm. The centres of the right hoop-leg and the two balls are in an exact line, making a normal sweep shot impossible with the ball so close to the hoop-leg.

The trick here is to bounce the ball off the left hoop-leg so that it will roquet the black ball. Again the target ball needs to be no more than a yard away, and the angle at which the blue ball will come off the hoop-leg will depend on the firmness of the hoop in the ground (which the player can ask the referee to check if desired before playing the shot).

This stroke is played with the player standing up, using a very sharp and hot-too-hard stop-shot action. The player must ensure that the mallet does not follow through far enough to hit the ball a second time.

The success rate in roqueting a ball by bouncing off a hoop-leg can be improved with practice. It may well be worth a try in a game, provided the ball you are attempting to roquet is your partner ball.

HAMPERED SHOTS—REBOUND SHOT

H ERE WE CONSIDER the difficult situation where the striker, playing blue, has roqueted or rushed the black ball which has finished centrally behind the hoop that blue wants to make, and less than half an inch (10 mm or about the diameter of a hoop-leg) from non-playing side of the hoop.

Taking off around to the front of the hoop is likely to be unsuccessful unless the player is prepared to run a long and rather sidey hoop. One solution, also unattractive, is to place the blue ball behind black and roll both balls through the hoop to the front, then run the hoop with blue (maybe needing a hammer shot action), and hope to be able to roquet black by hitting blue back through the hoop once more. We have not illustrated this method because we do not recommend it.

Instead, we suggest using a "rebound shot" after placing the blue ball in the hoop and touching a hoop-leg as shown in Diag. 1—a position from which blue cannot run the hoop in the croquet stroke. The mallet will hit the ball fractionally before the mallet contacts the hoop-leg, as hitting the hoop-leg first would result in a fault.

The hoop-leg will hopefully stop any further forward movement of the mallet and so avoid double-hitting the ball or "crushing" it on the far hoop-leg. (Note that the ball is hit away from the hoop-leg it is touching.) The ball is not contacted in the centre of the mallet-face, but with the right-hand edge of the face so that the left-hand edge will contact the hoop-leg.

Diag. 1
overhead view

(starting position)

mallet contacts ball before contacting hoop

Diag. 2
overhead view

(finishing positions)

mallet hits hoop and stops

Diag. 3
overhead view

mallet swings around a curve, contact ball and then hoop-leg

If he can master it, the player is recommended to use a curved swing as illustrated in Diag.3, which ensures that the mallet is moved well out of the way after contacting ball and hoop-leg, thus making a fault less likely.

If the black ball is not centrally placed behind the hoop (see Diags 4 and 5), the ball should be placed against the hoop-leg furthest from the black ball. This seems contrary to common sense, in that the blue ball is further in the hoop; but placing it against the leg nearest to the black ball will result in the blue ball rebounding at such a wide angle that the hoop may not be able to be made in the following shot (see Diag.5). However, with the black ball not centrally placed behind the hoop, taking off around the hoop is usually a better option.

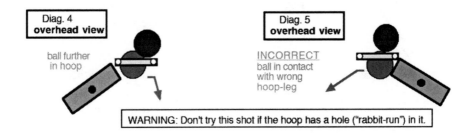

Diag. 4
overhead view

ball further
in hoop

Diag. 5
overhead view

INCORRECT
ball in contact
with wrong
hoop-leg

WARNING: Don't try this shot if the hoop has a hole ("rabbit-run") in it.

HAMPERED SHOTS—THE BRUSH STROKE

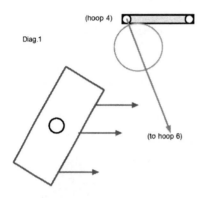

(hoop 4)

Diag.1

(to hoop 6)

THIS STROKE INVOLVES swinging the mallet across the front of the hoop from west to east as illustrated in Diag.1. The idea is to make the hoop with a ball that is (for example) in contact with the left leg of hoop 4 in the direction of hoop 6. There is often no double-hit when the stroke is played this way, so many referees will pass it as a legal stroke.

However, if you watch the position of the mallet when it contacts the ball, you will find that it is as illustrated in Diag.2.

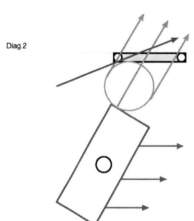

Diag.2

The green arrows show the direction in which the ball is actually hit, since it will come off at a right-angle to the mallet-face, or so close to a right-angle as to make the difference indistinguishable.

The green arrows indicate that the ball has actually been hit into the near hoop-leg, and for that reason the stroke will be a fault. In other words, the ball is hit in a direction very different from that in which the mallet is moving.

It is possible to rotate the mallet further in a clockwise direction so that the green arrows would not pass through the near hoop-leg; but the sideways movement of the mallet will then tend to drag the ball almost directly into the far wire, causing the ball to rebound into the centre of the hoop and contact the mallet again, due to the easterly direction in which the mallet is moving, which is towards the far hoop-leg. In this case the strike will be a fault for a different reason—a double-hit.

This does not prove that it is impossible to play such a stroke legally, but it is very difficult to do so.

The important thing for the referee is to understand that when the mallet contacts the ball, it must be pointing in a direction such that a ball moving away from the mallet-face at right-angles will be moving away from the near hoop-leg, not into it.

To judge this (as best you can), note where the 'V' between the ball and hoop-leg is pointing—i.e. the direction the ball will have to go in to be hit away from the hoop-leg (see red arrow)—and take careful notice of the orientation of the mallet head as the mallet contacts the ball. It is not easy, because you must also be aware that even if the ball is hit away from the near hoop-leg, there is also the double-hit possibility when it rebounds from the far hoop-leg. As a referee you should try it yourself a number of times to familiarise yourself with what can and cannot happen.

HAMPERED SHOTS—REVERSE BRUSH

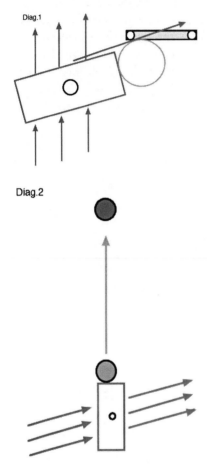

Diag.1

Diag.2

I F THE STROKE is played in the "reverse" direction, by "brushing" the mallet across the back of the ball from right to left instead of from left to right (see Diag 1), and the mallet when it contacts the ball is pointing outside the line of the common tangent between the ball and the hoop-leg (shown by a red arrow), then a competent player who has practised it can get the ball to pass through the hoop and make the hoop legally.

There will be no double-hit because the mallet remains well outside the near hoop-leg and can never get close enough to the ball or the far hoop-leg to contact the ball a second time.

A referee who has not played and tested such strokes may well be inclined to fault this stroke because he could imagine that the mallet, travelling in the direction shown by the arrows, will drag the ball into the near hoop-leg. Similarly, he may pass the stroke illustrated on the previous page in the belief that the mallet has dragged the ball away from the hoop-leg.

In order to convince himself about this, the referee should try the experiment shown in Diag.2. He will find that the ball always leaves the mallet-face in the direction the mallet is pointing, i.e. at a right-angle to the mallet-face, regardless of the direction in which the mallet is moving.

This is quite surprising to many people (especially to coaches who imagine that swinging across the line is a bad error of technique). If there is any "pulling" effect of the ball to the right, it is too small to be discernible.

In actual fact, the blue ball may well move to the left of the red target ball rather than the right. This is caused because there is a tendency for the contact to be made near the left-hand edge of the mallet-face rather than in the centre, thus causing the mallet-head to rotate anti-clockwise.

It all means that the referee must position himself so that he will be able to clearly see the direction in which the mallet is pointing when it contacts the ball, and he must be able to tell whether it is pointing inside or outside the common tangent between ball and hoop-leg as shown in Diag.1 by the red arrow. It should be noted that although the mallet does not "drag" the ball noticeably, it does impart a clockwise spin to the ball which will help it curl though the hoop after it hits the far hoop-leg.

THE PIRIE POKE

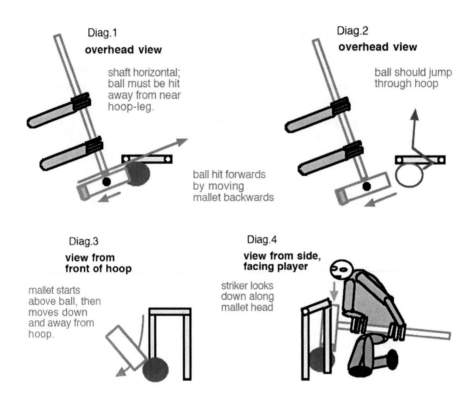

Diag.1
overhead view

shaft horizontal;
ball must be hit
away from near
hoop-leg.

ball hit forwards
by moving
mallet backwards

Diag.2
overhead view

ball should jump
through hoop

Diag.3

**view from
front of hoop**

mallet starts
above ball, then
moves down
and away from
hoop.

Diag.4

**view from side,
facing player**

striker looks
down along
mallet head

I N THIS STROKE the player is kneeling down and swings the mallet downwards and backwards, away from the ball, but the swing starts with the mallet vertically above the ball and sloping forward at a steep angle (the mallet shaft is horizontal). The ball is actually hit forward although the mallet is moving backwards, due to the ball being squeezed between the mallet face and the ground as in a jump-shot, and in fact if the shot is played correctly the ball will jump as it passes through the hoop. The striker should position himself as for the "sweep shot" so that he is looking straight down along the mallet-head, and the ball should be contacted very close to the higher edge of the mallet-face (see Diag.3).

The mallet can be lined up parallel to (or just outside) the 'V' between the ball and the near hoop-leg (see red arrow on Diag.1), so as to ensure that the mallet face is perpendicular to that line and the ball will therefore be hit away from the near hoop-leg.

By the time the ball contacts the far hoop-leg, the backward-moving mallet will have moved further away from the far hoop-leg (see Diags. 2 and 3), making a double-hit very unlikely. This means that, provided it is lined up correctly, the Pirie Poke is not likely to be a double-hit fault, nor will the ball be hit into the near hoop-leg. However it may still be a fault if the stroke is not a "distinct" hit. This should be judged in the same way as any jump-shot or pass-roll, since the same law applies to all strokes. The squeezing of the ball onto the ground does not constitute a fault in itself, and if the ball slides or rolls across the mallet face (or the mallet-face slides across the ball), that does not in itself constitute a fault either.

The shot should be practised using both a right-handed grip as shown, and also with a left-handed grip for use when the ball is in contact with, or very close to, the other hoop-leg.

The main thing for the referee to check is that the stroke is lined up (and that during the swing the mallet remains) such that the ball is hit away from the near hoop-leg, then watch and listen for any sign of an indistinct hit.

• **Which Grip Should I Use?**

This is a question that every novice will ask almost immediately.

Whilst there are many World Class players using every grip style, you can easily see from these 2 diagrams that the arc described by the Solomon Grip (with knuckles of both hands forward) is not as flat as that described by the Standard Grip.

As a flat, long swing is highly recommended, I encourage most players to try the Standard Grip at first.

CROQUET
NEXT BREAK STRATEGY

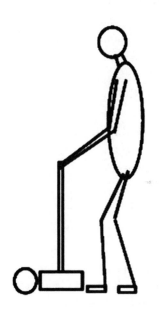

CONTENTS

First published in 1991 as "Croquet Tactics" by
John Riches, 26 Bowman Crescent, Enfield, S.A.
Digital edition v1.2 2004 by cleinedesign.
email *jballant@smartchat.net.au*

DEFINITIONS

1. STRATEGY involves the setting of aims and making of plans.
2. TACTICS involves the practical execution of such plans—the means by which the aims are achieved.
3. TECHNIQUE is the way in which specific shots are played.
4. TEMPERAMENT determines the player's psychological approach and the way he reacts to pressure.
5. THEORY is the player's general knowledge of the game, including rules, equipment, conditions, styles of play and how to combat them, etc.
6. STYLE is the way in which the player plays the game, and involves all of the above things taken together.

NOTE: For the sake of consistency and clarity, the male pronoun is used throughout the text in preference to the more awkward "he/she" or "s/he". In all instances the feminine gender should be understood as included.

CROQUET STRATEGY

THE BOOKLET EXPLAINS ideas which are only vaguely understood by most players and yet which are of basic importance to players who wish to achieve success at the higher levels. Most players at all levels tend to rely on instinct and natural flair, rather than an objective assessment of the given situation. Those of us who are not gifted with such flair and natural sporting instinct have traditionally been left in despair of ever being able to bridge the gap. We attempt to copy the things we see the leading players doing, without understanding why or when they should be used.

The best illustration of this is the fact that almost all players, from the top levels to beginners, use the same method of starting the game which was developed to suit the abilities of leading international players.

Starting the game
The first player hits his ball to the west border near hoop 4, then the second player 'lays a tice', etc. Few of us have ever seriously asked why this is done, or whether there could be an alternative method of starting the game which is better suited to our level of ability. Perhaps the raw beginner may dare to ask such a question. but he is quickly informed that the leading players start their games that way, so it must be the best method.

This ignores the fact that at top level the first player intends, if the 'tice' is missed by his opponent, to set up a break. To do this he will rush his partner ball the length of the lawn. take off to the opponent's ball in the second corner, play a pass-roll which places the opponent's ball at hoop 2 while going to his other 'tice' ball, and then (usually) again passroll for hoop 1. The second player intends, if he roquets the 'tice', to set up a break by splitting it to hoop 2 while simultaneously going to the first player's balls near the fourth corner and then rushing one of them back to hoop 1.

An unjustified assumption?
Why do we assume that such a method will also suit those of us who have little chance of playing such shots successfully, or who would have no intention of attempting them; and on lawns or in conditions where even international players may hesitate to attempt them?

I do not intend to consider other methods of starting the game, but wish to make the point that the correct course of action for a player to take in a given situation will depend on his own level of expertise and that of his opponent, as well as lawn and weather conditions, psychological factors and often other considerations as well. It is necessary to make a judgement based on all such relevant factors. and the judgement must be as accurate and objective as possible if we are to give ourselves the best possible chance of winning the game.

The fundamental aim

This brings us to the most basic and fundamental principle of all—THE CORRECT THING TO DO IS WHATEVER WILL GIVE US THE BEST CHANCE OF WINNING THE GAME. This may seem so obvious as to be hardly worth stating, yet we shall see that it carries with it implications which are far from obvious and are very often overlooked. Such a principle needs, of course, to be translated into more immediate short-term aims, and ultimately into concrete action ("So which shot will I play?") and it is here that the problems arise.

SHORT-TERM AIMS

ASK A PLAYER who has not been watching the game what he aims to do when it is his turn. His answer (apart from the obvious "roquet a ball") will reveal much about both his level of ability and his approach to tactics.

1. THE BEGINNER will answer that he plans to do whatever he decides will give him the best chance of making a hoop. This seems to be a reasonable aim, as the object of the game is to make hoops. However, if we watch him translate this aim into action, we may see him roll for hoop 1 with an opponent ball and then, not quite reaching a position from which the hoop can be made, sit in front of the hoop so that he is wired from the opponent's ball. Then, of course, the opponent removes his ball from the vicinity and our beginner proceeds to make his hoop with no ball to use afterward.

His action has been completely in harmony with his aim: he gave himself the best possible chance of making his hoop. Indeed, he may well be aware that if he passes up such an opportunity it could be a long time before he again has as good a chance of making the hoop—if ever!

It is not likely to help such a beginner if a well-meaning coach tries to convince him that his tactics are wrong. In fact, if his opponent is also a beginner then what he did may have been absolutely correct—that is, he may have not only given himself the best chance of making a hoop, but also the best chance of winning the game! If we manage to stop him from making hoops in such situations he is quite likely to lose to an opponent who does exactly what we have forbidden him from doing; and he will have good reason to look elsewhere for advice in future!

In trying to help such a beginner it is far more important to show him how to take-off, rush and approach hoops more accurately so that he becomes confident of being able to make a hoop without having to start a turn with a ball sitting six inches in front of it. When he plays against opponents with similar ability and confidence he will find out soon enough that his short-term aim was too short-term and too simplistic.

2. THE C-CLASS PLAYER will realise that the beginner's stated aim needs qualification, and will probably say something like: "I aim to make hoops, but not if it means losing the innings." He argues that only the player with

the innings can normally make hoops, and therefore if he can manage to keep the innings for two-thirds or three-quarters of the available time he will almost certainly make more hoops than his opponent.

Thus he may take off from his partner ball in the first corner to the opponent's balls in the fourth corner and try to rush one of them to hoop 2. If his approach is unsuccessful he will not, of course, sit in front of the hoop as the beginner may have done, but return to his partner ball in the first corner. Then, after the opponent has joined up again in the fourth corner, he will try more or less the same thing again—and again—until he either plays a poor take-off (and goes out or fails to roquet), or he ends up making hoop 2 and rolling (probably unsuccessfully) for hoop 3, after which he returns to his partner ball and begins the process again in the hope of making hoop 3.

In this manner he may succeed in hanging on to the innings for considerable periods of time, and against an opponent of similar ability his tactics may again, like those of the beginner against a beginner, be correct and justifiable. In addition to achieving his aim of keeping the innings for as long as possible he may also be giving himself the best possible chance of winning the game.

Once again, the way to help such a player improve is not to decry his boring and negative 'Aunt Emma' tactics. With his level of ability and the range of shots he can play there may be no other course of action which would increase his winning chances. Instead we must teach him to play the stop-shots and split-shots needed to bring his opponent's balls out from the border and place them where they will be of advantage.

This means that we are asking him to go against his stated immediate aim, since with both balls out in the lawn the opponent will be faced with a shorter roquet than from hoop 2 to the fourth corner, so our player will have decreased his own chance of retaining the innings. He will not be able to appreciate the wisdom of this until he realises that his short-term aim is insufficient.

3.   THE B-CLASS PLAYER has reasonable command of a full range of shots, though perhaps without full confidence in all of them. He is capable of playing breaks competently when he has the four balls available in the lawn, or where they can be brought into the break without undue difficulty.

He is aware, therefore, that there is more to croquet than merely playing to keep the innings. He knows that it is entirely possible to have the innings for three-quarters of the available time, but lose the game to an opponent who finally gets in and in half an hour makes two or three big breaks. Therefore his aim must be to make breaks himself, and he will occasionally be prepared to forgo the making of a hoop or (more rarely) risk losing the innings in pursuit of this aim.

He realises the need to get the opponent's balls out from the border to increase the chance of being able to use them in setting up a break, but will usually not know the BEST places to leave them. He will still tend to leave them as far apart as possible so as to minimise the chance of immediately losing the innings, rather than leaving them so as to maximise his own chance of obtaining a break.

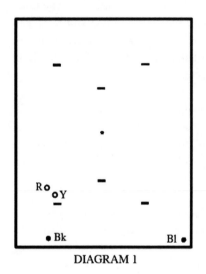

DIAGRAM 1

Let us assume that this player has rolled unsuccessfully for hoop 1 and set both balls near it, with one opponent ball at hoop 2 and the other in the fourth corner. The opponent shoots from hoop 2 at the balls set alongside hoop 1 and misses, finishing on the boundary in front of hoop 1 (see diagram 1). The B-class player may now decide not to simply make hoop 1 and rush or roll for hoop 2. Instead he will roquet his partner ball, take-off to the opponent ball on the boundary, and stop-shot it to hoop 2 while trying to simultaneously gain position to run hoop 1. Note that this course of action actually decreases his chance of making hoop 1 and also decreases his chance of keeping the innings, since if he is unsuccessful the opponent will be given another chance to roquet.

He takes these risks because he is thereby increasing his chance of setting up a break. There would be little sense in taking such risks if he were not able to play the break once it set up, e.g., if he could not confidently split a ball from hoop 1 to hoop 3 while going to the ball which he has stop-shotted to hoop 2. Once again, the tactics he is using may well be the best available to the B-class player, given his level of ability and that of his opponents.

It is only when he plays against a player who obstinately refuses to allow him ready-made breaks (by sticking in hoops, going out on take-offs, missing short roquets, etc.) that he may begin to realise the need to not simply wait hopefully for a break opportunity to come his way, but to set about deliberately creating it. Unfortunately, it may be only rarely that he gets to play against such an opponent, and even then he is likely to put his loss down to bad luck or his opponent's superior shots, rather than more correctly ascribing it to the inadequacy of his own strategy. Perhaps it is this type of player that the ideas in this booklet can most help. It is possible that they will inspire him to further develop his technique to the stage where he is no longer presenting his opponent with ready-made breaks, and no longer needs to rely on his opponent providing him with such unintended assistance.

4.   THE A-CLASS PLAYER has confident command of a full range of shots and will rarely break down while playing a break once he has it properly set up. He has the ability to play a three-ball break and pick up the fourth ball from any position on the lawn, and has at least some idea of where to leave the balls at the end of a break so as to give himself a good chance of obtaining another break to follow. He knows how to go about deliberately wiring his opponent's balls at the peg or at a hoop if he should decide that such a leave would be advantageous. But unfortunately, most players who have achieved such expertise are left with strategy still at the 'B-Class' level. They do not modify their short-term aim to suit their level of expertise and that of their opponents, and play much the same sort of game as the 'B-Class' player.

At this ('A-Class') level it is important to realise that it is very seldom possible to win a game without making sizeable breaks, and it is insufficient therefore to merely aim to make hoops and hold on to the innings, waiting to take advantage of any break opportunity which fortuitously presents itself. Even the ability and willingness to get the opponent's balls off the border and play stop-shots while making position to run hoops will seldom be enough. Instead, the whole aim must be to set up breaks.

The A-class player must adopt the attitude that EVERY TIME HE WALKS ONTO THE LAWN HE WILL DO WHATEVER WILL GIVE HIM THE BEST POSSIBLE CHANCE OF OBTAINING THE NEXT BREAK.

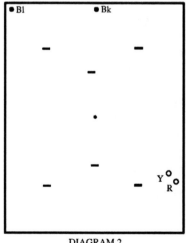

DIAGRAM 2

He must be prepared to take calculated risks to achieve this end, realising that in taking such risks he is actually minimising the risk of losing the game. This is a particularly difficult principle to grasp, due no doubt to the apparent contradiction which it involves. I must be prepared to decrease my chance of making a hoop or keeping the innings, in order to increase my chance of obtaining the next break and winning the game. Furthermore, note that the aim as stated is to achieve the NEXT break, which will not necessarily be an IMMEDIATE break.

I must be prepared to decrease or forgo my chance of making an IMMEDIATE break in order to increase my chance of making the NEXT break—that is, of getting a break before my opponent does. There is no contradiction here, and the point being made is an essential one. It is not important that I get a break going right now: what matters is that I get one going before my opponent does, and I must do whatever maximises my chance of achieving this.\

Imagine a situation (diagram 2) in which the red ball is for hoop 4, and is on the east border alongside its hoop. The yellow ball, which is for hoop 2, is about two feet in the lawn from red and slightly north of it, so that red has a rush toward hoop 6. Blue is in the second corner and black is on the border at about the mid-point of the north boundary. The obvious play would be to cut yellow into the lawn a bit and roll for hoop 4. A good player may well hope to make two, three or even more hoops by starting in this manner and obtaining a rush to the next hoop each time after making the current one. But for the A-class player there are two good reasons why he should not do this.

Firstly, although his skill level gives him a better chance than most of successfully making several hoops in a two-ball break, he is merely taking unnecessary risks for no real gain. If he fails in any of the approaches or hoop attempts. he is presenting the opponent with a 'free' shot along the north border, involving a likely break if he roquets, and still not conceding any immediate real chance of a break if he misses. Secondly, and more importantly, it gets him no closer to achieving his aim of obtaining the next break. In fact, if it results in him leaving one or both of his balls in the middle of the lawn and allowing the opponent the 13-yard shot along the north border, it is very likely to DECREASE his chance of obtaining the next break.

Note that the possible two-ball break is not to be regarded as the 'next break' for which we are aiming. The top international player, who can play two-ball breaks with near certainty and can also count on being able to eventually pick up the two balls from the north border and bring them into the break, may well see things differently; but I doubt that anyone in the world could claim with confidence that this would give him the BEST POSSIBLE CHANCE OF OBTAINING THE NEXT (three or four-ball) BREAK. And when he does obtain his next break it is not going to make much difference whether he starts it from hoop 4 or hoop 5 or hoop 6. In fact, it is easier and less risky to set for a break when his clip is on a corner hoop than when it is on one of the centre hoops, so by attempting the two-ball break he may not only be taking risks with nothing to gain, but also making it harder to find a leave that gives a good chance of achieving the aim of obtaining the next break.

Nor is there anything he can do with yellow that seems to help. He could roquet red and take off to blue in the second corner, send it to hoop 3 while going to black, and pass-roll with black for hoop 2. This would at least offer him SOME chance of obtaining an immediate break (the two-ball break attempt offered practically none), but few would expect to succeed in this more than, say, three or four times out of ten. If you doubt this, try it and see, bearing in mind the risk you are taking if you attempt any unlikely hoop. Even a player who is perfectly happy about playing the long take-off and confidently makes long hoops could hardly claim that this would give him much better than an even (50%) chance of obtaining the next break.

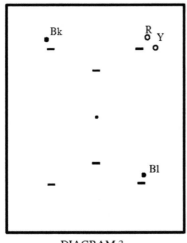

DIAGRAM 3

What, then, should he do? He should play red, rushing yellow to a point between the two opponent balls and then sending it about a yard past hoop 3 while running a similar distance past black. Then he can use a cut-rush and/or roll to place black a yard or two behind hoop 2 while going to roquet blue in the second corner. Lastly, he should send blue right down to hoop 4 while returning in the direction of yellow, and leave red so that it has a cut-rush down the west boundary on yellow for the next turn (diagram 3). This presents the opponent with just one chance to roquet, but if he takes any shot and misses there will be an excellent chance of quickly setting up a four-ball break, and if he chooses not to shoot there will still be at least a three-ball break set up. Since no-one can claim to consistently hit 17-yard shots under pressure more than three or four times out of ten, this gives at least a 60-70% chance of obtaining the next break.

It is clear that no other possible course of action would yield any higher percentage chance of obtaining the next break, so this is beyond doubt the correct strategy for the 'A-class' player to choose.

A matter of no concern
It also follows that an A-class player should not be concerned if his opponent starts to make progress by means of a two-ball break, or by making one or two hoops at a time while keeping the balls widely separated without really trying to get them into play. No opponent is likely to succeed in winning the game by any such strategy—in

fact, by anything except deliberate and well-judged "next-break" strategy—unless we accommodate him by playing particularly poorly.

Why don't they do it?
It also follows that an A-class player should not be concerned if his opponent starts to make progress by means of a two-ball break, or by making one or two hoops at a time while keeping the balls widely separated without really trying to get them into play. No opponent is likely to succeed in winning the game by any such strategy—in fact, by anything except deliberate and well-judged "next-break" strategy—unless we accommodate him by playing particularly poorly.

Why don't they do it?
Why, then, would so few A-class players do what we have just seen is correct? There are several possible reasons:

(1) They do not realise the importance of "next-break" strategy.
(2) They are thinking only of trying to establish an IMMEDIATE break.
(3) They are unable to work out, within a reasonable time, the correct (= best) leaves in situations such as the one under consideration. If they cannot visualise the final position of the balls and how easily it can be achieved, then they will fail to appreciate that such a leave is available to them, and how advantageous it could be.
(4) They cannot appreciate the mathematical approach involved in the reasoning that leads us to conclude that this is the correct thing to do. They argue something like: "But every time I play to set up a break my opponent roquets" (remember that he also is an 'A-class' player), and cannot see that by taking the risk of the opponent roqueting they are in fact maximising their chance of winning the game.

It is the difficulties involved in points (3) and (4) that I hope to be able to help overcome in what follows. As a mathematician I find the estimation and calculation of percentages quite natural, and have much greater faith in strategy and tactics based on this (i.e. "the law of averages", as some would express it) than in my own intuitive judgement which tends all too often to be subjective rather than objective.

The remainder of this booklet is devoted to the translation of this "NEXT-BREAK" principle into actual practice in concrete situations, and is intended for those who have achieved, or aspire to achieve, the 'expert' level in shot-making technique and wish to improve their strategy and tactics to a corresponding level.

TACTICS

TACTICS IS THE process by which players set about achieving their strategical aims. The tactics we use will (or at least SHOULD) be determined by our strategy. When our strategical aims change (e.g. when we start to adopt 'next-break' rather than 'keep the innings' strategy), we will also need to change the tactics we have been employing.

The tactics which give us the best chance of achieving one strategical aim cannot be expected to also give us the best chance of achieving a new and different aim. This seems rather obvious when it is pointed out, but many A-class players who realise that they have little or no chance of winning without making sizeable breaks and therefore acknowledge the importance of getting the next break, nevertheless appear to have given little thought to the changes in tactics needed to maximise their chances of doing so. Even when a tactic is pointed out to them which will clearly increase their chance of obtaining the next break, they are surprisingly reluctant to adopt it. Perhaps at this stage I should remind the reader that I am using the term 'A-class' to mean any player who has reasonable expertise in playing the full range of shots normally required in a game of croquet.

For example, in a doubles game which I played recently my yellow ball was left at hoop 1 which still had all four clips on it, and my partner's red ball was on the east border alongside hoop 4. Blue and black were on the south border almost directly behind hoop 4, and about two yards apart, as shown in diagram 4. I suggested that my partner take the turn and roquet blue. He flatly refused, saying, "I could easily miss that and they'd have a break all set up! You'll have to move. We can't leave your yellow ball at their hoop!"

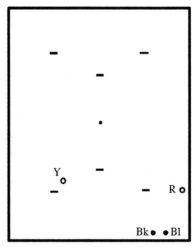

DIAGRAM 4

After the game I pointed out to him that he could have made the six-yard roquet at least eight times out of ten, and he agreed with this. I also challenged him to suggest any other course of action which would have given us the same 80% chance or better of obtaining the next break, and of course he could not do so, since I would clearly have a less than 50% chance of making a roquet with yellow, and if I hit away into a far corner or returned wide of red the opponents would be in possession of the innings and so must be conceded at least a slightly better than even chance of getting the next break. Although he agreed with the 'next-break' strategy in principle, he ended the conversation with, "It's all right for you—you roquet better than I do and are no doubt confident of hitting such a shot", and insisted that nothing I could say would ever persuade him to play red rather than moving yellow in such a situation.

His answer showed that he completely misunderstood my whole point. In most situations there is nothing you can do that will absolutely GUARANTEE you the next break. There will always be some sort of risk involved, but you must do whatever gives you the best CHANCE of getting the next break, because this also gives the best chance of winning the game. I would be no more likely to hit a six-yard roquet than he would, nor play the break any better after making the roquet, but in a singles game I would not hesitate to play red in a similar situation. I do not need to be CERTAIN of making the roquet. Since any other course of action offers LESS than a 50% chance of getting the next break, my strategy requires that I play red even if I believe that my chance of making the roquet is no better than 50%. Therefore I would attempt a roquet of even ten yards since I believe I would normally roquet at least five times out of ten over such a distance.

Examples such as this, of which I could quote many, illustrate how difficult it is for many players to think objectively in terms of percentages, and how unreliable their subjective intuitive) judgement can be. One of my friends replies to my arguments with, "It's no good saying you can hit it eight times out of ten. You are not going to get ten shots at it. You will only get one shot, and you have to hit it—that means you need to hit 100%!" I have given up trying to convince him, as I would apparently need to give him a course in the theory of mathematical probability, which seems somewhat impractical.

Importance of psychological factors
I must acknowledge, however, that my reasoning in the above example does ignore psychological factors which are very real. If in attempting the six-yard roquet your mind is filled with the thought that you are taking an enormous risk and will suffer dire consequences when it does not come off, then your chance of roqueting may well be much less than the 80% you would normally score on roquets of similar length. If your nerves go completely to pieces, your chance may well be less than 50%, and so by my own argument I would have to admit that the correct thing to do, which gives the best chance of getting the next break, would be to move yellow.

It is essential, therefore, for the 'next-break' player to have faith in his strategy. In attempting the six-yard (or ten-yard) roquet he is secure in the knowledge that he is giving himself the best possible chance of winning the game. In fact, any other course of action would amount (in part) to throwing the game away, since he would not be giving himself the best possible chance of winning.

The player who attempts such a shot should not be regarded as a 'gambler'. Next-break strategy does not require the player to possess a temperament which predisposes him to take risks. Quite the opposite! As I intend to make clear later, the whole purpose, intention and aim of 'next-break' strategy is to MINIMISE the risk of losing the game. By definition, the 'next-break' player will resolutely resist the temptation to undertake any course of action, no matter how superficially attractive, which unnecessarily risks allowing the opponent to obtain the next break.

The six-yard roquet is quite the SAFEST shot to play, as anything else entails a far greater risk of losing the game! This is not merely a psychological ruse: It is a mathematical fact! But for many players it requires not only a change in strategy and therefore in tactics; it also requires a change in the whole psychological way they approach the game and think about it, and this is by far the most difficult change of all to make.

IMPORTANCE OF CORRECT TECHNIQUE

HERE IT IS necessary to emphasize once again the importance of developing and maintaining correct technique in playing our shots before we can expect to be successful in employing 'next-break' strategy in our games. The whole justification for taking risks in order to set up breaks can be negated if, for instance, our hoop-running technique is such that we are likely to stick in a hoop and present the opponent with a break already set up; or our hoop-approach technique frequently creates the need to attempt hoops from awkward positions in order to keep the break going. This does not mean that a player must wait until his technique is near perfect before starting to introduce into his game many of the tactics arising from 'next-break' strategy. But it does mean that in some cases the taking of certain risks will be less clearly justifiable, and so the strategy is less certain to prove more effective than the alternative strategies which the player could instead use, or which his opponents may be using.

It is also necessary to remember that the tactics which are correct for one player to use in applying his 'next-break' strategy may not always be equally correct if used by another player adopting the same strategy. Differences in technique, temperament, ability of opponent, state of the game, lawn and weather conditions, etc., all need to be taken into account when assessing the risks involved and possible gains from each of the various alternative courses of action at every stage. What matters is that the assessment is made as objectively as possible, and that it is made with the aim of finding the course of action which gives the best chance of obtaining the next break, rather than simply aiming to make a hoop, or gain and keep the innings, or leave the opponent with the longest possible roquet, etc.

In actual practice everyone will make errors of judgement in assessing such chances, but the player with the aim of obtaining the next break fixed firmly and uppermost in his mind should gradually learn to make reliable assessments more and more often. This learning process need not be a slow one. It will proceed much more rapidly if the player takes time after a game to think back through the choices he made—at least the ones he was in any way doubtful about—and reassess them without the pressure and tension of battle clouding his judgement. Ideally, he should resort to a mathematical analysis of the situation when he is still in doubt, or enlist the help of someone else to do it for him, as this is the best way of ensuring that the choice is made with the greatest objectivity.

It would be foolish to suggest that players should actually perform mathematical calculations during a game before deciding between the various possible shots on offer (although on occasions I have found myself doing just this), but calculations made after the game can clearly reveal that in assessing the risks and possible benefits we are giving too much weight to one factor and too little to another. I do not seriously entertain the thought that many players will have the ability, interest or desire to engage in such mathematical post-mortems, but I believe that those who do will improve most rapidly. They will quickly develop the ability to reliably assess the various possibilities and arrive at the course of action which gives the best chance of obtaining the next break in any given situation.

I am also confident that such players will be at the forefront of the future development of croquet theory, which at present is most certainly only in its infancy compared with the research-based and scientifically developed body of theory being built up in many other areas of sporting endeavour.

In order to make the point of the previous paragraph more clearly, I offer the following example:

At the start of a turn I found myself in the position shown in diagram 5, with my opponent's blue ball in the first corner, my red ball 7-8 yards away along the west border in a shortish 'tice' position, yellow about 3 yards in front of hoop 5 and slightly west of it, and black about half way between hoop 3 and the peg. The red clip was on hoop 5, yellow on rover, blue on 2-back and black on 4-back.

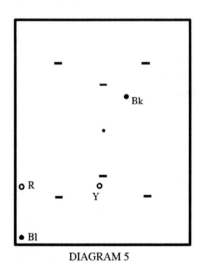

DIAGRAM 5

Thus I was one hoop behind, and bearing in mind my 'next-break' strategy, I tried to decide on a course of action. I decided to attempt the 7-8 yard roquet on blue, as I considered that I had a better than even chance of roqueting, with a good chance of a break to follow. I could not think of any other course of action which offered as good a chance of getting the next break. Of course, I realised that if I missed I would be giving my opponent the same break, but it seemed a chance that ought to be taken. As it happened I made the roquet and went on to win the game.

After the game my opponent commented that he had expected me to move the yellow ball which was out in the lawn and not far from blue's hoop. I explained that I did not want to make any more hoops with yellow, and if I shot with it at red and missed he would have been odds-on to make the 7-8 yard roquet with blue, while a missed shot at black would allow him the further option of shooting with black at blue, so that at best I would need to still make the 7-8 yard roquet but would then no longer have the easy break that I gained by making the roquet immediately.

He was still doubtful, and said, "Yes, but you put yourself under a lot of pressure to make the roquet, and a miss would have made things fairly easy for me", and went on to imply that the taking of such a shot was more likely a sign of foolhardiness rather than wisdom, even though on this occasion the attempt was successful.

In order to satisfy myself that my reasoning and judgement were sound, I went home and did some mathematical calculations (these are set out in appendix A for those who are of similar mathematical bent—"twisted" is more accurate than "bent", according to one of my friends) from which I concluded that the shot I took with red had offered approximately a 57% chance of getting the next break, while the longer shot with yellow at black offered only a 47% chance, assuming that if I missed he would correctly shoot with blue at red.

Then it suddenly occurred to me that there was a third option which I had not considered at all during the game. The 12-yard shot with red at yellow would have given me a 58% chance of getting the next break, and was actually the correct shot to play, even though it was a longer shot and involved a better than even chance of leaving yellow out in the lawn near the opponent's hoop! Of course, the difference between 58% and 57% in calculations with estimated probabilities is much too small to be significant, but this and similar calculations based on positions from other games quickly led me to realise that in making my assessments of the various options available to me, I was at that time giving too little weight to the importance of using the ball with which a break is possible, and worrying too much about the danger of leaving balls out in the lawn.

I do not wish to imply that one should always use the ball whose clip is backward, nor that one should leave one's balls out in the lawn with gay abandon. I am merely saying that the percentages tend to favour using the backward ball to a greater extent than my intuitive judgement had suggested, and the likelihood of leaving a ball out in the lawn is not sufficient reason to reject a course of action without further consideration.

My purpose in quoting this example was not to convince the reader of the need to play the backward ball and cease being concerned about leaving his balls out in the lawn. Rather, I wanted to show the most effective way for a player who adopts 'next-break' strategy to improve his tactics and ensure that the choices he makes are, in fact, giving him the best possible chance of obtaining the next break. It is also possible for him to gradually modify his tactics over time, based on experience and the awareness of which tactics and choices tend in practice to be successful.

Unfortunately it is very difficult to think back objectively (i.e. without bias) about the tactics we have used in our games, and I will demonstrate later that there are psychological factors which cause us to lay the blame for a loss (or the credit for a win) elsewhere than where it should rightly be laid. Mathematical probability calculations avoid most, but not all, of such difficulties.

In order for croquet theory to develop further along these lines in future it is neither necessary nor practical for everyone to spend time during or after their games performing mathematical calculations, but it is desirable that someone consider objectively the tactics of our leading players and assist them to make more reliable assessments of the chances offered by possible alternative courses of action. Then the rest of us can simply follow the leaders, as we have always done.

Before leaving diagram 5, let us see what would happen if yellow shot at black and missed, then blue roqueted red, rushing it along the west boundary to a point about level with the peg, producing the situation shown in diagram 6. Most players would then probably roll for blue's 2-back hoop with the red ball. Some would attempt to set up a break by splitting red to 3-back while trying for a rush on their black partner ball to 2-back. The first of these options leaves black near the middle of the lawn where joining up would be risky if the roll is unsuccessful. The second, if unsuccessful, allows red to be withdrawn from play so that, with yellow also on the border the chance of obtaining the next break would be little better than 50%.

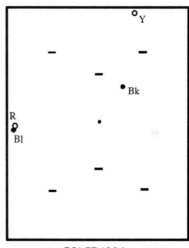

DIAGRAM 6

The correct play is to split red to 3-back and rush black not to the 2-back hoop, but to the yellow ball on the north boundary. If successful, yellow can then be rushed to 2-back to continue the break. If blue does not get the rush on black, then after roqueting black he can roll both balls toward yellow on the north border. After roqueting yellow, he can use a stop-shot to place it a yard or two west of 2-back and set blue with a rush on black to either 2-back or 3-back. This gives an excellent (at least 80%) chance of getting a break going on the next turn whatever the opponent does.

By setting up his break in this manner the player of blue covers the possibility that he may not be immediately successful by ensuring that the balls are left in a position which still gives him an excellent chance of a break on the following turn. It is a clear practical example of how "next-break" strategy should be translated into tactical moves, and also serves to introduce the next section in which we deal with the need to plan for the final position of the balls well before the turn is likely to end.

IDEAL LEAVES

R EADERS WHO ARE still with me may have been saying to themselves, "What is so new about all of this? Perhaps it is being explained in a way I haven't heard before, but surely every player capable of making breaks walks onto the lawn with the intention of trying to get the next break!"

This is no doubt true, but with many of us this aim is not always foremost in our thinking, and even if it is, we frequently fail to find the course of action which gives the best chance of achieving the aim.

A common tactical problem
When I first realised this, I was often left wondering whether I should play a cut-rush and roll to try to make my next hoop, (as most others would when the opponent's balls were widely separated), or instead try to place the balls so that if my opponent did not roquet I would have a break set up on my next turn. I also found that when I chose to set for a break which in those days was only when the chance of making a hoop was very remote indeed), found myself unsure of the best way to do so. I frequently discovered afterward that there were other places I could have left the balls which could have been more easily achieved and would have given me a better chance of getting a break.

A possible solution
In an effort to reduce mistakes of this type, I decided that it would help if I had in mind at least one or two 'ideal leaves' for each possible position of my clips. So I set myself to working out and recording the best place to leave the balls when my clips were both on the 1st hoop, and again when they were on the 1st and 2nd hoops, then 1st and 3rd, 2nd and 3rd, and so on.

I tried to find more than one good leave for each clip position, in case the first one turned out to be impractical in a particular position. There is little sense in playing to obtain a position which would give me a 50% chance of obtaining the next break, if in order to reach the position I need to take risks which involve a better than even chance of making an error and giving the break to my opponent. I wanted to find sufficient 'ideal leaves' so that for any position of my clips, and no matter where the balls were placed to start with, I could expect to achieve at least one of them with relative ease and safety. If it were possible to achieve more than one 'ideal leave', then I could select the one most easily reached, or the one which offered the maximum chance of getting the next break.

It was not long before my diagrams and notes filled many pages of the exercise book I was using, which was not surprising in view of the fact that there are 91 different possible positions of my two clips and I wanted more than one leave for each.

It was obviously going to be impossible for me to remember hundreds of positions from which to make a selection during a game. However, I realised that even if I remembered only a few of the best leaves for a few of the most commonly occurring clip positions I would be able to bring about considerable improvement in my tactics.

Helpful patterns
I also discovered that there were very strong patterns emerging as I worked out the leaves. The 'ideal leaves' with both clips on the 'return' hoops (e.g. 1-back and 3-back) were mostly mirror-images of the best leaves for the first six hoops (i.e. hoops 1 and 3), etc. In addition, the 'ideal leaves' for hoops 1 and 2 were very similar to those for hoops 3 and 4. and those for hoops 4 and 5 were similar to those for hoops 6 and 7, etc. All in all, I found that there were less than twenty 'ideal leaves' which I considered really important and useful, and the task of remembering these was not too difficult.

I do not propose to include here a set of diagrams showing the 'ideal leaves' which I worked out for myself. I refrain from doing so, not because I wish to keep some of my 'secrets' to myself, but because as a teacher I believe it is highly desirable for the student of the game to go through such an exercise for himself rather than copy those worked out by someone else. He is far more likely to remember them that way, and he will gain some understanding of the subtleties involved. In addition, the leaves he works out for himself may well differ from mine, since he may be more confident than I am in playing long rolls, or less confident with certain split-shots, etc.

An ideal leave
I will, however, discuss one of the 'ideal leaves' here by way of example, and in order to show that a player who has not given the matter prior consideration is unlikely to arrive at such a leave after only the few seconds thought he can allow himself during a game. Other 'ideal leaves' will be mentioned later in order to illustrate further tactical points, so from this the reader should gain sufficient idea of what he is to look for in searching for such leaves.

Diagram 7 shows an 'ideal leave' (which is not necessarily THE ideal leave) for a player who has his red clip on hoop 1 and his yellow clip on hoop 2. The black and blue balls have been placed at hoops 1 and 3 (not hoop 2!), and yellow has a 1-yard rush to the front of hoop 2. The balls are set up out near the hoop rather than nearer the border, so that if blue shoots at them and misses it will finish in a position where it will be a simple matter for yellow to run through hoop 2 to the boundary and roquet it, bringing it into the break immediately.

Notice that if the opponent attempts any shot with black or blue and misses, either red or yellow will be presented with a simple 4-ball break; while the removal of either black or blue into a corner (a "finesse" as the English players call it) leaves a 3-ball break with good prospects of soon picking up the fourth ball as well. In each case the break can be achieved without the need to play a long, accurate rush before a hoop is made. The most difficult shot would be a take-off with red from near hoop 2 to the black ball in the first corner if black had missed a shot at blue, but this should involve little risk even for a player well below 'A-class' level.

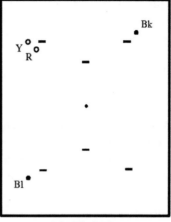

DIAGRAM 7

Wiring not required

If the placement of the opponent's balls can be such that they are wholly or partly wired from shooting at red and yellow, so much the better, but I decided to omit all wired leaves from consideration when working out my 'ideal leaves' because I found that to be certain of the wiring I needed to have such control of the balls that I could almost always play a break immediately, instead of setting up. This is not to say that I do not use wired leaves in my games. On the contrary, many of my opponents claim that at times I seem to be doing nothing other than deliberately wiring their balls from any reasonable shot.

Wired leaves can be of great importance at the end of a break when you have made as many hoops as you wish to make with the ball you are using, or when you have roqueted with a ball which is already around and you need to set for your partner ball.

Such leaves, however, are commonly understood (although chances to achieve them are also commonly missed), and are explained in croquet textbooks. Most A-class players, for example, are already familiar with several wired leaves designed for use after having taken the first ball around to 4-back. These may be designed to give good chances of a triple peel, or simply to allow the opponent a minimal chance of roqueting while retaining a reasonable chance of a break with the second ball if he fails to roquet.

My 'ideal leaves', however, are positions which I can hope to achieve when I do not have sufficient control of the balls to give myself a good chance of an immediate break, so I set for a break in the next turn and hope that my opponent fails to roquet.

Thinking about percentages

Returning to consideration of the diagrammed 'ideal leave', I would give most of my opponents no more than a 30% chance of roqueting red or yellow with blue or black, and less chance still if one opponent ball shoots at the other. Of course, I would not claim for myself any better chance of roqueting over such distances. This means that if I can achieve the diagrammed leave, I am giving myself at least a 70% chance of getting the next break. Against some opponents this becomes in effect 100%, since they choose not to shoot at all, allowing me the 3-ball break "for free".

The purpose of bringing percentages into consideration once again now becomes clear: whenever I make hoop 1 at the start of a game but do not have a ball waiting at hoop 2, I ask myself whether I can think of any course of action which would allow me to continue the break with 70% probability. That is, supposing I see a chance to take-off to my opponent's balls and send one of them to hoop 3, then cut-rush and roll the other for hoop 2. I ask myself whether I would expect to do this successfully 7 times out of 10. If not, then I decide whether I can instead achieve the diagrammed 'ideal leave' position without undue risk, and if so, I would choose to go for the leave.

After all, why should I choose a course of action in which I believe I have less than a 70% chance of getting a break, when there is an alternative which I know will yield a 70% chance or better?

Incidentally, the choice (if it were available) of taking off to my opponent's balls and merely rushing one of them to try to make hoop 2 while the other balls are nowhere near hoop 3 would hardly be given any serious consideration at all by a 'next-break' strategist. This is probably the tactic used by the vast majority of players in such situations (assuming that it is not practical to rush or split the partner ball to hoop 3), but we have already seen that it is quite contrary to the principles of 'next-break' strategy to take any sort of risk unless by taking it one is increasing the chance of obtaining the next break, or decreasing the opponent's chance of doing so, which amounts to the same thing. Playing to make hoops with the opponent's balls when there is little chance of being able to continue the break afterward definitely comes into the "taboo" category.

Having it both ways

Sometimes it is possible to have it both ways to ascertain extent. In diagram 8 yellow has just made hoop 1 with his partner ball, but without getting a good forward rush, and has managed to cut-rush the red ball to a point about half-way along the west border. The blue ball is on the border alongside hoop 2, and the black ball is on the border behind the same hoop. Playing yellow, I could now take off to blue, send it to hoop 3 while going to black, and pass-roll or take off for the 2nd hoop. I would rate my chance of succeeding as certainly no better than 70%, probably less.

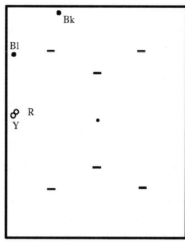

If I do not gain position to run the hoop my opponent can shift whichever ball would be of most assistance to yellow in the next turn, and may well choose to attempt the medium-distance roquet on one or both of my balls after I return to red half-way along the west border.

Alternatively, I could split red to hoop 3 and try to make hoop 2 from either of the

DIAGRAM 8

opponent balls. Again I would rate my chance of success as not much better than 50%, and the leave if I fail would have to be far from 'ideal'.

With the previously considered 'ideal leave' position in mind, I would do neither of these things, but instead would roll red to a position about 1 yard west of hoop 2 while going to roquet blue. This shot entails virtually no risk, as there is no need to try to obtain a rush on blue. I can keep yellow well in the lawn and only need to get close enough to blue to be certain of roqueting it. Then I would send blue a yard or so past hoop 3 while going to black, and use a stop-shot to place black at the 1st hoop while trying for position to run the 2nd hoop. In this manner I give myself a fair chance (say, about 40%) of continuing the break immediately, and retain the possibility of setting the 'ideal leave' which still gives me a further 70% chance if I am not immediately successful. Note that there is an added bonus in that if I decide to attempt to make hoop 2 then I am doing so with my partner ball present, rather than an opponent ball.

No doubt there are other players who would think of this course of action and adopt it during a game, but there are also certainly many who would not. An understanding of 'ideal leave' positions almost GUARANTEES that the player will think of it, and will also find many other far less obvious ways to improve his chances of obtaining the next break. I must have used this leave at least a hundred times in my games, but cannot recall it ever being used against me.

Preserving options
Another point to be made is that even if you decide to try for an immediate break, it is often possible to set it up in a way that allows you to keep in reserve the option of obtaining a good leave if you find yourself unable to continue. This was the reason

for rolling red to the 2nd hoop in diagram 8 instead of leaving it halfway along the west border, and also for sending black to hoop 1 rather than to hoop 4 or the peg. As a further example, consider the position in diagram 9. Here the yellow clip is again on hoop 2 and red on hoop 1. Playing yellow, you have roqueted black at hoop 3. You can take off for a rush on red to hoop 2, but this risks leaving the opponent balls fairly close together when you cannot be certain of making the hoop. So you take off instead to blue in the 3rd corner, and where do you place it?

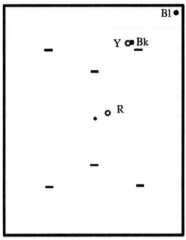

DIAGRAM 9

Now that you have been introduced to the 'ideal leave' position, the answer is obvious. Although most players would split blue to hoop 4 ("into forward play") as they try for a rush on red to hoop 2, it is better to place blue at hoop 1 on this shot. If you then get a good rush on red you will be able to place red to the left of hoop 2 on the approach shot and in running the hoop obtain a rush toward hoop 1. A "backward" rush is the easiest rush to give yourself after running a hoop, and you should not then find it difficult to get red to hoop 4 and bring blue back into the break before making hoop 3 with yellow. If you do not get the original rush on red you can roll for hoop 2 with the same intention, or get the 'ideal leave' position of diagram 7 if yellow does not gain position to run the hoop.

This idea of loading the partner's hoop, instead of putting both opponent balls into forward play during the setting up of the break, is well known but also often overlooked. A player who is accustomed to thinking in terms of 'ideal leaves' is likely to find many such opportunities to improve his tactics, when the player who thinks only of playing a break with yellow would miss them.

Pressure producing frustration
In this way you can frequently reduce the opponent to a state of frustration and exasperation, as whenever it is his turn to play he is faced with the need to move both of his balls at once, which is impractical, and must attempt a roquet which he cannot afford to miss. Most players find this far more difficult than roqueting in a shot where a miss is less likely to prove immediately disastrous. In addition to having to cope with the constant pressure, he will usually be in considerable doubt about whether or not he is doing the right thing. The psychological advantage gained in this way is not to be lightly dismissed.

In recent times the value of playing to set up an 'ideal leave', rather than taking risks trying to establish a break which is far from set up, has become more and more apparent to me, especially early in the game when I have not yet "got the feel" of the lawn. I now often find myself planning for an 'ideal leave' well before making hoop 1, instead of waiting until after I have made it.

Plan your leaves early

For example, in a recent game I split the black ball to hoop 2 and then rushed and rolled with my red partner ball for hoop 1, but my approach shot was poor and my yellow ball stuck in the hoop. My opponent then shot with black at red and missed, so that the black ball was then on the border in front of the 1st hoop. The blue ball was on the border near the 4th corner. This left me with the position shown in diagram 10, and I realised that the obvious play (since I could not count on roqueting yellow with red) would be to gently make hoop 1 with yellow and then rush red to hoop 2.

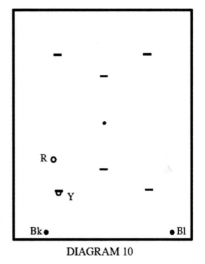

DIAGRAM 10

There would be little risk involved in this, but it offered no way to increase my chance of getting a break. Therefore I chose instead to hit yellow slightly harder on the hoop shot, obtaining a rush on red back to the first corner. From there I played a stop-shot which sent red past hoop 4, leaving it 2-3 yards in from the east border; and roqueted black.

Then a thick take-off put black in near hoop 1 as I went to blue, and another stop-shot sent blue to hoop 2, with yellow running up to red. I finished the turn by placing yellow so that it was the same distance out from the east border as red (i.e. 2-3 yards), with the balls just over a yard apart. This position (diagram 11) was another of my 'ideal leaves' with clips on hoops 1 and 2.

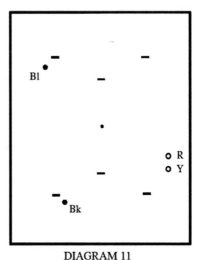

DIAGRAM 11

It is better to have my balls slightly in from the border rather than right on it, so that if the opponent shoots at my balls with either of his and misses, I will more easily be able to roquet his ball and get it in from the border while retaining a rush on my partner ball. It is also best to set my balls equidistant from the border as shown, rather than setting a rush to hoop 1 for red.

There are three reasons for this. Firstly, it reduces the chance of presenting a 'double' target to the opponent's black ball. Secondly, it tends to discourage many opponents from shooting at my balls because they reason that I have not set a rush for myself and they do not wish to risk making things easier for me by giving me one, together with the fourth ball. Thirdly and most importantly, it allows me an excellent chance of a break with either red or yellow no matter what my opponent does.

If he moves black, then yellow has a slight cut on red to hoop 3, followed by a take-off to blue at hoop 2; while if he moves blue, then red can cut-rush yellow to the south boundary and split it to hoop 2 as red goes to black at hoop 1. If either of the opponent's balls shoots at the other and misses, then there is a relatively simple 4-ball break offering.

A more 'ideal' leave
This leave tends to be more easily attainable than the 'ideal leave' which we first considered for the same clip positions (see diagram 7 again), as my two balls could be placed almost anywhere near the east border from near hoop 3 to the fourth corner. However, it does presuppose a readiness to play a split shot if necessary, from the south border behind hoop 4 to hoops 1 and 2. The A-class player should have no qualms about playing such a shot, but a player who is unhappy about it is faced with the need to set a rush for red to the 1st hoop, intending to play red whichever ball the opponent moves. If black then misses blue, he must depend on an accurate rush to the 1st hoop so as not to place himself under pressure in having to roll for it with the opponent's balls only 6-7 yards apart. He must also risk allowing black to shoot at his rush with a 'double' target as mentioned earlier.

Let us now return to the game we were following. On being faced with the leave in diagram 11, my opponent shot with black at blue and roqueted. I have used this leave on even more occasions than the first-mentioned 'ideal leave' of diagram 7; and on every occasion when both of his clips were still on hoop 1 the opponent has moved the ball at that hoop. Some of them shoot at the partner ball as in this game, others shoot at my balls, and many prefer to play the ball from hoop 1 out of play into either the first or fourth corner.

This seems strangely inexplicable to me, unless perhaps they reason that if I am forced to use the yellow ball I will be able to make one less hoop than with the red ball! If I were the opponent, I would certainly play the ball at hoop 2, since a roquet with it on red or yellow would give a break much more certainly than a similar roquet with the ball from hoop 1. On the other hand, if I thought that the player of red and yellow was of timid temperament and less than happy to play long split shots, I may decide not to shoot at all, but would play blue into the second corner in order to discourage the opponent from splitting red right to hoop 2 as he still ought to do.

The 'defensive' roll

Returning once more to the game: after my opponent roqueted blue with black he took off to my balls and rushed one of them to make hoop 1. This he succeeded in doing, but he did not get a forward rush, and since blue was no longer at hoop 2 he did not manage to continue the break. There followed a few turns in which neither of us succeeded in making a hoop, until eventually I got in with red and rolled with yellow for hoop 1, after having sent black to hoop 2. Blue was once again near the fourth corner. In rolling for hoop 1 I sent yellow about 2 yards from the hoop toward the first corner (I will explain later the reason for this, when we consider diagram 16), but failed to get red to a position from which it could run the hoop, so I set it about 1 yard behind yellow with a simple rush to the front of hoop 1 as shown in diagram 12. This time my opponent elected not to shoot at my balls with black, as a miss would allow me a 3-yard roquet followed by a break, so he returned to his partner ball in the fourth corner.

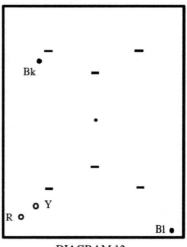

DIAGRAM 12

If at first you don't succeed . . .

Then, instead of making the 1st hoop with red, I rushed yellow to a point about halfway along the east boundary, took off (thickly) to black in the fourth corner, used a sharp stop-shot to send it to hoop 1 while staying near blue, and another to put blue at hoop 2 while going near red. I finished by setting exactly the same leave as before (see diagram 11 again), except that my balls were set a few yards further up the east border. This time my opponent missed the roquet with black on blue, allowing me to play yellow, rushing red to hoop 3 and taking off to black to set up a straightforward 4-ball break and take yellow around to 4-back. The opponent commented to spectators that he could not understand why I had "run away from hoop 1" instead of making it, because I was "worried about his balls together in the fourth corner".

The actual reason why I chose not to make hoop 1, of course, was that I saw an alternative course of action involving setting an 'ideal leave', which I believed would give me a better chance of obtaining the next break. The fact that he had roqueted on the previous occasion when presented with the same leave meant nothing. I would have set it (or a similar leave) again and again if necessary, as nothing else I could have done would have given me as good a chance of winning the game. There was certainly the remote possibility that he would keep on roqueting every time in such situations, in which case he would probably (but still not certainly) win the game. As noted previously, the adoption of 'next-break' strategy carries no guarantee of winning the game—it just gives you the best possible chance.

A principle to remember
It is worth pointing out in reference to the above example that if I had made hoop 1 with red I would then have had both clips on the same (2nd) hoop, which would have made it considerably more difficult to find an 'ideal leave'. There is a principle here worth remembering: it is easier to set for a break when your clips are not on the same hoop. This will also explain in part why experienced players tend to avoid "making a double" by peeling the partner ball through hoop 1 as they make it—a feat which beginners take great delight in.

A matter of percentages
In the position of diagram 12, after black has joined blue in the fourth corner, many A-class players would have made hoop 1 with red and then rushed yellow back to the middle of the south boundary. From here they could use a wide-angled stop-shot to place yellow at hoop 3 while going to the opponent balls in the fourth corner. If they could then rush either black or blue to hoop 2 they would have succeeded in obtaining an immediate break. This is the correct line of play to adopt, provided that you rate your chance of success as about 60% or better. If you are not confident of succeeding at least 6 times out of 10 then your best chance of obtaining the next break is to set an 'ideal leave' as I did in the game.

A dilemma for "Aunt Emma"
This may also be as good a time as any to draw the reader's attention to the fact that 'nextbreak' strategy involving the use of 'ideal leaves' is most effective when used against the legendary 'Aunt Emma', who although traditionally described in female terms can equally well haunt our lawns in male guise. When faced with an ideal leave she can almost always be relied upon not to shoot at all, but to retire instead into a corner. She does this because although she can take-off, rush and roll accurately, she does not play many split-shots and therefore rarely makes more than two or three hoops in a break. She knows that if she misses a shot which allows her opponent a simple 4-ball break she is instant history, as she ill be unable to match the nine or more hoops he will make. This means that the odds are so far weighted in favour of the 'next-break' strategist that unless he plays his shots very poorly indeed it will hardly be a contest.

Position of opponent's clips

The reader may have noticed with some surprise that in the foregoing discussion of 'ideal leaves' I have omitted all mention and consideration of the position of the opponent's clips. Is it not true that their position could make one leave more risky, and therefore less 'ideal', than another? This is no doubt true, but at present I have not seen the need to take account of the opponent's clip positions when deciding which leave to use. Occasionally it may influence my choice of which opponent ball to place at which hoop, but it is unlikely to lead to a choice of a different leave from the one I decide (before looking to see where the opponent's clips are) will give me the best chance of getting the next break. Perhaps someone else will refine the theory of 'ideal leaves' by taking the opponent's clip positions into account, or maybe I will one day see the need to get around to doing it myself.

An advantage of omitting the position of opponent's clips from consideration is that you have the whole of the time while your opponent is playing his previous turn (or turns) in which to work out one or more 'ideal' leaves for the position of your clips. Then when you get in you will be ready to decide whether to try for an immediate break or play to set up an 'ideal leave'.

MAINTAINING THE BREAK

WE HAVE ALREADY seen that many players tend to be too conservative in their judgement of the advisability of taking a risk in order to get a break started. The situation explained in diagram 4 was one example. The same is true when players make judgements about the risks involved in keeping a break going when things start to go wrong.

In a game I was watching recently the position shown in diagram 13 arose. The player of red had tried to run through hoop 4 to the blue ball on the boundary, but had finished only one yard behind the hoop. Black was about three yards from red in the

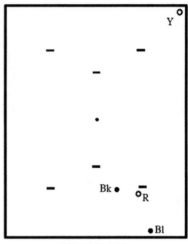

DIAGRAM 13

direction of hoop 5. After gazing longingly at the 5-yard roquet on blue, he elected instead to take the 3-yard rush on black to the next hoop. He approached and made hoop 5, but did not get a forward rush, so he rolled for hoop 6, with red finishing about 5 feet directly in front of the hoop and black behind the hoop. I expected him to then return red to his yellow partner ball in the third corner, but to my great surprise he attempted to make the hoop! If this does not sound strange to you, then like him you need to rethink the way in which you assess the risks involved.

Assessing the risks
I am sure that although he could not have been CERTAIN of roqueting blue on the border after making hoop 4, he could have made the 5-yard roquet at least 8 times out of 10. But I would find it hard to believe that he could have made hoop 6 from 5 feet directly in front more than 5 times out of 10. This means that he refused to take a risk which would have given him about an 80% chance of continuing his break, but decided a few shots later to take a risk which offered only about a 50% chance of making his next hoop with nothing set up to follow!

In both cases failure would have given away the innings, but not an immediate easy break. He deservedly failed to make hoop 6, and after the game blamed his loss on the fact that he "kept sticking in hoops". In actual fact, he lost because of the very poor tactics he used in refusing to take the risks he should have taken, and taking risks which even if they came off would have assisted his cause very little.

Different risk, but same principle
It is worthy of note that even if the black and yellow balls in diagram 13 were interchanged, the decision not to attempt the roquet on blue after making hoop 4 would still have been wrong. The player may feel happier about making the centre hoops with his partner ball rather than an opponent ball, but the position is similar to that described in diagram 2. He is taking the risk of having to leave his balls in the centre of the lawn where his opponent can take free 'pot-shots' at them. Such a risk may be justifiable if it represents his best chance of getting a break going, but here it can only reduce his chance, for the mere sake of making one or two additional hoops.

I have observed so many instances of some of our leading players making similar incorrect judgements, that I have come to believe there are very few players who would not benefit from a reappraisal of the types of risk which should, and should not, be taken.

Would you make it?
As another illustration of this point, let us consider the position shown in diagram 14. Imagine that you are playing red, and have rolled with the black ball for hoop 1, but the approach was poor and your red ball is now about 4 feet in front of the hoop on a 50 degree angle. Your yellow partner ball is 3 yards in front of hoop 2, and the blue ball is in the fourth corner. You must decide whether or not to attempt the hoop, realising that failure is almost certain to give your opponent a ready-made break. What % chance would you give yourself of making the hoop? What % chance would you NEED to have before you would be inclined to attempt the hoop? How reliable do you think your intuitive judgement is in such situations?

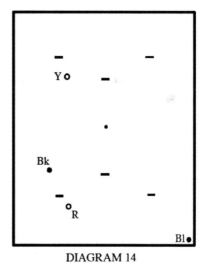

DIAGRAM 14

Do you find yourself electing to attempt such hoops and later concluding that you should not have taken the risk? Most players answer 'yes' to this last question, but hardly ever elect NOT to make the hoop and later realise that they SHOULD have taken the risk. Would it be helpful if you had some way of being confident of making the correct decision?

I have found that most experienced players believe they have a fair idea of their chance of making a hoop from various positions. For example, they would say, 'I reckon I could make it from there about 6 times out of 10. I am sure that I would have a better than even chance, but I certainly wouldn't expect to make it 8 times out of 10, and probably not even 7 times." I do not normally ask them to put this judgement to the test, as it would prove little. The point is that they are satisfied that their judgement of the chance of making the hoop is reasonably reliable, and it probably is.

Surprising vagueness
However, when asked what % chance they think a player ought to have of making the hoop in diagram 12, before they would consider him justified in attempting it, their answers are surprisingly vague. The percentage they suggest will depend largely on temperament, and may vary from: "You have the chance of a break if you make the hoop, so you ought to go for it unless the hoop is impossible", to: "you would need to be almost certain of making it, as you are giving a break to your opponent if you miss." Some may say: "There's no need to take such a risk. You can go back near yellow and the opponent is not likely to roquet", while others would say, "You can hardly sit both balls out in the lawn near the second hoop and give the opponent a free shot at them, so I guess the hoop should be attempted".

It seems amazing that there should be such vagueness and wide divergence of opinion among experienced players on such a straightforward question of tactics. Each of them must have been forced to make such decisions on many hundreds— probably thousands—of occasions, yet although the decision is very likely to be of great importance in deciding the result of the game. they apparently have no way of knowing whether or not they are making correct decisions in such situations.

Some have said: "If you decide to take a risk and it comes off, then the decision was correct. If it doesn't, then it was wrong!" This may be said jokingly, but it is a very dangerous and invalid line of argument. It says nothing about how you can know whether you were right or wrong if you decide NOT to take the risk; and it ignores the fact that players frequently take risks which come off, but which nevertheless

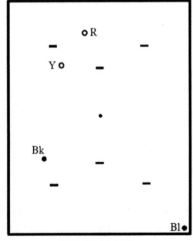

DIAGRAM 15

John Riches and Wayne Davies

should not have been taken. The fact that they took the risk and were successful on this occasion probably guarantees that they will take similar risks on future occasions and lose many games because of doing so.

Mathematics to the rescue!

Once again we must turn to mathematics for an objective and definitive answer. Although based on statistics and estimates, this is likely to be far more reliable than depending on the intuitive judgement of even the most experienced and accomplished player. A relatively simple calculation (see appendix B if interested in the mathematics involved) reveals that in a game between 'A-class' players you will be conceding to the opponent at least a 53% chance of obtaining the next break if instead of attempting the hoop you place your red ball near yellow in the lawn, or level with yellow on the west border, or behind hoop 2 to 'cover' the north boundary in case black shoots at yellow. There is little to choose percentage-wise between the three options if you decide not to attempt the hoop.

In view of this, it is correct to attempt the hoop provided you give yourself an even (50%) chance of making it, or even fractionally less. How accurate would your intuitive judgement have been? If you fail to attempt the hoop when you would have a 50% chance of making it, then you are not giving yourself the best possible chance of winning the game. It follows that the hoop shot is the SAFEST shot you can play, since it minimises your chance of losing. By doing anything else you would be taking a GREATER risk of losing the game! Unfortunately, I have no answer to the problem of how to convince your doubles partner of this fact, unless perhaps you give them a copy of this book to read, and since most players are likely to place more reliance on their own intuitive judgement than the result of a mathematical calculation, it may well prove to be a waste of time anyway!

What now?

Before we leave this position, we shall consider the correct course of action for the opponent if we decide not to attempt the hoop, and instead play the red ball to a position about 2 yards behind the 2nd hoop, so that it is 5 yards from yellow and 4 yards from the north boundary (diagram 15). When calculating the advisability of choosing this alternative to the hoop attempt, we had to take into account the fact that we were by no means certain to get the red ball exactly as described, covering the north boundary against a shot by black at yellow, but still close enough (hopefully) to roquet yellow if black returns to blue in the fourth corner. If you were now the player of black, what would you do?

The correct play for the A-class player is to shoot at yellow, even if you do not have a 'double' target with red behind it, and even though red is almost certain to roquet black on the north boundary if you should miss. I will not give the mathematical calculation which supports this, but the main point is that the player of red and yellow would have about the same chance of getting a break with his two opponent balls in the fourth corner as he would if black missed the shot at yellow. In the former case he would roquet yellow with red, take off to the opponent balls in the fourth corner and rush one of them to make hoop 1, with yellow hopefully not too far from hoop 2.

If black is on the north border after shooting at yellow and missing, then red can roquet the black ball and roll it to hoop 2 while getting a rush on yellow to hoop 1. If anything, the chance of getting the break going may be slightly better with black and blue in the fourth corner, as the rush should be easier to obtain accurately.

Black is more likely to roquet yellow at 16 yards than blue at 21 yards, and the chance of red getting a break going is about the same whichever shot is missed, so he should shoot at yellow. However, the great majority of players at all levels would return to the partner ball without hesitation, as they are unwilling to "give red an extra ball in forward play".

A hard-to-face fact?

This reinforces the statement made above that the natural intuitive judgement of players is frequently astray. It is unfortunate that apart from objective mathematical calculations there is no way for them to discover just how inaccurate many of their judgements are. Even when such judgements regularly result in games being lost, most players tend to attribute the losses to missed roquets or poor take-offs rather than poor tactical judgement. They happily ignore the fact that the opponent also made similar errors. It seems easier for us to accept that we have been out-played (or better still, 'out-fluked') than to face up to the fact that we have been out-thought!

COVERING THE BOUNDARY

T HE TACTIC OF using one of your balls to 'cover the boundary' behind your other ball in order to discourage the opponent from shooting at it is well known and widely used. However, most players use it only when setting up at the end of a break, or when they have only one shot left and find themselves unable to make the hoop they need in order to continue the turn.

We have already seen that 'next break' strategy is aimed at maximising your chance of getting the next break, and this also amounts to minimising your opponent's chance of getting the next break. It is impossible to do one without also doing the other, as they are merely two different ways of saying the same thing. Therefore, when we urge a player to choose tactics which will increase his chance of obtaining the next break, we are also saying that he should adopt tactics which will decrease his opponent's chance of doing so. From this point of view, it will not be surprising that 'covering the boundary' is an important consideration for the 'next break' strategist.

A matter of balance
t is important to realise that correct balance must be maintained between tactics whose sole intention is to increase your chances, and those whose intent is to decrease the opponent's chances. The favourite 'Aunt Emma' tactic of sending the opponent's balls to the far corners of the lawn and setting her own balls as far from them as possible is designed to decrease her opponent's chances, but unfortunately also serves to decrease her own chances of getting a break, so cannot be seriously entertained by the 'next break' strategist.

In fact, Aunt Emma's short-sightedness prevents her from seeing that although she is reducing the chance of her opponent obtaining an IMMEDIATE break, she is actually INCREASING the chance of him obtaining the NEXT break. This follows from the fact that with the opponent's balls well out of play, Aunt Emma has only a marginally better chance of getting a break going than the opponent has, since neither has much chance in the immediate future. Therefore, each player has a close to 50% chance of getting the next break, with Aunt Emma being conceded a slight advantage (say, 55%-45%, or at best, 60%-40%) by virtue of the fact that she retains the innings.

Instead of sending her opponent's balls out of play, there must almost always be alternative tactics available to her which would increase her chance of getting the next break to well above 60%. These are tactics which, however, involve taking a short-term risk in the hope of making a longer-term gain, so her short-sightedness would not allow her to see the value of them even if she thought of them.

In adopting the tactic of 'covering the boundary', the next-break strategist must similarly bear in mind the need to ensure that he is doing it in a way that enhances, rather than detracts from, the achievement of his overall aims. In using it to discourage his opponent from shooting, he will often be forgoing the opportunity to set himself a rush; or in some other way he will be making his next hoop less certain. These things need to be carefully weighed up in order to be sure that you are retaining the best percentage chance of getting the next break, and not merely playing to prevent the opponent from getting an immediate break.

With all this in mind let us see how the 'next break' player may use the idea of 'covering the boundary' while SETTING UP a break, and not just at the end of it, or when the break has turned out to be unachievable.

In diagram 16 all clips are still on hoop 1. We are playing the red ball, and have placed the black ball about 3 yards in front of hoop 2, with blue about half-way along the north border. We are about to roll for hoop 1 with our yellow partner ball from a point between hoops 4 and 5. It is normal to roll so that yellow finishes 3-4 yards behind hoop 1, hoping to obtain a forward rush after making the hoop.

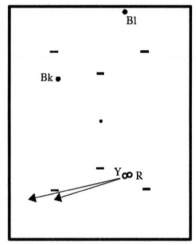

Defensive roll for hoop 1
DIAGRAM 16

What if the roll is unsuccessful?
If we fail to gain position to run the hoop, however, it will be difficult for us to adequately 'cover the boundary' in order to prevent or discourage black from shooting at yellow. By placing the red ball near enough to the south boundary to be reasonably sure of roqueting black after it misses yellow, we will be allowing black the alternative of shooting at blue, since we will then need to play a by-no-means-certain roquet under pressure, with no assured way of getting a break going even then.

Therefore we should consider the advisability of rolling so that yellow finishes a yard or two from hoop 1 in the direction of the first corner. This forgoes all chance of obtaining a forward rush if the hoop can be made, but if the hoop cannot be attempted it allows us to easily 'cover the boundary' behind the yellow ball. Since we have ensured that we can easily make hoop 1 in the next turn and probably obtain a forward rush, the opponent may also be discouraged from trying to roquet blue, because a miss would almost guarantee us a break by making hoop 1, then rushing or splitting yellow to hoop 3 and using the two opponent balls.

This tactic of rolling for a hoop so as to retain the option of covering the boundary is sometimes referred to as a "defensive roll". [After this booklet was first published I was taken to task by a reader for advocating defensive tactics rather than aggressive tactics. In actual fact the use of the "defensive roll" is usually a very aggressive tactic, allowing you the option of setting up in a situation where you are daring the opponent to shoot at your balls. In order to avoid this misunderstanding, in my later booklets I have changed "defensive roll" to "trap-line play" or "setting a trap"—a term I borrowed from other writers.]

Considering the disadvantages

The disadvantage of rolling yellow as suggested is that if we roll successfully and make hoop 1, we will have no forward rush, so we have reduced our chances of continuing the break without mishap. For many players this would outweigh the advantage of being able to 'cover the boundary' if the hoop cannot be attempted, so they should roll normally.

Importance of practice

I believe, however, that if the 'next-break' strategist can practise splitting balls to hoops 2 and 3 from a point 2-3 yards IN FRONT of hoop 1 rather than behind it, and become reasonably proficient in such shots, then he should be able to continue the break with almost as much certainty as if he had a forward rush. In this case the advantage of being able to retain the option of covering the boundary may well outweigh the slight additional risk involved in continuing the break if the hoop is made. This applies even more strongly if the hoop for which we are rolling is hoop 2 (diagram 17) instead of hoop 1, as the opponent will have a shorter roquet if

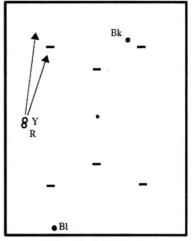

Defensive roll for hoop 2
DIAGRAM 17

we fail to cover the boundary and the split-shot to which we are committing ourselves in order to continue the break is less difficult. The 'next-break' strategist should strive to develop confidence in playing such split-shots so that he can use this 'covering the boundary' tactic, when forced to roll some distance to his hoop with his partner ball. This requires the ability to split to hoops 3 and 4 from 2-3 yards west of hoop 2, and (hardest of all) to roll for hoops 4 and 5 from 3-4 yards in front of hoop 3.

Hoop 4 most important

The most important time of all to cover the boundary is when making a longish roll for hoop 4 with the partner ball. Assume that an opponent ball has been placed at hoop 5, or preferably about 2 yards west of it (diagram 18). Unless you are certain of making hoop 4 you should roll for it so that your partner ball finishes 2-3 yards from the hoop toward the fourth corner. This allows you to cover the boundary if needed, and in this case you still have a relatively simple split-shot to continue the break if you are successful in making the hoop.

What if the opponent is also a 'next-break' strategist?

Before passing on, there is another point to be made: if your opponent is also a 'next-break' strategist, then on many occasions he will shoot at your balls even if you have the boundary covered. Let us return to diagram 16 and suppose that we have played as suggested, rolling yellow to a point about a yard from hoop 1 in the direction of the 1st corner. Then, red not being in position to attempt the hoop, we placed it halfway between yellow and the first corner spot. What will black do? We have already seen that a missed shot at blue would give us an excellent chance of an immediate break.

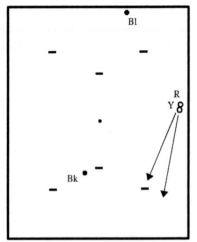

Defensive roll for hoop 4
DIAGRAM 18

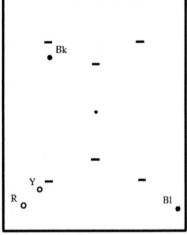

DIAGRAM 19

Even if blue were differently placed, in (say) the fourth corner as shown in diagram 19, the 'next-break' strategist would not be keen to return to it because he realises that we could make hoop 1 with red and rush yellow to almost any point along the east boundary, then proceed to set up an 'ideal leave'. If he returns wide of blue he would make it still easier for us to do this. And if he finesses into a far corner (e.g. the third), he is removing all pressure from us and we are still likely to get to an 'ideal leave' before he gets any better or safer chance to roquet than he has right now. Since allowing us to set up an 'ideal leave' would give us at least a 70% (and therefore him less than 30%) chance of a break, he loses nothing by shooting immediately. He knows that if he misses we will have the break immediately, but his chance of

John Riches and Wayne Davies

roqueting should be 25-30%. By finessing or returning to his partner ball he is in most situations giving us an even better chance of getting the next break, although he may succeed in delaying it for a turn or two.

Of course. this reasoning will only apply to a player who understands 'next-break' strategy and knows that his opponent also uses it. In such a game the tactics are likely to be very different from those seen when only one of the players is using 'next-break' strategy, and will probably be completely incomprehensible to most 'normal' players!

THINKING AHEAD

BECAUSE 'NEXT-BREAK' STRATEGY is often concerned with longer-term gains rather than immediate ones, it is essential for the player to develop the habit of thinking ahead instead of considering only his (or his opponent's) immediate turn. A clear example of this is seen in diagram 20, which was taken from a game between a leading state player and a visiting international player.

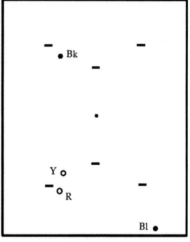

DIAGRAM 20

With all clips still on hoop 1, the state player had placed the black ball in front of hoop 2 and rolled unsuccessfully with red and yellow for hoop 1. Not being a 'next-break' strategist, he had not rolled so as to retain the option of covering the boundary as explained in the previous section. Blue was on the south border about four feet from the fourth corner. With yellow three yards behind hoop 1 in the direction of the peg (too far out in the lawn for red to cover the boundary behind it), he had to decide what to do with red on his one remaining continuation shot. He was unwilling to set both balls out in the lawn, since his opponent, being an international, was likely to roquet one of them and make a break. Therefore, he hit red into the first corner. His opponent shot with black at blue and failed to roquet, but finished predictably with a rush along the south border.

A self-created problem
Now what was he to do? He must move the yellow ball, but could not risk a shot at red in the first corner to which the opponent had a rush. A missed shot at the opponent's balls in the fourth corner would allow a cannon there, followed probably by another cannon in the first corner and an easy break.

So he played yellow into the third corner. The international player rushed blue toward the red in the first corner, but did not succeed in creating a cannon. Then, instead of trying for a rush on red to make hoop 1 with nothing set up ahead, he used a gentle stop-shot to send blue out to a point just short of hoop 1, roqueted red and sent it to hoop 2 while successfully making position to run hoop 1. He continued with a break to 4-back.

Option retained

Note that if he had not gained position to run hoop 1, he had retained the option of covering the boundary, so red (in accordance with the strategy he was using) would still have had no shot he could afford to risk. Even shooting at yellow in the third corner would risk allowing his opponent to make hoop 1 with a forward rush and two balls together in forward play.

Next break rather than immediate break

The point of all this is that the state player was so afraid of the opponent roqueting and setting up a break, that he gave him a break without him having to roquet at all! Instead of thinking ahead, he was trying only to prevent his opponent from getting an IMMEDIATE break, and he did not even succeed in doing this for long. A 'next-break' strategist would scarcely need to perform any calculations before concluding that the state player's tactics gave him very little chance of obtaining the next break.

A pointless postponement

In croquet games between players of this standard there is really no sense in playing merely to 'postpone the evil day' when the inevitable break is set up. In diagram 20 he should have set the red ball in the lawn near yellow, with a rush to hoop 1, and taken the chance of the opponent roqueting. Nobody consistently hits 50% of roquets under pressure over such a distance, but even if the opponent could hit 80% this would have given a better chance of getting the next break than the way he played. The later shot with yellow at the opponent's balls in the fourth corner, although they were too far apart to offer a 'double' target, was also a better chance than finessing into the third corner.

THE ART OF MANOEUVRING

WE HAVE ALREADY mentioned in passing that the 'next-break' strategist will learn, once he has the innings, to manoeuvre his way around the lawn until he gets a chance to play a break or set an 'ideal leave'. It does not matter how many turns this takes, provided that in the process the opponent is not given any chance to roquet which he considers to be worth risking. The way in which the manoeuvring proceeds will depend on the opportunities offering in the position, and is learnt gradually by experience.

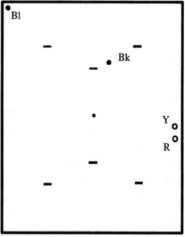

DIAGRAM 21

I have not developed any real principles which could guide the inexperienced player in how to go about it. These may come at some later time, but until then the main thing is not to settle for less than you are entitled to. In most positions it is possible to manoeuvre your way to either a break, or an 'ideal leave' which offers at least a 70% chance of a break. Therefore, you should not abandon the manoeuvring process in pursuit of a different line of play which offers (say) a 30-40% chance of an immediate break, but allows your opponent one or more "free" shots if you do not succeed in getting the break going.

No 'free' shots

A "free" shot in this sense is a shot which, if missed, still gives you little chance of an immediate break. Every shot you allow your opponent should cost him a break if he misses. By ensuring this, you keep him under pressure (and very few players roquet as well under pressure as they do when taking a "free" shot), and also you will on most occasions dissuade him from any attempt to roquet.

In order to give the reader a better idea of what is involved, let us follow the moves of an actual tournament game between a next-break strategist playing red and yellow, and a safety-first strategist playing with black and blue. With yellow already on 4-back and red still for hoop 2, the nextbreaker gained the innings but could only manage the much-less-than-ideal leave shown in diagram 21. The safety-firster decided not to shoot with black because shooting at blue in the second corner would leave two balls near his opponent's hoop; and a missed shot at red or yellow would allow red to get a rush to its hoop, which it did not at present have. Therefore he played black to 'safety' in the 1ˢᵗ corner.

This gave the next-break strategist the chance to try for an immediate break with red by cutting yellow to hoop 3, taking-off to blue and rolling for hoop 2. However, he apparently did not rate very highly his chance of succeeding in this, and chose instead to play yellow, rushing red to the south boundary behind hoop 4 and taking off to black in the first corner. Then he split black to hoop 3 and returned to red, setting a rush for it toward a point about half-way along the west boundary. This produced the situation in diagram 22.

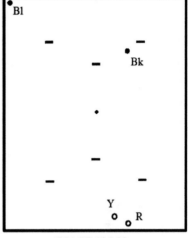

DIAGRAM 22

Obviously, black would not risk a shot here, since he has as much to lose as in the previous diagram, and less chance of gaining anything because the roquet is longer. Once again he did not wish to join blue in the corner near red's hoop, but a shot at yellow would allow red to get a rush to its hoop. So again black went to 'safety' in the first corner.

Finesse after finesse
Then red played a cut-rush, sending yellow about half-way along the west border. From here he could have taken off to blue and rolled for the hoop. Or, better still, he could have used a pass-roll to put yellow near hoop 2 while going to blue, and then sent blue to hoop 3 while trying for position to run hoop 2. But why should he risk either of these courses of action when he can without risk improve his chances of getting the break? Instead, he took off again to black and again sent it to hoop 3, trying unsuccessfully to wire it from yellow. He finished this turn by placing red on the west border about 2 yards from yellow as in diagram 23. Since red had a cut-rush to hoop 2, the opponent again had to move black, and had no more reason than previously to risk shooting, so for the 3ʳᵈ time black 'finessed' into the first corner.

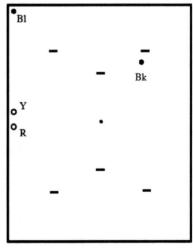

DIAGRAM 23

Extracting the maximum

The next-breaker thought he could do better still, so instead of using red, he played yellow, roqueting red gently and taking off again to black. This time he made sure that red was left where it would be easy to wire black from it behind the 3rd and 6th hoops. Black was again sent to hoop 3, and this time yellow could be hit out so as to give red a six-inch rush along the west border to blue.

This produced the situation shown in diagram 24, in which black would no doubt have shot at the double red-and-yellow target, except that he was wired from it! So for the fourth consecutive turn black was hit into the first corner. This gave red the chance to play the six-inch rush and create a cannon with blue in the 2nd corner, followed by an easy break.

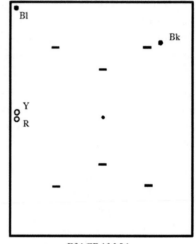

DIAGRAM 24

Unfortunately, he played it poorly and failed to create the cannon, so he used a stop-shot to place yellow a yard west of hoop 2 and sent blue to hoop 3, trying for position in front of hoop 2. This also failed, so he covered the boundary behind yellow (diagram 25). At last the opponent could afford a shot—albeit a very long one—with blue from hoop 3 at black in the first corner; except that he turned out (not so surprisingly) to be near enough to wired from it! The shot at yellow was out of the question for a safety-firster, so he played blue to the south boundary in front of hoop 1, wide of his partner ball.

Take the first shot

In all of this lengthy manoeuvring red has had two excellent chances to establish a break, and still has the innings. He has not had to take any noticeable risk, since it would have been quite out of character for his opponent to take any of the shots offered. It is apparent

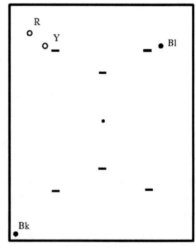

DIAGRAM 25

in hindsight that at the beginning (diagram 21) the player of black should have taken the shot at red and/or yellow, as he was not going to be given a better chance of roqueting before red had the break set up.

I asked a friend with whom I play practice games why he now seldom 'finesses' or returns wide of his partner ball. preferring to take a shot on every turn in spite of the risks involved. He explained: "Against others I wouldn't always shoot, but against you I know that things are not going to get any better; they'll only get worse. I know that if I pass up any chance to shoot, you will see to it hat I don't get any better chance, and you'll end up getting a break anyway. I always find myself later wishing I'd taken the shot in the first place."

And this is exactly how it should be. My friend did not really understand my tactics, but e knew they were different from those normally used against him. He realised that in order to have much chance of winning a game he would have to do things differently himself.

This further illustrates the point made previously that a 'next-break' strategist is not necessarily an aggressive player with a gambling temperament. An observer watching the manoeuvring process may conclude that he is very timid or conservative or even 'negative' n his play. He seems to be passing up possible chances to establish breaks because of the moderate risks involved. And indeed he is—but only because he sees a way to give himself n even better chance involving fewer risks.

It is unsafe to play safe!

It is also clear that the tactics used by the 'safety-first layer are in fact anything but safe! All he did as guarantee his opponent a 'safe' break, without giving himself any chance whatsoever of preventing t or gaining the innings, since he never at any stage made any attempt to roquet! It is the 'next-break' strategist who is using the safest possible tactics, as e is at all times playing to minimise the chance of is opponent getting a break.

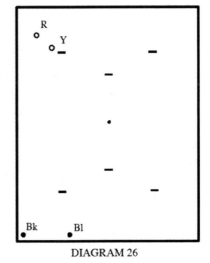

DIAGRAM 26

It is worth following the progress of this game a little further, as we can use it to illustrate another point worth making. We have already seen that in diagram 25 blue was played to the boundary in front f hoop 1, about 6 yards wide of his black partner all, resulting in the position of diagram 26.

This allowed red to make hoop 2 and obtain a backward rush toward the opponent's balls in the first corner. Then he left the yellow ball between the first corner and hoop 1, sent black to hoop 4 while running his red ball a yard or so past blue, cut blue back toward the first corner and used a stop-shot to end it to hoop 3. He finished by setting red a 2-foot rush to hoop 3 (diagram 27), more or less wired from blue. Blue shot at black and missed, then red rushed yellow to hoop 3 and this time got the 4-ball break going without further difficulty. Even without the wring red would have had an excellent chance of a beak.

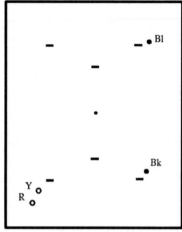

DIAGRAM 27

Returning wide is seldom correct

Notice that if blue could have shot at black in diagram 25 he would have probably done so, and although this would have placed the black and blue balls together in the first corner, red's task in setting up a break would have been slightly more difficult. He could have still rushed yellow to the boundary alongside hoop 1, but there would be at least a small risk involved in stop-shotting one opponent ball to hoop 4 while staying close enough to be sure of roqueting the other. The alternative would have been to send yellow to the 4th hoop while going to the opponent's balls in the first corner, and rush one of them to hoop 3. In this way he may have succeeded in establishing the break immediately, but an inaccurate rush would find him having to approach hoop 3 and make it with an opponent ball, and with his yellow ball out in the lawn. This is why it seldom pays to return wide of your partner ball when playing against a 'next-break' strategist. It not only passes up a chance to roquet, but often makes it easier for him to set for a break than if your balls were together. For similar reasons, a ball on the border in forward play is less likely to be of help to a 'next-break' strategist than it would to many other players. Unless the break is already set up with the other three balls, a border ball in forward play would seldom offer the 70% or more chance of a break that he is looking for. He can probably use it to manoeuvre his way to an 'ideal leave', but no more easily than if it were almost anywhere else.

A misleading term

Perhaps this is as good a time as any to register my dislike of the term "finesse". Although I have used it in this book, I believe it is misleading to the extent that it implies there is some degree of subtlety or cleverness involved in such a move. I have made clear my view that this is very rarely the case. The only alternative term I have heard was at a small country club where a player told me that his opponent was "egging out". I commiserated with him, assuming that he meant "pegging out", but he explained, "No, he is chicken—just keeps running off and laying an egg in the corner!"

EXCEPTIONS

I T MUST BE said that in a game of croquet there will at times occur positions in which the theories and principles discussed in this book do not apply. The idea of playing for an 'ideal leave', for example, is often of great value in the early part of the game, but is harder to use when one clip is already on or past 4-back. When both clips are on the rover hoop the 'next break' strategy is likely to be pointless, since a break is no longer possible. In such positions it may well be advisable to set yourself a rush and leave the opponent's balls as far apart as possible. And there may be little sense in covering the boundary when there is nothing you would want to do with your opponent's ball if he should shoot at your balls and miss.

Ideal leaves not always needed

I was reminded forcibly of this in a recent game when I had my red clip on rover and had just made penultimate and rover with yellow. I wired my opponent's balls at the rover hoop and rolled my two balls into the third corner where I set a rush for red to its rover hoop (diagram 17). This inevitably meant that at least one of the opponent balls had better than a single-ball target in shooting at my balls. My opponent roqueted, and too late I realised that I had not needed to risk setting a rush to rover, since one of the opponent's balls would still be at the rover hoop. All I needed was a rush for red to any place from where I could roll yellow toward

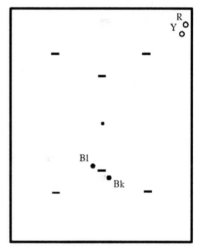

DIAGRAM 28

the peg while going to the ball at the rover hoop. I paid the penalty for making the leave too 'ideal'! Most A-class players would not have made this mistake, but by now I am used to thinking almost automatically in terms of 'ideal leaves', and it is easy to overlook the fact that the idea does not apply in all positions.

Similarly, if one or two balls have been pegged out, then the 'next-break' and 'ideal-leave principles will apply, if at all, to only a limited extent. In such situations the player should still, of course, aim to do whatever will tend to maximise his own chance of winning the game and minimise the chance of his opponent doing so. Percentages will continue to be an important consideration—perhaps even more so than in more common positions. Calculations will often still be the basis for checking whether or not a particular course of action is objectively correct, but the translation of the aims into action will probably no longer involve tactical moves of the type we have been considering at length.

Intuition versus calculation

I am aware that some players will not take seriously the need to base tactical decisions on the estimation and calculation of percentages. If you can trust your intuitive judgement to consistently give the correct answers, then perhaps you can manage to win games at A-class level without giving your tactical moves the sort of consideration recommended in this book. However, I believe that it will become increasingly difficult to survive on natural ability alone, as more and more opponents will realise the importance of playing the 'percentage game'.

The aggregation of 'slight' errors

It may not seem to matter much if in a particular situation you choose to allow your opponent a 45%, rather than 40%, chance of obtaining a break. If this occurred only once during each game, then about once in every twenty games your opponent will get a break that he would not have got if you had given more thought to your tactics. In actual fact, however, a player who does not consider the percentages is likely to do this sort of thing not just once, but many times in each game. Even if he only made five or six such "slight" tactical errors in each game, there is mathematically a better than even chance in every game that his opponent will get at least one additional break. Of course, the break still has to be played, and does not necessarily guarantee that the game will be won by the opponent even if played faultlessly. But it cannot be denied that a player who is unwilling to consider percentages is giving each of his opponents a sizeable advantage which he need not give them.

PSYCHOLOGICAL CONSIDERATIONS

EVERY SERIOUS CROQUET player is aware that psychology plays an important part in almost every game. There are many facets of the game where psychological factors are relevant. some well known and others rarely understood. Here I will mention only one such area: the psychology of risk-taking.

Some years ago I entered my first top-division tournament, and in one game I had a clip on 2-back while my opponent's clips were on 4-back and hoop 1. I established a break with my other ball and took it around to the peg. My opponent got in and later managed to peg out the ball I had taken to the peg, while my other clip was still on 2-back; and I ended up losing the game. Afterwards, several onlookers suggested that I had been most unwise to go right to the peg while the partner ball was still on 2-back, as I was "simply asking to be pegged out".

Was I 'asking for it'?
I was more inclined to blame my loss on the fact that after my ball was pegged out I had three excellent chances to make a three-ball break with my remaining ball and finish the game, but ruined them all by making elementary errors. I was not convinced that stopping short of the peg would have improved my winning chances. Since a single peel and peg-out would not have been difficult for my opponent, I would presumably have had to stop at penultimate. This would have reduced the chance of my ball being pegged out, but also required me to do a double peel or take additional turns in making the final two hoops. It worried me that my judgement seemed so much out of line with the insistence of several very knowledgeable players that it is far too dangerous to go to the peg in such a situation.

I went home and decided to try a percentage calculation of the various possibilities and probabilities (the first I ever did) in order to satisfy myself one way or the other. I convinced myself that in this instance I was right, although there have been many instances since in which a percentage calculation has forced me to admit that my judgement has been in error. Why, then, do so many others maintain that going to the peg is incorrect? This puzzled me until I realised that they are victims of a common psychological illusion.

A dangerous illusion exposed
When a player goes right to the peg and his opponent manages to peg out the ball and goes on to win the game, there is a very strong tendency to blame the loss

on the fact that you went right to the peg. Because this is the most obvious and distinctive feature of game, it is the thing that sticks in your mind. You may have also missed short roquets, gone out on take-offs and stuck in simple hoops, but these are all more or less normal, so you do not tend to blame them for your loss. Most players can quote several instances in which they "learned the lesson" that going right to the peg is likely to result in loss of the game after the opponent pegs your ball out. But no-one ever quotes an instance where they lost because they DID NOT go to the peg.

Is this because such instances do not occur? I believe that in fact more games are lost by players not going to the peg when they should have done so, than by going too far in a break. The results of my percentage calculations support this. It just seems natural to blame a loss on something you did wrong, rather than something you did not do. Similarly, you often hear a player say in explanation of why he lost "It serves me right—I knew I shouldn't have attempted that hoop. I should have gone back to my partner ball." But you never hear him say "I should have had a go at that hoop—there was a fair chance I could have made it". In reviewing his games, the 'next-break' strategist must learn to think objectively and realize that the loss of a game is just as likely to result from sins of omission as from sins of commission; or in other words from things you didn't do as from things that you did do.

There are many other more common situations where the 'next-break' strategist's assessment of risks will differ from that of a player who uses the standard strategy. The difference arises from the fact that the assessment made by the next-break strategist will tend to be objectively based and will involve estimation or calculation of percentages. Each risk will be considered in the light of his aim of obtaining the next break and/or winning the game. He will tend to take risks which others would avoid if he believes that in so doing he is increasing his chance of achieving these aims. and will avoid risks which others would take when they do not offer any such increase. Here we will consider briefly only two examples:

(The psychology of risk-taking is considered in much greater detail, together with many other ways in which psychological factors are involved in the game of croquet, in my booklet "Croquet: The Mental Approach". Some players seem to be temperamentally incapable of bringing themselves to take risks, even when they have been forced to agree that by taking the risks they are improving their chances of winning the game. It is noticeable that in croquet this problem occurs on average in women players far more often than in men. People may disagree as to the reason for this difference in the sexes, but its existence is indisputable. I know of no other field of activity where it is so pronounced.)

John Riches and Wayne Davies

HITTING IN

D IAGRAM 29 SHOWS a position from a doubles game in which the yellow and black clips were both on 4-back. Blue was for hoop 3 and red (my partner) was for hoop 1. Black and blue are together about halfway along the west border, with red on the south border and yellow in the lawn about a yard in front of hoop 5. My partner thought I was crazy when I suggested that he shoot with red at yellow, and wanted me instead to 'hit out' by shooting with yellow at red.

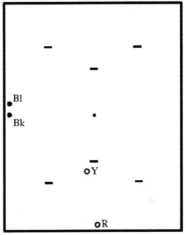

DIAGRAM 29

I pointed out that if I succeeded in roqueting red I could only set up for him, and with my clip already on 4-back I would not expect to get a leave which offered much more than a 60-65% chance of getting the break. I suggested that he would have almost the same chance of making the 8-yard roquet, after which he could send yellow to hoop 2 while going to the opponent balls, and so had an excellent chance of an immediate break.

On the other hand, if I missed the shot at red, blue could rush black to the first corner and send it to hoop 4, then use our balls to get a rush to hoop 3. If my partner shot with red at yellow and missed, then (provided he hit hard enough to reach the north boundary) blue may still be able to get a break going by sending black to hoop 4 and rushing yellow to hoop 3, but his task would be slightly more difficult.

A convincing argument?

Thus, if we were going to roquet we would much prefer to be using red; while if we missed it would still be better to have done so with red. My partner thought there had to be something wrong with my reasoning, as he had been told many times by experienced players that in most situations you should hit out rather than in. Since he could not find an immediate answer to my argument, he reluctantly agreed to hit in, and fortunately roqueted yellow. Had he not roqueted, I doubt that he would ever have taken my advice again.

In this case almost any player who thinks, whether he is a 'next-break' strategist or not, should be able to see the advantage in playing the ball with which a break can be made. In many situations, however, the advantages are less clear. The player (and there are many) who does not think for himself, but relies on generalised advice ("Don't hit in"; "never leave balls out in the lawn where your opponent can use them", etc.) is more than likely to make the wrong choice. He is also likely to later blame his loss on the fact that he "couldn't hit a roquet when he needed it", when the real reason was his poor tactics.

PLAYING THE BORDER BALL

IN DIAGRAM 30 all clips are still on hoop 1. Red has sent his yellow partner ball to hoop 2 while going to the opponent's balls in front of hoop 3. He had intended roqueting blue on the border and sending it into the lawn (say, to hoop 3) while getting a rush on black to make hoop 1 and establish a break. However, red has finished about 4 yards from blue and about a foot from black. I have seen many players in such positions still roquet blue and rush black to hoop 1.

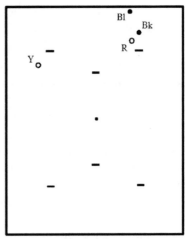

DIAGRAM 30

This seems to me a case of taking an unnecessary risk. The rush can be obtained more certainly by taking black out to the border near blue. There is no need at this stage to get the fourth ball off the border. It can easily be brought into the break after making hoop 2. By bringing it into the lawn immediately you are making it easier for your opponent if your rush and approach shot are such that you cannot attempt hoop 1.

In addition, the roquet of just over 4 yards probably cannot be regarded as a certainty. The risk of missing it may only be slight, but why take any risk at all which does not increase your chance of obtaining the next break? Onlookers may gain the impression that your decision not to attempt the roquet on blue results from a lack of courage, but objectivity rather than courage is more likely to win croquet games.

CONCLUSION

T HE READER MAY be wondering about the possible implications for the future of the game if the ideas presented in this book become widely accepted. There is probably no need for concern, since few players are likely to understand the ideas, let alone agree with them; and even those who accept them in principle may find that they are unable to change the way they have been taught to think about the game. However, I cannot resist the temptation to indulge in a bit of crystal ball gazing, even if it amounts to nothing more than wishful thinking.

I believe that as the game becomes more professional and games are played for higher stakes, players will be forced to approach it more objectively. Gut feelings and intuition may be fairly reliable at times, but for your next meal and money to pay the rent you like to depend on something more substantial and more objective.

The ideas I have presented here have covered only a few of the more obvious tactics arising from 'next-break' strategy. There are many important ideas and principles waiting to be discovered and explained. Some of these will apply to situations which occur only rarely, but others may well turn out to be of more general use. Many of my ideas will in time be refined and modified. Some will no doubt be proven wrong. Perhaps I will have at least succeeded to some extent in laying the groundwork and pointing out the way in which the theory of the game can be developed. I am certain that it must be based objectively on percentages.

In order to increase the objectivity, it is desirable that accurate statistics be available, as the results of percentage calculations are more reliable if based on accurate statistics rather than estimations. How often, for example, would you expect an A-class player to be able to play a stop-shot from the first corner which sends the croqueted ball to hoop 2 and also gains position for the striker's ball to safely run hoop 1? How often are games won by a player after one of his balls has been pegged out, leaving various clip positions? Until the game becomes fully professional there will be little incentive for anyone to spend the enormous amount of time and effort required to record, interpret and publish the statistics from which authoritative answers to such questions can be derived. As I observed earlier in the book, the theory of croquet is still very much in its infancy.

I do not believe, as some of my friends have suggested, that if these ideas are widely adopted the game will become little more than a type of mathematical exercise, and will lose much of its interest and challenge. On the contrary, I believe that the standard of play would improve dramatically and games between opponents who are both trying to apply these ideas will offer more interest and excitement than most of the games we see at present. The calculation of probabilities, understanding of strategies and adoption of 'percentage-game' tactics are all important, but the game has to be won out on the lawn with a mallet, not sitting at home with a book or calculator.

Finally, I look forward to (but will probably not live to see) the day when the rules are altered to allow coaching of players during an opponent's turn. This would be analogous to the role of a Davis Cup tennis coach who discusses tactics with his players during change of ends. It would provide a valuable and active role for our leading players when they become too old to continue in competition at top level. and enable them to pass on the benefit of their experience to younger players in the most effective manner possible. This could only lead to a rapid improvement in the general standard of play, but as one experienced player to whom I explained the idea observed: "It seems too logical a step to be given serious consideration!"

SUMMARY

1. A player who adopts 'next-break' strategy (or 'NBS') will not find himself taking greater risks than he was before, though it may appear this way to others who do not understand NBS. He will certainly be taking DIFFERENT risks, some of which he would not have taken before; and he will be taking them for different reasons. He may, for example, take a greater risk of immediately losing the innings, but only because by doing so he is REDUCING the risk of losing the game. On balance, NBS is the SAFEST possible way to play.

2. Although many of the ideas involved in NBS can be used by players at all levels, its real relevance is best seen in games between players at A-class level. A player whose skill level is below this class should give first priority to improving his technique.

3. NBS involves 'playing the percentage game'. Actual calculation of percentages during a game is usually impractical, and to a large extent unnecessary. Many players will be able to get by on their intuitive judgement, provided they always bear in mind the aims of NBS and are prepared to allow their judgements to be modified by experience.

4. NBS is designed to give the player at all times the BEST POSSIBLE CHANCE OF WINNING THE GAME.

5. NBS as outlined in this booklet is based on the assumption that in maximising your chance of getting the next break, you will also be maximising your chance of winning the game. This is true for players who can make breaks, once they have them set up, with only a small chance of breaking down. There will be certain situations and conditions in which this assumption is not valid, and a different strategy is therefore desirable.

6. NBS is aimed at obtaining the NEXT break, as distinct from an IMMEDIATE break. It may be necessary to sacrifice any chance of an immediate break in order to maximise the chance of getting the NEXT break.

7. The tactical moves by which a player implements his NBS will depend to some extent on his particular strengths and preferences.

8. The adoption of NBS will for most players involve placing greater emphasis on the desirability of playing the ball which, if a roquet is made, will give the best chance of a break.

9. NBS involves the avoidance of taking even the slightest of risks if it does not stand to increase the chance of obtaining the next break.

10. The understanding and use of 'ideal leaves' will be an important part of NBS for any player. These will at times differ from the leaves commonly

adopted by most players, as it may involve setting your balls out from the border, not giving yourself a direct rush to a hoop, etc.

11. The 'ideal leaves' are based on the position of your own clips, and can be worked out during the opponent's turn. It is useful to have always in mind certain leaves for commonly occurring clip positions, and these can be worked out at home. A player who is unwilling to do this would have to rely on his ability to find good (if not 'ideal') leaves on the spur of the moment, or else copy the leaves of another NBS player.

12. In order to be of regular use, an 'ideal leave' must be achievable without necessarily having full control of the balls. For this reason, leaves involving wiring are generally omitted from consideration in this context.

13. The NBS player should have some idea of the percentage chance which an 'ideal leave' offers him of getting the next break, and he should play to set it up unless he sees an alternative which clearly offers a better chance.

14. Even when a player decides to play for an immediate break, he may do well to bear in mind the 'ideal leaves' for the position of his clips. It may not be difficult to retain the option of setting an 'ideal leave' in case the immediate break is not finally achieved.

15. The setting of an 'ideal leave' may take more than one turn. The NBS player will learn to manoeuvre his way to the desired position without allowing his opponent any roquet worth risking in the meantime.

16. An 'ideal leave' is usually easier to find and achieve when your clips are on corner hoops and not on the same hoop.

17. When one ball is already around you will have fewer options in finding a leave which gives the best chance of a break with the other ball regardless of what the opponent does. It is therefore more likely that you will need to depend on an accurate rush, but also more likely that by then you will have a better 'feel' of the lawn.

18. NBS is an almost perfect answer to Aunt Emma strategy, provided, of course, that you are not likely to break down too often once you have the break set up.

19. The NBS player is also aiming to MINIMISE the chance of his opponent obtaining the next break, and to this end he should play so as to retain the option of 'covering the boundary' while getting a break started, as well as at the end of it.

20. NBS players will tend to shoot at a ball on almost every turn, rather than 'finesse' by hitting a ball out of play into a corner. The reason for this is simply that positions are rare in which finessing actually gives the best possible chance of obtaining the next break.

21. NBS players will also tend to avoid returning wide of the partner ball instead of shooting at it. If the opponent is also an NBS player he will usually find it easier to achieve an 'ideal leave' from a position where your balls are a

few yards apart than if they were together. However, you need to assess his chance of getting an immediate break if your balls are together.

22. The NBS player will not mind giving his opponent the opportunity to rush a ball to a hoop and make it, provided that in doing so there is no easy way for him to get a break started. This underlines the need for the NBS player to be constantly thinking ahead to the next turn, or even the one after that.

23. The NBS player will not be unduly concerned about taking shots which put his balls into the opponent's 'forward play', provided the balls are on the border and there is no break set up. In general, balls on the border in forward play are just as likely to hinder the opponent in setting up a break or achieving an 'ideal leave', as they are to assist him.

24. The use of NBS means that the opponent will commonly feel himself to be under constant pressure. For psychological reasons the NBS player should usually strive to MAINTAIN the pressure. This is another reason why he will at times be prepared to leave both of his balls out in the lawn in preference to taking one of them out of play; and will avoid tactics involving 'finesses' and 'returning wide', which are designed to frustrate rather than pressure the opponent.

25. In reviewing his games, the NBS player must remember that a loss can result from failure to take risks that should have been taken, as well as from the taking of unnecessary risks.

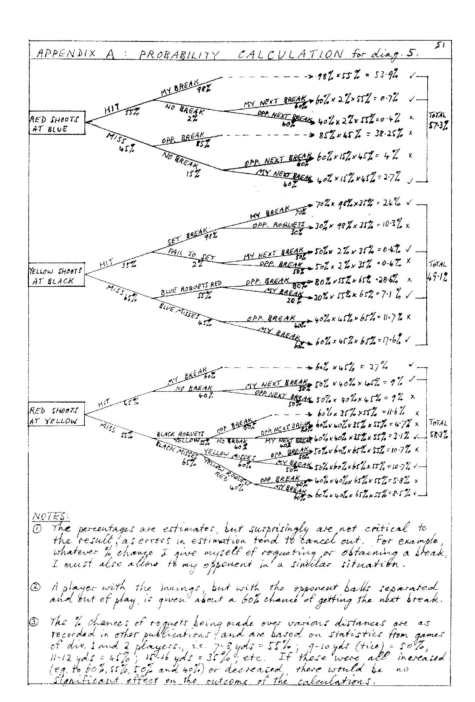

APPENDIX A : PROBABILITY CALCULATION for diag. 5.

RED SHOOTS AT BLUE

HIT 55%
- MY BREAK 98% → 98% × 55% = 53.9% ✓
- NO BREAK 2%
  - MY NEXT BREAK 60% → 60% × 2% × 55% = 0.7% ✓
  - OPP. NEXT BREAK 40% → 40% × 2% × 55% = 0.4% ✗

MISS 45%
- OPP. BREAK 85% → 85% × 45% = 38.25% ✗
- NO BREAK 15%
  - OPP. NEXT BREAK 60% → 60% × 15% × 45% = 4% ✗
  - MY NEXT BREAK 40% → 40% × 15% × 45% = 2.7% ✓

TOTAL 57.3%

YELLOW SHOOTS AT BLACK

HIT 35%
- SET BREAK 98%
  - MY BREAK 70% → 70% × 98% × 35% = 24% ✓
  - OPP. ROQUETS 30% → 30% × 98% × 35% = 10.3% ✗
- FAIL TO SET 2%
  - MY NEXT BREAK 50% → 50% × 2% × 35% = 0.4% ✓
  - OPP. BREAK 50% → 50% × 2% × 35% = 0.4% ✗

MISS 65%
- BLUE ROQUETS RED 55%
  - OPP. BREAK 80% → 80% × 55% × 65% = 28.6% ✗
  - MY BREAK 20% → 20% × 55% × 65% = 7.1% ✓
- BLUE MISSES 45%
  - OPP. BREAK 60% → 40% × 45% × 65% = 11.7% ✗
  - MY BREAK 60% → 60% × 45% × 65% = 17.6% ✓

TOTAL 49.1%

RED SHOOTS AT YELLOW

HIT 45%
- MY BREAK 60% → 60% × 45% = 27% ✓
- NO BREAK 40%
  - MY NEXT BREAK 50% → 50% × 40% × 45% = 9% ✓
  - OPP. NEXT BREAK 50% → 50% × 40% × 45% = 9% ✗

MISS 55%
- BLACK ROQUETS YELLOW 55%
  - OPP. BREAK 60% → 60% × 35% × 55% = 11.6% ✗
    - OPP. NEXT BREAK 60% → 60% × 40% × 35% × 55% = 4.7% ✗
    - MY NEXT BREAK 40% → 60% × 40% × 35% × 55% = 3.1% ✓
  - NO BREAK 40%
- BLACK MISSES 65%
  - YELLOW MISSES 60%
    - OPP. BREAK 50% → 50% × 60% × 65% × 55% = 10.7% ✗
    - MY BREAK 50% → 50% × 60% × 65% × 55% = 10.7% ✓
  - YELLOW ROQUETS RED 40%
    - OPP. BREAK 40% → 40% × 40% × 65% × 55% = 5.8% ✗
    - MY BREAK 60% → 60% × 40% × 65% × 55% = 8.5% ✓

TOTAL 58.3%

NOTES:

① The percentages are estimates, but surprisingly are not critical to the result, as errors in estimation tend to cancel out. For example, whatever % chance I give myself of roqueting or obtaining a break, I must also allow to my opponent in a similar situation.

② A player with the innings, but with the opponent balls separated and out of play, is given about a 60% chance of getting the next break.

③ The % chances of roquets being made over various distances are as recorded in other publications, and are based on statistics from games of div. 1 and 2 players, i.e. 7-8 yds = 55%; 9-10 yds (tice) = 50%; 11-12 yds = 45%; 15-16 yds = 35% etc. If these were all increased (eg. to 60%, 55%, 50% and 40%) or decreased, there would be no significant effect on the outcome of the calculations.

52

APPENDIX B : PROBABILITY CALCULATION for diag. 12.

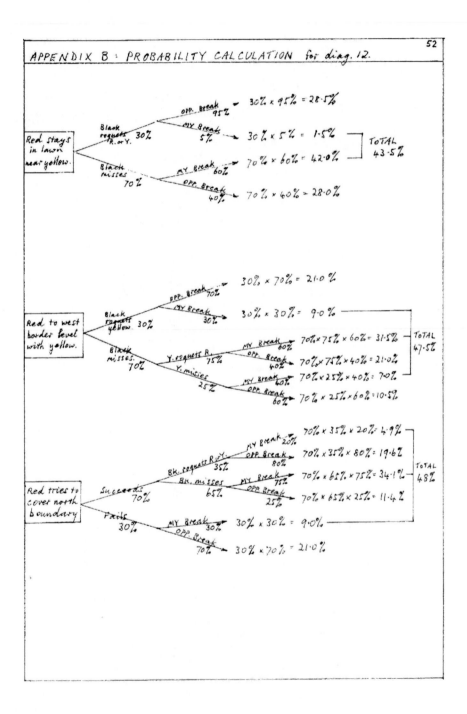

Red stays in lawn near yellow.

Black requets R. or Y. 30%
- OPP. Break 95% → 30% × 95% = 28·5%
- MY Break 5% → 30% × 5% = 1·5%

Black misses 70%
- MY Break 60% → 70% × 60% = 42·0%
- OPP. Break 40% → 70% × 40% = 28·0%

TOTAL 43·5%

Red to west border level with yellow.

Black requets yellow 30%
- OPP. Break 70% → 30% × 70% = 21·0%
- MY Break 30% → 30% × 30% = 9·0%

Black misses 70%
- Y. requets R. 75%
  - MY Break 60% → 70% × 75% × 60% = 31·5%
  - OPP. Break 40% → 70% × 75% × 40% = 21·0%
- Y. misses 25%
  - MY Break 40% → 70% × 25% × 40% = 7·0%
  - OPP. Break 60% → 70% × 25% × 60% = 10·5%

TOTAL 47·5%

Red tries to cover north boundary

Succeeds 70%
- Bk. requets R.+Y. 35%
  - MY Break 20% → 70% × 35% × 20% = 4·9%
  - OPP. Break 80% → 70% × 35% × 80% = 19·6%
- Bk. misses 65%
  - MY Break 75% → 70% × 65% × 75% = 34·1%
  - OPP. Break 25% → 70% × 65% × 25% = 11·4%

Fails 30%
- MY Break 30% → 30% × 30% = 9·0%
- OPP. Break 70% → 30% × 70% = 21·0%

TOTAL 48%

CROQUET

LESSONS IN TACTICS

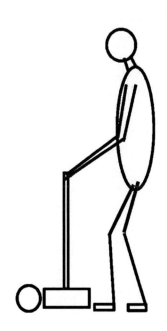

CONTENTS

INTRODUCTION

THIS BOOKLET WAS written in an attempt to help players realise the importance of tactics in the game of Croquet, and encourage them to improve the tactics they use regularly in competitive play. It was first written as a series of magazine articles, most of which have been published in either the Australian Croquet Gazette or the Queensland Croquet Newsletter.

Most of the explanations are aimed at players well below the top levels of play, though some of the topics dealt with later in the booklet will apply mainly to those who are capable of making sizeable breaks.

The justification for all tactical moves lies in the consideration of percentages. This is alluded to in various places, but for a fuller treatment the reader is referred to my booklet on "Next Break Strategy".

In this booklet I have concentrated on those tactical points which are not clearly explained in most other treatises on the game. Nor are they to be found in most coaching manuals. Here you will not find any mention of standard leaves or triple peels. The correct ways of playing 3-ball and 4-ball breaks can be found in many other books. The tactics of openings, endings and pegged-out games (i.e. one ball against two, or one against one) are outside the scope of this booklet, and may possibly provide material for a later booklet aimed at more advanced players.

Cannons, promotion shots, and other 'trick' shots belong in a booklet on advanced technique rather than one on tactics.

Despite these omissions which may cause disappointment to some, I am confident that even the strongest of players will find in this booklet much of interest, and many things that will help him to improve his own game.

If you believe that I have made omissions, oversights or errors in the material I have attempted to cover, please let me know. I am always looking for better ways of helping to raise the standard of Australian Croquet, and have been greatly encouraged in the pursuit of this aim by the expressed appreciation of many who claim to have learned from my previous four booklets.

Note: I have used the term "finesse" as meaning a shot in which at the start of a turn a ball is played (usually into a corner) without making any attempt to roquet another ball. The term is in common use by British writers, but has the disadvantage of carrying with it the suggestion that some degree of subtlety is involved, which is seldom the case. In most situations its use amounts to nothing more than plain foolishness.

. . . John Riches.

THINKING AHEAD—PART 1

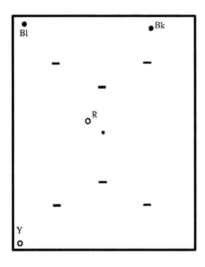

THE DIAGRAM SHOWS a position where blue has just missed a rush on red to hoop 2 (it occurred in a major South Australian tournament—I'm not sure whether such things ever happen elsewhere!). The red and black clips were on 4-back and yellow was on hoop 3.

Red shot at yellow in the 1st corner, as 99 out of 100 players would have done. He missed, and in his next turn was faced with the need to play a long left-side take-off to the opponent's balls with little chance of getting a break going. When I later replaced the balls in the diagrammed position and asked him why he shot at yellow with red, he expressed surprise, saying that surely there was no sensible alternative.

I asked him what he would have done if he had succeeded in roqueting yellow with red, and he said that he would probably have set a rush for yellow. Where to? "Oh, probably to its hoop (hoop 3)", he replied.

It took me some time to convince him that a rush for yellow to hoop 4 would be better than one to hoop 3, and that there was no point in trying to roquet yellow at all—he should have simply hit red out on the south boundary a foot or two from yellow so that yellow would have a rush (slightly cut) to hoop 4.

This will help explain why I strongly oppose any move to introduce a time limit of 45 seconds (or any other length of time) on each shot. Most players put far too little thought into the game as it is.

Players often blame the loss of a game on the fact that they "stuck in hoops which they should have made", or they missed a couple of short roquets, forgetting that the opponent made similar errors. It seldom occurs to them that the real reason they lost was failure to think ahead.

The player mentioned above would certainly not have realised his error if it had not been pointed out to him. If these few articles can encourage someone to think longer before hitting a ball, the time taken to write them will have been well spent.

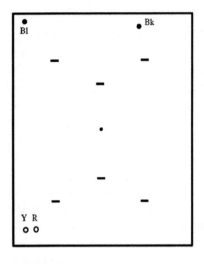

The position shown in the diagram immediately follows the one considered in part 1. The yellow clip is on hoop 3; the blue clip is on hoop 2; red and black are both on 4-back. Red, from near the peg, has correctly played to give Yellow a cut-rush to hoop 4 rather than trying to roquet yellow.

Here we consider how to best continue if the opponent shoots with one of his balls at the other and misses.

If he shoots with black at blue then yellow should simply rush red to hoop 4, take off to the opponent's balls in the 2nd corner, rush one of them to hoop 3 and set up a 3-ball break, planning to bring the 4th ball into the break later on.

If blue shoots at black and misses, yellow may similarly rush red to hoop 4 and take off to blue in the 3rd corner, though he will be less certain of getting a rush on black (6 yards away on the border) to hoop 3 and will not want to leave black too close to blue if the hoop cannot be attempted.

In this case, it is usually better to rush red not to hoop 4, but to a position somewhere behind hoop 4 and 1-2 yards in from the boundary. Then you can take off to blue in the 3rd corner and roll it out to hoop 3 (preferably alongside it rather than behind it) while going to the black ball without needing to try for a rush on it. After roqueting black you use a stopshot to send it about three-quarters of the way to hoop 4 while trying to gain position for yellow to run hoop 3.

If the hoop cannot be run, then yellow can be hit back to the south boundary near red. This leaves the opponent with the chance of a 14-yard roquet, but it would be one he could not afford to miss.

It is well worth taking the time to set up the balls in the position of the diagram and play through these moves on the lawn in order to fix them in your mind and gain an appreciation of how the second method is superior because even if the hoop cannot be attempted it keeps the opponent under pressure.

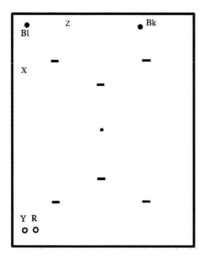

The diagram is the same as in part 2. The yellow clip is on hoop 3; blue is on hoop 2; and red and black are both on 4-back.

In part 2 we looked at the correct way for yellow to continue if one of the opponent balls shoots at the other and misses. Here we consider what to do if black goes wide of blue.

If black is hit out on the side (west) boundary at point x on the diagram, then red should take the turn rather than yellow. After roqueting yellow, red should take off to black at point x, and use an angled stop-shot to send black toward hoop 3 while going to blue in the 2nd corner. Then blue can be hit through to hoop 4 and red hit out again on the south boundary so that yellow again has a cut-rush to hoop 4 (and now also to the blue ball). Black then must move from hoop 3, and wherever it goes (unless it roquets) yellow has a good chance of a break on the next turn. If the wide-angle stop-shot of black to hoop 3 seems too difficult, then red could have gone to blue first and sent it to either hoop 3 or hoop 4 before placing black at the other hoop.

If black is played instead to point z on the north boundary, then yellow can rush red to hoop 4, take off to blue in the 2nd corner, and from there have a good chance of getting a rush on black to hoop 3 with an immediate break.

Note that there is no safer place for the black ball. In the 4th corner yellow would have a rush to it, and in the 3rd corner yellow could roll with it for hoop 3 after rushing red to hoop 4. Nor does it make sense to play blue without shooting.

We have seen that yellow has an excellent chance of quickly getting a break under way whatever the opponent does, which would not be true if the rush for yellow were (wrongly) set for its hoop. If the player of red and yellow is capable of taking off with reasonable accuracy, then black should shoot at red and yellow.

Unfortunately most players do not think far enough ahead to realise that this is the best option available, even though yellow does not yet have a rush to its hoop.

MAKING A DOUBLE

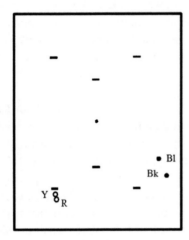 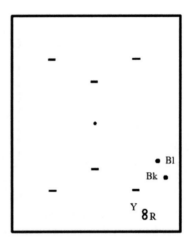

IN THE FIRST diagram red and yellow are both for hoop 1. Red has rushed or roqueted yellow about a foot in front of the hoop and has an opportunity to "make a double" by peeling yellow through the hoop and then making the hoop with red.

Players in lower divisions often take great pride and pleasure in doing this, but stronger players tend to do it only when they are more or less forced to because yellow is partly in the hoop.

"Making the double" involves taking the risk that yellow will not go cleanly through the hoop, or red will run too far and slightly off line so that it cannot easily make the hoop. Red is not even likely to succeed in getting a forward rush without the hoop impeding the backswing. Good players are not willing to take even a slight risk for the sake of only one hoop.

Red should resist the temptation to peel yellow and instead try to make the hoop with a rush toward the 4th corner, achieving the position shown in the second diagram. From here it is relatively easy to send yellow to hoop 3 and then rush one of the opponent's balls to hoop 2; whereas after "making a double" it would have been far more difficult to get a break going.

Another reason for not "making a double" is that it puts both of your clips on the same hoop, making it much harder to get a good leave if you cannot continue the break. The rule on "making doubles" is: In general, forget it; unless the peel will save a 'lift', or (at rover hoop) enable you to peg out, or you have only a few seconds left in the game.

CONCEDING A HOOP

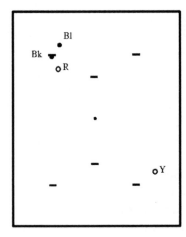 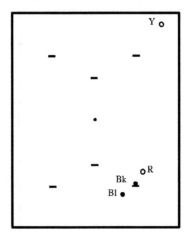

THIS SIMPLE IDEA will be further considered in a later article on "Balls in Hoops", but it is so often overlooked by players that it deserves an article of its own, with different examples. The first diagram shows a position from a tournament game in which red was quite a strong player. The red clip is on hoop 3 and red has taken off from yellow to the opponent's balls after black had stuck in hoop 2.

The obvious way for red to continue is to roquet the black ball, sending it just through the hoop, and then use it to get a simple rush on blue to hoop 3 with a break to follow. However, the player of red was unwilling to concede the hoop to the opponent, and roqueted blue first, giving himself little chance of making even one hoop for himself. The second diagram shows a similar situation in which red is for 4-back while yellow is still for hoop 1. After roqueting yellow, red has taken off to the black ball which had stuck in hoop 4. If he roquets blue he will not be able to do anything useful with black, but by conceding hoop 4 and rushing black through the hoop to the border he can then stop-shot it toward hoop 1 while going to blue, then send blue to hoop 2 and finish by hitting red out to the north boundary just left of yellow.

This gives yellow a cut-rush to the blue ball at hoop 2 after black moves from hoop 1, and allows an excellent chance of a break on the next turn. In addition, the black clip will now be on a centre hoop, making it more difficult for the opponent to find a good leave.

RETURNING TO PARTNER BALL

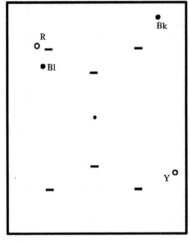

I N A PREVIOUS article we mentioned the need to think carefully before playing even the most obvious shot.

The diagram shows a position in which red is for 1-back and his yellow partner ball is for hoop 2. The player of red has roqueted black, taken off to blue, and rolled with blue for 1-back, but did not gain position to run the hoop. The obvious thing to do now is to return to the yellow partner ball on the east boundary near hoop 4. Since the yellow ball has not yet been used, most players in such situations would shoot at it, perhaps intending if the roquet is made to take off back to 1-back, hoping this time to gain position to run the hoop.

A few moments' reflection will suggest that the chance of this coming off is very small indeed. It is far better to hit red out to the left (north\side) of yellow, ensuring that as a result yellow will be left with a cut-rush to a point on the north boundary just to the right of the black ball. This places the opponent in an awkward position and gives an excellent chance of a break in the next turn unless he roquets, since wherever the blue ball goes you will be threatening to play yellow, rushing red to the 3rd corner and using it to load hoop 3 before rushing the black ball to hoop 2 with at least a 3-ball break set up.

Many players who complain about an inability to get breaks going are frequently missing such little tactical moves, because they have not developed the habit of thinking ahead to their next turn.

It seems elementary once it is pointed out, but if you watch you will be surprised how many players shoot at the partner without thinking, and in doing so forfeit any real possibility of giving a rush to the partner ball on the next turn. The principle to follow is that whenever you are forced to allow your opponent a chance to roquet you should try to ensure that if he misses (or 'finesses') you will have an easy break on the next turn. Thus he has only the one chance to roquet and is under pressure.

This is worth doing in most situations even if it means that the opponent's roquet will be a shorter one.

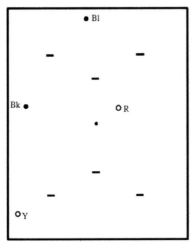

In the diagrammed position the red clip is on hoop 4 and yellow still on hoop 1. As red, you would no doubt decide to return to your yellow partner ball, but would you stop and think for a moment before doing so?

Most players would shoot at yellow, without any clear idea of what they would do if they roquet. In fact, there is little chance of getting a break going with red; and if the shot is missed black can then shoot at blue with reasonable safety, since it would be risky for yellow to roll for hoop 1 with the opponent's balls together on the north border. Therefore if black misses the roquet on blue, yellow would probably have to play a long take-off and rush one of the opponent's balls back to hoop 1, still without having loaded hoop 2.

Now consider the difference if red does not attempt to roquet yellow, but simply plays to stop just short of yellow so that yellow has a rush to hoop 1. This makes any shot by the opponent extremely risky, especially the shot with black at blue which could leave yellow with two balls in forward play and an excellent chance of setting up a break.

If the opponent decides to shoot at one of your balls with black then a miss would allow yellow to roquet black on the south border and use a stop-shot to send it toward hoop 2 while holding a rush on red to hoop 1. It is obvious that if the opponent shoots at any ball with blue he would be taking an even greater risk.

Thinking ahead like this is far more likely to affect the result of the game than missed roquets or sticking in hoops. It is an unfortunate fact that errors in shot-making seem to stick in our minds and receive the blame for many lost games when the losses are more correctly attributable to tactical errors that we were not even aware of.

A coach usually faces a difficult problem in persuading his students, especially if they have been playing for some years, that they need to spend time improving the tactical side of their game.

The diagram shows a position where black has just failed in an attempt to run hoop 1. The red and yellow clips are both on hoop 2. What should red do?

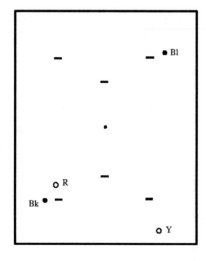

He could roquet black and roll for hoop 2, but if unsuccessful he will then have to hit back to yellow on the south border, with little chance of obtaining an accurate rush.

For many players a better option would be to rush black out to the first corner and then play a big wide-angle split shot in which the black ball is sent to hoop 2 while the red ball goes over toward its yellow partner ball on the border behind hoop 4.

Little accuracy is required with this split shot as you do not need to roquet yellow on the next shot. You only need to set yellow a rush up the lawn to either hoop 2 or (preferably) hoop 3.

As a general rule, the best rush to set for a ball is not a rush to its current hoop, but to the following hoop. This is often true regardless of where the opponent's balls are, as it makes it dangerous for the opponent balls to go together, since you can use the rush to load your next hoop, then take off to the opponent balls and rush one of them to make your current hoop.

Very few players seem to realise this, and most will set the rush for their current hoop without thinking. In many cases by setting a rush for the following hoop you can prevent your opponent from shooting at all, since he will realise that if you are capable of playing breaks then he would be taking a considerable risk in returning to his partner ball; and if you have set your rush the correct distance out from the border then a shot at your balls is also likely to give you an excellent chance of an immediate 4-ball break.

If you are capable of playing breaks but have difficulty getting them, try this in your next game and notice the difference. Players commonly complain that they were unable to get breaks going; or that the opponent roqueted "every time they had a break set up". In most cases closer analysis will show that they have been setting up poorly, allowing the opponent shots which he would have been unable to risk if the balls had been set properly.

COVERING THE BOUNDARY

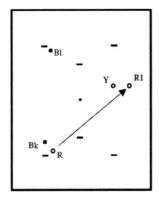 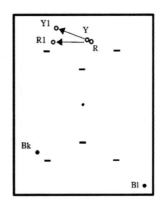

M OST PLAYERS ARE familiar with the idea of "covering the boundary" in order to discourage a shot by the opponent, yet it is not uncommon to see experienced players failing to do it, or doing it very carelessly.

In the first diagram all clips are still on hoop 1 and red has unsuccessfully approached hoop 1. In returning to the yellow partner ball red should be placed about halfway between yellow and the east boundary at point R1.

Many players would hit red right out to the boundary opposite yellow, but this is incorrect as (if the opponent fails to roquet) red would have no controllable rush and with the balls 6 yards apart even the roquet would not be a certainty.

In the second diagram red is on 4-back and has roqueted yellow which is still for hoop 1. Red should set for yellow as shown, by rolling to positions Y1 and R1. Even if the balls are not hidden from black behind hoop 2 a shot at them by the opponent would be too risky with the border correctly covered in this manner.

The red and yellow balls should be set about 3 yards and 2 yards respectively in from the border. They should not be less than 2 feet apart so that (if black shoots at them and misses) red will not hamper the attempt by yellow to roquet black on the border. It is incorrect to place them closer to the border as black could then shoot at them, knowing that if he misses there would not be room for yellow to load hoop 2 and keep a rush to hoop 1.

The balls are set behind hoop 2 rather than hoop 6 so that if black returns to blue yellow can load hoop 2 with red and take off to the opponent's balls.

TWO RUSHES ARE BETTER THAN ONE

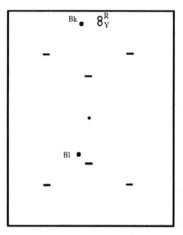

T HE DIAGRAM SHOWS a common type of position in which red has just made hoop 3 and rushed its yellow partner ball back to a position near black on the north border.

In playing the approach shot for hoop 3 red had planned to continue in this manner rather than trying for a forward rush to hoop 4 or to the blue ball.

There are two reasons why the backward rush to the black ball is to be preferred:

(1) A backward rush is usually easier to obtain with accuracy than a forward rush, and
(2) It will enable the fourth ball to be brought in—even if only a yard or two—off the border.

Now, in order to continue the break, red will use a stop-shot to send yellow as far in from the border as he can comfortably manage while also getting behind black so that he can rush it down the court to either hoop 4 or to the blue ball near hoop 5.

Many players do not realise that in such situations the rush to the ball is generally preferable to rushing direct to red's hoop, even though it necessitates another rush (of blue from hoop 5 to hoop 4) before the hoop is made.

Here two rushes are better than one because the second rush is a relatively short one which allows the ball to be sent to hoop 4 with greater accuracy.

This is another case where you will often see players choosing the wrong tactical option and later incorrectly blaming a poor approach or hoop shot for breaking down.

A similar situation occurs when the striker's ball has just made hoop 1 and there is a ball at hoop 3 but not at hoop 2. After making hoop 1 it may be possible to rush to the fourth ball near the 4th corner, and then get another rush not to hoop 2, but to the ball near hoop 3.

In almost all cases where there is an unused ball closer to your hoop than the one you are to rush, it is correct to organise a rush to the ball rather than to the hoop.

HITTING IN

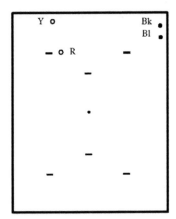 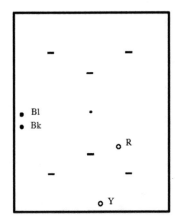

T HE FIRST DIAGRAM shows a position in which the red clip is on hoop 2, yellow and black are both on hoop 3, and blue is still on hoop 1.

Many players would now shoot with red at yellow without even considering anything else. However, if the opponent is capable of playing sizeable breaks then yellow should shoot at red. The shot should be hit so that if the roquet is missed yellow will finish on the far boundary behind hoop 4.

Even though this is putting a ball into black's "forward play" it is much safer than the shot with red at yellow, which if missed would allow black to rush blue to a position near hoop 4 and take off to red and yellow to easily set up a break. Whether the shot is hit or missed, it is preferable to have played yellow rather than red.

Of course, in the majority of cases it is correct to hit out rather than in, but situations where hitting in is preferable occur (and are overlooked) with sufficient frequency to make it well worth giving the possibility a moment's thought before automatically hitting the in-lawn ball out.

The second diagram, with all clips on the first hoop, is another example where the correct play is to "hit in" by shooting with yellow at red. Consideration of what is likely to happen afterward will reveal that if the roquet is made with yellow it will be easier to continue than if it had been made with red, and a miss with yellow would make it harder for the opponent to set up a break than a miss with red. Therefore, hit or miss, yellow is the ball to play.

RUNNING AWAY

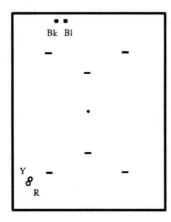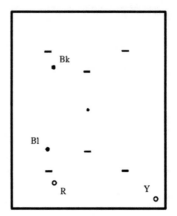

THE FIRST DIAGRAM shows a common type of situation where all clips are on hoop 1 and red has rushed yellow to a point 4-5 yards from the hoop. Many players would now take off to the opponent's balls and separate them rather than "risk" trying to make the hoop.

When both players can make breaks this is a very poor tactical move as it gives only a slightly better than even (say, about 60%) chance of getting a break going before the opponent does. Any player who believes he can successfully roll for hoop 1 and make it more than 6 times out of 10 from this position should not hesitate to do so immediately. On some occasions the attempt will be unsuccessful and you will then be leaving at least one ball at the opponent's hoop; but the alternative would have given him about a 40% chance of obtaining the next break anyway, though perhaps not immediately.

In the second diagram all clips are again on hoop 1 and red has played a poor approach shot with an opponent ball. For similar reasons he should attempt to run the hoop instead of returning to yellow provided he believes he could make it more than 6 times out of 10 from that position.

Even when the opponent's clips are on different hoops so that failure to make the hoop does not present the opponent with an easy break, players will frequently "run away" from such hoops in the mistaken belief that they are taking the safer course of action. Passing up a 70% chance of an immediate break is almost certain to be foolish rather than safe, as it is unlikely that you will get a better chance of establishing a break before your opponent does.

THE RIGHT BALL

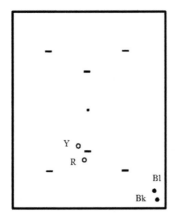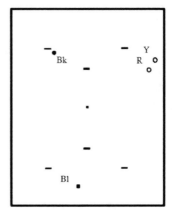

E VEN OUR LEADING players at times choose the wrong ball to play.

The first diagram shows a position in which red is for hoop 5 and yellow for hoop 4. In a top division tournament game red had failed to gain position to run hoop 5, and had sat in front, after which black had missed the roquet on blue near the 4th corner.

Now the player walked out and simply made hoop 5 with red, only to discover that there is no easy way to continue the break. It should be obvious that yellow is the correct ball to play, as it has at least an easy 3-ball break on offer by gently roqueting red and taking off to make hoop 4 with one of the opponent's balls.

The second diagram shows another position from the same tournament. Red and yellow are both for hoop 2. Blue had run hoop 2 right through to the boundary and missed the return rush on black.

The player of red and yellow now played with red, roqueted yellow and took off to make hoop 2 with black. Once again the continuance of the break had not been given sufficient consideration. Correct was to play yellow and rush red to the south border somewhere near the blue ball. Then a stop-shot could be used to send red into the lawn (preferably to hoop 4) while gaining position to rush blue anywhere up the lawn to a position from which it can be sent to load hoop 3 as yellow goes to black at hoop 2.

You should prefer to play the ball that has the best chance of establishing a break rather than just making one hoop.

PLAYING THE BORDER BALL

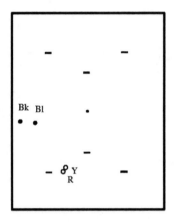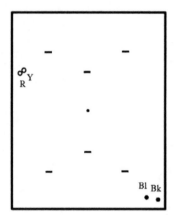

I N THE FIRST diagram red has just made hoop 1 and roqueted yellow. In using the opponent's balls the standard procedure is to go to the border ball (black) first, allowing black to be sent into the lawn with a stop-shot which gains position to rush blue to hoop 2. However in this situation it would not be possible to send black all the way to hoop 3, so it is necessary to load hoop 3 with the yellow ball in order to ensure the continuance of the break.

Therefore yellow should be sent immediately to hoop 3, and on this shot it is best to aim at getting red to a position where it can rush blue out to black, rather than going to the border ball first. There are 3 reasons for going to blue first: it is a safer shot; you can give more attention to placing yellow accurately; and you will be more certain of getting a good rush to hoop 2.

The one disadvantage is that the blue ball will be left near the border 'out of play' and will need to be later brought back into the break.

In the second diagram all clips are on hoop 1 and red has roqueted yellow near hoop 2. Red should take off to the opponent's balls and rush blue out to black rather than trying to go to black first. Again the shot will be safer and a good rush to hoop 1 will be more certain. It is worth taking risks in order to get your break established, but a 3-ball beak (at least for the time being) is sufficient. You should aim to bring the 4th ball into the break as soon as you can, but without taking further noticeable risks. You should practise playing 3-ball breaks and picking up the fourth ball from various positions, so that you learn various ways of doing it, and also learn to correctly estimate the seriousness of the risks involved.

PERCENTAGE PLAY

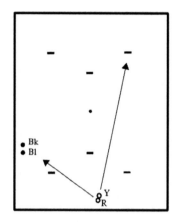 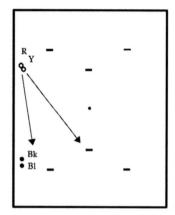

I N THE FIRST diagram red is for hoop 2 and has roqueted yellow on the South boundary. The best way to establish a break is to send yellow to hoop 3 with a long angled split shot in which red goes to the opponent balls on the West border, after which one of them can be rushed to hoop 2. Many players who are quite capable of playing the split shot will refuse to do so because they consider it risky. They would explain, "The red ball could fall short or go out or hit hoop 1 etc."

It is true that there is a certain risk involved, but you cannot expect to win games of croquet without taking risks. In this case, even if you would expect to roquet one of the opponent balls only 7 times out of 10 after playing the split shot, you should take the risk. Taking off may give you almost 100% chance of roqueting an opponent ball, but very little chance of establishing a break.

In the second diagram red is for hoop 4 and has rushed yellow to the border near hoop 2. The percentage play now is to roll yellow to hoop 5 while going to the opponent's balls. Again there is a risk involved, but it is one which most players should willingly take, since it offers an excellent chance of establishing an immediate break.

A player who merely takes off to the opponent's balls in such positions is likely to make only one or two hoops, and will usually not realise that he is losing games by passing up chances to establish breaks. Aggressive "percentage play" involves taking risks which will not always prove successful, but will result in many more wins than would otherwise have been achieved.

COVERING THE DOUBLE

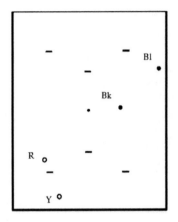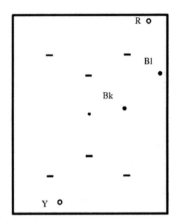

WHEN PLAYING AN opponent who is considered far stronger than themselves many players tend to hit into corners without shooting because they feel that they "cannot afford to give the opponent anything". They imagine that they are "playing safe", but in reality they are playing into the opponent's hands. It is a demonstrable mathematical fact that shooting at a ball will almost always give a better chance of winning than "playing safe" by "joining wide" or hitting into a remote corner.

The first diagram shows one of the rare exceptions to this rule. All clips are on hoop 1 and red is wired from yellow. As red, you consider quite reasonably that a shot at either of the opponent's balls is too risky, but what would you do? Black is likely, though not certain, to roquet blue, so hitting red into the 1st corner can hardly be described as "playing safe".

The best place for red is shown in the second diagram—on the north boundary about 3-4 yards from the 3rd corner. This puts considerable pressure on the opponent, as a missed shot with black at blue will almost certainly give red an inviting double target on the next turn; and if black does roquet he will still need to play some accurate shots to get a break going.

"Covering the double" like this is a tactic which few players have ever thought of, and fewer still have ever used, yet it is much better and more aggressive than, say, hitting red into the second corner which removes all pressure from the opponent. Some would play red right into the 3rd corner, which would also put the opponent under some pressure but only give red a single-ball target on the next turn.

THE THREE-ONE PRINCIPLE

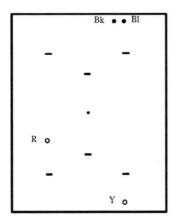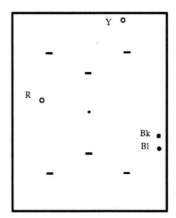

B EFORE READING FURTHER, examine the two diagrams carefully. In each diagram all clips are still on hoop 1 which is in the bottom left corner of the diagram. You are playing with red and yellow and your opponent has just returned about 4-5 feet wide of his partner ball on the yardline. What would you do?

In both situations most players at all levels would immediately shoot with red at the yellow partner ball. However, if red fails to roquet yellow the opponent has an excellent chance of a break. In the first diagram blue can rush black to hoop 2 and take off to your two balls, then rush one of them to hoop 1. In diagram 2 blue can rush black up the border toward the third corner, then send it to hoop 2 and continue similarly. It is far better to shoot at your opponent's balls as a miss is only likely to allow him to make one hoop.

"Finessing" into a corner or returning wide of yellow would also be futile against a thinking opponent who can make breaks, since he should at least be able to bring about a situation where your balls are at hoop 1 and hoop 2, and he has a rush to one of them (preferably the one near hoop 2). Then another finesse would leave him with a break anyway; and any missed shot would be far more disastrous than if you had shot at his balls in the first place.

The 'principle' is that it is usually harder to get a break going with three balls together and one separate than with two and two, assuming all are border balls. This, rather than their expectation of roqueting, is why good players prefer to shoot at the opponent's balls in many situations rather than return to the partner ball.

LOADING THE NEXT HOOP

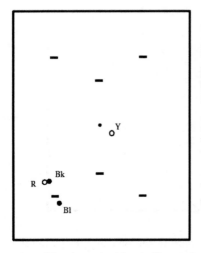

THE MOST COMMON tactical error seen on a croquet lawn is failure to load the next hoop as early and accurately as possible before making the current hoop.

In many cases there is little or no risk involved. In the diagram all clips are still on hoop 1. Red has shot from near hoop 2 and roqueted the black ball near hoop 1. There is a strong temptation to make hoop 1 immediately, but it is imperative to play a split-shot which sends black to hoop 2 while red goes to yellow near the peg. Then red can take-off back to the blue ball and make hoop 1.

The reason why this is so important is that it sets up a break which gives an excellent chance of making not only the current hoop, but several others as well.

Even if loading the next hoop involves taking a risk which renders the making of the current hoop less certain, the risk is often well worth taking. A 60% chance of making two (or more) hoops is better than being certain of making just one hoop; and the player who is prepared to take such chances will consistently beat a player who refuses to do so and imagines that he is 'playing safe'.

In croquet there is nothing safe about refusing to take any risks, except that it is usually a way of safely losing the game!

Sometimes a player fails to load the next hoop because of the risk involved, but there are also many situations where the hoop could have been loaded in a way he just didn't think of. There will often be more than one way of loading the next hoop, so that a choice must be made between them. It is important to consider all reasonable possibilities before making the choice. In the diagrammed position, for example, red could also take off to yellow and either rush it to hoop 2 and take off back to blue; or rush it to the south boundary in front of hoop 1 and use a stop-shot to send it to hoop 2. In the remaining articles on this topic we shall look at situations where the best way of loading the next hoop may be easily overlooked.

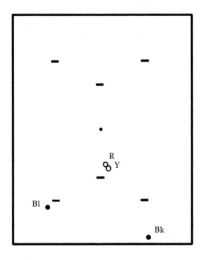

The diagram shows a position from a recent match where all clips are still on the first hoop and red had roqueted yellow near hoop 5. The player of red, who was an experienced and quite capable player, took off from yellow to make hoop 1 from blue. When asked why he had not tried to load hoop 2, he pointed out that the angle was too wide to allow yellow to be sent to hoop 2 while red went to blue at hoop 1. Therefore he planned to make hoop 1 and possibly then go to black which could be sent to load hoop 3 while getting a rush on yellow to hoop 2.

He apparently gave no thought to the possibility of going to black immediately and sending it to hoop 2 while going to blue at hoop 1; yet this shot, although a long one, is not a difficult one as it does not require extreme accuracy. He would not need to worry too much about getting a rush on blue, as long as he got close enough to roquet it; whereas the method he used of setting up the break required getting an accurate rush on yellow at the same time as sending black to hoop 3.

The correct shot in the diagrammed position is actually a pass-roll which places the yellow ball about a yard outside hoop 4 while going to black which will then be used to load hoop 2. (This allows you to 'cover the boundary' behind the yellow ball if anything should go wrong and you need to return to your partner ball.) Then hoop 1 should be made with a rush toward yellow.

There is a strong psychological desire in many players to "play safe" and make certain of the first hoop as did the player of red in this game. However, this involves giving the opponent additional chances to roquet, and is less "safe" than taking the slight risk involved in going to black immediately.

The recommended line of play does depend on your ability to keep the break going after having set it up. Test yourself by setting up the above position on the lawn 5 times and going to black immediately. Then try it another 5 times making hoop 1 immediately. Keep count of the total number of hoops made in order to determine which method gives the best chance of making the most hoops.

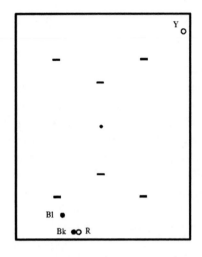

In the diagram red is for hoop 1 and has roqueted black. Many players would now send black as far as possible into the lawn with a stopshot which holds position to rush blue closer to hoop 1 so as to be certain of making it. It will not be possible to send black more than a few yards past hoop 1.

More experienced players will usually prefer to use a stop-shot which sends black right up to hoop 2, even though red will run past blue and require them to turn around and roquet blue, then roll for hoop 1 from 3-4 yards out.

It is less certain that hoop 1 will be made this way, but if it is made then the 3-ball break is fully set up. This is the correct way to play in the diagrammed position provided that you can play the split shot from hoop 1 to hoops 2 and 3 which will be necessary if you do not get a forward rush. The ability to confidently play such basic splits from any hoop to the following two is an essential pre-requisite for correct tactics.

If black is sent only part of the way to hoop 2, then after making hoop 1 you must do two things at once: load hoop 3 and get a rush to hoop 2. While a good player would expect to be able to do this on a reasonably high percentage of attempts, he will if possible avoid the need to do it. It is somewhat paradoxical that weaker players who cannot expect to do it so often tend to commit themselves to the attempt by not properly loading hoop 2.

There are two important principles of tactics involved here: (1) If possible, avoid committing yourself to having to do two things accurately in the one shot; and (2) In setting up a break it is better to take one immediate risk than commit yourself to later taking several smaller risks.

The recommended method may give only a 70% chance of establishing the break by making hoop 1, but the alternative (though hoop 1 can be made with certainty) commits you to having to play 4 or 5 (or more) accurate shots each of whose success rate would be no greater than 90%. Overall it is more likely that one 70% chance will come off than four 90% chances, as any mathematician will tell you.

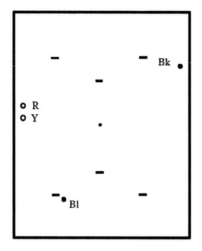 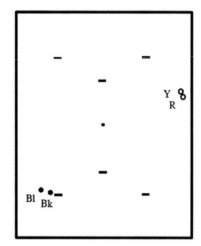

In the first diagram red is for hoop 1. The only way to load hoop 2 accurately is to rush yellow right out to the south boundary, then use a stop-shot to send it to hoop 2 while going to blue at hoop 1.

This may seem a patently obvious play to many of us, but it is amazing how many players in such positions will simply roquet yellow and take off to blue. Even a thick take-off to put yellow some distance into the lawn is just not good enough.

In the second diagram red is again for hoop 1 and has roqueted yellow. It should again be obvious that in taking off to the opponent's balls red should make certain of finishing on the northern side of them so that one of them can be rushed to the south boundary and then sent accurately to hoop 2. But here also many players will simply aim in the take-off to finish anywhere near blue or black.

The need to give yourself room to load the next hoop is often overlooked until it is too late.

This is also the reason why in the first diagram, after correctly loading hoop 2, the player of red should endeavour in making hoop 1 to get a rush to the outside of the lawn (i.e. to the boundary alongside hoop 2), rather than to the inside (to the peg or hoop 3) as in a 4-ball break.

In general, it is easier to load a hoop accurately with split-shot (especially a stop-shot) than with a rush or thick take-off.

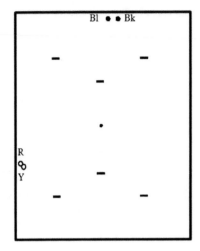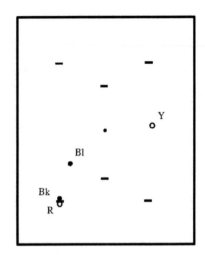

In the first diagram red has made hoop 1 and cut-rush yellow to the west boundary. From here the ideal shot would be a long roll which places yellow at hoop 3 while red goes to the opponent's balls on the north boundary.

For many players this long roll would be too difficult and risky, and it is understandable that they would be unwilling to chance it.

However, they should at least take off to the opponent's balls and roquet blue, not black. This allows hoop 3 to be loaded with blue in a stop-shot which also gains position to rush black to hoop 2. The stop-shot may involve a small risk, but it is one worth taking, since there is no satisfactory way to load hoop 3 if black is roqueted first.

The player who roquets black instead of blue may be more certain of making hoop 2, but will find it far more difficult to get a break going.

In the second diagram red is again for hoop 1 and has rushed black into the back of the hoop. The correct continuation is one that few players would think of: call the referee to check that black is partly in the hoop, then place red in the hoop against it and play a croquet shot that sends black all the way to load hoop 2 while red runs through to a position where it can roquet blue. The blue ball can be used to load hoop 3 before making hoop 2 with black—which has not been used since making hoop 1!

When shown this idea one experienced player remarked, "I could kick myself when I think how many such opportunities I have missed!"

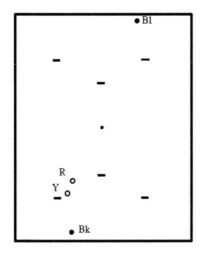 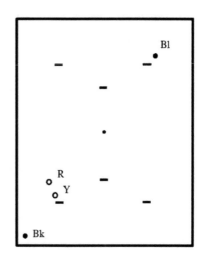

In diagram 1 all clips are on hoop 1. Black has just shot from hoop 2 at the opponent's balls and missed. If the blue ball were in, say, the fourth corner, then for most players the best way of trying for a break with red would be to roquet yellow, take off to black, and use a stop-shot to load hoop 2 with black while making position with red to run hoop 1.

With blue on the border in front of hoop 3 as shown a reasonable alternative would be to make hoop 1 from yellow, being careful to obtain a backward rush (much easier than a forward one) to black, which should then be rushed not to hoop 2, but to the north boundary near the blue ball.

The second diagram shows a similar position, but the black ball is now in the first corner which makes the stop-shot less attractive than when it was more directly in front of hoop 1. Also, blue is now at hoop 3. This makes the stop-shot an unnecessary risk in any case, as it is relatively easy to make hoop 1 from yellow and in so doing obtain a rush back to black in the corner. Black can then be rushed either to hoop 2 or to the blue ball at hoop 3 to set up the break.

In situations such as those shown here the position of the opponent's balls needs careful consideration in determining which option offers the best chance of getting a break under way.

In some cases the player of red should also consider the possibility of making hoop 1 and setting so that he has a guaranteed break (unless the opponent roquets) on his next turn. This will be considered further in future articles.

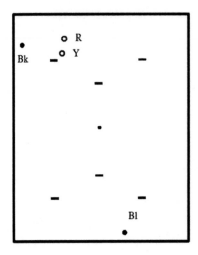 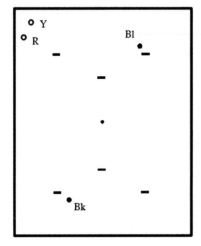

The first diagram shows a common situation where black has shot from hoop 3 at the opponent's balls near hoop 2 and missed. The red clip is on hoop 2 and yellow on hoop 1. How should red now play the turn?

He has four options:

(1) Roquet yellow, make hoop 2 and rush or roll to hoop 3, ignoring the black and blue balls.
(2) Roquet yellow, take off to black and use a stop-shot to send black to hoop 3 while making position to run hoop 2.
(3) Roquet black immediately.
(4) Make hoop 2 from yellow with a rush to black. Leave yellow there and rush black toward hoop 1. Leave black near hoop 1 and go to blue. Send blue to hoop 3 and return to set up near yellow as shown in the second diagram.

Although frequently used, option (1) gives no chance of getting a break going and should not be seriously considered. Options (2) and (3) both involve loading hoop 3 before making hoop 2. Which of them is preferable depends on which shot (6-yard roquet or stop-shot for position) the player is most likely to play successfully.

Option (4) involves little or no risk and gives at least a 70% chance of a break on the next turn, since few players of blue and black would roquet 3 times out of 10 from the position of the second diagram. Therefore one of the other options should only be chosen if the player of red believes that it would be successful at least 7 times out of 10. We shall further consider leaves such as the one in diagram 2 in a later article.

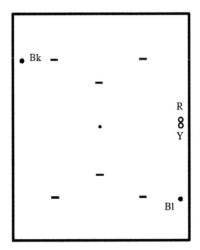
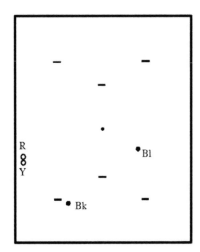

In the first diagram red is for hoop 4 and after making hoop 3 has cut-rushed yellow to the east boundary. How would you continue? Loading hoop 5 with yellow before rolling with blue for hoop 4 is too risky because if the roll is unsuccessful it could mean setting up in the middle of the lawn.

Many players would take off from yellow to blue, but this gives little chance of continuing the break.

The correct play is to roll both balls to a point about half way between hoop 4 and the blue ball, then roquet blue and send it just past hoop 5 while trying for position to run hoop 4. (In a later article on the "Trap Line" we shall consider this tactic in greater detail.) If the roll is unsuccessful it allows red to cover the boundary behind yellow to discourage a shot by blue.

In the second diagram red is for hoop 1 and has just taken off from blue and roqueted yellow. It is not possible to load hoop 2 with yellow while going to make hoop 1 with black. Where should yellow be placed? In the croquet stroke yellow should be sent as close as possible to the blue ball.

Such a move would never occur to most players, yet it is clearly the correct thing to do and involves very little risk. After making hoop 1 black can be used to load hoop 3 while going to the two balls you have conveniently left together. Then it will be a simple matter to use one of them to get an exact rush behind the other to hoop 2. No other shot from the position of diagram 2 gives as good a chance of continuing the break. If you can't load the hoop the next best thing is to leave two balls together.

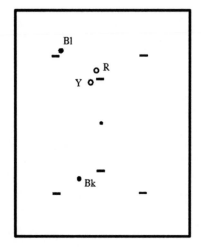
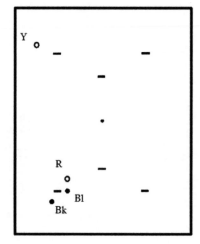

In an earlier article we mentioned the need to load the next hoop as early and accurately as possible. Players are often satisfied with placing a ball three or more yards from the hoop. The stronger and more experienced the player is, the less likely he is to be satisfied with placing a ball anywhere except right at the hoop.

One would expect it to be the other way around, with a weaker player needing a ball to be more accurately placed. It is somewhat paradoxical therefore that in the position shown in the first diagram most inexperienced players as red, having just made hoop 6 in the process of a 4-ball break, would simply roquet yellow and take off to blue at the 1-back hoop.

For a stronger player this would not be good enough. He would rush yellow down and place it accurately a yard in front of 2-back, then rush black back up toward blue before making 1-back.

In the second diagram red is still for hoop 1. He has used a split-shot to load hoop 2 with yellow while coming to the opponent's balls at hoop 1. However, yellow has gone too far and finished about 3 yards away from hoop 2. Now he should rush blue out to the south boundary and use a stop-shot to place it right at hoop 2 before making hoop 1 with black. Sending it only part of the way to hoop 2 is not good enough.

If your first attempt to load a hoop is not sufficiently accurate then you should not miss an opportunity to improve it, as in the first diagram, or else put a second ball there as well, as in the second diagram.

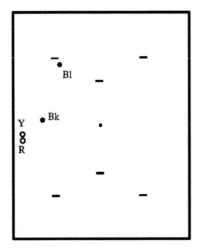 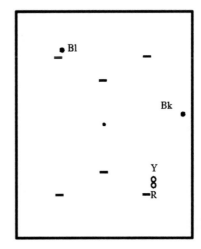

In the previous article we stressed the value of loading the next hoop as accurately as possible. Now we shall re-emphasise the importance of loading it as early as possible.

In the first diagram red has made hoop 1 and rushed yellow to the west boundary. Many players would now send yellow toward the peg while getting position to rush black closer to blue at hoop 2. However, this gives only one chance of accurately loading hoop 3. A better method is to use a stop-shot to put yellow at hoop 3, even though it means running past black so that you have to turn around and roquet it back toward the boundary. Then roll black into the middle while going to blue, or, if yellow did not go accurately to hoop 3, you have another chance to load it more accurately.

In the second diagram red is for hoop 2 and should send yellow to hoop 3 rather than leaving it at hoop 4. Players often take off to black in such situations, committing themselves to probably needing to do two things accurately in the one shot: place black at hoop 3 while also getting a rush on blue to bring it to the front of hoop 2.

It is surprising how many players, even at top level, miss such opportunities to give themselves a second chance at loading the next hoop. Remember, load the next hoop as early as is reasonably possible, and in so doing try to position the striker's ball so that if the first attempted loading is inaccurate you can rush the pivot ball to a position from where you will be able to make a second attempt at accurately loading the hoop. Players who follow this principle rarely fail to complete their breaks.

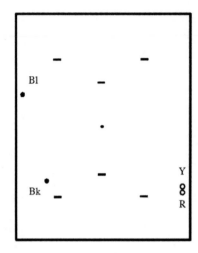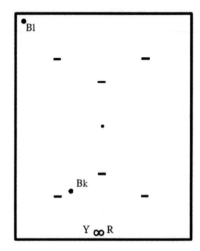

In the first diagram red is for hoop 1 and has roqueted yellow. It would be fairly easy to take off to black and make the first hoop, but hoop 2 cannot be considered "loaded" with the blue ball which is on the yardline.

A confident player may consider using a split shot to send yellow to hoop 2 while going to black with an immediate 4-ball break. If black were placed right at hoop 1 this could be the correct play, but with black placed as shown it would involve an unnecessary risk. Red should take off to blue and then use a thick take-off to put blue into court while going to black. There may be some risk in taking off right across the lawn to a border ball, and the loading of hoop 2 may not turn out to be really accurate, but this sort of small risk should always be taken.

In the second diagram the take-off to blue involves a slightly increased risk, and more importantly it would allow hoop 2 to be loaded only by playing a very difficult pass roll. In this situation yellow should be sent right to hoop 2 immediately as red goes to make hoop 1 from black. With blue in the 2nd corner some players tend to send yellow only about three-quarters of the way to hoop 2, but there is nothing "safe" about such chicken-hearted play. If hoop 1 is not made and red has to return to yellow the opponent will want to move the black ball rather than blue on the next turn, even if red and yellow are in the lawn close to hoop 2.

If red does not obtain a forward rush after hoop 1 he can simply take off to the blue ball and use it to load hoop 3, thus continuing the break.

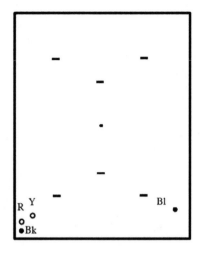 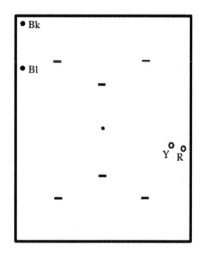

In the first diagram all clips are still on hoop 1, and black has just missed a shot from near hoop 2, finishing in the 1st corner. It is common to see players in this situation either ignore black and take the immediate rush to make hoop 1 from yellow, or else roquet black with red and use a stop-shot to send it 4 or 5 yards out of the corner before rushing yellow to hoop 1.

The blue ball is of little use, but the correct procedure is to play yellow, rushing red into the 1st corner to create a cannon which will allow the easy loading of hoop 2 with red while rushing black to hoop 1 in the same shot.

There are many different cannons which can be used to load hoops and set up breaks. Some are much harder than this one from the 1st corner for hoop 1. Good players practice them regularly and look for chances to create cannons at every opportunity.

In the second diagram red is for 1-back. A common continuation would be to rush yellow to the peg, take-off to black in the 2nd corner, and use a stop-shot to send it to 2-back before rolling with blue for 1-back. Trying to get a rush on blue in the stop-shot would be very risky.

A far better method is to rush yellow to blue and then rush blue into the corner to create a cannon with black. Another reasonable method is to rush yellow to a point between blue and black, then use a stop-shot to send yellow to 2-back while obtaining position to rush blue back toward black, in which case the break may be set up even if you do not succeed in creating the cannon.

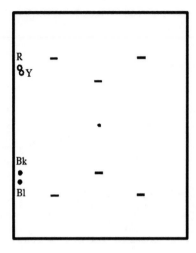 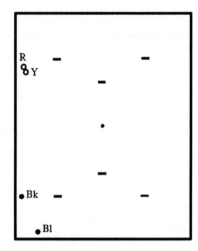

Players are sometimes afraid to load the next hoop correctly because it may involve putting the partner ball into the lawn. They fear the possibility of having to "set up" in the middle of the lawn if they do not succeed in getting the break started.

The first diagram shows a situation where red is for hoop 4 and has roqueted yellow on the border alongside hoop 2. Since the opponent's balls are together and accessible, the yellow ball should be sent to load hoop 5 with a roll shot in which red goes to a position where it can roquet one of the opponent's balls and use it to get a rush behind the other to hoop 4. As long as the roll shot is played so that red finishes well inside the boundary, this involves little risk.

Even when there is some risk involved, it may be well worth taking. It is really a matter of correctly weighing up the percentages. If the risk "comes off", you have an immediate break which could not have been obtained any other way. As long as you give yourself a noticeably better than 50% chance of getting the break started, the risk should be taken.

In the second diagram the opponent's balls are several yards apart, so the player of red would be far less certain of being able to rush one of them accurately to hoop 4. In this case he would be well advised to leave yellow where it is and take off to the opponent's balls with the idea of putting them both into the lawn in such a way as to give an easy break on the next turn provided the opponent does not roquet. This idea will be explained further in later articles.

THE TRAP LINE

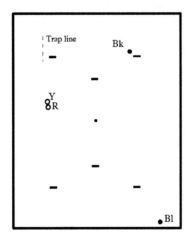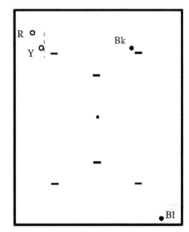

IN THE FIRST diagram the player of red is about to roll for hoop 2 with his partner ball. The normal thing, if making a short approach, is to send yellow to the right (or inside) of the hoop so that after making the hoop you can hope to rush the yellow ball toward either hoop 3 or the peg.

However in this case the approach shot will be a longish roll and the making of the hoop is no longer a near certainty, so it is wise to consider the possibility that you may not gain position to run the hoop.

For this reason it may be preferable to roll yellow to the left (outside) of hoop 2, placing it on what some English players refer to as the "trap line". For most players this imaginary line is situated between one and two yards to the left of the hoop, and is parallel to the west boundary. The yellow ball placed on this line meets the following conditions:

(1) it is near enough to the hoop to be easily roqueted after the hoop is made.
(2) if the hoop cannot be attempted, red can retire behind it as shown in the second diagram to a position about halfway between yellow and the side boundary, thus "setting a trap" for the opponent.
(3) If the opponent plays black to join up with blue (wherever it is—here we have placed it near the 4th corner), then red has a simple rush on yellow and can make hoop 2 before continuing.

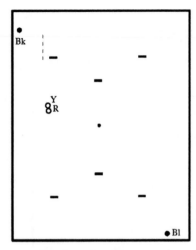

(4) if black shoots at yellow or red and misses, then red is close enough to the border to immediately roquet black.

(5) yellow is far enough from the border so that after black is roqueted by red it can be sent right back to hoop 3 with a stop-shot which still allows red to hold a rush on yellow to make hoop 2.

Most experienced players realise the importance of "covering the boundary" to make a shot at your balls risky for the opponent, but many are not aware of the ways in which you can use the concept of this particular "trap line" to not only cover the boundary, but achieve the best possible "leave" if the hoop cannot be attempted. For example, in the second diagram on the previous page the boundary could have been covered by placing red right out on the border, or with yellow in various other positions; but then if black joined up with blue you may no longer be certain of roqueting yellow and making your hoop. Only if yellow is placed on the correct "trap line" will it be possible to meet the whole five desired conditions given above. It is useful to get out on the lawn and practise using this concept until it becomes an automatic part of your thinking in situations where the success of the approach shot is in doubt, until the exact position and length of the line is firmly fixed in your mind.

Note that you must be prepared to pay a price for using the "trap line", since if your approach happens to be successful and the hoop is made, you will have forgone the chance of obtaining a useful rush, and committed yourself to playing a longer split shot to send yellow to hoop 4 while going to the black ball at hoop 3. This split shot also needs practice. The diagram on this page shows another use of the line. Here black could be on the border anywhere within several yards of the 2nd corner. By placing yellow on the "trap line" with a slight pass roll as he goes to black, red can then send black to hoop 3 while trying for position to run hoop 2. Thus he gives himself a reasonable chance of establishing an immediate break, and retains the option of the leave shown in the second diagram on the previous page if necessary. (Previously the term "defensive line" was used, but led to some misunderstanding. The use of the "trap line" is in fact a very aggressive move.)

In part 1 we looked at two situations, in which the concept of an imaginary "trap line" could be used to ensure the best possible leave if you are forced to play a long approach shot to hoop 2.

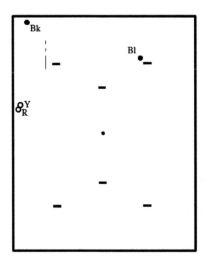

The diagram shows a third case, and here we assume that red has just made hoop 1 and sent the blue ball to hoop 3, but failed to get a rush on yellow either to hoop 2 or to the unused black ball near the 2nd corner. The other three clips are still on hoop 1.

Many players in this situation would take off to either hoop 2 or the black ball, but a far better idea is to play a short pass roll which places yellow on the trap line while going to roquet black. Then the black ball is sent with a stop-shot to hoop 1 while trying for position to run hoop 2 with red.

Note that sending black to hoop 1 (where your partner clip is) is better than placing it at hoop 4 or near the peg, as it gives the opponent a longer roquet and gives you a more certain break on your next turn if he misses. If the yellow clip were on hoop 4 or hoop 5, then black could be sent to one of those hoops. If yellow is already around on 4-back then there would be no better option than placing black at hoop 4.

If you cannot run the hoop, then you place red about halfway between yellow and the side boundary, so as to "cover" the boundary against a shot by blue, but being careful not to give it a double target.

You are then threatening to play an already set up 3-ball break with either ball in your next turn unless your opponent roquets. In fact, any missed roquet attempt will also allow you to have the fourth ball in your break almost immediately.

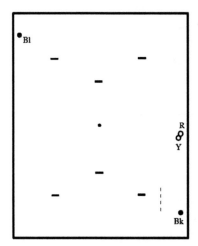

In this case you should place yellow near the in-lawn end of the trap line as shown on the diagram by the unbroken part of the line. This is so that if you gain position and are able to make the hoop, you can rush or cut yellow back toward hoop 1 and immediately bring the black ball into your continuing break.

In parts 1 and 2 we looked at how the concept of an imaginary "trap line" near hoop 2 can be useful when making an approach to the hoop from a distance at which success is uncertain.

Here we consider the same idea in relation to hoop 4, where it is even more often likely to be of advantage.

The imaginary line near hoop 4 (see diagram) is further from the hoop and closer to the boundary than the trap line for hoop 2. This is due to the fact that the next hoop is closer, so you do not need as much room to send a border ball (e.g. from the position of black on the diagram) to hoop 5 with a stop-shot which still allows you to hold a rush on a ball from the trap line to hoop 4. In the diagram the black ball can be either at hoop 5 or somewhere near the border within 6-7 yards of the 4th corner. Red is for hoop 4, having just made hoop 3 and managed to cut-rush the yellow partner ball to the position shown. This type of situation seems to occur frequently. Many players would simply take off to black, perhaps risking going out in an attempt to get a rush, and then roll with black for hoop 4.

There is a far better alternative at any level of play. You should play a roll which places yellow on the "trap line" while going to roquet black (do not try for a rush on it). Then use a half-roll to send black to hoop 5 while trying for position to run hoop 4. If you succeed, the split of yellow to hoop 6 while going to black at hoop 5 should not prove difficult. If you do not gain position to make hoop 4, then you can place red so as to give it a rush on yellow to hoop 4, and "cover" the boundary at the same time.

Most players prefer to send black a yard or two past hoop 5, hoping to wire it from yellow on either hoop 4 or hoop 5. For this reason it is worth trying to put yellow so that it is not only on the trap line, but also on a line through the two hoops, to make the wiring easier.

The shots mentioned above need practice, with yellow and black starting from various positions. In some cases the position of blue may also be relevant.

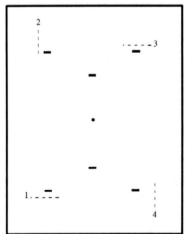

In parts 1 and 2 we examined the concept of an imaginary "trap line" to the left of hoop 2. In part 3 we saw that the "trap line" near hoop 4 is even more important, and is situated about a yard closer to the side border. The partner ball should be placed on this line when:

(1) using a long roll to approach the hoop with your partner ball and the next hoop is loaded with an opponent ball.

(2) the long roll approach with the partner ball would be too dangerous because there is an opponent ball "sitting over" the hoop on or near the border within 7-8 yards of the corner.

The same concept is sometimes useful at hoops 1 and 3, where it involves placing the partner ball behind the hoop instead of in front as you would if you were more certain of making it; and therefore it means sacrificing any chance of obtaining a forward rush if the hoop is made. The diagram shows the approximate position of the "trap line" for each of the corner hoops.

Placing the partner ball on this line enables you to "cover the boundary" if the approach is unsuccessful, by leaving your striker's ball about halfway between the partner ball and the boundary. This makes it extremely risky for the opponent to shoot at your balls with his ball which you have sent to your next hoop.

It should be noted, however, that if you succeed in making the hoop then the following split shot from the border in front of hoop 1 to hoops 2 and 3, or from the front of hoop 3 to hoops 4 and 5, will not be an easy one. The position of the fourth ball can be an important consideration here. For example you can use the hoop 1 "trap line" more happily if the fourth ball is near hoop 4, since if you make the hoop you can send your partner ball to hoop 3 and go to the ball at hoop 4, then take off to the ball at hoop 2.

Note also that there is no effective trap line for the centre hoops. For the 'return' hoops (1-back to 4-back) the "trap lines" will correspond in position to those shown in the diagram, but their use may be complicated by the fact that the opponent could be entitled to a 'lift'.

BALLS IN HOOPS

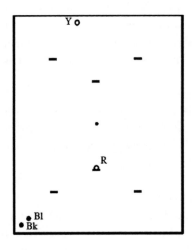 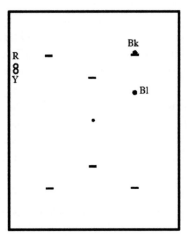

I N THE FIRST diagram all clips are still on the first hoop. The player of red and yellow has accidentally put his red ball into the jaws of hoop 5 and the opponent has since set up in the 1st corner. What should red do now? The main rule is: Don't panic. The red ball is actually in quite a safe position.

Yellow should now shoot at red, or even at the opponent's balls. Red can be left in the hoop for several turns, provided yellow has a shot which will not give the opponent an easy 3-ball break, and the opponent is not likely to make hoop 5 in his next turn. In the second diagram black has failed in an attempt to run hoop 3, and red, whose clip is still on hoop 1, has roqueted yellow on the west border near hoop 2. Black could easily run hoop 3 on its next shot, so has to be removed from the hoop.

There are two principles which apply here but are often ignored:

    (1) If possible go to the ball in the hoop (black) first.
    (2) Do not hesitate to concede the hoop if there is anything at all to be gained.

Many players would take off to blue, then to a position just behind hoop 3. They would succeed in removing the black ball from the hoop, but without any way of continuing the break. The correct play is to take off to the playing side of hoop 3 and rush black through the hoop toward the blue ball.

This gives black the hoop, but also allows red to get a rush on blue to hoop 1 with a reasonable chance of getting a controlled break under way.

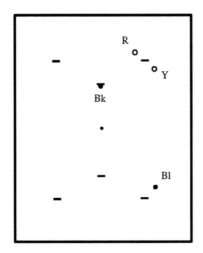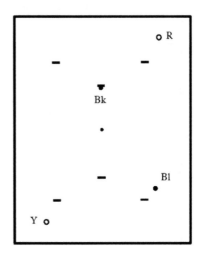

When you have unintentionally put an opponent ball into a hoop there may be little you can do if there is a ball near a baulk, unless you can continue the break.

The first diagram shows a situation taken from a tournament game between 1st division players. Red had left the black ball partly within the jaws of hoop 6 and then failed to gain position to run hoop 3. Red had only one shot remaining, and a "saving" shot was impossible because red was wired from yellow. With the black clip on hoop 4, red could see his opponent taking the black ball to B-baulk and roqueting yellow, sending it at least part of the way to blue with an easy break to follow.

After some thought, he hit his red ball to a position one yard east of the blue ball! The opponent could still have taken the baulked black ball to either baulk, but with red threatening to continue its break he did not have the nerve to do so. He reluctantly played blue, which was still for hoop 1 and had little chance of making a break.

Blue's correct play here would have been to set up the position shown in the second diagram by rolling red toward B-baulk while going to yellow, and sending yellow toward A-baulk before returning to hoop 4 where the black clip is. Unless red or yellow makes a roquet, black can claim the baulk on his next turn with an easy break. Any shot taken and missed would immediately give black the fourth ball as well.

If you had been red or blue in these two positions, what would you have done?

THE FOURTH BALL

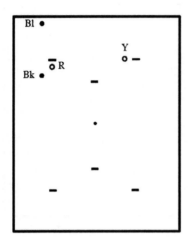 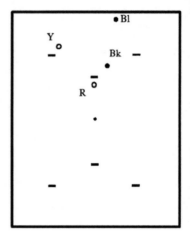

A 4-BALL BREAK is easier to play than a 3-ball break, so it is desirable to convert a 3-ball break into a 4-ball break whenever a suitable opportunity presents itself.

If the fourth ball is on the yard-line behind an even-numbered hoop then the most obvious way of 'picking it up' and bringing it into the break is to run right through to the border in making the hoop.

In the first diagram red is about to make hoop 2 and will run through to the border before roqueting blue. Notice that on the approach shot black has been left in front of hoop 2 rather than behind it. This will allow blue to be sent all the way down to hoop 4 with a stop-shot in which red holds position to rush black closer to the yellow ball at hoop 3.

In the second diagram red is about to make hoop 6. It is quite common for players to miss the opportunity to run right through to the north border and roquet blue, which can then be used to load the 2-back hoop.

Instead they make hoop 6 and roquet black, then send it only part of the way to 2-back while going to yellow. After making 1-back they suddenly discover that they must do something about the blue ball because they have given a 'lift'.

Somewhat better would have been to take off from black to blue and split blue to 2-back while going to yellow; but this requires you to do two things accurately in the one shot. While a good player should not find this shot difficult, he will avoid the need to play it when there is a simpler alternative as described above.

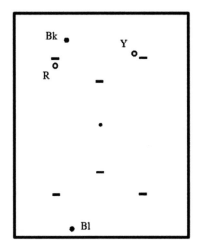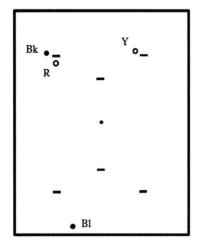

Players are sometimes advised to play a 3-ball break until they have loaded the hoop nearest to the fourth ball, then think about bringing it into the break. In the first diagram this would involve red making hoop 2 and splitting black to hoop 4 before making hoop 3 with yellow. Then yellow can be used to load hoop 5 before making hoop 4 with the black ball, which can then be rolled to load 2-back while going to blue which can be sent to hoop 6 while going to yellow at hoop 5.

An alternative after making hoop 3 would have been to take off from yellow to blue and use a slight pass-roll to load hoop 5 with blue while going to black at hoop 4. Then hoop 4 should be made with a rush on black to yellow in order to immediately bring it back into the break.

It is important that a player should learn to do all this if necessary, but a good player should also consider the advantages of trying to bring blue into the beak immediately, by placing black alongside hoop 2 to the left in the approach shot as shown in the second diagram.

After red makes the hoop black can be rushed to any point on the south boundary between blue and the 1st corner, then sent to hoop 4. Blue can often then be cut-rushed into the lawn, or else brought a yard or two out in a take-off to yellow.

For most players there is nothing to lose by attempting to bring the blue ball into the break immediately, and it offers a good chance of making things easier for yourself. Players should practise both methods in order to find out which one best suits their range of shots.

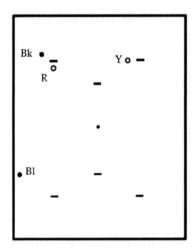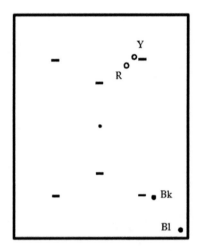

In the first diagram red is about to run hoop 2, and on the approach shot has placed the black ball to the left of the hoop in order to begin the process of getting the blue ball into the break. After making hoop 2, red will rush black about half-way to the blue ball, and from there use a stop-shot to load hoop 4 with black while going to blue, which can be sent a few yards into court toward the 2-back hoop as red takes off to yellow.

After making hoop 3 red would again be hoping to get a rush to blue so that he can bring it fully into the break. If he does not get the rush after hoop 3 he should still be able to get behind blue with a take-off. A player who does not follow this procedure will be forced to play a 3-ball break for quite some time, with an increased chance of breaking down at some stage.

In the second diagram the fourth ball (blue) is in the 4th corner. After making hoop 2 red has correctly sent black to a position outside hoop 4 and slightly behind it. Many players wrongly place black between hoop 4 and the peg, but find that if they fail to get a forward rush on yellow after making hoop 3 and have to take-off to blue, the shot needed to load hoop 5 with blue and get a rush on black to hoop 4 is far more difficult than if black is placed correctly as shown in the diagram.

This particular situation seems to occur in games with surprising frequency, but the correct placement of the black ball is rarely seen. After making hoop 2 the player had to think six shots ahead in order to appreciate the value of placing black so as to give himself the chance of bringing blue into the break in the simplest and safest way.

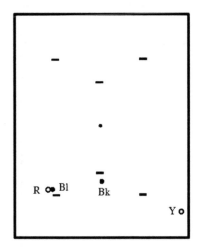 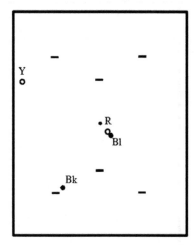

Some quite strong players fail to bring the fourth ball into a break when it is their partner ball. They prefer to play a 3-ball break with the opponent's balls, leaving the partner ball near the border so they will have "somewhere safe to come home to" if the need arises.

This is foolish and negative thinking. By leaving the fourth ball out of play they almost guarantee that the need to return to it will arise, and unfortunately this only serves to strengthen their conviction that they have done the right thing.

In the first diagram red is for hoop 5 and has roqueted blue near hoop 1. Red should immediately take off to yellow in the 4th corner and split it to hoop 6 while going to black at hoop 5. This is far better than sending blue to hoop 6 and leaving yellow on the border.

The second diagram shows a similar situation where red is for 2-back and has roqueted blue near the peg. Instead of sending blue to 3-back he should take off to yellow and send yellow to 3-back while going to black.

Apart from making the break easier, another excellent reason for having your partner ball in the break is that it enables you to achieve more accurate placement of the balls (including, of course, the partner ball itself) after making the final hoop.

This may all seem rather obvious, but I have seen a player start a 4-ball break and deliberately convert it to a 3-ball break by rushing the partner ball to the 4th corner and leaving it there! When he insisted that this was tactically correct, I could only say, "I hope you do it when you play me!"

WIRING

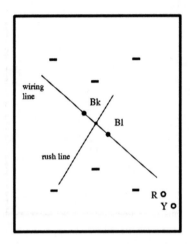
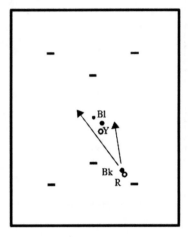

WHEN A PLAYER has learnt to make regular breaks with only a small risk of breaking down, he should try to not only complete the break but achieve the best possible "leave" at the end of it. The first diagram shows a situation where red has wired the opponent's balls at the peg so as to give his yellow partner ball an excellent chance of a further immediate break if the opponent fails to roquet.

This leave is quite strong if the yellow clip is on hoop 1, and better still if it is on one of the centre hoops. Note that the wiring line is approximately at right-angles to the line joining the peg to hoop 1 so that yellow will not have the peg interfering with a rush of either blue or black to hoop 1. The best way to achieve this leave is as follows:

Before making the final hoop (say, 3-back) with red, place the yellow partner ball and one opponent ball together near the peg. The best place for them at this stage is on the wiring line and on the side of the peg nearest 3-back.

After making 3-back with red (see 2nd diagram), send black past the peg and go to the two balls. Roquet blue and use a gentle croquet shot to wire it from black. In this shot blue should be sent, as much as possible, in a direction along the wiring line rather than across it, so as to allow a greater margin for error. Then roquet yellow, which was left close to blue so that in positioning blue you did not have to worry about getting red over to it, and roll both balls to set a rush near the fourth corner. If the rush is also set on or near the wiring line you will have an exact rush to whichever ball the opponent leaves in the middle.

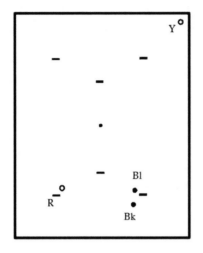 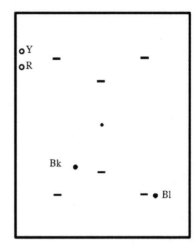

In the first diagram the red clip is on hoop 1 and yellow on hoop 3. Blue has just failed to make hoop 4. As red you may shoot at black, but what will you do if you roquet it? Most players would try for a rush on blue to make hoop 1 with little chance of continuing the break. In doing so they would be missing an excellent chance to almost guarantee a break for yellow on the next turn.

It should be a relatively simple task to leave the opponent's balls wired at hoop 4 with a couple of gentle croquet shots, then hit red back to give yellow some sort of rush to hoop 3.

The player who wishes to improve his wiring skills should work out wired positions for himself and practise obtaining them. Some are difficult to achieve and others may be achieved much more easily, especially if you start planning for them early enough.

Diagram 2 shows an excellent "leave" when the yellow clip is on hoop 4. Because there are two hoops between the opponent's balls the wiring is easier to achieve, and even if blue and black turn out not to be properly wired from each other any shot the opponent takes will be very risky.

Experienced players get to know the places on the lawn where wiring is easy to achieve, and learn to keep the possibility in the 'back of their mind' at all times so that whenever a situation arises where there will be a lot to gain by wiring the opponent's balls they can start working the balls into position as early as possible.

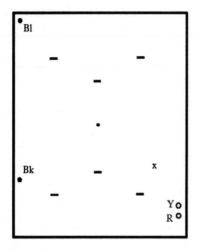 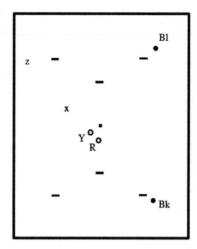

The position in the first diagram is commonly seen at the start of a game, after blue has missed the shot at black which had been set as a 'tice'.

On a strange or difficult lawn some players would then play red and simply cut-rush yellow to point x which is wired from both opponent balls, and there set a rush for hoop 1. (Note that either blue or black should shoot at the rush unless both are wired from it.) Then the opponent will probably think of removing his black ball from the vicinity of your hoop, but would be taking a considerable risk if he chose to shoot at blue and give you two balls in forward play.

In the 2ⁿᵈ diagram red is already on the peg and is setting up for yellow to make 3-back. He has sent black to 3-back and blue to 4-back and now is about to rush yellow out to the 2ⁿᵈ corner and set a rush for it back to 3-back. This is a reasonable course of action, but he should at least consider the possibility of rushing yellow instead to point x where he can set the rush wired from both opponent balls.

It is true that if the opponent happens to roquet, the balls left in the middle of the lawn may make it easier for him; but if he misses then yellow will find it easier to rush the shorter distance to his hoop with accuracy.

An alternative wiring position could be near point z, which is further from yellow's hoop, but has the advantage that wiring from blue is no longer necessary. A good player will be aware of such doubly-wired spots so he can use them to advantage when there is a good chance to do so.

RUSH-LINE THEORY

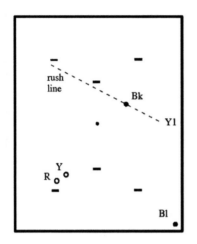 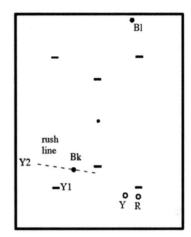

T HIS THEORY STATES that the best way of obtaining a rush to a hoop is to play the preceding croquet shot from a point along the line of the desired rush.

In the first diagram red has just made hoop 1 and will need to rush black to hoop 2. Yellow should be rushed therefore to point Y1 which is on the desired rush line drawn from hoop 2 through black.

The theory arises from the idea that if the croquet shot is played from on or near the rush line, the striker's ball will travel along this line as it approaches the black ball. Therefore there is a greater margin for error than if the striker's ball were rushed only to a point near the peg and had to travel across the rush line.

When approaching along the rush line you can aim to get 1 yard from the black ball, and if the red ball goes 1-2 feet further or falls 1-2 feet short then you will still have a reasonable rush. A ball travelling across the rush-line has a much smaller margin for error.

In the second diagram red has just made hoop 4. Many players would rush yellow to point Y1 near hoop 1 and load hoop 6 with a stop-shot in which the red striker's ball travels across the rush line almost at right-angles. The rush-line theorist would instead rush yellow to point Y2 on the rush line and play a split shot with a wider angle in which the red ball approaches black along the rush line. The wider angle may make the split slightly more difficult, but in compensation for this there is a greater margin for error as explained above.

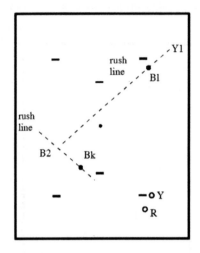 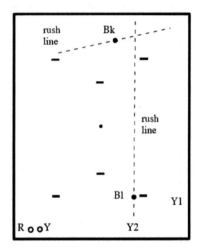

The rush-line theory explained in part 1 can be extended to involve a second rush-line in some positions. In the first diagram red has just made hoop 4. The yellow ball should be rushed to point Y1 from which yellow can be sent to load hoop 6 while red gets a rush on blue to point B2. Notice that point B2 is on the rush-line of black to hoop 5.

By rushing each ball to the rush-line of the next ball in this manner red can maximise his chance of getting accurate rushes and continuing the break.

The second diagram shows another example where two rush-lines are involved. Red is for 1-back and many players would rush yellow to the blue ball, then rush blue to 1-back. It would be better to rush yellow to point Y1 on the east boundary so that yellow can be used to load the 2-back hoop; and the rush on blue would be better made to the black ball rather than the 1-back hoop.

Better still is to follow rush-line theory, and rush yellow to point Y2 on the south boundary. From here also there is room to send yellow to 2-back while approaching blue along the rush-line to point B2 which is on the rush-line of black to the 1-back hoop.

Finding the best place to rush yellow to thus requires thinking six shots ahead. This may sound impressive, but a player who makes a habit of thinking in terms of rush-lines will learn to see it all in a flash. He will even learn to think further ahead and leave his balls at the end of the previous turn so as to be able to take advantage of the rush-lines if the opponent plays as expected and fails to roquet.

John Riches and Wayne Davies

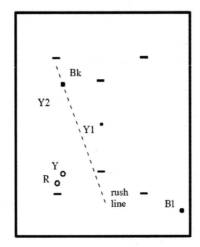 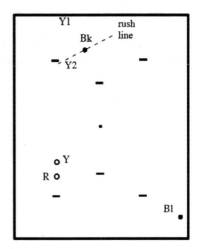

The extent to which a player accepts and adopts rush-line theory will depend on the range of shots with which he is comfortable.

There are many situations where it will be desirable to rush a ball closer to a hoop, but I is impossible to load the next hoop with a croquet shot played from the rush-line. In other cases the shot may be possible but of dubious value.

In the first diagram, rush-line theory would recommend that red, which has just made hoop 1, should rush yellow to point Y1 on the rush-line of black to hoop 2. However, loading hoop 3 from point Y1 requires a wide-angle split in which the difficulty in controlling the direction of the striker's ball may outweigh any gain in the margin for error as regards distance.

For this reason many players would have preferred a rush on yellow to point Y2. This would involve loading hoop 3 with a stop-shot in which the red ball travels across the rushline and so has only a small margin for error in distance; but with both balls travelling in the same line the stop-shot is likely to be easier to control than a wide-angle split.

Similarly, if black were placed as in the second diagram many would prefer the stopshot from point Y1 rather than the split from point Y2.

Note that from point Y2 the red ball would travel as nearly as possible along the rush-line. There is no point beyond black on the rush-line from which it is possible to load hoop 3 and keep a rush on black to hoop 2.

IDEAL LEAVES

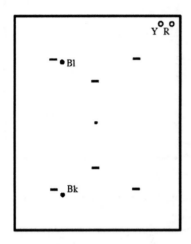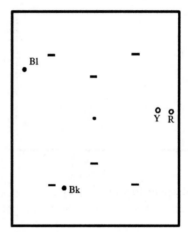

WHEN A PLAYER has developed the ability to make consistent breaks he should start planning "ideal leaves". The planning is done while your opponent is in play. You know where your clips will be when it is your turn, and you ask yourself, "If I cannot make a hoop next turn, but could place the balls wherever I want to, where would be the ideal places to leave them?"

The diagrams show two "ideal leaves" when red is for hoop 1, and yellow is also for hoop 1 or is already on 4-back. Notice that in neither of them are the red and yellow balls anywhere near hoop 1, nor is there a rush set for hoop 1.

If allowed to place the balls anywhere they wish, (barring wired positions), most players would choose a 'leave' inferior to those shown here.

In the first diagram red can cut-rush yellow to the blue ball at hoop 2, then rush blue to hoop 1; or if black shoots at blue and misses then the first rush can be to black.

In the second diagram blue is 1-2 yards in from the border to the side of hoop 2. This allows red (after black moves) to rush yellow out near blue without having to worry about judging the strength of the rush, then put yellow in near hoop 2 while getting a rush on blue to hoop 1.

Either leave gives red about 70% chance (since black has less than 30% chance of roqueting) of a break on the next turn. When it is your turn, unless you can see at least a 50% chance of an immediate break, you should set up such an "ideal leave."

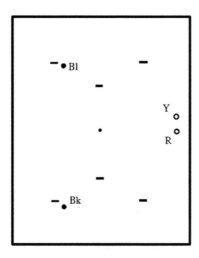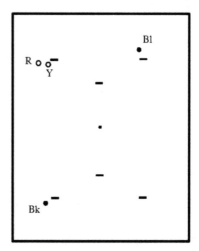

The first diagram shows an "ideal leave" when the red clip is on hoop 2 and yellow is still for hoop 1. Unless the opponent roquets, either red or yellow has at least a 3-ball break on the next turn. After making hoop 1 in any game, if the other balls are placed so that you have a less than even chance of continuing the break, then it is wise to aim instead at achieving a leave such as this.

The red and yellow balls are set parallel to the east border, and preferably 1-2 yards in from the border so that if the opponent shoots at them and misses you will be able to roquet his ball and get it out some distance into the lawn immediately. It is better still if red and yellow are partly wired from one or both of the opponent's balls, but "ideal leaves" should be planned without any thought of wiring, since it is likely that if you have sufficient control of the balls to achieve wired positions, you should have been able to continue the break.

An alternative "ideal leave" for the same clip positions is shown in the second diagram. Here red and yellow are set near hoop 2 rather than on the boundary. This is so that, if black shoots at them and misses, red can run through hoop 2 to the border and immediately bring black into the break. Notice that the 'ideal' position for black in these two leaves is slightly different.

In practice sessions it is good to place the balls in such "ideal leave" positions, shoot with black or blue at any ball, then play the break with red or yellow.

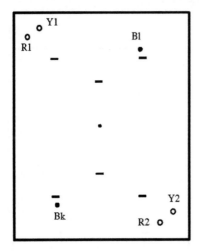 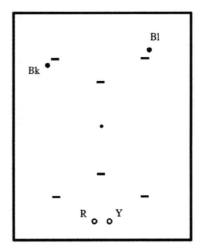

When you have clips on hoops in opposite corners the "ideal leave" is to place an opponent's ball at each of your hoops. In the first diagram red is for hoop 3 and yellow is for hoop 1. The red and yellow balls can be set in either of the other two corners, and are best placed 2-3 yards from the corner on an angle diagonally across the corner as shown.

If red and yellow are in the 4th corner (positions R2 and Y2) then red should be able to rush yellow to a point on the east boundary opposite hoop 4 from where a thick take-off will put yellow in near the hoop while red goes to blue at hoop 3. Alternatively yellow is also threatening to cut-rush red to the south border and send it to hoop 2 with a split-shot in which yellow goes to black at hoop 1.

The second diagram shows another "ideal leave" for the same clip positions. Yellow can cut-rush red to make hoop 1, or red can similarly put yellow at hoop 4 before taking off to the blue ball at hoop 3. The red and yellow balls should be set 2-3 yards in from the border to make the cut-rushes easier, but still allow an opponent ball to be roqueted immediately on the south border if the opponent shoots and misses.

With clips on 2-back and 4-back, or on the other two diagonally opposite corner hoops (i.e. hoops 2 and 4, or 1-back and 3-back) there are corresponding leaves similar to these two. A player with such positions in mind is able to choose whether or not to set up the leave rather than make an unlikely attempt to establish a break immediately in any given situation, and will often succeed in reducing the number of opportunities the opponent has to roquet, which will also increase his own chances of getting a break established before the opponent does.

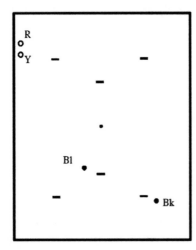 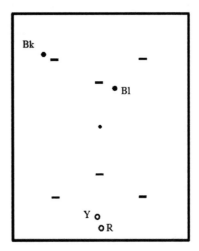

When the two clips are on the same hoop, or one ball is already around, it may be harder to find an "ideal leave" which will guarantee you an easy break if the opponent fails to roquet.

In the first diagram red is for hoop 4. If black is not wired from blue and shoots at it, then a miss will allow red to rush yellow to black, followed by black to blue and blue to hoop 4. Red can cut-rush yellow to blue at hoop 5 in any case.

In this leave the opponent's balls may seem closer together than is desirable. They could be left further apart, but that would decrease your chance of getting the break fully established if, say, the opponent retired with black into the 3rd corner. Therefore it is likely that you would have to allow him further chances to roquet.

It is more aggressive to allow him only the one chance to roquet, and it is also sound tactically as the percentages favour aggressive play.

The second diagram shows a very similar leave if red is on hoop 6 and yellow is on the same hoop or already around. In this case the rush is best set to the black ball at the 1-back hoop.

As explained above, clips on the same hoop usually make it harder to find an "ideal leave". This is one reason, among others, why experienced players tend to refrain from "making a double" by peeling the partner ball through a hoop as they make the same hoop with the other ball.

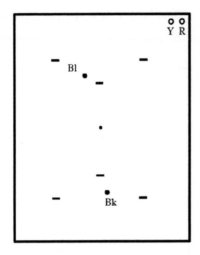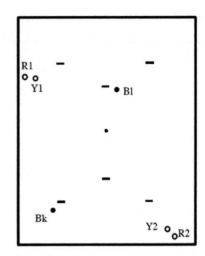

When your clip is on a centre hoop it can be more difficult to find a good leave. In the first diagram red is for hoop 5 and yellow is either already around or is also for hoop 5. The rush could be set to either of the opponent's balls, or, as shown, to the position where black will finish if it shoots at blue and misses. If black plays into the 4th corner then red will have to cut-rush yellow to a position near the blue ball and rush blue to hoop 5.

There is a good chance of wiring black from blue with two centre hoops and the peg in between, but there is also the possibility that blue could take the shot, and with the opponent's balls at the centre hoops you cannot leave your balls more than 15 yards from one of his.

If the yellow clip is still on hoop 1 (and red on hoop 5 as in the first diagram) then a leave such as the one shown in the second diagram (positions R1 and Y1) makes the break simpler to establish provided the opponent does not roquet. Again the rush could be set to hoop 5 instead of to the blue ball at hoop 6. Setting at positions R2 and Y2 leaves the opponent with a longer roquet, but if blue is played into either the 2nd or 3rd corner then yellow will need to play a long split shot from near the 4th corner to put red at hoop 2 while going to black at hoop 1.

A comparison of these two diagrams with those we have given previously will explain why some experienced players try to avoid having their clips on the centre hoops. They achieve this by not making hoop 4 (or possibly even hoop 3—instead they would set an "ideal leave") unless they can keep going and make the centre hoops as well; and by either stopping at 4-back or continuing the break right to the peg.

John Riches and Wayne Davies

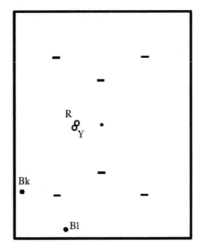 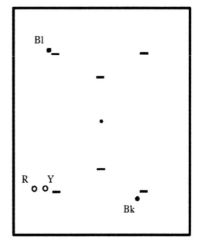

The planning of one or more "ideal-leaves" for the position of your clips during your opponent's turn will enable you to give yourself the best possible chance of getting a break on your next turn in the following situations:

(1) When you have little chance of continuing the current break because balls are out of play.
(2) When you have roqueted with a ball which is already around.
(3) When you wish to set for your partner, especially in handicap doubles if you are the stronger player.

It is surprising how often players reduce their own chances by setting a leave which is clearly inferior because they had not worked out the best possible positions to leave the balls.

In addition to the above uses, you can sometimes go about setting up a break in a way which reserves the option of reaching an "ideal leave" if your attempt is unsuccessful. In the first diagram red is for 2-back and yellow for 1-back. Red has roqueted yellow and should now roll it to a position just west of 2-back while going to black on the border. Black can then be placed at 3-back while red goes to blue, which should be sent to 1-back (yellow's hoop) as red tries for position to run 2-back. If red cannot then make the hoop it can give itself a rush behind yellow, setting up the "ideal leave" shown in the second diagram and giving an easy break on the next turn if the opponent does not roquet. Most players can appreciate the value of this, but it requires the player to have the position of the second diagram clearly in mind at the start of the turn.

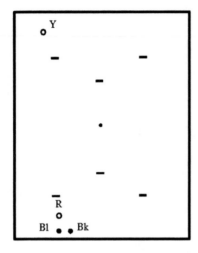 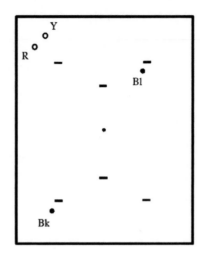

While the practice of working out and using "ideal leaves" may not enjoy universal support among leading players, many have made it an important part of their tactical play.

At international level, where the opponent is likely to roquet almost everything, there is more pressure to go for even the slightest chance of a break rather than electing to set an "ideal leave". For us mere mortals, however, there are several different types of situation, as explained in parts 1-6, where deliberately playing for an "ideal leave" can increase our chances of winning the game.

In fact, one of the most interesting uses is when you know you are not playing well. Perhaps you have not been able to practise recently, or you just do not seem to have the "feel" of the lawn.

In such a state you have arrived at the position shown in the first diagram. The yellow clip is still on hoop 1, but you have muddled your way through two hoops with the red ball, which is now for hoop 3, and have taken off from yellow to the opponent's balls on the south boundary. If you were playing well you may roquet blue and rush black to hoop 3, hoping afterward to get a rush to either yellow or blue and somehow set up a break.

Today you decide instead to roquet black, put it at hoop 1, then send blue to hoop 3 while returning to yellow to set up the "ideal leave" shown in the second diagram. Unless the opponent roquets there will be a ball at one of your hoops on your next turn and a good chance of loading the following hoop. Even when out of touch you should be able to make some progress from here.

NON-STANDARD LEAVES

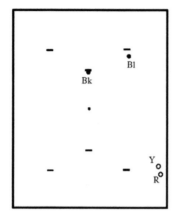
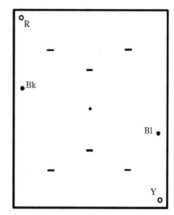

THERE ARE VARIOUS recommended "standard leaves" used by players at top level after they have completed the first nine-hoop break to 4-back or the second 12-hoop break to the peg. They can be found in almost any croquet textbook, together with an explanation of how to arrive at them, how to continue afterward, and what to do when the opponent uses them.

Some are set mainly to give the best chance of a triple peel on the next turn. Since these articles are not intended for players at the top level I will only mention two non-standard leaves which may prove useful.

In the first diagram red is for 4-back and yellow has just gone to the peg and set up as shown. It is not hard to leave black in or on the penultimate hoop if you put 2 balls at the hoop before making 4-back. The only danger is that the opponent will now pick up black and roquet blue, but few players below top level would risk leaving blue at your 4-back hoop.

The second diagram shows what I call the "gala day" leave, since it is particularly useful on small lawns when you have gone around to 4-back and your opponent has a 'lift'. Black and blue should be left about six inches in from the border so that if one of them shoots from where it is at the other and misses you will have an attractive double target.

The distance of blue and black from your balls depends on the ability of your opponent, but should be slightly greater from the ball you have taken to 4-back, since that is the one the opponent will prefer to shoot at. You would need to practise reaching this position, and must start working for it immediately after making 1-back.

FOR THE COACH

I BELIEVE IT is of utmost importance that the ideas covered in this booklet should be passed on as widely as possible to Australian Croquet players. However, many will be unable to learn from diagrams and explanations such as those I have given. Those interested in coaching will face many problems in the teaching of this material.

First of all, and probably most difficult, the players will need to be convinced of the need to spend time doing things which will result in an improvement in their tactical play. Then a judgement must be made as to which tactical ideas a particular player is ready to receive, understand and incorporate into his play, given the level of skill he possesses.

Effective methods of teaching the ideas must also be found. Some coaches have tried using a magnetic board drawn up as a croquet lawn, with coloured markers (glued to small fridge magnets) to represent balls. It seems, however, that only about 30-35% of players (even of those who are keen to learn) are able to transfer the concepts from the magnetic board to an actual game situation.

The most effective way may be to set up positions on the lawn similar to those given in this booklet, then ask a player what he would do if it were his turn, and allow him to do it. This takes time, but he may then be willing to enter into discussion of other possibilities, and try them out. Positions such as those given in the sections on Thinking Ahead (pages 3-5) and Returning To The Partner Ball (pages 8-10) have been found to be particularly effective in convincing players that there is much to learn in the area of tactics. It is important to allow the player to practise the correct tactical moves in as many different ways as possible, in order to fix them in his mind and increase the chance that he will think of them in a game when under pressure.

As one experienced player has commented, the player who understands and adopts tactical moves such as these should never again need to worry about opponents who use the legendary "Aunt Emma" tactics, as the odds will be weighted so much in his favour (given that the difference in shot-making skill level is not too great) that the result will not be in doubt.

On this page I have raised many problems and answered few of them. The answers belong in a coaching manual which may one day become available to coaches. It seems that until now most such manuals have concentrated on technique. Some have tried to set out some basic tactical ideas (and some more advanced ideas, e.g. detailed explanations of triple peeling), but I am not aware that anyone has yet given much consideration of the most effective ways to teach such ideas to players who need to know them.

Digital edition v1.2 2004 by cleinedesign.
email jballant@smartchat.net.au

CROQUET
THE MENTAL APPROACH

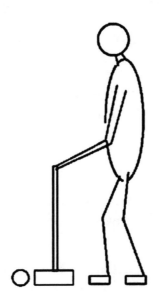

CONTENTS

NOTE: For ease of comprehension I have used male pronouns throughout this booklet when referring to the croquet player in general. It should be understood that the female gender is in all cases included.

ACKNOWLEDGEMENTS: I wish to express my thanks to those who assisted with proofreading of this booklet. Carolyn Spooner, Colin Pickering, Tom Armstrong, Rod Brown and Jane Lewis have all given encouragement and advice which I have greatly appreciated.

Digital edition v1.2 2004 by cleinedesign.
email jballant@smartchat.net.au

INTRODUCTION: PSYCHOLOGY IN CROQUET

A LEADING PLAYER recently remarked to me that in his estimation the winning of croquet matches depended about 70% on mental approach, with the other 30% divided more or less equally between technical skill, tactics, and theory.

Perhaps many of us, particularly those who compete at less exalted levels, would estimate the percentages somewhat differently; but most would agree that psychological considerations play a very important part in the game.

It is surprising, therefore, that few croquet textbooks deal with this topic other than by giving it a brief, passing mention; and few coaches make any attempt to pass on knowledge in this area in any planned or organised manner.

My own understanding of psychology is unfortunately limited. Although I did study the subject for three years, the courses concentrated mainly on the psychology of teaching and learning. This is partly transferable to croquet, especially in relation to coaching, but there are many areas where my knowledge is far from comprehensive. Thus in attempting the task of explaining what I believe to be some of the most important ways in which psychology intrudes into our game, I am aware of my limitations and cannot claim to be making any sort of definitive statement. However, I am also aware that if do not attempt it, it may be a long time before anyone else does. It seems that the passing on of incomplete knowledge in this area to our students of the game may be better than passing on none at all. At least it will be a start which others can develop further.

I have made contact in some detail with professional sports psychologists. They tend to deal, as expected, with established methods of relaxation, maintaining concentration, goal setting and visualisation, risk-taking, etc., as used in the coaching and playing of other sports. However, they readily admit that they are uncertain about the extent to which these things apply in the game of croquet; and they have no knowledge at all of various psychological considerations which are peculiar to our game.

I hope that the reader will use what follows as a suggested starting point in the search for the correct mental approach to the game of croquet.

PSYCHING DOWN

I CAME TO croquet after many years of playing competitive sports such as football, tennis, squash and basketball. It is commonly accepted that maximum performance in these sports depends largely on the ability of coaches to ensure that players are "psyched up" before a game. This involves developing in the player a mind-set of absolute determination, readiness to give 100% effort, continuous concentration, and a competitiveness that borders on desperation.

It did not take me long to discover that such a mind-set is largely counter-productive in the game of croquet. For my first tournament of any consequence I was invited down from the country to play against others who were under consideration for state selection. In talking to the other players at the start of the tournament I was surprised to learn that none of them gave himself any chance of winning the tournament, for various reasons which they explained at length. Furthermore, it did not seem to concern them at all, because they were not interested in getting into the state team anyway! Apparently they had all only entered the tournament to gain experience or in order to make up the numbers.

In view of this, I decided that if I really tried hard and gave it my best effort I should have an excellent chance of winning almost every game. My opponents in several games reaffirmed before we started that they expected me to beat them quite easily.

It will not surprise the experienced croquet player to learn that I hardly won a game in that tournament. My opponents, regardless of what they said, were all hoping to win the tournament. They were not trying to 'con' me with what they told me, but were going through an essential process of 'psyching themselves down'. They were actually trying to convince themselves that there was nothing of importance riding on the games. This was all an attempt to overcome nervousness, reduce tension, and allow themselves to approach the games in a relaxed frame of mind.

In the more active sports mentioned above a player who starts to relax during a game is hardly likely to be successful. If he is on a football field, the coach may quickly remove him from the game. However, there are sports such as golf, darts, snooker, archery, rifle shooting and croquet where a relaxed approach is essential to maximum performance, and the ability to psych yourself down, rather than up, is highly desirable.

It is not certain that this applies to all players. I have heard of a player, for example, whose opponent reportedly made a remark which she thought was deliberately calculated to upset her. She claimed, however, that it actually made her all the more determined to win. She started to grit her teeth and tell herself that there was no way she was going to lose to such an ill-mannered opponent. She played the game of her life and won handsomely. She certainly did not seem to have relaxed in any way, but played better than ever before.

If I knew more about psychology I may be able to explain this. All I can say is that the great majority of players need to be relaxed before they can expect to play well. Perhaps there is a distinction to be made between relaxation and nervelessness. The player was apparently not relaxed, but neither was she nervous. She had great determination, which is a good thing as long as it can be dissociated from nervousness. The determination may have led to greater than normal concentration.

Relaxation can be overdone and taken to a point where it breeds a degree of carelessness which can be just as disastrous for the croquet player as nervous tension. A balance is needed, and relaxation need not entail any lack of concentration. Indeed, it is likely that most players can concentrate better and for longer when relaxed than when tense.

OVERCOMING NERVOUSNESS

THE FIRST IMPORTANT thing to understand about nervousness is that there is no sense in getting worried about the fact that you are nervous, as this will only make things worse. All croquet players experience some degree of nervousness before and during important games. With some it has a more severe effect and lasts longer than with others. One comforting thought is that nervousness tends to decrease with experience. As you enter more tournaments and play more important games you tend to be less nervous because you instead begin to feel that you have "been there, done that" so many times before. This allows you more chance of overcoming the nervousness before its effect has been disastrous. However, some nervousness will always be there in most players.

The main effects of nervousness are seen at the start of a game, but many players find that the nerves can return at a later stage of the game after they had seemed to have settled down. This is particularly likely to occur in a tight finish where every shot becomes critical. An attack of nerves can come upon the player all of a sudden. Some players "suddenly freeze" when faced with making, say, a four-foot hoop which could decide the game.

It is evident that nervousness has both physical and mental effects on the player. The muscles are affected so as to lose coordination, and the limbs tend to twitch, shake and move jerkily. In addition, timing is affected so that rhythm is destroyed, and the player is likely to experience a 'mental blank' which may cause him to play the wrong ball, run a wrong hoop, forget that he has given a 'lift', or overlook an essential element of shot technique.

The techniques used by players in attempting to overcome an attack of nerves are many and varied. We can mention here only a few of the most common and more interesting methods.

2.1 Exercises and breathing

Some have found it helpful to go through a warm-up (or psych-down) programme before starting a game. This can involve such things as taking a light jog or a warm shower, silent meditation, imagining yourself in tranquil surroundings, listening to soothing music, walking around the lawn to view it from all angles, sitting or lying absolutely still for a few minutes, physical exercises designed to loosen and stretch muscles, etc. Others have resorted to chewing, smoking, drinking, eating particular foods, fasting, or taking tranquilisers.

2.2 Specific relaxation programmes

Many players go through a specifically designed programme in order to promote relaxation and reduce the effect of nervous tension. Sports psychologists are able (for a fee) to assist players in preparing various types of relaxation programme which may involve mental imaging, concentration on relaxing particular sets of muscles, etc. For example, the player may be advised to practise at home going through a series of simple relaxation exercises in which groups of muscles are tightened, then relaxed. This may culminate in, say, the clenching and then relaxing of the right fist, by which time a state of near total relaxation has been achieved. The intention is to create in the player's mind an association between total relaxation and the unclenching of the right fist, so that during a game the clenching and unclenching of the fist is sufficient to bring about a similar state of relaxation.

Some players wear headphones attached to a small portable cassette player carried in the pocket. On the tape they have relaxing music or soothing voices. This also serves to minimise distraction from traffic and other noises, but makes it rather difficult for the opponent to forestall a shot in cases where he is entitled or expected to do so. One could question whether this could amount to receiving assistance contrary to the rules of the game, and there is the possibility that a tape could contain specific instruction on points to remember when playing the shots.

The famous violinist Yehudi Menhuin once explained the secret of how he managed to appear so relaxed when performing in public.

"When I walk on stage I simply imagine what everyone in the audience would look like if they were all sitting there in their underwear. The image brought to mind is so amusing that it is impossible to continue to feel nervous, no matter how important the personages in the front row may be."

We will probably never know whether or not such an approach works in croquet, as no-one (including me) is ever likely to admit to having used it.

Apart from tranquilisers and the occasional shot of brandy which some players use in an attempt to steady their nerves, there is the possibility that beneficial effects can be obtained by giving special attention to diet before an important match. Some claim that it helps if they eat, or avoid eating, particular types of food. There is so little agreement on this point that it is difficult to pass on any useful advice. Some say that if they eat anything at all immediately before a game they are likely to feel churned up inside once the game starts; while others share my own theory that the more food there is in your stomach, the less room there is for the 'butterflies' to fly around.

2.3 Dress

Experienced players are aware of the importance of dressing in a way that allows you to feel as comfortable and relaxed as possible. New shoes and tight shirts, belts or skirts should not be worn in important matches. Some wear gloves which keep their hands warmer in cold weather, and hats or eye-shades which enable them to feel more comfortable when out in the hot sun. Women may feel more comfortable in a divided skirt or shorts than in either trousers or a dress. By giving some thought to the matter of what you should wear, it is possible to reduce (or at least not add to) the nervous tension felt during a game. Whenever the National championships are held in Hobart players from the mainland states should consider the advisability of practising wearing gloves beforehand. In past years some have discovered that the bitingly cold winds can make their hands and fingers quite numb, but gloves worn for the first time in an attempt to overcome the problem are likely to create new and unforeseen problems of their own and thereby increase nervous tension.

When discussing these things at a country tournament some time ago, one attractive young lady said that on one hot day she had gone out to practise with a friend without wearing a bra, and was surprised at how relaxed she felt, and how well she played. While we do not suggest that such drastic measures should be generally adopted, we do re-emphasise the importance of wearing clothing in which one can feel comfortable and relaxed.

2.4 Relaxing activities

During a game, some players are prone to whistle or talk to themselves (or to others) as a means of promoting relaxation. Others may smoke, walk up and down, or go for a short jog.

It was my good friend Tom Armstrong who first pointed out to me the importance of visiting the toilet after making a break under pressure. At the time I wondered whether he was joking, but he most certainly was not.

"You can't play good croquet with a full bladder," he said, "The removal of excess fluid will reduce nervous tension and take at least three bisques off your handicap". I can testify that for me personally he was correct on both counts. Perhaps there is a case to be made for refraining from drinking too much before or during a game.

The cups of tea associated with croquet from time immemorial may be having a detrimental effect on the standard of play!

2.5 Outside influences

Players are often affected by external things which can increase nervous tension. Some claim that they cannot play well when their spouse, or some other person from their club, is watching. The spouse can usually be banished if he/she is causing a problem, but other spectators are less subject to direct control. Anyone has a right to watch any game, so you need to find a way of preventing their presence from affecting your play.

The only real answer to this is to make up your mind that you are not going to LET it affect you. This can certainly be done, and can be possibly the most effective solution to the problem of nervousness in general. A dramatic example occurred recently at our club, with a player who played well in practice games and club matches, but when he played in tournaments or matches at the S.A.C.A. headquarters against players from other clubs, his nerves "went to pieces", and he was constantly missing short roquets and sticking in the easiest of hoops. He would not attempt shots that he could play with ease on our home lawns, for fear that he would mess them up. I had suggested various ways of dealing with the problem, but nothing seemed to work, and I had concluded that he would probably never be able to play well under pressure.

Then, one day, he entered another tournament and told me that he was simply not going to let nerves affect him—he was going to go out and play the shots that ought to be played, and not worry about it, whether they turned out as desired or not.

"I have suddenly realised that if I miss a shot the earth is not going to open up and swallow me," he said, "so from now on I'm just going to go out and enjoy myself."

I was sceptical about whether he could do this, but in fact he played quite well and won the tournament. I am not sure how many players would be able to overcome nervousness as he apparently did, by sheer willpower alone; but for those who can do it, it is certainly the most effective and immediate solution to the problem that I have seen.

Conversation and comments from spectators can also upset and/or distract a player, possibly making him more nervous. For this reason, some officials at important events have attempted to prevent spectators from sitting with players or talking to them at all. However, some players tell me that they welcome conversation with spectators as it tends to help them relax and take their mind off the stupid thing they did in the last turn. Explaining your actions and joking about it with a sympathetic listener does indeed seem a useful way of removing tension in such situations, but it is also important to be able to then dismiss the thing from your thoughts and prepare to concentrate fully on the next turn.

If you tend to be more nervous in unfamiliar surroundings, arrive early at a competition venue with which you are unfamiliar, so you can walk around the lawns and survey them from every possible angle, looking for slopes, rough areas, patches of heavy grass, etc. Even for those not particularly prone to nervousness this seems like good advice; and if you are one of those struggling to cope with nervous tension it is essential that you do everything you can to help yourself feel more comfortable and familiar with the game situation.

2.6 Technique

There is a definite connection between technique and nervousness, and players should be able to modify their shot-making technique so as to lessen the harmful effects of nervous tension.

The nervous player usually finds that during the swing he is involuntarily lifting his head and shoulders ("coming up for a look"), and this is accompanied by shaking or twitching in the hands and possibly knees. This can partly be overcome before starting the swing by ensuring that your stance is comfortable and well balanced, toes are relaxed, and shoulders also relaxed instead of being "hunched up".

The shaking in the hands and wrists is more difficult to overcome, but it is at least possible to take some measures to lessen its effect:

(1) A heavy mallet is less likely to shake as much as a light one, simply because a greater force is needed to move it off line.

(2) A lighter than normal grip should be used. Unfortunately, a player who is nervous and tense usually tends to grip the mallet more tightly than ever, thus transmitting the shaking of the hands directly to the mallet head.

(3) You may find it helpful to move both hands together well down the mallet shaft when nervous, especially for hoop-running. With a long grip a slight movement of the hands can tend to be magnified as it causes a corresponding movement in the mallet head, so that a small sideways movement of, say, half a centimetre in the hands can cause the mallet head to move several centimetres to one side and hit the ball well off centre or miss it completely. The shorter grip tends to lessen this unwanted effect and also makes it easier to swing directly (and only) from the shoulders. There are certainly disadvantages also associated with shortening the grip, such

as loss of power and difficulty of maintaining alignment; but the nervous player may well find that, at least until he "settles down", the advantages outweigh the disadvantages.

2.7 "Desperado" effect

Most players are familiar, in one way or another, with what I call the "desperado" effect.

This occurs when a player is convinced that he has nothing whatever to lose, so he may as well relax and "go for everything". A player in such a frame of mind can be a very dangerous opponent, as the fact that he is completely relaxed makes him tend to play exceptionally well.

In the first round of a country tournament I recently played a game in which this phenomenon was particularly noticeable. It was the first round of the championship singles, with divisions 1 and 2 combined. My opponent was a lady to whom I would have had to give six bisques in a handicap event. She convinced herself before we began that she had no chance of winning, so she may as well relax and enjoy herself.

She started by roqueting everything she went for, and running several ridiculously long hoops from near impossible angles; and continued in such fashion to make three sizeable breaks while I had not managed to hit a roquet. I knew what was happening and was starting to wonder whether she was likely to keep it up for the whole game, when I received some unexpected help from one of her clubmates who came over and asked her how she was doing.

"Oh, I've started quite well", she said, "I'm on four-back and one-back and he hasn't started yet."

"That's great", said the clubmate, "If you are careful you should have a good chance of winning."

This was exactly the advice my opponent did not need. Once she realised that she did indeed have a chance of beating me, she started to play more carefully and did not make another hoop.

The trouble with using the "desperado effect" as a cure for nervousness is that it only works in situations where there genuinely is nothing to lose. However, it is important to understand it, and so avoid becoming nervous yourself when your opponent is playing as mine did.

Other situations where this effect is frequently seen include turns after the bell (which for this very reason I believe are unfair), and games in which one of the players is left with a single ball.

2.8 Role of partner in doubles

In a game of doubles a player may say or do things which can have a dramatic effect on the state of mind of his partner.

It is important to do everything you can to encourage your partner and help him to relax. Some players like to be left alone during their turn to make their own decisions and play their own game.

This is rather foolish of them, as two heads are better than one, and the partner may suggest things which otherwise would have been overlooked. However, the suggestions should always be made in a way that will increase, rather than undermine, the player's confidence in his own game.

In general, it is good psychology to suggest that your partner go for shots that he seems a bit hesitant about attempting, rather than saying, "Well, if you are not confident of getting it, you'd better play safe." This is especially true when there is much to gain if the shot is successful. Similarly, it is poor psychology to attempt to dissuade a partner from taking a risk, unless it is apparent that he has overlooked something such as a 'lift' which the opponents will be entitled to.

Thus in almost any situation it is most likely to increase your partner's confidence if you encourage him to take risks rather than play safe. In many cases this will also prove to be the best move tactically, as 'selective memory' (which will be explained later) causes the great majority of players to avoid taking risks which should be taken, while very few are guilty of taking risks which should not be taken.

For similar reasons it is usually unwise to follow your partner around the lawn during a turn, supervising him in every little detail, unless he is a raw beginner.

2.9 The out player

Another important factor in overcoming nervousness is knowing what to do when you are the "out player". The out player is the one who does not have the innings. In most cases this means that you are watching your opponent make a break, or while he manoeuvres for position. Instead of worrying about the number of hoops he is making and how far behind you are getting, you should use the time to concentrate on noticing and thinking about things such as those listed below, that will be of use to you when you finally manage to gain the innings. The result will be that you have already thought about many of the things that can tend to prevent your shots from turning out as intended. This can have an important effect on your mental approach to the game, as nothing increases nervousness more than shots which go astray for no apparent reason.

Some of the things the out player should concentrate on are:

(1) The speed and slope of the lawn.

By watching the opponent's shots carefully you should be able to see whether they are falling short, going too far, or curving off to one side. This will give you an indication of the speed of the lawn and whether it slopes inward or outward in certain areas.

(2) Playing conditions.

If, for example, there is a strong wind blowing, you should try to gauge its effect on your opponent's shots and work out ways of minimising its effect on your own shots when you get in. If it is raining you should look for parts of the lawn which show signs of becoming waterlogged. You should also take note of whether the lawn surface is hard and firm, or sandy or spongy, as jump shots may be difficult and inadvisable on the softer type of surface.

(3) The ability and style of the opponent.

As he makes his break you should note the accuracy (or lack of it) with which he plays his shots; his willingness to take risks to keep the break going or tendency to avoid risks by playing safe wherever possible; his ability to take off or rush accurately across the lawn and play very sharp stop-shots or long rolls, or cut-rushes, etc. This knowledge can help you decide on the risks you can afford to take when it is your turn to play.

For example, if he has left both of his balls near his hoop you may need to decide whether to shoot at them, knowing that a miss would allow him to attempt a five-yard roquet on your ball and set up a break. Against a player who has shown that he does not like taking risks, and whose roquet action looks a bit suspect, such a shot may be well worth taking. Similarly, if the opponent leaves his two balls together on the border it may be worth shooting at them and giving him three balls together if you know that he cannot play the stop-shot required to send one of them across the lawn to a hoop while staying close enough to turn around and be certain of roqueting the other ball. Without such a shot his chance of setting up a break may be small enough to make the risk worth taking.

(4) Possible leaves.

It can be very helpful to look at the position of your own clips and work out one or more "ideal leaves" which you may be able to use when you get in. In many cases you may manage to make a roquet, but your chance of making a hoop or getting a break going may be extremely remote because the other two balls are on the border in remote parts of the lawn. The best you can hope to do is to go and get them off the border and leave them out in the lawn where you may be able to use them to set up a break next turn, provided your opponent does not roquet.

Unfortunately, many players have little idea of the BEST places to leave the balls in such situations, and realise later that they should have left them differently. The time to work out the best leave is during the opponent's previous turn, since you already know where your clips will be when your turn comes around. This is much better than relying on your ability to think of a good leave on the spur of the moment, or worse still leaving it until you have already played some of your shots and no longer have any chance of controlling the positions of some of the balls. (This topic of 'ideal leaves' is explained in much greater detail in my booklet "Croquet: Next Break Strategy". but is mostly outside the scope of a booklet on psychological aspects of the game.)

In addition to improving your tactics, concentration on such positive thinking will take your thoughts away from things which would increase your nervous tension.

CONFIDENCE BUILDING

O NE OF THE main problems with nervousness is that it is associated with lack of confidence. In some situations the nervousness may CAUSE a lack of confidence in your own ability to play shots successfully in a match which you know you can play in practice. At other times it may be the other way around, so that the nervousness may be CAUSED BY a lack of confidence which results from some other factor. In the latter case it may be possible to find ways of overcoming the lack of confidence and thus removing the cause of your nervousness.

For example, you may be about to play an opponent who is recognised as a much stronger player than you, or in conditions with which you are unfamiliar. It may be helpful to "psych yourself down" or adopt the "desperado" approach or remind yourself that your opponent has to cope with the same conditions. Perhaps the best piece of advice comes from a world-class chess player who was noted for his confident, attacking style, although his general manner gave an impression of retiring timidity. When asked how he managed to do it, he explained, "Even when I am not confident, I try to play as if I am!"

This advice seems more relevant to croquet than to chess, since confidence probably plays an even greater part in determining the results of many games. Some players are apparently able to play cautiously at the start of a game and then start to play more adventurously after they have settled down a bit, but this approach is less likely to be successful as your standard of play, and that of your opponents, improves. The danger is that you may never be allowed to settle down against an opponent who takes full advantage of the early opportunities offered by your "cautious" approach, and is able to keep you under pressure from then on.

From a psychological point of view it would seem more advisable to "play as if you are confident" in the early stages of the game when your opponent may not have "settled down" sufficiently to take full advantage of any mistakes. Far more games are lost by failing to take risks which should have been taken than are lost by taking risks that should not have been taken.

3.1 Coping with pressure

An area in which many players can improve their mental approach is their ability to play "pressure" shots with confidence. A longish hoop that HAS to be made, or a five-yard roquet which you SHOULD make, but will give an easy break to your opponent if you miss, are common examples of shots which need to be played confidently. How is it possible to be confident when you know that you are by no means certain to make the hoop; and although you should expect to make the roquet, it is also quite missable?

In such situations you do not need to attempt to hypnotise yourself into believing that you WILL run the hoop or make the roquet. Some players may be able to achieve such a happy (and unrealistic) mental state, but most of us are too experienced to be able to fool ourselves so easily.

It should be possible, however, to at least convince yourself that by attempting the shot you are giving yourself the best possible chance of winning the game. There is no certainty involved certainties in croquet are as rare as they are in politics, economics or horse-racing—but you know there is nothing else you could do to give yourself any better chance of winning than what you are doing. Perhaps there is a similarity to the 'desperado' mental approach here, but without the drawback of it being difficult to sustain. Such a mental approach should allow you to play the shot confidently, even though you are well aware that success is not guaranteed.

Your confidence may be further increased by the well-founded belief that against most opponents if you keep on attempting the things that give you the best possible chance of winning, the odds will be weighted enormously in your favour. It is like playing a coin-tossing game with an opponent who, in order to win, must call correctly on seven or eight tosses out of ten. There is no certainty that he won't be able to do it, but there is plenty of reason for you to be quietly confident.

3.2 Coping with frustration

Against some opponents you will find yourself having to cope with tactics designed to frustrate you rather than pressure you into making errors. Instead of placing his balls so that he is ready to take advantage of any slight error you make, this type of opponent will place them so that you have difficulty doing anything with them. In playing most of your shots you will not be under the pressure of knowing that failure will lead to certain disaster; but you will be under a different type of pressure which arises from the frustration of not being able to make much noticeable progress when you feel that you ought to be getting somewhere.

It is usually a bad policy to try making hoops one at a time with your own two balls when your opponent's balls are out of play and well separated. This allows him to keep shooting at your balls, or occasionally at his partner ball. His shots can be taken in a relaxed frame of mind, since in most cases a miss is unlikely to cost him anything more than allowing you to roll to the next hoop. When he does succeed in roqueting he is likely to be able to use your balls to make more hoops than you have been able to make with only two balls. Worse still, the roquet he makes always seems to come at a time when you at last have the balls well placed for a possible break; and this adds to your frustration.

The answer to this problem lies in the realm of tactics. There is no need to allow play to continue for turn after turn in which you can only hope to make one hoop at best. Consider the position shown in diagram 1 where you are playing with the red and yellow balls which are both in the fourth corner. All clips are on hoop 1 and the opponent's balls are together in the second corner. Take off to them but do not simply try to rush one of them out and make your hoop while the other opponent ball and your partner ball are both left near the border out of play.

There is the risk that you will stick in the hoop with the opponent ball handy, or that you will have to return to your partner ball in the fourth corner and allow him the chance of roqueting his partner ball as he goes back to it in the second corner. Even if he fails to roquet, you again have to play a long take-off followed by a roquet which in many cases will be far from a certainty. Such risks are simply not worth taking when all that you stand to gain if they come off is one hoop!

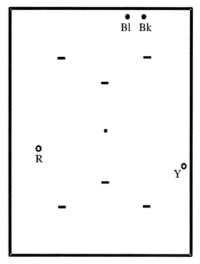

Diagram 2

Instead, stop-shot one opponent ball out into the lawn, then turn around, roquet the other and send it also out to a place where you will be able to use it. In this case you could place them at hoop 2 and hoop 1. When you return to your partner ball in the fourth corner, be sure that in doing so you leave one of your balls with a useful rush. Your opponent will have one chance to roquet, but he can move only one ball, and if you have placed the balls carefully then a miss should allow you to use his other ball to make several hoops with the three balls in play.

If the opponent's balls are left on the border but well apart, it may still be possible to get them both out into the lawn by taking off to one of them and sending it into the lawn while going to the other. If this is too difficult. then you should at least be able to put the first opponent ball into the lawn and return to your partner ball with a rush set to the other opponent ball. This will make it dangerous for him to join up, and if he again places his balls well apart you can take the rush to one of his balls and then rush it out into the lawn, after which a take-off to the other opponent ball will allow you again to achieve the desired situation. There will often be other and possibly better ways of going about things; but the thing to remember is that if you find that the tactics of your opponent are starting to frustrate you, then you should think of a way to prevent him from continuing them. In the situations described where you have the innings this should not be too difficult to do.

A different type of frustration arises when it is your opponent who has the innings and is content to make one hoop at a time, keeping your balls widely separated but usually out of play in the style of the legendary "Aunt Emma".

The best answer is to keep the opponent under pressure by placing your balls so that you are threatening to take advantage of any error he makes. It is important to retain confidence that when you do at last manage to make a long roquet you can expect to make more hoops than your opponent has been able to make. You must also be prepared to take risks in order to give yourself the best chance of obtaining the innings as early as possible. In many cases you should shoot at his balls rather than returning to your partner ball, especially if they present some sort of double target, but often even if they are both on the border without a useful rush.

In diagram 2, for example, with all clips on the first hoop, suppose that you are playing with the red and yellow balls. Your opponent had roqueted red and taken off unsuccessfully for hoop 1, then hit out near his partner ball on the north border as shown.

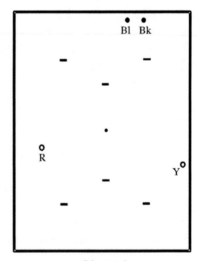

Diagram 2

Even though he has no rush to his hoop, you should shoot with red at the opponent's balls. This is far better than "finessing" by hitting the red ball out of play into either the first or fourth corner. Note that shooting with red at yellow is too dangerous because a miss would allow your opponent to play black, rushing blue to hoop 2, then taking off to your balls and rushing one of them to hoop 1 to set up a break. A player who adopts the "Aunt Emma" style is unlikely to be able to make effective use of the third ball in most situations, so it is usually worth taking the risk of attempting whichever shot you are most likely to roquet.

The positive mental approach involved in your adoption of such tactics will tend to bring its own dividends in other ways as well. Hitting your ball into a corner without making any attempt to roquet takes pressure off the opponent and allows his nerves to become more settled.

3.3 Visualisation

As in many other sports, visualisation can play an important role in the mental approach of the croquet player.

Just as a high jumper prepares to jump by imagining himself sailing over the bar, the croquet player can build confidence by pausing before playing a shot and forming a mental image of the shot being played successfully. This could involve "seeing" in your imagination the striker's ball running straight across the lawn and making a perfect roquet or making a hoop with the greatest of ease. Many players can also "see" the ball as it comes off the mallet face with a particular type of spin, enabling them to better judge the amount of 'pull' or 'roll' that will be imparted to the ball.

Visualisation also provides a means of correcting errors before they become serious. If you form a clear mental picture of how both balls will behave in a split shot, for example, you can then check whether or not the balls do, in fact, behave as expected. If not (e.g. one falls short and the other goes too far) then you should ask yourself why, and work out the adjustment needed the next time you play a similar shot. A player who has no clear mental picture of what he expects the balls to do will have no way of knowing whether or not they did it, so is likely to continue making the same errors in future shots of the same type.

To facilitate visualisation of the type of swing you intend to use, you could practise the swing alongside the ball before playing the shot. For hoop shots in particular many players find this helpful.

3.4 The uncertainty principle

In croquet the "Uncertainty Principle" bears no relation to the similarly named principle in mathematical probability and quantum physics.

It simply says that a shot is less likely to be successful if the player is unsure about whether he should be playing it. Some players are extremely skilful at taking advantage of this principle, and when playing against them you continually find yourself in considerable doubt about which shot you should play and whether or not you should be taking a particular risk.

After missing a shot you keep thinking, "I knew I shouldn't have tried that". Consequently it is difficult to approach any shot with confidence and soon your whole mental approach can become tentative and timid.

Many players cope better if they are left with longer roquets, provided they at least know they are doing the right thing in attempting them. Then they may still miss, but they will not blame themselves for having made a wrong decision, so their future play is not affected.

In order to overcome the problem of uncertainty leading to doubt, self-blame, and increased tension, it is necessary to pause before playing a shot and give yourself time to consider the situation from every angle. You need to assess the chance of the various shots on offer being successful, and the extent to which an unsuccessful shot would be disastrous. Then you must make a definite decision about which shot you will play. If two or more shots seem equally attractive after careful reflection, then choose one of them and be done with it. In general, if there is no other clear way of deciding, it pays to choose the shot which if successful offers the greatest gain.

Do not in any way prepare to play a shot until the decision has been finally made. Then, once the choice is made, DO NOT go back over it. Turn your whole attention to the things (stance, grip, swing, follow-through, etc.) which you need to get right to make the shot you have chosen successful. If you happen to miss, simply tell yourself that the shot had to be attempted in that particular situation. By all means ask yourself what made the shot unsuccessful and try to correct it in future shots, but do not dwell any longer on whether or not you should have done something else. We can certainly learn from our mistakes, but the time to look back and reassess your decisions is after the game is finished, not while it is still in progress.

There are many situations in life when a decision has to be made based on incomplete information and a largely subjective assessment of the likely outcomes of the alternatives. The fact that a decision has resulted in disaster does not prove that it was a wrong decision at the time it was made. If further information had been available then a different decision may have been made, but the decision made was the only reasonable one in view of what was known at the time.

So it is in croquet. You may have assessed the risk involved in playing a particular shot as worth taking, but after missing it you find that your opponent proceeds to make an all-round break which he starts by playing two or three shots that you did not think he was likely to be to play successfully. This does not mean that your decision was wrong, and there is no sense in blaming yourself for having taken the wrong shot. Perhaps in future you may assess risks differently when playing against the same opponent, but in all probability he could not do it again and your decision was, in fact, correct in the sense that by attempting it you were giving yourself the best possible chance of winning. The fact that you in fact lost proves nothing, as no other course of action would have GUARANTEED a win. You could have lost as easily—in fact more easily—if you had made a different choice.

On the other hand, if your opponent takes advantage of your miss by adopting a simple course of action which you had failed to take into consideration, then perhaps it is in order to give yourself a quick mental kick in the pants to ensure that the pain felt is sufficient to encourage you to be more careful in future when making the assessment of which shot to play.

3.5 Destroying confidence

We have already seen that one way of destroying your opponent's confidence is to create uncertainty in his mind about which shot he should be playing. This requires careful planning. For example, suppose that your clips are still on the first hoop and you have made a roquet but have virtually no chance of making an immediate break, so you decide to get the opponent's balls from the border and leave them out in the lawn, hoping to be able to use them in a break next turn.

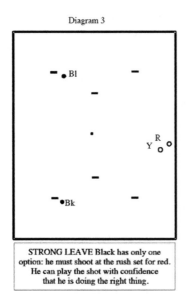

Diagram 3

STRONG LEAVE Black has only one option: he must shoot at the rush set for red. He can play the shot with confidence that he is doing the right thing.

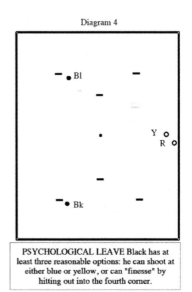

Diagram 4

PSYCHOLOGICAL LEAVE Black has at least three reasonable options: he can shoot at either blue or yellow, or can "finesse" by hitting out into the fourth corner.

The obvious leave is to send his balls to hoop 1 and hoop 2, and place your own balls somewhere near the east border between hoops 3 and 4, with a rush set to hoop 1 (see diagram 3). Then he is forced to move the ball at hoop 1, and unless he roquets you will be able to play your rush to hoop 1 with at least a three-ball break.

However, there is a danger that such a leave can be TOO good. Your opponent is more or less forced to shoot at your balls, even if your rush is set perfectly and he has only a single-ball target. There is no sense in him playing the ball into a corner to take it out of play, since you have a three-ball break anyway. Therefore he can shoot at your balls with certainty that it is his only chance of preventing your immediate break, and knowing that if he misses he will be giving you little more than you already have. This allows him to approach the shot in a relaxed, nothing-to-lose frame of mind.

By setting your rush for the boundary behind hoop 2 instead of for hoop 1 (diagram 4), you can produce an entirely different situation. Now a shot at your balls by the opponent, if missed, will give you a rush to hoop 1 which you do not already have. He must also consider shooting at his ball near hoop 2 and so must assess your chance, if he misses, of rushing to his ball on the border behind hoop 2, rushing that ball out to hoop 2, and rushing the ball from hoop 2 to hoop 1 to set up a four-ball break. Finally, he has to decide whether it would pay him to hit his ball into, say, the fourth corner, which would allow you to rush to his ball at hoop 2 and then rush that ball to hoop 1. In this case you would still have a three-ball break and he has passed up a chance to roquet.

Most players find it difficult to decide on the correct course of action in such a situation, so the uncertainty principle comes into operation. If they decide to attempt a roquet they are less likely to hit it than in the previous situation when they had virtually nothing to lose. This psychological consideration may well outweigh the fact that if the opponent misses you are committing yourself to playing two good rushes instead of one in order to start your break.

Apart from such legitimate use of tactics to undermine your opponent's confidence, there are numerous more devious and less ethical ways.

One player I knew would always make a point of asking about his opponent's health before starting a game, and would sympathise fervently over every slight condition mentioned. This served to encourage the opponent to believe that he could not hope to play good croquet with his health in such a precarious condition, and would keep him thinking about his aches and pains rather than his playing technique. Perhaps there is a danger that the sympathy could be overdone to the extent that the opponent becomes convinced he has no chance at all, bringing a "desperado" mindset into operation.

On another occasion I heard a player at the start of a game commenting on the "difficult cross-wind which would make good croquet almost impossible". After the game I suggested that he was in danger of talking himself out of any chance of playing well. He assured me, however, that he was not really worried about the wind which was not all that strong anyway. The comment had been entirely for the benefit of his opponent, who was known to be a slow starter.

"He always takes some time to get his shots sorted out", I was told.

"If he thinks that the wind is mainly to blame for his misses he will be less strenuous in his efforts to discover the real problem, which would almost certainly be a minor error in technique."

I am sure that the number of such psychological ploys designed to help destroy an opponent's confidence is limited only by the imagination, and possibly the ethics, of the player using them.

3.6 Psychological effect of wiring, peeling, etc.

Tactics such as wiring, peeling and pegging out the opponent's balls can also have a noticeable psychological effect.

Some years ago I was taught by an older player to wire the opponent's balls at the peg after making a break to 4-back. Later I realised that it would be far easier to simply leave one of the opponent's balls east of the peg and the other ball two or three yards south-west of hoop 2. In practical terms the result was the same, since he would inevitably lift the ball near hoop 2 and shoot with it from baulk.

However, by then I had also come to realise that the wiring seemed to have a psychological effect on many opponents, producing a sense of frustration or defeatism that was not in evidence when they were faced with the simpler but equivalent leave.

I discovered that peeling can also be used psychologically, when on one occasion I was playing a doubles match in which an opponent stuck in the penultimate hoop with my partner's ball present and the other two balls out of play. My partner roqueted the opponent ball gently and then peeled it through penultimate before hitting out near my ball on the border. I asked him why he had chosen to assist the opponent by making a hoop for him which he had been trying unsuccessfully to make, and whether he was intending to try to peel the opponent ball again through rover and peg it out.

"Probably not", he replied, "But I want him to think that I might." And for the rest of the game the opponents went to great lengths to keep the peeled ball out of play. If the opponent himself had succeeded in taking his ball to rover or even the peg, I doubt that they would have been so worried about the possibility of us pegging the ball out; but the peel seemed to convince them that we would be desperately trying to do so. They managed to prevent us from pegging the ball out, but hardly made any further hoops. We won the game far more easily than I imagine we would have done without the psychological penultimate peel.

Most players are aware that the pegging out of an opponent's ball can itself have a pronounced psychological effect. Some players foolishly adopt the attitude that once their ball has been pegged out they no longer have any chance of winning, so they give up trying and stop thinking, merely going through the motions while awaiting the inevitable end of the game. Others decide that they have nothing to lose, so they go for everything in more or less desperado fashion. This is certainly preferable to giving up, but the best approach must surely lie somewhere in between.

3.7 Realistic aims

If they miss two or three longish roquets, there are players who instead of trying to work out why the roquets are missing, say "I just can't roquet today", and resign themselves to accepting the inevitable result. Their confidence has been destroyed because they seem to have set themselves the aim of making every roquet, and are expecting too much of themselves. It is far better to set realistic aims which enable you to maintain a positive approach when things start to go wrong. A preferable attitude is the one used by a player I once partnered in a doubles tournament. After missing two 14yard roquets he said, "I average one out of three at that distance, so there should be no worries about the next one—I'm due for a roquet!" His reasoning may be mathematically unsound, but from a psychological viewpoint it is commendable. He did not get another chance at such a roquet, so I do not know how he would have reacted if he had missed yet again.

In my early playing days I used to set myself the aim in any match I played of making no more than six "errors". I would count it as an error if I missed a roquet of less than 5 yards, or stuck in a hoop that should have easily been made, or went out on a take-off, or on a take-off finished more than 5 yards from the target ball and missed the subsequent roquet. I did not count a poor take-off if I still managed to roquet the target ball, and I did not count poor hoop approaches or split shots, though perhaps I should have.

This meant that I was accepting the fact that I could expect to make a few errors of the type that one "should not make", and so when an error occurred I was less likely to blame myself and dwell on my stupidity to the extent that it affected future shots. Fortunately, my opponents at that level usually made more than six errors, and by maintaining a more positive approach I was able to win many games even when I made more than my allowance of errors. As I improved I was able to realistically reduce my allowance of errors, until eventually it seemed to be no longer needed. It is worth noting that even at the top level it is considered that a player can reasonably allow himself three errors per game and still expect to win most games.

In addition to the times when we set ourselves aims which are too high and unrealistic, there are also times when the goal we set for ourselves is too vague, and so too easily achievable. Many years ago I used to practise with Robert Bartholomaeus, who moved to New Zealand and became one of their leading players. When playing a roquet of 2-3 feet or making a hoop from a similar distance directly in front, he was not content to simply hit the ball in the general direction and make the roquet or hoop. He always aimed to roquet the target ball dead centre or make the hoop without touching the sides. If he succeeded in achieving his aim, his confidence increased because he knew he had played the shot well. If he did not, then he was able to start thinking about how to correct the slight error in his swing. Such failure did not adversely affect his confidence because he could tell himself that he had still managed to make the hoop or roquet, so in that sense his shot had been successful.

RHYTHM OF SWING

PERHAPS IT IS not obvious to all that there is a particular rhythm which must be achieved in correctly swinging a croquet mallet. For most shots the correct type of swing is one that resembles (but only approximately) a simple pendulum of fixed length (arm plus mallet-shaft) with the force provided by the weight of the mallet and not by the hands, wrists or elbows. "Let the mallet head do the work" is the standard coaching principle.

The laws of physics tell us that once the length of a pendulum is determined, its period (or rhythm of swing) is also determined. There is a fixed time, measurable in seconds, which the pendulum will take to move from the highest point of its swing to the lowest. If the mallet is moved more quickly or more slowly than this set period, then it is no longer operating as the desired simple pendulum. If a player changes the length of the pendulum by moving his hands up or down the mallet shaft, then he should also change the rhythm of his swing. A longer grip requires a slower swing.

4.1 Physiological influences

Our study of nervousness and the mental approach to croquet would be incomplete if we failed to consider the effect of physiological influences. This is most noticeable in relation to the rhythm of swing.

When a person experiences nervousness his body produces more adrenalin which results in various measurable physiological changes in his body. The most noticeable of these changes is a change in the rhythm of his heartbeat. As everyone knows, when you are nervous your heart beats faster.

The school at which I teach is a special music school, and the music teachers tell me that this change in heart beat rhythm due to nervousness is a major problem for performing musicians. The accepted theory is that we unconsciously take our natural rhythm (whatever that is) from our heartbeat. For this reason a nervous performer tends to play a piece of music much faster than he would if he were relaxed. They are quite unaware that they are playing at a different speed from the one they have been using in rehearsals, and wonder why their fingers get tangled up. To counteract this unconscious reliance on heart rhythm the students are advised to spend a few seconds just before a performance listening to a metronome or the ticking of a watch, and from that derive the correct speed or rhythm of the piece they are about to play. Famous musicians and conductors are also reported to have used such means of establishing rhythm, as well as using an actual pendulum or regularly flashing light, etc.

As a musician myself, and having been involved in many performances, I have long been aware of the tendency to unconsciously play faster when nervous, and the need to counteract this tendency by consciously and deliberately slowing down the "natural" rhythm when nervous. This 'heartbeat theory' is the only explanation I have heard which seems to adequately explain the effect.

It seems likely that in croquet the rhythm of swing will also be affected by a change in heart rhythm, and experience suggests that indeed this is so. When nervous, most players tend to hurry the swing. The backswing is shorter than when they are relaxed, and in order to still achieve the required force they tend to push the mallet handle forward with their hands in a 'jabbing' motion instead of letting it swing forward under its own weight. The reason for the shorter backswing, which necessitates the disastrous push or jab, seems to be that in practice sessions they have developed the habit of moving the mallet backwards for a fixed period of time which is measured internally and unconsciously in terms of heartbeats.

Let us assume, for example, that the backswing normally takes two heartbeats, after which the mallet pauses momentarily and then begins its forward swing. If the heart is beating faster than normal it is obvious that the backswing will be shortened (unless the mallet is moved back at a much greater speed than normal, which does not seem to happen). This means that on the backswing the mallet will not reach its normal height, so will move forward with less gravitational force than normal. The only way to overcome this loss of force and still move the ball the required distance is to provide additional force by pushing with the hands and wrists. Unfortunately, with the hands necessarily in different positions on the mallet shaft it is difficult to co-ordinate their pushing so that the mallet still swings along the desired line of aim, especially since it is something that has not been practised because it is not normally part of the swing. This also explains why judgement of length, as well as direction, is affected by nervousness.

Now that we are aware of the problem and its cause, what can be done about it? I do not know whether there are drugs available which would slow down the heart beat, but in any case they would be undesirable, unnecessary and probably illegal under the new rules governing the use of performance-enhancing drugs in sport.

For most players the problem can be at least partially overcome by reminding yourself at the start of a game, or at any other time when you are aware of feeling some degree of nervousness, that it is necessary to consciously SLOW DOWN AND LENGTHEN the backswing. This should enable you to re-establish the period of the correct simple pendulum swing, thus rendering pushing and jabbing unnecessary.

4.2 mechanics (length of lever)

I have already mentioned above that the period or "rhythm" of swing is determined by the length of the pendulum. This suggests a second possible advantage of shortening the grip slightly in a nervous situation. If the timing of the swing is taken from a faster beating heart, then the shortened period is likely to be closer to correct for a shorter than normal pendulum. The first advantage was explained earlier when we considered ways of coping with nervousness and saw that with a shorter grip any wobbling or shaking is less likely to be magnified in the mallet head. It should be borne in mind that there will be disadvantages of a shorter grip which must also be taken into account before deciding to use it as a partial answer to problems arising from nervousness.

Some players use a swing which resembles the operation of a double (or "compound") pendulum in which the hands swing in pendulum fashion from the shoulders, but the wrists are bent backward during the early part of the swing so that the mallet lags well behind the arm movement. Then as the hands reach a position above the ball the wrists are rapidly bent forward so that the mallet head moves very fast through the ball, swinging in a separate pendulum movement from the hands. It is possible to generate additional force from this 'dual pendulum' type of swing provided the timing is correct; but the reliable synchronisation of the two pendulums can present considerable difficulty.

A nervous player may tend to hurry the swing of the arms so that the second pendulum (the mallet) whose timing is not altered, will tend to lag further behind the hands than normal. This causes the hands to reach a position directly above the ball while the mallet is still in its downswing, resulting in loss of power and causing the ball to jump because it is hit downward onto the ground. You can miss a rush completely due to mistiming if you use this type of swing.

RHYTHM OF BREAK

WHEN PLAYING A break, another type of rhythm can be established. This is a less regular rhythm, but it is a rhythm nevertheless which a player will do well to understand. It comprises the timing of the various actions that are involved in playing the break, such as the speed at which the player walks between shots, the time taken to line up and stalk the shot, the number of practice swings, the length of pause before the player quits his stance after playing a shot, etc.

When I first started watching croquet players in action, I was fascinated by the way some of them seemed to play their breaks in a trance-like state, with a slow-motion robotic type of movement. Everything was done at the same mechanical, unhurried pace. Players like Neil Spooner, Mavis Giles and the late Joyce Gehan spring immediately to mind, and all of these told me in later years that while playing a break they are almost completely oblivious to things going on round about them. Movement becomes more or less automatic as the shots almost seem to "play themselves". The rhythm of the break was quite obvious to even a very inexperienced observer, although I understood nothing of the reasons for it.

Others have little or no established rhythm when making a break. They hustle from one shot to another, then pause in apparent uncertainty, and give the general impression that the break is made up of a series of somewhat jerky and unrelated stop-start movements. A third group tend to start slowly and gather momentum as they go, so that if the break continues long enough (which becomes less and less likely), they end up almost running from shot to shot. Generally, the best players do have their own rhythm, but some good players do not.

I cannot help believing that a definite break rhythm is desirable and should be carefully developed, even though it is certain to be interrupted at times by actions of spectators, opponents, players and balls from the other set, etc. Contrary to expectations, the players with the definite break rhythm are the ones who apparently are best able to cope with such unwelcome interruptions. They seem able to simply snap out of their trance, wait until the interruption has passed, then resume the break rhythm as if nothing had happened. Perhaps their ability to resume the break so easily arises from the fact that they have a definite, established rhythm to return to.

In determining the correct break rhythm for a player to use, there are several factors to be considered:

5.1 Tension release

With the majority of players there is a build-up of tension during a break, especially if a series of shots is played which involve a certain degree of risk. It is important that the break allows sufficient time between shots for all or most of the tension to drain away, so that it does not accumulate to the point where it seriously affects future shots.

5.2 Mental programming

It is also important that the rhythm contain a particular established mental programme for each type of shot. This will involve thinking one at a time through the various things that are essential to ensure the success of the particular shot being played.

For example, when playing a roquet shot of any distance from six inches to right across the lawn, the player will work through a programme such as:

Prepare to stalk the ball.
Check that the grip is correct.
Walk in steadily with eyes fixed on ball.
Take up a comfortable stance.
Check foot positioning.
Check squareness of mallet face.
Observe distance and determine length of backswing.
Practise backswing and check straightness.
Fix eyes on contact point on ball.
Relax shoulders and keep them still from now on.
Take a long, relaxed, slow backswing.
Ensure that hands move forward in correct line.
Reach forward in long, low follow-through.

This may seem like a ridiculously long checklist, especially for a six-inch roquet. However, it is only necessary to DO these things. It is not necessary to think them through and say all of them to yourself before each stroke. With practice, most of these things become automatic so that the player need think consciously about only a few of the points which he is most likely to get wrong. The programme is very much an individual thing, and will be different for each different player. For a croquet shot the player will have a completely different programme of things to consider, check and do. When things are going well the programme can be run through in just a few seconds, but sometimes the player will need to take more time in order to alter something that seems to be not working well enough, or to take into account additional things such as wind, pools of water, slope of lawn, etc., which are not part of his regular programme.

If anything distracts him during this process, the player should stop, pause, and then begin the programme all over again.

It is also important that the same programme be followed in its entirety for even the simplest of shots, for instance the six-inch roquet already mentioned. Why is this necessary when it is hardly conceivable that such a roquet could be missed, even without such detailed preparation? There are at least three good reasons.

Firstly, it is not impossible for even the best of players to miss a six-inch roquet. Secondly, it preserves the break rhythm by ensuring that each similar shot is prepared for and played in the same way. Thirdly, it reinforces the programme in the player's mind so that he is less likely to overlook something on a later shot when it may be more critical.

The player is actually using the six-inch roquet to practise his future shots. If he takes the trouble, for example, to check the squareness of his mallet face before EVERY roquet, then it will become an automatic part of his break rhythm, and he will not forget to do it at times when he could easily be distracted by such things as having given a "lift", or a ball left in a hoop, or a spectator's remark, or the approach of the time limit, etc.

5.3 Correction of errors

Before beginning his mental programme and playing any type of shot, the player should form a clear picture in his mind of exactly what he is expecting the ball(s) to do. Then he should pause after playing the shot and reflect briefly on whether or not the shot turned out as expected. If not, he should consider the likely cause of such deviation, even though it may not have had any serious consequence in that particular shot. In this manner he is able to start correcting any slight errors (e.g. the striker's ball going further than expected on croquet shots) before a disaster occurs. The break rhythm, therefore, should include a brief pause for this purpose after playing each shot and BEFORE moving away to play the next shot. This ensures that the player will not be still thinking about what went wrong with the previous shot while playing the current shot. Many a hoop has been missed because the player was still thinking about the not-quite-perfect approach shot; and many a roquet has been missed because the player is still trying to work out why his take-off fell short.

Such errors must certainly be noted and corrected in future shots, but while you are playing the next shot is definitely NOT the time to be thinking about error correction.

5.4 Bearing

Another aspect of break rhythm worth considering is its psychological effect on an opponent. When watching the way that Joyce Gehan, for example, walked onto the lawn, played her break (or one single shot), and walked off again, I could not help being impressed by her 'regal' bearing. She walked around the lawn as if it were her private domain and invariably gave the impression that she had everything under perfect control. Even when she was many hoops behind and had just missed a four-foot roquet she could manage to walk off the lawn in a manner that suggested it was exactly what she had intended to do. Perhaps a modern psychologist would explain this in terms of 'body language'.

Other players have also succeeded in creating an aura of being in complete command, and the psychological effect on an opponent can at times be devastating. I am sure that break rhythm is an important element of the overall effect, as I have never gained such an impression from a player who hustled or hesitated his way around the lawn without establishing a regular rhythm.

5.5 Distractions

We have already noted with some surprise that players with a well-established break rhythm are better able than others to cope with distractions which can interrupt the rhythm.

Such distractions may be deliberate (for example, the opponent calling out, "Did that ball move?" or "haven't you already used that ball?" or "would you get the referee to watch that hoop shot, please?") or accidental (for example, a player or ball from the other set, a wandering dog, etc.). There is no reason why you should allow such interruptions to upset you in any way. Provided you have established a set rhythm, you should be able to pause and take time out for something else, then return to it later. This is similar to the way in which a musician playing a piece with well-established rhythm can easily return to it after a pause; but if the piece has an obscure, jerky ("syncopated") rhythm he will find it far more difficult to get under way again.

It is important, however, that after any interruption the break is not resumed until the cause of the distraction has been completely dealt with and dismissed from the mind of the player. This is why experienced players often ask a player from the other set to play first once the break has been interrupted, even though they were in a break and according to the rules should have been given priority. It can be quite amusing when two such players are both insisting that the other play first, and their insistence is understandable when it is realised that some players find it harder to dismiss the distraction completely from their mind when there is a player from the other set standing alongside waiting for the shot to be played.

PSYCHOLOGY OF TACTICS

A LTHOUGH MOST OF our attention has so far been given to the effect of mental attitudes on stroke production and the playing of breaks, there is little doubt that for the more advanced player it will be in the realm of tactics that wrong mental attitudes do the greatest harm. This is all the more unfortunate in that it is very rare for a player to have any awareness of what is happening. In the case of nervousness the player is at least aware that he has the problem, even if he has no satisfactory solution to it. When a player is using poor tactics resulting from a poor mental approach it can be very difficult to convince him that there is anything wrong with either.

6.1 Risk taking and selective memory

If one is to learn from experience, it is necessary to correctly assess the success or otherwise of tactics used in the past. It is unfortunate that few players are able to make accurate judgements when attributing blame for failure or credit for success, because we are all prone to suffer from what is known as "selective memory".

I became aware of this years ago when I played in my first important tournament. I had a clip on 2-back and started a break with the other ball, taking it all the way to the peg. Later the opponent managed to get in and go to the peg, then peg out my ball, leaving me with the one ball still on 2-back. I eventually lost the game and walked off the lawn to be immediately set upon by a group of old ladies who sympathised with my loss, but explained that in going right to the peg with the second break I was clearly inviting the opponent to peg my ball out, and the result was only what I should have expected.

They were able to quote examples of their own similar experiences, to impress on me that they also had to "learn the hard way" that such a tactic was rash in the extreme.

I was quite unable to follow their reasoning, since I attributed the loss not to the fact that I had gone to the peg, but rather that I had later made several elementary mistakes when I had relatively easy chances to finish the game.

I have come to believe that in such a situation, where a game is lost after going to the peg and having a ball pegged out by the opponent, there is an almost overwhelming tendency to attribute the loss to the fact that you went too far in the break. This is in complete disregard of numerous other factors (for example, poor approach shots, sticking in hoops, missed short roquets, etc.) to which the loss could equally well—in fact far more reasonably—have been attributed.

The problem seems to be that these other factors are relatively commonplace, so do not stick in the mind. The one memorable feature of the game was the all-round break, so that is selected by the mind as the cause of what happened. It is rather curious that when a player in a similar situation stops at rover or penultimate and subsequently loses the game, he never seems to attribute the loss to the fact that he failed to make the hoops when he could have done so. This is true even when he loses by only the one or two hoops.

I am certain that I am far more likely to lose a game by NOT going to the peg when I could have, than by going to it when I should not have done so. I am also convinced that provided my other clip is past 1-back (so that my opponent will not receive contact and stands to receive only one more 'lift'), I give myself the best possible chance of winning the game by going right to the peg, regardless of the position of my opponent's clips. This may not be true for players in lower divisions, but is certainly true for those who are capable of playing all-round breaks.

There are many other situations where selective memory is in evidence. It is quite common for a player to attempt a slightly angled hoop, stick in it, and later blame this for the loss of the game. This is in spite of the numerous other errors made by both sides. "I knew I shouldn't have attempted it", he will say, and you know that next time he is faced with such a hoop shot he will elect to run away from it. The trouble with this reasoning is that when he in future chooses not to attempt the hoop and still loses, he will not attribute his loss to his failure to try the hoop, and say, as indeed he ought, "I should have tried the hoop when I had the chance."

Thus we always tend to attribute blame to the risks we took (unsuccessfully) rather than to the risks we failed to take. This is no doubt due to the fact that the effect of the failed risk is usually immediate and graphic, whereas the equally serious effect of running away from a risky shot is often only seen in the longer term and is easily attributable to the opponent's good play rather than our own poor tactics. It is also less damaging to the ego to admit that we have been outplayed (or better still, out-fluked) rather than out-thought!

Selective memory plays a part in colouring our assessment of the tactics used by other players as well as our own tactics. When watching a game, we tend to attribute a loss to the poor tactics of the loser, and a win to the good shots of the winner. Thus we say of the loser, "He shouldn't have set up near the opponent's hoop", or "He should have used the other ball"; while we say of the winner, "He was able to hit a couple of long roquets at critical times", or "He ran his hoops extremely well". Even here we are not really commending the winner on his willingness to attempt the roquets and hoops—we are merely commenting on his good fortune that the risks came off.

It is because of these and many other similar ways in which selective memory affects our assessment of risk-taking tactics that most players become more cautious in their play as they gain in experience. Unfortunately such caution is derived from fallacious reasoning and leads to the spurious conclusion that the way to win is to play good shots and avoid taking risks. While the first half of the conclusion is undeniably true, the second half is certainly not. How, then, is the problem of selective memory to be overcome? Perhaps in the future there will be professional players with paid coaches who record in detail every move of a game so that it can later be analysed with complete objectivity. Until then, we must continue to depend on our memories. We should at least realise the dangers involved so that we can try to be more objective and take everything into account before apportioning credit or blame.

To further illustrate these points, let us consider the common type of position shown in diagram 5.

All clips are still on the first hoop, and you are playing with the black and blue balls. Your opponent has just approached the hoop with your blue ball, but did not gain position to run the hoop, so has hit out about three feet from his partner ball on the east border. Your black ball is on the north border roughly in front of the third hoop. What will you do? Even if there is a good double target on offer, few players would seriously entertain the thought of shooting at it with the black ball, because of the obvious risk involved. A miss would present

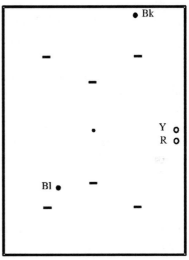

Diagram 5

the opponent with an easy nine hoops. Neither would most consider shooting at the opponent's balls with blue, since he does not at present have a rush to his hoop. A missed shot with blue at black would allow the opponent to play red, rushing yellow to the third corner and sending it to hoop 2 before rushing one of your balls to hoop 1, again with nine hoops as the likely outcome.

Most elect to play for "safety" by hitting blue into the first corner. But what is likely to be the outcome of this "safety" play? The opponent will play red and cut-rush yellow to a position on the north border near black. Then he will rush black to hoop

2, being careful to leave yellow about six inches (15cm) in from the yard-line. This will be followed by a take-off to blue in the first corner and a roll for hoop 1. The roll may not be successful, but in this case he can hit back to the north border near yellow with a rush set to black at hoop 2.

(Note that he could have done the same if blue were in the fourth corner, or any other "safe" place, as well as having the option of playing yellow instead of red.) This would leave you in a worse position (diagram 6) than you were in originally.

Now the opponent is threatening to make a 3-ball break on his next turn whichever ball you move, and any missed attempt at a roquet will give him the fourth ball as well. There is little sense in again playing blue into a corner and sitting down to watch him make the nine hoops, so you are forced to take a shot and hope for the best.

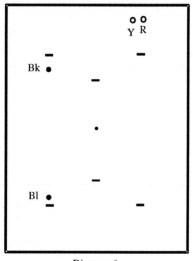

Diagram 6

In retrospect it becomes obvious (to us, but probably not to a player in a game) that you should have taken a shot in the original position instead of playing for so-called "safety". We can now see that there was nothing "safe" about hitting the blue ball into a corner. It merely served to delay the opponent's break by one or two turns, but made it all the more certain, because you are passing up one or more chances to roquet and allowing him to eventually get the break going without having been subject to any risk at all.

If both players are capable of making breaks, then in the original position a roquet should certainly have been attempted. It would be reasonable to shoot with black if you assess your chance of hitting the double target at better than 50%. Otherwise you should shoot with blue at yellow. (There is more to be considered than we have covered here, and the reasons for shooting at yellow rather than red belong in a book on tactics rather than one on psychology.)

For our purposes, the position just considered illustrates the fact that many players feel they have achieved something if they have managed to "put off the evil day" when the opponent achieves his break, even if in so doing they have made it more certain.

Suppose that in the position shown in diagram 5 you had played blue into the first corner, after which your opponent had been successful in rolling for the first hoop and making the nine hoops as suggested. Would you recognise your error in failing to shoot with blue at yellow? Probably not. You are far more likely to attribute the nine hoops to the opponent's skill (or good fortune) in gaining position to run hoop 1 on the roll from the corner. This is an excellent example of the type of trick our memory can play on us in assessing the reason for a disaster, as it completely overlooks the fact that he had an excellent chance of making the nine hoops, whether the roll was successful or not.

What, then, should be our attitude to risk-taking? Should we simply go out and take each and every manner of risk regardless of the possible consequences? Not at all. Such an approach in most players would lead to a desperado-type, 'devil-may-care' attitude which results in carelessness and inability to concentrate. We frequently see players taking risks that should definitely NOT be taken. A full consideration of the intricacies of this topic is outside the scope of this booklet, but we can at least state two clear and reliable general principles:

1. When you have the innings, be prepared to take any reasonable risk which if successful will give you a break, but do not take risks from which you stand to gain only one hoop with nothing set up ahead.
2. Conversely, when you do not have the innings, take any risk which could gain you the innings provided that if it is unsuccessful the opponent stands to gain only one hoop, or in order to set up a break he will have to play a series of difficult or very accurate shots.

In the position considered previously (diagram 5), a player who follows the second of these principles would correctly opt to shoot with blue at one of the opponent's balls, without having to reason his way through the long process of justification given above.

Perhaps we should again emphasise that the two principles given above apply only when both players are likely to make large breaks if given a reasonable chance. There is little point in taking a risk to set up a break if you do not have the shots necessary to keep it going, nor to prevent a break which the opponent is unlikely to be able to sustain for long.

6.2 Acceptance of percentage play

Another area of tactics where psychology plays a part is the ability of a player to accept the concept of basing his tactics on percentages. The way in which percentages should be estimated or calculated and used as a basis for developing a tactical approach is explained in detail in my booklet "Next Break Strategy" which deals with advanced tactics. Here we will consider only some interesting facts about the way in which players view, and often reject, the idea of percentage play.

Some years ago The Australian Croquet Gazette published an article by Stan Hall, a leading N.S.W. player and theoretician and a professor of mathematics, in which he proved that when shooting at two balls up to 18 inches apart and 15 or more yards away, you should aim at a point midway between the two balls and actually try to go through the gap. This gives you a better percentage chance of roqueting than if you aim at one or other of the balls.

Although they accept Stan's conclusion, I have found that many players are unable to make themselves do it at a critical stage in an important game. Somehow it does not seem right to be trying as hard as you can to do something that you do not really want to succeed. One player explained, "If I did manage to go through the middle I would be mentally kicking myself for the rest of the game." Being a mathematician myself and able to follow through in detail Stan's argument, I find no such difficulty about deliberately aiming to go through the middle. If I happen to achieve the unwanted success, I tell myself that at least it was an accurate shot, and aiming differently would have given less chance of roqueting.

We have already noted that many players have a mental approach which makes it difficult for them to take risks, even when it can be clearly demonstrated that in taking the risk they are giving themselves the best possible chance of winning the game. It seems impossible to convince them that in fact "playing safe" is more risky than taking a chance in many situations.

On many occasions when playing doubles games I have had difficulty convincing my various partners that in positions such as that shown in diagram 7, with all clips on the first hoop, they should shoot with red at the black ball in the first corner. They insist that the shot is "too risky" and instead want to "play safe" and make the hoop immediately from yellow.

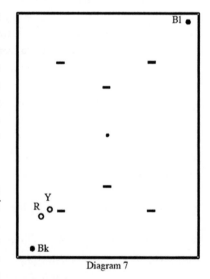

Diagram 7

I point out that they could expect to make the 5-yard roquet at least 8 times out of 10, and they usually agree on this point. Then I argue that if they make the hoop immediately they will have virtually no chance of setting up a break before allowing the opponents one or more roquets which we could expect them to make at least 2 times out of 10. Therefore by taking the shot at black we give ourselves, say, an 85% chance of an immediate break, while making the first hoop immediately cannot be expected to give us more than about a 60-70% chance of getting a break going before the opponents do. The logic is irrefutable, but even so my partners are frequently unconvinced that shooting at black is much the safest course of action, in the sense that it minimises our chance of losing the game.

A friend with whom I sometimes practise is also dubious about taking chances such as the one described, but for a different reason. When I explain to him that he could expect to hit the roquet at least eight times out of ten, he says, "Yes, that may be so, but I am not going to get ten chances to hit it. I will only have one chance which I have to hit. I need to be able to make one roquet out of one, which is 100%!" Unless all croquet players are required to pass an examination in the laws and applications of mathematical probability, there will always be players whose psychological makeup leads them to erroneous conclusions like this one.

Betty Roberts, a strong player at the Broadview club where I am a member, has her own unique method of using percentages. When faced with the need to make a somewhat risky roquet she says, "Well, I can either hit or miss, so at least I have a 50% chance!" Her reasoning is fallacious from a mathematical point of view, but psychologically it is of value if it allows her to attempt the shot in a more relaxed frame of mind.

We have noted earlier the fact that a player who uses tactics based on an objective assessment of percentages has a ready-made element of confidence built into his mental approach. I may not have any great confidence in my ability to make correct subjective judgements, nor in my ability to swing a croquet mallet in a straight line, but there is no doubt that my confidence in the laws of mathematical probability is well founded!

PSYCHOLOGICAL DISTRACTORS

THERE IS MUCH scope for research into the effects which certain physical perceptions can have on the brain of a croquet player.

(My wife, who strenuously resists all temptation to play the game, cannot think of anything more futile than attempting research into the brains of croquet players, and suggests that "search" would need to come before "research".)

Here I will suggest two of the many areas in which I believe, in spite of my wife's opinions, that research could prove fruitful and of benefit to players.

7.1 Distraction by a ball

An interesting situation commonly occurs in which a player has sent an opponent ball to hoop 2 and plays an unsuccessful approach shot for hoop 1 with his partner ball. With the partner ball behind the hoop and a little to one side, the first thought is to cover the boundary against the opponent's shot with his ball from hoop 2. If this is not practical, the usual procedure is to sit in front of the hoop so that there is only one ball that the opponent has a chance of roqueting.

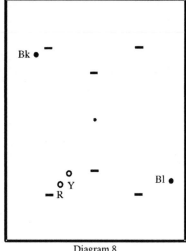

Diagram 8

However, one player I know prefers to give himself a rush with both balls open to the opponent's shot and 4-5 feet apart as in diagram 8. He claims that the second ball tends to act as a "distractor", so that the opponent is less likely to roquet with two balls to choose from than with only one, provided they are set the right distance apart. I do not know whether or not this theory is true. It does not seem altogether unreasonable, so should not be dismissed out of hand. Perhaps the answer depends to a great extent on the ability and mental approach of the opponent. In any case, it seems that it ought to be possible to conduct tests which may enable some more definite statement to be made on the question of whether or not balls can be useful "distractors" in certain positions.

7.2 Distraction by a line

My friend Tom Armstrong once pointed out to me that in certain situations a line can also act as a distractor. You can test this out yourself by measuring a target ball onto the yard-line on the south border in front of hoop 1 and asking a number of friends to play a roll shot from the same yardline directly behind hoop 4, as shown in diagram 9. They are to send the croqueted ball to hoop 1 and the striker's ball as close as possible to the ball on the border in front of hoop 1. It is amazing how many players will roll the striker's ball out of court. If they were asked to play the same shot in a different part of the lawn they would not experience the same difficulty.

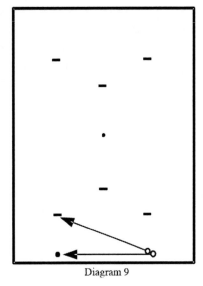

Diagram 9

I gained an insight into why this may be so when one day I was playing a tennis match on unfamiliar courts and found that every time I tried to hit a backhand passing shot up the sideline it finished well out of court. Even though I knew it was happening I found it very difficult to correct the error. Then I realised that there was a clubhouse which ran fairly close alongside the court, and it was built so that it ran almost parallel to the court, but not quite. The building was about 3 feet further from the sideline at the far end of the court than at the near end. Somehow, I was unconsciously using the line of the clubhouse in lining up my passing shots, and it was acting as a distractor, tending to drag the balls out of court. It transpired that many visiting players experienced the same problem with backhands from that end of the court.

This suggested to me that the boundary line on the croquet court may be acting as a distractor for the player lining up the roll shot. He needs to take note of the angle between the directions in which the two balls will travel and choose his point of aim (that is, direction of swing) accordingly. However, it is not easy to ignore the boundary line which is fairly close to one of the arms of the required angle. This tends to make the angle look wider than it actually is, and can cause the player to choose a point of aim halfway between the hoop and the boundary, instead of halfway between the hoop and the yard-lined ball. All of this may be merely my imagination, but nevertheless it has made me particularly wary of roll shots in which the striker's ball is to travel parallel to and close to a border. Whether the explanation is correct or not, there is no doubt that the striker's ball has an unnerving tendency to finish out of court unless particular care is taken to ensure that the line of aim is correct.

I have a suspicion that there are many other situations in which balls, lines, hoops or the peg can act as distractors. Most of us are aware that hoops often seem to have a strange magnetic attraction for a ball that is not supposed to go anywhere near them—or is this just another example of selective memory?—and many players find that when they line up an angled hoop shot and concentrate on making sure that the ball misses the near hoop leg, this very concentration seems to affect the line of swing. The hoop leg seems to act as a distractor. For this reason they may need to use a different method of lining up the hoop shot, and avoid fixing any attention on the hoop leg at all.

ILLUSIONS

A NOTHER WAY IN which the mind of a croquet player may be misled can perhaps best be described under the heading of 'illusions'.

(a) judgement of distance

There has been controversy since time immemorial concerning the correct method of choosing the point of aim (i.e. direction of swing) in croquet shots. Some insist that you should "halve the angle" between the directions in which the two balls are to travel. Others are equally adamant that you should "halve the distance" between the positions where the two balls will finish. When the balls travel roughly equal distances there is no problem, since both methods yield approximately the same aiming point. For stopshots or pass-rolls, however, as well as for other croquet shots in which one ball travels noticeably further than the other, there is quite a difference, and both cannot be correct.

From the laws of physics "parallelogram of forces" and mathematics "the diagonals of a parallelogram bisect each other" there is no doubt that halving the distance, rather than the angle, is theoretically correct. Why, then, do players still persist in "halving the angle"?

The answer lies in the fact that there is a type of optical illusion which makes it difficult to judge accurately distances along a line which slopes diagonally across our field of vision. To test this, remove the peg from the lawn and while standing at hoop 2 try to pick out a point which is midway between hoop 3 and hoop 4. Even with the peg there to help them most players choose a point much closer to hoop 3 than hoop 4. This is because if the correct mid-point is marked, the nearer half will appear greater than the half which is further away. Everyone realises that although the sun and moon appear about the same size in the sky, the sun appears smaller than it really is because it is so far away, and the moon appears larger than it should in relation to the sun because it is closer. But not everyone is aware that the same illusion affects our judgement of distances on the croquet lawn.

For this reason a player who plays a split shot from hoop 2 to hoops 3 and 4 and SAYS he is choosing his point of aim by halving the distance between the hoops will often actually be aiming at a point which is close to that chosen by someone else who claims to be halving the angle. Thus the illusion causes both players once again to aim at roughly the same point. This turns out reasonably well, since the striker's ball is affected by 'pull' (caused by follow-through) to a greater extent than the croqueted ball. To allow for this 'pull', which the aforementioned laws of physics did not take into account, it is necessary to move the point of aim from the midpoint a little toward the finishing point of the striker's ball.

However, in pass rolls the illusion will work in reverse, causing the player who 'halves the distance' to move his aiming point AWAY from where the striker's ball is going, when the allowance for 'pull' requires that it should be moved TOWARD the finishing point of the striker's ball. If he is not aware of what is happening this could make the player start to lose faith in the laws of physics at least inasmuch as they apply to the behaviour of croquet balls. His only consolation will be that his friend who insists on halving the angle will in this case be even further astray in trying to find the correct aiming point.

(b) double targets

A similar effect, caused by the same type of illusion, is seen when a player takes his ball to a baulk and places it so as to have a double target on two balls, one of which is further away than the other. He will normally try to place the ball so that if it travels in a straight line it will not quite be able to pass between the two target balls without hitting one of them. However, we frequently see that the striker's ball does, in fact, somehow manage to fit through the impossible gap. Players often explain this by claiming that the ball jumped or curved due to irregularities in the lawn; but the true reason is more likely to lie in the fact that when we are placing the striker's ball on the baulk it is much closer to us than either of the two target balls, making it appear larger than the gap between them. Perhaps the player should place his striker's ball alongside the nearer of the two target balls and then view it from the baulk in order to select a suitable position which he could 'mark' by leaving his mallet there while he retrieves his ball. I have never tried this procedure, and am not sure of its legality since it could possibly be construed as using a ball as a "trial" ball. In any case, it may well not turn out to have any noticeable advantages.

(c) cannons

In connection with cannons there are two 'illusions' worthy of mention. The first is in the judgement of the strength required. As with cut-rushes, there is a very strong tendency to underestimate the force required, so that the balls fall far short of their intended finishing places. This may be caused by overlooking the fact that there is a third (striker's) ball which has no desired finishing position, but nevertheless requires force to move it. Most players, at least until they have practised the shot many times, tend to use the same amount of force that would be needed for a split shot in which two balls only are sent to the same places.

The second illusion arises from a method used in teaching players how to arrange the balls for various cannons. It is now common to refer to coin sizes in order to convey an idea of the correct gap between the two non-touching balls, and I think this was another of Tom Armstrong's innovations. However, it is forbidden under the rules of the game to actually use a coin when arranging a cannon, so the size of the coin has to be judged. For some reason which I have not yet been able to adequately explain, players seem to invariably underestimate coin sizes. If you ask a player to arrange the balls so that there is a "ten-cent gap" between them, you will almost certainly find that the gap he produces will not even go close to accommodating a ten-cent piece. This phenomenon need not present a problem, provided the teacher allows for it by naming a coin larger than the gap he actually wants, but if the student then decides to use actual coins when practising the various arrangements, he may find that the balls do not behave as expected.

PSYCHOLOGY OF CHEATING

THIS MAY SEEM a strange topic to deal with, but there is no doubt that cheating can have a marked psychological effect on the opponent, if not on the player who is cheating.

(a) guilt feelings

For most players the knowledge that you have gained an unfair advantage, even inadvertently, leads to feelings of guilt and concern as to whether there may be lasting damage to a hitherto good reputation. In a semi-final of the 1990 Port Pirie championship singles tournament I was playing against Dean Paterson, a member of the state team, and found myself in such a situation. I had left Dean's balls near hoop 2 and the peg, and had roqueted my red partner ball in the first corner. I decided to set a rush on the south border, wired by hoop 1 from the ball near the peg. I rolled the short distance along the border from the corner, but red went too far and came to rest where it was not wired, so after some deliberation I placed yellow so that red had an exact rush to the ball near the peg, which therefore would have only a single ball target.

Dean, who had been sitting at the far end of the lawn behind hoop 2, came onto the lawn and decided to shoot at my rush, even though there was no double target. He missed, but on measuring his ball in found that my red ball was misplaced. We consulted the referee, who ruled correctly that Dean had played with a ball misplaced, and there is no remedy. This seemed rather hard on Dean, who could hardly have been expected to walk right down and check that I had correctly yard-lined the balls at the end of my turn. The fault was entirely mine and I had gained an unfair advantage, yet under the rules nothing could be done about it.

I then asked the referee whether, with my agreement, he would allow us to replace the balls correctly so that Dean could play the shot again. He readily consented to this and complimented me on my display of good sportsmanship. Dean roqueted on the second attempt, but I still managed to win the game fairly easily.

In actual fact I must confess that my action in requesting that Dean be allowed a replay was prompted by psychological considerations rather than good sportsmanship, although I would like to think that a sense of fair play would have led me to take the same action even without psychology being a factor.

I did not wish to play the remainder of the game with the knowledge that I had gained an unfair advantage which everyone would have been talking and whispering about. In such a situation it would be almost impossible to relax and play well. I preferred to play with the warm feeling that came from having earnt everyone's respect (even if not entirely deserved) for my "fairness and good sportsmanship".

The unfortunate incident thus affected Dean more than it affected me; but this would probably not have been so if I had simply accepted the referee's ruling and played on as I was entitled to do. The great majority of experienced croquet players are quick to declare that they have left a still ball or made a double tap, etc., and would prefer to be placed at a disadvantage rather than have someone think they had gained an unfair advantage even unintentionally. In most cases this preference arises from an appreciation of psychology, and does not necessarily support the contention that croquet players possess any greater sense of honesty than other members of the community.

(b)   inadvertent cheating

Another type of inadvertent cheating occurs when a player is completely unaware that he is committing faults by pushing ('shepherding') his rolls, double-tapping on hoop approaches, leaving still balls, etc. Perhaps it should not be termed "cheating" when the player genuinely does not realise he is doing it, but this is little consolation to an opponent who believes that the player in question is gaining an advantage from such actions.

It is quite rare for players at higher levels to complain about opponents committing such faults. This is not because such things do not occur at the higher levels of play, but because the player knows full well that there is little to gain by making a complaint, and there is much to lose psychologically. Some years ago an experienced player commented to me during a game that her opponent was 'shepherding' her ball on most hoop approaches. I watched for a while, and there was no doubt that many of the approaches did involve a rather blatant 'push'. I asked why she had not complained to the opponent about it and asked that all future hoop approaches be watched by the referee.

"There is little point in doing that", she explained, "It is probably due to the fact that this is a much faster lawn than she usually plays on. She is not aware that she is doing it and would probably think I am complaining simply in order to upset her. She is not gaining any advantage from it, anyway. She is quite capable of playing hoop approaches without pushing, and if the referee is called to watch it would only make her take greater care over her shots. She is experienced enough not to be too upset by having a referee standing nearby, and it would probably end up affecting my game more than hers. After the game I will suggest that she consider changing her action slightly in case someone queries her shots."

This attitude is a particularly wise one, and I recommend it as objectively the best way of handling any similar situation. Players who 'double tap' also rarely gain any advantage, since it is hard enough to control one hit in a stroke without introducing a second one to complicate things. Players who leave still balls often find their take-offs going too far and are unlikely to play them with greater control, since they are expecting the croqueted ball to move. If you understand this you will be able to prevent yourself from getting worked up about such faults committed unknowingly by your opponent. When you realise that the opponent is actually putting himself at a disadvantage in most cases, you can see why most experienced players prefer to say nothing and avoid creating tension whose effect on both players may be unpredictable. If the opponent who is leaving still balls is about to play a long diagonal corner takeoff, you can ask him to have a referee watch it because in this case there could be a considerable advantage if the croqueted ball does not move; but all such long corner takeoffs should be watched by a referee anyway.

(c)   deliberate cheating

We have seen that in croquet there are good psychological reasons to support the old adage "cheats never prosper". However, it must be acknowledged that there are exceptions to the rule. On rare occasions you can expect to encounter a habitual cheat. Such players are so few that they are well known, and their reputation usually precedes them. They are able to cheat deliberately in a way that has become more or less automatic, so that they apparently no longer experience feelings of guilt about the unfair advantages they are gaining. This can present you with a real problem in how to handle the situation, as they will hotly deny any claim you make about their unfair actions. The resultant unpleasantness is almost certain to affect your game adversely while the cheat has become hardened to such accusations which, of course, he has heard many times before.

If you believe that you are capable of beating such a player in spite of his cheating, then it may be best to say nothing until the game is over, but make sure that the referee and as many influential people as possible are aware of what is happening so that he can be warned not to try the same sort of thing in future games. If you believe the advantage he is gaining is such that it must be stopped, then you face the difficulty of finding a way of dealing with it without creating a situation in which you are likely to become worked up and tense.

In some cases a referee may be available to witness what is going on, and willing to step in and say something, so that you can remain aloof from the situation. On other occasions it may be possible to deal with it in a semi-humorous manner.

I once played a tournament game on a lawn which had many tufts of grass and shallow depressions, particularly along the edges. Every time I took off to my opponent's balls and tried to rush one of them, it would be in a depression so that it was almost impossible to rush properly. I wondered why my opponent did not seem to encounter the same difficulty with his rushes. He was an older gentleman and seemed rather unsteady on his feet as he walked around the lawn, which surprised me since I had not noticed him walking in such a stumbling fashion at other times.

It took some time before I realised what was happening. Whenever he measured one of his balls in, he would make sure that it was placed in a depression. Later, when he himself wanted to rush one of his balls, he would 'accidentally' fall over it or kick it, then have to replace it. The ball would be replaced so that the rush presented no problem. I watched in fascination as this occurred several times. The next time I needed to rush a ball from a depression I 'accidentally' fell over it myself. "I must be getting clumsy in my old age", I remarked, as I replaced the ball where I could rush it to my hoop. He realised that I was aware of his little game, and from then on made sure that his balls were measured in correctly and remained as placed.

On another occasion I was watching a game played by a lady who was a reasonably strong player, well known for her failure to declare still balls and her regular claiming of roquets that in fact missed by several inches. She shot across the lawn at a ball near where her opponent and I were sitting. The ball missed by an inch or so, but as the opponent stood up to begin her turn, the player called out, 'That was a roquet. Didn't you see it? It just tickled the blue ball.'

"If you say so, dearie", said the opponent as she resumed her seat, "I would never doubt the word of someone with such wonderful eyesight!" The cheat was suitably embarrassed and seemed unable to get her game together from then on.

Unfortunately the right thing to say does not always come to mind. The important thing is that if you do decide to take action about your opponent's deliberate cheating, you must do it in a way that will leave him embarrassed and unable to continue with what he was doing, while avoiding the generation of any heat which could affect your own game.

I have been the victim of deliberate cheating on several other occasions, as have most players. A comprehensive list of such unfair tactics would make interesting and educational reading, but is not within the scope of this booklet. When it is a one-off thing and you have no evidence to support a complaint to the referee, you can do nothing more than put it down to experience.

On one occasion, for example, I carefully wired my opponent's balls at my partner ball's hoop, checked that he had no possible chance of roqueting one with the other, and rushed my partner ball to set up in a far corner. While I was doing this a player from the other set lifted one of the balls I had wired, although the shot she played did not go within yards of the lifted ball. Then she replaced the ball and my opponent, who by coincidence happened to be her husband, walked onto the lawn and roqueted the ball dead centre. I was flabbergasted, and could only stammer, "I thought I wired them". Since that time I have watched the actions of that husband and wife team very closely whenever they were playing on the same lawn.

(d) time wasting

Perhaps this should have been dealt with in the section on 'illusions'. I have frequently heard players complaining that their opponent is wasting time toward the end of a time-limited game, but in at least 90% of such cases I could not see any evidence that the opponent was taking more time than he was entitled to. The normal actions of a player just SEEM to be taking longer when you are behind, the scores are close, and you can almost hear the seconds ticking away. Perhaps the quickened heart rate that we mentioned previously also affects our judgement of time.

It is in fact reasonable in such a situation for the opponent to take more care over his shots than he was doing previously, since any slight error at this stage is likely to decide the result of the game. It is similarly understandable that he should give more thought to his tactics before deciding on a course of action.

Your best chance when you are behind in such a situation is to simply grin and bear it. If there is evidence that the time wasting is blatant and deliberate, then the referee is able to warn the offender and, if necessary, add time on to that allowed for the game. However, a referee should be very wary about taking such action for reasons we have mentioned in the previous two paragraphs.

If you are the player who is ahead, you must not allow yourself to be hustled into error or distracted by your opponent's comments to the effect that time is short. If my opponent does make such a comment, I always make a point of taking longer over the next shot in order to allow any tension to drain away. I usually stop and say, "Please keep your comments to yourself, or make them so that I cannot hear them. I will not be hustled. I will take as much time as I need to work out what I want to do and check through the things I need to take into consideration when playing the shot. I am USING the time, not WASTING it. If you are not happy about it, please call the referee, and if he thinks I am gaining an unfair advantage he is welcome to add extra time on to the game."

It is my personal belief that almost all complaints about time wasting simply display the ignorance of the complainer as to the many things that a player should take into consideration in a tense situation. Those who complain about an opponent 'wasting time' are almost always high-bisquers. Leading players understand the situation and accept it unhappily, but without complaint.

My personal attitude is that the way to prevent your opponent from deliberately wasting time is to be in front. If I am behind and my opponent seems to be taking longer than might be expected over some of his shots, I simply put it down as the well-deserved penalty for my previous bad play. This seems far preferable to allowing the pressure of disappearing time to become uppermost in my mind, so that even if I am given another chance my nerves will not be in any suitable state to cope with it.

Similarly, do not allow yourself to be upset in any way if your opponent, who is behind in the scores, starts to hurry and run between shots. He is quite entitled to do so if he thinks there is more to gain than lose by it. There is no justification for regarding his actions as a display of poor sportsmanship unless he also tries to force you into hurrying your shots.

PSYCHOLOGY OF PRACTISING

W HEN PLAYERS ARE questioned about the subject, we find that their psychological approach to practice varies considerably. Some have a psychological makeup which seems to preclude all except the most casual and brief type of practice, while others spend many hours each week alone on the croquet lawn.

While it is tempting to regard a player as lazy when he has the time to practise but seems to lack the inclination, we should bear in mind that if they became serious about practising some players would find it impossible to remain relaxed during matches. They need to adopt a casual type of approach to the game as a whole, which includes and affects their attitude to practising.

It is hardly surprising that players who play the game for social reasons, rather than as a serious competitive sport, usually do not practise at all. There are, however, some points to be made which may be of importance to those who wish to improve their game for whatever reason.

(a) Set definite goals.

Practice should be planned to at least some extent, in order to ensure that real benefit is derived from the time spent. It is an interesting fact that many players are only willing to practise the things they can already do well. One player explained the reason: "By practising the things I am good at I can build up my confidence. If I keep trying to do things I can't manage very well I become frustrated and lose confidence in my game."

We have already seen how important a factor confidence is in any croquet game, but it seems that the confidence developed by adopting this sort of approach to practice will only be in evidence when the player is playing shots of the type he has practised. Thus it is likely to lead to the development of a style in which the player relies on a very limited range of shots which he can play quite well, and avoids all temptation to play shots of the type he has not practised.

Improvement is far more likely to be evident in the player who is aware of the weaknesses in his game and sets about remedying them; although in order to maintain confidence he should also spend time quickly running through the things he is good at. It is important to enlist the aid of a competent coach to ensure that you are practising things the right way. There are many players who have spent years practising shots with incorrect grip, stance or swing. In this manner they have managed to develop bad habits which are very difficult to eradicate.

Practice sessions should not be too long. Three sessions per week of about 45 minutes each will be far more effective than spending one whole morning per week practising. If the session becomes too long it is impossible to maintain full concentration. Some of the shots will inevitably be played carelessly, and again bad habits can be developed.

I know of a leading player who would spend a whole day practising one shot. He would run a hoop 200 times from one foot directly in front, then 200 more times from two feet, and 200 more from three feet, etc. There was little noticeable improvement in his hoop running under pressure in matches as a result of this. I cannot help but think that such inordinately lengthy practice sessions are likely to be counter-productive. He would have done better to set himself a definite and achievable goal, e.g. to run the hoop ten times out of ten from one foot out, nine out of ten from two feet, eight out of ten from three feet, etc., up to five feet. Even this would involve 50 practice shots at a hoop, which may well be too many for most players in the one practice session. An alternative goal could be to run the hoop five times out of ten from two feet out, without touching the sides. As soon as concentration begins to wane the player should end the session or change to practising a completely different skill. There is little point in practising hoops longer than five feet. The time would be better spent in practising approach shots to ensure that in a match you do not need to attempt hoops longer than five feet.

(b) Practise success, not failure

Colin Pickering, who could lay claim at the time of writing to being the strongest player in Australia, regularly practised roquets. He did this by placing balls a few yards apart and roqueting one with the other dead centre. He concentrated on developing a perfectly straight swing (including backswing and follow-through). He did not practise longer roquets, or shooting at the peg from the edge of the lawn as many players did, as he said that such players were 'practising failure', since they will miss the peg more often than they will hit it. There is much sense in his approach. If you wish to practise longer shots, then you should at least set yourself an achievable target, e.g. of hitting the peg three times in ten shots, so that if you manage to do this there will be a clear sense of having succeeded.

(c) Practise the right things

After a game in which they stuck in several difficult hoops, players will often spend time practising their hoop shots. In actual fact the problem may not lie in their inability to run hoops, but in one or more of the shots played prior to the attempt at running the hoop. The approach shots may have been unsatisfactory, or the rushes may have been poor, causing the approach to be made from too far out. More importantly still, it may be that the player needs to practise split shots in which he concentrates on accurate placement of the croqueted ball at future hoops, so that when he later comes to make the hoop he will not need to rush a ball to it or play a long approach shot.

One of my favourite practice exercises involves playing a continuous three-ball 'break' in which I make the four corner hoops several times around, without going up the centre of the lawn. I concentrate on placing the croqueted ball accurately at each hoop, instead of concentrating mainly, as most players do, on the striker's ball. When running each hoop I try to get a rush to the next hoop, but I do not take the rush, preferring to roquet the ball gently and practise the split shot from each hoop to the next two. In a match, of course, I would take the rush and regard it as a bonus, which seems to help develop a confident mental approach.

(d) Use repetition to ensure retention of skills

We have already mentioned the need for repetition in order to ensure that the skill being developed becomes firmly fixed in the mind. Many players 'practise' by simply going out and playing a game with themselves, playing all four balls. This seems to be an inefficient use of time, as no particular skill is being developed, other than possibly establishing a 'break rhythm'.

It is surprising that players give so little thought to planning their practice sessions, but complain about having insufficient time available for practice. It would seem that if their available time is as limited as they claim, then they should be taking far more care to ensure that the time they do spend on the lawn is used to the greatest possible advantage. Take-offs are never deliberately practised, stop-shots rarely, and only one or two cannons are practised occasionally. The take-off from a corner to the diagonally opposite corner needs regular practice, as does a stop-shot which sends one of two yard-line balls to a distant hoop while staying close enough to be sure of roqueting the other. A player should run through his whole repertoire of cannons at least once per month.

(e) Use variation to maintain interest

In addition to varying activities during the practice session, it is useful to practise under varying conditions. I make a point of occasionally arranging a practice session on a different type of lawn, and as explained in a previous section, at times I deliberately practise when it is raining or windy or the temperature is around 40 degrees Celsius. This allows me to practise handling strong wind, wet balls and grip, soggy lawns, sweaty hands and extreme heat. Practice sessions can be organised early in the morning, when it may be necessary to find ways of getting the muscles working and coping with dew or frost; or at night under lights, when the shadows of the balls may present a whole new problem in lining up take-offs and peels.

(f) Practise break rhythm

In an earlier section we looked at the importance of developing a regular break rhythm. The player who has available the shots needed to keep a break going should give some practice time to practising the break rhythm exactly as he intends to use it in matches, taking the same time and care over every shot. Even when you are practising the one shot over and over it is possible to use most of the elements of your break rhythm so that you are practising the shot under conditions which duplicate those in a match.

(g) Practise seriously

In addition to individual practice sessions where you work on particular skills, you should try to arrange regular practice games. It is important to find an opponent who will take the practice games seriously, as these games provide the opportunity to practise your skills under pressure. For this reason you must be playing to win, even though there is nothing hanging on the result. Do not play any shot which you would not play in an important match. Do not tell yourself that "it's only a practice game" so you can afford to take risks which you would not normally take. Do not bend the rules or allow your opponent to bend them. Treat the games seriously and play to win as convincingly as you can. Do not take pity on the opponent and do things designed to 'give him a chance'. If the opponent does not do his utmost to beat you every time, then find another practice partner. The reason for this advice is that both your shot-making technique and your tactics need to be practised UNDER PRESSURE, and if you are not feeling yourself under pressure in the practice games then you would be better off spending the time in some other way.

It is not necessary for this purpose that the opponent be your equal in ability, though it can be helpful from a coaching point of view if he is stronger than you (but not so strong as to destroy your confidence completely) and can offer advice from time to time. Practice against a weaker opponent can still give the pressure you need, provided you play the whole game as you would against a stronger opponent and put yourself under mental pressure to do as well as you possibly can. You can also provide the pressure by offering bisques to your opponent, provided this is agreed upon BEFORE the game commences and NOT after you are well ahead; or by adopting some particular game plan. For example, you could decide to try to win after giving contact in your first break, or after pegging out one of your own balls, or after completing a number of peels you have set yourself. If you use such an artificial means of creating additional pressure on yourself, you must still take the game seriously, and if your opponent has to know about it then make sure that he also knows you are still hoping to win.

On the other hand, if an opponent offers you bisques which you feel you do not need, do not be offended. Take them and beat him. He is unlikely to offer them again. If you cannot beat him then you have no reason to feel slighted. I once asked Tom Armstrong what to do when my opponent went right to the peg and gave me contact. "Say 'thank you very much' under your breath", said Tom, "Then go right to the peg yourself and peg him out. The problem will not arise a second time." If I could not manage to do as Tom suggested then I had no reason to be critical of the opponent's tactics.

PSYCHOLOGY OF COACHING

H ERE WE WILL briefly consider only a few psychological factors of which a coach should be aware. A more detailed study of this topic belongs more rightfully in a book on coaching.

(a) encouragement and the need for success

Tom would never forgive me if I did not at least mention the fact that almost every new player needs to experience success as early as possible, and should be encouraged at every opportunity. Experienced players sometimes joke about the way Tom tells every newcomer that they have a "wonderfully straight eye", a "remarkable natural aptitude for the game", and are "certain to be pressing for selection in the state team within a short while". (With me it was the national team, so he must have decided that I needed more than the normal amount of encouragement.) However, it is not a joke to the new player. He realises, of course, that Tom's tongue is firmly in his cheek; but the warm feeling is there all the same. And whether we regard it as a joke or not, there is no doubt that the method works. Monumental evidence of this is provided by the remarkable success rate achieved by Tom and his wife Jean in getting newcomers to move from the stage of vague interest in what the game is about, to the stage of being well and truly 'hooked' on it.

Tom has also pointed out that the game of croquet provides its devotees with far more than mere sporting competition and recreation. Many newcomers have other psychological needs that should be considered. He has made the interesting observation that most people who express interest in taking up the game are unhappy. After all, if they are fully satisfied with what they are currently doing, why would they be interested in taking up something different? If, for example, they appear to be lonely and in need of someone to talk to, then instead of teaching them hoop approaches it may be better to spend time listening to them talk about their problems—or better still, find someone else to do the listening and sympathising.

(b) avoid quantum leaps

The coach must be wary of trying to teach too much too soon. Some players can assimilate more than others due to greater intelligence and longer concentration span, but it is better to leave them eager to hear more next time than to leave them weary and confused. I have long been concerned that the leap from Golf Croquet to Association Croquet is too great for many newcomers to cope with happily, and for this reason I have advocated the use of "Ricochet" as a means of avoiding some of the psychological problems (of befuddlement and defeatism) that can accompany the aforementioned quantum leap and cause some players to simply refuse to make it.

Ricochet is a version of croquet which involves only single-ball shots. All rules of croquet apply, except that when a roquet is made the striker does NOT pick up his ball and place it against the roqueted ball. He has two further shots, but plays the first of these from where his ball finishes after making the roquet. It is normal to rotate turns as in golf croquet, and two or three additional balls can be thrown onto the lawn before starting the game in order to make it easier for the newcomers. If an experienced player is joining in, he can be 'handicapped' by being allowed to use only a few of the balls. The movement from Ricochet to Association Croquet is far less painful than the jump from Golf Croquet to Association Croquet.

(c) acceptance of change

A problem which many coaches encounter is the tendency of players to reject recommended changes in technique (i.e. grip, stance, swing, etc.) unless they are immediately successful. It seems unfair to expect to immediately be as successful with a new correct style as you have been with the incorrect one you have practised for years; but unless they experience such immediate success the great majority of players will return to the incorrect style with which they are more comfortable.
For this reason the coach must give careful thought to the time and manner of introducing the recommended change. In general, a change in technique should only be recommended when the player is thoroughly convinced of the need to change and has a high level of confidence in the coach.

(d) be wary of "principles"

I believe that a coach should be wary of teaching the game by means of general "principles" which tend to become inscribed in the learner's mind alongside the Ten Commandments and other such never-to-be-broken laws. In fact it has been observed that certain croquet players are more prone to break some of the Commandments than they are to break ingrained principles such as "Never set up in the middle of the lawn", or "Always play the border ball first", or "Always keep your balls together at the beginning and end of a game", or "Leave your partner ball near a border so you will always have somewhere safe to come home to", etc.

Even when the player in later years is well aware that such principles have exceptions, he will often find that failure to adhere to them gives rise to feelings of guilt and betrayal of past coaches who passed on the advice.

(e) do not patronise

It is also important to recognise the difference when a newcomer, instead of being interested in the game for mainly social reasons, is of truly competitive instinct. Such newcomers are sufficiently rare in some clubs for their needs to be overlooked.

Such a player must be continually presented with new challenges, or he will rapidly lose interest. As soon as he shows that he has improved to a level where he can beat the players he is regularly playing with, he must be provided with stronger opponents.

When such a player is still in the 'beginner' stage, it is vital that well-meaning club members understand they must NOT allow him to play shots again when he makes mistakes, or overlook faults, or give him additional turns, or deliberately miss so as to give him more play. Members who do such things are no doubt well intentioned and trying to be kind, but they are also being 'patronising' and taking away from the beginner any possible sense of achievement. If he is truly competitive then losing will not discourage him. Instead it will spur him on to improve as quickly as he can. But winning a game in which he was given additional turns or allowed to replay missed shots will not have any appeal or interest for such a player.

CREATE YOUR OWN DISTRACTION

ONE OF THE most effective means of overcoming nervousness, especially when running a hoop or playing a short roquet, is to concentrate on examining the milling pattern on the ball in the place where you expect the mallet to contact it.

The mind recognises certain "danger" situations and the body responds by producing an increased adrenalin flow (or a "rush of blood"). In many of life's situations this can be an appropriate response which promotes alertness and gets the muscles "ready for action"; but it tends to result in a mental state which is the opposite of relaxation. It can cause muscles to jerk and twitch involuntarily as the mallet swings forward, destroying the alignment of the mallet head and lessening the chance of the stroke being successful.

The theory is that concentrating on the milling (or for that matter on anything other than the hoop you 'have to run' or the roquet you 'cannot afford to miss') will distract your mind from thinking about the "danger" associated with the stroke you are playing, since although there may be an involuntary nervous reaction to the prospect of running an awkward hoop or hitting a missable roquet, there should be no such involuntary reaction associated with studying the milling on the ball. Note that in order to be effective this requires you to actually study the milling pattern and take an interest in it; not just to look at it.

You should begin to study the pattern as the mallet starts to move forward to hit the ball. There is no need to look at the hoop you are running or the ball you are roqueting once the forward swing has started, as the result of the swing has already been pre-determined by your brain telling the muscles how they are to coordinate; and if you were to see the mallet going off line your reaction time would be too long to allow you any chance of altering things before the mallet reached the ball anyway. In fact, once the forward swing has started you can shut your eyes without affecting the success of the stroke in any way—something most players find hard to believe until they try it for themselves (although we are not recommending that you do it in a game situation). However, there is still time for an involuntary muscular reaction to affect the stroke, as it does not need to pass through the conscious brain in the same way as something you have noticed.

So line everything up, relax your foot muscles (and also those in your wrists and forearms), feel where your shoulders are in space (and feel that they are not going to move during the swing), and then, as the forward swing starts, take your mind off the stroke and simply study the milling pattern on the ball.

TURN NEGATIVES INTO POSITIVES

AN IMPORTANT PART of psychological preparation for a croquet game is to quickly consider the various things which may possibly affect your play. If they are things which you can control and alter (e.g. muscle stiffness, feeling ill, uncomfortable clothing, cold fingers becoming numb, perspiration fogging up your glasses, etc.), then you can do something about them either before starting the game or as soon as they start to become a problem. However, there will also be things such as rain, strong wind, patches of different types of grass (or bare earth), very tight and difficult hoops, uneven or sloping lawn, etc., over which you have no control. It is vital to see these things as 'positives' rather than 'negatives'.

Firstly, remember that your opponent will have to cope with exactly the same things, so there is no reason why you should be disadvantaged by them. Secondly, realise that such things can actually be turned to your advantage if you can "outwit" your opponent by correctly assessing their effects and suitably modifying (where necessary) your technique, tactics and strategy.

Perhaps the art of turning 'negatives' into 'positives' is at its most effective in dealing with interruptions and distractions during a break; e.g. a dog running onto the court, interference by the players or balls of a double-banked game, spectator noise and movement, etc. An experienced player will learn to view such an interruption, not as a frustrating annoyance, but as a welcome opportunity to pause, take stock (again) of the conditions and state of the game, relax, and think through things like lifts, intended leave, time remaining and any strokes that have not been turning out quite as intended. Then, when the distraction has passed, he will turn his full concentration back to the next stroke that has to be played and set about re-establishing his regular break rhythm.

Do not let things worry you that are not under your control. Do not blame them for a poor stroke you have just played—instead blame your own failure to cope with the conditions, and note what you will need to do in future to make your strokes successful. Try to devise ways of using the less than ideal playing conditions to help you beat your opponent. In other words, see them as 'positives' rather than 'negatives'.

CONCLUSION

I BELIEVE THAT much could be said about the way psychological considerations affect other areas of the game such as refereeing and administration but these can wait until some other time, and may well prove too hot to handle. It is my hope that the ramblings, anecdotes, experiences and occasional insights presented above will encourage players to become more aware of psychological influences in the game. I trust that others will use this booklet as a starting point for their own researches and observations, and that the game will become even more fascinating to people as they realise that it contains psychological elements to a far greater extent than is found in any other game.

ADDENDUM

Coping with excitement

Carolyn Spooner has suggested that I should have included a section on what she calls the "fear of winning". There is no doubt that some players seem almost psychologically incapable of defeating a particular opponent, to the extent that one could quite reasonably conclude that they are somehow "afraid" of winning.

At times I have been aware of this in an opponent who has only to complete the final three or four hoops of a simple four-ball break in order to score an unexpected victory. This is something he would do with ease at most other times, yet I have somehow sensed that he was almost certain to break down and let me in again.

This is a quite different psychological phenomenon from that described in section 2 as the "desperado" effect, as the player has quite likely been playing good, sound croquet without taking abnormal risks or adopting any type of devil-may-care attitude.

I believe that the problem can be best described as a type of excitement which comes upon the player when he suddenly realises that he is about to beat an opponent against whom he had given himself little chance of winning.

This state of excitement has physiological effects on the player similar to those caused by nervousness. There is a rush of adrenalin, more rapid heart-beat, and jerky muscle movements which result in a lack of muscular co-ordination. Together with these is the psychological effect of confused thinking so that the player becomes more likely than before to play a wrong ball, run a wrong hoop, forget about a 'lift', or commit some other "inexplicable" error.

As with nervousness, the shots most commonly affected are hoop-running, rushes and short roquets; and the answer seems to lie in being aware of the danger and the first warning signs, then deliberately slowing down all movements. This includes walking more slowly between shots in order to give you time to relax, clearly visualising the next shot before playing it, concentrating fully on playing one shot at a time, using a longer, slower backswing, and (perhaps most important of all) ensuring that each stroke is played with the weight of the mallet alone, and without any additional force from the hands.

It may also be possible to develop psychological 'tricks' designed to avoid the onset of such excitement, for example by telling yourself that you have already achieved more than anyone had expected, so any further hoops can be regarded as a bonus; or thinking in terms of percentages, e.g. "From here I must have at least a 90% chance of winning. Nothing is ever a certainty, however, and all I can do is play each separate shot to the best of my ability. If that's not good enough to win this particular game, then at least it should be on the next nine or so times I get myself into a similar situation."

I would be interested to hear from players who have discovered other ways of coping with this difficulty, which is one of the few problems I cannot remember having affected me personally; or indeed about any of the other topics considered in this booklet.

CROQUET
FINER POINTS

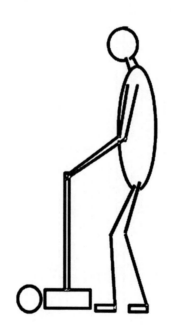

AUTHOR'S NOTES

1. Although male pronouns are used throughout for the sake of clarity, they are intended at all times to include the feminine. In fact, many of the players alluded to in the various articles were female. The gender-inclusive male pronouns serve to protect anonymity and seem appropriate in cases where the sex of the player has no relation to the point being made in the article.
2. Any reader who considers that the author has made certain points with insufficient clarity and justification is invited to enter into correspondence with him on such matters. I will be interested to hear from anyone who is willing to take the time to inform me of their opinions, especially concerning ways in which the material or its presentation can be improved.
3. This booklet, like the author's previous booklets, has been written, typed, illustrated, photocopied, assembled, stapled, bound and published by him alone. For this reason print-runs are necessarily small, usually of about 20-30 copies. It is quite likely that errors found after one print-run will be corrected in the next, with the result that copies of the booklet may not be identical to each other. The electronic versions introduce further layers of cruft that biblioarchaeologists may wish to annotate at some stage in the future.

First published: January 1995

John Riches

Digital edition v1.2 2004 by cleinedesign.
email *jballant@smartchat.net.au*

CONTENTS

INTRODUCTION

M Y AIM IN writing this booklet, as with the previous booklets, is to make people think by presenting to them some ideas which they may not have previously considered. In this way I hope to make a small contribution toward raising the general understanding of the game, and the standard of play in this country.

As with the other booklets, I have tried to avoid the temptation to merely repeat things which are adequately explained in other books on the game of croquet. Here you will find no detailed explanation of peeling or wiring or standard openings or the standard leaves after the first nine hoops have been made. Instead, I have largely endeavoured to update and extend the material introduced previously in relation to technique, strategy, tactics, coaching and the psychology of the game.

Those who have not read the previous booklets may encounter a few unfamiliar terms such as "trap lines" and "ideal leaves", but this should not hinder them from understanding the main points I am trying to make.

The booklet consists of about 100 separate articles organised into sections which deal with various aspects of the game. Some of the articles could have been placed in more than one section, and occasionally there will be a small amount of overlap from one article to another, where an idea is repeated and explained in further detail.

Some of the articles (about 20 in all) have been previously published in the Australian Croquet Gazette, or the Queensland Croquet Newsletter, or the SACA Coaching Committee's newsletter. They are repeated here in order to make more complete the coverage of the particular topics under consideration, and for the benefit of readers who may not have had access to the above mentioned publications.

. . . John Riches

TECHNIQUE

MY FIRST BOOKLET "Croquet Technique" was an attempt to explain in some detail the way in which each of the basic shots should best be played, and the reasons for using the particular method recommended for each shot. The following few articles take things further, covering some of the finer points which a player needs to know in order to achieve greater consistency with his shots, and so that he will more quickly be able to put things right when they start to go wrong.

The reader may note that not every shot is covered here. For a fuller explanation of right-angled splits and the basic splits and rolls he is referred to the above-mentioned booklet.

Take-offs and hoop approaches are covered from the coaches' viewpoint in section 8.

I thank the National Coaching Director, Jane Lewis, for some of the ideas in the article "Swing high, swing low".

BACK TO BASICS: THE ROQUET

I N PREVIOUS ARTICLES I have stressed the importance of working on improving your tactics, as it is in this area that most games are won and lost between players of roughly equal ability. However, it is also important that a player knows how to discover quickly what is going wrong with a shot that is not working satisfactorily, and how to put things right.

This requires a sound understanding of the basic elements needed to ensure the success of each different type of shot, and a good coach can be of tremendous help, since the player is unable to watch himself to find out what he is doing wrong.

The science of "Error Correction" is probably the most important part of a coach's training, and is the reason why a player seeking help should always go to a trained and accredited coach rather than to just any good and experienced player. The likely causes of errors will vary from player to player, and the coach must not only be able to diagnose the error (which can require a great deal of expert knowledge), but must also know how to go about correcting it. Simply telling the player what he is doing wrong is not good enough, unless you can also tell him how to ensure that he puts it right.

For the roquet, there are many things to be considered, but the elements most likely to be the cause of error for most players are the following:

(1) Grip: Must be relaxed, not tense. There is a strong tendency, especially when nervous, to tighten the grip during the swing. The player is usually unaware that he is doing it, and the coach cannot see it happening; consequently it is an error which can be difficult to detect. When the grip is tightened the alignment of the mallet is almost always altered, so that it will no longer be in line with the direction of swing.

(2) Aim: When you have "stalked" the ball (to ensure that hips and shoulders are square to the line of swing) and checked that your grip and stance are correct, fix your eyes on the exact centre of the target ball. Then transfer your attention to the point on back of the ball where the mallet will contact it, and concentrate on hitting that point in the centre of the mallet face.

(3) Backswing: Must be slow, deliberate, straight and long. Many players use a backswing which is hurried and far too short. A short backswing means that the falling weight of the mallet will be insufficient on its own to provide the force needed to send the ball the required distance, so the player has

to push with wrists and forearms to give additional force, and this reduces control of direction.

(4) Swing: The arms must swing freely from the shoulders, without any jerky use of wrists or forearms. The shoulders must remain still, and while body movement may not necessarily be disastrous, it is usually dangerous and represents a source of possible error. Many of the older books on the game warn of the danger of "lifting up your head" during the swing; but it is the shoulders, rather than the head, that you must concentrate on keeping still.

(5) Foot placement: It is vital for good roqueting that the player be able to achieve consistency of foot placement. The feet must every time be placed the same distance back from the ball, and the same distance out from the line of swing (see diagram). It is also necessary that the toes are always pointing in exactly the same direction in relation to the line of swing. In the diagram the toes are shown pointing parallel to the line of swing (see thicker arrows). This is not a necessity: many players have them pointing either outward or inward. The important thing is that you find a way of ensuring every time that they point in the same direction. just as a consistent ball toss is essential for a tennis player to serve well, so consistent foot placement is an essential precondition for consistent roqueting.

(6) Follow-through: The forward swing must be relaxed and unhurried, with a long, low follow-through. You should feel that you are trying to keep the mallet-head moving forward along the ground, maintaining contact with the ball for as long as possible. Avoid the type of follow-through in which the mallet finishes above your head. If your roquets have been a bit "off" lately, work through these basics one at a time, with an accredited coach if one is available, and it is likely that the problem will be discovered somewhere along the way.

Distance from ball

Distance from line of swing

BACK TO BASICS: THE STOP SHOT

YEARS AGO IT was common to see stop-shots with a ratio of 1:10 or even 1:12, but nowadays players seldom seem to achieve better than 1:6 or at most 1:8.

The main reason for this change is that the Dawson Mk 2 balls are noticeably less elastic (i.e. less "lively") than the older Jacques balls, and in order to cope with this change players are tending to use heavier mallets.

It is far more difficult to play good stop-shots with a heavy mallet than with a light one, but players feel that with the Mk 2 balls the extra weight has advantages which outweigh any reduction in stop-shot ratio.

Some have wrongly suggested that the switch to more rigid shafts, rather than the older flexible cane or metal shafts, which has accompanied the increase in weight, can be considered as another factor; but such thinking is misguided. In fact, it is easier to play a good stop-shot with a rigid shaft than with a flexible one; and one reason for having a more rigid shaft is just this—it is necessary to allow the playing of a reasonable stop-shot with a much heavier mallet head. The error in thinking that the older flexible shafts permitted one to play better stop-shots seems to have arisen from the fact that the flexible shafts were usually fitted into lighter heads, and the weight of the head was the dominant factor.

Here are some hints which may help you to improve your stop-shots, even if you do have a mallet weighing well over 3 pounds:

(1) Try placing the striker's ball so that the roughest part of the knurling (i.e. the milling pattern on the ball) is in contact with the roqueted ball.

(2) This idea is difficult to convey in words without a demonstration; but try lifting the mallet up by hunching your shoulders, then jabbing it sharply downward at the back of the ball as if attempting to impart some backspin to the ball. However, do not slope the mallet forward so that you are hitting down on the ball. Keep the mallet head flat or else tilted up very slightly at the front.

(3) You could also try having a rough face on the end of your mallet. Years ago it was fashionable to have milling on your mallet face similar to the milling on the ball, instead of the smooth, shiny end faces we see today. This would also have a negative effect in that it would make rolls and splits more difficult. If none of these hints work. you can always learn to plan ahead and play your breaks so that you do not need to play any

sharp stop-shots, as some of our leading players are doing. However, the usefulness of stop-shots in getting balls into play and setting up breaks cannot be denied.

(4) In a game, is it wise to avoid wide-angle stop-shots as far as possible. When the angle between the directions of the two balls opens out toward a right-angle it becomes more and more difficult to stop the striker's ball short, and it also becomes correspondingly more difficult to control both the distance and direction of the striker's ball.

Appearances can be rather deceptive. The diagram below shows a wide-angle stop-shot played from the 1st corner, in which the player of red tries to send the black ball in front of 2-back and obtain a rush to 1-back on the yellow ball in position Y1. It seems that, because of the shorter distance involved, this should be considerably easier than obtaining the same rush if the yellow ball were instead at position Y2, which would make the shot into more of a roll rather than a stop-shot. In both cases the red ball would need to finish inside a small imaginary "target triangle" in order to create an acceptable rush.

In actual fact, the margin for error is greater for the roll shot to Y2 than for the stop-shot to Y1, and it is more likely that the rush will be obtained when the striker's ball travels the longer distance. The physics and mathematics which supports this

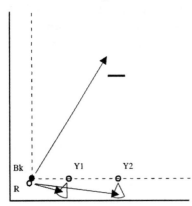

conclusion is too complicated to explain here (those interested are invited to write to the author for a copy of the fuller explanation), but it means that in a match situation it is usually wiser to compromise and send black, not in front of 2-back, but 2-3 yards behind it, so as to narrow the angle of the stop-shot and allow a greater margin for error. This should be remembered in any situation where one needs an accurate rush and may be tempted to use a wide-angle stop-shot to obtain it.

SWING HIGH, SWING LOW

I T IS IMPORTANT for the beginner to understand that for most shots the height of the mallet BACKSWING should determine the length of the shot (i.e. how far the ball goes). Too often players try to limit the height of the backswing because they believe that a high backswing makes them inaccurate with their roquets. There are several points to consider here:

If the player wants to hit a ball the longest possible distance, but only has a low backswing, then the extra strength needed for the desired result must come from the player's own muscles and body movement, instead of from the natural fall and follow-through of the mallet. Many players grip the mallet with their hands apart, which in itself may cause the mallet to be pushed off line, while the extra force used in hitting at the ball can cause jarring and tendon damage above the wrist. Sudden body movement forward can make the player unbalanced and tense. How tiring!

If the player feels that control is lost during the forward movement of the mallet, then PROVIDED THAT THE HANDS STAY TOGETHER, he could try moving them a short distance down the mallet handle. Keep the backswing high for long shots, reducing it for short shots. To move the ball only 12 inches, the backswing need only be about 6 inches. To move the ball fast across a distance of 35 yards, the backswing must be as high as the player's stature allows.

Well-meaning players often observe someone else (frequently their doubles partner) using a high backswing, and it is obvious that the mallet is being turned off line at the top of the backswing. They then suppose that this is a source of error, and suggest that a shorter backswing may enable the player to swingstraighter and more accurately. In actual fact, very few players maintain a straight mallet line throughout the whole of their swing. While there is likely to be some advantage for the player if he can manage to keep the mallet head pointing in the right direction at all times, the only thing that really matters is the direction in which it is pointing (and travelling, which is not necessarily the same!) at the instant when it contacts the ball. The player will usually straighten the mallet well before the mallet reaches the ball, so the turning of the mallet at the top of the backswing need not be a cause for concern. It is also important to realise that a high backswing does not necessarily mean that the shot must be hit hard.

The principle to remember as a coach is that an unnecessarily high backswing is far better than one which is not high enough. It is quite possible to play even the shortest of shots with quite a high backswing, simply by bringing the mallet forward more slowly; but to play a long shot with a short backswing would require the player to provide force with the muscles in his forearms and wrists, diverting these muscles away from their more important task of maintaining the direction of the swing. Players should be encouraged to develop a high backswing and an unhurried forward swing. There should be no additional force imparted from the forearms and wrists as the mallet contacts the ball. The timing of the correct, unhurried swing can be practised quite easily by swinging the mallet with the top hand only. The bottom hand should play no part in pushing the mallet forward or hurrying it through. This hand should be used only to guide the direction of the swing. The grip should not be tight or tense, but should be light and comfortably relaxed. Some players think that a tighter grip will prevent the mallet from twisting if the ball is contacted off-centre; but it is far better to ensure that the ball is hit in the centre of the mallet face, which is achieved more easily by using a relaxed grip. The tension of the grip should be felt as a light pressure in the finger tips, and this tension should be evenly maintained during the swing without any tightening of the grip. When practising, the player should make himself aware of this tension and concentrate on maintaining it evenly, so that he will learn to do it automatically in a match situation. All coaches are therefore urged never to suggest that a player shorten his backswing for single-ball shots such as roquets, rushes or hoop running. Even stop-shots should be played with a high backswing. The only possible exceptions are pass-rolls, and hampered shots where a high backswing is impossible.

John Riches and Wayne Davies

WIDE-ANGLE SPLITS

 I N MANY SITUATIONS the best way to establish an immediate break is by playing a wide-angle split-shot. Unfortunately, one frequently sees players failing to take advantage of the opportunity because they lack confidence in their ability to control the shot, so they resort to a take-off or simpler type of split-shot which fails to load the following hoop accurately before making the current hoop.

This often means that they do not succeed in getting the break fully set up, and it is even more unfortunate that they later tend to attribute the loss of a game to missed roquets or failed hoop attempts instead of their unwillingness to play the correct shots.

The left-hand diagram below shows a situation where the player of red has made hoop 1 from his yellow partner ball and roqueted it at point R. Now he is about to send it to point Y near hoop 3 while the red ball goes to point B so that it can rush the blue ball to hoop 2. Most players do not find this shot difficult, but when confronted with the situation shown in the right-hand diagram it is a very different matter. Here the only difference is that the blue ball is in a different place, making the angle of the split much wider. The reason why many players would now hesitate to attempt the wide-angle split is that they do not understand the difference that the wider angle makes to the way the shot has to be played. The dotted lines on the diagrams are intended to give an idea of strengths of the forces involved in shots of this type.

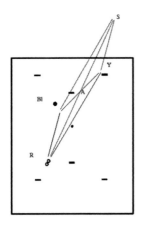 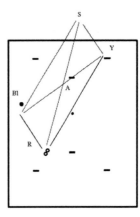

Strength: The strength of the shot is represented roughly by the length of the line RS on each diagram. Though the red and yellow balls travel the same distances in each of the two shots, the line RS is shorter for the wider angle shot, so the shot does not need to be hit as hard as if the angle were more normal (i.e. narrower).

Direction: The mallet should be swung straight along the line RS in each case. Players often find this difficult because there is a strong psychological temptation to follow through around a curve, ending up in the direction the red ball is to travel. This temptation must be strenuously resisted if you hope to keep accurate control of both balls.

The simplest way to get the correct direction is to find point A, which is halfway between where you want the two balls to finish. It is far easier to find this point on the lawn than it is to imagine a parallelogram with its furthest corner (S) out on another lawn or behind a fence! Since RAS is a straight line, aiming at point A is the same as aiming at point S. Note that this line of aim does not halve the angle of split. Note also that in the first diagram the line of aim is about 2 yards to the right of hoop 6, while in the second diagram it is about 1 yard to the left of the same hoop. In addition, the direction will usually need to be adjusted slightly to allow for "pull" and spin on the balls.

This involves swinging not directly at point A (or S), but a few degrees from this line on whichever side the striker's ball will go. In these examples the red ball is going to the left of the line RAS and yellow to the right, so the line of swing, allowing for "pull", will be slightly to the left of the line RAS.

Mallet slope: The most difficult and vital adjustment for the wider angle shot is that you must get back off the shot, so that your mallet has much less forward slope than for the narrower angle. (If you use the alternative method of accelerating through the balls instead of sloping the mallet forward, then you must use far less acceleration.) In the examples shown, the red ball travels almost half as far as the yellow ball, which requires a slight roll for the narrower angle. However, the wider angle shot in the right-hand diagram must be played as a very sharp stop-shot, with a flat mallet and the mallet stopping instead of accelerating. The reason for this is that when the angle is wider the yellow ball is no longer so squarely in front of the red (striker's ball), which will now go too far unless a stop-shot action is used.

ADJUSTING SPLITS

IN ORDER TO play accurate split-shots, the player must first learn the simple mechanics of the shot, including:

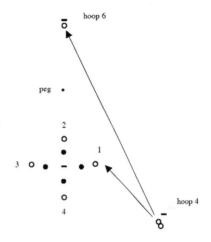

*   How to line it up, allowing for pull.
*   How to control the relative distances the balls will travel, either by tilting the mallet forward, or (less desirably) by accelerating the swing.
*   How to find the correct point of aim for the swing, and how to swing in this required line, without turning the mallet or curving the swing toward the destination of the striker's ball.

In addition, it is necessary to practise regularly the commonly occurring split-shots, e.g. the split from hoop 4 to load hoop 6 while going to a ball near hoop 5 as shown in the diagram at right, which is for most players the simplest of the basic splits. The player must understand the type of adjustment that needs to be made when the (black) 'target' ball is placed in different positions around hoop 5. Four positions are shown in the diagram, but other positions between the ones shown need to be practised as well, and the same should be done for other split-shots, from any other hoop to the following two hoops.

For position 1, most players will need to aim about a yard to the left of the peg, and have the mallet tilted slightly forward. This should be practised until good position for both balls can be achieved consistently.

   Then the player should be able to adjust the stroke for position 2 by keeping the same line of aim, but increasing noticeably the forward slope of the mallet, which must be maintained as the mallet contacts the ball. This will give the striker's ball more forward roll, so that it goes further than previously. (An alternative method would have been to increase the acceleration through the ball.) The additional distance also requires that the stroke be played with a little more force, which is obtained by using a slightly higher backswing.

   For position 3 it will be necessary to change the aiming point (i.e. line of swing) by moving it another yard or two away from the peg and toward hoop 5. The forward slope, backswing and strength of the shot should all be similar to those needed for position 2.

Position 4 can be achieved by using roughly the same aiming point as for position 3, or perhaps a very slight further adjustment away from the peg; but requires the player to use much less forward slope of his mallet (i.e. "get back off the shot"), and needs less force than the shot to position 3.

The player who wishes to achieve a high standard of accuracy should practise playing these shots, with the striker's ball going to any of the four (or more) positions, until the adjustments become more or less automatic. Then he can proceed to some of the harder splits, e.g. from hoop 2 to hoops 3 and 4; or from hoop 1 to hoops 2 and 3, learning to make similar adjustments for various positions of the 'target' ball.

Note that in a game it may be necessary to make a further adjustment for the fact that the shot is being played from somewhere other than just behind a hoop, and this also needs to be understood. The split from hoop 5 to hoops 6 and 7 is complicated by the possibility of the peg interfering, and the split-roll from hoop 3 to hoops 4 and 5 will be hardest of all to control and adjust with any degree of accuracy.

After thus learning to adjust the splits for the required finishing position of the striker's ball, the player should be able to concentrate on more accurate placement of the croqueted ball which is being used to load the next hoop. Contrary to the belief of most players, this is actually the ball whose accurate placement is most critical to the continuance of the break.

Only after the type of adjustment needed in each case is fully understood will the player be able to play these shots with complete confidence that the balls will actually go where he wants them to go.

BACK TO BASICS: THE RUSH

B ESIDES POSSIBLY ROQUETING and hoop running, the rush is a shot which can go wrong more easily than any other. In order to play good, consistent rushes and immediately correct any error that creeps in to the rushing technique, a player needs to understand and keep in mind the following principles:

1. Use a long grip. Any player who has developed the habit of playing rushes with one or both hands down the handle should be able to bring about an almost instantaneous improvement by re-learning the shot with both hands together at the top of the handle.

2. Use a flat swing. In particular, as the mallet moves through the ball, the bottom of the swing should be more or less parallel to the ground, and the follow-through as low as possible. Do not bring the mallet upward in the follow-through so that the head of the mallet finishes above head height, as some tend to do. The need for a flat-bottomed swing is the reason why players who use a short-handled mallet or a shorter grip than necessary will usually not rush as consistently as those with longer mallets and grips. (However, there are other considerations as well that must be taken into account when determining the optimum mallet length and grip for any particular player.)

3. Use a stance that allows a long, straight backswing from the shoulders, not from the wrists; and also a long, low forward swing without overbalancing. Avoid any unnecessary body movement such as bending of the knees or trunk. The weight should be back, more or less on the heels, and most players are helped by standing a little further back from the ball than they would for a roquet.

4. Use the weight of the mallet alone to provide the necessary force. Any hurrying of the forward swing, by using muscles in the wrists and forearms, is likely to be even more disastrous in a rush than in other shots. The strength should come entirely from the weight of the falling mallet, and is controlled by the height of the backswing. It is an interesting fact that, depending on the grip and stance, a shorter mallet may in some cases actually allow a higher backswing which can partly compensate for the physical shortness of the 'pendulum' from shoulder to ball.

5. All muscles in fingers, hands, wrists and arms should be relaxed. This may need to be done consciously during preparation for the swing. There is always a temptation to tighten the grip during the swing, which can twist the head of the mallet off line and ruin the shot completely. This temptation is harder to overcome in the rush than in other shots, and may be another aspect of technique that requires conscious concentration in order to counter it.

6. Do not look up at the ball you are rushing. After having lined the shot up, fix your eyes on the place where the mallet will contact the striker's ball, and keep them there. Simply allow the mallet to swing through of its own weight in its own time, with confidence that if you get these basics correct, everything will turn out as desired.

7. When attempting a cut-rush, remember Tom Armstrong's dictum that "90% of cut-rushes are under-hit". To counter the fact that only a fraction of the force from the striker's ball will be imparted to the ball that is being rushed, use a noticeably higher backswing than you would for a straight rush of the same length; but be even more careful not to hurry the forward swing.

8. Some players may be helped by realising that, for example, in order to cut the black ball to the hoop in the diagram at left, it is necessary to use at least sufficient force to send the striker's ball, if the black ball were removed, to the position shown by the dotted ball at the top of the diagram. This position is obtained, for those geometrically minded, by imagining a right-angled triangle with its right-angle at the hoop, and its longest side ("hypotenuse") following the direction in which the striker's ball is to be hit.

9. By aiming your swing through the centre of the striker's ball and the edge of the rushed ball, you should in most cases obtain a "cut" of 30 degrees from straight ahead. Players who are adept at judging the actual sizes of angles can make use of this fact in lining up their cut-rushes.

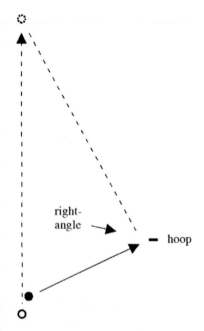

10. Of all these pieces of advice, the most important needs to be re-emphasised: Use the weight of the mallet, don't tighten the grip, and don't hurry the forward swing.

BACK TO BASICS: HOOP RUNNING

ONE OFTEN HEARS players attributing the loss of a game to the fact that they "kept sticking in hoops". The problem is usually best rectified by working on improving their hoop approaches, rather than their hoop running; but nevertheless there are several points that the player must get right in order to be able to run hoops confidently and consistently:

1. **Take a proper backswing**. Some players deliberately shorten the backswing when running hoops, and some misguided coaches have even advised it, but one of the most important principles of good hoop running is that the backswing must be high enough to provide all the force needed, without the player having to make any use of muscles in his fingers, hands, wrists or forearms. The mallet must be swung smoothly from the shoulders. It is far better to use a longer backswing than necessary, rather than one which is in any way shortened.

2. **Do not tighten the grip during the swing**. The mallet should be held with the desired grip tension—a comfortably relaxed grip—while the shot is being lined up. The player who has problems in this area should consciously "feel" the pressure of his fingertips against the handle of the mallet, and then maintain the same even pressure throughout the swing.

3. **Do not hurry the forward swing.** The tendency to "jab" is difficult for many players to cope with, and is best overcome by concentrating on maintaining an even grip tension as explained above.

4. **Swing down through the ball with the mallet tilted slightly forward.** This will give the ball topspin which will help it "kick" through the hoop if it hits the sides. Do not use a flat forward "push", and do not try to hit upward at the ball, or through the top of the ball.

5. **Follow through low toward the hoop.** Never attempt to run a hoop with a stop-shot action.

6. For fairly sidey hoops aim your swing through the centre of the ball **at the inside edge of the far hoop-leg.** This is much better than thinking about the need for the ball to miss the near hoop-leg. For very sidey hoops, learn to play jump shots with a relaxed, smooth, unhurried action.

7. It has been suggested that when you need to run through the hoop and right down to the other end of the court, the best way to do it is with a smooth, accelerating swing. I am not certain of the validity of this advice, but it is worth trying, at least in practice situations.

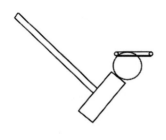

8. A shot developed by the author in conjunction with the late Vern Potter at Port Pirie (SA) and christened the "Pirie Poke" is worth passing on, though it is difficult to explain it in words without an actual demonstration. It allows hoops to be made from what may seem to be almost impossible situations, where the ball is in contact with a hoop leg, or less than 1 mm from it, in a position as illustrated in the top diagram at left.

The "Pirie Poke" (side view)

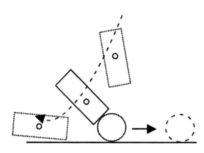

The mallet is used sideways, with the handle almost parallel to the ground, and as it contacts the ball the mallet is moving both downward and backward. It may seem surprising that it is possible to hit a ball forward by moving the mallet backward, but this is actually what happens, and this fact ensures that the ball will not be "crushed" against the far hoop leg. Because the mallet is moving backward away from the hoop leg, it cannot be still in contact with the ball when the ball hits the hoop leg!

It is important to select a line of aim which ensures that the ball is hit away from the near hoop leg. This is easier to do if the player can contrive to have his arms in what seems a rather awkward position, so that he can sight along the mallet head, which is directly in front of his eyes, as he contacts the ball. The shot is played while kneeling on one knee, and with one hand quite close to the mallet head.

Readers who are interested in this shot are urged to use the information given here as a basis for experiment, but will probably still need the assistance of a coach who has been shown the shot and can demonstrate it competently.

UNUSUAL CANNONS

1. **Triangle cannon:** This is illustrated in the top diagram, and has replaced the older "banana" or "worm" cannon as the correct shot to use when you simply want to obtain an accurate rush to your hoop, leaving the roqueted ball behind rather than trying to use it to load the following hoop. For example, if you are playing the red ball which is for hoop 6 or 1-back, and have created a cannon in the 4th corner as shown, there is little you can hope to do except get a good rush on black to your hoop. If, for example, the yellow ball has been rushed into the corner where black was a corner ball, then the balls should be arranged as shown, in a tight triangle, except that there is a tiny gap, as required by the laws, between the red and black balls. The red ball is then hit with a gentle stop-shot action so as to move the yellow ball out of the way (even after it is yardlined) and simultaneously place red where it has a perfect rush to its hoop on the black ball **which does not move.** Note that the laws do not require that the third (black) ball in the cannon has to be moved, and it is easier to ensure that you get an accurate rush on it if you know exactly where it will be.

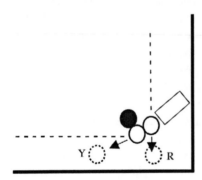

2. **Promotion cannon:** The second diagram shows a situation which occurs not infrequently near the start of a game, and where players often fail to find the best way to continue. Red, which is for hoop 1, has a cannon on the east border, and will send the third ball (blue) to hoop 1 without roqueting it in the cannon shot. Instead, red will go to the nearby yellow ball, which can then be roqueted and split to hoop 2 while red goes to make hoop 1 from the unused blue ball. The yellow ball may even have been placed there deliberately so as to facilitate such a cannon, as described in the later article on Opening Ideas. It should be realised that this type of shot needs to be practised, as the "feel" of the stroke is very different from a split-shot, in that the red ball has the full weight of two balls in front

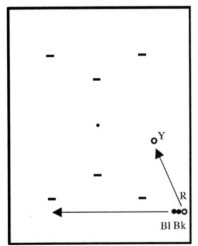

of it, making it come off at a wider angle and travel a shorter distance than one might expect.

3. **Delayed cannon:** This possibility is also frequently overlooked. The third diagram shows a situation where the player of red has tried to create a cannon, intending to promote blue to hoop 1 as described above, but just failed, since when measured onto the yard-line the black ball was not quite in contact with blue. In this case he can use a stop-shot to send black to hoop 2, and roquet blue in the same shot. Then he can play a croquet stroke in which red obtains a rush on yellow to hoop 1, again with a break set up.

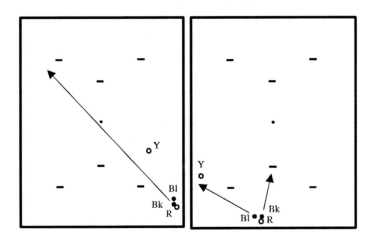

Another type of delayed cannon is shown in the fourth diagram. Here red is for hoop 4 and has roqueted black very close to blue on the south border. Black should be sent to load hoop 5 by using a shot in which blue is at the same time rushed out of court near the yellow ball on the west border.

Then yellow can be rushed to hoop 4 to establish the break.

CANNON WITH A used ball. The first diagram shows a situation where red is for hoop 5 and yellow is for hoop 2. The player of red has taken off from yellow to the opponent's balls in the 3rd corner. He has roqueted blue, and had hoped to create a cannon by rushing it into the corner where black was on the corner spot; but blue did not finish in the corner as intended. Now he can take off from blue trying for a rush behind black to hoop 5, but sees little prospect of setting up a break in this fashion. He could also send blue to hoop 2 with a stop-shot, turn around and roquet black (a roquet of 4-5 yards which may not be a certainty), and then place black at hoop 5 before returning to yellow with an excellent leave in which there is an opponent ball at each of red and yellow's hoops. There is yet another option which most players would overlook. He can use a gentle stop-shot or roll to send blue into the 3rd corner square, yardline it so that it is in contact with black, and then roquet black gently without disturbing blue, so as to create a cannon in the 3rd corner in which black is the roqueted ball, and the third ball is blue, which has already been used. He can now move blue (he can indeed, though people who do not understand the laws may dispute this) and arrange a cannon in which black is split to hoop 2 and blue is simultaneously rushed to a position near hoop 5.

Note that he cannot claim the roquet on blue, because he had used it previously, so he will finish the turn by hitting red out near yellow, and make a break on the next turn unless the opponent roquets. The player of red needs to be careful when playing the cannon to ensure that the red ball stays in the lawn, and also that he does not double-hit the red ball. Neither of these things would matter in a normal cannon, but either would end the turn when blue is a ball which has been already used.

In the second diagram the player of red wants to set up for yellow, which is for hoop 1. He would like to place the opponent's balls near hoops 1 and 2, and set yellow a rush to either of these two hoops. Once again, the best way, provided you have practised it, is by rolling blue into the corner square, then roqueting black to create a cannon with the used ball. Once this idea is understood, and has been practised, other situations in which it can be used will readily come to mind. The hardest part is to actually think of it in a match when you are under pressure!

Roll cannon. In the third diagram red has created a normal cannon in the 2nd corner by roqueting black. However, red is for hoop 6, and there is no way a normal cannon can be used to load 1-back while rushing blue to hoop 6. Instead of leaving black behind in the corner, red can set up a break by playing a "roll cannon". This shot is arranged by placing the three balls in almost a straight line (actually, black, which is the middle ball of the three, should be about 1mm to the right of the line through the centres of the other two balls when viewed from the corner), and using a pronounced pass-roll action to roll both red and blue to hoop 6. Black should finish near the 1-back hoop if the shot is arranged and played correctly. The shot is actually easier than it at first may sound, but the player will need some practice at it in order to convince himself that it requires much more of a pass roll than one might think, due to the weight of two balls, rather than one, in front of the striker's ball. Red may possibly roquet blue on the way to hoop 6, but most times it will at least finish close enough to make the roquet on the following shot. Note that it is difficult to fault this shot by "pushing", as the weight of the third ball causes red to remain in contact with black for quite some time.

MALLETS

F OR SOME YEARS I had the privilege of working with a mallet craftsman, advising him from the point of view of a croquet player on various aspects of mallet design. We tried out just about every idea you could think of, and some that would probably never occur to you. We discovered all sorts of things that do not work, including things like putting all the additional weight at one end, fitting the handle off centre in the head, sloping the handle at various angles, shaping both the handle and the head in various eccentric ways, and many more.

One of our ideas that did work—the "Magic Mallet"—was written up in the Australian Croquet Gazette and drew little comment or interest, until I won the SA Division 1 medal in 1990 using such a mallet. Suddenly there were protests about the legality of the "Magic Mallet", and when it was established after much argument that the design did not in fact contravene the Laws, moves were immediately made to have the Law relating to mallet construction (then Law 2 (e), now Law 3(e)) altered so that the "Magic Mallet" became illegal.

Most of the many things we discovered about mallet construction would be of little interest to anyone other than a maker of mallets, but in the following few articles some points are explained which may be of value to coaches and players.

PERIPHERAL WEIGHTING

COACHES ARE FREQUENTLY asked for advice on the ideal type of mallet, and there are many things which should be taken into account before giving such advice to a particular player. What is "ideal" for one player may be of little use to another whose height, strength, grip, stance and type of swing are all quite different.

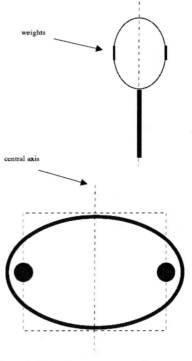

Instead of dealing with these things here, which would require many pages of complicated information, I will pass on one idea which arises from recent researches in sports technology.

The Level 2 Coaches Manual contains an interesting section on "peripheral weighting". One problem in sports such as tennis, squash, cricket, badminton, etc., is that it is difficult to always hit the ball in the middle of the racquet or bat. When the ball is hit off-centre the racquet tends to twist in the hands and the ball goes in some direction other than the one intended. By distributing the weight as far from the central axis as possible it has been found that the effect of off-centre impacts can be considerably reduced. Those with an understanding of the laws of physics regarding momentum and inertia will readily understand why this is so, and will probably wonder why it took the experts so long to think of it.

The top diagram shows a latest-style tennis racquet with additional weight distributed on the sides of the frame. The same idea has been applied to other racquet sports, and both cricket bats and golf clubs are being produced with a scooped-out centre at the back of the bat or club, and additional weight added to the sides.

Does it work? We can only offer the player's personal opinion that it does indeed serve to enlarge the "sweet spot" on the mallet face and increase the likelihood that the ball will travel in the desired direction even when struck slightly off-centre. He has not conducted any objective tests or come up with any evidence to support this opinion, except that he claims to roquet much better (most of the time!) than he did with previous more conventional mallets. This, of course, may well be due to factors other than the design of the mallet head, but the idea of using peripheral weighting in the design of croquet mallets is at least worthy of further consideration and experiment. The concept can be carried to a far greater extreme than in the mallet described above. e.g. by making the mallet head hollow, or of very light wood, and adding weighted strips along the sides of the head away from the central axis. We would be interested to hear any further ideas on this matter, or on any other aspect of mallet design which may help improve the general standard of play.

Some years ago, well before the Coaches Manual was published, one of our leading players had a similar idea and designed a mallet head with a flat, oval cross-section as shown (approximately) in the second diagram. A comparison with a standard square-faced mallet (dotted lines) will show how the weight has been removed from the corners of the square and redistributed on the sides, further from the central axis. The mallet head was made of very heavy Mulga wood and did not require the addition of lead weights, but if it had, then he presumably would have asked that they also be placed at the sides as shown by the small dark circles, rather than in the centre of the mallet face or with holes drilled in the bottom of the mallet head along the central axis as has commonly been done in the past.

BAD WRISTS AND HEAVY MALLETS

I N RECENT YEARS there seems to have been an increase in the number of players with wrist problems. The reason for this increase is not clear: some believe that the less elastic Dawson Mk 2 balls have been a contributing factor, while others suggest that it could have resulted from the trend to more rigid mallet shafts instead of the older more flexible metal or cane shafts.

With almost all players being taught to use centre-style and play long rolls with the bottom hand well down the handle, flexibility in the shaft is no longer considered so desirable. Although the rigid shaft may possibly result in a little more jarring on some shots (this is debatable, as many insist that they get no jarring from their rigid shafts), the rigidity is preferred because it allows greater control and accuracy in rolls and split-shots, as well as a better stop-shot ratio. A player with a rigid shaft has one less variable—the whippiness of the shaft and its effect on the ball—to control, and this is what makes possible the greater accuracy.

Whatever the reason, coaches are likely to be approached by players with weak or injured wrists seeking advice on whether they should continue trying to play the game, and if so, what changes they should make in order to better cope with the problem.

While it does not come with any authority from a medical viewpoint, our suggestion is that the coach should consider offering the following two pieces of advice:

(1) If the player has been using an Irish or Standard grip, then he or she could be advised to try changing to the Solomon grip, and ensuring that the hands are together at the top of the handle. The Solomon grip has its own problems from a coaching viewpoint, but these will be compensated for by the fact that it tends to place far less strain on the wrists, even in shots that need to be hit with considerable force. This is because (a) the wrists are in a more relaxed position, and (b) the grip allows a higher backswing so that greater use can be made of gravitational force rather than muscular force from the wrists and forearms.

(2) Try using a heavier mallet. This may seem like strange advice to give to a player with weak wrists, and some may protest that they find it hard enough with their weak wrists to control a light mallet. However, contrary to their expectations, the fact is that a heavier mallet will put less strain

on the wrists than a lighter one—provided it is swung correctly from the shoulders. This again is because the additional weight allows greater use of gravitational force.

The heavier mallet will also tend to swing more smoothly through the ball—similar to hitting a tennis ball with a croquet mallet or a croquet ball with a sledge-hammer—and this alone can markedly reduce wrist strain.

We suggest that instead of the average type of mallet which weighs under 3 pounds, the player could try one weighing around 3 pounds 4 ounces. Three and a half pounds would be an absolute maximum, as there are also disadvantages inherent in the additional weight: the player will find it harder to play stop-shots and harder to retain accurate control of "touch" shots such as long take-offs and delicate hoop approaches. These disadvantages should be offset by an improvement in roquets and rushes; and most importantly less strain on the wrists. Several players with wrist problems have tried this out and found that they were able to continue playing good croquet when it had appeared that they may have had to consider giving the game away.

For very long rolls on heavier lawns the player could try using a side-style swing. This is not normally to be recommended (though some leading players do it) because the additional force gained from the higher backswing which the side-style allows, is accompanied by a reduction in accuracy due to the increased difficulty of keeping the eyes and weight directly behind the shot, and achieving a straight swing and follow-through. A player without wrist problems, regardless of stature and strength, should not need to resort to a side-style swing for any type of shot. However, the player may find it necessary at times to trade off some of the accuracy he would otherwise be able to achieve in order to lessen the risk of worsening his problem.

John Riches and Wayne Davies

ON BEVELLED EDGES

MANY YEARS AGO mallets were made with wide bevels on the end faces and usually also with brass strips around them. The purpose of both the bevels and the brass strips was simply to stop the wood from splitting or chipping when the ball was struck near the edge of the mallet face.

In recent times hard plastic ends have come into common use, but many players and manufacturers have failed to realise that the bevels and brass rings are now neither necessary nor desirable. There are various hampered shots which will occur in games from time to time and can only be played satisfactorily if the mallet has no bevelled edge, so in such situations the bevels can be a distinct disadvantage. Brass strips are unobjectionable, except for the additional cost—but why pay for something you do not need?

WHERE SHOULD A MALLET BE BALANCED?

MALLETS HAVE TRADITIONALLY been made so that they will "balance" horizontally when supported at a point about one-sixth of the way from the bottom of the head to the end of the handle. There does not seem to be any compelling reason why the fraction one-sixth should be better than any other fraction, and in fact some leading players have used mallets with additional weight added to either the head or the handle, causing it to balance at a quite different point.

The advantage for a manufacturer in balancing all mallets similarly is two-fold: (a) The construction process is made more standard and therefore simpler; and (b) When a player switches from an old mallet to a new one he will be able to adjust to the feel of the new mallet more quickly if the balance is the same, even though the total weight may be different. Thus it is more likely he will be immediately satisfied.

It is also worth noting that in recent years there has been a trend toward heavier mallets, and this seems to have been a response to the reduced elasticity (or apparent "deadness") of the Dawson Mark 2 balls.

Most players have found that the increased weight needs to be accompanied by a more rigid handle in order to allow the playing and accurate control of stop-shots and certain split-shots.

THE END: ROUND OR SQUARE?

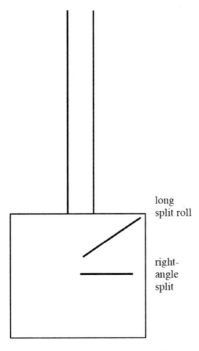

long
split roll

right-
angle
split

SOME PLAYERS USE mallets with round ends, while others have a square, octagonal, 'half-round' or 'three-quarter round' shape. Since most shots are (or should be!) hit near the centre of the end face, it would seem that there is little reason to prefer one shape rather than another. As with many other things, it was Tom Armstrong who first drew my attention to the fact that if the balls were covered with wet paint, most croquet shots would leave a line on the mallet face starting near the centre and going toward the edge, as shown by the heavy lines in the diagram at left.

The mark would in many cases end before reaching the edge, as the ball would have parted contact with the mallet by then; but for long split rolls, e.g. from hoop 1 to hoops 2 and 3, played (as they should be) with the mallet sloping well forward, the contact between ball and mallet may continue to the edge of the mallet face. The result of such a shot can vary markedly according to whether the ball leaves the mallet face at a point on the side face just below the corner as shown on the diagram, or a point on the top face, or at the corner itself. A rounded face avoids the problem, if there is one, of having to cope with this difference in the way the ball comes off the mallet for shots which in other respects are very similar. I suspect that this is at least part of the reason why, before changing to the oval mallet shape shown in the article on Peripheral Weighting, I found the split from hoop 1 to hoops 2 and 3 much easier to control than from 1-back to 2-back and 3-back.

My swing, like that of most players was probably not quite straight and symmetrical; and this perhaps caused the ball to come off the mallet face at slightly different points with noticeably different consequences. If the mallet face has to be square, then at least some rounding of the corners would seem to be justified by these considerations.

SECTION 3

LAWS

THE MATERIAL IN this section drew a considerable amount of interest when published in the Autumn 1994 issue of the Australian Croquet Gazette. In addition to the amusement it provides, it may prove helpful to others who have not already seen it.

I must point out that the explanations in no way represent the official views or interpretations of the ACA Laws Committee, and the blame for any errors or misleading statements rests squarely on the shoulders of the author alone. For this reason the reader is encouraged not to take all of them too seriously, and to check them out for himself in the Laws book if he is in any doubt.

For those interested more seriously in the Laws and refereeing I have available a "Croquet Referees Guide" which was published in October 1994 and used by the SACA Laws Committee as a basis for their Referees Training Course. Further details are given on the final page of this booklet.

NOTE: Since this section was written the Laws of Croquet have been revised so that "folk-laws" 2 and 4 no longer apply.

It is now not possible for a hoop point to be scored in any faulted stroke unless the limit of claims has been passed before the fault is discovered (see "folk-law" number 2); and a fault will end the turn in some 'compound error' situations where formerly the turn would not have ended (see "folk-law" number 4).

There is now a 'five-second' rule which applies in determining whether or not a ball had come to rest before it moved (see "folk-law" number 16); but it applies only when the ball was stationary for 5 seconds or more in a position where it did not require testing.

FOLK-LAWS

THE GAME OF croquet abounds in folklore, which is a body of advice, rules, principles and experiences derived from the accumulated wisdom of players from the past and passed on by word of mouth to each succeeding generation.

There are sayings which relate to technique, tactics, equipment, administration, clubs, lawns, and any other aspect of the game you care to think of. The following is a collection of folklore items which relate to the laws and refereeing. See if there are any you have not heard before:

1. A ball in hand cannot commit a fault.
2. If a stroke is faulted, no point can be scored in it.
3. If your ball is interfered with by a moving ball from the other set, you have the option of a replay provided it had not reached its objective.
4. A fault overrides an error.
5. Crushes only apply when you are making a hoop.
6. It you pick up one of your balls in the mistaken belief that you have a lift, it must be replaced and you are committed to playing that ball.
7. A shot which damages the lawn is a fault.
8. It is a fault if you hit the hoop with your mallet.
9. A hammer shot is a fault if your arm touches any part of your leg.
10. You cannot claim a roquet on a misplaced ball.
11. If you play with a ball misplaced you have condoned its position.
12. Failing to place a clip correctly is an error.
13. A referee called to watch a hoop shot should not tell the player if he plays the wrong ball or makes the wrong hoop.
14. When moving balls in because you do not have a stance, you must have your back to the lawn.
15. The peg can only be straightened if the position is not critical.
16. If the ball rolls back into the hoop after you have removed your clip (or counted to four), you can count the hoop as having been made.
17. Spectators are not permitted to talk to players during a game.
18. You are not permitted to run onto the court (or between shots) to save time.
19. In a time-limited game a player may not retrieve the adversary's ball if it leaves the court.
20. If you hit your ball during a practice swing it is a fault (or you have played your stroke).

---

21. A ball must complete the running of one hoop before it can begin to run the next hoop.
22. If you take croquet from the wrong ball you must go back and take croquet from the correct ball.
23. If you play a ball from the other set your turn ends.
24. If you have pegged a ball out you are not entitled to claim a wiring lift.
25. You can claim a baulked ball if your adversary has used your ball and there is no ball you can possibly roquet with it.

You will probably have heard almost all of these sayings many times. Perhaps you will be able to add to them many other common croquet platitudes. One could probably make a similar list covering other areas of the game, e.g.

Technique: "To give your ball topspin when running a hoop, lift your mallet up through the ball."

Tactics: "Never set up in the middle of the lawn."

Handicapping: "You are likely to ruin a young player if you bring his handicap down too quickly."

And most famous of all: If you can't roquet, you can't play croquet", meaning that if you want to win more games, you should concentrate mainly on improving your roqueting ability.

The fascinating thing about the "Folk-Laws" is that not a single one of them is true; and many players will be surprised to learn that the four pieces of "advice" at the bottom are incorrect also!

EXPLANATION

(1) The first one is technically true, but not the way that people mean it. They mean that if the striker's ball makes a roquet and then comes back onto your foot, or onto the bevelled edge or side of your mallet, it is not a fault because the ball has made a roquet, and so has become a "ball in hand". This is nonsense!

Firstly, the ball does not become "in hand" until it comes to rest, and secondly, the situations described in the previous sentence are indeed faults, notwithstanding that a roquet has been made.

(2) If the fault occurred in a croquet stroke, and the striker's ball went through its hoop while the croqueted ball crossed the boundary, then the opponent has the right to waive the fault and the point would count, even though the stroke in which it was scored was a fault. [Note: under the revised laws this no longer applies.]

(3) The replay is never an option. Either the shot must be replayed (whether you want it or not), or else there is no replay permitted.

(4) This is hardly ever true. A fault is, in fact, merely one kind of error. For example, if a player in a singles game has two balls in contact at the start of a turn, picks up one, then replaces it and plays the other, he has played a wrong ball under the old Law 28(a). If he also leaves a still ball in this stroke, then in addition he has committed a fault. The old Law 26(f)(1) makes clear that the only law to be applied is Law 28: the player replaces the balls and continues by taking croquet with the correct ball. [Note: under the revised laws this no longer applies.]

(5) 'Crushes' are not mentioned in the Laws. However, most people know what they mean by the term, and a 'crush' will be a fault (so a referee should be called to watch any awkward shot near a hoop) whether you are making the hoop or not.

(6) Under the Laws the ball is replaced, but there is no requirement to play it. You have not nominated it as the striker's ball under the new Law 9(b)(1) and the new Law 27 (h) allows play of either ball. On the other hand, if you were entitled to lift the ball, then once you do so you are committed to playing it.

(7) It is only a fault if the shot was deliberately played and was a type of shot considered likely to damage the court.

(8) There is no such rule. The only way that hitting a hoop with your mallet can be a fault is if by doing so during the striking period you cause another ball to move or shake.

(9) It will only be a fault if during the striking period your arm rests against any part of your leg (old Law 32(a)(4), new Law 28(a)(3)). Touching your leg is irrelevant.

(10) On the contrary, unless the stroke was forestalled by the adversary, the roquet stands and you continue by taking croquet (old Law 29, new Law 27(i)).

(11) The position of a misplaced ball can never be condoned. There is no mention of condoning in the old Law 29 or the new Law 27. The wrong position of a ball can never become its correct legal position.

If a player plays when a ball is misplaced, one of two things can happen:

(a) The misplaced ball is affected by the stroke. In this case its new position now becomes its legal position; but the incorrect position was never its legal position.

(b) The misplaced ball is not affected by the stroke. In this case it must be replaced correctly. By playing while it was misplaced the player did not in any way "condone" its incorrect position.

(12) The error is not "misplacing a clip" or "failing to place a clip correctly", but "playing when misled". Thus the error may be committed many turns after the clip was misplaced, and always by a player who did not misplace the clip.

(13) A referee called onto the court has the same powers and duties as a 'Referee in Charge' (Reg. 6) for the time he is on the court acting as referee. Thus he is required to act as an 'ever-vigilant adversary' (old Reg. 5(b), to 'be ever-vigilant' new Reg 5(b)), and accordingly he not only can, but must declare any error (old Law 45(b), new Law 48(b)). [Caution: regulations on referees may be changed in 2004]

(14) You must have your back to the court when measuring balls onto the yardline (old Law 47, new Law 12(e)), but there is no requirement to do so when measuring them in because you do not have a stance.

(15) The peg can be straightened at any time (old Reg. 5(h), new Law 3(a)(3)).

(16) In order to make the hoop the ball must have come to rest (see old Law 14. The new Law 14 differs). Old Law 22(b) explains when a ball is deemed to have come to rest, and gives only four situations in which the hoop would be allowed after the ball rolled back. The equivalent new law is 6(b). Whether or not the clip has been removed has nothing to do with it. Neither does the distance the ball went through the hoop before rolling back. Nor is it sufficient for the striker alone to have looked at it and decided that it was through the hoop.

(17) There is no such rule. Nor did the old Laws say a spectator cannot give advice to a player. They only said that the player was not permitted to receive any such advice or take advantage of it. The new Law 50(a) allows spectator input on errors and interference and lays down the appropriate responses to it.

(18) There is nothing in the Laws to prevent you from running as fast as you can at any time for any purpose, whether or not you have been running previously.

(19) Again, there is nothing in the Laws to prevent you from saving time by retrieving the opponent's balls for him. You are quite entitled to do this, whether the opponent wants you to or not.

(20) It will not be a fault if it was only a practice swing, because you were not "swinging with intent to hit the ball" (old Law 31 (b), new Law 5(a) altered that wording, and added 5(g)). Therefore the 'striking period' had not commenced, and a fault can only be committed during the striking period.

(21) A ball does not complete the running of its hoop until it comes to rest (old Law 14(b)(2), new Law 14(c)). If it goes through two hoops in order in the one shot, it will begin running the second hoop before it has completed the running of the first.

(22) Under old Law 30, the adversary had an option and could interchange the balls instead of asking for a replay. This disappears under the new law (27 (d) and (e)) and either a replay is granted or turn ends.

(23) Playing a ball from the other set has nothing to do with the game. The ball you hit, and any other balls roqueted or moved, should be replaced. Then you continue by playing a ball from your own set.

(24) You cannot claim a lift under Law 36 (advanced play) after pegging out any ball; but a lift under Law 13 (wiring lift) can still be claimed.

(25) There are possible situations (although very unusual) where your swing is hampered, not by a hoop or peg, but by another ball. It may well be quite impossible to imagine any way in which a roquet could be made, yet the player is not entitled to a wiring lift.

Technique: By trying to lift your mallet up as it contacts the ball, all you are likely to do is make the ball skid and so give yourself less chance of making the hoop. The way to give a croquet ball 'topspin' is to tilt the handle of the mallet slightly forward.

Tactics: One frequently sees players reducing their chances of winning by following this misguided advice. Certainly, you should not normally leave your balls deliberately in the middle of the lawn by choice. But in a situation such as the one shown in the diagram at right, where the player of red has played a poor hoop approach shot and cannot make the first hoop, he should sit red in the lawn near yellow so that the opponent at least has to hit a roquet in order to get the innings. Hitting red out of play to the border somewhere concedes black the innings without him even having to hit a roquet, and (depending on the positions of the opponent's clips) will probably also make it risky for yellow to shoot at any ball on the following turn if, say, black shoots at blue and misses.

Handicapping: This silly idea has been used as justification for deliberately retarding the development of many a promising young player, when he has achieved results which clearly show that his handicap should be rapidly brought down. An improving player should actually be brought down ahead of his actual results, since the results will inevitably lag behind his improving ability. The handicap he plays on now is based on results achieved some time in the past, and since then he will almost certainly have continued to improve.

Most Famous: This foolish saying ("If you can't roquet, you can't play croquet") causes problems for coaches, by making the player think that the main thing he has to do in order to win more games is improve his roqueting ability. At any level of play, with the possible exception of international competition, the ability to control split-shots and hoop approaches is far more important than the ability to hit roquets. If you want to win more games you should concentrate on improving your croquet shots and your tactics, rather than spending hours trying to bring about a small increase in the number of long roquets you are likely to hit. Many top-level games are won without the winner having to hit a roquet longer than 2-3 yards; but the ability to play controlled split-shots is essential.

GAMESMANSHIP

MANY AND VARIED are the dodges tried by players in an attempt to gain some sort of psychological or tactical advantage. Some of them are perfectly legitimate, e.g. in a doubles game leaving the ball of the stronger opponent, or the one who is not yet around, right out of play. Others may be such that they do not contravene the Laws, but would be regarded by certain people as highly unethical. Still others amount to downright cheating. You and I would naturally never engage in dubious practices. We mention a few here merely so that we can be well prepared to counter them when we encounter opponents whose ethical standards are not as high as ours.

(1) At the start of the game one player wins the toss and chooses to hit in first. The other chooses red and yellow. The first player plays blue to the east border as usual. The second player takes two balls to the 1st corner and plays red to a 'tice' position. When the first player goes to play his second ball, it "happens" that the yellow ball is waiting conveniently near the in-lawn end of A-baulk, while the black ball is over near the 1st corner. Many a time an unwary player has fallen for the trap of playing the yellow ball without realising that it is not his partner ball, and had to end his turn by removing it and placing the black ball on a baulk.

(2) The player of red and yellow has pegged out his yellow ball, but missed the peg with red. The opponent roqueted, sent red to a far corner of the lawn, and set up in the 1st corner. The player of red takes his ball to the baulk, "inadvertently" forgetting that he is not entitled to a lift because he has pegged a ball out. Unless the opponent realises it in time to forestall, it will be too late. Some have been known to deliberately wait until the opponent's attention has been momentarily distracted before having the unfortunate mental lapse.

(3) The yellow ball had been pegged out by the opponent, and red still has several hoops to make. The opponent has left the red ball so that it will risk giving away an immediate 3-ball break if it shoots at the opponent's balls or sits in front of its hoop. The player of red can think of no noticeably better place for the red ball than where it already is, but if he plays it or declares his turn he will become responsible for the position of the red ball and the opponent will be able to wire both balls from it on the next turn, not allowing him a shot. The player of red walks onto the lawn and plays the blue ball! When the opponent protests, he readily admits to having played a wrong ball. The blue ball is replaced and it is the opponent's turn.

The player of red is now responsible for the position of the blue ball, but not for the position of his own red ball! The opponent now has to allow him a shot on the next turn.

(4) Before running a somewhat sidey hoop, the player notices that on the approach shot the balls finished so that his ball is wired from the opponent ball behind the hoop. In running the hoop, he ensures that the mallet follows through gently into the hoop so that if the ball happens to stick in the hoop the mallet will hit it a second time and it will have to be replaced in the wired position. This seems to happen remarkably often in play at higher levels. There is no way of knowing whether or not the second hit was deliberate, as good hoop-running technique can involve a long, low, gentle follow-through in the exact line in which the ball travels.

(5) Near the start of the game a player starts a turn with touching balls in the 4th corner and is faced with a long diagonal take-off to the opponent's balls in the 2nd corner. He picks up yellow, places it against red, then replaces yellow and plays the red ball instead. If the opponent notices, the only penalty is that he must go back and take off correctly with yellow, having had a practice shot. If the opponent fails to notice what has happened, and the take-off is a good one, he will continue the turn accordingly. If the take-off falls short or goes out, or yellow is a still ball, he can declare his own error of playing the wrong ball. According to Law 26 (f) the fault (if there was a still ball) is overridden by Law 28 (a). In any case, the balls are replaced and the player starts his turn again by taking off correctly with yellow from red.

If you know of other good ones I can use—in my articles, of course—please write and let me know. [Later note: When the Laws were revised in the year 2000, changes were made so as to prevent all of the above underhand "tricks" except the first. However, it will probably not take long for players to think up new ways of taking advantage of an unwary opponent—particularly one who is not familiar with the laws. The above can still usefully illustrate the type of thing one needs to be alert for.]

John Riches and Wayne Davies

SECTION 4

COACHING

SOME OF THE following articles have been published in the SACA Coaching Committee's Newsletter during the past three years, and include ideas contributed by other members of the committee, to whom I am grateful for their assistance.

Since the Newsletter has a very limited circulation the articles are included here, together with others, in the hope that both coaches and players in the wider Australian croquet scene will benefit.

Once again it must be stressed that coaching is far from an exact science. The committee has been giving a lot of consideration during the past three or so years to solving not only the problem of how things should be done, but also how they should be taught.

The results of all our work can be seen in the booklets of notes for the coaches training courses at various levels. These are available, or in the case of levels 2 and 3 will become available in the future, through the National Coaching Director. Those interested should in the first instance seek the advice of their State Coaching Director, as other material may be preferred for various reasons in some states, or provided in addition.

It is also likely that in some states there may be a policy of making the material available only to accredited coaches, and there can be sound reasons for such a policy.

THE ROLE OF THE COACH

THE ROLE OF the croquet coach has been traditionally seen as one of showing the player how to play the various shots, and when things are not working out as desired, telling him what he is doing wrong. In recent years we have come to realise that as coaches we need to be involved in such things as establishing practice drills, psychological preparation, teaching tactics, planning the competitive programme of a player, and goal-setting for competitive events, as well as developing the correct attitude toward risk-taking, ways of coping with unusual or unfavourable conditions, most effective use of hit-up time, etc.

As just one example, let us return to consider a player who is missing roquets because he was hurrying his forward swing. (See the later article "More on error correction" on page 74 for further discussion of this particular problem.) After diagnosing and correcting the error, the task of the coach is far from finished. He still needs to set practice drills for the player, and establish a means of assessing whether or not the problem has been satisfactorily remedied. Then he needs to help the player set goals for competitive play, e.g. concentrate on unhurried swings during the hit-up before a game, then hit both balls into play and (later) run hoop 1 without hurrying the forward swing. There may need to be other times during the game as well, e.g. on the first stroke of every turn, where the player will find it necessary to consciously think through the idea of a higher backswing, relaxed arm and wrist muscles, and unhurried forward swing.

Very few errors can be corrected with any degree of permanency without this type of goal-setting for match play. No matter how much time the players spends at practice, and how many times he repeats a perfect, unhurried swing, he will still be likely to revert to his old habit of hurrying the swing in match play under pressure, unless he makes a deliberate and conscious attempt, at one or more specific times during the match, to ensure that he puts into effect the things he has learnt while practising. The player needs to play the shot with a changed goal: instead of thinking, "I must make this roquet (or hoop or rush)", he thinks, "I must use an unhurried forward swing", and even if the shot is missed he can consider that he has to some degree succeeded if he did in fact manage to achieve this more basic goal. He may lose a game or two at first, but he would probably have lost them anyway, and it is more important to ensure the winning of future games by correcting the error in technique, rather than to win the current game.

After the competition the coach should seek feedback from the player, e.g. "Did you remember to use a high backswing and not hurry the forward swing as you hit the balls into play? And did this help to establish the timing for later shots?"

If the problem remains, then more work on it is needed, and if not, then attention can be given to a different problem. It may also be necessary for the coach to assist the player in planning a particular programme of practice sessions and competitive play. The timing of such things is not always entirely under the control of either coach or player, but it will usually be possible to designate certain periods of the year, when there are no competitions of supreme importance, in which attention can be given to correcting any slight errors in technique and the practising of unusual shots such as roll-cannons, very long pass rolls (e.g. from the fourth corner, to load hoop 4 while going to a ball at hoop 3), jump shots, hampered shots, etc.

As a major competition approaches attention can be diverted to the fine-tuning of basic shots such as gentle roquets over 5-6 yards, wider than usual rushes, take-offs from corner to corner, hoop running, and other shots where any error is likely to be one of judgement and timing rather than one of technique. Psychological preparation is another important factor, and can include preparedness to cope with or counter the style of play of particular opponents, or ways of assisting your partner in doubles, as well as ways of handling specific lawn and weather conditions.

It all leads up to one incontrovertible fact: every player competing at top level, as well as every player who wishes to improve rapidly, should have a personal coach who is both accredited and trusted. In others sports such as tennis, golf, athletics, etc., no-one would expect to be competitive at a high level without the regular services of a competent coach. Why is it that leading croquet players in the past seem to have adopted the attitude that it is beneath their dignity to seek specialised coaching advice? Fortunately, this attitude is gradually changing, and before long everyone who plays at or near state level will be forced to have regular coaching sessions in order to remain competitive. Such a change can only be for the good of the game, and lead to a general increase in the standard of play.

WHAT IS RIGHT-HANDED?

CROQUET COACHES AND players seem to be in no doubt as to what constitutes a right—or left-handed stance and grip. In a right-handed grip the left (non-dominant) hand is placed at the top end of the handle, and the right (dominant) hand is placed underneath. In a right-handed stance the left foot is forward of the right foot.

I assume that I am not the first coach to have noticed that the percentage of croquet players using a left-handed grip and stance seems to be far higher than the percentage of left-handed people one would expect to find in the general community. This has led me to wonder whether or not the traditional idea of what is "left-handed" is in fact correct. There is no doubt that when most players were playing side-style the above description of a right-handed grip was correct, as this method involved having the hands well apart and providing most of the force with the bottom hand. However, most right-handed side-style players actually use what (going by the above) would be termed a "left-handed" stance—that is, they have their right foot forward.

Nowadays most players are taught to play centre-style, keep their hands together, and swing the mallet with the top hand rather than the bottom one. Perhaps there is a need to rethink the traditional ideas concerning the grip and stance that as coaches we automatically recommend to players, depending on whether they are right or left-handed.

This question has arisen in my mind, partly because, like many others, I am very right-handed at everything else, but play croquet "left-handed" because to me it seems more natural. In fact, to me it seems that I am playing right-handed, since the strength of the shot comes from my right hand, and the left hand is used only to guide the direction of the swing.

What, then, would be the effect if when the next person who asks me to teach him the game and says that he is right-handed, I were to suggest that he adopt a "left-handed" grip and stance as I myself do? I have always regarded the fact that I am left-handed at croquet and nothing else as one of my many idiosyncrasies, which like the others should not be passed on to those I coach. But now I am no longer so certain that I am doing the right thing. I do not have the nerve to go against all the accumulated wisdom of the centuries and recommend a "left-handed" grip to a right-handed player, as it could well prove to be disastrous and ruin any chance he may have had to ever become proficient at the game. Then I would blame myself forever after, and deservedly so. No coach should recommend anything other than what he knows is most likely to be of greatest benefit to the player. At present I have no evidence to support or even suggest that a right-handed person is likely to benefit from being taught to play left-handed; but all the same I cannot help wondering whether there may be more for us to learn as coaches in this area. A further complication arises from the fact that almost all right-handed people are also right-eye dominant.

This means that if they are taught to play with a left-handed grip and stance, they will suffer (as I do) the minor disadvantage of needing to swing the mallet vertically below the eye which is on the same side as their front foot. This causes the thigh on that front leg to interfere somewhat with a straight backswing, unless the stance is a very wide one, or the front foot is consciously placed at what seems an unnatural distance from the line of swing. This is something I must keep on consciously reminding myself of, and is a source of error on those occasions when I forget and place my right foot too close to the line of swing which should be directly under my dominant right eye.

It would be possible, but probably not desirable, to explain all this to a newcomer and suggest that he experiment, hoping that he will work out for himself the way of doing things that will best suit him. However, this is in general not a satisfactory teaching method. The newcomer is likely to learn far more quickly if he is not confused by being shown a number of alternative methods and having to choose between them on the basis of ignorance and no experience. Most players will get on best if the coach makes one clear recommendation as to the grip and stance that is most likely, in the judgement of the experienced coach, to suit that particular player. No doubt there will be rare occasions when we get it wrong. In such cases it should become evident fairly quickly that the player is not coping satisfactorily with the things we are asking him to do in the ways we are asking him to do them, and at that stage the player may be advised to experiment with different grips and stances in the hope that he will find something that suits him better.

In my experience, however, a player who cannot cope at all with the standard grip and stance is not likely to get on well with any other; and once a player is managing reasonably well it will be very difficult to change him, which again raises the question as to what we should be teaching him in the first place.

JUMP SHOTS

WHEN TEACHING JUMP SHOTS, be aware that the different types of grip (standard, Irish, Solomon) probably will have a bearing on where the student places his hands. A player with the Solomon grip needs to hold the mallet at the top of the handle. However, a player with the standard grip is likely to get on better if he shortens the grip somewhat; and a player with the Irish grip will probably need to use a shorter grip still in order to achieve similar results without placing undue strain on the wrists. A coach should be wary of assuming that the way of playing a shot which he finds best for himself will also be best for any particular student.

WISHFUL THINKING

WHEN PLAYERS ARE asked to perform a series of set drill exercises, (e.g. play 5 stop-shots from the 1st corner to load hoop 2 and gain position no more than 1m in front of hoop 1) and record the results, their recorded percentages will usually need to be considerably reduced in order to provide a true indication of current ability. This fact was reinforced recently when one of the exercises mistakenly set as "homework" for a group of players being coached was to play a 'right-angle split' from 1m behind hoop 1, sending the croqueted ball to within 2m of hoop 4 and the striker's ball to within 2m of hoop 2.

Everyone recorded success rates of 60-80% on this shot, although the shot is extremely difficult, if not virtually impossible. It seems that they were very generous in their estimation of the 2m distances involved!

It is probably a good thing to think positively, and have confidence in your ability to play difficult shots with a reasonable success rate; but if you base too many of your tactical choices on such wishful thinking instead of on an objective consideration of percentages, things are likely to come unstuck somewhere.

The most reliable way for the coach to find out whether or not the student has mastered a shot is to have the student perform the tests with the coach present. On many occasions players have insisted that they can take off from one corner to within 3m of a ball in another corner almost every time; but when given a strict test their success rate is less than 30%, which shows that they definitely need more instruction and further practice.

HANDEDNESS AND DOMINANCE

I N ADVISING PLAYERS about stance, grip and swing it is important that a coach begin by asking such questions as:

(1) Is the player right-handed, left-handed or ambidextrous?
(2) Which, if any, is his dominant eye?
(3) Is there any physical condition which may need to be accommodated?

The correct positions for the player's feet and hands will depend on the answers to these questions, yet we could all probably quote experiences where a coach has tried to give advice to a player about his stance or grip without realising that the player is, say, right-eyed and left-handed; or right-handed but has no dominant eye.

The coach needs to know how to check such things, as the player may not know whether he is right- or left-handed, nor which, if any, is his dominant eye. A full explanation of the effects of handedness and eye dominance on stance and grip would require far more space than is available here. We advise coaches who wish to be better informed on these matters to seek detailed advice from a member of the state coaching committee. For now, we will simply state the following general principles without further elaboration:

(a) Most (but not all) players find it most comfortable to use a grip with the non-dominant hand at the top of the handle. For single ball shots this hand should move directly forward during the swing, with the dominant (underneath) hand just "going along for the ride" to help guide the direction of the swing without supplying any additional force.

(b) If possible the front foot in the stance should be on the same side as the top (non-dominant) hand. That is, a right-handed player will stand with his left foot forward. Some players prefer to adopt a stance with their feet level, in which case they will probably need advice as to how they can prevent themselves from over-balancing and "walking" forward during the swing.

(c) The mallet should swing directly underneath the dominant eye, with the shaft vertical, not tilted to one side, as a tilt can impart spin to the ball, making it tend to curve off line. This means that even with a level stance the mallet will not be exactly midway between the two feet, unless, perhaps, the player is one of the rare breed who do not have one eye more dominant than the other.

(d) A player whose dominant eye is on the opposite side from his dominant hand is likely to experience difficulty in developing a straight backswing, especially if he uses the "Irish" grip, and may need further advice in this area.

TEACHING THE TAKE-OFF

ONE OF THE problems facing a coach is that most players think they already know how to take-off, and are not really interested in receiving further instruction on the subject. It is interesting to ask them how close they would normally expect to get when taking-off to a ball at the far end of the lawn, without going out. Most will be confident of "usually" finishing within 2-3 yards of the target ball, but when put to the test (using slightly differing distances and directions across the lawn) they are likely to succeed only about 3 times out of 10! This exercise should at least convince them that there is room for improvement.

It is unfortunate that many players have been given poor advice in past years and this is part of the reason for the inconsistency in their take-offs. This highlights the danger of accepting coaching from untrained coaches, as one still hears advice such as the following being passed on by well-meaning but ill-informed club-mates:

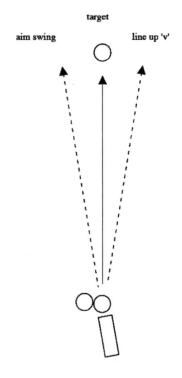

1. "Turn your mallet face a little inward toward the croqueted ball to make sure that it moves!"—this will indeed ensure that the croqueted ball moves, but it involves hitting with the mallet face not at right-angles to the line of swing, which creates 3 problems: (a) the distance travelled by both balls is harder to control; (b) the player will find it difficult to take off from the 'other' side; and (c) it requires the muscles to co-ordinate in a way which will cause disaster if transferred into the swing used for other shots.

2. "Line up the V to where you want to go, then move your striker's ball back a little . . . about half an inch."—this advice is less harmful, but is only likely to prove accurate for one particular distance, and omits mention of the correct line and type of swing. It is also likely to cause the striker's ball to go out in certain situations, e.g. a take-off from behind hoop 4 to the opponent's balls on the border alongside hoop 3.

3. "Try playing your take-offs like I do, with a stop-shot action."—This makes distance more difficult to judge accurately, as it introduces into the swing

additional and unnecessary variables (rate of deceleration and timing or 'sharpness' of stop action) which have to be controlled. The take-off action does, however, have one virtue in that 'pull' is reduced and in some cases may no longer need to be taken into consideration.

We do not have room here for a full consideration of the many finer points of this shot, but the accompanying diagram and the following principles will give some idea of the correct teaching method:

1. Line up the V to one side of the desired finishing point so as to allow for 'pull' (or "mallet-drag").
2. Select a point of aim about the same distance the other side of the desired finishing point.
3. The distance of these points either side of the desired finishing point will depend on the length of the take-off.
   For the full length of the lawn a beginner should allow about one and a half yards, and the allowance is correspondingly reduced for shorter shots.
4. Ignore the croqueted ball, and swing through with the mallet face square, as if attempting to roquet an imaginary ball at the aiming point.
5. Use a higher backswing, rather than a push with the hands, to provide the additional force needed in a very long take-off. Do not hit down on the ball. The swing should be flat, with a normal follow-through.

CIRCLE METHOD FOR HOOP APPROACHES

T HIS METHOD OF lining up and playing hoop approaches was explained in my booklet "Croquet Coaching:
Error Correction" and has been incorporated into the official course notes for the training of coaches. In comparing the Circle Method with the standard method of playing and teaching hoop approaches, the following should be noted:

(1) The standard method involves deciding upon the desired finishing positions of the two balls (usually about two feet in front of the hoop and two yards behind it) and recognising the type of split-shot which will be needed to get them to these positions. This could be a stop-shot, half roll, equal roll, pass roll, thick take-off, (etc.), and the player then needs to know the correct grip, stance and type of swing he must use to play whichever of these shots is required. He must also be able to adjust the grip, stance and swing according to the wideness of the angle of split. Most of this is well beyond the understanding of many players, at least until they have been playing the game for some years. By this time they will often have developed the undesirable habit of playing most hoop approaches as take-offs, since it is the only method they can cope with.

(2) The Circle Method has the great advantage that it can be taught to a beginner right from the start, without the need for him to understand, or be able to play, any type of split-shot or roll.

(3) It also has the advantage that it allows the player to develop a greater degree of consistency (and with it confidence) than any alternative method.

(4) A disadvantage is that the Circle Method will not always result in the player obtaining a forward rush in order to facilitate the continuance of his break. However, at an early stage of his development the difficulty in achieving accurate control of the timing of the more desirable stop-shot (when more or less directly in front of the hoop) may still mean that the Circle Method is a good option. At a later stage, when he can play stop-shots with accurate control of the striker's ball, he can vary his hoop approach method as he considers desirable. It is worth noting that several leading players are now using the Circle Method, sometimes with slight modifications, for almost all hoop approaches; and most of these find it so consistent that they will only vary it when the alternative shot involves no risk at all.

(5) The term "Circle Method" was coined in order to explain the method to coaches. It is not necessary for the player to think in terms of circles, but it

is useful when teaching it for the coach to place markers around the hoop in a circle so that the learner can practice lining up the shot and playing it from various positions around the circle. The reason for this is that every position on the circle is the same distance from the hoop, so the player will use the same aiming points for both the croqueted ball and the line of swing; and these can be marked by the coach with small objects such as corner pegs as a guide for the player. The method is described as follows: (see diagram)

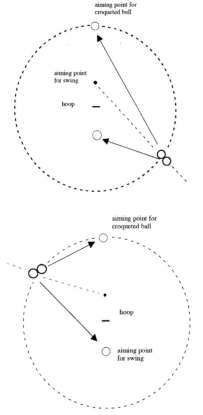

1. Observe the distance of the ball you have roqueted from the hoop (i.e. the approach distance).

2. Find a point on the lawn this same distance directly behind the hoop, and place your striker's ball against the roqueted ball in line with this point. That is, you are aiming the croqueted ball to go to the point you have selected directly behind the hoop.

3. Find another point which is also directly behind the hoop, and about one-third of the way from the hoop to the first point you selected. This second point will be the aiming point for your swing. In playing the shot, you will 'stalk' this point, keep your mallet face square to it, and swing your mallet through directly in line with it, avoiding all temptation to "shepherd" the swing around toward the hoop. You will try to ignore the croqueted ball and swing as if you are hitting your striker's ball to make it roquet an imaginary ball at this second aiming point.

4. The shot must be played with the mallet sloping forward, but only slightly, at an angle of about 15 degrees from the vertical. This degree of forward slope can be learnt with considerable accuracy over time, as it is exactly the same for every hoop approach using the Circle Method, whether you are approaching the hoop from in front, alongside, or behind as shown in the diagram at left.

5. The swing is also the same, except for strength, for all positions around the circle. It is often referred to as a 'stab-roll', but this is not an entirely accurate description. In this case the mallet should be neither stopped

(decelerated) nor pushed forward (accelerated) as it contacts the ball. The player merely endeavours to maintain the movement (i.e. speed) of the falling mallet as it 'passes through' the ball. This takes some time to learn, but is actually easier for newcomers than for those who have developed the habit of "rolling" from such positions, or of "stabbing" at hoop approaches with a flat mallet.

6. The strength of the shot is the only thing that is not automatic and has to be judged for each separate hoop approach. However, the player will be helped if he realises that it is determined by his distance from the second aiming point, not his distance from the hoop. (In fact, about the same force is required as if he were hitting a single ball twice the distance to the second aiming point toward which he is swinging; and he should soon learn that less force is required as you move around the circle to a position behind the hoop, because you are then closer to the aiming point, which means that the total of the distances travelled by the two balls will be smaller.) The strength should be controlled by lifting the mallet back higher for a longer hoop approach, rather than by providing any force from the wrists or forearms. That is, you simply let the mallet 'fall' through the ball from a greater height, again maintaining its speed through the ball. This, also, allows the player to eventually achieve surprising consistency.

7. Another surprising aspect of the Circle method is that there seems to be a considerable margin for error. Even when the shot appears to have been somewhat mis-hit, the hoop is often still possible to make.

8. For a longer hoop approach the imaginary circle will be larger, and a higher backswing is needed, but otherwise the shot is played in exactly the same way. Note that (allowing for pull) the distance the striker's ball finishes in front of the hoop will be about the same as the distance from the hoop to the second aiming point, or about one-third of the circle radius. This means that in a longer hoop approach you will expect to finish further from the hoop, which maintains the margin for error. However, players who use this method for hoop approaches of six yards or more (e.g. from the border near a hoop) may wish to slightly increase the forward slope of the mallet in order to achieve a narrower angle of split, so that the striker's ball finishes closer to the hoop.

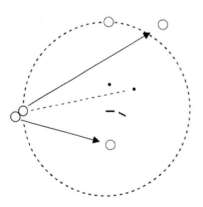

9. At a later stage, when the player finds it desirable to not only make the hoop, but try for a rush in a particular direction after

making it, he can do this by simply imagining the hoop in a slightly different position. This will, of course, alter the size of the circle (not shown in the diagram at left) and the positions of the two aiming points, and means that the shot will need to be hit a little harder or softer, depending on whether the rush and imaginary hoop movement are to the far side or the near side of the hoop.

FINE ADJUSTMENTS TO THE CIRCLE METHOD

1. If the balls are placed correctly, and the mallet is swung in the correct way and in the correct line with the correct slope, then as the balls move across the lawn to their destinations they should remain on a line parallel to the side border of the court. The only variable (provided the things which you organise before playing the shot are correct) is the strength of the hit, which is controlled by lifting the mallet higher in the backswing and dropping it through the balls from a greater or lesser height as necessary. This means that if something goes wrong, it should be easy to see what it is, and to correct it in the next attempt, e.g.—If you hit *too gently*, the two balls will fall short of their desired destinations as shown by the positions labelled '1' on the 1ˢᵗ diagram at right, and the next time you should take a higher backswing. If you hit *too hard*, they will both go too far as shown by the positions labelled '3', and next time should use a shorter backswing. If you get it *just right* the balls should go to the positions labelled with a '2'. The dotted lines indicate that if the only error is in the strength of the shot (i.e. amount of backswing), then the balls will finish on an imaginary line parallel to the side border.

2. If the balls do not finish on a line parallel to the border, then it is because one ball has gone too far in relation to the other. This can be corrected by changing the mallet slope as follows:

    (a) If the striker's ball falls short and the croqueted ball goes too far, then stand a little further over the balls and increase the mallet slope slightly for the next attempt. (See 2ⁿᵈ diagram)

    (b) If the striker's ball goes too far and the croqueted ball falls short, then stand back a bit and use less slope next time.

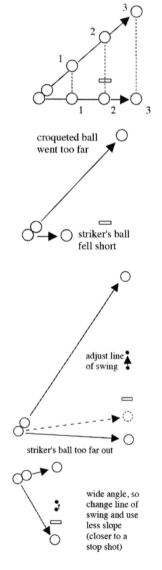

croqueted ball
went too far

striker's ball
fell short

adjust line
of swing

striker's ball too far out

wide angle, so
change line of
swing and use
less slope
(closer to a
stop shot)

3. As you get more proficient and confident with the circle method you will probably find yourself using it for longer approaches, perhaps up to 6 yards or more from the hoop, e.g. when approaching a corner hoop from the border. Using the method as described for this distance will result in the striker's ball finishing 4-5 feet in front of the hoop. If you want to try to get the striker's ball to finish in closer to the hoop than this, you should be able to achieve it by using a little more forward slope and changing the line of swing a little more into the croqueted ball, i.e. a little more than a third of the circle radius behind the hoop. (See 3rd diagram)

4. When you are approaching from positions on the circle behind the hoop you will find that the angle between the directions in which the two balls are to move becomes wider, until when you are almost directly behind the hoop it becomes a right-angle and the shot is more or less equivalent to a take-off.

As the angle becomes wider you will find that the striker's ball starts to slip across the surface of the croqueted ball, instead of the ball surfaces gripping on each other (and the balls immediately moving apart) as they do for narrower angles.

This slipping of one ball against the other in wide-angle shots means that the striker's ball will tend to go too far and the croqueted ball will fall short of the desired destinations. To correct for this, stand a little further back and use less mallet slope while also changing the line of swing a little more into the croqueted ball to lessen the slipping effect and make it go further. Most players who have used the method for some time will learn to make this adjustment almost automatically whenever they are approaching from a position so far around behind the hoop that the angle of split between the desired directions of the two balls exceeds 60 degrees or so. (See 4th diagram)

WHERE IS THE V?

C OACHES AND PLAYERS often talk to beginners about where to point
the V between the balls in order to line up a take-off. Unfortunately, it
will often be far from clear to the beginner just what the coach is talking about,
and where the 'V' is. The left-hand diagram below shows how most players see the
V as a shape above the two balls; but how can it be said to "point" in any direction
except possibly straight down?

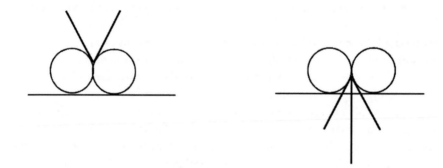

It seems more sensible to look at an upside-down V underneath the balls as shown
in the right-hand diagram, and imagine the central line added to make an arrow
shape which does indeed point somewhere.

We should never assume as coaches that because a concept is perfectly clear to
us, it will be equally clear to those we are teaching!

HELPING YOUR PARTNER

S OME GOOD PLAYERS are very adept at not only making hoops themselves, but assisting much weaker doubles partners to do so as well. Others do not know how to go about helping their partners, and instead of seeing it as an interesting challenge, they see the task as a frustrating one leading to despair.

Here are a few hints that may help you when you find yourself in such a situation:

(1) Always encourage the weaker player to take reasonable risks, instead of advising him to play safe. He needs to think that you have some degree of confidence in his ability, whether you have or not!

(2) Find out what shots he is capable of playing confidently, and set so that he will be able to use those shots. There is little point in putting the opponent's balls at hoops 1 and 2 when your partner is on hoop 1 and setting him a rush in the 4th corner, if he is not capable of rushing a ball across the lawn with reasonable accuracy.

(3) Do not leave the opponents' balls as far apart as possible, expecting your partner to break down. This would also make it harder for him to use them. Set them closer and take the risk of them roqueting, in order to ensure that when they do miss a roquet your partner will be able to get somewhere.

(4) Remember that setting the best possible leave for your partner is more important than making hoops yourself, which you can easily make later on. Even in a handicap game you should not make 4-back until your partner has reached the peg. This is so that if one of the opponents gets to rover or the peg, you still have the opportunity, and sufficient shots in your break, to peel him (if necessary) and peg him out.

MORE ON ERROR CORRECTION

O NE OF THE most common errors committed by players is hurrying the forward swing in single ball shots (roquets, rushes and hoop running). This is often most noticeable when the player is a bit nervous or out of form, which results in the shot being mistimed. The backswing is shortened and the forward swing is hurried, with the mallet being pushed forward by wrist and forearm action instead of being allowed to swing smoothly through under its own weight.

In most cases the player will be unaware that he is doing this, and when the coach points out the error to him, he will not know how to go about putting it right. As a coach, you will need to do more than simply tell the player what he is doing wrong. One excellent way of attacking the problem is to place a ball on the yardline and ask the player to roquet it from about 6-7 yards away without any ball crossing the boundary. The shot must be played very deliberately, with a fairly high backswing, and repeated many times until both distance and direction are adequately and consistently controlled. Then, when the correct (slower than before) timing is well established, the player can try longer roquets with the same deliberate action, trying to feel that he is keeping the mallet on the ball as long as possible, and 'sweeping' it rather than 'hitting' it. He should also concentrate on keeping the shoulders still during the swing, and should practise running hoops with a similar deliberate and unhurried action.

Most players find that the shot in which they are most likely to hurry the forward swing is the rush. Whenever rushes are played at practice or in matches, the player should consciously try to maintain an even grip tension throughout the swing, relax the muscles in his wrists and forearms, and use a long, flat swing from the shoulders. The distance of the rush should he controlled by the height of the back-swing. For a very long rush, use a maximum back-swing, firm grip, and still let the weight of the mallet do all the work.

PERCENTAGE PLAY

A S YOUR COACHING Committee, we are constantly seeking to find better ways of teaching the things a player needs to know, so that we can pass the information on to our coaches. The most difficult area to teach is undoubtedly tactics, and we have been giving it our attention for some time now, especially since we have been working on ideas for the new Level 2 and Level 3 syllabuses.

We have decided upon satisfactory ways of teaching such tactical ideas as the theory of trap-lines and ideal leaves, when to peg balls out, the tactics of pegged-out games, and many others. However, there are some topics which we are still trying to discover an effective way of teaching.

One of these is the idea of percentage play. This is of major importance, since the justification for all tactics must lie ultimately in percentages.

The need for it is illustrated by the position in the left-hand diagram below, which occurred in a recent division 1 game. Red had made hoop 3, then had taken off to black on the border near hoop 4 and played an unsuccessful approach shot for hoop 4. Now red was hit to "safety" near the 4th corner as shown by the arrow, since the player considered it too risky to return near yellow and leave both balls out in the lawn, because the black clip was on hoop 3.

This allowed black to shoot at blue. The shot missed, and when black was measured in by the opponent, black and blue were touching balls as shown in the right-hand diagram. In this situation the player decided to shoot with yellow at red, and missed, with yellow finishing in the 4th corner.

On the next turn, black took off to red and yellow, rushed red into the corner to make a cannon, and without much difficulty was able to set up a break.

What the player of red and yellow failed to realise is this: By playing as he did he not only gave the innings away without the opponent having to even hit a roquet, but also created a situation from which the opponent could reasonably expect to get a break established 7 or 8 times out of 10. If he had left both his balls in the lawn, the percentage chance of the opponent roqueting would have been far less than 70-80%; in fact only about 40%. What can a coach do to get players thinking in terms of percentages and choosing the best percentage option, rather than following misleading "principles" such as, "Never set up in the middle of the lawn"?

Level 2 coaches should also have realised that after making hoop 3 with red, and with black on the yardline alongside hoop 4, the player should have used "trap-line theory" instead of leaving yellow out in the lawn; and in the position of the second diagram he should have applied the "three-one" principle and shot with yellow at the opponent's balls. If this shot was missed, the opponent could get a rush to hoop 3 for black, but the chances of establishing an immediate break would hardly have been more than 3-4 out of 10, and would certainly have been far less than the 7-8 out of 10 that he was given in the game.

We need to be able to convince players that there is nothing safe about hitting balls out of play. On the contrary, in most situations it considerably reduces your chance of winning the game.

Most games are won and lost, not through missed roquets or failed hoop shots, but because of poor tactical choices which the player is quite unaware of because he or she does not think in terms of percentages.

Are we aware of this as coaches? And if we are, how do we go about getting players to change the way they think about the various options available to them during a game?

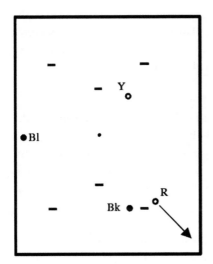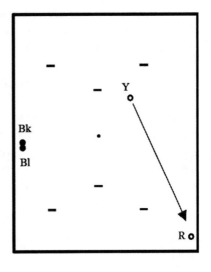

THE MOST IMPORTANT ADVICE

I F YOU WERE asked as a coach to give the one most important piece of advice that a player should remember and follow, what would it be?

Some would say, "Keep your head down (or your shoulders still)", or "watch the back of the ball", or "always stalk the ball", or "take a long, slow backswing", etc. These are all excellent pieces of advice, but there is one even more important and fundamental. It is, "Let the mallet do the work!"

This means that in all single-ball strokes and most croquet (two-ball) strokes the shot should be played using the weight of the mallet only, with no additional force supplied from muscles in the forearms, wrists, hands or fingers. Almost every leading player—and certainly every player with fluent shots that make the game look easy—follows this basic principle.

In order to achieve this, most players will need to have their hands together at the top of the shaft for all single-ball shots, so that both hands can move forward with the mallet. A few manage to do it with one hand down the shaft separated from the other, but the temptation to retard the forward movement of the top hand and push with the bottom hand is so great that the majority of players with hands separated are unable to resist it.

For long shots (e.g. a rush right across the lawn) a long and high backswing is necessary so that the gravitational force of the falling mallet head will be sufficient to provide the power, without any additional force from the muscles. The grip should be firm enough to ensure that as it contacts and moves through the ball the velocity (speed) of the mallet head due to gravity is maintained. There is no need to accelerate the mallet head through the ball, except in equal rolls, pass rolls and some unusual cannons, but neither should the resistance of the ball be permitted to slow down the forward movement of the mallet, unless the shot is a stop-shot or stab-roll.

Even when players learn to use only the weight of the mallet in their roquets, many are still unable to make themselves do it in rushes and hoop shots, especially when under pressure in a tense game situation.

The great value of following the principle lies in the fact that it allows all muscles (including the brain if it can be so described) to be co-ordinated for the task of guiding the swing in the desired direction, to ensure that the ball is hit in the exact centre of the mallet face.

When you are asked to assist a player whose roquets (and inevitably his other single-ball shots) are giving cause for concern, your first thought should be to encourage him to remember and follow this "first commandment"—Thou shalt let the mallet do the work. If you can get him to do this, you will have solved most of his problems automatically. If he is quite unable, as many are, to achieve the ultimate in this regard, then you will need to look for other ways of bringing about small improvements in his swing; but a long, hard, slow process can be expected.

As one experienced coach explained it, swinging a mallet is like riding a motor-bike: there is no need to push.

"DON'T COPY ME—DO WHAT I SAY"

IT IS ALWAYS a concern when we see, or hear of, a coach teaching learners to do things the way the coach does them, without knowing whether or not the method is likely to be correct for that particular learner. We trust that our accredited coaches will not fall into this trap, as we stress in our courses that we must vigorously resist the temptation to pass on our own idiosyncrasies unless we are certain that we are doing the right thing. Common examples of things we should avoid teaching, even if we do them ourselves, would include stop-shot take-offs, side-style rolls, flat hoop approaches, and many others.

JUST A THOUGHT to fill up a small space: "You don't stop playing because you get old; you get old because you stop playing!"

SWINGING OVER THE BALL

ALMOST ALL OF the MacRobertson Shield players would swing the mallet several times above the ball while lining it up. Some then rested the mallet head momentarily on the ground before starting the final swing, but most simply took a larger final backswing and hit the ball without touching the mallet on the ground at any time.

There is a suspicion that to some extent they may be following the latest fashion and copying each other—this does happen in top-level croquet to a greater extent than one might imagine. However, in recent years the practice has become remarkably prevalent and persistent, and one must conclude that most of them really believe it helps them ensure that the final swing will be more exactly in the desired line.

There are sound reasons for believing that the practice swings help train the muscles to co-ordinate in the required manner with the correct timing, and therefore result in a straighter hit, but there is also a price to be paid for this advantage. On the final swing the mallet must be lowered just the right amount to contact the ball in the centre of the mallet face. The lowering should be achieved by straightening the elbows slightly, rather than dipping the shoulders down. However this introduces an additional variable (the amount of lowering) which must be correctly judged in order to avoid either hitting the ground or 'topping' the ball.

Our current inclination is to recommend that learners should avoid copying the experts in the adoption of this practice, though we would not discourage a more experienced player who wanted to try it out.

It should be noted that resting the mallet on the ground when addressing the ball also has a disadvantage, whether or not it is preceded by practice swings: if the mallet head and stance are aligned while the mallet is resting on the ground it is very difficult to ensure that the handle is exactly vertical at the time, and if it is not exactly vertical then by the time the mallet has swung backward and forward, and is now hanging vertically below the hands, it is likely that the ball will no longer be hit in the centre of the mallet face.

HANDLING DIFFICULT CONDITIONS

THE DIFFICULT CONDITIONS could include strong winds, pools of water, a lightning-fast lawn, or one with a very uneven surface.

Such conditions are likely to affect a player who relies on roquets, rushes and take-offs more so than one who can play accurate split-shots. It is important to see that before you make your current hoop the following one is accurately loaded. If the first attempt at loading finishes more than a metre or so from the hoop, then try to send a second ball there as well.

There is a tendency to think, "the difficult conditions make it more likely that I will break down, so I will keep the balls widely separated in case something goes wrong." This is very poor strategy. The correct approach is to keep the balls close together so that you are less likely to break down because you will not need to play any long shots, and will have plenty of options.

The difficult conditions can be viewed positively as giving you a chance to out-think your opponent and so defeat him even if his shots (roquets, take-offs and rushes) are normally more accurate than yours. Even if you do break down with balls together the opponent may not make much out of it, especially if he follows the misguided separate-for-safety strategy.

For the serious competitor, it is important to arrange practice sessions under varying conditions. This may include practising in pouring rain, 40-degree heat, howling gales, or bitingly cold conditions, as well as deliberately visiting lawns that are known to be very fast, heavy, bumpy, or double-paced. People will no doubt question your sanity if you go out to practise in such situations, but when matches have to be played in similar conditions you will have the great advantage of already having worked out how to cope with them mentally, technically and strategically. Thought should be given to such things as clothing (hat, gloves, water on glasses, etc.) and the provision of suitable fluid intake. When required to play in freezing weather conditions, a player whose fingers are blue and numb, and who has never practised wearing gloves, will almost certainly be unable to play good croquet. Similar problems can arise if you come from a dry climate and suddenly find that your rain gear (including shoes) is less waterproof than you thought, or restricts your movement to the extent that you cannot swing the mallet freely.

Once again, it is the role of the coach to see that the player is properly prepared to cope with whatever climatic conditions prevail, and ensure that his mental approach remains positive at all times.

ON WORKING TOGETHER

I T IS AN understandable but unfortunate fact that many coaches develop a type of jealousy regarding the players (particularly beginners) they are coaching. "I am coaching George, and I don't want anyone else interfering or confusing him with differing advice", is a common attitude.

As coaches we should not feel threatened by the idea that someone else besides us may be able to help the beginner.

Players (beginners or experienced) should be advised to seek help from other sources—particularly from other accredited coaches—whenever possible. Someone else may say exactly the same thing we have been saying, but say it in a way which the player is suddenly able to grasp; or may present new ideas that turn out to be extremely helpful. The player will need to learn to discriminate between good and bad advice, but he has to do this anyway in almost every game of doubles that he plays, when he will no doubt receive plenty of advice from his partner about which shots to play and how to play them!

We should always be ready to learn from someone else, so it is wise to enquire later how the beginner got on with the other coach. Sometimes even unaccredited people come up with good coaching ideas, and they could then be complimented and encouraged to consider taking an accreditation course.

Some players have in the past considered the idea of suggesting to their club that the club should invite a particular coach to visit the club and take group coaching sessions, but have been afraid that such a suggestion could be perceived as a vote of no confidence in those (accredited or unaccredited) coaches at the club who are presently trying to assist players.

Good coaches are aware of how much there is to learn in the area of coaching, and would never claim to know it all, or to be able to present it in a way that will be ideally suited to the needs of everyone. They will therefore welcome any assistance from an "outside" coach, and will see it as an opportunity to learn something themselves, even if they themselves have had more experience and have a higher coaching accreditation than the "outside" coach. In fact, every club coach should be actively seeking such opportunities to invite other coaches whose methods they know are sound to take sessions with the players they are endeavouring to help. It is especially helpful if you can take note of things you have tried to explain that the players do not seem to have "cottoned on to" particularly well, and ask the visiting coach to concentrate on some of these areas.

MAKING SIDEY HOOPS

WHEN TEACHING A player to make sidey hoops it is common to teach him to make sure that his ball misses the near hoop-leg. We believe that concentration on the near hoop-leg is counter-productive, and suggest that instead he aim the centre of the ball at the inside edge of the far leg and swing straight in this line.

As players we have been training ourselves for years to look at a target and swing the mallet toward it.

It will now be very difficult for us to look at something and swing correctly in some other direction. If you fix your eyes on the near hoop leg in order to ensure that you miss it, you are actually increasing the chance that you will hit it. For all sidey hoop shots, and also when attempting to roquet a ball which is partly hidden behind a hoop, you should avoid looking at the hoop leg. Instead, work out exactly where you want the centre (not the edge) of your striker's ball to go, and concentrate on that point, rather than on the hoop.

Perhaps this is a good place to emphasise again the fact that for the coach, the main difficulty in teaching a player to run hoops well from any position is usually the problem of getting him to avoid shortening the backswing, and use a relaxed and unhurried forward swing.

SHOT SEQUENCES

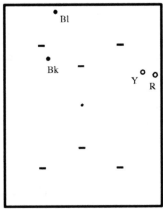

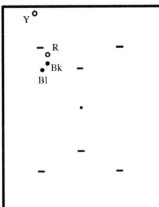

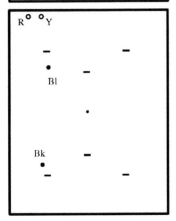

F OR PLAYERS CAPABLE of making breaks, an important part of their training and coaching programme should be the working out and practising of particular "shot sequences". These will usually follow particular leaves that the player regularly makes, or positions he is likely to encounter.

Suppose that you are faced with the situation shown in the first diagram, where all clips are on hoop 1 and blue has just shot at black and missed, after you had left one of his balls at each of the first two hoops and set yourself (correctly) a rush to hoop 2 rather than to hoop 1. What is the best way to continue—i.e. the way which will give you the best chance of establishing a break before your opponent does? Most players cannot be relied upon (or rely on themselves) to be able to work out the best line of play in such situations under pressure on the spur of the moment; and even if they could, they would gain a considerable psychological advantage from having worked it all out previously and knowing that what they are doing does in fact give them the maximum chance of winning the game. The confidence that comes from knowing you are doing exactly the right thing is a very valuable asset.

Many players would play red, roquet yellow gently, take off to blue, and roll blue out to hoop 2, at the same time trying for a good rush on black to hoop 1. In similar situations the correct procedure will often depend on the particular shots the player can play successfully, and this is why the shot sequences should be worked out with the assistance of an experienced coach, and will not always be the same for all players.

In this case, however, almost every player would do better to rush the yellow partner ball to the north boundary, as close as possible to blue, and preferably a yard or two toward the 2nd corner from where blue is. Then a short take-off should allow you to follow by rushing blue to black, and a simple croquet shot will then give you a "Dolly" rush on black to hoop 1, while making a vague attempt if possible to leave blue wired from yellow (see second diagram).

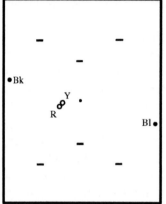

If hoop 1 is made, but without a forward rush, then one satisfactory way of continuing the break is to take off to yellow and use it to load hoop 3 before making hoop 2 from blue. This is why it was better to rush yellow slightly to the far side of blue in the first diagram, rather than the near side (would you have realised this in a game?)

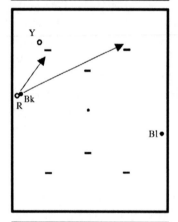

If the hoop cannot be attempted, then red can return to a position near yellow on the north border (third diagram), leaving the opponent in a very awkward position. Even if blue is not wired from your balls, most players would consider it far too risky to shoot with blue and leave black at hoop 1. But any shot with black, if missed, would also give you an excellent chance of setting up a break; and if black is hit away into (say) the 4th corner, you can roquet yellow and roll it out to hoop 2 (preferably just behind the hoop rather than in front, so that if necessary you can return and cover the border behind it), and rush blue to hoop 1.

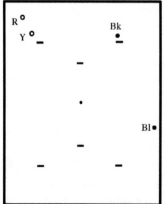

Thus, this method of proceeding from the first diagram gives you easier shots than if you had taken off and left yellow near the east border, or at hoop 3; and also keeps greater pressure on the opponent if things go wrong. It is just one example of the type of shot sequence that should be part of the preparation and knowledge of every player who wishes to succeed at the higher levels of competition.

The idea of working out shot sequences is not really a new one, as most players have at least some idea of what to do in the standard opening if the opponent varies his play at various stages. (See the article on Opening Ideas for some further information.) But in situations such as the one in the first diagram below, where red is for hoop 2 and has roqueted or rushed yellow to a point between hoops 1 and 2 as shown, many would be unsure of the best way to continue. Yellow should not be left out in the lawn, and an attempt to get a rush behind black on the west border would be risky and unlikely to succeed.

The best plan for most players is to make use of the "trap-line" concept explained in my booklet "Croquet: Lessons in Tactics", and send yellow 1-2 yards to the left (outside) of hoop 2 while going to black, then send black to hoop 3 while trying for position in front of hoop 2, as illustrated in the second diagram. If red does not gain position to run the hoop, then it can cover the border against a shot by black as shown in the third diagram.

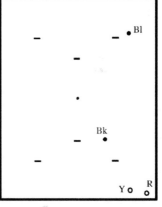

Now it will be the opponent's turn, and depending on what he does, the player of red could have the following shot sequences prepared.

(1) If black shoots at yellow and misses, red will roquet black, send it back to hoop 3, and make hoop 2 with (if possible) a rush to blue.

(2) If black shoots at blue and misses, red will make hoop 2 from yellow, trying for a rush to hoop 4 (not hoop 3), and then rush one of the opponent's balls to hoop 3.

(3) If black is hit wide of blue (say, into the 4th corner), then red has two good options—

   (a) Instead of making hoop 2, rush yellow right down to the 4th corner, then send black to hoop 3 and blue to hoop 2, setting up as shown in the top diagram at right.

   (b) Make hoop 2 from yellow with a rush to black in the 4th corner, then roll black out past hoop 4 and rush or roll blue to hoop 3, returning if necessary to yellow as shown in the fifth diagram.

(4) If black goes anywhere else, make hoop 2 with a rush to black, send it to hoop 3 and set a rush for red to hoop 4.

These are not the only possibilities, but the player will do well to have a clear idea in mind of at least one good answer to whatever black decides to do. Working out shot sequences to suit the shots you are confident with, and practising them, must help improve your game.

COACHING PRINCIPLES

A GOOD COACH needs to know many things. For example, in relation to just the technique of playing one particular shot, he needs to know:

* The correct things to do.
* Things that need to be avoided.
* The level of the player's development at which they should best be taught.
* The order in which they should be taught.
* The best way to teach each of them.
* The types of error that can occur in the stroke being taught.
* The possible causes of each type of error.
* How the error can be corrected.

In previous articles (e.g. "The role of the Coach") we have seen that he also needs to know how to devise practice drills, organise a training programme, assist the player in setting goals, and assess the effectiveness of the programme. All of this may be involved in the correction of just one error in technique in one shot, and covers far more information than can be given in even a long series of articles.

Here we shall simply consider two basic principles which apply to the best way of teaching the various aspects of technique:

1. **Eliminate variables.** This means that the coach needs to be aware of the various different methods that good players may use to play the particular shot in question, and should choose a technique which eliminates unnecessary variables that would only serve to complicate things and involve additional things that the player would have to learn to control.
2. **Isolate elements.** Wherever possible, the coach needs to find an approach such that the player can concentrate on learning just one or two aspects of the stroke at a time, and get them right before moving on to incorporate other aspects.

Suppose, for example, that the player has reached a stage where he wants to learn to play accurate split-shots, and the coach also agrees that the time is right for this.

Firstly, the coach will decide on the technique that he will encourage the player to use. This may depend to some extent on the player's grip, stance, physical capabilities, etc.; some of which the coach may decide need to be changed, and some of which he may decide not to attempt to alter at this stage. In most cases he would recommend a technique which involves no unnecessary body movement and does not require the mallet to be accelerated through the ball, as these are factors which would vary (i.e. "variables") for different split-shots, and so if they are part of the player's technique, he will have to learn to control each of them. A method of playing the shots without introducing such variables will be easier to teach and will allow the shots to be learnt more quickly and played more accurately.

Secondly, having eliminated body movement and acceleration during the swing as unnecessary variables, the coach should consider the elements of technique which remain and cannot be eliminated because they are essential to the shot; i.e. how to line up the balls, how to find the correct line of aim (or "line of swing"), and how much forward slope to give the mallet. These elements, of course, will need to be varied for each different type of split-shot, and this is what the player must learn to do. The coach should then realise that the most effective way of teaching these things will not be to try to teach them all at once. By starting with right-angle splits, which resemble thick take-offs to a certain degree, the player can learn to line up the balls (allowing for "pull") and find the correct line of aim, without needing to consider mallet slope at this stage, since right-angle splits are always played with an upright stance, long grip and flat mallet. After the player has learnt how to find the correct line of aim (by "dividing the line" between the desired finishing positions of the two balls—see my booklet "Croquet Technique" for a more detailed explanation), he can proceed to other types of split-shot in which the additional element of mallet slope also has to be judged and controlled. One way of doing this is indicated in the article on Adjusting Splits in the section of this booklet that deals with Technique.

Whatever area of the game you are teaching, or in fact when you are teaching anything at all in any area of knowledge, these two principles will be relevant and can prove valuable. A good and effective teacher is always looking for ways of eliminating variables in order to simplify what has to be taught, and isolating elements in order to reduce confusion and facilitate learning.

John Riches and Wayne Davies

SECTION 5

JUST FOR FUN

A S A LIGHT-HEARTED interlude, I have decided to include the following skit which was presented in dramatic fashion many years ago by members of the then SACA Strategy Task Force to a meeting of officials from various clubs, and afterward was published in the Australian Croquet Gazette. The purpose of the Task Force was to discover ways of developing and improving the game in our state, and to assist clubs in implementing such ideas.

In addition to providing some light-hearted entertainment, the skit contains some valuable food for thought concerning the way in which our clubs operate.

Most of the names are completely fictitious, and any resemblance to any person living or dead is purely intentional, but will be denied by the author. The exceptions are Gert Maslen, Marian Magor and Mrs Tucker, who were real and highly respected past stalwarts of the SACA—so much so that they deserve to be immortalised by having their names left unaltered in this piece of deathless prose. Rod Brown, who was President of the SACA at the time and also chaired the Task Force, is at the present time (January 1995) serving as ACA Treasurer. I hereby declare him also to be immortalised, but to a lesser extent, since I am not sure how well he could cope with being both mortal and immortal at the same time. I express here my gratitude to some other members of the Task Force who contributed ideas that I could make use of.

The title of the drama parodies the name of the South Terrace Croquet Club, which is the oldest club in SA and is situated in Adelaide's beautiful South Parklands, about 100m from the SACA's Hutt Road Croquet Centre. The title was chosen because some members of that club happened to be on the Task Force at the time and participated in the presentation.

Of course, the things portrayed bear no relation to happenings at that club or any other club. Things like that only occurred in the dark and distant past, and could never happen at a meeting of any present day club . . . or could they ??

MONTHLY MEETING OF THE
MOUTH TERRACE CROQUET CLUB

CHARACTERS: Fred—President
Joe—Secretary
Peggy—Div. 3 captain
Ernie—Lawns supervisor
Muriel—Daughter of foundation member
Una—Association Publicity and Development Officer
NOTE: "Hutt Road" is the headquarters of the SA Croquet
Association.

SCENE: The clubhouse of the Mouth Terrace Croquet Club.
The time is 11.15 on a Saturday morning.
Fred is seated, looking at his watch.
Enter others, except Peggy.
General conversation ensues.
Fred finally gains their attention.

Fred: May I remind everyone that our meetings are supposed to begin at eleven
o'clock. We have a lot of business to attend to, and
Ernie: Hutt Road sent out another lot of rubbish, I suppose. All they ever do is
ask for money. They must think that we spend our time sitting around here
with nothing to do but raise money so that our state team can have cheap
inter-state trips and nice lawns to play on. Why can't they do something
to help struggling clubs like ours? All they do is sit in at Hutt Road and
talk. I'd like to see a few members of the state team come out here and get
on the end of a shovel or a wheelbarrow for a few hours. I had to spread
three tonnes of loam on my own last week, and
Fred: Yes, well I'm sure we all agree that you do a great job on the lawns, Ernie,
but we have an agenda to get through, so . . . Where's Peggy? I thought I
saw her car pull up earlier.
Joe: She's outside talking to a new member. At least, I think she's a new member.
I never saw her before, and she looks too old to be Peggy's daughter.
Muriel: I remember once when we had a new member. 1972 it was. Quite a nice
young man, too. Only came for four weeks, though. Can't understand him
leaving like that—I enjoyed having him for a partner each week. He had a
lot to learn, of course. Kept wanting to do split-shots and put my ball out
in the middle of the lawn. He even peeled me through some of my hoops,

but I told him I was quite capable of making hoops for myself, thank-you very much. One time he got five hoops ahead of me! If I hadn't stopped him he probably would have gone right around to the peg. Still, he was quite good at setting me up at my hoops. I got onto the return twice, and if I hadn't stuck in the sixth

Fred: Well, someone had better go and tell Peggy that we've started the meeting. *(Ernie goes)* People like her think nothing of keeping everyone waiting as if we've got all the time in the world. To me it's just plain bad manners. Surely it's not too much to expect . . . AH . . . Peggy—we've been waiting for you.

Peggy: I'm sorry, but I've been outside talking to a nice young lady who's interested in learning the game. Says her husband and two teenage children would probably be interested too, and if

Fred: Yes, well that's all very well, but if we don't get through our meetings we won't have a club for her to join.

Peggy: But couldn't you carry on without me while I at least show her how to hold a mallet, and put some hoops out so that she can

Fred: We need you here. You are our division 3 captain, and it's division 3's turn to organise the afternoon tea for our gala day next month. How can we do it without you?

Muriel: I remember when we had only division 3's and 4's, and we had to do the afternoon tea every second month. We used to

Fred: Are there any apologies?

Joe: How can there be? We're all here!

Fred: I know that, but it's on the agenda so we have to do it. We've always done it that way, and while I'm president we're going to keep on doing it that way. Joe—record in the minutes, please, that there are no apologies.

Joe: I've already done it. The last time we had an apology was at the last August meeting when Muriel sent an apology because she had to take her cat to the vet, but then she managed to get to the meeting anyway, so she apologised for apologising, and I

Peggy: I think I'd better go and explain to the lady outside. Perhaps we should invite her to come back this afternoon?

Joe: This afternoon? But I thought you said she doesn't know how to play.

Peggy: She doesn't, but if she came this afternoon I could show her

Joe: You know the rules. Beginners have to come out to at least six coaching sessions on Thursday mornings and pay their membership subscription before they can come out on Saturday afternoons.

Fred: We've never been allowed to bring beginners out on Saturdays.

Muriel: Five times, not six. I remember when old Mrs Archibald had three people at once, coaching them on Thursday mornings. 1957 it was, and that's when Ernie here joined the club, wasn't it, Ernie?

Ernie: That's right. I had to come out five times on Thursdays before I could come on Saturdays.

Peggy: But this woman and her husband both work, so

Joe: No, it was six times on Thursdays, not five! I'm sure I'm right about that. It'll be here in the minutes somewhere.

Ernie: Well, I only came five times. Mrs Archibald said I was the best student she ever had. I played at Hutt Road in less than four months, and lost a bisque, too!

Joe: Here it is. Moved by Eve Adam, seconded Mrs Noah—"New members who have not been members of any other club shall be required to attend six coaching sessions with Mrs Archibald on Thursday mornings and pay the annual subscription of thirteen shillings and sixpence before joining in play on Saturday afternoons."

Muriel: When I used to help Mrs Archibald with the coaching we only made them come five times. Mrs Archibald said if they couldn't pick it up in five sessions, they'd never learn.

Ernie: That's right. Five times I came on Saturdays, not six!

Joe: Well, you're out of order then. You've been out of order for 28 years! You've still got one Thursday to go!

Ernie: Since Mrs Archibald has been dead for 14 years, I don't see how she's going to coach me now. Mind you, she'd probably still be as helpful as some coaches I've seen.

Peggy: Couldn't we allow them to come out this afternoon, just this once? The lawns won't be full, and I wouldn't mind teaching them. They seem such a nice family, and we've been saying that we need new members. They can't come on Thursdays, and anyway, since Mrs Archibald died there hasn't been anyone coming out on Thursdays to do any coaching.

Fred: We're wasting our time having meetings and making rules if we're not going to keep to them.

Peggy: But why do we need such a rule?

Fred: Because . . . er . . . because it's always been done that way—well, for at least the last 28 years anyway. We can't just go changing things around whenever we feel like it. No-one would know what was going on if we did that, would they?

Peggy: Er—no, I suppose not. But it seems such a pity that we can't find some way for them to

Joe: It just doesn't work to have beginners coming out on Saturdays. We've tried it before!

Muriel: Yes, 1952 it was . . . or maybe 1953. I remember that it was just before my poor old mother's eightieth birthday. She was a foundation member of the club, you know, and I remember her telling me about the problems they had in the twenties with beginners. Of course, hardly anyone knew

Joe:	how to play when the club was started, so they were nearly all beginners, except for Mrs Archibald. She was a foundation member too, you know.

Joe: how to play when the club was started, so they were nearly all beginners, except for Mrs Archibald. She was a foundation member too, you know.

Joe: Besides, it's just not fair on our members. They come out and pay their lawn fees to play a game, not to help coach beginners.

Ernie: I agree that beginners should come out on Thursdays like we've always done. Most of them only come once or twice and we never see them on Saturdays anyway. It's just as well, too—if we keep on getting more people coming out on Saturday afternoons, before long our lawns will be full and we won't get a game. With two lawns we can only accommodate sixteen players, and we've got eleven already.

Fred: Yes, that's true . . . although it's not often that everyone turns up on a Saturday afternoon. At the rate we are growing—2 members every 28 years—it will be like Ernie says, and we won't be able to get on the lawns by the year . . . 2078!

Joe: If they really want to learn the game they'll come out on Thursdays like the rest of us had to.

Fred: Is there any correspondence?

Joe: The usual stuff from Hutt Road. They want to know what our plans are for the next "Life. Be in it." campaign, so they can assist us with publicity and

Muriel: "Life. Be in it."?! That's all that jogging around and exercising stuff isn't it? Well I can tell you that I'm not going to come out in a leotard and prance around like that girl on television, no matter what Hutt Road says. Why are they wasting time and money on that sort of rubbish?

Joe: They say it's designed to help clubs get new

Muriel: There's some exterior motive behind it, you mark my words! We don't need their help. In the old days when Gert Maslen and Marian Magor and Mrs Tucker were running things we had to do everything ourselves. What we need is not advice from Hutt Road. We need new members! Mind you, when I was club captain in 1964, we almost got three new members, but two of them decided to join the Fitzroy club instead, and the other was killed in a car accident two days before she was going to be accepted. An iron girder fell off the back of a truck, came through the car windshield and cut her head clean off! No-one told us she had died, so we nominated her and accepted her. It was four months later that we found out through her sister—and we had already paid her capitation fee, too!

Ernie: They should have called it a DE-capitation fee, by the sound of it.

Joe: Hutt Road has also sent us a notice about a meeting of working players

Peggy: None of us work, and we haven't had any working people in the club for years.

Ernie: No. What a pity. We could certainly do with some more workers in the club.

Peggy: Don't you think I should go out and say something to the new member? She said she was interested in

Fred: Later on. We still have a meeting to get through. Was there anything else from Hutt Road?

Joe: Yes. They want to know if we have anyone interested in attending a seminar on improving club administration and better ways of introducing new players to the game.

Fred: Well, I'm afraid we haven't time to deal with that now.

Joe: What are we going to do about the "Life. Be in it." campaign and working players meeting?

Fred: They will have to wait until our next meeting in June. We still haven't organised the afternoon tea for the Gala Day, and

Peggy: Don't you think we should let the members know about some of those things? June will be too late, and some of them may want to

Fred: No, we don't want our members going in there, anyway. They'll only come back full of weird ideas and start telling us how we should be running the club. It's all right for Rod Brown—he's got plenty of other people to do all the work for him. I'd like to see how he'd get on as President of this club. Never enough money to keep the lawns in respectable condition, and all of us over seventy and on the pension.

Muriel: I remember when we had to raise money to pay for the carpet. Old Maudy Anderson and I cooked for four days, and made

Peggy: I really think I should see to the new member . . . (*looks outside*) . . . That's strange—she seems to have gone!

Fred: Never mind. She probably wouldn't have been a good club member anyway. Most of them never turn up to meetings and aren't interested in helping build up the club at all.

Muriel: I remember when that young man came in 1972—or was it 1973?—He came to a meeting. That was just about the time he left. I still can't understand why he left. Such a promising young player he was. Had a lot to learn, though

Fred: Yes. Well now, about the afternoon tea . . . (*Fred is interrupted by a loud knocking at the door. Una enters.*) Oh . . . er . . . Hullo, what can we do for you? We are just in the middle of a clubmeeting.

Una: Is this the Mouth Terrace Croquet Club?

Fred: Yes. Who are you?

Una: I thought you were expecting me. My name is Una. The Croquet Association recently appointed me to the new position of Publicity and Development Officer, and has asked me to visit your club and explain some ideas on how to attract new members. I'm from the Newtown Club, and we've been successful in gaining several new members recently, mainly younger working people. We thought that other clubs like yours may be able to gain something from our experience.

Fred: I see—er—well—what a good idea! At last the people at Hutt Road are starting to do something to help struggling clubs like ours. We were only saying a few minutes ago how much we need new members, weren't we, Joe?

Joe: That's right. That's exactly what we said.

Muriel: Especially younger working people. None of us is getting any younger, you know. I remember when that young lad came in 1964—or it may have been 1965—he was working. Had an engineering degree, he told me. Had a lot to learn, though

Fred: Yes, well what have you got to tell us? I hope it won't take long. Our meeting finishes at 12 o'clock!

Peggy: But surely we could go on a little longer if we need to.

Fred: We've always finished our meetings at 12 o'clock, and I don't care what Hutt Road do, while I'm President

Una: I won't take long. Since you've already agreed that your club needs new players, you've already taken the first step. The rest of your members agree too, of course?!

Fred: Er—yes. Well, as a matter of fact we haven't discussed it yet with the others. But we all agree, don't we? *(all nod)* In fact there's a motion in the minute book to that effect, if I remember rightly.

Joe: That's right. Here it is . . . moved Peggy, seconded Ernie—"That we have a drive to attract new members, and that we begin as soon as we have completed the current project of raising money for our new curtains." That was passed in . . . April 1977!

Peggy: We still don't have the new curtains, either.

Una: After you agree that new members are needed, you should make sure that all members of the club understand the need and the reasons for it, and are willing to give it a high priority.

Muriel: Old Mrs Archibald was going to make the curtains when we raised enough money to pay for the material, but she died before we finished raising

Una: You should also think about exactly how many you would like to have and could adequately cater for. Set a definite target and aim to achieve it by a definite date. A club needs more and more money each year just to keep it going, and the best way to raise money is to gain more members—especially working players who are not trying to make do on a pension and will eventually share in the work of running the club. Do you realise, for example, that if you had gone ahead with your membership drive back in 1977 instead of waiting until you had new curtains, and if you had gained just four new members, by now their membership fees alone would have amounted to the equivalent of about $8000 additional revenue for the club, and you could have bought the new curtains many times over!

Ernie: When I seconded the motion I said we ought to go ahead with it, but Muriel and Mrs Archibald insisted on getting the curtains first.

Muriel: Well, curtains are important. As Mrs Archibald said at the time, you won't attract new members if your clubrooms look like the Black Hole of Calcutta!

Una: I agree. That's a very good point you've made, but as I said, it really gets down to a matter of priorities. We decided at our club to aim at building our membership up to at least 32 active players as quickly as possible. We tried several ways of inviting non-players to try the game—advertisements in the local paper, accompanied by a photo of an attractive young player; letter box drops; leaflets handed out in the local shopping centre; invitations to local organisations to come to a barbecue and 'Fun Night'; posters in hairdressing salons; Adult Education classes in the evenings at our club; open days in connection with "Life. Be in it." . . .

Muriel: We tried a letter box drop once, in 1951—or was it 1952?—I walked down three streets, both sides, putting a leaflet in every letter box. We had to pay six shillings to get the leaflets printed, and it was all wasted. Only two people came out. Mrs Archibald took them for two sessions, but then she was to go away on holidays, so I said I'd come out with them while she was away, but they never came again!

Una: Unfortunately there is no single method that can be guaranteed to work in any particular area. You need to be persistent and keep trying first one method, then another. The only guarantee is that if you don't try anything you won't get any response!

It's equally important to see that you do everything possible to keep and encourage people when they do show some interest. The main thing here is that you need to be flexible—work out what their needs are, and be ready to fit in with them. This may mean being prepared to change the way you do things, and as many members as possible should be willing to share the load of keeping in touch with enquirers and arranging the sort of help they need.

Fred: Since Mrs Archibald died we haven't really had anyone to do the coaching.

Una: Beginners don't need a highly qualified coach. They need someone—the right sort of person—to take an interest in them. If and when you decide they do need coaching, that doesn't mean you have to do it yourself. Just make sure that someone capable is organised to do it. You could even arrange, as we did, for someone from another club to assist.

Peggy: That would be a good idea.

Una: And you could do other things as well to encourage them. If they are working you could arrange play for them of an evening, or on Sunday afternoons if they play another sport on Saturdays. Some clubs have even successfully run early morning "Come and Try" sessions three days a week aimed at business people.

Joe: I don't know about Sunday afternoons. Mrs Archibald always objected to the lawns being open on Sundays.

Ernie: Mrs Archibald again! She's been dead for 14 years and she still runs our club! Perhaps she'll register her vote on Sunday play at the same time as she comes back to give me my final Thursday coaching session!

Una: You could also do other things to make it more likely they will want to stay. You could make sure the club has a couple of good mallets to lend to new players so they won't have to try to learn with old-fashioned awkward monstrosities that make it impossible to play shots correctly and compete on equal terms with those who have decent mallets; and you could consider a reduction of, say, 20% on their membership fee for the first year

Muriel: Why should we do that? If they are working players they can afford to pay the full amount better than we pensioners can. Remember we have to pay more for Gala Days now, and if Joe: Still, if it encourages them to join and makes them think we're really keen to have them as members, it may be worth it.

Peggy: Yes, 80% may be better than nothing at all!

Una: Exactly! And remember that working people have much less opportunity to play than the rest of us do, so they're really getting a lot less for the money anyway. One word of warning—don't be too quick to start talking to new members about working bees, wash-up and cleaning rosters, uniforms, raffles, meetings, and all that sort of thing. It is important for a start that they simply come out and enjoy playing the game. Try to work out whether they are interested in the game mainly from a social point of view, or whether they see it as a serious competitive sport and are keen to improve. Try to arrange the sort of competition they will appreciate most. After they have progressed a little it may mean arranging a low-level "competition" against another club which also has some beginners, even if some of you others have to play as well to make up a team.

But I can see that you really are on the way to starting a successful membership drive, and I'm sure you will think of many more useful ideas. I'll leave you to discuss it further, and don't hesitate to contact me or someone else in the Association if you think we can be of further help.

Fred: Thank you for coming. *(Looks at watch)* Now we have just one and a half minutes left. What are we going to do about—

ALL: THE AFTERNOON TEA AT THE GALA DAY!!

PSYCHOLOGY

THIS SECTION CONTAINS ideas which further develop some of the themes introduced in my booklet "Croquet: The Mental Approach". As explained in the introduction to that booklet, there is no doubt that psychological considerations play a greater part in croquet than in any other sport. At present the knowledge available in this area is fragmentary. Much research is still to be done. Psychological principles need to be established, documented, and explained. Both coaches and players need to be educated in ways of applying such principles.

As yet the experts in sports psychology seem to have given little attention to our game, doubtless because the application of their expertise requires funding at a level which is unavailable in the sport of croquet. The thoughts presented here are not offered with any pretence of authority. The author will readily admit that he knows no more about the subject than many other people—and probably a lot less than some—so the ideas in this section, like those in the above mentioned booklet, are designed merely to start people thinking in an area of the game to which many players and coaches give insufficient attention.

PSYCHOLOGY OF DOUBLE TARGETS

I N MY BOOKLET "Croquet: The Mental Approach" I raised the question of whether or not there may be situations in which an opponent is less likely to hit a double target than a single one. In the first diagram red has rolled with yellow for hoop 1, but finds himself unable to make the hoop. It has been suggested that instead of placing the red ball in front of the hoop where it would be hidden from black, it may be better to leave it open to black with the red and yellow balls a carefully judged distance apart, depending on the roqueting ability of the opponent. The idea is that the second ball could act as a distractor, and increase the likelihood

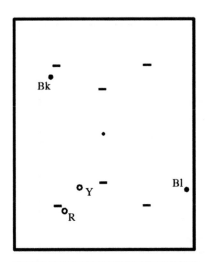

that the black ball will go through the gap between the two balls rather than roqueting one of them.

This idea is interesting because if there is any truth in it at all, then it would apply, paradoxically, against a strong opponent rather than a weak one. A poor roqueter is quite likely to aim at one of the balls and hit the other; but a good player is far less likely to do so, therefore the idea may be worth consideration against a strong opponent, but not against a weak one. Also paradoxically, the gap left between the balls should be smaller if the opponent is a better roqueter!

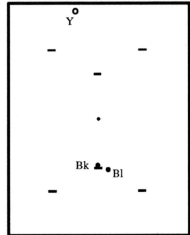

Of course it can be argued that the opponent simply needs to completely ignore one of the balls and shoot only at the other one; but I am not sure that many players would be psychologically capable of doing this if the gap is the right size.

The second diagram shows a position from an important tournament game in which my red ball had been pegged out, my yellow ball is for the peg, and my opponent had failed at the rover hoop with his black ball.

His two balls offered me a double target with a gap of just over a foot, so instead of shooting at the peg, I shot at the double and went straight through the middle of the gap. He made rover with black and cut blue toward the peg, producing the situation of the third diagram.

Here, he realised that the 3-4 yard peg-out could not be considered a certainty, so he played the croquet shot as a gentle roll in order to try to leave the blue ball wired from yellow if he failed to peg it out. This is in fact what happened, and he pegged out his black ball. Now, in the position of the fourth diagram, I had only a shot at the peg, which I took and hit it, winning the game 26-25. I am sure that if I had been him in the situation of the fourth diagram, I would have done the same thing, yet I could not help thinking at the time that if the rover hoop had been removed I probably would not have won the game.

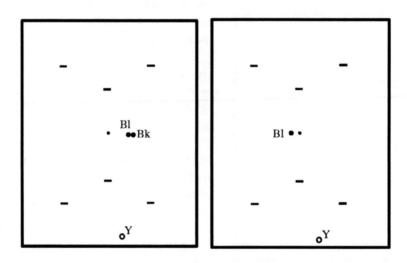

I would have shot at the blue ball if I had not been wired from it, and with the peg acting as a distractor it would have been difficult to make myself shoot straight at the ball without allowing a little bit on the side where the peg was. Should he have wired blue from yellow? It is likely that all of us would have tried to do the same, though perhaps not so successfully.

But I wonder whether I would have been as likely to hit the double target with about a two-foot gap?

John Riches and Wayne Davies

PSYCHOLOGY OF TRIPLE PEELS

WHEN A PLAYER reaches the stage of attempting triple peels, which usually means that he is close to being considered for state selection, he encounters and must learn to overcome psychological problems of a type he has probably not had to deal with previously.

The first is that if he is not careful, he can develop a strong sentimental attachment to the triple peel which he is attempting, to the extent that he wants to try to keep it going at all costs. This seems to involve, at times, a strange lack of objective judgement which causes the player to take risks that are far greater than those he would normally take, and which can be seen, when viewed calmly and logically, to considerably reduce his chance of winning the game.

Whether or not a triple peel should be attempted at all in a game that you really need to win, is a point worthy of consideration. An article published in an English magazine in the 1990s dealt with the question of when a triple peel should, and should not, be attempted; and concluded that it will only be objectively feasible if the player has about a 50% chance of completing it successfully, and in addition there is a better than even chance that the opponent, if he gets in, will be able to complete an all-round break. If you are interested in trying triple peels you can test the first of these conditions for yourself by setting up a leave such as the one shown in the diagram below, and seeing how often you can complete the triple peel. If you cannot do it 5 times out of 10, then by attempting a triple peel in a game you are likely to reduce your chance of winning instead of increasing it. It should be remembered that at best the triple peel will serve to deny the opponent just one turn in which he is entitled to a lift shot, and against most opponents the allowance of this shot will not be of sufficient consequence to justify the taking of noticeable risks which could have been avoided by playing instead a simple 4-ball break.

The second psychological problem is that it is possible to get carried away with the excitement of the fact that you are about to complete a triple peel! This can result in increased tension, causing failure in even the simplest of shots required to complete the break after all of the harder and riskier work has been done. For some players this psychological difficulty is very real, and it takes them many attempts in competition play, all with the triple peel almost completed but not quite, before they finally manage to complete one.

The third problem, and a very difficult one to overcome indeed, is in the player's psychological approach to the remainder of the game when he has failed in an attempt to triple peel. For some players, once the triple has failed there is no longer sufficient interest for them in the game to maintain the intense concentration they had been applying to every shot before things went wrong, and so they start to play well below their best and are likely to lose the game when they may well have been able to win it.

Perhaps the best answer to all of these psychological problems associated with triple peels is to do so many of them that they become common-place and no longer seem to assume any great importance.

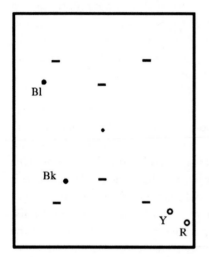

However, this is not so easy for most of us to achieve, and the best we can do is to at least be aware of the psychological dangers, and be ready to meet them. Things are not helped by the unfortunate tendency of others to overrate the triple as an achievement. For example, many still consider that a player who triple peels his opponent's ball and pegs it out, but then loses the game, has achieved more than the player who won the game!

A fourth psychological danger is the tendency for the player to suffer a mental let-down after the third peel. Sometimes the three peels are completed even before the 2-back hoop is made. Because the player knows that all the hard work has been done, he can find it difficult to maintain full concentration and so can break down in what should be the most straight-forward part of his break.

If you wish to give yourself the best chance of doing a triple peel without being greatly concerned about whether or not it will increase your chance of winning the game, then you should try (as the player of red and yellow and having taken yellow to 4-back) setting the leave shown in the diagram. The opponent will almost certainly lift the black ball, and although his lift shot will not be a particularly long one, if he misses it you should have a better chance than any other leave would give you of finishing the game with a triple peel which involves little risk in getting it going.

John Riches and Wayne Davies

PSYCHOLOGY OF LEAVES

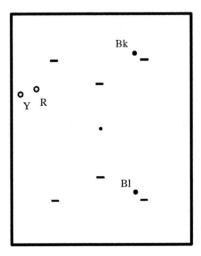

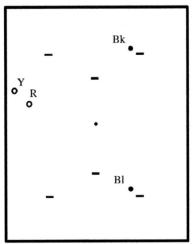

I N EACH OF the diagrams on this page we shall suppose that the player of red, which is for 4-back, has set up for his yellow partner ball, which is for hoop 3. Note first of all that, unless the player of yellow is incapable of rushing a ball across the lawn, it would be incorrect to set up with the red and yellow balls in the 3rd corner or near yellow's hoop. The first diagram shows a very strong leave, but apart from the difficulty of setting the rush for yellow without leaving black a double target, some players would see as a disadvantage the fact that black is more or less forced to shoot at red, even though there is only a single ball target, since yellow already has a perfect rush to its hoop. By setting the rush as shown in the second diagram, to the blue ball instead of to hoop 3, you can raise considerable doubt in the minds of many opponents about whether or not they should shoot at all, since a miss would give yellow "more than he has already got". The reasoning is fallacious, since in both situations yellow, if he is a competent player, would clearly have a better than 75% chance of establishing at least a 3-ball break. Black should have around a 25% chance of roqueting either red or blue, so the correct play for black is to shoot at the ball he considers himself most likely to hit.

However, even opponents who realise this may not find it easy to cope with the psychology of the situation.

The third diagram shows a similar leave in which the player of red has sought to take advantage of an opponent who likes to adopt a "safety-first" approach and avoid risks wherever possible. His correct shot is with blue at red or yellow, but such a

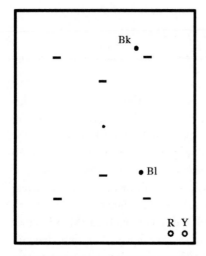

player will find it very hard to bring himself to "risk" leaving black at yellow's hoop, even though it actually would be by far his safest course of action.

He is likely instead to hit black away into a corner and leave yellow with a good no-risk chance of establishing a break.

The fourth diagram shows a situation where red had conceded a 'lift' to the opponent before setting for yellow, and has set a "reverse rush" in order to discourage black from shooting at red or yellow.

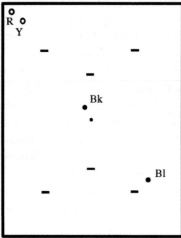

The English player and writer Keith Wylie has correctly pointed out that this idea should be seen as nothing more than a "con", since there can never be anything to gain by setting the rush in reverse against an opponent who is capable of correctly and objectively deciding on the best reply. Black can always do whatever he would have done if the rush were set the right way round, so his percentage chance of getting the next break cannot have been reduced by the backward setting of the rush. In fact, in many situations his chance will have been increased by the offer of more attractive alternatives.

Against some opponents there may at times be something to gain by setting a weaker leave for yourself than you could have done, but only if you know the opponent well enough to rely on him to succumb to the psychological pressure and do the wrong thing.

"NEVER CHANGE A WINNING GAME"

THE OLD SPORTING adage referred to in the title of this article has some interesting applications to the game of croquet. Coaches sometimes are frustrated by it, when they can see that a player is adopting a facet of technique, or a series of tactical choices, which will lead to increasing problems and the loss of games as the player moves on to play at higher levels. If the current technique and tactical play seem to be working and enabling the player to win games, then it will be difficult to persuade him that there is any need to change. Later, when the player finds that the coach was right and he is no longer having the success he had experienced at lower levels, it may be much harder to make the change because the incorrect methods have become ingrained habits reinforced over a considerable length of time. The fact that you are winning should not be taken as absolute proof that all is well with your game, and a wise player will seek the advice of a competent and trusted coach to peruse the tactical choices and technical expertise displayed in games he won, as well as trying to ascertain the reasons why other games were lost.

The idea of not changing a winning game can, however, be quite important in some other areas of the game of croquet. On many occasions players have been observed to have built up a considerable lead by using a particular strategical or tactical approach, only to change that approach later in the game for no apparent reason, and allow the opponent back into the game. Examples are the attacking player who, by taking risks that happen to come off, reaches a stage where he suddenly realises that he has a real chance of beating an opponent he did not expect to beat, and starts to play more carefully because he "does not want to risk losing his lead"; and the player who has been succeeding in getting the opponent more and more frustrated by keeping the balls where they cannot easily be used, until he (or more often his partner in a doubles game) unaccountably gets a "rush of blood" and takes the risk of attempting a five-foot angled hoop with the opponent's ball present, thus presenting the opponent with a ready-made break.

Many years ago I was watching the final of a country tournament in which an experienced state player was in trouble against a player who had recently been promoted from division 2 and was playing extremely well. There was no sign that the pattern was likely to change until the state player missed a roquet, measured his ball onto the yardline, and was challenged by his less experienced opponent on the grounds that the ball had actually gone out a foot or so from where it was measured in. "Oh dear, he shouldn't have done that," commented an old and wise lady sitting next to me, "He probably would have won the game anyway." At the time I did not understand the point of her remark, but sure enough, the state player, stung by what he saw as a challenge of his honesty, started to concentrate harder and suddenly began to play like a winner. I learnt from this, and other similar incidents, that it simply does not pay to change the psychology of a winning game. Whether the state player had measured the ball in correctly or not, his actions should have been ignored by the less experienced player. Even if the challenge was justified, it was far too dangerous from a psychological viewpoint to risk changing the mental approach of an opponent who was at that stage not playing well.

On another occasion a young and very strong player was playing well against a more experienced opponent in the best-of-three-games final of the SA Open Championship. The younger player had won the first game and was well ahead in the second, when he made a serious mistake of a type which I am sure in later years he will not make. He apparently considered that some of his opponent's hoop approaches looked suspiciously like double-taps, and so asked the opponent to have a referee watch all his future hoop approaches. While the young player was perfectly entitled to take such action, it was another case where it was most unwise to risk changing the psychology of a winning game. The opponent, instead of becoming upset at the request, saw it as an opportunity to think through his hoop approach technique and ensure that he got everything exactly right. The greater concentration resulted in his hoop approaches, and other shots as well, being played with a care and accuracy that had not been in evidence previously, so that he won that second game and went on to rather easily win the third game as well.

Perhaps a case can be made to support the idea that during a game you should never challenge an opponent's shots in this manner, since if he is indeed double-tapping his hoop approaches (or leaving still balls on take-offs, etc.) it is only likely to reduce his control of those shots anyway. It is hard enough to control the balls in one hit, let alone two hits in the same swing! On the other hand, if you are well behind and look like losing, then any such action you take is hardly going to make things worse, and may be worth a try. But if things are going well and you look like winning, forget it!

SECTION 7

PEGGED-OUT GAMES

VERY FEW PLAYERS seem to deliberately practise playing with two balls against one, one ball against two, or one ball against one. It is another area in which many poor tactical decisions are made, even at the highest levels of play. Some players avoid entering pegged-out games when they could have increased their chances of winning by doing so, simply because they have little idea of what to do in such situations.

There is an enormous amount of information for coaches to pass on and for players to learn and practise. Only a small fraction of it can be covered here, in order to give some idea of what there is to learn.

Many players are unable to adjust their thinking to the fact that percentages and tactical principles change drastically once a ball has been pegged out. They use more or less the same tactics and play the same shots as they would in a game with all four balls, as if one of the balls is out of play temporarily. By doing this they allow the opponent numerous chances that he should never have been given. Unfortunately, they usually later blame the loss of the game on anything but the fact that their tactical choices were foolish in the extreme, and it is far from easy to convince them that they need to spend time improving their knowledge in this area.

In pegged out games wiring assumes far greater importance, leaves can become really critical, and correct placement of balls (which means knowing the right places to put them stroke by stroke, as well as being able to get them there) becomes vital.

Readers who take the trouble to think through the examples given in this section, either keeping track of the balls mentally or setting up the position on a pin-board (or better still out on the lawn) cannot help but improve their understanding of the types of situations that can arise, and what to do in them.

WHEN TO PEG A BALL OUT

A COACH WILL often be asked by players whether or not it is correct to peg out a ball in a particular situation. Such a question can be very difficult to answer with any real conviction, as the answer will usually depend on the skill levels of both the player and the opponent. As a general guide we recommend the following principles for players who are below international level, but are capable of playing sizeable 4-ball and 3-ball breaks.

1. **Pegging out your own ball.**

   (a) You should peg out your own ball when you have missed the peg with your partner ball in attempting to peg it out, unless the partner ball has gone well out toward a boundary and the opponent's balls are separated. Leaving yourself with one ball is more likely to win the game than leaving both of your balls in the middle of the lawn. It is also better than leaving your partner ball in the middle and hitting your ball out of play, as your opponent then is likely to gain the innings and with all four balls still in play will have greater opportunity to set up and complete an all-round break.

Exceptions to this rule may occur when the opponent also has both clips on the peg (or on rover or penultimate) and his balls are close enough together to make it very likely that he will roquet.

   (b) Also peg out your own ball when your opponent has only one ball left in the game and your partner ball is five or more hoops ahead of him. The chance of losing a 2-ball game from such a position (except at international level) is so slight that your best chance of winning will almost certainly be to peg out your forward ball. This is true even if you have an alternative possibility of playing a 3-ball break with your partner ball and finishing the game immediately. Unless your partner ball has made 4-back the chance of something going wrong with the 3-ball break is greater than the chance of losing the 2-ball ending.

2. **Pegging out an opponent ball**

   (a) You should peg out one of the opponent's balls any time you can, provided his partner ball has not yet made 4-back. This applies even if your own partner ball is still on the first hoop, assuming that you know how to play with two balls against one. If the opponent's remaining ball will be on penultimate then your own partner ball would need to have made 1-back, as otherwise you would probably do better to keep all four balls in the game and take the risk of the opponent roqueting, having ensured that if he fails to roquet you will have a reasonable chance of setting up a break for your partner using the ball the opponent has left out in the lawn. If your opponent's remaining ball will be for rover or the peg (so that he needs to take only one ball into the lawn in order to give himself an excellent chance of finishing the game), then the peg-out will be inadvisable unless your partner ball has made 4-back.

(b) As a corollary to the above, peg out BOTH the opponent's ball and your own ball when your partner ball will be five or more hoops ahead of the opponent's remaining single ball.

P.S.—Don't forget that after you peg a ball out your opponent will still be entitled to lifts, but you will not.

WHEN TO MAKE 4-BACK

YOU WILL OFTEN see a player make a nine-hoop break, then later get in with the same ball and go to rover or the peg when his partner ball has hardly started. In most situations it is tactically wrong to make 4-back before your partner ball has at least made 1-back. The reason for this is not so much the possibility of your opponent going right around and pegging your ball out (although at the highest levels that may indeed be a relevant consideration), but rather the far more important point that by giving the opponent a 'lift' you will have made it more difficult to obtain a leave which gives your partner ball the best chance of setting up a break.

The setting of a really good aggressive leave is far more important, and far more likely to result in your winning the game, than the making of one or two (or three) additional hoops with your forward ball.

It is curious that some players will make their all-round break with the second ball noticeably more difficult by attempting a triple peel whose main purpose is to deny the opponent one lift shot; yet if it fails (say, at hoop 3 without the peel having been made) and they get in again with the forward ball, they will make 4-back and so give him the shot, simply for the sake of making a hoop or two.

They may argue that they are giving themselves the opportunity of finishing the game in one more turn; but why should it be any more difficult for your opponent to go right around and peg your ball out (peeling it through rover if necessary) than for you to do so?

For players below international level, and one suspects at international level also, percentages surely favour setting properly for the partner ball, and ensuring that you will peg out in the turn in which you make 4-back with the ball whose clip is already there, so that you avoid conceding the 4-back 'lift'.

THREE-BALL GAMES

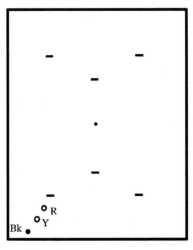

WHEN A BALL has been pegged out, so that only three balls remain in the game, the tactics can involve making a series of decisions which are far more difficult than those faced in a normal game. Part of the difficulty can arise from the fact that few players actually practise three-ball games on a regular basis, so they have very little experience on which to base estimates of percentages.

The first diagram shows a position which occurred in one of my recent games, which we knew was likely to be the deciding game in the 1994 South Australian inter-club premiership series. The blue ball has been pegged out (the player of blue, a much stronger player than his partner, had made the first break to 4-back, then I had managed to triple peel his ball and peg it out). Yellow (my partner) is for 2-back; my red clip is on the peg, and black is for hoop 3.

Black has just taken a shot at our balls from the far end of the lawn and missed. We are now faced with three options:

(1) Yellow can roquet black and play a three-ball break. This involves the risk that if he breaks down at any point, black will almost certainly have all three balls out in the lawn, with an opportunity to himself finish the game with a 3-ball break.

(2) Ignore the black ball and try to make one hoop at a time, always leaving our balls wired from black, or in a distant part of the lawn so that he will have to hit a long roquet and then play some difficult shots in order to get a 3-ball break going. This sounds like a safer strategy, but is not so easy to do in practice. There is also the consideration that when 4-back is made, black will be entitled to a 'lift'.

(3) I could play the turn with red, rush yellow out to black, then send black to a distant part of the lawn and peg my red ball out, leaving my partner to play a 2-ball game with 5 hoops lead. Five hoops ahead is normally considered the minimal number in order to ensure a higher percentage chance of winning the game than if the three balls were all kept in the game.

In this case, however, I would not be sure of leaving yellow in a position to run its 2-back hoop, and it is likely that black would gain position to run hoop 3 before yellow could get in front of 3-back. Thus yellow may have to wait until black had made hoops 3, 4 and probably 5 as well before he could try for position in front of 3-back, and would then be only 3 or 4 hoops ahead.

It is also possible to try to combine these options, e.g. by using option (2), but hoping at a later stage to switch to option (3) by pegging out the red ball when, for example, the yellow clip is on 4-back. The choice between these various options, especially in the heat of battle, is a perplexing one, and it is not helped by the certain knowledge that whatever choice you make will be severely criticised if you happen to lose the game.

The "correct" choice is probably option (1), but in this instance my partner did not feel confident about the idea of playing a 3-ball break under so much pressure, so we chose option (2). History records, sadly, that a few turns later black managed to hit one of our balls when we thought they were both completely wired from him, and played a rather awkward 3-ball break which he somehow managed to keep alive long enough to win the game.

One factor in 3-ball games not to be underestimated is the fact that the player of the single ball is in a situation where he has nothing to lose. All pressure has been removed from him, at least for the time being, and he may as well go for everything. Many players can seem to play 'above themselves' in such situations, while the player with the two balls is under constant pressure.

We went home trying to work out what we could and should have done differently in the above situation, and at various other stages of the game. There was no shortage of helpful advice offered by spectators, but the main thing we concluded is that in future we need to give ourselves a lot more practice at playing with two balls against one, or one against two. The textbooks seem to give little definite advice, other than to state that the majority of 3-ball games are won by the single ball. However, the reason for this may well be that few players know how to play the two balls correctly, so the player of the single ball is given far more chances than he should be given; and in many cases players only peg out an opponent's ball when they are already in a somewhat desperate situation.

When playing with one ball against two, the first important principle to follow is: **Always shoot at the opponent's balls** (whichever one, if you roquet, would give the best chance of establishing the 3-ball break) regardless of what you would be giving him if you miss. Against a capable opponent there is little point in sitting in front

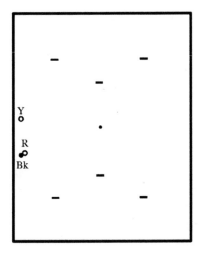

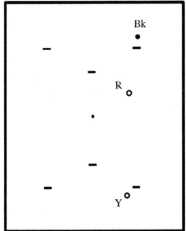

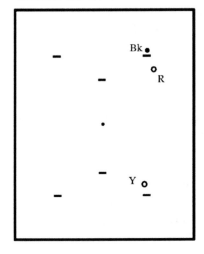

of your hoop as many players like to do, or trying to "sit over" him in the hope that he will make a mistake. Secondly, it is important to **take every chance of establishing a 3-ball break.**

Playing to make hoops with only one of the opponent's balls in play is for most of us a waste of time, unless we have only one or two hoops to make. This principle is illustrated in the first diagram, where the player of the single black ball is for hoop 3 and has roqueted red after his opponent had set wide on the west border.

Many players as black would now take off from red, trying for a rush behind yellow to hoop 3. A better plan is to send red to a position about one third of the way from hoop 3 to hoop 4 without making any attempt to get behind yellow. Then yellow can be split to a position a yard or two behind hoop 4 as black goes to hoop 3.

The chance of getting right in front of the hoop and being able to run it is remote, but black can instead sit in front of the hoop, with a strong position as shown in the second diagram. Any shot taken and missed by the opponent will now give black a good chance of setting up the 3-ball break that he needs. The placement of the red and yellow balls is important. Yellow is placed behind hoop 4 rather than in front so that it is further from red, but mainly so that if red is hit away to a far corner, black can run hoop 3 right through to the south border without having to worry about controlling the strength of the shot, and then be in a good position to roquet yellow and continue. In similar situations players tend to load hoop 4 (if that can be done first, e.g. if black had roqueted yellow instead of red in the first diagram), then approach hoop 3 with a long roll in which the opponent ball is placed only 1-2 yards behind the hoop as illustrated in the third diagram. If the roll is unsuccessful and the hoop cannot be made, it is then difficult for black to sit in front of the hoop without allowing the nearby red opponent ball any part of the black ball to shoot at. This is why the hoop should be approached with a shot that places the opponent ball several yards behind the hoop, so that even if black is not properly wired from red, the shot will be too risky for the opponent to contemplate.

Note also that it is wrong, as some would do, to sit black at a distance of only one foot or less in front of hoop 3. This could give a better chance of completely wiring it from the opponent's ball, but if even the tiniest bit of the black ball is showing, the opponent can safely shoot at it because the hoop will hamper any attempt by black to turn around and roquet the red ball on the north border if it misses.

The black ball needs to be set about a yard in front of hoop 3 as shown in the second diagram, and then if red shoots at it and misses, black will not make the hoop immediately, but will roquet red on the border and send it back to where it came from—again several yards behind the hoop—with a reasonable chance of getting the 3-ball break established, and again keeping the player of red and yellow under pressure by setting once more as shown in the second diagram if the hoop cannot be made. An understanding of exactly where to place the balls when you get the chance is essential if you are to give yourself the best possible chance of winning with one ball against two.

It is not possible in the space available here to cover all of the possibilities that can occur in three-ball games, but some understanding of the type of thinking involved can be gained from a careful consideration of tactical ideas starting from the position shown in the first diagram, where black is for 1-back and has just failed to make the hoop, and has finished in a position from which he will not be able to make it on his next shot.

Let us suppose that red is on the peg and yellow is for 3-back. Red will not want to risk shooting at black, as a miss would give the player of black a better opportunity than he ought to be given. Shooting with red at yellow, as some would do, also involves unnecessary risk, as a miss would allow black to either shoot at red and yellow, or sit in front of his 1-back hoop.

If red is hit away into the 3rd corner, then black will shoot at it, since red is already for the peg. Therefore, red should be played into the 4th corner, to a position where (if possible) it is wired from black, since black will shoot at it wherever it goes unless it is wired.

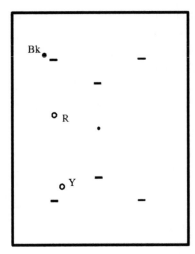

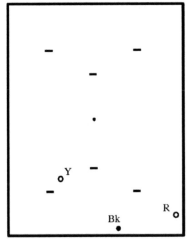

The best place for red, especially if it would be wired from black there, is right on the corner spot. If red goes a yard or two out of the corner then black (if wired from red) can go wide of it on the other border, as shown in the third diagram, keeping pressure on the player of red and yellow, who will again have to move red and leave yellow out in the lawn.

Supposing, then, that red is played into the 4th corner. If black now sits wide of it, then red can shoot at black with relative safety, so black is likely to sit in front of its 1-back hoop, allowing yellow to be played on the following turn. However, to play yellow near red in the 4th corner would again be dangerous, allowing black to run 1-back and shoot at red without giving yellow an immediate break if the shot is missed, unless the position is such that yellow can create a cannon in the fourth corner, which is a possibility that both players should always bear in mind.

There is no need for the player of red and yellow to go together and allow black to shoot at his balls in a situation where a roquet would allow black to rush the other ball to his hoop (or set up as in the previous article), until a

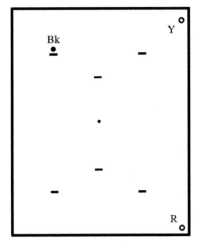

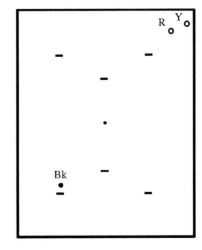

position can be created such that a miss by black will give yellow an immediate break. After yellow is played into the 3rd corner (this time there is no need to try to get it right on the corner spot), black might make 1-back and sit in front of 2-back. In this case red should not shoot at yellow, but should be played to a position as shown in the fourth diagram, so that after black makes 2-back he will not be able to sit near 3-back, and a missed shot at the opponent's balls will allow yellow to finish the game with a 3-ball break.

If black sits in the 4th corner after making 2-back, then yellow can rush red to a position where it can set a completely wired rush to 3-back for itself, having regained the innings and the initiative without undue risk.

TWO-BALL GAMES

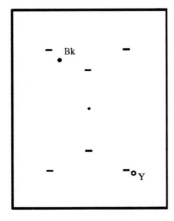

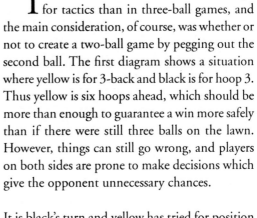

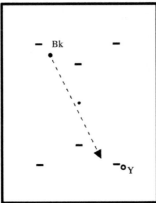

IN TWO-BALL GAMES there is less scope for tactics than in three-ball games, and the main consideration, of course, was whether or not to create a two-ball game by pegging out the second ball. The first diagram shows a situation where yellow is for 3-back and black is for hoop 3. Thus yellow is six hoops ahead, which should be more than enough to guarantee a win more safely than if there were still three balls on the lawn. However, things can still go wrong, and players on both sides are prone to make decisions which give the opponent unnecessary chances.

It is black's turn and yellow has tried for position to run 3-back, but has finished too close to the hoop and has no chance of making it in the next turn. The player of black has a choice of three interesting possibilities:

(1) He can shoot at yellow, even if partly wired from it. In order to regain reasonable winning chances black must catch up at least three hoops on yellow, and the only way he is likely to do this is by making a roquet at some stage. If the shot is missed, yellow will be unable to sit in front of 3-back and would not want to risk a shot at black, even if it has one without a hampered backswing. However, there is the risk of black hitting the hoop to be taken into account, as if black finishes within easy roqueting distance of yellow, the game is as good as finished. Even so, this is probably black's best chance.

(2) He can play black to a position where it is wired from yellow and prevents yellow from going to position in front of 3-back (see second diagram). This avoids the risk of hitting the hoop, but requires accurate judgement of distance in

order to ensure that black finishes in the correct wired position. The result can be a sort of "stalemate" where the players creep around the hoop a few centimetres at a time, keeping their balls wired from each other, and on occasion declaring their turns when there is no better place for the ball than where it already is. If the game has a time limit, then the onus will be on black to eventually do something. He will probably choose a suitable moment, when yellow cannot run the hoop, in which to hit his ball out to border and invite yellow to risk the 6-8 yard roquet on it.

(3) He can try for position in front of hoop 3. If he succeeds then yellow may have to go right away from its hoop and allow black to catch up two or three hoops before yellow can again go near 3-back, but if black does not get position to run hoop 3, then yellow can simply sit in front of 3-back (almost certainly wired from black) and once again the game is as good as over.

The reason for needing to be five or more hoops ahead before willingly entering a two-ball endgame (assuming that you are not already past 4-back) is that with a little luck it is possible for the opponent to catch up one or two hoops by following you around from hoop to hoop, and you need to be at least three hoops ahead when you get to make rover. In the third diagram, for example, black is still to make 4-back. Whoever has the turn, black can give himself a reasonable chance (say 25%, which is too much if you are yellow) of winning by making 4-back and sitting in position to run penultimate. Then yellow will not be able to safely sit near the peg, so will have to attempt the peg-out from a longer distance. If yellow is already near the peg when black makes 4-back, then of course black would shoot at it, expecting to hit the 15-yard roquet 3-4 times out of ten, which is a better chance than you would want to give him.

SECTION 8

TACTICAL ERRORS

T HE FOUR ARTICLES in this section were published in the Australian Croquet Gazette during 1994, and illustrate the type of incorrect tactical thinking which is evident even at the highest levels of play. Examples similar to those given could be found in the games of almost every player at any level. We cannot hope to completely eliminate such errors from our play, but we can at least try to learn from them, and so reduce their number.

A famous chess player once pointed out that there is no need to keep on repeating the same errors, as there are plenty of new ones waiting to be made! I think that the same can fairly be said in reference to the tactical errors we make in games of croquet.

HOW TO LOSE A GAME OF CROQUET

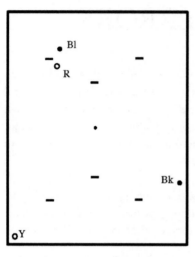

A COACH WILL usually experience great difficulty in convincing players that most of their games are lost through poor tactics rather than through missing roquets or sticking in hoops. The diagram shows a position at the start of a game played during the recent Australian Championships.

Red had made hoop 1 and played a long roll with blue for hoop 2, but failed to gain position to run the hoop. The other three clips were still on hoop 1. The player of red now shot back at his partner ball in the 1st corner.

When the roquet was missed, red and yellow became touching balls in the corner. This allowed blue to shoot at black, and although this roquet was also missed, the player of red and yellow had no clear way of setting up a break on his next turn, unless he was prepared to split his partner ball to hoop 2 while going right across the court to the opponent's balls on the far boundary, then rush one of them back to hoop 1. He elected instead to take off to the opponent's balls, succeeded in making hoop 1, but had nothing set up ahead and had to allow the opponent another chance to roquet before there was any real chance of establishing a break.

If red had succeeded in roqueting yellow it is most unlikely that he could have found a way to establish a break in that turn anyway. There were at least three options available to red which would all have been preferable to shooting at yellow in the diagrammed position:

(1) Red could have played to stop in the lawn a yard or two short of yellow, giving yellow a rush to hoop

    1. This is not easy to do accurately, but if successful would make it dangerous for blue to shoot at black, since yellow can then make hoop 1 with a rush to either hoop 3 or the 4th corner, setting up at least a 3-ball break.

(2) Red could have been hit out a yard or two up the west border from yellow, giving yellow a rush to hoop

2. This also more or less "prevents" blue from shooting at black, since yellow could rush-load hoop 2 then take off to the opponent's balls and rush one of them to hoop 1. However, it is likely that blue would have a rather inviting double target in the 1ˢᵗ corner.

(3) Better still, red could have been hit out on the south boundary, about a yard from yellow so that yellow has a cut-rush to the black ball. Once again the opponent would be taking a severe risk if he shot with blue at black, as yellow can then rush red to the 4ᵗʰ corner and use a stop-shot to send it to hoop 2 before rushing an opponent ball to hoop 1.

Option (3) has the added advantage that if the opponent plays blue to the east boundary wide of black as shown in the second diagram (which would have been a reasonable answer to either of the first two options), then yellow can cut-rush red toward black and without difficulty place the opponent's balls at hoop 1 and hoop 2 before setting himself a rush to either—preferably to hoop 2 rather than hoop 1 unless the rush is wired from the opponent ball at hoop 1.

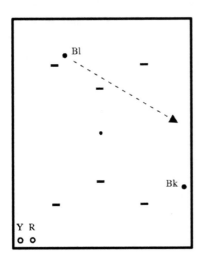

This again faces the opponent with a situation in which any missed roquet will prove very costly, but there is now a good chance of establishing at least a 3-ball break whatever he does.

There is little doubt that the player of red and yellow is still blissfully unaware that he greatly reduced his chance of winning the game by shooting at yellow in the position of the first diagram. This is what makes it so difficult to convince players, even those well below state team level, that although it is important to get out on the lawn and try to improve their roquets and hoop-running, etc., it is even more important to take deliberate steps to improve your tactics.

The stronger the player becomes, the more it is that tactics, rather than improved shot-making, becomes the main key to winning more games.

The moral is: MAKE SURE THAT YOU LEARN FROM THE MISTAKES OF OTHERS. YOU DON'T HAVE TIME TO MAKE THEM ALL YOURSELF!

HOW TO AVOID MAKING HOOPS

I T IS OFTEN difficult for a coach to convince players that there are times when it is wrong to make a hoop.

Even at the highest levels of play it is not uncommon to see players making hoops without thinking. The positions shown here occurred during the National Championships in Adelaide, and involved some of our leading players; but players at less exalted levels can also learn much from the errors that were made.

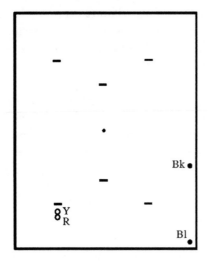

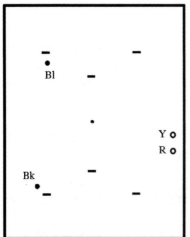

In the position of the first diagram all clips were still on hoop 1. Red had rushed yellow to about one foot directly in front of hoop 1, and now made a "double" by peeling the yellow partner ball through the hoop before making it with red. As often happens when this is attempted, the result was that after making the hoop red had a hampered roquet on yellow, and then elected to take off to the opponent's balls, leaving yellow in the lawn near hoop 1 with very little chance of continuing the break.

The correct play was to avoid making the hoop for yellow, and simply place the yellow ball to the right of the hoop so that after making the hoop red would have a rush toward the opponent's balls. Then it does not require much skill or accuracy to place the balls roughly as shown in the second diagram, with one of the opponent's balls at each of your hoops. Your red and yellow balls can be placed anywhere along the east boundary, but should be set parallel to the boundary and slightly in from the yardline, so that you are threatening to make at least a 3-ball break with either ball, and a missed roquet attempt by the opponent will immediately give you the fourth ball as well.

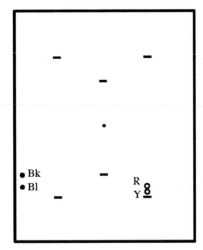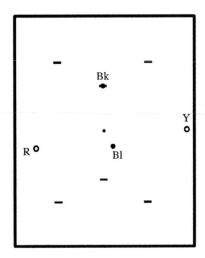

In the third diagram we see another example of the same error, where the player made hoop 4 with both balls, then was not prepared to play the big split-shot needed to load hoop 6 with yellow while going to the opponent's balls, so decided to take off to them and could only manage to rush one of them to hoop 5 with little chance of continuing the break. The correct play was to make hoop 4 with red only, placing yellow so that after making the hoop red has a rush to the 1st corner. From there it is relatively easy to send yellow to hoop 6 while going to the opponent's balls with a break set up. A reasonable, not quite so good alternative was to play to rush yellow to hoop 6 after making hoop 4.

The fourth diagram shows another example where a hoop was made when it should not have been. Black had stuck in hoop 6, then red had shot at it but missed. Now black made the hoop and shot at blue. When the shot was missed, the opponent could shoot at blue with either ball, and even if he missed, blue would have no safe shot to follow.

Here the black ball is in a very safe position, so blue is the ball to move. Blue should shoot at black, and if it misses finish just short of the yardline.

Then on the next turn black can run through the hoop to the boundary, getting a rush on blue to 1-back.

HOW TO ENSURE A LOSS

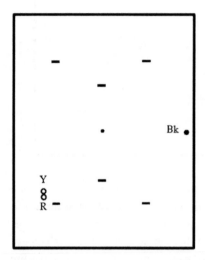

T HE POSITION SHOWN in the first diagram was taken from an important game between two of our leading players in the National Championships in Adelaide. Blue has been pegged out and black is for the peg. The yellow clip is on 4-back and red has just made hoop 1. The opponent had pegged out blue, leaving black near the peg; but yellow had roqueted black, sent it away to the 4th corner, and set up in the 1st corner for red to make hoop 1. Then the black ball was played to the middle of the east boundary as shown, from where it has a relatively short shot at the peg. This idea of using a turn to place the single ball (which is for the peg) in the middle of a side boundary, instead of shooting at either the peg or the opponent's balls, is sometimes used by experienced players, but should prove futile against a thinking opponent.

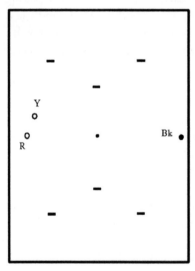

The player of red and yellow made hoop 1 with red, but did not obtain a forward rush, and after roqueting yellow had reached the position shown in the diagram. From here, red rolled with yellow for hoop 2 and set up there. Then black shot at the peg and missed, after which red made hoop 2 and rolled to hoop 3, again setting up. Again black shot at the peg and missed. Red made hoop 3, after which black was permitted another shot at the peg, which this time was successful.

In the diagrammed position the player of red and yellow was obviously in a desperate situation, with only a slight chance of winning the game. However, with players capable of making all-round 3-ball breaks, as these were, the result is certainly not a foregone conclusion if correct tactics are used. It is clear that the policy adopted by the player of red and yellow, of making hoops one or two at a time and allowing the opponent to continue shooting at the peg from side to side, is an almost certain way to lose the game. Sooner or later black will hit the peg. The chance of black missing the peg eight or ten times in a row, even with players well below state level, is extremely remote.

Therefore the correct play is to allow black only one shot, which if missed will give red a 3-ball break on which it should go to the peg. Then another shot (from the 1st corner, if possible wired from the peg and with yellow set in the 3rd corner for 4-back) must be allowed, and if this is missed then yellow should finish the game. Black will not be entitled to any lifts since blue has been pegged out.

This means that in the first diagram, after making hoop 1, red should not have rolled with yellow to hoop 2. Instead, the correct tactic is to set up as shown in the second diagram, on the opposite side of the peg from black. Then, if black shoots at the peg and misses, red will have an excellent chance of setting up the 3-ball break required. This will be true whether black shoots hard at the peg, or just dribbles in to stay near it. If black shoots at red or yellow and misses, then red again should be able to set up a 3-ball break without any great difficulty. For this reason it is important that the red and yellow balls are set, not too near the border, but a carefully chosen distance in from it.

If black refrains from shooting, then red can make hoop 2 and if it does not get a good rush to hoop 3 it should again set up so that any shot black takes and misses will give a 3-ball break.

From a coaching viewpoint it is unfortunate that some players, particularly those who consider themselves to belong to some sort of elite class, seem to resent any suggestion that their tactics can be improved. This highlights the fact which is accepted in almost every other sport, but not generally in croquet: Every serious competitive player should have regular sessions with a coach, and the higher the level at which he or she plays, **the more vital it is.** For example, every top tennis player or golfer (or athlete in almost any other sport) has his or her own individual coach. It is also worth noting that in almost all cases the coach cannot play anywhere near as well as the player who is being coached.

HOW TO LOSE THE INNINGS

T HE POSITION SHOWN in the first diagram is taken from a game played in the English Silver Medal tournament at the National Championships in Adelaide, between players who had won the gold medals in their respective states. We shall see that even at this level players can be seen giving the innings away and losing games through poor tactics.

Yellow is for hoop 5 and red for hoop 3. The opponent has his blue clip on 4-back, while the black clip is still on hoop 1. Before reading any further, work

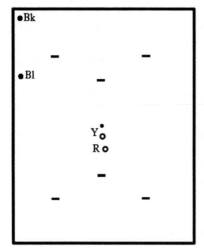

out clearly in your mind what you would do if you were playing red and yellow in this situation.

Players at all levels frequently make wrong tactical choices in such situations because they do not think past the making of their next hoop. In lower divisions such thinking may be excusable, but when the players are capable of making consistent breaks, as these certainly were, they cannot afford to make serious tactical errors.

The player decided to play yellow and make hoop 5. He managed to do this after an anxious moment or two, since his cut to the hoop did not finish particularly close and he had to make a somewhat sidey hoop shot.

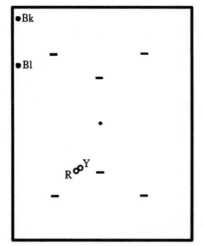

After making hoop 5, yellow, instead of getting a forward rush, had a rush toward hoop 1. At this stage red should have been rushed out to a position near the border, since it is obvious that yellow has much less than an even chance of continuing the break. The principle involved is straightforward and easily understood, but frequently overlooked (as it was here) in actual play: **Do not leave your partner ball in the lawn unless you**

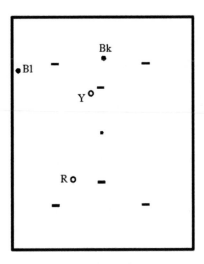

have a better than even chance of making the next hoop.

However, the player decided to simply roquet red instead of rushing it, and so reached the position shown on the second diagram. In this situation he again should have realised the danger of leaving his partner ball out in the lawn, and should therefore have played a thick take-off to send red within four yards or so of the border, so that if things went wrong he could return to it without allowing the opponent a safe shot. Instead, he took off to blue, leaving red out in the lawn. His error became more apparent when he had taken off from blue to black, almost (but not quite) managing to get a rush on it, then cut black part-way into the lawn and pass-rolled unsuccessfully for hoop 6. He found that in the position of the third diagram he could not afford to leave both balls out in the lawn, and was unable to make the hoop, so he hit yellow out to the border in front of hoop 1. Then black shot at blue and missed, and red could not afford to risk shooting at yellow, since the black clip was on hoop 1. Therefore red had to retire into the 4th corner, giving away the innings without the opponent even having had to make a roquet!

It would not be fair to criticise too strongly the player of red and yellow, as most players would have done more or less the same sort of thing, which indeed could prove successful on some occasions.

In the next article we shall consider in detail what the player should have done in order to greatly increase his winning chances, and try to discover some tactical principles which will assist us to avoid making such tactical errors. One principle has already been quoted above and concerns leaving your partner ball out in the lawn.

Many players who are aware of this principle err in the opposite direction by leaving their partner ball near the border at all times.

But the converse is also true: **You must be prepared to put your partner ball into the lawn when you have a better than even chance of establishing a break.**

GENERAL TACTICS

B Y FAR THE MOST difficult task which lies ahead for our coaches is to bring about a desperately needed improvement in the standard of general tactics used by players at all levels in Australia. Even at inter-state level there are few players who think objectively in terms of percentages, yet apart from the calculation (or at least accurate estimation) of percentages there is no other way of justifying tactical choices, or of knowing whether or not you are making the correct decisions. The fact that you make a particular tactical choice and then go on to win the game does not mean that your choice was the correct one—not even in that particular instance, let alone on future similar occasions—and neither does the adoption of a line of play by leading players provide convincing testimony of its correctness.

The tactical approach espoused and advised in this section is not without its controversial aspects, and may not suit every player's temperament; but I am certain that those who do succeed in understanding and adopting the various ideas and principles of tactical play will win far more games than they otherwise would have done.

DEFEATING 'AUNT EMMA'

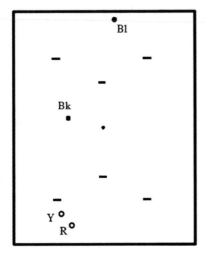

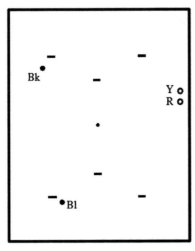

THE LEGENDARY "AUNT Emma", who may also haunt our lawns in male guise, is noted for ultra-defensive play. She will make as many hoops as possible from her partner ball while keeping your balls as far apart as possible. She rarely thinks to put your balls where she will be able to use them later, as she is more concerned to make sure that you are unlikely to roquet. For this reason she rarely makes more than one or two hoops at a time, and in positions such as the one shown in the first diagram where you are playing red and yellow and all clips are still on hoop 1, she will not be prepared to risk shooting with black at either your balls (since a miss would give you an easy break), or at her blue partner ball (which would give you two balls together in forward play).

Therefore, not having read our previous article "Why Not Shoot?", she will probably hit the black ball into, say, the 3rd corner.

Many players become frustrated by this type of opposition and end up taking foolish risks in an effort to end a situation in which neither side is making any apparent progress. Others try to 'play her at her own game', which is almost always a mistake because she is very good at the limited range of shots needed to play the way she does.

What is the best way to defeat her? Firstly, you must realise that in order to defeat her you must learn to play breaks. If you do not possess the range of shots (particularly splits) needed to set up and maintain a break, then you must set about acquiring these skills as rapidly as possible, and this will probably require the assistance of a good coach. Until you have done this you must expect to continue losing games to a good "Aunt Emma"—and make no mistake, some "Aunt Emmas" are indeed very good players who win a lot more games than one would expect.

Even players who are capable of playing breaks, however, do not always go about things in the right way when playing against the venerable Aunt. For example, in the first diagram above, after black is hit into the 3rd corner, you should not attempt a two-ball break with red while her balls remain out of play. In making hoop 1 you should try to get a rush toward the east border somewhere between hoops 3 and 4, instead of a rush to hoop 2. Then you can take off to black in the 3rd corner and send it to hoop 2 while going to blue; then send blue to hoop 1 and hit red out near yellow to achieve the set-up shown in the second diagram. Here it is once again unlikely that Emma will risk shooting at a ball, but you will have an excellent chance of getting at least a 3-ball break under way whatever she does.

The main principles involved in beating Aunt Emma-type play, therefore, are:

1. Learn to play split-shots and maintain breaks.
2. Be patient and always shoot at a ball, with confidence that once you succeed in roqueting you will easily be able to make more hoops than she has done while playing simply to keep you separated.
3. Do not play to make hoops with your own balls while hers are out of play. Get her balls and put them where you will be able to use them, and if possible where she will not be willing to risk shooting.
4. Accept the fact that nothing you can do will guarantee that you will beat her. If she hits every roquet and you play poorly enough you will still manage to lose to her; but if you go about things as recommended here and refuse to allow her tactics to upset you, the odds will be weighted overwhelmingly in your favour.

Perhaps, after everyone has read and applied this series of articles, Aunt Emma will at last be laid to rest!

THE ANSWER TO RETURNING WIDE

I HAVE MADE the point in previous articles that there are very few situations, if any, where it pays to 'return wide' of your partner ball against a thinking opponent who is capable of making breaks. Yet this ill-advised tactic is still seen quite frequently in play at all levels. The first diagram shows a position in which the red clip was on hoop 5. The player of blue considered that shooting at the opponent's balls (a single-ball target) was too risky, since a miss would allow red to roquet blue and send it to load hoop 6, then rush yellow to hoop 5. He also chose not to shoot at black, because it could allow red to set up a break by rushing yellow to hoop 6, taking-off to the two balls on the south border, and rushing one of them to hoop 5.

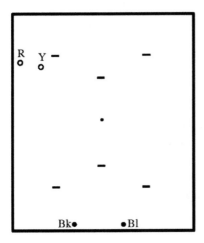

Therefore the player decided to 'return wide' by hitting blue out on the south border about 8 yards away from black. His idea was to avoid presenting the player of red with the opportunity to set up an easy break, which any missed shot would have allowed him to do.

THE WRONG REPLY

Having left his opponent with the balls placed as shown in the second diagram, the player of blue now expected red to roquet yellow, possibly rushing it to hoop 6, then take off to black, roquet it, and play another take-off, trying to get a rush behind blue to hoop 5. This way red may be able to get a break established, but it would take some accurate shots and would involve leaving yellow out in the lawn where red would be unable to safely return to it if anything went wrong. If the player of red is foolish enough to attempt this line of play, then blue's tactic of 'returning wide' would be justified; but look at what happens if blue's opponent plays correctly:

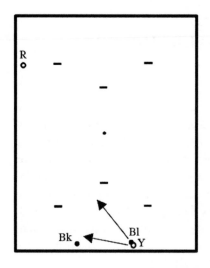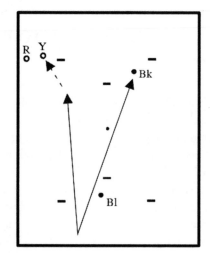

THE CORRECT REPLY

In the position of the second diagram, the turn should be played not with the red ball, but with yellow. After roqueting red, yellow should take off to blue (easier than black because the line of the take-off to blue would meet the south boundary at a more acute angle), then roll blue to the front of hoop 5 while going to black, as illustrated in the third diagram. There is no need to try to get a rush behind black, so the yellow ball can be kept safely away from the border, going to a position from which black can be easily roqueted. Then black should be sent to a position between hoops 3 and 6 as shown in the fourth diagram, and yellow can then be hit back near red, giving red a rush into the lawn. These shots do not require any great accuracy and entail little risk.

This would leave the player of black and blue wishing that he had taken a shot in the first place (which is exactly what should always be the consequence of 'returning wide'), as any shot he now takes and misses will give red an easier break than he would have had then; and if he again fails to shoot red will in any case have a good chance of establishing a break without needing to take any undue risk.

The first diagram shows a situation where the red clip is on hoop 2 and yellow is on hoop 1. The player of red and yellow has set a rush for red in the 2nd corner, with the opponent's balls widely separated. The player of black and blue felt that if he shot at either of his own balls with the other, a miss would make it too easy for either red or yellow to set up a break, so he played black into the 1st corner as shown by the arrow, thinking that this would make it difficult for either red or yellow to get a break established on the next turn. The fallacy in this sort of thinking lies in the fact that the player of red and yellow does not need to try to establish a break

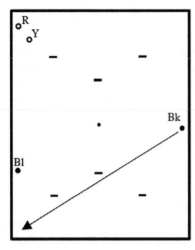

on the next turn, and the player of black and blue has passed up the chance of a possible roquet.

THE WRONG REPLY

In the game the player of red decided to make hoop 2, attempting to get a rush to hoop 3. However, he ran too far through hoop 2, and could only manage to roquet yellow into the lawn instead of rushing it anywhere useful. This brought about the situation of the second diagram, where red is faced with the need to get his partner ball out of the middle of the lawn while going to the opponent's balls, with little chance of being able to set a good leave, let alone continue the break. Thus the negative strategy adopted by the opponent in hitting his black ball out of play has been fully justified.

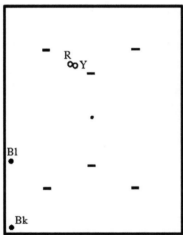

THE CORRECT REPLY

In approaching hoop 2, yellow should have been placed on the left (outside) of the hoop, in order to obtain a rush either to the opponent's balls, or to a position on the "trap line" behind hoop 2.

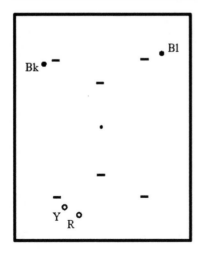

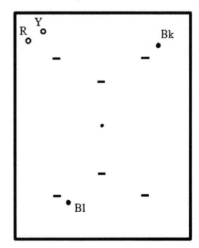

This would allow him to set up an 'ideal leave" as shown in either the 3rd or 4th diagrams. If you bear in mind that red is now for hoop 3 and yellow for hoop 1, you will see that if the opponent now misses any shot, he will be giving an even easier chance of establishing a break than before. In the position of the 4th diagram he does not even have a reasonable option of hitting out to a corner again, as either red or yellow should have little difficulty establishing a break anyway. This shows that against a thinking opponent, returning wide of your partner is pointless, and black should have shot at a ball (presumably blue) in the first diagram.

The answer to such negative play is to make only one hoop (or none at all, as after black was hit into the 1st corner, red could have rushed yellow right down to the south border and immediately set a leave somewhat similar to the ones shown, but with the red clip still on hoop 2), and then go and get the opponent's balls and place them to advantage. This is actually easier to do when they have been placed several yards apart than if they were together.

Against a thinking opponent, returning wide of your partner almost always reduces your chance of winning the game.

Unless you were wired from one or more of the three balls, there should have been at least one ball you could have shot at which would have given a better winning chance.

PERCENTAGE PLAY

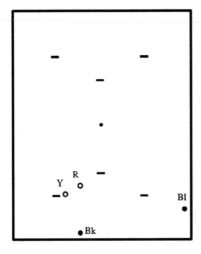

IN CROQUET, THE justification for all correct tactical moves must lie in percentages. Consider, for example, what you would do as the player of red and yellow in the first diagram where all clips are still on hoop 1 and black has just shot at red from near hoop 2 and missed. There are five possibilities:

1. **Two-ball break** Make hoop 1 with red, then rush or roll to hoop 2, etc. This would probably be the choice of the majority of players. However, it is a very poor choice when both players are capable of making reasonable breaks, as the game will not be won by making odd hoops. With this method your chance of getting a break established before your opponent does must be little better than even—say, 55-60%.

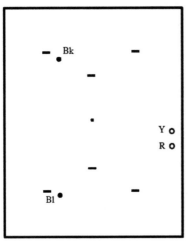

2. **Stop-shot for position:** Roquet yellow and take-off to black. Send black to hoop 2 with a stop-shot in which you also gain position to run hoop 1. This method gives you an immediate break if the stop-shot is successful, but allows black another chance to roquet if not. It is only justifiable when you can claim for yourself a success rate (in playing the stop-shot and making the hoop) of around 50% or better.

3. **Set up an "Ideal Leave":** Make hoop 1 with red and rush or split yellow to a position anywhere near the east boundary as you go to blue in the 4th corner. Roll blue to hoop 1 while going to black (keep red well in court—no need to risk going out). Send black to hoop 2 while returning to yellow to set up the position shown in the second diagram. This allows the opponent one chance to roquet, but guarantees a break if he misses or fails to shoot. On such a long roquet very few players would expect to hit more than one in four (25%), so this method gives you at least a 75%

chance of a break on your next turn, making it far preferable to either of the two methods so far considered. (A detailed consideration of such "Ideal Leaves" and their use is given in my booklet on 'Next Break Strategy'.)

4. **Immediate break:** Make hoop 1 with a rush back to black.
    Rush black to blue and put it a little way into court while obtaining a rush on blue to hoop 2. Make hoop 2 with a rush to either hoop 3 or one of the other two balls, etc. You may succeed in establishing an immediate break this way, but if anything goes wrong you will be allowing the opponent at least one chance to roquet, and if he misses it is still unlikely that you will have an immediate break set up, so you may well have to give him further chances to roquet. To justify this method you would once again need to give yourself a 50% or better chance of establishing the break immediately, as otherwise method 3 would give you a better chance of winning the game.

5. **Immediate roquet:** Red also has the option of roqueting black, with an immediate break if successful, but a break for the opponent if not. In the light of what we have already seen, this method will be the correct one to use provided red has an 80% chance or better of roqueting black. Note that he does not need to be certain of making the roquet. If he is convinced that he could hit it at least 8 times out of 10, then the roquet should be attempted as it gives the best possible chance of winning the game.

You can obtain a reasonably accurate assessment of your potential success rates (i.e. percentages) for the various methods by trying them out in practice sessions. However it must be remembered that your success rate in matches when under pressure may differ somewhat from the percentages you can achieve in relaxed practice sessions, and this should be taken into account. In general, it seems that although it is seldom seen, method 3 should be chosen by most players in such situations.

A RUSH TO WHERE? *by John Riches*

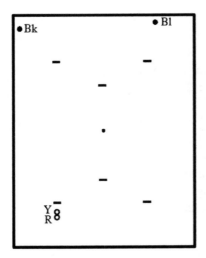

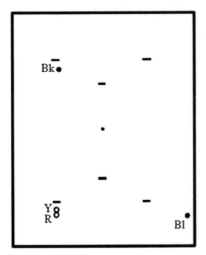

ONE OF THE common tactical errors seen on our croquet lawns is the failure to rush a ball to the best possible place, so as to maximise the chance of setting up or continuing a break. Many players give little thought to the question of finding the correct place to rush to, and even those who do give it some consideration usually wait until they are about to play the rush, when it is often too late.

Test yourself by examining the three diagrams and determining where you would hope to rush the yellow ball to after you make the first hoop with red. This assumes, of course, that you would make such a decision before approaching the hoop, if not earlier. In these cases you are approaching from about 1 yard directly in front of the hoop, and it should not be too difficult to organise the approach shot so that after making the hoop you will have a rush to wherever you wish.

In the first diagram yellow should be rushed to the 3rd corner so that a stop-shot can be used to send it near hoop 3 before rushing blue to black (or to hoop 2) to set up at least a 3-ball break.

In the second diagram yellow should be rushed to the 4th corner. Then a stop-shot can be used to send it to hoop 3 before roqueting blue and taking off to black at hoop 2. This allows you to get blue in off the border a yard or two by playing a thickish take-off, and will make it easier to continue the break later. An alternative would be to put yellow at hoop 4 and rush blue to either hoop 3 or (better still) the boundary alongside hoop 2 from where it can be used to load hoop 3 in the croquet stroke.

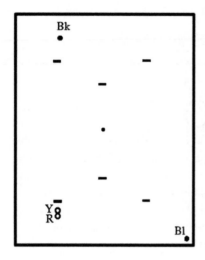

In the third diagram there is little point in going to the blue ball after making hoop 1, unless you are approaching the hoop from so close that it will not be possible to obtain a forward rush. It is better to try for a rush to the 2nd corner, from where yellow can be sent to hoop 3 with a stop-shot while getting behind black to rush it out to hoop 2. This is much better than rushing yellow to hoop 3, or hoop 2, or the north border behind black. You need to think about not only making hoop 2, but continuing the break afterward. Note also that after accurately loading hoop 3 with yellow you should make hoop 2 from black and then rush black to the border in front of hoop 3. It would be a serious mistake to rush it into the middle of the lawn as many players do, since from there it cannot be used to properly load hoop 4 before making hoop 3.

In fact the position of the blue ball in the 4th corner requires that the black ball should be sent right to hoop 4, and it is better to send it a yard or two past hoop 4 than to leave it short. Then, after making hoop 3 with yellow, even if you do not get a forward rush, you will be able to take off to blue in the 4th corner and proceed to set up a 4-ball break. If black is left short of hoop 4 (i.e. more than a yard or two in front) it will not be so easy to get blue into the break. Try it and see!

John Riches and Wayne Davies

INTO THE CORNER

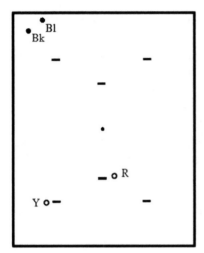

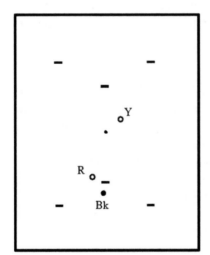

THERE WILL BE times when even the most aggressive player is forced to play a purely defensive shot which will usually involve hitting a ball out of play into a corner.

Such occasions will hopefully occur only rarely, and usually when you are forced to play a ball which is already on the peg or 4-back, so you would not want to make any hoops with it even if you managed to make a roquet. It will usually mean also that the ball you have to move is wired from at least one of the other three balls, since if all three are open it is almost certain that taking one of the three available shots would give a better chance of winning the game than "finessing". (In croquet the term "finessing" or "retiring" means hitting a ball out of play without attempting a roquet. The former term is widely used in England.

In one sense it is unfortunate in that it suggests there is something subtle about the use of such a tactic, when in most cases the exact opposite is true.)

In the first diagram yellow and blue clips are both on the peg, and black is for 1-back. Yellow is wired from red but must move, and cannot afford to shoot at the opponent's balls, so will 'retire' or 'finesse' into a corner—probably the third, anticipating a 'lift'. Many coaches pass on the advice which is to be found in various textbooks on the game: "In such cases, never hit your ball right into the corner. Instead, go a foot or two away from the corner spot on the side border!' There are two main reasons for this—

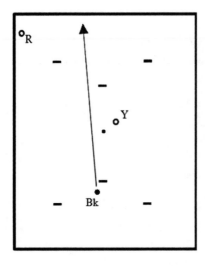

(1) It denies the opponent the chance of making a cannon by rushing another ball into the corner.

(2) If you later shoot at it with your other ball and miss, you will then have a potential rush rather than touching corner balls.

However, there are situations when a ball which is hit out of play should be placed right on the corner spot. See if you can think of such a situation before reading further.

In the second diagram yellow is on the peg, and red and black are both on rover. The blue ball has been pegged out and black is not entitled to a lift. Red has just approached rover, hoping to make it and peg out. However the approach shot was poor and red cannot make the hoop. Black is wired from yellow and must be given a shot. What should red do?!

Having read the first part of this article, you may already have worked out that this is a situation in which red should not only 'retire' into a corner, but it is important that red is placed right on the corner spot.

To illustrate this point, suppose that red makes the tactical error of going not right into the second corner, but a foot or two down the side border as shown in the third diagram. This allows black to play to the north border as indicated by the arrow, choosing a distance which prevents yellow from returning to red, but makes it very risky for red to shoot at black. By playing in this way black gives himself an almost even chance of winning the game, which is far better than he should have had.

Notice also that if red now shoots at yellow, then so can black, achieving a similar position (if both miss) at the other end of the lawn. It would also be very risky for red to sit near yellow in the middle of the lawn.

If red is placed right on the corner spot instead of on the yardline just out of the corner, there is no opportunity for black to use such a pressure tactic, as red would be able to shoot through black safely into another corner.

John Riches and Wayne Davies

"A HOOP IN THE HAND IS WORTH . . ." *by John Riches*

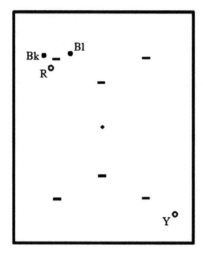

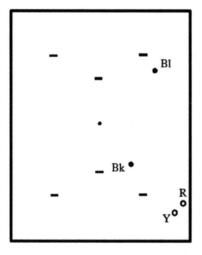

PERHAPS THE MOST common tactical error seen on our croquet lawns, and the one to which the loss of most games can be attributed, is the failure to set up a break when it was possible to do so. The failure usually results from an unwillingness to take a short-term risk in the hope of achieving a long-term gain.

In the position shown on the first diagram red is for hoop 3 and has taken-off from yellow to the opponent's balls after the opponent had failed at hoop 2. Many players of red would now roquet black gently and make certain of obtaining a simple rush on blue to hoop 3. However, for a player who is past the 'beginner' stage it is far better to rush black right out into the 2nd corner and use a stop-shot to send it as far as possible toward hoop 4 while trying for the rush on blue to hoop 3. The reason why players fail to do what they should is that they realise they would no longer be certain of getting as good a rush on blue, and so would be less likely to make hoop 3. Therefore they forgo a chance to set up a four-ball break in order to make certain of one hoop. When stated in this way the foolishness of such a choice seems rather obvious, as when both players are capable of making breaks, games are not likely to be won by making odd hoops. Foolish it may be, yet almost every game in lower divisions and also many at higher levels could be used to provide instances where players fail to obtain breaks because they do not even attempt to set them up for reasons similar to those just explained.

It is not easy to convince players that there is nothing "safe" about refusing to take the risk of possibly not making the one certain hoop.

The more experienced and advanced player sees it differently, and knows that there is no point in making hoop 3 unless he can either continue the break, or at least set up a position such that unless the opponent hits a long roquet he will have a break on the next turn.

If the player of red plays correctly, and sends black toward hoop 4, but fails to get the rush on blue to hoop 3, then he will have to roll both balls (red and blue) to the hoop, and if he does not gain position to run the hoop he can return to his yellow partner ball near the 4th corner, obtaining the position shown in the second diagram. It is important to realise that there is no real danger (at least below international level) in having the black ball only 9-10 yards away from your own balls, as the opponent would be taking a great risk if he now elected to shoot with black instead of moving blue—and this is a type of risk which in most cases should not be taken!

In fact the position of the second diagram is a very strong one for the player of red and yellow, because any shot with blue also entails giving you both of the opponent's balls where you should be able to make use of them. In situations like this players also find it hard to accept the fact that having the black ball close as shown in the diagram is stronger and safer than having it further away—say, 2-3 yards left of the peg, where the opponent would be able to shoot at it with blue quite safely.

It is this sort of thinking that sorts out the top players from the also-rans. There are many who can play all the shots accurately and consistently, but who can be counted on to lose game after game because they refuse to take what they see as a "risk" involved in setting up a break when they had the opportunity.

Instead of taking the small risk of missing out on making one hoop, they take the much greater risk that such an opportunity may not be presented to them again. After losing the game it is common to hear them complaining that they missed roquets and could not get going properly, when a closer analysis of the game would reveal that they did not need to make any more roquets than they had made—they lost because they did not make use of the opportunities they had to set up breaks.

This is a theme which I have mentioned in one way or another on previous occasions. I do not apologise for returning to it, and will continue to do so until there is evidence that players are beginning to take notice of it.

John Riches and Wayne Davies

WHEN NOT TO MAKE A HOOP

I N THE FIRST diagram we see again the position which we considered in the previous article (page 62).

Yellow is for hoop 5, red is for hoop 3, black for hoop 1 and blue for 4-back. We saw that the player of red and yellow played the yellow ball, made hoop 5, and found himself with very little chance of continuing the break. From there he ended up giving away the innings without the opponent having to make a roquet.

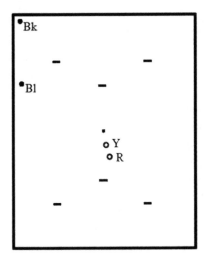

His first mistake was that he should have used the red ball, rather than yellow, in this turn. The making of one hoop for yellow is irrelevant, and in fact, as we shall see, actually places the striker at a disadvantage.

There are times when you are better off not making a hoop, and this is one of them.

Red should rush yellow toward the opponent's balls and simply set up as shown in the second diagram, with one of the opponent's balls at each of red and yellow's hoops. This allows the opponent one chance to make a long roquet, which he stood to get anyway, and guarantees an easy break if he misses. Since even the best players cannot claim to roquet 50% of their shots over such distances, this gives red and yellow a much better than even chance of getting the next break. It is important to note that by making hoop 5 with yellow, the player actually harmed his own cause. The reason for this is that with clips on hoops 3 and 6, instead of 3 and 5, it is much harder to find a good leave which will guarantee a break on the next turn if the opponent fails to roquet. With clips on hoops 3 and 6 it is

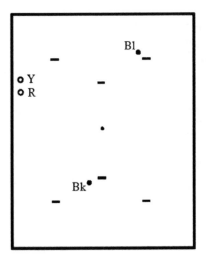

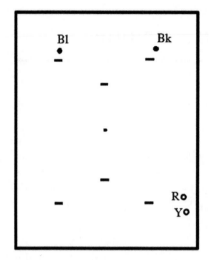 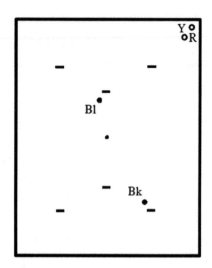

too risky to leave an opponent ball at each of your hoops, because these two hoops are too close together.

Clips on the same or nearby hoops are almost always a disadvantage. The best leave you could hope for would be something like those shown in the third and fourth diagrams. A few moments' thought should be sufficient to convince anyone that the position shown in the second diagram is much stronger for red and yellow than either of these two. In addition, if you go back to the first diagram and imagine yourself playing yellow, it is far from easy to work out a satisfactory way of making hoop 5 and placing the four balls as shown in the third or fourth diagrams (note that an accurately set rush is needed in each), so you would probably have to settle for a leave which is far weaker again.

Therefore, if you were red and yellow in the position of the first diagram, and the opponent generously offered you the chance to move your yellow clip on from hoop 5 to hoop 6, the offer should be politely declined, as you are far better off with it on hoop 5!

Yet players in such situations insist on making the easy hoop with nothing to follow and imagine that they have achieved something.

Instead of playing to make a single hoop with nothing set up ahead, it is almost always better to set up the lawn accurately in the first place. The exception to this is when your clips are already on the same or nearby hoops, so by making one hoop you can separate them and set a stronger leave.

WHEN TO RETURN WIDE OF PARTNER

I N THE FIRST diagram all clips are still on hoop 1. The game was played at inter-state level, and the player of black decided that shooting at blue would be risky, as if the shot was missed red need not try to make hoop 1, but could rush yellow to the fourth corner and then use the angled stop-shot illustrated in the second diagram to load hoop 2 before rushing either black or blue to hoop 1 with a break set up. Therefore he elected to return wide of blue as shown on the third diagram.

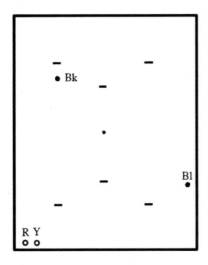

This tactic is frequently seen at all levels of play. It is arguably a legitimate tactic when used by players who are not capable of making consistent breaks, although against such an opponent the shot with black at blue is relatively safe, since he is likely to have difficulty playing the two rushes and angled stop-shot needed to set up the break as in the second diagram.

However, at higher levels of play the tactic of returning wide of partner, instead of shooting at a ball, should be seen in most cases as nothing more than an attempt to "con" the opponent by relying on him to commit an elementary mistake in tactics or shot-making, or both. A competent opponent simply will not make such mistakes, and black would have been better off attempting a roquet in the original position.

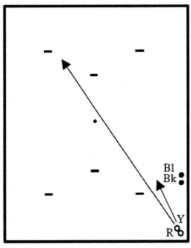

In the game the "con" trick worked, as after black returned wide of blue the player of red and yellow played red and attempted to make hoop 1 by cutting yellow in slightly, then rolling for the hoop. This involves taking risks with little prospect of getting a break established. It justified the tactic of returning wide in this particular instance and

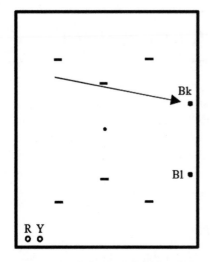 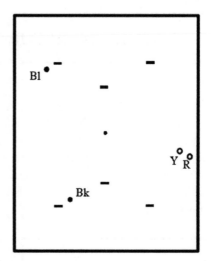

was what the player of black and blue was hoping for. Red actually succeeded in making hoop 1, but did not get a forward rush and had to take off to the opponent's balls with little chance of establishing a break; and neither was there any satisfactory way of obtaining a strong leave in order to give himself a good chance of a break on his next turn.

In the position of the third diagram red should have cut-rushed yellow toward blue and proceeded to set up the position shown in the fourth diagram. This allows the opponent one chance to make a long roquet, and gives an excellent chance of setting up a break if he misses. Any shot he takes will be "riskier" than the shot he refused to take in the original position.

Note that by returning wide of blue, black not only passed up a chance to roquet (he should actually have shot at yellow in the position of the first diagram), but also made it very easy for the player of red and yellow, if he had stopped to think, to set up for himself an "ideal leave".

The position of the second diagram is actually less risky for black and blue against a thinking opponent than that of the third diagram.

When the opponent can be relied upon to think, and play percentages, the answer to the question in the heading of this article is "Almost never"!

LEAVING BALLS TOGETHER

M ANY PLAYERS AT all levels of play seem to have a phobia about leaving balls together. An important breakthrough in the development of a croquet player comes when he or she manages to overcome this fear and starts regarding balls left together as a welcome advantage rather than a source of danger.

The first diagram shows a position which occurred in a doubles game in which I was involved. All clips were still on hoop 1. Our opponents had set their black and blue balls about 2 yards apart on the south boundary as shown, and my partner had played red, rushing yellow also to the south boundary.

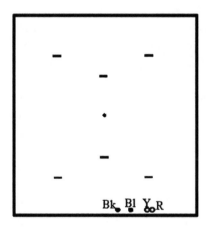

He asked me whether I thought he should (a) stop-shot yellow into the lawn a few yards past hoop 4, then make hoop 1 from the opponent's balls, which would risk leaving at least one of our balls in the lawn if anything went wrong; or (b) send blue to hoop 1 and then split black to hoop 2, trying at the same time to get position to run hoop 1, with the option of returning to yellow on the border if unsuccessful; or (c) stop-shot yellow to hoop 1, roquet blue, rush black along the border in front of hoop 1, and stop-shot black to hoop 2 while trying for position to run hoop 1.

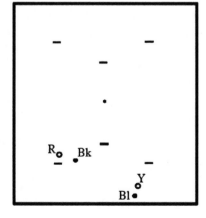

After making hoop 1 with alternative (a) he would have the situation shown in the second diagram. From here he could go to blue and send that ball to hoop 3 while trying for a rush on yellow to hoop 2 His chance of succeeding in this may be reasonable (say, about 60-70%), especially if he could rush black accurately to blue after making the hoop. Alternatives (b) and (c) offered a better chance of continuing the break if hoop 1 could be made, but the

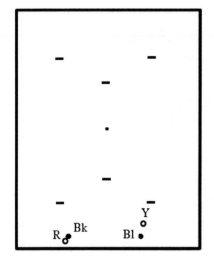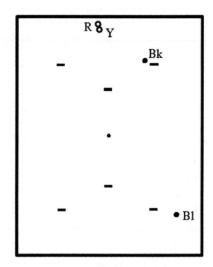

likelihood of making the hoop was considerably reduced to probably no more than an even (50%) chance. I suggested as a fourth alternative that he send yellow only a yard or two into the lawn, leaving it near blue, and rush black to make hoop 1. He could expect to do this about 9 times out of 10, and also get some sort of backward rush to the border in front of hoop 1, which is almost always the easiest rush to get after making a hoop. This would bring him to the position shown in the third diagram, and from there it is not difficult to send black to hoop 3 while going to the two balls that have been left together. In most cases you would rush yellow out to blue (ignoring the common advice to go to the border ball first), and then get a rush on blue to hoop 2. Because the two balls have been left close together the getting of an accurate rush is relatively easy. It could be an interesting exercise to set up the original position at your club and ask players of various levels how they would continue as red, and why.

The correct continuation will depend to some extent on the shots which the player can play confidently, as well as his degree of "togetheraphobia". Another example is shown in the fourth diagram, where red is for hoop 3 and should send yellow right to hoop 4 (near blue), rather than only part-way as is frequently seen.

HOW TO CHANGE THE LENGTH OF A SHOT

THE POSITION SHOWN in the first diagram occurred in a recent tournament game between two good division 2 players. The player of red had roqueted his partner ball on the west boundary, with the red clip on 3-back and yellow on the peg. He decided to take off to black, trying for a rush to his 3-back hoop.

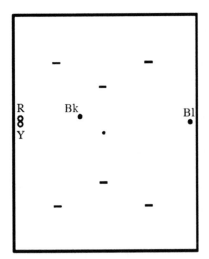

The rush was not a particularly good one, and he had to approach the hoop with a pass-roll from near hoop 5. When he failed to gain position to run the 3-back hoop, he returned red to the west boundary near yellow, reaching the position shown in the second diagram.

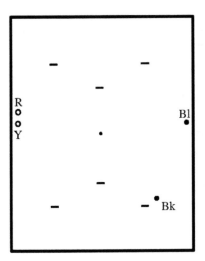

The opponent then shot with black at blue and made the 14-yard roquet. Later I discussed the game with the player of red and yellow, and asked firstly why he did not try to rush black to blue, instead of to the hoop. It turned out that although he was quite an experienced player, this course of action had simply not occurred to him. He could now see that it would have been easier, given the direction he was coming from, to get a good rush to the blue ball rather than the hoop; the black ball could be rushed right out of court anywhere near blue without having to judge the strength of the shot, the black ball could be put advantageously into the lawn a yard or two when getting a rush on blue to 3-back, and the rush to the hoop would be a shorter one, which could therefore be judged more accurately.

This idea of converting a long rush into a shorter one is frequently overlooked.

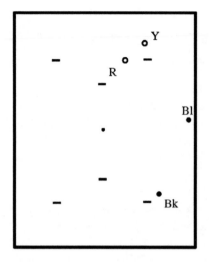

Secondly, I asked why he had taken off from yellow, instead of sending it to load the 4-back hoop. He explained that he was not certain of getting the rush and making 3-back (as indeed happened), so did not want to put his yellow partner ball too close to blue, in case he had to return to it. So we set up the position shown in the third diagram, which was the situation he wished to avoid, in which yellow is at 4-back and red has returned near it, presuming that as in the game he had been unable to make 3-back. I asked him what he considered the opponent should do in this position, and he realised that the shot with black at blue was now very risky for the opponent, since a miss would allow red to roquet yellow, take off to the two opponent balls, rush one of them to 3-back, and very likely finish the game. (Note that in diagram 2 this same shot entailed little risk.)

Therefore he said that black should shoot at red or yellow, and the opponent's 14-yard roquet had been converted to a 21-yard roquet! Whether he was able to make his 3-back hoop or not, he was better off with yellow at 4-back, yet he had considered this course of action too risky!

Better still, when sending yellow to 4-back he could have tried for the rush on black to blue instead of to the hoop, as we have already seen; and yellow could be placed a yard or two behind 4-back so that if necessary red could return to a position about halfway between yellow and the north boundary, thus "covering the border" and making any shot at all by the opponent extremely risky.

An analysis of almost any game, up to and including those played at state level, will reveal that games are won and lost as a result of tactical errors such as these, and not because (as the player of red imagined) the opponent managed to hit a good roquet with black at a critical time. Below international level the ability to hit long roquets has little effect on the outcome of a game; but tactical choices have a very great effect.

Unfortunately, it is almost impossible for a coach to convince most players that if they want to win more games they should be spending time improving their tactics rather than their roqueting ability.

John Riches and Wayne Davies

OPENING IDEAS

M OST PLAYERS HAVE some ideas concerning how to continue if the opponent varies at some stage from the standard opening. Here are some points which may prove helpful:

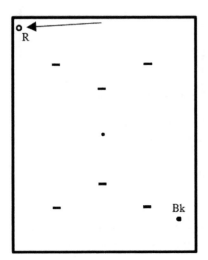

(1) If the opponent's first ball of the game (black) falls just short of the yardline near hoop 4, as shown in the first diagram, it is not a good idea to hit your first ball to the normal 'tice' position, as blue, instead of shooting at black, can be played so as to obtain a rush to your 'tice'. The best plan is probably to hit your ball (red) in from B-baulk, to a position about one foot up the side border from the 2nd corner spot as shown. Then, if the opponent shoots at red with blue, he risks giving you an easy double target with yellow; and if he plays to the border near black, you can (in fact, must) shoot at his balls from either B-baulk or (if they present a good target) from A-baulk.

(2) If (on the second turn of the game) you had shot with red at black and missed, the most aggressive continuation for the opponent would have been to place blue as shown in the second diagram, where he is threatening, unless you roquet with yellow, to play black on the 5th turn, use a stop-shot to send red to hoop 2, and rush blue to hoop 1. Care needs to be taken in placing blue to ensure that yellow will not have an inviting "triple" target from the in-lawn end of B-baulk. Any shot taken by yellow from A-baulk will risk making it very easy for

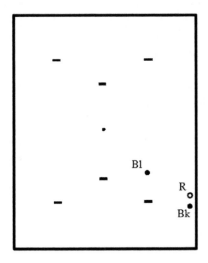

black by giving him the fourth ball to use as well.

(3) If you had roqueted black with red on your first turn, there are three reasonable possibilities—

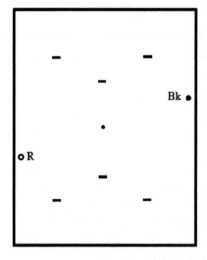 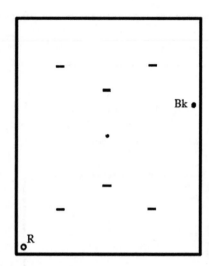

(a) Roll both balls (red and black) to the peg and leave them cross-wired there. Both balls should be left within 2 yards of the peg so that the opponent has no safe shot through toward a corner. However, he can risk putting his third (blue) ball also in the middle of the lawn, allowing you the chance to roquet and set up a 4-ball break; but giving him a 3-ball break if you miss.

(b) Send black up the east border to a long 'tice' position from B-baulk, and hit red out on the west border in a similarly long 'tice' position from A-baulk, as shown in the third diagram. Then, if the opponent shoots diagonally at either ball, he risks leaving you a double target to shoot at with yellow on the fourth turn.

(c) Place black as in (b) above, but hit red out in the 1st corner as shown in the 4th diagram. This is a very aggressive option, and unless the lawn is very fast and the opponent is very good at playing long pass rolls, is likely to cause him considerable embarrassment.

There are many other similar ideas which are frequently overlooked by players who have not thought through and prepared themselves to meet any opening variations the opponent may decide to try on them.

A DIFFERENT OPENING

ARE YOU GETTING bored with starting games in the same old way every time? Why not try an aggressive new start which has proved effective at interstate level (although at that level it may be considered somewhat risky) ?

In the first diagram the player of red and yellow won the toss, elected to start, and hit his first (red) ball from B-baulk as shown by the arrow to a point on the south boundary about 2 feet from the 4ᵗʰ corner spot.

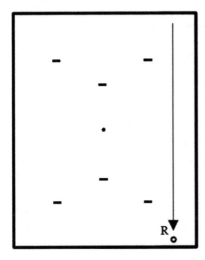

Then his opponent played black to a "tice" position as normal, and yellow was played into the 4ᵗʰ corner, making no attempt to roquet red. This results in the position shown on the second diagram.

If blue then misses the tice and finishes in the second corner, yellow has a cut-rush either to the tice or to hoop 1, giving a better than usual chance of establishing an immediate break. If blue had roqueted the tice he would be no better off than in a standard opening. If blue shoots at the balls in the 4ᵗʰ corner he risks giving red a cannon (which needs practice), again with an excellent chance of a break.

If black (on the 2ⁿᵈ turn) shoots at red and misses he risks giving yellow a double target, or else allowing yellow to be placed as shown in the second diagram. Here red is threatening to at least roquet black and send it to hoop 2 while getting a rush on yellow to hoop 1.

A missed shot by blue at yellow will give him the 4ᵗʰ ball as well, while a missed shot at red would allow a simple promotion cannon as illustrated in the fourth diagram (in which

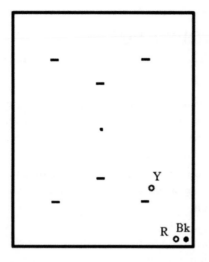 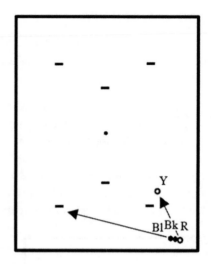

the blue ball is sent to hoop 1 without being roqueted, while red finishes near the yellow ball, which can then be roqueted and split to hoop 2 as red goes to the unused blue ball at hoop 1), followed by an immediate break.

In the third diagram yellow should be placed so that it does not allow blue too inviting a "triple target" from B-baulk; and at international level one would need to bear in mind that if the opponent does succeed in making a roquet with blue on the fourth turn, he is likely to have an easy nine-hoop break. However, even at that level the risk he is taking in shooting at any ball is considerable, since any missed shot will give you the same break even more easily. There is also the consideration that to set the break up immediately the opponent will often need to play either a promotion cannon, or a delayed cannon, or a cannon from the fourth corner to load hoop 2 while rushing a ball to hoop 1.

These cannons are not straight-forward, and it is unlikely that the opponent will have spent much time practising them; whereas you, if you plan to use this opening, can ensure that you know how to play them accurately and confidently.

On the whole, this opening seems to offer you a better chance of getting a break established before your opponent does than most other openings; and there is also the psychological advantage of getting him confused and wondering what he should be doing in reply.

HITTING THROUGH TO BORDER

IN THE POSITION shown on the first diagram red has a good, but not certain, chance of roqueting black. It is common for an experienced player of yellow to advise his inexperienced partner, "Have a go at black, but make sure you go right through to the border if you miss". In most situations this is very good advice, but in the situation shown here red should pause and consider what the opponent is likely to do on his next turn, and it is obvious here that black is likely to shoot at blue. If black does not succeed in roqueting blue, the opponent's two balls will be on the south border, and the ideal place for red would then be 2-3 yards in from the border so that the opponent's balls present a double target as shown in the second diagram. Therefore, it may be better to play red so that if it misses black it will not quite reach the border.

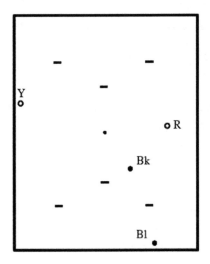

Note that if red were on the border in the second diagram then the single-ball target presented by the opponent's balls would be far less inviting for red. Of course, the roqueting ability of the opponent must be taken into account, and also the possibility that he will be able to use red more easily if he does roquet blue with black. But you should at least give a thought to tactics such as this, rather than simply shooting through to the border without thinking, then later complaining that you lost the game because you "couldn't get a roquet", when you actually lost because you did not think!

This idea is an example of the many situations in which players tend to shoot at a ball and go right through to the border without thinking.

A slightly different version of the same idea is illustrated in the third diagram. With all

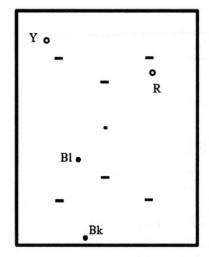 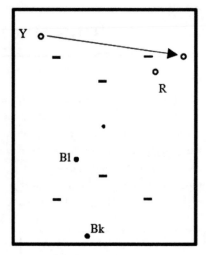

clips still on hoop 1, most players would shoot with yellow at red. This is good if the roquet is made, but there were two alternatives worth consideration:

(1) Red could shoot at blue, and finish on the west border a few yards from the first corner. This would allow red a likely double target if blue then shoots at black and misses, but would allow black a (risky) shot at red, and would probably commit you to shooting at black with red if blue is hit out to the south border wide of black.

(2) Yellow could, instead of shooting at red, be played so as to cover the border against a shot by blue at red (see fourth diagram). This would place the opponent under considerable pressure, since with both your clips on hoop 1 a missed shot with blue at black would give you a good chance of setting up a break, and a missed shot at your balls would allow yellow to roquet blue, send it to hoop 2, and rush red to either the black ball (which is the best way to go about things) or to hoop 1. Once again, the choice of shot depends on the roqueting ability of both you and your opponent; but the alternatives should at least be given consideration.

One suspects that the number of games lost simply through lack of thought is far higher than most players would admit—especially in regard to their own games!

John Riches and Wayne Davies

PLACING THE PIVOT BALL

O NE OF THE keys to playing consistent 4-ball breaks is accurate placement of the pivot ball. This requires not only the ability to play confidently a considerable range of croquet strokes, but also a clear understanding of exactly where the pivot ball should be placed. In the first diagram red is about to send blue into the lawn for use as a pivot ball in the break before making hoop 1 from black. The correct place for blue is not just anywhere near the peg, but as close as possible to a specific point which is found as follows:

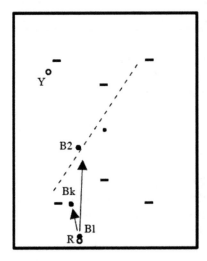

Imagine a straight line drawn from just behind the hoop you are about to make to the hoop you will load after making it (i.e. hoop 1 to hoop 3 as shown by the dotted line).

Find a point one-third of the distance along this line and from there go one yard toward the ball at hoop 2. This will bring you to point B2, which is the ideal place to send the pivot ball. Following this "one yard from one-third" principle in placing the pivot ball will allow you to load hoops more accurately with straight, simple croquet strokes (mostly "natural" 1:3 drives) which also give you a rush on the pivot ball toward the ball waiting at your next hoop.

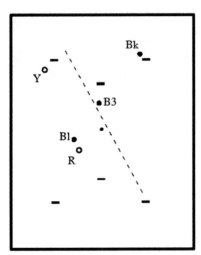

However, before roqueting or rushing the pivot ball, you need to find its next pivot point (B3 on diagram 2) by imagining a point behind hoop 2, going one-third of the way to hoop 4, then one yard toward the black ball at hoop 3.

The blue ball in diagram 2 must be rushed or roqueted to a place from which it can easily be sent to point B3 while red goes to yellow at hoop 2. This usually involves

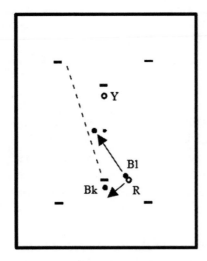 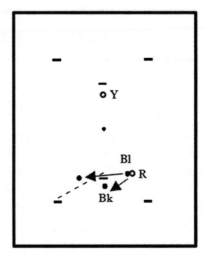

rushing the pivot ball (blue) out past the ball at the hoop (yellow) and then using either a 1:3 drive or a stop-shot to send it to point B3. A break continued in this manner is easy to maintain and should seldom get out of control. There is no need to attempt to get a rush in any particular direction after making each hoop, so you can concentrate on simply ensuring that the hoop is made. A useful rush, if you get one, can be considered a bonus.

After making hoop 4 and having loaded hoop 6 with yellow as shown in the third diagram, there are two alternatives. If you intend to load 1-back with black after making hoop 5, then continue the previous pattern of "one yard from one third" and place the blue pivot ball near the peg as shown, using an angled stop-shot.

Some players, however, prefer to load 2-back at this stage of the break, and so they should send the pivot ball to the point shown on the fourth diagram, which is one-third of the way from hoop 5 to 2-back. Note that placing the pivot ball right at 2-back, as many players do, is incorrect because it makes the break slightly harder to continue unless you can rely on getting a rush on black after making hoop 5.

The exact position of each pivot point will vary a little according to the shots the player prefers to play, but it is important to keep placing the pivot ball not just anywhere, but in the best possible position to make future shots easy.

PRACTISING DURING THE GAME

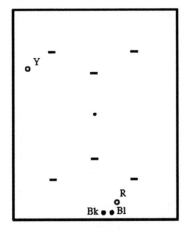

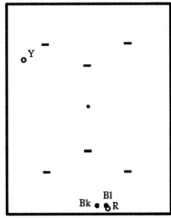

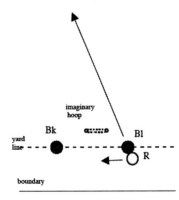

W̲HEN I SUGGESTED this idea to a player I was coaching, he said, "Oh, they'd never allow that at our club.

They won't even let you practise on the lawns before play starts!" I explained that what I had in mind was something quite different. When you are faced with a very simple shot, or one of little consequence, it is easy to treat it carelessly, and so miss out on an opportunity to practise the shots you will need to play later.

One obvious example is the situation where you are hitting your first ball into the game. The wise player will take great care in checking his grip; positioning his feet; selecting his line of aim; effecting a high, straight backswing and smooth, flowing forward swing; and judging the strength of the shot required to send the ball (probably) over the boundary to an exact point outside the lawn.

This enables him to practise getting right the timing of his swing and all these things which he may possibly overlook in later shots when he could have other things on his mind. It should also assist him in gaining some appreciation of the speed of the lawn.

In the first diagram red is for hoop 1, and has taken off from yellow to the opponent's balls on the south border. He is about to play a roquet of less than one yard on the blue ball. This is an excellent opportunity to practise either the rush or the hoop-running which he will be playing in the next few shots. If he wishes to practise his rushing, he will stand a little further back than for a normal roquet, lean his weight back a little, and use a long, flat, smooth swing to actually rush the blue ball firmly out of court, noticing whether his striker's ball jumps slightly or fails to hit the blue ball dead centre, so that he can correct such slight errors when he plays the forthcoming rush.

If he wishes to practise hoop-running, then he may instead stand slightly further forward than for a normal roquet, take a perfectly straight backswing, and use a smooth forward swing to gently roll (rather than hit) his ball, again expecting to roquet the blue ball absolutely dead centre and looking for any slight error that may need correction.

After roqueting blue, the player of red will have reached the position shown on the second diagram. Here he will send blue a short distance into the lawn and get a rush on black to hoop 1. This involves playing a fairly simple croquet stroke which can be used to practise the hoop approach he will soon be playing. The third diagram gives an enlarged view of the three balls at the bottom of the second diagram, and shows an imaginary hoop near the yardline. By imagining a hoop in the right place and playing the croquet stroke as if he were approaching it, the player of red is able to practise the grip, stance, backswing, forward swing and strength of a fairly simple hoop approach. In most cases this will increase, rather than lessen, his chance of getting a good rush on black to hoop 1. He can then proceed to play the rush, hoop approach, and run the hoop using the shots he has practised, and correct any slight errors he has noticed.

These are merely examples. The astute player will be aware of the things he needs to concentrate on getting right when playing the various shots, and will find many such opportunities to practise them so that he can correct any likely errors before disaster strikes.

This is why most of our leading players seem to be painstaking in their approach to shots which a less experienced player would see no need to be so concerned about. They are practising during the game, and it is perfectly legal under the Laws!

HOW TO PLAY AGGRESSIVELY

I N MY BOOKLETS on Strategy and Tactics I explained in detail the point that aggressive play is tactically correct, in that it almost always gives the best percentage chance of winning the game. It is unfortunate that many players, whose shot making has developed to the stage where they can make consistent breaks, fail to adopt the more aggressive tactical approach that their skill level (and that of their opponents) now not only allows, but demands. It seems that they fail to realise that if both you and your opponent can make sizeable breaks, you cannot expect to win

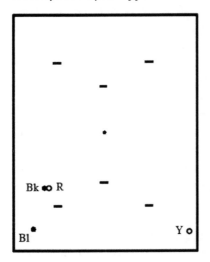

games by making one or two hoops at a time. The game will be won by the player who gets breaks established before his opponent does; and your whole strategy should geared to ensuring that it is you, and not your opponent, who does this. The making of one or two hoops here or there is irrelevant; in fact, until 1-back is made, even a break of six is largely irrelevant, since it will still take you at least three turns to finish the game, assuming that you cannot afford to concede contact. At the highest level, a break of six can even be a disadvantage, because if your clip was still on hoop 1 you would have the opportunity to finish the game in two turns by doing a triple peel; but with it already on hoop 6 this would be far more difficult, and in most cases not worth trying.

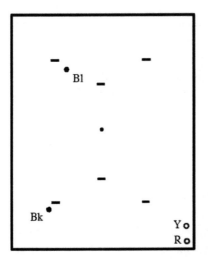

The first diagram shows a position at the start of a game where red has just made hoop 1 and roqueted black. How should the player of red continue? Most would take off from black to blue, trying for a rush to either hoop 2 or the yellow ball. However, there is no way of loading hoop 3 or even hoop 4 before making hoop 2, so the chance of getting a break established is very small indeed. We have just seen above that it is largely pointless to try to make one or two hoops with little chance of establishing a break. Taking risks by making odd hoops with an opponent's ball when there is no break to follow is usually not aggressive; it is foolhardy. The truly aggressive player is willing to take risks, but only when, if they come off, he will have a break set up.

The correct play (for a player who can make breaks) is to use a small pass roll to position black near hoop 1 and obtain a rush on blue to yellow in the 4th corner. If the rush is not obtained, blue can simply be sent to hoop 2 and red then hit out into the 4th corner, obtaining the leave shown in the second diagram.

Even if blue can be rushed right to yellow, it should be sent with a stop-shot to hoop 2 and the same leave made. It is pointless to try to rush yellow to hoop 2 and make it, as the great majority of players would do, since it involves leaving blue out of play and very likely allowing the opponent a relatively safe shot on his next turn. In the second diagram, the opponent gets one long shot, but a miss will give you an easy break. This is real aggression! It says to the opponent, "Shoot if you dare, but you'd better not miss, because if you do, I'm going around!" It is always tempting, especially against a very strong opponent, to take the opportunity to make another hoop or two while you can; and who knows?—if you happen to play several good shots in a row, or fluke a long roll that ends right in front of your hoop, you may even succeed in getting a break established immediately. Such happy possibilities are pleasant to contemplate, but in reality the odds are very much against them. You are far more likely to end up having to allow the opponent a chance to roquet in a position where even if he misses, you will still be a long way from setting up a break.

This is why it is tactically far better to recognise right from the start that your chance of setting up an immediate break is very small, and take the first opportunity to set up an "ideal leave" as explained in my previous books, allowing your opponent one long chance to roquet, and one only, before you have your break established. Note also that in the second diagram, if the opponent chooses not to shoot, and instead hits a ball away into a corner, you will still have at least a 3-ball break.

Aggressive play involves the willingness to take a reasonable risk which, if it comes off, will give you a break, especially when the opponent will not have an immediate break if it fails to come off.

In the first diagram blue, which is for hoop 2, has just missed a shot at red, which had stuck in hoop 3.

The player of red can now hit red through the hoop and down to yellow near hoop 4. Most players would do this without stopping to think. But the aggressive player thinks of making breaks, not hoops. He will realise that the chance of setting up a break after making hoops 3 and 4 is extremely remote, and if something goes wrong there is a fair possibility that he will have to leave one or both of his balls out in the lawn and allow the opponent to take a relatively safe shot at them. A risk such as this should not be taken, since the only thing you stand to gain is one or two somewhat meaningless hoops. Correct is to make hoop 3 gently and then roquet blue, provided you can play the fairly long split roll from near the 3rd corner to load hoop 5 with blue while going to yellow at hoop 4. The roquet may be far from a certainty, but if you hit it you have a good chance of a break to follow; and if you miss it blue can do little. This type of risk is the sort that should definitely be taken, although far too many players, even at state level, would prefer a "safer" course of action which in fact gives them less chance of winning the game. Suppose, for example, that you believe you can roquet blue (after making hoop 3) eight times out of ten. Is there any other way you can assure yourself an 80% chance of getting a break established before your opponent does? If you simply make hoop 3 and then hoop

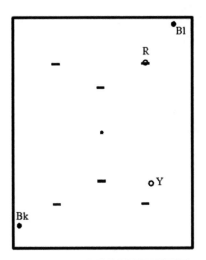

4 with both opponent balls out of play, you are soon going to have to give him a chance to roquet, which he could expect to hit, say, one time out of four. That gives him a 25% chance, and you only a 75% chance, even in the unlikely event that you only have to allow him the one chance. The 80% chance you could have taken in the first place was clearly your better option.

In the fourth diagram all clips are on hoop 1 and red has roqueted yellow in the 4th corner. The aggressive play is to split yellow to hoop 2 while going to the opponent's balls in the 1st corner. Once again, you do not need to be certain of getting to the opponent's balls without going out, and then roqueting one of them.

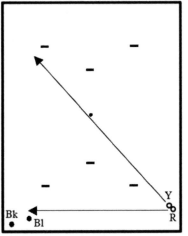

If instead you take off to the opponent's balls, you will almost certainly have to give the opponent another chance to roquet before you get a break established. No matter where you put the balls, he should have a 20% or better chance of roqueting. In order to ensure that he gets only the one chance, you would need to leave them so that if he misses you can make an immediate break yourself, and this means that you must leave his balls near hoops rather than out on the borders, giving him more likely about a 30% chance of roqueting. All of this means that failure to attempt the big split-shot needed to immediately set up your break involves conceding a 20-30% (say, 25%) chance to your opponent. Therefore, if you would expect the split to be successful 4 times out of 5 (i.e. 80% of the time) or better, you are reducing your chance of winning the game by not attempting it. In addition to this, the psychological advantages of playing aggressively are not to be dismissed lightly.

Note that if you rate your chance of playing the split-shot successfully at noticeably less than, say, 75%, then you would be incorrect to attempt it. In that case, you should take off to the opponent's balls, make hoop 1 from one of them, and set up a leave similar to that shown in the second diagram on the previous page.

This gives the opponent the one (approx. 25%) chance to roquet, so it is preferable to attempting the split if your success rate would be less than 75%. Also note that the fact that the opponent would have an immediate break if the split is unsuccessful does not matter.

Allowing him a 20% chance of a break, and yourself an 80% chance, is pretty good odds, and better than you are likely to obtain by pursuing any other course of action. Such chances should be taken without hesitation!

MORE ON THE 'THREE-ONE' PRINCIPLE

T HE 'THREE-ONE' PRINCIPLE, as explained in "Croquet: Lessons in Tactics", states that when all four balls are on or near a border, it is usually harder to establish a break with three balls together and one separate, than with two and two. Therefore, when you have one of your balls out in the middle of the lawn, it is usually safer to shoot at the opponent's balls when they are together near the border, instead of shooting at your partner ball. This applies regardless of the fact that the opponent may not have a useful rush, and if you miss you will allow him to get one, since he will able to rush only one ball to his hoop, without having loaded the following hoop. When players are capable of playing reasonable split-shots and making breaks, allowing the opponent to make one hoop is of little consequence. However, returning to your partner ball (unless both his two balls and your two balls will be in different corners and he has no useful rush) is likely to allow him to use a rush and/or split-shot to load the following hoop with his partner ball while coming to your two balls, then rush one of your balls to his current hoop with at least a 3-ball break set up.

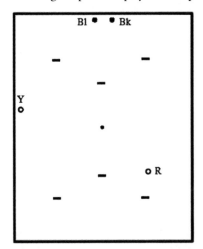

We have also seen in other articles that against a thinking opponent it is almost always suicidal to "return wide" of your partner ball, as there is no reason why the opponent should allow you any safer chance to roquet, before he gets a break established, than the one you passed up by returning wide.

It is surprising how often one sees some of our leading players, as well as those at lower levels but still capable of making breaks, who either do not understand this principle or fail to apply it in their games, and so greatly reduce their winning chances.

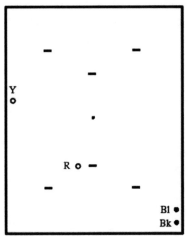

The first diagram shows a situation where black is for hoop 3 and blue is for 4-back.

Although black does not have a useful rush, and there is no double target, the only sensible thing for the player of red to do (in a game where both players are capable of making sizeable breaks) is to shoot at the opponent's balls. A useful exercise is to work out which of the two opponent balls red should shoot at. Players may argue either way, e.g.—

(a) "If I shoot at black and miss, the opponent will probably have to leave my red ball on the border and take his partner ball to hoop 3. If he cannot make the hoop, he will then be unable to set up safely, and will have to leave at least one of his balls out near the hoop. If he takes my ball to his hoop, he has the blue ball to return to if anything goes wrong."

(b) "If I shoot at blue and miss, it will be harder for black to create a cannon, which is probably his best chance of getting a break established. He would in any case be having to make hoop 3 with my red ball, so that if he fails at the hoop he will immediately let me in."

It seems that the second of these two arguments is the stronger one. The possibility of the opponent creating a cannon should be taken into consideration, and he is likely to be less happy with a cannon in which he must send his blue partner ball into the lawn to load the next hoop and make his current hoop from your red ball, than if the red and blue balls were interchanged.

In the second diagram black has now made hoop 3 and is for hoop 4. Here again red should shoot at the opponent's balls rather than at yellow, for reasons similar to those given above.

Very few players, it seems, are willing to "risk giving the opponent an extra ball", and so most prefer to shoot at their yellow partner ball or 'return wide' of it. As with other tactical considerations, they mostly have failed to realise the dramatic change in the level of risk they are taking once they start playing opponents capable of maintaining breaks. Tactics which were rightly considered fairly safe against weaker opponents now become extremely risky, and vice versa; and defensive tactics become far less likely to prove successful.

RISK TAKING

A LTHOUGH MANY REFERENCES to this topic have necessarily been made in other sections, it is of sufficient importance, and so little understood, as to warrant separate consideration in a section of its own.

Some of the ideas are difficult to explain clearly in words, and really need to be reinforced by demonstrations out on the lawn. Even when they are understood by a player, he may well experience difficulty in bringing himself to adopt them, think of them in a match situation, and actually put them into practice.

The series of articles on 'manoeuvring' in particular will require a considerable amount of persistence from the reader if he is to fully grasp its importance and usefulness, and be able to apply it in his own games. Perhaps the point should again be made here that many of the ideas explained in this section, as well as some in other sections, will mainly be relevant when both players are capable of making sizeable breaks.

PRINCIPLES OF RISK-TAKING

THE MOST DIFFICULT part of teaching and learning correct tactical play is that which deals with the type of risk which should, and should not, be taken during a game. All such decisions should ideally be based on the estimation and calculation of percentages, but there are some principles which can often prove helpful:

1. **The stronger your opponent, the more risks you should be prepared to take.** For example, suppose that I am offered the possibility of playing a shot which I would expect to hit 4 times out of 10, and if successful would give me an all-round break, but if unsuccessful would give the same break to my opponent. I would take the shot and grab the 40% chance against an international player, because in general play his superior shots and greater experience would assure him of a much better than 60% chance of beating me. But if the opponent is weaker I would not want to allow him a 60% chance, and would wait hopefully for a better chance later on. This is in direct contrast to the common and incorrect idea that when you play a strong opponent you cannot afford to give them any chances, so must play safe. Such negative play will perhaps make the game longer and more boring, but will guarantee the stronger player will eventually win.

2. **Be prepared to take reasonable risks at the start of a game,** especially if it is the first game of the day for both you and your opponent. Some players have a habit of "playing dry", which involves (in their opinion) playing safe and refusing to take any risks, until they have "got the feel of the lawn and played themselves in". In fact, there is nothing "safe" about the adoption of such tactics, except that on percentages it is a safe way of allowing your opponent to get a long way ahead before you get started. The best time to take risks is when your opponent also does not have the "feel of the lawn", so is less likely to be able to profit if anything goes wrong. In addition, if the risk happens to come off, then it will give you a valuable boost in confidence.

3. **Take any risk which offers you a 60% or better chance of setting up (or continuing) a break.** You do not need to be certain of succeeding before attempting a hoop or roquet which, if unsuccessful, will let your opponent in and (even) give him a break. You should chance it, provided you estimate that you would expect to succeed more than 6 times out of 10. Refusing to take such chances is not playing safe; it is simply reducing your chance of winning the game. However, in most situations there is no

point in taking even a much smaller risk if, when it comes off, it allows you to make only one hoop with nothing much set up ahead.

4. **When you are the out-player, take any risk which gives you a 40% or better chance of gaining the innings.** This means that you should attempt a roquet which you would expect to hit only 4 times out of 10, even though a miss will allow your opponent to set up an easy break. Both this principle and the previous one follow from the fact that the player with the innings has at least a 60% chance of getting the next break, regardless of where the balls are. By (for example) hitting a ball out of play without attempting a roquet, you give yourself no better than a 40% chance of getting a break established before your opponent does, and are immediately conceding him at least a 60% chance of getting the next break. Therefore any 40% chance of making a roquet is preferable.

5. **Shooting at a ball is almost always safer than not shooting.** The percentages greatly favour aggressive play. In most situations hitting away into a corner will allow your opponent much better than the minimum 60% chance of getting the next break mentioned in the previous paragraph. It is usually closer to 70% or 80%. Therefore you should attempt a roquet when you give yourself only 20% or 30% chance of making it, even if a miss will give the opponent an immediate easy break. I sometimes lie awake at night trying to think up positions where shooting at a ball may not give the best percentage chance of getting a break established before the opponent does, and so may not be the safest thing to do. Such positions are very rare, and almost always involve a situation where you are wired from one or more of the balls, and the ball you have to move is already around, so you do not particularly want to roquet with it anyway. If there are three balls you could shoot at, then there should be at least one of them which you would expect to hit 3 times out of 10, or which if you miss will require the opponent to play some accurate and not-so-straight-forward shots in order to set up his break. The player who is prepared to take such risks will not expect to win every game, but will certainly win more games than if he refuses to take them. Occasionally the risk will not come off, and after losing the game you are tempted to say to yourself (or more likely have someone else say to you), "I should have played safe!" But it is important to remember that there is nothing safe about "playing safe" in the way that most people mean it. What reason could you give for supposing that you would have won the game if you had not taken the risk which failed to come off? In actual fact, you would have been even more likely to end up losing. Of course, if you knew you were going to miss, that would be a different thing; but you could well have made the roquet and ended up winning. That is what makes the study of croquet tactics, and playing the game, so fascinating: there are no certainties or guarantees. All you can ever do is maximise your chances and hope they come off.

RISK TAKING

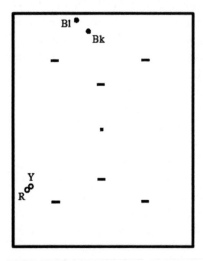

THE FIRST DIAGRAM shows a common type of situation in which all clips are still on hoop 1 and red has roqueted yellow about 5 yards from the hoop. The player of red now must decide whether to play an approach shot and attempt to make the hoop, or instead take off to the opponent's balls near the north border.

The second diagram shows a similar situation, except that in this case the opponent's balls are near the 4th corner instead of near the north border. What would you do if you were red in each situation?

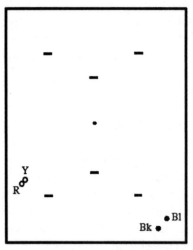

On what basis would you make the decision—what things would you take into account in these or similar situations? Would the position of the opponent's balls (assuming they are together) make any difference?

The answer, of course, depends on the ability of both players, and particularly on whether or not they are capable of making sizeable breaks. If they are, then it is also likely that they are capable of making the hoop with a 5-yard approach at least 7 times out of 10—maybe even more often. If this is the case, then the correct tactical move for the player of red in the first position is to make hoop 1 immediately, even though the opponent's clips are also on hoop 1 and a failed attempt at the hoop would give away an immediate break.

However, he would be wrong to attempt the same thing in the second position, even if the opponent's clips were on other hoops. This will no doubt surprise many readers, as for most players the change in position of the opponent's balls would seem to make little difference. Why is it correct to try to make the hoop in one case and wrong in the other?

The answer lies in the fact that if the hoop is made in the first position the player of red will be able to continue and easily set up a break. Even if he does not get a forward rush after making the hoop, he can take off to blue and use a stop-shot to send it toward hoop 3 before making hoop 2 from black. However, in the second position the chance of setting up a break after making hoop 1 is very small. For most players the best way would be to hope to obtain a rush on yellow to hoop 3, then take off back to the opponent's balls in the 4th corner and rush one of them to hoop 2. The chance of succeeding in this case is probably no better than 20% (if you doubt this, set up the position on the lawn and see if you can establish a break—that is, reach a position where you have made a hoop and have the next hoop already accurately loaded—more than two times out of ten), whereas in the first position, once the hoop is made, the player of red should be able to set up a break about 9 times out of 10.

This leads us to the principle on which we should base almost all decisions about whether or not to take any particular risk: **Any better-than-even (say, 60%) chance should be taken if its success will result in an immediate break, but even a 90% chance is normally not worth taking if it is likely to result in the making of only one hoop**. Although it may seem rather obvious when stated like this, it is surprising how few players think this way during a game. Many would consider it too risky to try the hoop in the first position, while others would attempt it in the second position—and then not realise that they are losing games, not because of missed roquets or hoops, but through poor tactics.

MANOEUVRING

W E HAVE SEEN already that one of the principles of risk-taking is that shooting at a ball is almost always safer than not shooting. The main reason why the out-player (i.e. the one who does not have the 'innings') should elect to shoot at a ball on almost every opportunity is that failure to do so allows the opponent to strengthen his position without risk by 'manoeuvring'. The manoeuvring process usually (but not always) begins when the opponent has turned down an opportunity to roquet, and instead has hit his ball into a corner or returned wide of his partner ball, imagining that thereby he is "playing safe".

The aim of the process is to strengthen your position without taking any undue risk or allowing the opponent any safer chance to roquet than the one he has already passed up. During the process you can hope to make hoops and /or work toward the establishment of a break. The idea is that your opponent can do nothing to prevent you from achieving one or both of these objectives unless he is prepared to risk a shot which, if missed, will give you an immediate break. Once they start hitting away without shooting at a ball, most opponents will find it difficult to bring themselves to attempt a shot which is obviously riskier than the one(s) they have already chosen not to attempt.

The break is usually achieved by eventually setting up a position where you will have at least a 3-ball break regardless of which ball the opponent moves, and in which any shot he attempts and misses will give you the fourth ball as well. It is important to realise that this should, and can, always be accomplished without taking any real risk of either losing the innings or allowing the opponent a "safe" shot.

The main principles of 'manoeuvring' are as follows:

(1) Until you can get the break set up, leave your partner ball within 6 yards of a border so that you can cover the boundary behind it, if necessary, to prevent the opponent from shooting at it with the ball he must move. Note that this is different from the "Aunt Ernma" idea of leaving your partner ball on the border "so that you will have somewhere safe to come home to".

(2) Do not risk making a hoop unless:

(a) you are sure you can make it with ease, or
(b) the opponent's balls are well apart, or
(c) after making the hoop you can fairly easily use his balls to set up a break.

(3) At the end of a turn, leave the balls so that any missed shot by the opponent gives you either:

(a) a ball near your hoop and another ball you can easily use to load the following hoop, or

(b) a rush to your hoop and two balls in forward play, or (c) a rush to a ball at the following hoop, so that you can leave your partner ball there and rush that ball to your current hoop. In each of these cases you would have an excellent chance of establishing a break, so it would be quite inconsistent for an opponent who has already passed up roquet chances to risk taking any such shot.

(4) Be prepared to play the 'other' ball—i.e. the one other than the ball you want to make hoops with.

(5) In general, prefer to set yourself a rush to the following hoop rather than to your current hoop. It may seem that these 'principles of manoeuvring' amount to a rather negative, "no-risk" strategy. In reality it is quite the opposite. It is a very aggressive process because it keeps the opponent under pressure, ensuring that any shot he attempts and misses will cost him a break. This is a far cry from the "take-off and separate" style of Aunt Emma, which is aimed at frustrating the opponent rather than pressuring him.

Emma does not plan her set-ups so as to establish breaks, and will not take the risks needed to maintain a break even when she has one started. She leaves the opponent's balls on the border as far apart as possible rather than placing them where she will be able to use them; and relies on the opponent missing roquets, instead of setting so that he cannot risk attempting them. She does not play (and would not risk) even the fairly safe split-shots involved in the manoeuvring process. In following articles we shall look at practical examples of the manoeuvring possibilities that are available, but often overlooked, in common game situations.

In the position shown on the first diagram the black clip was on hoop 1 and blue on hoop 6. The player of red needed to move his ball from its position in the lawn and realised that if he shot at yellow and missed he would leave two balls near black's hoop.

Black could have then rushed blue to hoop 2, taken off to red and yellow, and set up at least a 3-ball break. Therefore he chose to hit his ball into the 4th corner. This allowed black to (at least) engage in a simple 'manoeuvre' by rushing blue to hoop 2 and setting a simple rush with the boundary covered as shown in the second diagram. Now if red shoots at yellow and misses there will again be two balls near black's hoop, while if yellow shoots at red unsuccessfully then blue has a reasonable

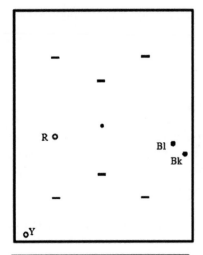

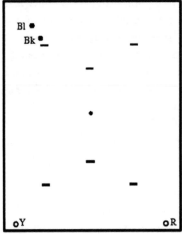

chance of making hoop 2 with a rush to hoop 3 and two balls near hoop 4.

The player of red and yellow, confronted with the situation in the second diagram, may well decide to shoot with yellow at red and hope that blue will not succeed in getting a good rush to hoop 3 after making hoop 2, and so have difficulty in establishing the break. This would certainly be preferable to again refusing to shoot at anything.

But it is obvious now that it would have been far more sensible for red to shoot at the opponent's balls in the position of the first diagram. "He doesn't have a rush to his hoop," is the common protest at this suggestion, "and a miss will make it easy for him to get one." This is indeed true—but how can he load the following hoop for either ball before making the current one? His best chance of establishing a break is to play black, rush blue to hoop 2, take off to yellow and roll for hoop 1. There is a chance of this succeeding, but few players could expect to do it more than 3 times out of 10, and black could always have tried this, even after red was played into a corner.

Most players of red could expect to roquet in the first diagram about 3 times out of 10, so by electing to shoot you are giving yourself as good a chance of achieving your objective as you are conceding the opponent of achieving his. Of course, the objectives are different—yours is to gain the innings, while his is to establish a break; but failing to shoot gives you no chance at all of gaining the innings, and makes it easier still for the opponent to set up a break. Yet players continue to hit into corners and later complain that there was nothing more they could have done because they never had the innings! A word of caution: the above reasoning applies only to games in which both players are capable of making breaks and consequently neither can expect to win by making one hoop at a time. If you are still at the stage where you regularly win or lose games with scores such as 11-9, then an unsuccessful shot with red at the opponent's balls could allow him to make one more hoop which may indeed be critical. At that level you should be spending your time out

John Riches and Wayne Davies

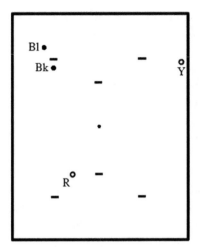

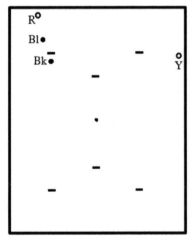

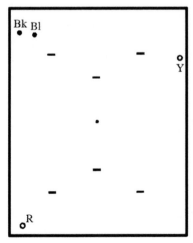

on the lawn practising the shots needed to establish and maintain breaks, rather than concerning yourself with advanced tactical considerations. The best advice is, "First learn to split confidently from any hoop to the next two; then start thinking about tactics." Both of these things require the assistance of a competent coach, and any player who wishes to improve his game in any way should realise that without the assistance of a good coach he cannot expect to progress as rapidly as he should.

The previous article showed that you should shoot at a ball when a miss would allow your opponent to make only his current hoop without being able to set up a break by first loading his following hoop. Now we shall see that you should also shoot even when a miss will allow the opponent to set up a break, provided that he has to play two or three good, accurate shots in order to do so.

The first diagram shows a position taken from a division 1 doubles tournament. The player of black had made hoop 1 and failed at hoop 2, with his ball rebounding to a position from which the hoop could be made on the next turn without undue difficulty. The other three clips were still on hoop 1. The players of red and yellow decided that they should move the red ball, since blue had enough of the black ball to make it likely that he would take the turn if, say, yellow shot at red and missed. However, a shot with red at yellow would put two balls into black's 'forward play', and a shot at the opponent balls would produce the position shown in the second diagram, where black can (probably) run through hoop 2 to the boundary and make use of the 'extra' red ball. Therefore the player of red elected not to shoot, and instead played his ball into the

1ˢᵗ corner. This allowed black to start 'manoeuvring'. He made his hoop and set a rush to hoop 3 wired from yellow, as in the third diagram.

Once again red and yellow decided they could not risk shooting, so yellow was played into the 4ᵗʰ corner. It is almost impossible to imagine red and yellow winning the game with such tactics (they lost 26-3), yet there are many players who are quite capable of playing all-round breaks, but who deny themselves much chance of getting in and making a break by refusing to shoot in such positions.

In the original position red should have shot at black, since although he would have an 'extra ball' in the position of the second diagram, black would need to play some accurate shots under pressure to get a break fully established. Note that if blue takes the turn from the second diagram he will be unable to rush black to hoop 1. In the first diagram even a shot by red at yellow would have been preferable to not shooting, as black's only immediate way of establishing a break after making hoop 2 would be to split blue to load hoop 4 while going to the opponent balls on the border near hoop 3—a shot which many players would find difficult and risky. Perhaps the principle involved can be explained this way:

In the first diagram red should expect to roquet black about 3 times out of 10, so the opponent has no better than a 70% chance of getting his break going even if he were certain of playing the accurate shots required on each of the 7 times that red misses. But with red and yellow refusing to shoot, the opponent must surely still have at least 70% chance of eventually establishing a break without having taken any risk at all.

Previous articles have shown that you should shoot at a ball in situations where a miss will allow the opponent to make only one hoop without being able to first load the following hoop; and also in situations where in order to establish a break he will need to play some accurate shots. Now we will see that even when the shots required by the opponent to set up a break are fairly straight-forward, taking the shot may still give a better chance of winning than any alternative course of action against a player who thinks.

In the position shown in the first diagram I was playing with red and yellow, and my opponent's blue clip was on hoop 2. I shot with red at yellow and roqueted, but an observer asked me later how I could justify the 'risk' I took, since a miss would have allowed blue to roquet black, take off to red, place red at hoop 3 and rush yellow to hoop 2—all fairly straightforward shots—with a break easily set up.

He suggested that instead of shooting I should have played red into the 1ˢᵗ corner (second diagram), as blue had no useful rush and would then not find it easy to set up

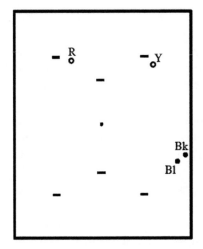

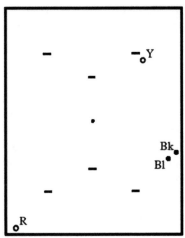

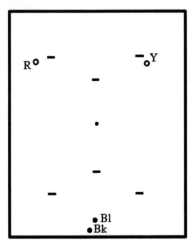

a break. I explained that my opponent would not have needed to play blue at all. Instead he could play black, rushing blue to a point about 2 yards in from the middle of the south boundary, then taking off to red in the 1st corner. Then he could send red back to hoop 2 with a split in which no particular accuracy is needed, and finish by setting blue a rush to the yellow ball at hoop 3 (third diagram), or, if he preferred, direct to hoop 2.

In this situation I would be faced with a (slightly) longer roquet than before, and the red ball may even turn out to be wired from yellow. Any missed shot would now give my opponent a 4-ball break which he could set up more easily than if I had missed yellow in the original position; and he would have at least the 3-ball break even if I again hit red away into a corner. Thus I had nothing to gain and stood to only make things worse for myself by failing to take the shot in the first place. A consideration of similar possibilities should convince the reader that hitting red into the 2nd, 3rd or 4th corners would have been no better, as in each case my opponent at the very least could without risk set up a position similar to the third diagram.

It is worth noting that in the first diagram I also seriously considered shooting with yellow at blue. Leaving the red ball at blue's hoop would not have mattered, since the long pass-roll placing black at hoop 3 while going with blue to red at hoop 2 may not have been all that easy for my opponent. However, yellow would have finished too close to the opponent balls, again allowing him to use it to set up an easy break for blue.

Alternatively, he could play black and set up a leave similar to the one in the third diagram,

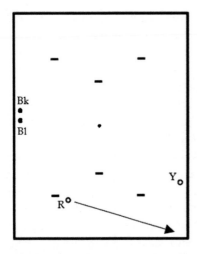

but with his balls near the 4th corner. The reader will by now be starting to understand why players at international level tend to follow the principle, "Walk onto the lawn and take the shortest shot—regardless!"

In previous articles we have seen that hitting a ball out of play into a corner, rather than shooting at a ball, is in almost all cases an ill-advised course of action. Part of the reason lies in the fact that it takes all pressure from the opponent and, if he is astute enough, allows him to improve his position without taking any risks. If he does this manoeuvring properly he should be able to end up with at least a 3-ball break without having allowed you any less risky shot than the one you passed up in the first place.

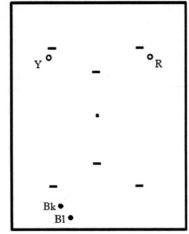

Some players, however, instead of hitting into a far corner, prefer to return 'wide' of their partner ball. This is intended to keep their opponent under some sort of pressure, since he will find it difficult to use the balls to set up a break, but they are close enough together to have a good chance of roqueting if he simply ignores them.

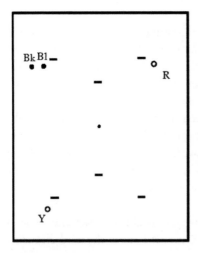

In the first diagram black was for hoop 2 and the other three clips were still on hoop 1. Red reasoned that shooting at yellow was too risky because if the shot was missed it would allow blue to rush black to hoop 2, take off to red and yellow, and rush one of them to hoop 1 with a break established. Therefore red was played into the 4th corner 'wide' of yellow. This sort of thing is seen frequently on our lawns, and the legendary "Aunt Emma" is particularly fond of it. However, it amounts to nothing more than giving the game away against a thinking opponent who understands the art and importance of 'manoeuvring'.

Such an opponent, as black and blue, will not make the mistake of going to red and yellow with the idea of trying to rush one of them to his hoop. Instead, he will 'manoeuvre' to improve his position in one of two possible ways:

(1) He could play black, rush blue to the boundary in front of hoop 1, take off to red in the 4th corner and use a stop-shot to place it at hoop 3 while going to yellow. Then yellow could be sent to hoop 2 while black returns to set a rush for blue as in the second diagram. None of these shots is difficult or requires any great accuracy.

(2) Or he could play blue, rush black to hoop 2, take off to red, again send it to hoop 3, and put yellow at hoop 1 before returning to set up as in the third diagram. The same result could also be achieved by going to yellow first.

In either case the player of red and yellow is now faced with a situation in which any missed shot would give more away than if he had shot with red at any of the three other balls in the first diagram; and if he elects not to shoot he will be leaving either black or blue with an immediate 3-ball break. Note that method (2) involves

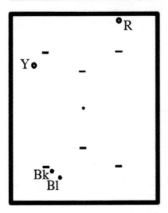

one long take-off to a corner ball, but results in an even stronger set-up. In diagram 2 yellow could choose to shoot at red, but would risk leaving both balls in the opponent's forward play.

It would make little sense for a player to do this when he was not willing to risk shooting in the first diagram. It is now apparent that in the first diagram red should have shot at a ball, as 'returning wide' only enabled the opponent to strengthen his position.

Yet so many players continue to do it!

In order to gain a deeper understanding of the 'manoeuvring' process referred to in previous articles, let us follow the moves in an imaginary game. In the first diagram, which was taken from a first division match, the blue clip is still on hoop 1 and black is already on 4-back. The yellow ball has just been played from near hoop 1 into the second corner because it was wired from blue and black, and the player considered that a shot at his red partner ball would have been too

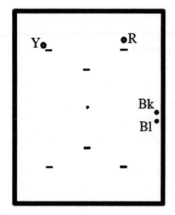

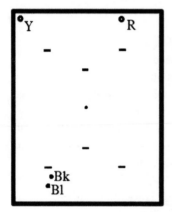

risky, since it would have given blue, which had a rush to hoop 1, two balls together in forward play. Now, if you are playing blue and black, you should start manoeuvring to set up a break for your blue ball. With the black clip already on 4-back the manoeuvring will be more difficult than if you could threaten to set up a break with either ball.

You can begin by playing the rush to hoop 1. If you do not get near enough to be almost certain of making it, then in approaching the hoop you should use the idea of placing the black ball within 6 yards of the boundary so that you retain the option of covering the south boundary against a shot by either yellow or red if the hoop cannot be attempted. With the boundary so covered, failure to make the hoop would not matter, since any shot by the opponent would give you either an immediate break or two balls in forward play; and so it is most unlikely that he would be willing to risk shooting.

If the hoop can be safely made, then you try to do it in such a way as to be able to rush your partner ball to the east boundary, between hoops 3 and 4. Then a take-off to red, followed by a thick take-off to yellow, will allow you to roll with yellow for hoop 2. If the roll is successful, then you have the break under way; and if not, then you can return to black with the set-up shown in the second diagram, where yellow must move but once more finds that any shot he attempts is riskier than the shot he passed up originally. If he again hits yellow into a corner (say, the 1ˢᵗ), then you still have a good chance of a break by rushing black to red and then red to hoop 2.

If on making hoop 1 you failed to get the desired rush to the east border, then you could have simply roqueted black and set blue a rush (preferably wired at least partly from yellow) near the south boundary to the red ball as shown in the third diagram. Although this set-up is not as strong as the one in the second diagram, it still gives you a reasonable chance of setting up a break by rushing black to red followed by red to hoop 2; and any shot taken by the opponent and missed will make the establishing of a break a simple matter.

Thus far, without taking any risk, you have made one hoop and given yourself an excellent chance (if you had got the desired rush and succeeded in setting up as in the third diagram) of establishing a break. Your opponent has had no better or safer opportunity to shoot at a ball than the one he turned down originally by hitting his yellow ball from hoop 1 into the 2nd corner instead of shooting at red.

If he is consistent in refusing to attempt such shots then by continuing the process in a similar fashion you can make hoop after hoop, until you finally succeed in establishing a break. It should be obvious that this 'manoeuvring' process, once understood and applied, is an almost certain way of beating the "Aunt Emma" style of the player who plays with the unrealistic aim of avoiding all risky shots.

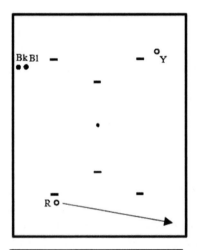

This series of articles may have given the impression that when it is your turn it is never correct to do anything except shoot at a ball. This is not true; but against an opponent who plays correctly, positions are very rare in which failure to shoot gives a better winning chance than shooting. As suggested in a previous article, such positions usually involve wiring.

In the first diagram blue and yellow are both for hoop 3 and black is for hoop 1. Red, whose clip is already on 4-back, is wired from both black and blue. It would be reasonable to decide that the one possible shot with red (at yellow) is too long and risky, and any shot with yellow even more so. In this case red could sensibly be played into the 4th corner. Then, in order to establish an immediate break, black or blue would need to play some rather difficult and accurate shots.

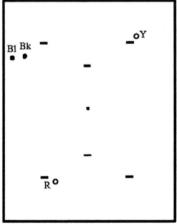

If the opponent understands how to 'manoeuvre' to improve his position, he may (for example) play black, roquet blue gently, take off to yellow, roquet it and take off to red in the 4th corner, try a long roll for hoop 1, and if unsuccessful return to blue with a set-up as in the second diagram. Note that black and blue are now set the other way round so that the opponent's position is now stronger in that he will now have an immediate break whichever ball (red or yellow) is moved, unless it roquets. However, a shot with either red or yellow is now no longer than in the first diagram, and will give no more away—there was an easy break for black or blue in either case. There was also the slight possibility that something could have gone wrong for black during the 'manoeuvring' process, which of course could also have been done in ways other than the one described.

In the first diagram the situation for red and yellow could hardly get any worse than it already is. By hitting red into the 4th corner you are more or less saying, "I am almost willing to concede you the break, but let's see you play a couple of long take-offs first."

The difference between this and the positions considered in previous articles where failure to shoot was incorrect, is that in those positions the opponent by 'manoeuvring' with little or no risk could bring about a situation in which you were left with a noticeably longer roquet than the one you could have attempted originally, and he had an easier break if you missed or chose not to shoot.

This 'manoeuvring' presupposes the ability to play and maintain a break once it is set up, and is facilitated by an understanding of 'ideal leaves' as explained in my booklets on Strategy and Tactics.

Hopefully the examples given in this series of articles will have made clearer the point of the whole process and the sort of way in which to go about it. It often means declining all chance (usually a low percentage one anyway) of making an immediate break, and often involves playing the turn with the ball other than the one with which you want to make hoops. However, against certain types of players the rewards

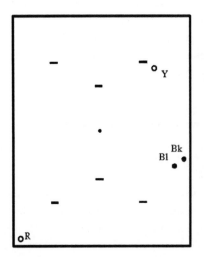

are considerable, and, if sufficient of our up-and-coming younger players can be assisted to understand the art, then the day may well arrive when "Aunt Emma" is nothing more than a dim and distant memory in the minds of those of us who played "B.M."—"Before Manoeuvring".

In an earlier article (see part 4) we looked at the situation shown in the diagram, where the blue clip was on hoop 2.

The red ball had been left at hoop 2, and has just been played from there into the first corner because the player considered it too

John Riches and Wayne Davies

risky to shoot at any ball. We saw that the decision not to shoot was ill-advised because it allows the opponent (black and blue) by 'manoeuvring' to strengthen his position without risk, thus forcing red to either allow blue a break without a roquet having even been attempted, or else attempt a roquet which, if missed, would give blue the break more easily than if the player had taken one of the shots on offer in the original position (when red was at hoop 2). This 'manoeuvring' process involved black taking the turn in the diagrammed position, rushing blue to the centre of the south boundary, taking off to red, and sending it back to hoop 2 while going to set a rush for blue to yellow at hoop 3.

Note that although it is an almost certain way of beating Aunt Emma, this type of manoeuvring, which is the correct play for the player of black and blue in the above situation, may not be advisable against an aggressive opponent. Of course, an aggressive opponent would have taken a shot rather than hitting red from hoop 2 into the 1ˢᵗ corner in the first place. However, there are other ways in which the same position could have arisen against an aggressive opponent. You must bear in mind that an aggressive player of red and yellow is almost certain to shoot after the player of black and blue has strengthened his position by manoeuvring as suggested above; and unlike Aunt Emma he would not have already passed up a chance of a shot involving less risk than the one he is now faced with.

If he does shoot and roquet, he is also likely to make more hoops than Aunt Emma, who obviously over-rates the risks involved in shooting, and so is almost certain to similarly over-rate many of the risks needed to keep a break going.

If you can now switch sides and imagine yourself playing black and blue against an aggressive opponent, you can see that it is necessary to consider the advisability of trying for a break immediately, without allowing him the extra chance to roquet. This involves playing blue, roqueting black and rolling both balls to hoop 3 in the hope of getting a rush on yellow to hoop 2 and making it. If you are confident that you can do this successfully under pressure about 5 times out of 10 (try it at practice not under pressure—the results may surprise you!) then this would be the thing to do. But against Aunt Emma, 'manoeuvring' will give a higher percentage chance of winning unless you can expect to roll successfully at least 8 times out of 10. By ending the manoeuvre with a rush for blue to yellow rather than to its hoop you can almost guarantee that Aunt Emma will again refuse to take any shot, so the success rate on the roll required to make it the better option would be close to 100%!

Note that it is necessary to estimate to some extent the likelihood of your opponent being willing to 'risk' shooting after you have strengthened your position by manoeuvring. (In actual fact we have seen that he is taking a greater risk by not shooting.) Against an aggressive opponent you will be forced to take greater risks in attempting to get a break going as early as possible; but against Aunt Emma there is no need to take such risks.

Even against an aggressive opponent the manoeuvring process may be your best option. (This would be the case if in the diagram you could not expect, as blue, to play the roll and get the rush to hoop 2 with 50% success rate.) Against Aunt Emma it will almost always be the best option.

STRENGTHENING YOUR POSITION

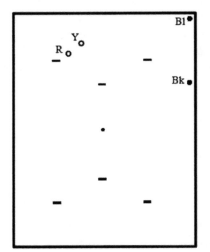

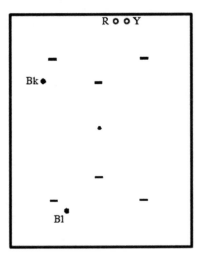

IN PREVIOUS ARTICLES we have seen how it is often possible strengthen your position without risk, especially against an opponent who has already passed up a chance to roquet by hitting a ball 'out of play'. Even when there is a small amount of risk involved, a manoeuvre to strengthen your position may be worthy of consideration.

The first diagram shows a position from one of my matches.

Red and black clips were both on 4-back. Yellow and blue were still on hoop 1. My opponent had just played blue from near hoop 1 (where I had left it after rolling unsuccessfully) into the 3rd corner. He had decided that shooting at my balls was too risky, as a miss would have given me an excellent chance of a break with yellow; and a shot at black, if missed, would have made it even easier for me as I could take-off to his two balls and rush one of them to hoop 1.

Now I considered the possibility of playing yellow, roqueting red, taking off to blue, and trying to get a rush on black to hoop 1, but felt that I was unlikely to succeed in this more than about 3 times in 10. Since there was a better than even chance that I would have to give my opponent another chance to roquet, I decided to make sure that he would get only the one chance, and unless he roqueted I would have a fairly easy break.

Therefore, instead of playing yellow I used red, cut-rushed yellow to the south boundary, then took off to blue in the 3rd corner. A long, but not difficult, stop-shot sent blue to hoop 1 while red went to black, making no attempt to get behind it.

Then I placed black near hoop 2 and hit red out near yellow, producing the position shown in the second diagram.

In this position my opponent now has another chance to roquet, but what are his choices? Any missed shot with blue would give me a break more easily than the one he had originally considered too risky to attempt. Black has a shorter shot, but it involves leaving blue at my hoop and playing the ball which he does not want to use because it is already on 4-back. But if he again takes blue 'out of play' into, say, the 4th corner, then I can cut-rush red toward hoop 2 and still have a good chance of establishing a break!

He elected to shoot with black at my balls, which was probably the correct choice in this situation, but it is not easy to roquet under such pressure when you are not at all sure you are doing the right thing by shooting anyway. He missed and I had a simple break for yellow under way.

I considered it worthwhile to take the risk of my opponent roqueting in order to give myself an easy break if he missed. If he had known what I would do, I am sure he would have shot at red with blue in the first place, instead of hitting into the 3rd corner. He had expected me to try for a low-percentage chance of an immediate break with yellow. When your opponent understands how to strengthen his position by manoeuvring in this manner, hitting balls into corners just does not make sense. We shall consider this theme further in the next article.

WHY NOT SHOOT?

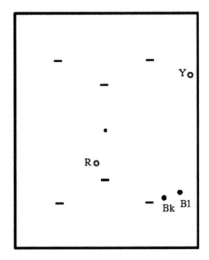

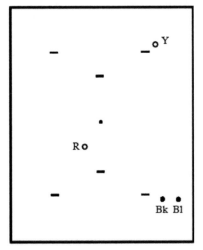

THIS ARTICLE IS a logical continuation of the previous article on 'Strengthening Your Position'. The first diagram shows a common type of position in which many players, as red and yellow, would consider it too risky to shoot at a ball. The opponent has his blue clip on hoop 4 and black on hoop 3. Some players would hit red into the 3rd (or some other) corner, hoping that the opponent will play the next turn with black and try to get a break going by using red and /or yellow to make hoop 3, which few players could succeed in doing more than 5 times out of 10. Or perhaps blue will try to make a 2-ball break up the centre, which would have an even lower chance of succeeding.

However, the opponent can simply make hoop 4 with blue and then take off to yellow and set up a yet stronger position such as the one shown in the second diagram. Here the player of red and yellow is faced with a shot at least as risky as the one he refused to take in the first diagram, but the opponent will have at least a 3-ball break even if no shot is taken.

In the clubroom at Broadview Croquet Club we have a sign which proclaims:

The Broadview Principle: When it is your turn, nine times out of ten you should shoot at a ball. On the tenth occasion, when a miss would allow the opponent an easy break you should pause to consider the possible alternatives—and then still shoot!

Of course, this is not a principle to be followed slavishly, but most of our members do accept the philosophy that attack is more likely to win games than defence.

In a position such as the one in the first diagram it makes little sense for red to do anything except shoot at a ball. There are several excellent reasons why shooting is almost always preferable to hitting a ball into a corner or returning wide of your partner ball:

1. It is an absolute necessity in a game of croquet to maintain a confident mental approach, which is much harder to do when you start conceding turns to the opponent without any resistance.

2. Even if you shoot and miss, you are practising your roquets and can set about correcting errors in your swing. If you hit 3 times into a corner, rather than taking 3 shots and missing them, you are less likely to roquet the next time when you at last decide to take a shot. For this reason it follows that if you do decide that there is no alternative to hitting a ball out of play (perhaps because you are wired from the only reasonable shot), you should pick a definite aiming point, such as a corner peg or flag, carefully stalk the ball, and play the shot with as much concentration as you would the most important roquet or hoop shot.

3. By refusing to shoot, you invite the opponent to find a way of strengthening his position without taking any noticeable risk, as explained in previous articles and above. He should be able to eventually get a break going without having allowed you any less risky shot than the one you should have taken in the first place.

4. From a percentage viewpoint, failing to shoot immediately concedes the opponent a better than even chance (say, 60%) of getting the next break. No matter how far apart you put your balls this must be true simply by virtue of the fact that he has the innings and you do not! Therefore, even if a miss gives him a certain break (and it rarely does) there is still usually at least a 10% chance that something may go wrong for him. You would therefore only need to have about a 30% chance of roqueting to make shooting the least risky course of action. If both players can play breaks, this will be true at almost any stage of the game.

John Riches and Wayne Davies

CROQUET

COACHING:
ERROR CORRECTION

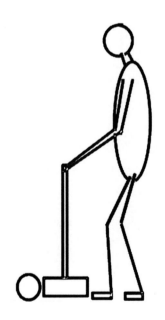

CONTENTS

CROQUET COACHING— RECOGNITION OF ERRORS

INTRODUCTION

T HIS BOOKLET IS intended to assist coaches in diagnosing and treating the problems of technique commonly encountered by croquet players.

There are other books which explain how the various shots should be played, but few mention how to put things right when the shots are not turning out as expected.

In playing a roquet, for example, the player needs to give attention to such things as the suitability of his mallet (length, weight, size of grip, etc), stalking the ball, correct grip and hand positioning, correct stance and foot positioning, slope of handle, type of swing (from hands or shoulders; pendulum swing or forward push, etc.), body movement, length of backswing, tightness of grip, acceleration of mallet head, squareness of mallet face, follow-through, etc. In addition to the many things he must concentrate on getting right, there are things to avoid; and on top of all this there is his mental approach which also plays an important part in determining the success or otherwise of the shot.

When things are going wrong, the player often is unable to determine which of these things is the cause of his difficulties. This is understandable, because he is unable to watch himself play the shot from the various angles needed to ascertain whether or not he is actually doing things the way he thinks he is.

The coach needs to be able to quickly discover what the player is doing wrong. He needs to then know what the player OUGHT to be doing instead, and most importantly of all, he needs to know how to get him to do it.

The information contained here has come from years of experience in teaching and coaching, and from an author who can claim to have made more errors than most, and to have many times gone through the difficult process of trying without help to find out the cause of an error and how to remedy it.

SECTION A—THE ROQUET

1. "I KEEP MISSING MY ROQUETS, ALWAYS ON THE LEFT HAND SIDE."

PROBLEM: EITHER THE alignment of the shot is incorrect, or—more likely—the mallet is being diverted from the alignment during the swing by the player pushing with his bottom hand.

CORRECTION:

(1) Check foot positioning. If the swing is parallel to the front foot as generally recommended, then this foot may be pointing slightly outward. Alternatively, the foot may be too far from the line of aim, so that the mallet does not swing directly below the right eye as it should, assuming the player is right-eyed. View from directly in front to check for these errors.

(2) Take a longer backswing so that the falling weight of the mallet will provide sufficient force without any need to push into the handle with either hand. Relax the bottom hand so that it is used as a guide only, cock the wrists backward so that the mallet head is pulled rather than pushed through the ball, and reach forward as far as possible ALONG THE GROUND in the follow-through. (A player who concentrates on achieving this type of follow-through will automatically tend to get closer to the correct wrist-cocking and mallet-pulling action.) View from the side to watch for these errors. In the ideal swing the hands should begin to move horizontally forward *just before* the mallet head has completed its backswing. This requires the wrists to be slightly flexible at this early stage of the swing. Practise short roquets using the top hand only, in order to develop the timing of a swing that does not require additional force from the bottom hand.

NOTE: Failure to stalk the ball is not likely to produce such consistency of error, nor is movement of head and shoulders, nor is nervousness.

FURTHER NOTE: This problem, and possibly the next one as well, can also be caused by the player tightening his grip during the swing. Unfortunately, there is no way for the coach to tell by observation that this is happening.

The player should grip the mallet with the desired tension (preferably fairly light) before lining the shot up, check that the mallet face is square to the line of aim, and then maintain the same tension during the swing. This is much easier to say than do. Many players can avoid squeezing the grip tighter during practice swings or when they are practising roquets under no pressure, but find it difficult to stop themselves doing it in a pressure situation. A valuable tip for game situations is to be conscious of grip tension when hitting the balls into play at the start of a game, and also when running the first hoop.

To convince the player of the need for this, ask him to hold the mallet still and tighten his grip. The mallet face will turn a few degrees, and it becomes obvious that if he does this during the swing it will destroy the alignment of the mallet. Players often learn to accommodate this loss of alignment by aiming slightly to one side of the target, but this is only likely to work at certain distances and cannot be recommended.

2. "MY MALLET KEEPS TWISTING IN MY HAND."

PROBLEM: The player is not hitting the ball in the middle of the mallet face. He is hitting it off centre to one side. It is the force of impact on the ball that is causing the mallet to twist in his hands.

CORRECTION: Line up the shot more carefully, keep the shoulders still, swing smoothly from the shoulders watching the exact point on the ball where the mallet will contact it, and REACH FORWARD along the ground in the follow-through to keep the mallet head moving along the line of aim. Getting these things right will usually result in fewer off-centre hits.

If the problem is still not corrected, the player is almost certainly tightening his grip just prior to impact. This tightening can destroy the alignment of the mallet. Check this by asking the player to hold his mallet still just above the ground in the position where it is about to contact the ball, and then tighten his grip. Watch for movement in the mallet head. Explain the effect of such movement, and ask him to line up his shots while holding the mallet with whatever firmness he feels is necessary for the shot (remembering that the firmness should be provided by the top hand rather than the bottom one), then try not to tighten his grip as he swings. A tight grip (as distinct from 'firm') is neither necessary nor desirable.

NOTE: A player who misses a roquet will sometimes say, "I twisted my mallet", imagining that he did it himself. This is never so. HE did not twist the mallet—THE BALL twisted it, as explained above.

3. "I KEEP MISSING REASONABLY SHORT ROQUETS OF 4 OR 5 YARDS. I FEEL I AM AT LEAST AS LIKELY TO HIT A ROQUET OF 10 OR 15 YARDS."

PROBLEM: The player is swinging around a curve instead of swinging through in a straight line. This is especially common in players who play side-style. It would not matter, provided that the mallet head is travelling in the correct line of aim at the moment of impact, but this is rarely the case. The player has learnt (unconsciously) to accommodate the curved swing by aiming (or at least lining up) the shot to one side of the target ball, and holding the mallet so that the face is turned slightly outward as compared with the curve of the swing. This may allow him to roquet quite well over a set distance, but for roquets of a different length—either shorter or longer—the set of the mallet face will no longer exactly counteract the curve of the swing.

CORRECTION: There may be no satisfactory answer. It would be necessary to change BOTH the swing and the alignment of the mallet head. In addition, his line of aim would need to be changed, which will be difficult because he is not aware that he is aiming other than at the target ball. Changing only one of these will make things worse than ever, and the player will probably reject all further advice. The player may not be able to learn to swing along a straight line, especially if he has had a curved swing for many years. In this case, it may be possible for the player to understand what he is unconsciously doing, and learn to consciously vary the set of the mallet head in order to accommodate the effect of the curved swing at various distances. However, it will probably be better to simply suggest that he try to reach forward further along the ground toward the target ball, particularly on the shorter roquets. This should produce a slightly straighter swing, reducing the amount of correction needed.

If the player is a relative beginner playing centre style, the curved swing will be evident when viewed from behind, and it is more than likely that the curve results from incorrect foot positioning. In some cases the player does not realise that he is placing his feet so that with a straight backswing he would hit himself in the ankle.

4. "MY ROQUETS SEEM TO START ON LINE, BUT TEND TO CURVE OFF BEFORE THEY REACH THE BALL I AM TRYING TO ROQUET."

PROBLEM: Assuming that the curve cannot be attributed to irregularities in the lawn, then somehow or other the player is imparting side-spin to the ball. As the ball slows down the spin starts to take effect and causes the ball to swerve to one side. This spin may be due to either the mallet face being very slightly turned so that it is not quite perpendicular to the line of aim, or the handle of the mallet being tilted to one side so that when it contacts the ball the mallet head is not vertically below the hands.

Neither of these need prevent the ball from being hit straight, but there will be some spin imparted to the ball, which is likely to curve off line as the player has noticed.

CORRECTION: It is possible to allow for the curve in selecting the line of aim, since the curve should always be to the same side. Many players actually do this, but it is hardly a satisfactory long-term solution for a player who aspires to reach the highest level. The alignment of the mallet face can be checked by using a few practice swings above the ball before striking it. It may not be sufficient to simply check the alignment before starting the swing, as the player may be altering the alignment during the swing.

If the mallet is leaning to one side during the swing, this will be apparent when viewed from behind. In this case it will NOT help to have the player reach further forward in the follow-through. The reaching forward helps keep the mallet moving along the line of aim, but this was not the problem, as the ball is already travelling along the correct line for most of its journey. In fact, reaching forward with the mallet tilted sideways is only likely to magnify the problem by imparting more side-spin to the ball.

One thing that may help is to ask the player to try lining up his shot with the mallet head NOT touching the ground, holding the mallet only lightly with the bottom hand so that the weight of the mallet makes it hang vertically below the top hand. Then the shot should be played essentially with the TOP hand (practise it without using the bottom hand at all) which must move directly forward in the line of aim. It may also help if the bottom hand is moved up closer to the top hand, even until the hands are interlocking or overlapping. Alternatively, if the player insists on keeping his hands apart then he could try placing the bottom hand more directly BEHIND the shaft rather than on one side of it. Most players who play with the shaft on a noticeable sideways tilt have their hands well apart and the bottom hand pressing against the handle from one side during the swing.

5. "AT TIMES I HIT THE GROUND WITH MY MALLET ON ROQUETS, OR MORE ESPECIALLY ON LONG RUSHES AND CANNONS."

PROBLEM: This is always caused by the player 'dipping' his shoulders as he swings, usually in an effort to impart more force to the ball.

CORRECTION: The player needs to concentrate on keeping his shoulders absolutely still on EVERY swing. It is important to do this even on shots where some shoulder movement would not seem to matter, so that it becomes an ingrained habit and will not be forgotten when he has to consider other factors as well. He must be convinced that shoulder movement will certainly not result in any additional force being imparted to the ball, and instead he could be encouraged to use a tighter grip (top hand only) on shots which require greater than usual force.

SECTION B—THE RUSH

6. "I CAN'T GET ENOUGH DISTANCE IN MY RUSHES, AND EVEN IN A ROQUET SHOT I HAVE TROUBLE REACHING THE FAR END OF A HEAVY LAWN. I DON'T HAVE THE STRENGTH FOR SUCH SHOTS."

PROBLEM: SINCE THE weight of the mallet alone, with sufficient backswing, is all that is required without any additional force, it is evident that the whole weight of the mallet is not being imparted to the ball. Bad timing could account for part of the problem, but more likely the player is not using a simple pendulum swing from the shoulders. He is probably using a DOUBLE pendulum in which he keeps his hands close in to his body and swings the mallet mainly from his wrists instead of from his shoulders. This will usually be accompanied by an obvious push with the bottom hand in an endeavour to provide the additional force which should be coming from the shoulder swing. It is also possible that the player is moving his shoulders during the swing in a further misguided effort to gain additional force, and thus hitting the ball with the very bottom of the mallet face, instead of in the "sweet spot". This can result in loss of force from mallet to ball.

CORRECTION: Take a firm (not tense) grip on the mallet and lock the wrists in a position which will have the mallet handle vertical at point of impact. Keep the hands further out in front (about a foot from the body) throughout the swing, and swing freely from the shoulders, which MUST NOT MOVE during the swing.

Observe from the side to check that at time of impact the hands are moving forward, not backward, and the shoulders are not moving at all. If necessary, place your hand on the back of his shoulders to stop them from moving upward until he gets used to the need to keep them still.

NOTE:

(1) There may also be a need to alter the position of the bottom hand, which may be too far down the handle to allow a free swing from the shoulders without any push. For the rush shot the bottom part of the swing and the follow-through should be as flat as possible, but this cannot be achieved with the bottom hand too low on the handle, because the length of the pendulum from shoulder to mallet head is too short.

(2) It will also probably be necessary to assure the player that his problem is certainly not lack of physical strength. Even on a heavy lawn a normal mallet swung freely from the shoulders has sufficient force to send any ball the full length of the lawn, provided all of the force is correctly imparted to the ball. However, on a very heavy lawn it may be useful to use a firmer, longer grip and a longer backswing.

(3) Loss of force in rushes can also result from the striker's ball jumping slightly and hitting the other ball above centre. This is not likely to be the problem here, as the player is saying that his roquets are also affected.

(4) With the sharp ridges on the new Dawson balls, it has become desirable to play rushes of three feet or less with a semi-stop-shot action, in order to make the striker's ball skid along the ground rather than roll for the first part of its journey. This is in contrast to a hoop shot where forward spin is desirable, and is one reason why it is recommended to stand further back from the ball on a rush than on a normal roquet shot, and use a long flat swing with the mallet approaching the striker's ball low along the ground. Forward spin on a ball with sharp ridging tends to make it ride up over the target ball, losing some of its force. If the balls are more than three feet apart, then the ball will have started rolling in this distance regardless of how the shot is played, so the player should concentrate on direction rather than spin.

7. "I HAVE NO CONFIDENCE WITH RUSHES LONGER THAN ABOUT TWO FEET. SOMETIMES I MISS ALTOGETHER WHEN I TRY TO RUSH A BALL ANY DISTANCE."

PROBLEM: The mallet is being taken off line during the swing, in a way that (presumably) does not happen in normal roquet shots.

Two things are likely to cause this

(1) The player is probably pushing forward with his bottom hand, and pushing the mallet slightly off line at the same time. This is particularly likely to occur on a heavy lawn when the player is not confident that his normal swing will produce sufficient force. It is very difficult to keep such a push in the exact line of swing, especially if the bottom hand is on the side of the handle rather than behind it.

(2) The player is lifting his eyes, and with them his head and shoulders, watching the target ball instead of the striker's ball. This will usually result in the ball being contacted OFF CENTRE on the mallet face, and the weight of the ball will push the mallet face off square.

CORRECTION: Observe from the side to check for pushing or shoulder movement, and from the rear to look for off-centre contact or swing being pushed off line. Then correct whichever of the two problems is evident as follows—

(1) Use a firm grip with the top hand and keep it moving forward throughout the swing. Relax the bottom hand so that it is placed only lightly on the handle, and use it to guide the direction of the swing without imparting any force.

(2) Keep the shoulders absolutely still and avoid any other body movement. A hand placed on the back of the shoulders is once again a useful aid.

8. "SOMETIMES MY BALL JUMPS WHEN I PLAY A RUSH SHOT. AT TIMES IT HAS JUMPED RIGHT OVER THE OTHER BALL."

PROBLEM: Unless the striker's ball is lying in a hole or just behind a tuft of hard grass, this can only be caused by the mallet head still being in its downward movement, with the handle tilted forward, when it contacts the ball. The player may be using a double-action pendulum swing in which the mallet swings mainly from the wrists, while the hands swing from the shoulders. The two pendulums thus created can easily get out of time (synchronisation) with each other so that the hands reach their desired contact position directly above the ball while the mallet head is still travelling downward.

CORRECTION: Stand a little further back from the ball and SLIGHTLY raise the front end of the mallet head. Swing smoothly from the shoulders with wrists locked and a firm grip with the top hand. This should produce a single pendulum with a long, flat swing in which the mallet head has passed the bottom of its swing and is just starting to move upward as the ball is contacted.

SECTION C—THE TAKE OFF

9. "I CAN TAKE OFF FROM ONLY ONE SIDE OF THE BALL. WHEN I TRY TO TAKE-OFF THE OTHER SIDE THE CROQUETED BALL OFTEN DOES NOT MOVE."

PROBLEM: THE PLAYER is swinging around a curve. It is also likely that he is turning his mallet face inward so that it is no longer perpendicular to the line of swing. He is probably not aware that he is doing either of these things, though some misguided coaches have actually taught players to consciously turn the mallet face inward on a take-off, in order to ensure that the roqueted ball moves.

CORRECTION: The curved swing may be difficult to change, especially if it is also evident in other shots, as is particularly common among side-style players. However, there is a strong tendency for all players—even those who swing straight through in roquets and rushes—to use a curved swing in a take-off, subconsciously endeavouring to 'shepherd' the striker's ball in the required direction. The player needs to develop confidence in the fact that if he swings perfectly straight with a square mallet face the striker's ball will still go where he wants it to (provided the line of aim is correct), and he will retain better control of the other ball as well.

One way to encourage the development of such confidence is to practise right-angle split shots, or "thick take-offs", choosing an aiming point midway between where he wants the two balls to finish (or more exactly, moving from this midpoint a little to the side where the striker's ball is going). He should concentrate on keeping the mallet face square and swinging directly at this point, following through in a straight line. Check that he finishes the swing with the mallet still pointing in this line and the mallet face still square. Then he can treat the normal take-off as merely a particular example of this right-angle split shot. Some players need to stand slightly further back than they would for a roquet, and use a flatter swing, to ensure that when it contacts the ball the mallet is moving forward rather than downward. It is difficult to control a take-off if you stand over the ball and hit down at it.

When he develops a straight, flat swing and knows which line to swing in, he will be able to take off from either side with equal ease.

10. "I FIND IT HARD TO CONTROL DISTANCE IN MY TAKE-OFFS. OTHERS SEEM TO BE ABLE TO JUDGE THEM FAIRLY WELL, BUT

I GO TOO FAR OR STOP TOO SHORT. I SEEM TO TAKE FAR TOO LONG TO GET THE FEEL OF THE LAWN."

PROBLEM: It is very likely that a faulty technique is being used. The player is probably turning the mallet face inward toward the croqueted ball and swinging slightly outward, producing a fairly thick take-off in most instances. He will have difficulty preventing the croqueted ball from going out on long corner take-offs, as it will not only be the striker's ball that gets out of control. The swing may or may not be curved, as it is possible to swing outward (away from the croqueted ball) with a perfectly straight swing, yet still move the croqueted ball provided the mallet face is turned inward. He is probably not consciously aiming the swing in any particular direction, and if asked where he is aiming will be forced to admit this, or will give some vague answer such as "where I want the ball to go".

CORRECTION: The player needs to learn a better method of choosing an exact point of aim for each take-off, then learn to swing directly at this aiming point with a square mallet face. A useful method for a take-off right across the lawn is as follows

(a) If you are taking off from the RIGHT hand side of the croqueted ball, then place the striker's ball so that the V between the balls is pointing about one yard to the RIGHT of where you want the striker's ball to finish. This allows for the fact that the ball will "pull" inward as it slows down.

(b) Aim your swing about one yard (or a little more for beginners with wobbly swings) to the LEFT of where you want the striker's ball to finish. This means that the croqueted ball will move (usually about one yard), as you are swinging well inside the V.

(c) When taking off only halfway across the lawn, allow only half a yard on each side, and if the distance is shorter still, make a correspondingly smaller allowance.

(d) If the striker's ball is consistently going to one side of the target point, the one-yard allowance for "pull" can be increased or decreased accordingly.

(e) When taking off from the LEFT side, aim the 'V' to the LEFT of the target point and select an aiming point to the RIGHT of it.

(f) Once again, the swing should be flat and straight. Do not stand over the ball or hit down on it.

NOTE: This method amounts to essentially the same thing as the recommended method of aiming for all split shots, i.e. aiming at a point halfway between where you want the two balls to finish, since a take-off is merely a particular type of split shot in which the striker's ball travels a large distance and the croqueted ball a small distance. It is important for the player to realise this so that he can learn to control the position of the croqueted ball when a thick take-off is desired. However, teaching normal take-offs in the manner described here has the advantage that the player is making a conscious allowance for "pull", and he is able to increase or decrease this allowance as he feels it is necessary to do so. By choosing an aiming point the same distance away as where he wants his ball to finish, he is better able to judge the correct strength of the shot. Some players find it very difficult to judge the midpoint between where they want the two balls to finish when the distances are so disproportionate, especially since they usually do not want the croqueted ball to finish in any particular place.

SECTION D—THE STOP SHOT

11. "MY STOP-SHOTS ARE NOWHERE NEAR AS GOOD AS THE ONES I SEE OTHER PLAYERS DOING. MY STRIKER'S BALL ALWAYS SEEMS TO GO TOO FAR."

P ROBLEM: TOO MUCH force from the mallet is finishing with the striker's ball instead of the roqueted ball. The forward movement is not being sufficiently checked. This can be caused by one of the following

(1) Mallet face not square.
(2) Swing not exactly in line through the centres of the two balls.
(3) The method used for stopping the forward movement of the mallet is not working satisfactorily.
(4) Type of mallet.

CORRECTION: (1) and (2) can be checked by observing from the rear, and can easily be corrected by stalking the ball, etc. (3) is more difficult to correct, as perfect timing is needed to achieve a really good stop-shot. It may be that the player is using one hand low on the handle to produce a flat forward jab with the mallet head horizontal. Stop-shots can be played this way, but it is difficult to stop the forward movement instantly, especially with a heavy mallet. Alternatively, he may be using a very light grip and swinging from the wrists only, contacting the striker's ball at the bottom of the swing and allowing the combined weight of the two balls to stop the forward movement. This is also a reasonable way of playing a stop-shot, but again good timing and a light mallet are needed.

Consistently good stop-shots can best be achieved with a very firm grip, lifting the front end of the mallet head ONLY SLIGHTLY and swinging downward. The ball is contacted AFTER the mallet head reaches the bottom of the swing, when it is starting on its way up, and at this instant the hands are moved vertically downward, or backward toward the body, in order to am the rear end of the mallet head onto the ground and 'stop it dead'. The hands should preferably be together, but need not be at the top of the handle.

NOTE: In teaching this shot there may be a danger that the backward movement of the hands could be inadvertently transferred to other shots, e.g. the rush, in which the front of the mallet head is also slightly raised, with disastrous results.

(4) If the player has a mallet with a very springy handle (e.g. cane or metal) then he may have to accept the fact that it will not be possible to play stop-shots with it as consistently well as another player with a more rigid handle. A light head on the mallet can help counteract the effect of a springy handle, so that good stop-shots are still possible; but a heavy head will make them even more difficult.

SECTION E—THE ROLL

12. "I CAN'T DO A PROPER ROLL OR PASS-ROLL. THE CROQUETED BALL GOES TOO FAR, OR ELSE THE STRIKER'S BALL DOES NOT GO FAR ENOUGH."

PROBLEM: THERE ARE three possibilities

(1) At the moment of impact the mallet handle may not be sloping sufficiently forward. It is possible that the player is starting the swing with the handle sloping forward correctly, but during the swing the top hand is moving backward toward the body, so that by the time the ball is contacted the handle is almost vertical.

(2) The player may be hitting forward along the ground at the ball, instead of using a downward swing to contact the striker's ball high up (the mallet head should be about an inch above the ground at time of contact) and 'squeeze' the striker's ball forward with the forward-sloping mallet face.

(3) Equal-rolls and pass-rolls require some degree of smooth acceleration during the swing, with a pronounced follow-through. The player may be failing to achieve this acceleration, or mistiming it.

CORRECTION: Observe from the side to see which of the problems is in evidence, then correct as follows

(1) Change the swing so that both hands, and particularly the top hand, are moving forward. This makes it into a sort of forward push rather than a swing, in which the mallet is translated (i.e. moved forward with the forward slope of the handle being maintained) rather than rotated in a pendulum-like swing as for most other shots. Practise many times without a ball. Start with the mallet held out away from the body, and the handle sloping forward as desired, with elbows straight. Draw the mallet back toward the body by bending both elbows, maintaining the forward slope. Then push the mallet forwards by straightening both elbows, again keeping the slope constant. This gives an idea of the type of 'swing' needed.

(2) In actual fact, the swing (or better, push) as described in (1) should be directed downward as well as forward, to produce the forward-squeezing effect on the striker's ball.

(3) The acceleration can be learnt by playing the shot several times from a position directly behind a hoop, so that the hoop hampers the backswing.

This forces a very short backswing which automatically results in acceleration during the swing. Then try it without the hoop, still using a very short backswing. Later the backswing can be lengthened, so long as the first part of the forward swing is very (almost painfully) slow. The degree of "pass" in the roll can be controlled by delaying the start of the acceleration to a greater or lesser extent. A firm grip is needed to ensure that the acceleration is smooth through the ball, and no fault is committed. This should all be done without any shoulder movement.

An alternative method is to use a very firm grip and keep the elbows stiff, but not necessarily straight. As the mallet head reaches the ball, swing the hips downwards, allowing your whole body weight to drop onto the ball. This produces a pronounced acceleration at, and just after, the moment of impact, and has the advantage of avoiding (in appearance, at least) the possible "pushing fault" which arises when the acceleration is produced from the elbows just AFTER contact. A disadvantage for some players is that the downward body movement finishes with the player squatting on his haunches, and thus may be physically demanding on muscles and joints.

SECTION F—THE SPLIT

13. "UNLESS I PLAY A TAKE-OFF, I FIND IT VERY HARD TO JUDGE APPROACH SHOTS FROM A YARD OR TWO TO THE SIDE OF THE HOOP. I CANNOT SEEM TO GET A FORWARD RUSH FROM SUCH POSITIONS EXCEPT BY SHEER FLUKE."

PROBLEM: THE PLAYER does not understand the mechanics of split shots, of which approach shots are one particular type. He does not appreciate the effect of mallet slope on the outcome of the shot, nor how to determine the correct slope and line of aim, nor how to adjust the slope for wideness of angle. He probably has been swinging around a curve on such shots, in order to 'shepherd' his striker's ball to the front of the hoop, but thus losing control of the other ball.

CORRECTION: A decision must be made whether to (1) explain and teach the mechanics of ALL split shots, or (2) find ways of simplifying things to enable him to cope with most hoop approaches without worrying about other splits for the time being. After making this decision, proceed in one of the following ways

(1) a. First practise using the forward slope of the mallet to control the relative distances of the two balls in straight croquet shots. Alter the slope as required by moving the hands up or down the handle.

  b. If the angle between the desired directions of the two balls exceeds 40 degrees, adjust the grip by moving the hands upward slightly so that the mallet is moved closer to vertical. If it exceeds 60 degrees, move up a little more, and for 80 degrees move right up to the top.

  c. Find a point on the lawn half-way between where you want the two balls to finish, then move it a little to the side where the striker's ball will go. (This adjustment is necessary because the striker's ball, but not the other ball, is affected by follow-through.) This will give you the correct aiming point, and you should swing the mallet (with correct slope) in a STRAIGHT LINE toward this point.

  d. If both balls fall short or go too far, hit harder or softer. If one goes too far and the other falls short, alter the mallet slope (by changing the hand positions) to change the relative distances. If the angle is too narrow or too wide, change the point of aim.

(2) a. Look at the distance of the roqueted ball from the hoop, and find a point this same distance from the hoop, but directly behind it. Line up the balls so that the roqueted ball will go to this point.

b. Choose a point of aim, which will also be directly behind the hoop. The aiming point is about one third (or perhaps slightly less to allow for 'pull' on the striker's ball) of the way from the hoop to the point where you intend the roqueted ball to finish.

c. Your distance from the hoop also determines the mallet slope needed for the approach shot. As you move back from the hoop, you move your hands down the handle to increase the forward slope of the mallet.

d. With this method everything is determined only from the approach distance. Thus for any approach shot from 3 yards, whether from in front of the hoop, behind it, to the side, or from any other direction, you will line up the roqueted ball to go to the same point 3 yards behind the hoop, aim your swing at the same point 3 feet (or slightly less) behind the hoop, and have the handle sloping forward at the same angle (about 15 degrees from the vertical, making an angle of about 75 degrees with the ground.) Accurate judgement of actual distances is required, but some people find this easier than the judgement of relative distances which is necessary for the accurate control of split-shots in general. Nor is there any need to estimate wideness of angle and allow for it, as this is taken into account in the method as given. In playing the shot the player can concentrate on judging the required strength, which is the only variable remaining.

The method described gives a straightforward and consistent way of approaching a hoop from any distance up to about six yards, and from any direction; and allows a surprisingly large margin of error, so that a slight variation in the position of the aiming point or the mallet slope will not greatly affect the success of the shot.

e. A disadvantage is that the player who learns this method will eventually also need to learn how to adjust the approach shot to give the best chance of obtaining a rush in some direction other than straight ahead after running the hoop, and will soon come to realise that even for a straight ahead rush from some positions improvements could be made. For example, in approaching the hoop from only one yard out, he may do better to aim the roqueted ball MORE than a yard behind the hoop and play an angled stop-shot.

14. "ON SPLIT-SHOTS I CAN USUALLY GET THE STRIKER'S BALL WHERE I WANT IT, BUT I DO NOT SEEM TO HAVE MUCH CONTROL OF THE OTHER BALL. IT USUALLY STOPS WELL SHORT OF WHERE

I WOULD LIKE TO PLACE IT. IN FACT, I NO LONGER TRY TO GET IT RIGHT DOWN TO THE NEXT HOOP."

PROBLEM: The player is probably using a roll action in which the mallet head is moving low along the ground as it approaches the ball and is being accelerated (or 'pushed') forward through the ball. He may also be 'shepherding' his striker's ball by swinging around a curve, and probably does not understand the need to adjust the mallet slope for wide angles. It is understandable that a player who has difficulty controlling split-shots will tend to concentrate on at least getting the striker's ball to the desired place, ignoring the croqueted ball.

CORRECTION: Check for these three errors by watching from the side (for horizontal approach and acceleration) and from behind (for curved swing) as he plays split shots at varying angles. Correct the errors as follows

(1) Explain that most split-shots should be played by hitting down on the striker's ball and contacting it well above centre. The grip should be firm and a semi-stop-shot action should be used, rather than a roll action which involves a much longer follow-through.

(2) Ask him to concentrate on developing as straight a swing as possible, realising that there is no need to 'shepherd' his striker's ball.

(3) Explain the need to alter the position of the hands on the shaft (and consequently the mallet slope) by moving the hands upward as the angle between the directions of the two balls becomes wider. He should practise making his striker's ball travel half (or later two-thirds or three-quarters) as far as the croqueted ball as the angle is gradually increased.

Then, when playing split-shots, he should concentrate on getting the CROQUETED ball exactly where he wants it. Contrary to popular opinion, the positioning of the striker's ball is usually less critical to the continuance of a break than the correct positioning of the croqueted ball. If the croqueted ball is going correctly to the desired place, then it is fairly easy to adjust either the line of aim or the mallet slope to ensure that the striker's ball also finishes close enough its desired place. It is much harder to make the adjustment the other way round.

15. "I CAN CONTROL SPLITS FAIRLY WELL IF THE ANGLE IS NOT TOO WIDE, BUT I AVOID A SPLIT IF THE ANGLE EXCEEDS 45 DEGREES, AS I'M NOT CONFIDENT THE BALLS WILL GO WHERE I WANT THEM TO."

PROBLEM: The player does not realise that the mallet slope must be altered for wider angles. This can be done either by moving the hands up the handle to lessen the forward slope of the mallet face, or by standing further back from the ball to achieve the same effect.

CORRECTION: Check that the player knows the correct hand positions for straight croquet shots, making the striker's ball travel, say, half (or two-thirds or three-quarters, etc) as far as the croqueted ball in the same line. If the foot positioning is not altered, then these hand positions will determine the forward slope of the mallet face for each shot, and should be satisfactory for all split shots where the angle between the directions of the two balls does not exceed 40 degrees.

With an angle wider than 40 degrees the striker's ball will start to slide across the surface of the croqueted ball as it begins to move. This results in less of the force being transferred to the croqueted ball, and more remaining with the striker's ball, so that the striker's ball goes further and the croqueted ball less far than they would in a straight croquet shot played similarly.

To counteract this, it is necessary to lessen the forward slope of the mallet face, which is usually achieved by altering the hand positions. Most players find that they need to move the bottom hand up about two inches if the angle exceeds 40 degrees, a further two inches if it exceeds 60 degrees, and further again if it approaches 80 degrees, by which time both hands should be together near the top of the mallet shaft.

16. "I CANNOT UNDERSTAND WHY I FIND SOME SPLITS, SUCH AS FROM 1-BACK TO 2-BACK AND 3-BACK, EASIER THAN THE MIRROR-IMAGE SHOTS, SUCH AS FROM HOOP 1 TO HOOPS 2 AND 3."

PROBLEM: Either the swing is curved or the handle of the mallet is tilted sideways, causing the striker's ball to come off one side of the mallet differently from the way it would come off the other side.

CORRECTION: Both of these errors would become evident when the shot is viewed from behind. The curved swing is best corrected by changing it to a forward push with both hands moving toward a carefully selected aiming point. The sideways tilt may result from the player endeavouring not to hit himself in the nose or face with the handle of the mallet during the swing, since he will be bent well over for these long split rolls. Here again it will help to develop more of a forward pushing action rather than a pendulum-type swing for these shots; or if he still wants to use a pendulum swing then he should keep his elbows straighter so that the mallet handle is further out in front his body and away from his face.

SECTION G—HOOP RUNNING

17. "I TEND TO STICK IN HOOPS ON ANY SHOT WHICH IS AT ALL SIDEY."

PROBLEM: THERE ARE three possibilities

(1) The player is lifting his eyes (and with them probably his head and shoulders) to look at the hoop during the swing, instead of keeping his attention focused on the point where he wants the mallet to contact the ball.

(2) He is not lining the shot up correctly. Some players fail to realise that you do not aim at the centre of the hoop when running it from a sidey angle.

(3) He is not imparting to the ball the forward spin needed to 'kick' it through the hoop after it contacts the hoop leg.

CORRECTION: After checking to see which of these is the main problem, proceed as follows:

(1) Since the eye-lifting and shoulder movement is usually caused by nervousness, the player needs to consciously relax his shoulders and arms before starting the swing. Then he should take a slightly longer backswing and let the weight of the mallet swing through without any push from the hands. He should keep his eyes fixed on the back of the ball and keep his shoulders still during the swing.

(2) As the hoop shot becomes more sidey the point of aim moves from the centre of the hoop toward the far leg. Players realise that the side of the ball must miss the near leg, but focusing attention on the near leg is unwise, since it is not in the desired line of aim. For a very sidey hoop shot (about 45 degrees) the line of aim should pass through the centre of the ball to the inside edge of the far hoop leg. If the shot is less sidey, the aim can be a little inside the far hoop leg and closer to the centre of the hoop. It should be noted that a sidey hoop shot needs to be hit more firmly than one from the same distance directly in front, to allow for the loss of forward momentum when the ball contacts the far hoop leg.

(3) It is a mistake to try to run a hoop by bringing the mallet head horizontally along the ground at the ball. This type of flat forward push with the mallet handle vertical will give little or no forward spin to the ball. Instead it will cause the ball to skid without rolling for the first foot or so, and it will

only just be starting to roll as it reaches the hoop. (Note that this skidding is desirable in a rush, but is the opposite of what you want in a hoop shot, because a skidding ball will tend to 'stop dead' if it makes any contact with the hoop.)

For hoop running a pendulum-swing from the SHOULDERS is needed, with the mallet sloping slightly forward and hitting slightly down on the ball. The hands must move forward, not backward, and the forward slope of the mallet should be only slight—just sufficient to press the ball lightly onto the ground as it begins moving. This causes the bottom of the ball to be held momentarily against the ground as the top of the ball starts to move forward, producing an immediate rolling motion or 'forward spin' instead of the ball skidding. Although it is not necessary to do so, some players accentuate the forward spin by lifting the mallet so that the head is about an inch above ground level when it contacts the ball, hitting through the top part of the ball. Care must be taken, however, to avoid hitting the ball with the bottom bevelled edge of the mallet face, as this would produce a misdirected mis-hit.

If the hoop shot is played from more than three or four feet out then there is less need to try to produce forward spin on the ball, since by the time it has travelled this far it should have stopped skidding and develop sufficient forward rolling motion. Thus for longer hoop shots the flat forward swing may be quite satisfactory, and direction rather than spin becomes the main consideration.

On all hoop shots the mallet head should follow through well past the point of contact. Players who use a stop-shot action for hoop running will find the ball sticking in the hoop not only on sidey hoop-shots, but on hoop-shots from straight in front as well.

18. "I CAN RUN HOOPS EASILY ENOUGH AT PRACTICE, BUT IN A MATCH THE BALL JUST WON'T SEEM TO GO THROUGH."

PROBLEM: The player's technique is adequate, but in a match his timing is affected by nervous tension.

CORRECTION: There are many things that can be done to reduce nervous tension, and ways of playing the first part of a game which take into account the need to avoid difficult shots until the player has started to relax a little. Such things are not within the scope of these notes, but we will mention a few things that can be done to make it less likely that nervousness will disastrously affect a hoop shot.

It should be realised that regardless of appearances almost all players are nervous when playing a game of any importance. It is necessary to accept the fact that some nervousness is unavoidable, and find ways to still play reasonably good shots. Some of the following advice may help

(1) Allow time for the tension of the previous shot to drain away before attempting the hoop. If you have just made an eminently missable six-yard roquet, or played a difficult hoop approach, your adrenalin level will be high for a short while and your heart will beat faster. This will affect your timing, as your body (according to one theory which seems reasonable) takes its timing unconsciously from the heartbeat.

(2) Even allowing such time, some tension will remain and the heart will still probably be beating faster than normal. This tends to make the player hurry the swing by taking a shorter than normal backswing and 'snatching' or jabbing at the shot instead of using a smooth pendulum swing from the shoulders. To help counteract this, the player should consciously take a longer backswing with shoulders relaxed (not hunched up).

(3) If the player's hands are shaking it is possible to lessen their effect on the shot by gripping the mallet more lightly (the natural tendency when nervous is to grip it more tightly, which transfers the shaking directly to the mallet head) with the hands closer together, preferably interlocking or overlapping. Some players find that a shorter grip, with both hands moved down the handle, also helps.

(4) Before swinging, check that the stance is comfortable (toes relaxed, etc.) and stable. During the swing, concentrate on keeping the shoulders still and avoiding all body movement.

19. "I KEEP RUNNING MUCH TOO FAR THROUGH HOOPS, GIVING MYSELF A LONG ROQUET BACK."

PROBLEM: Obviously, the player is imparting too much force to the ball.

CORRECTION: This can be a real difficulty for some players, and although the problem is obvious the solution is not. It is unlikely to help if the player simply tries to hit more gently on hoop shots. There are several things that can be tried

(1) Play the hoop approach differently, so that the striker's ball finishes closer to the hoop and the croqueted ball further behind the hoop. A player who consistently runs hoops from three or four feet in front should not complain

about going too far through, as he is fortunate to consistently run them at all from such distances. It may also be necessary to concentrate on getting the previous rush shot to a better position, so that the different type of approach shot is facilitated.

(2) When it is important to run no more than two or three feet past a hoop on the hoop shot in order to obtain a desired rush, some players find it helpful to shorten their grip on the mallet by moving both hands well down the handle. This seems to allow more delicate control of distance, but the effect on direction also needs to be considered, as the hoop-running may be jeopardised if it becomes more difficult to swing in a straight line.

(3) The force imparted to the ball can be lessened by shortening the backswing, but this cannot be recommended as it is more difficult to establish that the mallet is moving in the correct line, and the timing is also affected. It is better to retain the length of the backswing but slow down the forward swing. A lighter grip with the hands can also help, and some players slope the mallet further forward on such shots, hitting more down on the ball so that more of the force goes into the ground.

(4) It is possible that the player is playing hoop shots with the mallet handle vertical, using a flat, low swing which will not produce any forward spin on the ball. For this reason he may feel he needs to hit them harder to ensure that they still go through after contacting a hoop leg. However, if the ball does not contact the hoop on the way through it will run much too far.

20. "NO MATTER HOW HARD I TRY, I CANNOT PLAY A JUMP SHOT THROUGH A HOOP. THE BALL JUST WON'T JUMP FOR ME."

PROBLEM: The mallet handle is not sloping forward sufficiently at moment of contact.

CORRECTION: Stand further forward and lock the wrists. Swing from the shoulders without moving the shoulders. Do not consciously try to hit down on the ball (if the contact is made before the mallet head reaches the bottom of the swing this will happen automatically). Play the shot confidently, not tentatively, contacting the ball well above centre. Keep your eye on the exact spot on the ball where you want the mallet to contact it, and give it a decent whack, as most of the force will be absorbed into the ground. Do not try to play it as a stop-shot, as it is important to let the whole weight of the mallet-head go right through the ball. Some control of follow-through is needed, however, in order to avoid committing a fault by damaging the lawn.

In some cases the lawn itself may be the problem. It is almost impossible to make a ball jump on sandy, spongy or soggy lawns.

As with other shots, the jump shot should be played with the weight of the mallet, without any additional push from the hands or wrists. This is important because direction is critical. There is normally little or no margin for error, and any push from the hands is likely to take the swing off line.

SECTION H

THE BREAK

21. "I PLAY SEVERAL GOOD SHOTS TO GET A BREAK STARTED, THEN WHEN I HAVE ALL THE BALLS SET UP WHERE I WANT THEM, I DO SOMETHING STUPID LIKE STICKING IN AN EASY HOOP OR MISSING A SHORT ROQUET."

PROBLEM: THE PLAYER is relaxing mentally as well as physically. There is a strong natural tendency to do this. In croquet physical relaxation is important, but mental relaxation can be dangerous.

CORRECTION: Be aware of the danger. The mental relaxation ("it should be easier from now on") can lead to failure to check all of the things necessary to ensure the success of the next shot. For example, the player may fail to check the squareness of the mallet face before playing a three-yard roquet, whereas on the previous more difficult shots he would have taken great care to check everything. He should develop the habit of taking the time to check EVERYTHING (body alignment, stalking, stance, grip, squareness, line of aim, shoulders still, etc.) before playing EVERY shot, even a gentle six-inch roquet. This is not because there is any likelihood of missing the six-inch roquet if he fails to check everything, but in order to develop an ingrained and automatic habit of getting it all correct, so that he is not so likely to inadvertently omit something when his mind is suddenly relaxed or distracted. In effect, he is using the six-inch roquet to practise for future shots.

ADDENDUM

S INCE THIS BOOKLET was first written, important advances have been made in various areas of croquet coaching. In recent years the SACA and ACA Coaching Committees have adopted what is known as the "DRAMA" error-correction programme, which is set out in summary form on the following page.

I have decided to add it to this booklet so that readers can gain an understanding of all that is involved in the very difficult process of correcting errors of technique. The material we have covered here deals only with points 2 and 3 of the error correction programme, i.e. the recognition of the error and the alteration of technique that is needed to correct it. Even in these areas there is much more that coaches, particularly those involved in higher levels of coaching, need to know.

It is important that we lay to rest for all time the old idea that coaching involves simply telling a player what he is doing wrong. That in itself is difficult enough, but even if done correctly it is no better than a doctor who diagnoses your illness but makes no attempt to treat it.

A good coach will realise that the correction of errors involves aspects such as determination, organisation and psychology; and the player will need help in each of these areas. Most errors are only corrected over a period of time, with repeated involvement of the coach and continuing commitment by the player.

The final stage, in which the new technique is successfully assimilated into game situations under pressure, is often neglected by coaches, and consequently the player will tend at those times to revert to his old error-prone technique.

There is no room here to explain in full each of the stages in the summarised programme. That should be part of the training programme for accredited coaches, and at higher levels of training will be covered in even greater detail.

One point that is worth making here is that a serious competitive player will never reach the stage where he no longer needs the services of a good coach. On the contrary, the stronger he becomes, the more vital it is that he has regular coaching sessions with a personal coach in whom he has complete confidence. The reader will no doubt be aware that in most other sports (e.g. tennis, golf, etc.) the leading players all have their personal coaches who usually travel with them, providing both technical and psychological assistance on a daily basis. It is also worth noting that in almost all cases the coach cannot play anywhere near as well as the player can. Croquet has a long way to go in accepting this attitude toward coaching.

The author, at the time of writing this addendum, is currently ranked no. 2 player in Australia on the official ACA player ranking list. I would never have achieved this position without the assistance of my coach Jane Lewis, who is currently the ACA National Coaching Director, and whom I pay to coach me on a regular basis.

I cannot watch myself, and so am often unaware of the small errors that may start to creep into my technique. The coach is able to recognise such errors long before I would realise that I have a problem, and at such an early stage the errors are usually easily corrected because they have not become an ingrained habit.

I recommend that coaches study the error correction programme, and for further assistance in implementing it I suggest that they approach their state coaching committee personnel. If this is impractical, then I would welcome correspondence and will be interested in trying to assist with any particular problems.

John Riches
26 Bowman Crescent
Enfield SA 5085
Phone: (08) 262 3657

CROQUET

TECHNIQUE

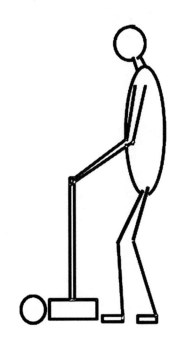

CONTENTS

INTRODUCTION

1. In the notes on croquet technique which follow, it is assumed that the player will be of medium height and build, and uses the centre style with a standard grip. An experienced coach dealing with a particular individual may well decide to vary some of the advice given here, though almost all of it will prove sound for any player, regardless of stature, style or grip.

2. No mention is made of the need to make adjustments for different types of balls. A learner should keep to one type of ball only.

3. It is hoped that these notes will prove useful not only to beginners, but also to coaches, and especially to experienced players wishing to correct some flaw or improve some weakness in their game.

    It is often difficult to find out exactly why a shot is not consistently producing the desired result, as you cannot easily observe yourself in action. A good coach who understands clearly the correct technique will be of inestimable help, but if you do not have access to such a person, a thoughtful perusal of these notes may at least prove second best.

4. If you have a shot which you wish to improve, you may discover on reading these notes that your technique is not as recommended here. You may have developed a reasonable alternative, or you may have developed bad habits which unless eradicated will prevent you from making any progress. The decision whether to change or not may not be an easy one; but if you do decide to make a change, do not look for an immediate and dramatic improvement. You should not expect to do as well with a good technique you have not practised as you were doing with a bad technique you have practised for years.

5. Unfortunately there are no illustrations accompanying these notes at the present time, as the author ('collator' would be a better term, as nothing here is original) is notoriously inartistic.

6. All basic shots are covered, but more advanced shots such as cannons, jump-shots, hammer shots, etc., are beyond the scope of these notes.

7. Strategy and tactics are also not mentioned, though they may be more important to the development of a player than technique. The notes will explain how to play a particular shot, but will not tell you which shot to play.

8. The purpose of this booklet is to fill what is seen as a void. There are croquet books available with much excellent information about how to play various shots, but none give in any comprehensive way the REASONS for doing things the way they recommend. Here you will find not only

the latest technique fully detailed, but also the REASONS explained at length—perhaps too much length for the beginner to fully comprehend—so that both coach and player can return to it again and again, and can make sound judgements about the value of alternative methods.

9. While these notes are believed to convey the latest and best techniques currently being used and taught, it is recognised that many players use alternatives which may be as good or almost as good.

10. New techniques are constantly being developed (or at least they should be) and evaluated. This booklet does not represent the last word on the subject by any stretch of the imagination.

John Riches and Wayne Davies

THE ROQUET

1. "Stalk" the ball by walking in along the exact line in which you will want the ball to travel, with hips and shoulders square to this line. Always do this, even for the shortest and easiest of shots.
2. Take a firm but comfortable grip on the mallet handle before beginning to move forward. Try not to move the hands up or down the handle from now on.
3. Walk forward toward the ball steadily and purposefully, with your eyes on the line of aim to ensure that you maintain the 'squareness' of your body.
4. If anything distracts you, start again.
5. Place your feet in the correct position. This will vary according to your style, height, grip, mallet, etc.; but you will need to know quite clearly the correct foot placement for your particular stance, so that you can achieve consistency of foot placement. Many (right-handed) players find it best to place the left foot about 4 inches (10 cm) from the line of aim, and 6 inches (15 cm) back from the ball, so that the toe is level with (or just behind) the handle of the mallet at the moment of impact. For most players this foot should be pointing in a direction exactly parallel to the line of aim. This provides a further check on squareness and consistency of stance. The position of the right foot is less critical. It need not be pointing parallel to the line of aim, but should simply be placed in any comfortable position out of the way of the backswing, so that 'body squareness' and balance can be maintained during the swing.
6. Next, test the 'squareness' of the mallet face to the line of aim by making a few practice swings above or behind the ball without hitting it. Concentrate on keeping your shoulders still during this, and if the face of the mallet is not 'square', correct it by re-aligning your body (feet, hips, shoulders) or by turning the mallet in your hands, but NOT by merely turning the mallet head while maintaining the same grip and stance. Do not place the mallet head on the ground at any time, as this makes it harder to maintain the alignment of the mallet.
7. Fix your eyes on the exact point where you want the mallet face to contact the back of the ball, and concentrate on making a SLOW, REASONABLY LONG backswing. The length of the backswing will depend on the desired strength of the shot i.e. how far you want the ball to go.
8. Allow the mallet to swing smoothly forward to hit the ball, again concentrating on keeping your shoulders still and watching the contact point on the ball.

There should be NO PUSH WHATEVER imparted to the mallet during the forward swing. Rather, it should feel as if you are merely GUIDING the forward movement of the weight in the mallet head, or even slightly PULLING it forward. The arms should swing freely from the shoulders so that the hands move FORWARDS throughout the swing, and until the instant of contact they should be slightly forward of the mallet head (hence the slight 'pulling' feel).

If you have a tendency to push (or worse still, 'jab') during the forward swing, the first thing to do is try taking a longer but slower backswing, and eliminate any shoulder movement.

Most players find (eventually) that they do better with the hands close together (or even interlocking as in golf) on the handle of the mallet, rather than having them apart, as the placing of the lower hand further down the handle usually results in pushing instead of pulling the weight of the mallet during the forward swing.

Your wrists should be kept firm, but not locked tight during the swing—a small degree of flexibility is desirable. Your stance should not be too cramped or crouched. A more upright stance usually allows a freer, straighter swing.

9.   The follow-through should be directly along the line of aim, and also as low as possible along the ground. Try not to lift the mallet head upwards before you are forced to do so because your arms will not reach any further forward.

10. It is vital to ensure that your grip tension is not changed during the swing. Many players, especially when nervous, increase the tension by squeezing the handle just before the mallet contacts the ball. This will usually tend to destroy the alignment of the mallet head. (You can test this by holding the mallet still and tightening your grip.) The best way to avoid this is to feel the tension in your finger-tips, rather than the palms of your hands, before commencing the swing. Then you can feel any change more easily because the finger-tips are more sensitive than the palms.

11. *EXPLANATION:*
     Many players fail to understand the importance of slightly pulling, rather than pushing, the mallet forwards. If you wish to appreciate the reason for this, take one end of a broom handle and try to PUSH the far end along a straight line. Then see how much easier it is to PULL it along the line. You may also like to consider why a horse pulls a cart rather than pushing it; why it is easier to maintain a straight line by pulling a wheelbarrow rather than pushing it; and why the rear wheel of a bicycle follows a straighter path than the front wheel during a 'slalom-type' manoeuvre.

12. **COACHING HINT:**

In order to learn the correct type of straight swing, it can be very helpful to practise playing short roquets and hoops using one hand only. Use your TOP hand on the shaft, with the bottom hand completely removed. This will force you to take a long backswing and move the top hand FORWARD throughout the swing, pulling the mallet-head forward rather than pushing it. You will also need to watch the ball closely and avoid all other body movement, or you are likely to miss the ball altogether. You should soon learn to control the movement of the one hand adequately and time the swing correctly; and you will probably be surprised at how well you can play one-handed roquets. Then the lower hand can be used as a steadying influence only, without imparting any additional force.

At the start of a game it can also be useful to try a few one-handed practice swings in order to get the correct timing. This hint applies especially to players who use the 'Irish' grip; but all centre-style players will find it helpful.

THE HOOP SHOT

THE REQUIRED TECHNIQUE is almost identical to the roquet, with the following additional considerations:

1. It is best to stand slightly further forward than for a roquet. This ensures that the ball is hit slightly downwards, as the mallet has not quite reached the bottom of its swing. The effect of this is that the ball is pressed lightly into the lawn surface, increasing friction on the bottom of the ball. Thus the bottom of the ball is held in check against the ground, while the top starts moving forward. This gives the ball a top-spin (or forward spin) which will tend to carry it on through the hoop if it touches the sides.

2. Hoop shots should not be hit harder than necessary to ensure that the ball passes through the hoop and finishes a yard or two clear on the other side. A slow backswing is essential, followed by a gentle forward swing without any semblance of a push in it. The follow-through should be forwards along the ground, as if you are putting the mallet head gently through the hoop, or would do so if your arms were long enough. You should feel that you are SWEEPING the ball gently through the hoop. Do not look at the hoop during the swing. Keep your eyes on the point where the mallet has contacted the ball, and keep your shoulders still.

3. For a hoop shot from directly in front of the hoop, give additional attention to lining up the exact centre of the ball and the exact centre of the hoop, ensuring that the mallet face is perfectly 'square' to this line of aim at all times. Do not be satisfied to merely hit the ball in the general direction of the hoop and hope that it goes through.

4. For a 'sidey' or angled hoop shot you can no longer aim at the centre of the hoop, but neither should you try, as some suggest, to make the edge of the ball miss the near leg of the hoop. You need instead to concentrate on hitting the CENTRE of the ball where you want THAT to go.

   Try aiming the centre of the ball just inside the far leg of the hoop, a little more or less inside depending on the angle at which you are running the hoop. Concentrate on this alone, and follow through 'along the ground' exactly in this line. Keep your shoulders absolutely still throughout. Angled hoop shots need to be hit slightly more firmly than shots from a similar distance directly in front, as the contact with the hoop will take a larger proportion of speed from the ball.

   With sidey hoops it is even more important to ensure that the ball is given a forward spin by hitting slightly down on it in the manner described above. A ball hit with a flat forward 'push' will tend to skid rather than roll for the first foot or so. This means that it will usually only just be starting to roll when it reaches the hoop, and may not have sufficient forward spin to carry it on through the hoop. For long hoops (more than 3 feet out) the ball will have stopped skidding and gained sufficient rolling motion regardless of how it is hit, so a flat swing should be satisfactory.

5.   As with the roquet, it is important not to increase grip tension by squeezing the mallet handle during the swing.

THE TAKE-OFF

1. For a long take-off to, say, a border ball, allow for the ball to 'pull' inwards by lining up the V about one yard to the right of the ball you are going to (assuming that you are taking off from the right hand side of the ball you had roqueted).

    Aim your swing, however, a yard to the left of the ball you are going to. That is, after lining up the V, forget all about the ball you had roqueted and play the shot as if you are attempting to hit a single ball to a spot one yard left of the target ball.

2. If you are taking off from the left hand side of the ball you have roqueted, then line up the V a yard to the LEFT of the target ball and aim a yard to its RIGHT.

3. In many cases you may not wish to aim your take-off directly at the target ball. For example, you may wish to obtain a rush on it to a hoop or to another ball; or if it is on a side border you may decide to aim your take-off a yard or two further in court to reduce the risk of going out over the boundary. In each case, line up the V about one yard to the right (or left) of the point WHERE YOU WANT YOUR BALL TO FINISH, and then aim the swing one yard the other side. The roqueted ball should move about a yard if you play the take-off in this manner, but this distance is usually not of any great importance, as long as it does move. For a shorter take-off the one yard allowance can be reduced.

4. As in other shots, a square mallet face (to the line of swing, NOT to the direction in which the V is pointing) is important. Do NOT turn your mallet face in towards the roqueted ball "to make sure it moves", as this makes it harder to judge the strength of the shot, and also harder to control the place where the roqueted ball will finish, which is sometimes quite important.

5. For a take-off from a corner spot to the diagonally opposite corner, line up the V as exactly as you can, but only about one FOOT to the right (or left) of the place where you want the striker's ball to finish. and take great care to hit your ball directly at a point one FOOT to the other side of the desired finishing point.

    The reason for only allowing a foot, instead of a yard, over such a long distance is to reduce the risk of the ball you are taking off going out over the boundary. It should move about one foot only, if the shot is correctly played in the described manner. It normally will not matter if your striker's ball 'pulls' more than the allowed foot, as you would hardly be trying to obtain a rush.

6. It is important that you learn to take off from either side of a roqueted ball with equal confidence. When taking off from your partner ball to go and use the opponent's balls you should try to leave your partner ball in such a place that you can easily obtain a useful rush for your next turn if you have to come back to it without having made any hoops.

7. All take-offs should be played with a follow-through action, allowing the mallet-head to swing through freely. The distance your ball travels can then be controlled very accurately by raising the mallet-head to a particular point on the backswing. It is not recommended to play normal take-offs with a stop-shot action, as this introduces an element of timing which needs additional control, and also may cause the ball to 'pull' in the wrong direction, curving outward rather than inward.

THE RUSH

T HE RUSH IS similar to a firm roquet shot, with the following additional considerations:

1. Before playing any rush, check whether one or both of the balls is lying in a small hole on the lawn. If so, the desired rush may be very difficult or even impossible. If your (striker's) ball is in the hole, it is quite likely to jump right over the ball you wish to rush if you hit with sufficient force to achieve the intended result.

2. Stand a little further back than for a roquet shot, and slightly raise the front mallet face. Both of these adjustments are designed to ensure, even if the swing is slightly mis-timed, that when the mallet head contacts the ball it is either travelling horizontally or has just begun to swing upward.

    It is essential to avoid any tendency to hit downward on the ball, as this can cause the ball to jump. Even a slight jump can cause your ball to hit above centre on the ball you are attempting to rush, losing some of the forward force of the shot. If you are attempting a fine cut-rush, a slight jump may result in a complete miss.

    Some players move both hands down the handle a little and take a very firm grip, with wrists locked. This allows a simple pendulum swing from the shoulders, which must be kept absolutely still. The intention of this method is to eliminate the 'slight pulling' effect when the hands move forward ahead of the mallet head as described in the normal roquet shot. (The raising of the front mallet face has changed the wrist position, and hence changed the timing of the 'slight pull', so perhaps the shorter grip also lessens the complications involved in correctly timing the different shots.)

    By doing this, they sacrifice a little accuracy of direction, which may not be so critical in a close rush, in order to further ensure that the ball does not jump. As suggested, the element of timing (and hence the possibility of mis-timing) in the shot is reduced, but the amount of force which must be imparted by the arms is increased, because the weight in the head of the mallet does less of the work.

3. When playing a straight rush, concentrate on swinging along the exact line of centres of the two balls. Again it is important to keep the mallet face square to the line of swing, as even a slight inaccuracy will result in a large error in the rush. In fact, an inaccuracy which would cause the striker's

ball (in a single ball stroke) to miss a hoop by only a few centimetres can cause the rushed ball to finish several yards from the desired hoop.

4. Take a longer backswing than you would if you were hitting a single ball the same distance, and let the mallet 'flow' forward. There is usually a great temptation to PUSH the mallet forwards because you are conscious of the weight of the second ball to be moved; but this temptation must be resisted if consistently good results are to be achieved. If additional force is required (for example, to rush right across a heavy lawn), this should also be achieved by taking a longer and higher backswing, rather than by trying to impart it with the wrists and forearms.

5. There is also a strong temptation during the swing to look at the ball you are attempting to rush, instead of keeping your eyes fixed on the place where your mallet will contact your striker's ball. This leads to shoulder movement, which can be disastrous.

6. If you have a tendency to hit the ground with your mallet on this (or any other) shot, it is because of head and shoulder movement dipping downwards during the swing, in an effort to impart greater force. With correct timing, long backswing and a firm grip, it is quite unnecessary to use any 'push' or body movement to rush a ball right across even the heaviest lawn.

7. The follow-through must be, as always, forwards along the ground. This is of even greater importance in a rush than in other shots, as it helps flatten out the bottom of the swing, ensuring that maximum force from the mallet is imparted to the ball.

8. If you are also 'cutting' the ball you are going to rush, you will need to judge the exact direction in which to hit the CENTRE of your striker's ball in order to cut the rushed ball at the desired angle.

   For a normal rush it may be worth remembering that by aiming the centre of your ball at, say, the right hand edge of the ball you are rushing, you can achieve a cut to the left at an angle of approximately 30 degrees from the line of aim, but 15% of the force is lost on impact of one ball on the other.

   This loss of force is the reason why most cut-rushes are not hit hard enough, and (if the desired direction is achieved) they tend to fall short of the desired finishing point. A cut-rush needs to be hit appreciably harder than you would hit a single ball to make it travel the same distance. The finer the cut, the more force is lost, and the harder you need to hit.

THE DRIVE

APART FROM THE take-off, in which the movement of the roqueted ball is more or less incidental, this is the first of the croquet (2-ball) shots in which the movement of both balls requires careful and accurate control.

1. Place your striker's ball against the ball you have roqueted, with the line of centres pointing exactly at the point to which you wish to drive the roqueted ball.

2. Use the same grip and stance as for a roquet, and play the shot in the same way. The direction of swing should be along the line of the desired drive, with the mallet contacting the ball at the bottom of the swing. The grip should be firm enough to ensure a smooth follow-through, in spite of the opposing weight of two balls, rather than one.

3. In order to drive the roqueted ball to a specified point, you will need to hit slightly harder than if you were hitting a single ball the same distance.

4. If the drive is correctly played, the roqueted ball should travel to the desired place, with the striker's ball following behind in the same line but travelling only one-quarter to one-third as far as the roqueted ball. The exact fraction will depend on the weight of the mallet and other factors such as firmness of grip, timing, and follow-through. Most players have little difficulty in achieving reasonably consistent results, as this is the most natural and easiest of croquet shots. For this reason it is common for a player making a break to deliberately set up a drive by playing the previous rush shot to a carefully selected position.

THE STOP-SHOT

THIS IS SIMILAR in appearance to the drive, but is played quite differently, in order to make the striker's ball stop short of the place it would travel to in a drive.

1. Place your striker's ball against the roqueted ball, as for a drive, with the line of centres pointing to the place where you want the roqueted ball to finish.
2. Stand slightly further back from your ball than you would for a drive or roquet, and raise the front face of the mallet slightly (about 1 cm). This is done, as in the rush shot, to ensure that you do NOT hit downward on the striker's ball and give it topspin or cause it to jump.
3. It is important to check that both your stance and your mallet face are 'square' to the line of swing, so that the maximum force is transmitted to the roqueted ball rather than the striker's ball.
4. The most important and distinctive feature of the stop-shot is that there should be NO FOLLOW-THROUGH at all, or as little as possible. This requires exact timing, and is far more difficult to achieve than it sounds. Very few players can play good stop-shots consistently. With practice you should be able to have the striker's ball travel no further than one-sixth, one-eighth, or even one-tenth as far as the roqueted ball.
5. The mallet itself can be an important factor in determining the fraction achievable in a stop-shot. A heavier mallet, springy handle, and 'soft' mallet face (e.g. wood, as compared with the harder bakelite plastic) all make it harder to play sharp stop-shots, though they may have advantages in some other shots.
6. The backswing should not be shortened for a stop-shot, but players use various methods of trying to achieve the required minimum follow-through:

    (a) Some achieve reasonable results by releasing (or relaxing) their grip on the mallet at about the instant of contact.
    (b) Some try to keep the hands still so that the arms do not swing from the shoulders. With both hands at the top of the handle, they use the wrists to swing the mallet fairly loosely from the hands.
    (c) Some keep a firm grip throughout, often with one hand part-way down the handle, and concentrate on achieving a sharp, flat forward 'jab' which ends at the point of contact between mallet and ball.

(d) Perhaps the best method, but a difficult one to master, is to move both hands well DOWN the handle, take a very tight grip, and jab the mallet firmly downward (still keeping the front mallet face raised slightly) so that it will contact the ground immediately after contacting the ball. This contact of the back of the mallet on the ground checks the forward movement of the mallet, preventing any further followthrough.

Players who manage to combine this method with a rapid BACKWARD movement of the hands just before the instant of contact (in order to jam the back of the mallet very firmly into the ground) seem able to achieve remarkable results with a fair degree of consistency.

Coaches should note that this backward movement of the hands should only be taught after careful consideration, since it can have disastrous results if transferred inadvertently into the swing used for other shots.

It is also important to be aware of the fact that different types of ball will allow quite different results which are very noticeable in the stop-shot. A harder, more elastic ball will allow a much more effective stop-shot.

THE HALF-ROLL

THIS SHOT IS also similar to the drive, but the intention is to send the striker's ball half as far as the roqueted ball. The differences are as follows:

1. Again place your striker's ball against the roqueted ball with the line of centres pointing in the direction in which you want both balls to travel.

2. Stand further forward over the balls, with your front toe level with the back of your striker's ball, and move your bottom hand down the handle. The position of the hands will vary for different players and different mallets, but you need to know the exact position that gives you the desired result. Most players place the bottom hand almost half-way down the handle for this shot, leaving the other hand at the top.

   This stance and grip should enable you to hit DOWNWARD on the striker's ball (rather than forward along the ground at it), striking it somewhat above centre.

3. During the shot the handle of the mallet should be sloping forward, making an angle of about 75 degrees with the ground. This causes the striker's ball to be squeezed forward, so that it travels further than in a drive.

4. It is most important that the forward slope of the mallet handle (and consequently the mallet face) should be MAINTAINED throughout the swing; and for this to happen both hands must move FORWARD at the SAME RATE.

5. The grip needs to be firm, with the mallet head following through the ball and onto the ground.

6. The head and shoulders must be kept still throughout the swing. There is a strong temptation to stand up as the mallet contacts the ball, but this alters the slope of the mallet and so the desired result is not achieved.

7. Long or short half-rolls are played in this same manner, but for long shots it is harder to keep the shoulders still and maintain the angle of mallet slope, as a longer backswing with more force is required.

THE THREE-QUARTER ROLL

T HIS IS AGAIN similar to the drive and half-roll, except that the striker's ball is to travel three-quarters as far as the roqueted ball.

1. Place the balls as for the half-roll, and use the same stance, placing your front foot level with the back of the ball.
2. Move your lower hand further down the shaft, until it is almost two-thirds of the way down (i.e. one-third of the way up from the bottom). The top hand will probably no longer feel comfortable at the top of the handle, and may also be moved a little down the shaft.
3. This change of hand position should produce a greater forward slope of the mallet handle, until it makes an angle with the ground of approximately 60 degrees.
4. The other aspects (firmness of grip, maintenance of slope, still shoulders, followthrough) are as for the half-roll; but the greater forward slope of the mallet will produce a more pronounced squeezing effect to send the striker's ball further forward.
5. Adjustments can be made to both the three-quarter roll and the half-roll by moving the hands slightly up or down the handle, giving a slight change in mallet slope, and causing the striker's ball to travel, say, just over half or just under three-quarters as far as the roqueted ball.
6. It should be obvious that if the roqueted ball is to travel the same distance as in a half-roll while the striker's ball travels further, the three-quarter roll will need to be hit slightly harder. Some players experience difficulty with long three-quarter rolls on a heavy lawn, but if a maximum backswing is used and the arms are swung confidently from the shoulders so that the full force of the mallet goes into the ball, any player should be capable of playing the shot quite easily.
7. Some players use a different technique for this shot, involving a forward push through the bottom of the shot rather than trying to maintain the pronounced forward slope of the mallet. This method sometimes gives rise to doubts concerning the legality of the shot, but should be regarded as legal provided that it is played with a single, smooth swing, rather than allowing the forward movement of the mallet to be checked on contact with the ball and accelerating the mallet head rapidly after the balls have moved apart. A SMOOTH acceleration throughout the swing, combined with a firm grip to ensure that the mallet is not checked when it contacts the ball, should produce a perfectly legal shot.

Some players tend to start the swing with a loose grip, and suddenly tighten it at the instant of contact. This again is likely to produce a shot of doubtful legality.

All questions of legality aside, this method cannot be recommended, as it introduces an element of timing which the 'forward slope and downward hit' method avoids, and which tends to reduce the achievable degree of consistent accuracy.

If you have a springy mallet handle, however, you may possibly achieve better results with the 'push through the bottom' method. The spring helps overcome any marked checking of the mallet head as it contacts the ball (this may be more apparent than real, as the flexibility allows the handle to continue its forward movement even if the head of the mallet is checked), and also tends to 'throw' the striker's ball forward as the deformation straightens out. The springy handle will also probably make it harder to control the accuracy if you use the recommended method, as the downward force tends to be used up in bending the handle rather than squeezing the ball forward.

8. On a soggy or sandy lawn the recommended method may be impractical, as the downward hit can tend merely to bury the ball in the surface, creating an indentation from which the ball can no longer be squeezed forward satisfactorily. This leaves the 'accelerated push' method as the only viable alternative in such conditions.

9. The downward hit (on a firm surface) will often cause the striker's ball to jump into the air noticeably. This is quite OK, and even desirable, as it means that less of the weight of the roqueted ball is preventing the striker's ball from moving forward.

THE ROLL

T HE FULL ROLL, in which the striker's ball travels the same distance as the roqueted ball, is again similar in some ways to the half-roll and three-quarter roll.

1. Again place your striker's ball against the roqueted ball so that the line of centres points in the direction in which you want both balls to travel.
2. Use the same stance once more, placing your front toe level with the back of the striker's ball.
3. Your lower hand should be placed at least two-thirds of the way down the handle, and your top hand will also need to be moved, to about one-third of the way down the handle.
4. This stance and hand position should produce an angle of approximately 45 degrees between the mallet handle and the ground, and this angle should be maintained to the greatest extent possible during the swing.

    In order to achieve this, most players need to start with their elbows bent, and then straighten them during the swing until both arms are reaching straight out in front.
5. It is also usually necessary, depending on the length of the roll and the speed of the lawn, to incorporate some degree of push and acceleration which, of course, must be smooth and combined with a firm grip in order to avoid suspicions of illegality. This introduces the element of timing which we have tried to avoid in the previous rolls, and thus decreases the consistent accuracy one can expect to achieve. The follow-through should be as long as possible, with the mallet head moving low along the ground.

    To the extent that the shot involves a pushing rather than squeezing action to send the striker's ball forward, it will be necessary to concentrate on swinging forward through the balls rather than downwards; but the mallet should still, as in any roll, contact the ball above centre.
6. Players who have difficulty with this shot are usually standing up markedly as they play the shot. This shoulder movement alters the angle of the mallet handle and prevents both hands from moving forwards at the same rate. They also tend to HIT at the balls rather than SWEEPING the two balls forward.

    The remedy is to keep your shoulders still (get someone to put a hand firmly on the back of your shoulders and physically prevent them from moving upwards), and to overcome the 'hitting rather than sweeping' tendency, try using a shorter backswing. If you find it hard to actually shorten the backswing, practise playing the roll from a position just behind a hoop, so that the backswing is hampered by the hoop.

7. Long rolls require considerable force, in order to move two balls (a total of 6 lb in weight) over a distance of up to 30 yards, and for this reason it is important that both arms swing freely forwards from still shoulders, with a firm grip and eyes fixed on the place where the mallet will contact the ball. Do not use body movement in an effort to get more "oomph" into the shot, as it will almost inevitably reduce, instead of increasing, the force transmitted to the balls; and will often result in a complete mishit.

THE PASS ROLL

I N THE PASS roll the striker's ball is made to travel FURTHER than the roqueted ball.

1. It should be obvious that a pass roll is impossible if the two balls travel in exactly the same direction, as the striker's ball cannot physically pass through the roqueted ball, and neither can it be made to jump over it.
2. For this reason it is usual, after placing the striker's ball as for a normal roll, to stand even further forward and aim the swing a few degrees to one side of the line of centres of the two balls.
3. The bottom hand should be placed at the very bottom of the mallet shaft for this shot, as close as you can get it to the head of the mallet without actually touching it (which, of course, would be illegal). The other hand will also be well down the handle, so that the handle slopes forward at least as much as for a full roll, or even more so.
4. The grip must be very firm, and the mallet head must be moved forward with a pronounced BUT SMOOTH acceleration.
5. Many players obtain best results by hitting through the TOP HALF of the two balls, with very little backswing but an exaggerated (low) follow-through.
6. The shoulders must be kept still while the arms swing forward, with elbows beginning in a bent position and being straightened as both arms reach forward during the swing.
7. As for the full roll, practice from a position where the backswing is severely hampered is a useful way of learning and perfecting the required technique.
8. Some players use an alternative method of hitting sharply downward on the striker's ball (rather than forward through the top half) and combining this with a noticeable forward rotation of the TOP of the mallet handle, to increase the forward squeezing effect. This will often cause the striker's ball to jump, which is not necessarily a bad thing; but it seems to work better when the balls are made to travel in two quite different directions rather than in almost the same direction.
9. In order to retain some control of direction it is important to ensure (as far as possible) that the follow-through is in a straight line and the mallet handle is not tilted to one side during the swing.

THE SPLIT SHOT

THIS IS SIMILAR to one of the previously considered croquet shots (stop-shot, drive, half-roll, three-quarter roll, full roll, or pass roll), with the important difference that the two balls may need to be sent in entirely different directions.

1. Place your striker's ball against the roqueted ball so that the line of centres points to exactly where you want the ROQUETED ball to go. (Or just 'outside' this point to allow for 'pull' as explained below.)

2. Look at the two places where you want the balls to finish, and consider the distance you want the roqueted ball to travel. Estimate the FRACTION of this distance (though in a different direction) to be travelled by the striker's ball, and grip your mallet accordingly (i.e. as for a stop-shot, drive, half-roll, etc.).

3. If the angle of split (between the two directions the balls will travel in) is less than 30 degrees, retain this grip; but if the angle is 30-60 degrees you will need to move your hands up the handle a bit and/or stand further back from the ball. This lessens the forward mallet slope, as there is less need to 'squeeze' the striker's ball forward when the full weight of the roqueted ball is no longer directly in front of it preventing it from moving freely away.

   If the angle of split is 60-80 degrees, you will need to move your hands up to near the top of the handle, and stand back as for a roquet or stop-shot. There is now very little or none of the roqueted ball in front of the striker's ball which can therefore move away freely in its required direction.

4. In a split shot, the friction between the two balls imparts a spin to each ball, causing them to deviate (or 'pull'—an overworked term in croquet) inwards as they slow down sufficiently to allow the spin to grip on the lawn surface. In a split shot approaching the full length or width of the lawn this 'pull' will commonly cause the balls to curve inwards towards each other, finishing about a yard inside the points where it was envisaged they would finish if no allowance for this 'pull' had been made. To make allowance for 'pull', therefore, you should line up the centres of the balls about a yard OUTSIDE the point where you actually want the roqueted ball to finish. For a shorter split shot less allowance need be made.

5. Now select a point, as near as you can judge, which is HALFWAY between the two places where you want the balls to finish, then choose another point a little closer to where to want your striker's ball to go (about a yard closer in a full length split), and aim your swing at this second point. Swing your

mallet straight through in this line confidently, resisting all temptation to curve the swing or turn your mallet face towards where you want your striker's ball to go. Most players find it difficult to get used to the idea of not hitting in the direction they want their own ball to travel; but there are two balls to be given EQUAL CONSIDERATION.

The reason for aiming slightly into the striker's ball instead of at the exact midway point is threefold:

Firstly, the striker's ball is usually more affected by spin (and therefore pull) than the roqueted ball.

Secondly, the striker's ball tends to slip a little on the surface of the other ball before it grips, especially in a wide-angle split.

Thirdly and most importantly, the follow-through of the mallet head affects the direction of the striker's ball, but not that of the roqueted ball.

This is true of all split shots, from stop-shots to pass rolls, though the amount of allowance that should be made will vary, depending on such things as the distances travelled by the balls, type of ball, type of lawn surface, and whether the balls are wet or dry, as well as the peculiarities of your swing and follow-through.

6. Most players find the wide-angled shots the most difficult to control, but for some reason they fail to practise them. Perhaps they fail to understand the need to adjust their stance and grip according to the angle of split.

7. Sometimes it is necessary or desirable to play a very sharp wide-angle stop-shot, in which your striker's ball travels a minimum distance in a direction almost at right-angles to the direction of the roqueted ball. This occurs, for example, when you have just made the sixth hoop without any useful rush, and want to send the roqueted ball to the eighth ('2-back') hoop while going to a ball near the seventh ('1-back') hoop.

    The best way to play this shot is to grip the mallet firmly and hit the ball as close as possible to the right-hand edge of the mallet face, using the sharpest stop-shot action you can manage. In this way you will minimise the effect of the mallet following through (as it must to some small extent) and preventing the striker's ball from moving away immediately to the right.

8. Because of 'pull' (the English call it 'mallet drag') the maximum achievable angle of split is not 90 degrees, but about 80 degrees. In this case the normal roquet-type swing and follow-through will cause the two balls to travel approximately equal distances. If you want your striker's ball to travel less distance than the roqueted ball in such a wide-angled shot you will need to use a stop-shot action. Wide-angle stop-shots, together with pass-rolls, are renowned as the most difficult croquet shots to control accurately; but if mastered they can become invaluable.

9. The basic splits from hoop 1 to hoops 2 and 3 (a three-quarter roll, or just over), and from hoop 2 to hoops 3 and 4 (a wider angle, so grip as for a half-roll and stand further back) are essential in order to keep breaks going, and need constant practice.

10. It is also important to learn to adjust these basic shots when the ball you are going to is not exactly placed just in front of your next hoop, or if you are not achieving the desired result.

   For example, suppose that you have just made hoop 1, and wish to split the croqueted ball to hoop 3 while your striker's ball goes to a ball near hoop 2.

   If the ball you are going to is a yard to the right of hoop 2, you will need your striker's ball to finish TWO YARDS to the right of the hoop in order to obtain a rush. Thus your half-way point and aiming point will be adjusted about a yard to the right. Similarly, if the ball you are going to is a yard to the left of hoop 2, you will need to adjust your aiming point correspondingly to the left.

   If the ball is behind hoop 2, the distance your ball needs to travel will be increased, so you will have to stand further forward and move your hands further down the handle to get more slope on the mallet and squeeze the striker's ball further forward; or else use an accelerated 'push'. If the ball is, say, 3-4 yards in front of hoop 2 you will not want your ball to travel so far, so you should stand back slightly and move your hands upward on the handle to reduce its forward slope.

   If your split shots are having unsatisfactory results, first check your technique to see whether you are correctly playing the required half-roll or three-quarter roll (etc.) Then if, say, the striker's ball is consistently falling short of its objective (or the roqueted ball is going too far), move your hands down the handle and stand further forward to increase both the slope of the handle and the fractional distance travelled by the striker's ball. An understanding of the mechanics of the split shot (technique and reasons for it) will enable you to correct other errors similarly.

11. *COACHING HINT:*
   Some players have found it helpful to remember the following mnemonic for split shots, using the letters of the word GRADE:

   > **G**rip the mallet with hand positions determined from the
   > **R**atio of the distances you wish the balls to travel.
   > **A**djust hands upward if the angle of split is wide.
   > **D**irect the swing at (approx.) the midway point.
   > **E**rrors must be noted and corrected for future shots.

THE APPROACH SHOT

THIS IS THE shot in which the striker's ball is placed in position to run its hoop, while the roqueted ball is placed where it can be used after the hoop has been made. The shot used will be one of the croquet shots we have already considered (a take-off, stop-shot, drive, half-roll, three-quarter roll, full roll, pass roll, or most often some sort of split shot). All of these need to be mastered before you can expect to be able to play the correct (i.e. the best possible) approach shot in any given situation. Some additional considerations are worthy of mention:

1. In most cases distances of only a few yards will be involved. This may lead to the false assumption that approach shots should not present much difficulty. However, a high degree of accuracy is required, and any error will usually have severe consequences.

2. First, decide where you would like (ideally) both balls to go. This means that your striker's ball will go into position to run its hoop, and the roqueted ball will be positioned so that after running the hoop you will have a good chance of being able to not only roquet it, but rush it to where you want to go.

3. The ideal position for most approach shots will be to place the striker's ball 1-2 feet in front of the hoop and the roqueted ball 2-3 yards behind it, possibly a little to one side to allow a rush in some desired direction.

4. Look carefully at the distances the two balls will have to travel to get to these positions, and at the angle between the two directions. Decide whether such a shot is possible, and if so, which of the croquet shots will be needed. Many learners find this difficult. The small distances are deceptive and the hoop is a distraction, causing them to (say) use a stop-shot action when a half-roll was needed, or vice-versa.

5. Assess the difficulty of the required shot, and also how confident you are of being able to play it accurately. If you are not confident, then settle for some less than ideal placement of the roqueted ball which can be achieved by a shot you can play with greater confidence.

   Your overwhelming desire, of course, should be to reach the stage of proficiency where you can play all such shots with equal and utmost confidence.

6. If you are playing the approach shot from further back (e.g. 4-5 yards instead of 1-2 yards) then you will usually need to be content to place your striker's ball 3-4 feet in front of the hoop rather than 1-2 feet, to allow a greater margin of error while still retaining a reasonable chance

of making the hoop. This means that the hoop shot will be played more firmly and the ball may well run further after passing through the hoop, so the roqueted ball should also be placed further from the hoop than in a shorter approach shot.

7. Because a longer approach shot requires that BOTH balls be placed further from the hoop, the point of aim for most approach shots (approximately halfway between where you want the balls to finish) varies very little. For almost all approach shots up to 4 yards from the hoop, you should aim at a point 1-2 feet behind the hoop. Swing through straight in this direction. Do not swing in a curve or turn your mallet face in an attempt to 'shepherd' your ball into better position, as this will lose your control of the other ball.

8. For approach shots involving half-rolls or three-quarter rolls, the 'forward slope and downward hit' method has a considerable advantage as compared with 'pushing through the bottom'. It allows better control of the striker's ball and easier adjustment to the speed of the lawn, as no timing is involved. Almost all leading players use this method, at least for approach shots; and most even prefer not to use a short drive as an approach shot, replacing it with a type of downward hit stop-shot referred to as a 'stab-roll'.

9. Remember to allow for such things as wideness of angle, pull, type of balls, and speed of lawn which may vary from hoop to hoop. In a short approach shot these things are no less important than in a long split shot.

10. In general, it is undesirable to hit the roqueted ball across the face of the hoop in an approach shot, or to take off from the 'inside' of a ball behind the hoop. In both of these cases the 'pull' on your striker's ball will tend to take it away from a line directly in front of the hoop, rather than along it. Because of this your margin for error will be reduced.

11. There is much more to learn about special types of approach shot, e.g. from very close to the hoop where the hoop itself may interfere with the shot, or from further away when allowance may have to be made for the possibility that the intended hoop shot may turn out to be impossible or too risky. Such finer points involve more than technique, and are beyond the scope of these present notes.

Author's note:

This booklet was my first effort, and was written several years ago. Since then, some new coaching ideas have been developed. In those days I was using the "Circle Method" for hoop approaches, but did not have the confidence to teach it or recommend it to anyone else. Instead, I regarded it as something unlikely to be of help to anyone but me. Every coach should be wary about teaching things which he has found helpful himself, but which are not used by other players, especially those playing at the top level. Since then, however, both the SACA and the ACA have investigated the "Circle Method" and have adopted it as their officially recommended way of playing and teaching hoop approaches; and some of our leading players are now using the method very successfully.

Therefore, I am now including here the following two additional pages which are copied from my latest booklet "Croquet: Finer Points". They explain the method in reasonable detail, and most players will find the method far easier to learn and play consistently than the alternative wide variety of strokes which can be used in hoop approaches as explained above.

CIRCLE METHOD FOR HOOP APPROACHES

This method of lining up and playing hoop approaches was explained in my booklet "Croquet Coaching: Error Correction" and has been incorporated into the official course notes for the training of coaches.

In comparing the Circle Method with the standard method of playing and teaching hoop approaches, the following should be noted:

(1) The standard method involves deciding upon the desired finishing positions of the two balls (usually about two feet in front of the hoop and two yards behind it) and recognising the type of split shot which will be needed to get them to these positions. This could be a stop-shot, half roll, equal roll, pass roll, thick takeoff, (etc.), and the player then needs to know the correct grip, stance and type of swing he must use to play whichever of these shots is required. He must also be able to adjust the grip, stance and swing according to the wideness of the angle of split. Most of this is well beyond the understanding of many players, at least until they have been playing the game for some years. By this time they will often have developed the undesirable habit of playing most hoop approaches as takeoffs, since it is the only method they can cope with.

(2) The Circle Method has the great advantage that it can be taught to a beginner right from the start, without the need for him to understand, or be able to play, any type of split shot or roll.

(3) It also has the advantage that it allows the player to develop a greater degree of consistency (and with it confidence) than any alternative method.

(4) A disadvantage is that the Circle Method will not always result in the player obtaining a forward rush in order to facilitate the continuance of his break. However, at an early stage of his development the difficulty in achieving accurate control of the timing of the more desirable stop-shot (when more or less directly in front of the hoop) may still mean that the Circle Method is a good option. At a later stage, when he can play stop-shots with accurate

John Riches and Wayne Davies

control of the striker's ball, he can vary his hoop approach method as he considers desirable. It is worth noting that several leading players are now using the Circle Method, sometimes with slight modifications, for almost all hoop approaches; and most of these find it so consistent that they will only vary it when the alternative shot involves no risk at all.

(5) The term "Circle Method" was coined in order to explain the method to coaches. It is not necessary for the player to think in terms of circles, but it is useful in teaching it for the coach to place markers around the hoop in a circle so that the learner can practise lining up the shot and playing it from various positions around the circle. The reason for this is that every position on the circle is the same distance from the hoop, so the player will use the same aiming points for both the croqueted ball and the line of swing; and these can be marked by the coach with small objects such as corner pegs as a guide for the player. The Method is described as follows: (see diagram)

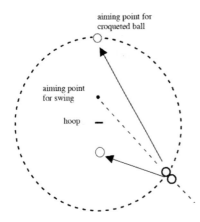

1. Observe the distance of the ball you have roqueted from the hoop (i.e. the approach distance).

2. Find a point on the lawn this same distance directly behind the hoop, and place your striker's ball against the roqueted ball in line with this point. That is, you are aiming the croqueted ball to go to the point you selected directly behind the hoop.

3. Find another point which is also directly behind the hoop, and about one-third of the way from the hoop to the first point you selected. This second point will be the aiming point for your swing. In playing the shot, you will 'stalk' this point, keep your mallet face square to it, and swing your mallet through directly in line with it, avoiding all temptation to "shepherd" the swing around toward the hoop. You will try to ignore the croqueted ball and swing as if you are hitting your striker's ball to make it roquet an imaginary ball at this second aiming point.

4. The shot must be played with the mallet sloping forward, but only slightly, at an angle of about 15 degrees from the vertical. This degree of forward slope can be learnt with considerable accuracy over time, as it is exactly the same for every hoop approach using the Circle Method, whether you are approaching the hoop from in front, alongside, or behind as shown in the diagram at left.

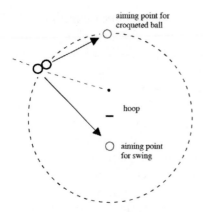

aiming point for croqueted ball

hoop

aiming point for swing

5.   The swing is also the same, except for strength, for all positions around the circle. It is often referred to as a "stab-roll", but this is not an entirely accurate description. In this case the mallet should be neither stopped (decelerated) nor pushed forward (accelerated) as it contacts the ball. The player merely endeavours to maintain the movement (i.e. speed) of the falling mallet as it 'passes through' the ball.

This takes some time to learn, but is actually easier for newcomers than for those who have developed the habit of "rolling" from such positions, or of "stabbing" at hoop approaches with a flat mallet.

6.   The strength of the shot is the only thing that is not automatic and has to be judged for each separate hoop approach. However, the player will be helped if he realises that it is determined by the distance from the second aiming point, not his distance from the hoop. (In fact, about the same force is required as if he were hitting a single ball twice the distance to the second aiming point toward which he is swinging; and he should soon learn that less force is required as you move around the circle to a position behind the hoop, because you are then closer to the aiming point, which means that the total of the distances travelled by the two balls will be smaller.) The strength should be controlled by lifting the mallet back higher for a longer hoop approach, rather than by providing any force from the wrists or forearms. That is, you simply let the mallet 'fall' through the ball from a greater height, again maintaining its speed through the ball. This, also, allows the player to eventually achieve surprising consistency.

7.   Another surprising aspect of the Circle method is that there seems to be a considerable margin for error. Even when the shot appears to have been somewhat mis-hit, the hoop is often still possible to make.

8.   For a longer hoop approach the imaginary circle will be larger, and a higher backswing is needed, but otherwise the shot is played in exactly the same way. Note that (allowing for pull) the distance the striker's ball finishes in front of the hoop will be about the same as the distance from the hoop to the second aiming point, or about one-third of the circle radius. This means that in a longer hoop approach you will expect to finish further from the hoop, which maintains the margin for error. However, players who use this method for hoop approaches of six yards or more (e.g. from the border near a hoop) may wish to slightly increase the forward slope of the mallet in order to achieve a

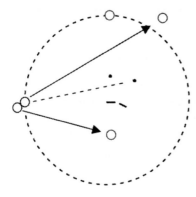

narrower angle of split, so that the striker's ball finishes closer to the hoop.

9. At a later stage, when the player finds it desirable to not only make the hoop, but try for a rush in a particular direction after making it, he can do this by simply imagining the hoop in a slightly different position. This will, of course, alter the size of the circle (not shown in the diagram at left) and the positions of the two aiming points, and means that the shot will need to be hit a little harder or softer, depending on whether the rush and imaginary hoop movement are to the far side or the near side of the hoop.

CONCLUSION

1. Expertise at croquet cannot be reduced to a matter of simply knowing the best technique for each shot. KNOWING and DOING are two very different things, but players who make the effort to find out and understand the correct technique should at least stand a better chance than most of being able to decide what is causing errors, and how to set about correcting them. They will also be in a position of being able to assist others with sound advice. Their reward will be a greater consistency, so that they seldom play badly; and also play well after having been away from the game for some time.

2. The extent to which the correct technique can be successfully applied will depend on the player's straightness of eye (to some of us things appear to be in line when they are not), co-ordination, timing, judgement, concentration and temperament. The old adage that 'practice makes perfect' seems to apply less in croquet than in many other sports. The importance of regularly practising particular shots cannot be denied, but simply playing game after game may not bring about any improvement. In fact, if poor technique is being used you may be developing bad habits which will make it harder to progress than if you had not been playing at all.

3. If you do decide to play practice games, and are serious about improving your game, then make most of the games serious contests in which your determination to win is as great as in any match or tournament game. Do not play shots carelessly or give only token thought to correct tactics "because it's only a practice game". Play only the shots that you would play in a tournament game, so that you develop the confidence to play them under pressure. Technique which is faultless when the player is relaxed can suddenly collapse under pressure, so it is essential to practise playing the shots under pressure.

4. Whether in a match or at practice, take sufficient time to consider carefully which shot should be played, and then the points of technique you need to get right. Refuse to allow anyone to hurry you in any way. A player who tries to pressure the opponent into playing hurriedly is at the very least displaying ignorance of the vast number of things that need to be thought through in relation to both tactics and technique, especially in a tense situation approaching the end of the allocated time for the game.

5. Lastly, if you have found these notes helpful, tell others about them, as a widespread interest in improving technique can only be good for the game. Be wary, however, of lending them your copy, since you will need it yourself to refer to whenever things start to go wrong, which for most of us is all too often.

Digital edition v1.2 2004 by cleinedesign.
email jballant@smartchat.net.au

CROQUET

COLLECTED ARTICLES

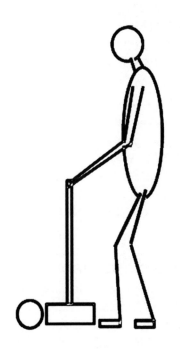

CONTENTS

Digital edition v1.2 2004 by cleinedesign
email jballant@smartchat.net.au

SITTING IN FRONT by *John Riches*

I T IS A common practice of players in lower grades, when they find themselves unable to make their hoop, to "sit in front". The diagram illustrates a situation where all clips are still on hoop 1, and the player of red has approached the hoop but is unable to make it. Many players would now sit the red ball in front of the hoop wired from black, reasoning that if black moves red will be able to run through the hoop and hopefully roquet blue.

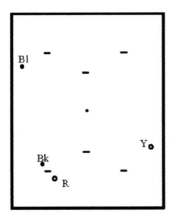

Firstly it should also be realised that the very first shot required, hitting the red ball a foot or so to an exact position in front of hoop 1 wired from black, is not simple and is fraught with danger.

Even then, if black is hit, say, into the 4th corner, the chance of red being able to establish a break is remote, and most times he would find it difficult to even obtain any sort of satisfactory leave. He will have made one hoop—possibly two if lucky—but the price is too high.

An alternative reply for the opponent, and usually the recommended one, would be to shoot with blue at black. This shot, if missed, again allows red to make the one hoop but with little chance of doing anything afterward; and if the opponent makes the roquet he will have an immediate break. Tactical choices which allow the opponent chances to set up an immediate break while giving yourself at best a chance of making only one or two hoops can hardly be correct for players capable of making breaks.

An experienced player will sit in front of the hoop very rarely if ever, preferring in the diagrammed position to hit red out near yellow with a rush to blue and a likely break next turn, whereas inexperienced players even sit in front of hoop 2 with one opponent ball behind the hoop and the other at hoop 3, giving away the innings as well for the chance to make one hoop.

WHAT IS YOUR ANGLE? *by John Riches*

It is interesting as a coach to note how few players, even at state level, are comfortable playing splits which involve wide angles. This is a great pity, because such shots will at times be the best or only way of setting up an immediate break. The ideal is for each player to be able to estimate the size of the angle involved in any split he is thinking of playing, and know how to adjust his stance, grip and swing accordingly.

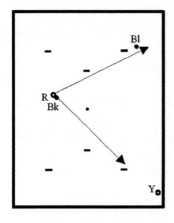

If estimation in degrees is asking too much, then at least he should be able to judge whether the angle is "narrow", "starting to open out", "fairly wide", or "very wide—approaching a right-angle".

A good trained and accredited coach will be able to explain how and why, as the angle opens out, you need to stand further back, take a longer grip, and swing flatter, as well as select your line of aim and adjust it to allow for changing amounts of pull and 'mallet drag' as the angle becomes wider.

An understanding of this will allow you to confidently load hoop 4 as you go the blue ball to make hoop 3 when you find yourself in the situation shown the 1ˢᵗ diagram, instead of taking off or playing the pass-roll shown in the 2ⁿᵈ diagram, which is in fact harder to play.

Loading hoop 4 accurately is the only way of ensuring that you will be able to bring the yellow ball into your break without difficulty.

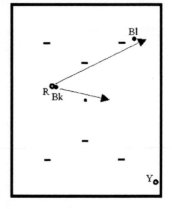

INSIDE THE RECTANGLE? *by John Riches*

When I learnt the game I was taught to play a 3-ball break by keeping the balls within the rectangle formed by the four corner hoops. This involved sending the croqueted ball about a yard short of the hoop when using a split or stop-shot to load your next hoop. In the diagram at left, after making hoop 1 you would send the croqueted ball to position 2 behind hoop 3 instead of position which is in front of

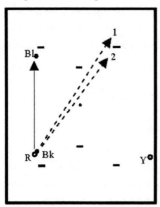

the hoop. Now we place less emphasis on this idea, and instead prefer to send the croqueted ball in front of the hoop to position 1. The reasons for the change are:

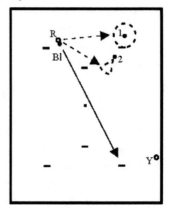

(1) As illustrated in the diagram at right, there is a much bigger (circular) area into which you can get your red striker's ball after making hoop 2, and still be able to easily make hoop 3, compared with the smaller wedge-shaped area for position 2.

(2) Loading the hoop within the rectangle often meant making the hoop from behind.

(3) It is easier to get a useful forward rush when approaching the hoop from the front. Against this we must weigh up the fact that some players will find the wider angle split harder to control.

The moral is: Learn to play wide-angle splits confidently, then load your hoops in front rather than behind. One exception in a three-ball break is the 1-back hoop which should still be loaded with a ball placed inside the rectangle and behind the hoop—if you do not understand why, ask your coach to explain it.

DO YOU HAVE THE RIGHT ADDRESS? *by John Riches*

One of the things we tell players who play centre-style as most do nowadays is that when you address the ball your hands should be well out in front of your body—in fact there should be a gap of about one foot between hands and body for most people, depending on stature and body shape. (I had one player who said "but my arms are not long enough for that. My body is a foot out in front already!") This allows plenty of room for a full backswing, so that the stroke can be played using the full weight of the mallet without having to jab or hurry the forward swing, and applies to all grips and stances, whether the hands are together or apart.

Many players address the ball with their hands much closer to the body, with elbows bent so that the back swing will be severely restricted, and a common reaction when they are told to comfortably straighten their elbows, so that their hands are further forward, is But if I do that I will not be able to see the ball as I hit it. They are often surprised when we tell them that you do not need to see the ball as you hit it, because they have been told in past years to fix their eyes on the back of the ball and keep them there during the swing.

This is good advice, and is essential during the lining up and the backswing in order to get the body square to the line of swing and ensure that the mallet is swung back in the correct line. Fixing the eyes on the ball and keeping them there also helps to keep the head and shoulders still during the swing, but as long as the shoulders do not move it is not essential that you be able to see the ball during the forward swing.

To illustrate this you can line everything up, swing the mallet back, then close your eyes as you start the forward swing. It will make no difference to your ability to roquet or run a hoop that your eyes are shut. In fact, if your eyes are open and you see something going wrong (e.g. your mallet starting to go off line) there would be nothing you could do about it anyway, because your reaction time is too long to make any correction after starting the forward swing. Your hands should come forward slightly ahead of the mallet head, and will usually block your view of the ball before the mallet impacts it, but this will not be a problem. So when addressing the ball remember to push your hands out away from your body and give yourself more room.

ROQUETING: SWINGING IN LINE *by John Riches*

One of the hardest things a croquet player has to try to do is swing the mallet in the correct line. It has been pointed out by other authors that the human body is very poorly designed as far as performing such an action is concerned, although one must admit that the design does have certain advantages for various other functions that may need to be performed. It would be far easier if we had one arm about six inches (15 cm) longer than the other and our eyes one above the other instead of side by side. Since we cannot change the design of our bodies, we just have to learn to do the best we can with what we have.

It is obvious that you will give yourself the best chance of roqueting consistently if you can train yourself to swing your mallet straight along the line in which you want the ball to travel, with the mallet head also aligned in this line. Note that similar considerations apply in sports like darts and snooker, but not so much in sports like tennis or table-tennis where you will often do better to swing across the line in order to deliver more power and impart useful spin to the ball.

Two things are important: the mallet should swing straight back and then forward along the correct line; and the mallet head should be pointing along this line before, during and after contact. These two things are very difficult to achieve—so much so that if you watch closely you will see that few players can do it—and require ideally (1) a stance that allows the mallet to swing freely back and forth under the dominant eye, and (2) a grip such that the bottom hand does not tend to "take over" and turn the mallet off line.

It may seem that it would not mailer if the mallet head goes off line or loses its straight orientation after contacting the ball, but in fact the follow-through seems to be the main thing you should concentrate on, as it makes you get the earlier part of the swing right as well. It is hard to tell where the mallet is pointing during the backswing and early part of the forward swing, but you can more easily tell whether or not the mallet head remains correctly in line after you have hit the ball. The grip should not be too tight (or 'tense), the shoulders should remain still, and the muscles in the wrists, forearms and shoulders should be completely relaxed. Practise getting these things right one at a time, and notice the gradual improvement.

DO YOU SUFFER FROM CRAMP? *by John Riches*

Any coach who takes the trouble to watch the roquet action of players at various levels will soon come to realise that one of the most common problems is that many of them bend over too far and so cramp their swing to the extent that they are unable to swing the mallet freely from the shoulders. Instead they swing mainly from the wrists and elbows, providing additional power from the muscles in the forearms instead of making full use of the weight of the mallet. Some are so bent over at the waist that their nose is only an inch or so from the end of the mallet handle, and their elbows are bent outwards so much that they resemble a pelican with its wings outstretched.

Some players manage to play quite well with such a restricted action, but it usually requires considerable strength in the forearms together with excellent judgement and co-ordination. Most will find it much easier if they stand up straighter—the elbows should be comfortably straight—and keep their elbows in, rather than out to the side. This allows the grip to be more relaxed, the weight of the mallet to be fully utilised so that the same result can be obtained with less muscular effort, and the body to remain steadier during the swing because it is better balanced.

Of course, there will be some shots such as pass rolls and equal rolls which require a bent-over stance with one hand down near the head of the mallet in order to accelerate the mallet smoothly through the ball, but most other shots can be played more easily and with greater consistency by standing up straighter and using a longer grip so that you can swing the mallet more freely from the shoulders.

The main time players tend to bend over too far and cramp themselves is when they are tense and lacking in confidence. You may need to recognise the times when tension is most likely to affect you, and train yourself to resist the urge to cramp yourself. Do this by consciously standing up straighter, straightening your elbows, and adopting an air of confidence—tell yourself that you will give yourself the best possible chance by using a long, flowing, relaxed swing from the shoulders instead of "huddling" down over the ball and jabbing.

GIVE YOURSELF A BREAK! *by John Riches*

One of the most frequently heard complaints by people I coach is "I can make breaks when I have them set up, but I find it very hard to get them started." It usually turns out they have had several opportunities, but have failed to grasp them because it would have involved playing a stroke in which they were not fully confident. I have recently seen players at state level fail to set up breaks as they should have done in the two positions illustrated below. In the first diagram all clips were on hoop 1 and the player of red, having roqueted his yellow partner ball, should have rolled yellow to hoop 2 while going to blue (see arrows), then taken off to black at hoop 1. Instead he took off to blue, did not get a useful rush, and ended up making hoop 1 without hoop 2 loaded.

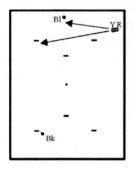
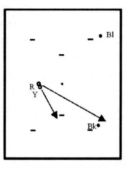

In the second diagram red was for hoop 4 and he should have pass-rolled yellow to load hoop 5 as shown but instead he took off to black and made hoop 4 without hoop 5 properly loaded. In each case the current hoop was well loaded and should be made with little difficulty, so before making it you should load the next hoop accurately. The two shots needed to do this in the diagrammed situations involved very little risk, but in any case you should be prepared to take a reasonable risk in order to make certain of the break. Don't be timid. Play confidently the shot needed to give yourself a break.

GENEROSITY MAXIMISED *by John Riches*

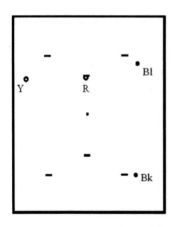

The diagrammed position arose in a recent game I was watching. The player of blue had taken off from red to the front of hoop 3, leaving red in the penultimate hoop. Blue succeeded in gaining reasonable position to run hoop 3, but played the hoop shot poorly and bounced off the hoop, finishing as shown.

The player of red and yellow (an experienced player, but well below state standard) now called me as referee and asked for a wiring lift with red, to which ruled she was entitled because red was partly in the penultimate hoop. She then quickly picked up red (which was also for hoop 3), took it to B-baulk and shot at yellow, but failed to roquet.

After the game I suggested that she could have left red in the hoop, and since the opponent had generously given her a wired ball, she could have played to gain maximum advantage from his generosity by simply playing the yellow ball to A-baulk (or even to a position on B-baulk wired from blue).

Then, unless the opponent roquets, on her next turn she could claim the wiring lift, take red also to the baulk, and give herself a simple rush to hoop 4 and the black ball, which in turn can be rushed to hoop 3. Or if she had placed yellow on

B-baulk she could take red there also and give herself a cut-rush to hoop 3, with hoop 4 already loaded.

The player admitted that she was so excited about being entitled to a wiring lift that she failed to consider retaining the option of taking it in a later turn. In fact, she was unaware that the laws allow this, and had assumed that the wiring lift had to be taken immediately.

Of course, my suggestion in this case would have involved taking the risk of the opponent roqueting, so a top player would no doubt take the lift and expect to roquet a ball from B-baulk.

SOMETHING AFOOT *by John Riches*

Much has been written about the importance of foot placement in roqueting. Some favour a level stance, while others find that a "step stance" gives a more stable base from which to swing, with less chance of overbalancing and stepping forward or otherwise introducing unwanted body movement during the swing. Some have their feet close together, while others prefer a wider stance. It is obvious that preferences will vary according to body size and weight, as well as mallet length and the type of grip used.

One aspect which is little understood is the need for the foot muscles to be completely relaxed during the swing, with the instep flattened down against the ground. Some players tend to tense the foot muscles into a tight ball, and this makes it very difficult to swing the mallet smoothly. They are helped immediately by the coach simply telling them to flatten their insteps onto the ground when they take up their stance. Others, of course, have always done this correctly without needing to be told.

To convince yourself of the benefit involved, try balancing on one foot like a flamingo, firstly lightening the muscles of the foot you are standing on, and secondly allowing them to relax so that a wider base of your foot is in contact with the ground. It will be apparent that relaxing the foot muscles gives a more stable base, making it easier to maintain balance.

Perhaps the main benefit is that the flattening of the insteps against the ground can be used as a simple relaxation exercise, since relaxing your foot muscles tends also to assist relaxation of muscles in other parts of the body, and helps overcome nervous tension. Thus the movement of muscles in the shoulders and arms can be more easily controlled, producing a smoother swing with less tendency to twitch and jerk—all this from such a simple exercise as flattening your insteps!

A minor coaching point such as this will not overcome flaws in technique such as a tendency to tighten the grip during the swing, or to take too short a backswing and hurry the forward swing; but it can make a difference to performance by helping the player "fine tune" his game, provided he remembers to do it during the 5-minute hit-up, and continues to do it throughout the game, even when distracted by such things as 'lifts' and time-pressure.

SMILE, BUT DON'T BREATHE *by John Riches*

There are many methods used by croquet players to help themselves relax and concentrate frilly on the task at hand. In addition to the simple ideas we will mention here, some adopt quite complicated visualisation and relaxation procedures which they have either developed themselves or 'borrowed' from other sports such as rifle shooting, golf snooker, archery, darts, high jumping and pole vaulting. In each of these activities it is desirable to relax all muscles other than those needed to perform the immediate task, e.g. pulling the bigger.

In a previous article we looked at the idea of flattening the insteps onto the ground. Here are three further things which may prove helpful:

(1) Years ago a leading player who was partnering me saw me walking onto the lawn to play my turn with a frown on my face. Not realising that it was in fact my 'normal happy look', she said "You can't play good croquet with such a frown on your face. Smile!" Her advice sounded rather trivial to me at the time, but in more recent years I have found that many players do in fact play better croquet if they simply smile to themselves and open their eyes wide before playing each stroke, particularly a critical one. Of course, you must be prepared to have people think you are a bit queer, but then again, it may get your opponent wondering what you are up to. If, for example, you find yourself tensing up and jerking when you attempt to run a slightly sidey hoop, why not give it a try?

(2) Suspension of breathing is widely used in the sports listed above, and can be helpful in croquet also. The idea is to expel all the air from your lungs, and then play the stroke (or pull the trigger) before you breathe in again. This avoids the slight shoulder movement produced by breathing, and allows the aims to swing from a slightly more stable base. It also assists relaxation, but don't get it wrong by taking a deep breath and trying to hold it while swinging! Deep breaths should be avoided just before a swing.

(3) When something goes wrong, never display any emotion such as disgust, annoyance with yourself, disappointment, etc. If you miss a four-foot rush, or stick in a hoop, walk off the lawn as if it was exactly what you intended to do and everything is under control. You may be able to fool yourself if no-one else, and enable yourself to remain relaxed instead of getting uptight.

WHEN RISK BEATS CERTAINTY *by John Riches*

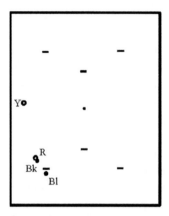

A common tactical error made by players, particularly in lower grades, is that they are not prepared to take reasonable risks. In many situations you are more likely to win by giving yourself a chance of making a break, even if in setting it up you are also taking the risk of breaking down, than by "playing safe" and making certain of just one hoop.

The diagram at left shows a situation with all clips still on hoop 1, where the player of blue had rolled with his partner ball to hoop 1, and finding that he could not make the hoop had sat just in front of the hoop. Then the player of red has shot from near hoop 6 and roqueted black. (Note that although it would have been a slightly shorter shot, shooting from near hoop 6 at the yellow partner ball would have been a tactical mistake because a miss would have left both red and yellow where blue could easily use them after making hoop 1.)

Having roqueted black as shown, there is for many players a strong temptation to immediately go to blue and make hoop 1. This is so simple and inviting that it is difficult to think of anything else, but experienced players will recognise it as a serious tactical error, because it will be far from easy to make more than just the one hoop.

The correct play, which seems obvious when pointed out but is frequently missed or ignored in matches, is to send black to hoop 2 with a half-roll which takes red near enough to roquet yellow safely, then take-off (there is no need to send yellow into the lawn unless you are really confident that you can do it without any further risk—for example of wiring red from blue) to blue and make hoop 1 having already loaded hoop 2 and given yourself an excellent chance of making several hoops instead of just the one. In such situations the chance of a break is almost always better than the certainty of one hoop. I am sure you know this, but do you do it?

CHOOSING THE RIGHT RISK *by John Riches*

In the diagrammed position red was for hoop 1 and had taken off from yellow intending to go to black. The player of red looked at the roquet on black, knowing that it would have given her the chance to set up a break by stop-shotting black to hoop 2 before making hoop 1 from blue, but also realizing that because the black clip was also on hoop 1, a miss would give the break to the opponent.

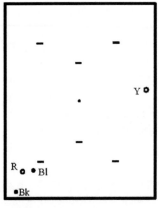

She decided not to take the risk and instead roqueted blue, made hoop 1, then rushed blue back out to black, got behind black and rushed it toward hoop 2.

After playing an approach shot for hoop 2 she found herself about 5 feet out and almost directly in front of the hoop. After more thought she decided to attempt the hoop but considered herself unlucky when she failed and let the opponent in.

Does this all sound reasonable to you? If so, you surely need to re-think the sort of risk you are, and are not, prepared to take in a game. The player was experienced and had a single figure handicap; so although it may not have been a certainty and she obviously did not think it was, her chance of making the 5-yard roquet on black was at least as good as, and probably better than, her chance of making a hoop from 5 feet out directly in front. In fact it would have been an interesting exercise to get her to have ten goes at each and see which she could do most often.

Yet she passed up the roquet chance when it would have given her a break, and instead attempted the 5-foot hoop with nothing set up ahead! The loss of the game was in no way the fault of bad luck, but of her poor tactical choices, when she neglected to take the risk that should have been taken and instead chose to take a greater risk that would have given her only the one extra hoop even if it had been successful. The lesson is clear: the key to good tactics is the correct assessment of which risks to take and which not to take.

WHY DO GOOD PLAYERS SHOOT? *by John Riches*

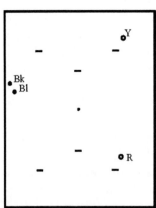

What would you do if you found yourself in the diagrammed position as red and yellow, when black is for hoop 3 and the other three clips are still on hoop 1?

Your first thought will no doubt be that you should move your yellow ball away from blacks hoop. However, if you shoot at red and miss you will give the opponent two balls in his forward play with a rush toward them, while a missed shot at his balls will allow him to use it to get a "dolly" rush to his hoop.

The average player may well decide in such a situation to hit yellow away into a corner, but if both you and your opponent are capable of playing breaks then you should not hesitate to shoot. If red has a good

John Riches and Wayne Davies

double target your best chance may be to shoot with red at the opponent's balls, but it is more likely that the correct shot will be with yellow at red. If this shot is missed players commonly assume that the opponent should have no difficulty setting up a break with your two balls in his forward play and a rush in that direction also; but in fact the percentages are not as good for him as they may appear. If he goes to yellow on the south boundary, he still has to roll yellow out to hoop 4 while getting a rush on red to hoop 3, then play the rush reasonably accurately.

Even at state level players tend to succeed in this and set up an immediate break no more than about 6 times out of 10, and in the diagrammed position there is also the possibility that hoop 4 will interfere with the rush. If yellow does shoot at red and miss, black should cut-rush blue as close as possible to yellow on the south border, then get behind yellow and rush it out to red in order to then get a really good rush on red to hoop 3. Many opponents would hesitate to do this because it can involve leaving blue rather close to yellow, so they adopt a line of play which gives them even less chance of setting up an immediate break.

WIRING DOES NOT ALWAYS HELP *by John Riches*

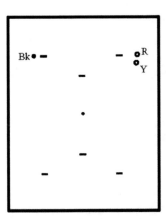

Although 3-ball games can happen at any level, this article is aimed at more advanced players, since at lower levels of play they tend to occur more rarely, and then by accident rather than by design.

In the diagrammed position the blue ball had been pegged out and black is for the peg. Red had just made hoop 3 and "cleverly" contrived after roqueting yellow to set a rush to hoop 4 with both balls wired from black. The opponent was responsible for the position of black, so he was not entitled to a wiring lift.

The player of red was pleased with himself for achieving a completely wired position, but in this case he is forcing black to take a relatively safe shot at the peg, and would have done better to roll his two balls to a position between hoop 4 and the east border, then set with red "covering the border"—not on the border—as shown in the second diagram.

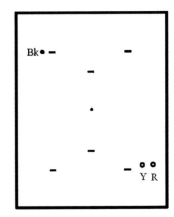

Now black can still shoot at the peg and/or the red and yellow balls, but a miss will allow red to roquet black and easily set up a 3-ball break.

It should be clear that even if yellow is already around, the only real winning chance for red is to play a 3-ball break, since making one or two hoops at a time will allow black to shoot at either the peg or a ball so many times that the chance of him missing every time is negligible.

In the second diagram black could, of course, shoot gently at the peg, but red should still be able to set up an immediate 3-ball break.

PLAYING THE ODDS *by John Riches*

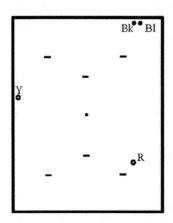

The diagrammed position shows a situation where black and yellow are both for 4-back, blue is for hoop 4, and your red ball (which you will want to move from the opponent's hoop) is still for hoop.

The only sensible thing to do is shoot with red at the opponent's balls, which are a yard or so apart on the north border. When this idea is first suggested to them many players protest: "But my opponent doesn't have a rush to his 4th hoop. If I shoot at his balls and miss it will allow him to get a good rush and easily make the hoop".

This is true enough, but if you shoot at yellow and miss he will be able to rush black over that way and use your balls to at least get a rush to his hoop and make it. If you return wide of yellow on the west border he will do the same, and you will have passed up a chance to gain the innings by roqueting. If you hit red away into a corner you will have gained nothing because he can simply set himself a rush to his hoop for next turn, or better still rush black over to yellow and put yellow into the lawn before selling himself a rush, thus forcing you to play the yellow ball in your next turn, so that even if you roquet it will not be with the ball you need to make hoops with.

The main point, however, is that if you shoot at his balls immediately and hit one, you have an excellent chance of an immediate break yourself. Taking shots which allow him to make one hoop if you miss, but give you the chance of a break if you hit, will tip the odds very much in your favour. You only have to hit about one in five of such shots in order to come out well ahead.

The moral of this little story is well expressed in the motto on display at the Broadview (S.A.) Club where I am a member, and which was borrowed from a basketball coach: "You miss 100% of the shots you don't take"

TAKE THE BREAK *by John Riches*

In a recent article I made the point that the only effective way to beat 'Aunt Emma' tactics is to learn to play the split shots needed to set up breaks and keep them going.

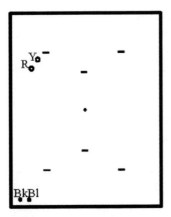

Sometimes players complain that they tried to set up breaks but were unable to do so; when in fact they did not take the opportunities which were presented to them.

In the diagrammed position red is for hoop 2 and yellow is for hoop 5. "Aunt Emma", rather than shooting with blue from near hoop 3 at the opponent's balls, has predictably (and in this case correctly) returned to her black partner ball in the first corner.

The player of red now made hoop 2, then tried to set up a break by rushing and splitting yellow to hoop 4 while going to Aunt Emma's balls in the first corner and rushing one of them to hoop 3. The idea was not unreasonable, and at least he was tying to set up a break rather than simply make the hoop and then separate the opponent's balls as Aunt Emma would have done; but the method he chose required him to play some long and accurate shots, and he did not succeed in setting up the break.

He had not even considered playing yellow instead of red in the diagrammed position, roqueting red, taking off to Aunt Emma's balls and then rushing one of them to hoop 5, after which a rush to either hoop 6 or one of the other two balls would give him the desired break. This is an easier and more likely way to set up a break, but of course he has passed up the chance to make an easy and "safe" hoop, when making hoop 5 instead of hoop 2 is not quite so easy and somewhat less certain.

It is hard to convince players that such "safety first" thinking in fact loses games. Ray Howell, a member of the S.A. state team, has been preaching the right attitude: "Winning without risk is victory without glory!"

THE HIT-UP *by John Riches*

In most tournaments nowadays a hit-up of at least 5 minutes is permitted before the start of each game. It is important that players know how best to use this time, and for this reason every club should allow a 5-minute hit-up before club games. In fact the really enlightened clubs encourage players to arrive as early as they can on club days and spend time practising before games start.

The way you should use your hit-up time will depend on whether it is a singles or doubles game, whether or not you have just played a game on the same court, whether there are changing weather conditions to cope with, whether you have a particular aspect of your game that you are working on and need to concentrate on getting right, and the mistakes you made in your previous game. A good coach should be able to advise you on ways of puffing the hit-up time to good use in each of these situations.

The main thing I insist upon with the people I coach is that they should never pass up the opportunity for a hit-up. Don't let your opponent or partner talk you out of it sure that you use the time wisely regardless of what they do.

In some places the hit-up time is optional and is taken out of the time allowed for the game by starting the clock before the hit-up begins. Don't fall for the trap of thinking that in this case it will be a disadvantage to spend the 5 minutes hitting up. It has been proven conclusively that with a hit-up games tend to finish quicker and scores are higher, as players take less time to get the feel of the lawn and establish breaks.

Some players like to hit a ball around the four boundaries during the hit-up, so as to find out where the border slopes in or out. Even on an unfamiliar court this is not a good use of a very limited hit-up time. It is more important to get your timing right by playing several short, gentle roquets, running a couple of hoops, then playing one or two take-offs, and rushes across the lawn. Do not start with the longer shots, as you need to get your timing right first—a long backswing and an unhurried forward swing using the full weight of the mallet.

There is much more to know about the use of hit-up time. Perhaps we will return to it in a future article. In the meantime watch what good players do, and plan beforehand how you will use the time to best advantage.

AUNT EMMA REVISITED *by John Riches*

It always disappoints a coach to hear the common complaint: "She played such a dreadful 'Aunt Emma' game—separated my balls from one end of the lawn to the other, made one hoop at a time off her own balls, made no attempt to load hoops ahead, and wouldn't try to run a hoop unless she was right in front or my balls were a long way apart. I find it so boring playing against people who refuse to use correct tactics and won't take any risks."

There are several points to be made about this sort of complaint:

First, it is hardly reasonable for you to expect an opponent to play a particular style of game just so that you will enjoy yourself more, or so that you will have a better chance of beating them. Surely you cannot blame Aunt Emma for trying to beat you in the way she believes will give her the best chance.

Second, such complaints are never made by people who have just beaten Aunt Emma; it always turns out that they have managed to lose to her in spite of her "bad and boring" tactics.

Third, the use of poor tactics by your opponent is something you should welcome, not something you should complain about, just as you should not complain (and no doubt won't) if they miss all their roquets.

Fourth, you should see it as a challenge to work out a way to take advantage of her poor tactics, and demonstrate that your style of game is superior to hers.

Fifth, the only chance of ever getting the Aunt to change her ways and play more adventuresome and enjoyable croquet is for her to keep on losing games until she comes to realise that she needs to do something different. This will not happen while people like you allow her tactics to frustrate and bore them into 'giving up' and allowing her to win the game because they cannot be bothered putting in the thought and care needed to counter her negative tactics.

It should be remembered that an accurate Aunt Emma can be a very strong opponent, and can present a real challenge. If you want to beat her the first thing to do is learn to play the split shots needed to set up breaks and keep them going. Accept the challenge and seek to play her as often as you can until you have learnt how to cope with her negativity. Soon she will start avoiding you and looking for other victims.

TIDYING UP by *John Riches*

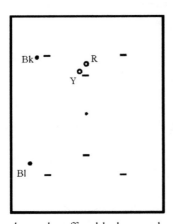

There are many players who know how to set out and play all-round 4-ball breaks, and have the shots to do it, but who break down because they fail to use simple opportunities to 'tidy up' the positions of balls which do not go exactly where they are wanted.

In the diagrammed position red has just made hoop 6. 1-back has been well loaded with black, and 2-back is reasonably loaded with blue. It is tempting in such situations to say that things are going well enough, so you simply roquet yellow a few yards to a position between 1-back and 2-back,

then take off to black to make 1-back. However, although blue is reasonably well placed at 2-back, it could be better, and it is important to realise that it will cost you nothing to improve the loading of this hoop. It will involve playing a few extra shots as compared with the 'simpler' way of making 1-back immediately, but the shots will be no more difficult and if the balls fail to go where you want them you will hardly be any worse off so there is something to gain and nothing to lose by taking the trouble to 'tidy up' the position of the ball from which you will later have to make 2-back.

Yellow should be rushed near to blue and then placed more accurately in front of 2-back as you get a rush on blue back toward 1-back. Then you can leave blue (instead of yellow) between 1-back and 2-back, and go to black to make 1-back with your next hoop loaded really accurately. It is such care in the little things that distinguishes the top players from the average ones, and ensures that they are able to not only complete the break without breaking down, but also get the 'perfect leave' they want at the end of the break. In such situations it pays to follow the old Cornish motto: "Near enough is not good enough. When you get it exact, that is near enough."

MAINTAIN THE BREAK *by John Riches*

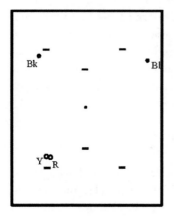

In the diagrammed position red has just made hoop 1. Black is at hoop 2, but blue is about 1 yard from the yardline and cannot be considered a satisfactory load of hoop 3. The player has several choices:

(1) Many would take off to black, make hoop 2, and hope to find some way of both loading hoop 4 and making hoop 3—perhaps with a dicey hoop approach from where blue is.

(2) Slightly better is to pass-roll yellow near to hoop 6 while going to black, and after making hoop 2 hope to send black to hoop 4 and get a rush on yellow to either hoop 3 or to the blue ball.

(3) Another possibility is to play a right-angle split which sends yellow vaguely toward hoop 4 while going to black, and after hoop 2 try for a rush on black to hoop 3 or to the blue hall.

(4) A fourth alternative is to take off to blue, hoping to rush it closer to hoop 3, or else place it there with a long pass-roll, before making hoop 2 from black.

(5) The best choice is to split yellow to hoop 3, so that after making hoop 2 you can send black to hoop 4 with either a rush or a split while going to either yellow or blue.

In making this choice you ignore the fact that yellow and blue will not be far apart. In fact you regard it as an advantage which will make it easier to continue the break after making hoop 2. If you cannot play confidently a split shot from any hoop to the next two hoops, then it is the most important thing you must learn to do as quickly as possible—far more important than improving your roqueting or your hoop running. There is no sense being concerned about leaving yellow close to blue if things go wrong, since if you fail to make hoop 2 black and yellow will almost certainly be together and your opponent will have the innings anyway. Assume that you will make hoop 2, and play the shot that makes it easiest to continue afterward.

DON'T SET UP IN YOUR OWN CORNER *by John Riches*

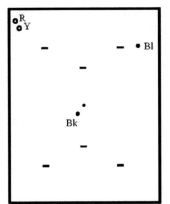

In the diagrammed position we can assume that yellow is already on 4-back and the player of yellow has again roqueted and set up as shown, hoping that in the next turn he will be able to get a break going with his red partner ball (or partner's ball in a doubles game) which is still for hoop 2.

Many assume that the best place to leave your two balls is near the border close to red's hoop, with a good rush in so that the hoop can be easily made.

However, if you (or your partner) are capable of playing breaks, then you should be looking to maximise the chance (if your opponent fails to roquet) of making not just one hoop, but a break.

The second diagram shows a far better leave from this point of view, provided the player of red is capable of rushing yellow to black and black to hoop 2.

Nor would the leave shown in the first diagram be any better if black were at hoop 4 instead of near the peg. Think through the shots the opponent may take and how you would continue as red, in order to convince yourself of this. You should work out and remember the ideal leave for each hoop, taking account of the shots you are capable of playing confidently and assuming that deliberately wiring balls will be impractical. Then be ready to use such a

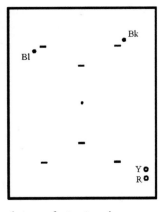

leave if the opportunity arises, and so maximise your chance of winning the game.

THE RIGHT SHOT *by John Riches*

In the diagrammed position the player of black had set up so that blue, which was for 1-back, has a good chance of a break in the next turn provided the player of red does not roquet. Regardless of where the red ball went, he should be able to rush black near enough to yellow, then leave black near 2-back and rush yellow to 1-back, with at least a 3-ball break.

The player of red elected to shoot at yellow and missed, thus making it even easier for blue to establish a 4-ball break by rushing black to red on the south border, then red to yellow and yellow to 1-back.

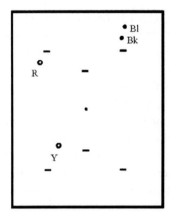

When asked why he had not shot at black, he replied that he thought he would finish too close to blue, who would turn around and roquet red, then get a rush on black to his 1-back hoop. This is a reasonable answer, and in fact there is not much to choose between shooting at black and shooting at yellow in the diagrammed position. (Of course, readers of my coaching articles will realise that the idea of not shooting at a ball, and instead hitting away into a corner, should not be given any consideration at all.)

In such a situation, where the two shots are of approximately equal length, it is a good idea to ask yourself which position you would prefer to face if you were to play the next turn with blue: would you rather have the red ball on the south boundary (having missed yellow), or in the 3rd corner (having missed black)? Not many would relish the idea of having to play a 6-yard pressure roquet; nor would they want to have red left near the baulk-line after making the 1-back hoop by rushing black to yellow and yellow to 1-back.

Whatever you do with red, you must accept that the opponent will have a good chance of selling up a break with blue unless you hit a roquet. Since you are equally likely to hit either shot, choose the one which, if missed, creates the situation you would least welcome if you were the opponent.

USE ALL THE BALLS *by John Riches*

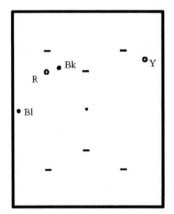

You are playing red in the position shown, and have just made 1-back. What will you do now? One possibility is to roquet black and send it to load 3-back (or worse still take off) while trying to get a rush on blue to 2-back; but with blue either on the yard-line or fairly close to it, it is likely that you would be faced with a rather long approach to 2-back after having given a 'lift'.

Even if blue were two or three yards in from the yard-line, where this shot would have a much greater chance of succeeding, you should not miss the opportunity to use the yellow ball which is about 4 yards from 4-back and cannot be considered a satisfactory load of that hoop. If you will have to end the break at 4-back to avoid giving contact, then it is even more essential to get yellow into the break immediately, to facilitate a good 'leave'.

Therefore the correct play is to rush black somewhere near the 3rd corner, use a stop-shot to send it to 3-back, and get a rush on yellow to blue (best) or to 2-back. It is rather too common for players to forget all about the yellow ball in such situations because it is outside their field of vision. They think only of how to make the next (2-back) hoop as quickly as possible. There is also a temptation, when stopping at 4-back, to be satisfied with simply making the remaining two hoops and not giving much thought to the need to obtain the best possible leave in order to maximise your chance of making another break with your other ball in your next turn.

There are several noticeable differences between Australian states in the way breaks are usually played, and one difference is that in SA our players strive to bring the 4th ball into a break as soon as possible, while in other states it is more common to play a 3-ball break and pick up the 4th ball later. There are reasons for such differences which could perhaps provide material for a future article.

DON'T LEAVE PARTNER IN THE MIDDLE *by John Riches*

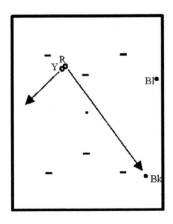

In the diagrammed position red has just made hoop 2, having run through to border, then roqueted yellow, sending it about half-way between hoop 2 and hoop 6. Many players would now take off to black, and try to continue the break by taking-off to blue, hoping to be able to rush it near enough to hoop 3. The problem with this method is that it leaves the partner ball out in the lawn when it is far from certain that you will be able to establish an immediate break.

A more conservative player may take off from yellow to hoop 3 immediately, or else roll both balls to the north border (possibly trying to get red in front of hoop 3) and set up there, allowing the opponent an extra attempt to roquet. An immediate take-off to blue is also possible.

In such situations the best option is to play a thick take-off as indicated by the arrows, sending yellow within 4-5 yards of the border while going to black to try to establish the break. Then it should not be difficult to bring yellow back into the break, for example after making either hoop 3 or hoop 5.

Most players give far too little attention to practising thick take-offs, and so are not confident in playing them. Perhaps they do not fully understand the mechanics involved, e.g. how to find the correct line of aim in order to allow for 'pull' on the yellow croqueted ball, 'mallet drag' on the red striker's ball, and the fact that in a thick take-off the red ball will tend to slide across the surface of the yellow ball in a way that does not happen in most other split shots. If you play the thick take-off and find yourself unable to make hoop 3 after approaching it with blue, you can return your red ball to the west border near yellow, possibly with a rush in the direction of hoop 4 so that blue would have no safe shot and you are threatening to establish the break in your next turn.

LOAD THAT HOOP *by John Riches*

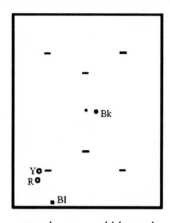

The diagram shows a situation where all clips are still on hoop 1, and blue has just shot from near hoop 2 at yellow, finishing on the south border in front of hoop 1. In such situations it is very difficult for a coach to persuade players NOT to immediately make hoop 1.

This would be incorrect (provided the player is capable of playing any sort of reasonable rush) because it guarantees only one hoop, when you should be thinking about establishing a break.

A slightly better line of play is to roquet yellow with red (or vice versa), take off to blue, and use a stop-shot to send blue to hoop 2 while trying to stop in position to run hoop 1. However such "load and hold" shots are not high percentage shots, and should only be used when there is no better alternative.

In this situation the best chance for most players to establish the break is to play red, rush yellow to hoop 2, and then take off to black near the peg, hoping to rush it either to hoop 1, or (better and easier still) near to blue on the south border, after which blue can be rushed to hoop 1. If you fail to get any sort of rush on black in the desired direction you can simply take off to blue and roll for hoop from the south border.

One final word: If for some reason you still prefer to make hoop immediately, then make it with a rush back to blue, which can be obtained more easily and certainly than a rush to black. Then blue can be rushed past hoop 5 toward black and sent to load hoop 3 before rushing black to hoop 2. This way you at least get both opponent balls out into the lawn.

As you walk onto the lawn to start your turn you should always be asking yourself not "How can I make my hoop?", but "How can I load the next hoop before I make the current one?"

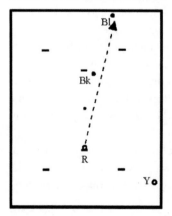

A MISSED OPPORTUNITY
by John Riches

When watching games it can seem to a coach that there are some players who "never miss an opportunity to miss an opportunity".

I am not referring here to the missing of short roquets or failure to make simple hoops, but to the failure to recognise an opportunity that has been presented to the player. Such failure is often due to an inability to think flexibly.

The first diagram shows a situation where red had almost—but not quite—made hoop 5. Blue, from near 2-back, shot at black and missed, finishing on the border in front of hoop 3. Many players would now run hoop 5 by hitting red near to black at hoop 6, failing to realise that they are missing an excellent opportunity to set up a 3-ball break by hitting red immediately to blue as shown by the arrow.

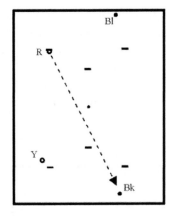

In the second diagram red had stuck in 1-back, and can make it by hitting down to yellow at 2-back, but will then face the problem of getting the opponent's balls away from the baulk-lines. If red had almost made the hoop, it is likely that he can complete the running of the hoop by hitting red through the hoop at an angle, so that it finishes near enough to black to roquet it and use it to load 3-back before making 2-back from yellow.

Such shots need some care—a good coach will be able to give useful advice about the best way to play it—and are well worth practising.

THINK BEFORE YOU HIT *by John Riches*

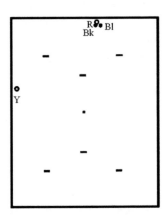

The 1st diagram shows a situation where red, which is for 4-back, has shot from near the peg and roqueted the black ball on the north border. When yardlined, the black ball is about 10cm from the blue ball. Most players would now leave black near the yardline and get a rush on blue to 4-back.

It is clear that they are likely to have difficulty continuing the break after making the one hoop, and they would make it much easier for themselves if they could somehow put the blue ball into the lawn before making 4-back.

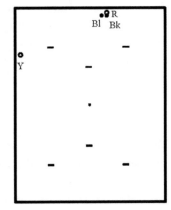

In this situation a little thought should suggest the idea of playing a disjoint cannon (or delayed or open or pseudo cannon, depending which book you read). This involves rushing blue to 4-back immediately in the croquet stroke, while also hitting into black sufficiently to send it toward penultimate. It sounds rather difficult, but after a little practice most players can play this type of shot quite confidently, and give themselves an excellent chance of continuing the break to the peg.

In the second diagram the blue ball is on the other side of black, but a disjoint cannon can still be used to send black to penultimate while rushing blue to yellow, and then yellow to 4-back. You will be surprised at the number of opportunities for disjoint cannons you can find if you start to look for them.

INVESTING IN THE FUTURE *by John Riches*

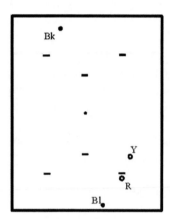

One of the most difficult tactical decisions that has to be made during a game is whether to take a low-percentage chance of continuing or selling up an immediate break; or to instead set up a good leave for your next turn. The correct answer will depend on the skill level of both you and your opponent, but in most cases (at least until you reach international level) the best advice is to set up so that your opponent gets one long shot, after which (provided he misses) you will have an immediate simple break. This policy will not work every time, but it will win you more games than attempting long, low-percentage rolls for your next hoop which usually result in giving the opponent one or more "free" shots after which, if he misses, you still do not have a break set up.

In the 1ˢᵗ diagram red is about to make 3-back, and the yellow clip is on 1-back. Although there would be no contact given, it is wrong for red to roll both balls to 4-back in the probably vain hope of making that hoop—and then having to get both opponent balls away from the baulk-lines. Instead he should simply set up the position in the 2ⁿᵈ diagram by puffing blue at 2-back and giving yellow a rush to black at 1-back. The principle is: Plan ahead, so as to make your future play as easy as possible.

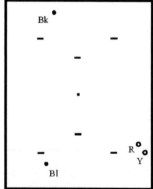

DIFFERENCES BETWEEN STATES (part 1) *by John Riches*

When watching players from different states I have noticed that SA players tend to go to more trouble than others to bring the 4ᵗʰ ball into a break as soon as possible. If playing red and approaching hoop 1 in the situation shown in the 1ˢᵗ diagram they would plan, after making the hoop, to rush yellow somewhere near the 4ᵗʰ corner,

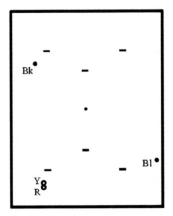

then use a stop-shot to load hoop 3 while going to blue, and play a thick take-off from blue to black, thus getting blue a few yards into court.

After hoop 2 they would again hope for a rush to blue, so they can immediately set up a 4-ball break. Players from most other states seem to prefer to make hoop 1 with a rush to the border near black, and load hoop 3 with a stop-shot, planning to bring blue into the break at a later stage.

In the second diagram SA players would usually make hoop 2 with a rush to the 1st corner, again with the idea of bringing yellow into play as soon as possible.

The reason for this difference is difficult to establish, but it may be due to the fact that in SA the hoops tend to be set very rigidly in the ground, which contains a lot of clay and dries out like cement (WA also has dry soil for most of the year, but it has less clay and more sand). With rigid hoops the 4th ball is necessary to ensure that you do not need to run any longish hoops.

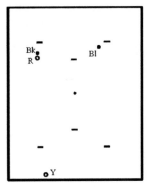

DIFFERENCES BETWEEN STATES (part 2) *by John Riches*

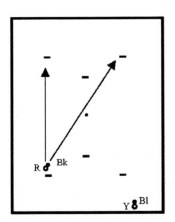

Another noticeable difference between players from various states is that SA players tend to play more shots with their hands at the top of the handle, using a lot of forward slope on the mallet shaft, while others tend more often to move one or both hands down the shaft, using less forward slope, and so make it a more definite "roll". Most of our players keep the hands at the top of the shaft when splitting from hoop to hoops 2 and 3 as shown in the first diagram, and also if they were playing yellow and approaching 3-back from the yardline in front of the hoop as shown.

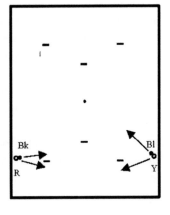

In the second diagram we would not use a narrow-angled roll to approach hoop 1 with red from the side border, but would keep the hands at the top of the shaft and use a wider-angled split approach, as shown with yellow approaching 3-back. The idea is that the hands at the top of the shaft allow better control (contrary to the intuitive feeling of many players), and the firmer ground due to our low rainfall allows the striker's ball to be confidently "squeezed" forward (quite legally) instead of needing to be "rolled". A hands-down rolling action can work quite well, but involves acceleration, and so introduces into the swing further variables which need to be accurately controlled.

DON'T LOAD TWO AHEAD *by John Riches*

One often sees players loading two hoops ahead, when it would be better to load only one hoop ahead and have the 4th ball as a "pivot ball". In the first diagram red

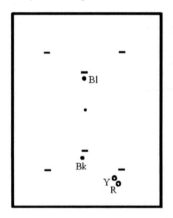

has made hoop 4, with hoops 5 and 6 already well loaded. The tendency of such players is to either roquet yellow gently and send it to 1-back with a stop-shot before making hoop 5, or (worse still) rush yellow to 1-back and take off back to black at hoop 5. It is better to roquet yellow 2-3 yards toward black, then place it either near the peg or between hoop 5 and 2-back.

The second diagram shows a position which can occur early in a game. Red is still for hoop 1, and blue has just shot from near hoop 1 at black and missed. Many players would now cut-rush yellow to hoop 3 and leave it there, taking off to blue, then rolling blue to hoop 2 while trying for a rush on black to hoop 1.

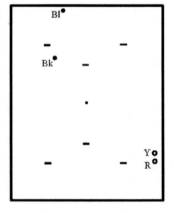

Yellow should have been rushed to the border in front of hoop 3 and left about 20 cm in from the yard-line when taking off to blue.

A third common situation where a hoop is loaded too early is when players load hoop 6 instead of hoop 5 after making hoop 3, and in the position of the first diagram it would actually be better to have blue not at hoop 6, but about one-third of the way from hoop 4 to hoop 6. However it is OK to load 2-back after hoop 5—if you are interested in the reasons for all this, ask your club coach to explain it to you.

THE PRIORITY BALL *by John Riches*

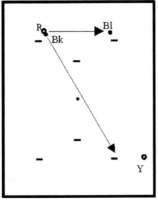

When using a split shot to load a hoop, in almost all cases you should give priority to the croqueted ball, in order to ensure an accurate load.

There is a common and understandable tendency to worry mainly about getting the striker's ball near enough to another ball to roquet it, and to merely send the croqueted ball anywhere vaguely in the direction of the hoop you are loading.

In actual fact it is the croqueted ball which needs to be placed more accurately than the striker's ball in order to ensure the continuance of the break. In the 1st diagram red is loading hoop 4 with black while going to make hoop 3 from blue. He will have little difficulty in making hoop 3 provided in the split shot red finishes within 3 yards of blue, but having black finish 3 yards from hoop 4 is not good enough, and is likely to make things much harder for himself after he has made hoop 3 and wants to bring the yellow ball into the break. In the second diagram red has made 1-back and is splitting black to 3-back while going to the slightly wayward blue "pivot ball". Again it is the blackball, rather than the red ball, which must be positioned accurately in the split. When playing such split shots, learn to concentrate on accurate placement of the croqueted ball.

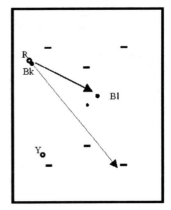

NO-MAN'S LAND *by John Riches*

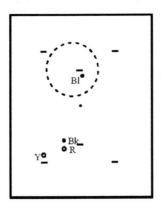

The first diagram shows a common situation where red is for hoop 6 and is about to rush black up the lawn, then use it to load 1-back while going to make hoop 6 from blue. In playing the rush it is important to realise that there are some places from which it will not be possible to accurately load 1-back as desired in the following stroke. In fact there will be a circular area of no-man's land" as indicated by the dotted circle, and it is helpful to picture this area so that you can avoid rushing the black ball into it and finding too late that you cannot load 1-back as planned.

In the 2nd diagram red is for hoop 5 and has obtained a good rush on black into the lawn, but must similarly avoid rushing it into the imaginary circle which is larger this time—because if he does so he will not be able to load hoop 6 accurately while going to yellow to make hoop 5.

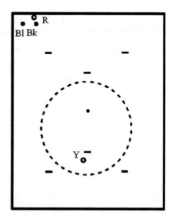

For those mathematically inclined, the diameter of the "no-man's land" circle extends approximately from the hoop you want to load to the ball you are going to use next, and then on past that ball for about an additional one-third of the distance. The same would apply if the ball you are going to use next is not at your hoop, and you need to get a rush on it while loading the following hoop; but of course the "no-mans-land' circle will be in a different position.

THE BEST PLACES *by John Riches*

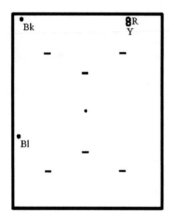

There are many situations in which players place balls incorrectly, often because they are unaware of the best places to put the balls.

In the 1st diagram all clips are still on hoop 1. In taking off from yellow to black, red should not try to send yellow in to hoop 3, but should leave it about 6 inches (15 cm) from the yardline; and when pass-rolling from the 2nd corner to blue I would encourage players, at least until they reach state level, to leave black about one yard behind hoop 2 rather than in front of it. The reasons for leaving the balls as described become apparent only if you think several strokes ahead, and realise that you are far from certain to make hoop 1 from such a situation, and so should give some thought to where the balls will be best placed for your next turn.

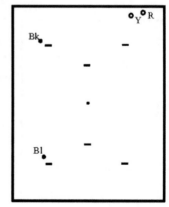

If you fail to gain position to run hoop 1, and have to return to yellow, you should aim to set up the position shown in the second diagram. Red has a rush to black, and if blue shoots at black and misses, then with black behind hoop 2 as shown it is easier to go to blue and put it at hoop

2 while getting a "dolly" rush on black to hoop 1 than if black were 1-2 yards in front of the hoop. If you are doubtful about this point, try it both ways and see how often you can do it. If you make hoop 1 at the first attempt, then making hoop 2 from a ball one yard behind it should not be too difficult.

SETTLING AN OLD ARGUMENT *by John Riches*

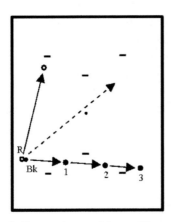

When lining up a split shot, many players still use the old, incorrect method of "halving the angle of split" in order to find the direction in which they need to swing the mallet. This method can work for splits in which the two balls are to travel roughly equal distances, but can be shown to be theoretically incorrect.

The 1st diagram illustrates a situation where red is going to hoop 2 and sending black to either of three possible points, all in the same line. Because the angle of split is almost a right-angle, the mallet will have to be swung flat through the ball in each case. How will you determine which of the three points the black ball goes to? If you "halve the angle", you will always swing in the direction of the dotted arrow, since the angle is exactly the same each time.

It is clear that people who claim they are "halving the angle" are in fact not doing so, since they would be able to send the black ball only to position 2. The correct method of finding the line of swing is shown in the 2nd diagram. You must swing at a point halfway between where the two balls are to finish. This point, for the three different shots, is indicated by an 'X', and the three different lines of swing are shown accordingly by the dotted arrows. Only the second dotted line is close to halving the angle of split as in this case the balls travel almost equal distances.

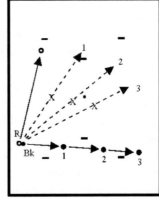

THE SAME OLD ERROR *by John Riches*

The first diagram shows a situation where red has just roqueted blue near hoop 5. With the red clip on 1-back and the other two balls unused, how would you continue?

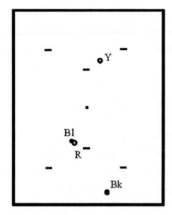

In such situations it is common to see players take off from blue to yellow, aiming to rush yellow to 1-back. While this would be a reasonable continuation, it involves making an error which we have seen many times before: failure to load your next hoop before making the current one. It is not difficult in this situation to put blue at 2-back while going to black, and this would be a far better thing to do even if black were on the yardline.

When black is a yard or more in court as shown, there is a good chance of getting a rush on it up the lawn and making it more certain that you will get a good rush on yellow to 1-back. If you have to take off from black to yellow, then getting the rush on yellow should not be much more difficult than if you had taken off from blue, and is a small price to pay for the advantage of having 2-back accurately loaded before you make 1-back.

A similar situation is shown in the second diagram, where red is for hoop 1 and had roqueted blue near the peg. He should not take off to black, but should send blue to hoop 2 while going to yellow, then take off back to black to make hoop 1 with hoop 2 already loaded.

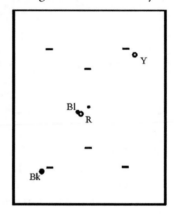

BUT IS IT COACHING? *by John Riches*

From time to time I still hear people express the idea that the main role of a coach is to (a) teach beginners how to play the game; and (b)tell you what you are doing wrong. Recently a player told me: "So-and-so is a good coach. He watched me play for a few minutes and told me exactly what I was doing wrong!"; and he was surprised when I asked: Did he tell you how to put it right?" A coach who merely tells you what you are doing wrong is no better than a doctor who diagnoses your illness but does not know how to treat it—you would probably have been better off not knowing! Further questioning of the above-mentioned player revealed that the "coach" had told him his backswing was crooked and out of line. This fact was obvious to anyone at all, whether they knew anything about coaching or not; but such a problem can be quite difficult to remedy, and it is unlikely that the player will be able to correct it on his own, as when he stands over the ball and swings the mallet back it will appear to him that his backswing is straight.

The real problem is that there is something in his swing which is causing the ball to go off to one side—possibly tightening the grip during the swing, or incorrect placement of the bottom hand, or cramped stance, or incorrect foot placement, or hurrying of the forward swing, etc.; and the coach needs to be able to sort out not only what the problem is, but what is causing it, and then how to remedy it. In fact, a crooked backswing on its own (which is rare) may not cause any actual problem at all.

The problem in the swing is almost certainly mechanical, and probably one of those listed in the previous paragraph, causing him to miss roquets fairly consistently on the same side. Over time the player has unconsciously learnt to "correct" for it by aiming a little to the other side of the target ball, which enables him to hit the roquets for awhile, but in the long run makes the problem worse. After doing this for some time his brain becomes conditioned to accept the incorrect idea that the line he is swinging in is actually the correct line—because it seems to work. His brain needs to be retrained, and that is where the real work of the trained coach begins. Then, of course, there are the various other aspects of coaching—psychology, tactics, training programmes, and so on, all of which need to be tailored to suit the individual player being coached. Be sure that the person from whom you accept advice really does know what coaching actually involves.

BALL SLIP *by John Riches*

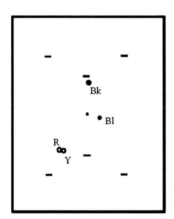

Most players are unaware of "ball slip" which affects the lining up, and consequently the result, of "thick take-offs". In the 1st diagram red wants to send yellow in front of rover while going to make penultimate from black; and in the 2nd diagram he wants to send yellow in to 4-back while going to the opponent's balls to make 2-back. Many players find that in their thick take-offs the croqueted ball falls short of its intended destination, while the strikers ball tends to go too far.

This is due to the fact that in a "thick take-off" or right-angle split the surfaces off the balls tend to slip against each other instead of gripping as they do in other split shots. (Ball slip also occurs in a normal 'fine' take-off, but is not noticed because of the different method of lining up.)

In order to allow for "ball-slip" you will usually need to select the line of swing by choosing a point halfway between where you want the balls to finish, and then adjusting the line a little more into the croqueted ball, instead of into the striker's ball as

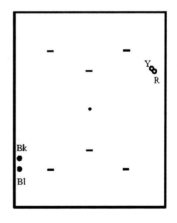

you need to do with other splits. This is because in most split shots "mallet drag" on the striker's ball more than counteracts "pull" on the croqueted ball; and significant ball slip occurs only when the angle of split approaches a right-angle. The amount of "slip" will depend on the condition of the balls and whether they are wet or dry.

PRINCIPLES OF LEAVES *by John Riches*

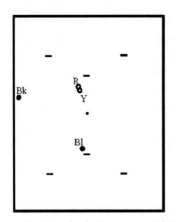

What considerations should be bone in mind when thinking about a good leave? The most important thing is to choose a leave such that if the opponent fails to roquet you will be able to set up an immediate break, before giving him a further chance to roquet and gain the innings. A second consideration is that the leave should be attainable without undue risk. Contrary to popular opinion, both of these things are usually more important than minimising the chance of the opponent roqueting.

One way to explain this is to consider the percentages involved. For example, you may be inclined to think that you could improve a leave by placing the balls so that instead of the opponent having (say) a 40% chance of roqueting he will have only a 35% chance.

This would be an improvement if everything else was unchanged, but the change is also likely to make it harder for you, if the opponent fails to roquet, to get a break established before giving him another chance to roquet. For example, your chance of establishing an immediate break may be reduced from 90% to 80%. To many players it will seem safer to reduce the chance of the opponent roqueting, but in this case the price you would have to pay is too high, and you would be better off allowing him a slightly shorter roquet, but ensuring that if he misses it is less likely that he will get another chance. In terms of percentages, 90% of 60% is better than 80% of 65% (the 60% and 65% are the chances of the opponent failing to roquet after the two alternative leaves). The problem is that many players tend to think only of the immediate future. They play to minimise the chance of the opponent roqueting, and then only after he has failed to do so will they give thought to maximising their own chance of setting up a break. By then it will often be too late. Tactical choices based on one stroke at a time will prove to be inadequate against an opponent who looks further ahead and sees the whole picture.

GETTING THE LEAVE *by John Riches*

This is an article for more advanced players who can make a break of nine hoops often enough to make it worthwhile for them to also consider the best leave, and how

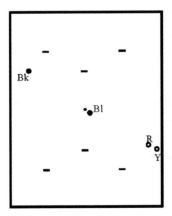

to get it, in order to give the best chance of making another break if the opponent misses the lift roquet.

There are various leaves possible, but in recent years the most frequently used one is the diagonal leave" illustrated in the first diagram, where red has gone around to 4-back and set for yellow which is still on hoop. Black and blue are wired by the peg, which also hampers a shot by blue at red and yellow; and in addition the short lift shot from the eastern end of A-baulk is hampered by hoop 4.

It is obviously a strong leave, but how do you get it? Many players try it, and some succeed, by leaving an opponent ball (black) in position near hoop 2 after making 1-back. However it is usually better to load hoop 3 with the opponent ball, and after making 2-back send both your partner ball and the other opponent ball just east of the peg as shown in the second diagram, before making 3-back from the same opponent ball you made 1-back from. After making 3-back it is easy to send that ball (black) near enough to the position shown on the first diagram while going to blue near

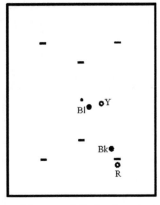

the peg. With yellow also close handy, you can position blue carefully in the wired position before rushing yellow to the east border to set up.

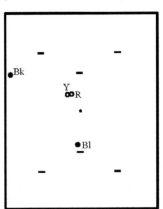

It is not uncommon to see quite good players missing opportunities to obtain the best possible leave at the end of a break because all they are thinking about is making the last one or two hoops.

In the diagrammed position red, which was for penultimate at the start of the turn, had roqueted blue and used it to load rover hoop before making penultimate from yellow. After making penultimate he has now roqueted yellow again as shown.

Now, if not even earlier, is the time when he should consider how he is going to leave the balls after making rover. He must check where the yellow clip is (in this case it was on 2-back) and work out the best places to leave the four balls at the end of his break.

In order to give himself the maximum chance of finishing the game in his next turn he will need to ensure that both opponent balls are left so that he will be able to set up a 3-ball break using whichever ball the opponent does not move. It is not good enough to leave the black ball out of play on the west border as it is at present. Therefore he should take off to black and send it to either 2-back or 3-back before making rover, after which the blue ball can be left at the other of these two hoops. This ensures that at the start of his next turn, provided the opponent does not roquet, there will be a ball either at yellow's hoop, or loading the next hoop. All he has to do in addition is rush yellow to (say) the east border near 4-back and set it a rush to either of the opponent balls.

An even stronger leave would be to wire the opponent's balls across the 2-back hoop; but this would also require red to get all balls into play, with black and yellow in this case placed near 2-back, before red makes the rover hoop. Don't leave it until after you have made the last hoop before you start to think about the leave.

SHOT SELECTION *by John Riches*

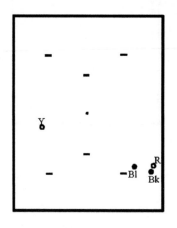

In the diagrammed situation the player of black and blue had failed to make hoop 4 with black. The player of red has just shot with red from near hoop 5 and roqueted the black ball. The red clip is on hoop 1. He will now play to get a rush on blue—but to where?

Some players will rush blue to hoop 1 and try to make the hoop without giving any thought to first loading hoop 2. They will usually struggle to make more than one hoop, and that is all they deserve to make.

Others will rush blue close to yellow, then rush yellow to hoop 1 so that they can make the hoop with their partner ball. These players will have similar difficulty making much more than one hoop. Many will rush blue to hoop 2 and then take off for a rush on yellow to hoop 1. At least these people are thinking about the need to set up a break instead of making just one hoop, but they have not selected the best tactical continuation.

The correct way is to rush blue to a position about halfway between hoop 1 and yellow, then use a stop-shot to load hoop 2 while getting a rush on yellow back to hoop 1. Most times you should be able to load hoop 2 with blue more accurately with a stop-shot than you can with a rush, and the stop-shot should also enable you to get a better rush on yellow to hoop 1 than you would have got if you had taken off from near hoop 2.

John Riches and Wayne Davies

The principle of loading hoops with croquet shots (preferably stop-shots) rather than rushes is constantly emphasised by coaches and just as constantly overlooked by players in lower grades—if they make any attempt at all to load hoops ahead. Players often blame the loss of a game on missed roquets or failure to run easy hoops, when the real reason they lost was poor shot selection in situations such as the one we have considered here.

THINK BEFORE YOU RUSH *by John Riches*

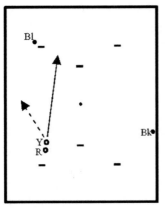

In the first diagram Red has made hoop 1 and has a forward rush on yellow, with black waiting just behind hoop 2. Many players will rush yellow to a position about halfway between hoops 2 and 6 as shown by the unbroken arrow, then find that they have no satisfactory way of loading hoop 3 before making hoop2.

If you cannot cut yellow right into the 2nd corner, then you should rush yellow only half-way to hoop 2, and preferably cut it a bit toward the west border as shown by the broken arrow, to a position from which you can split yellow accurately to hoop 3 while going to black to make hoop 2.

In the position shown on the second diagram red is again for hoop 2 and has taken off from yellow to black. Now it is again important for red to rush black to a position from which black can be sent to load hoop 3 before making hoop 2 from blue. The best place to rush black is as close to the 2nd corner as you can get it, since from there it will require only a simple stop-shot to achieve the desired result.

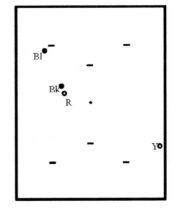

A top player, instead of taking off would have split yellow to hoop 3 while going to black. This long split roll may be seen as risky by some players, but he will want to load the next hoop and bring the fourth (partner) ball into his break as early as possible and would consider that a certain amount of risk is worth taking if it will make it easier for him to continue the break. The moral is: If you are not prepared to load hoops ahead, you must expect to get beaten by opponents who are.

TIME FOR A BREAK *by John Riches*

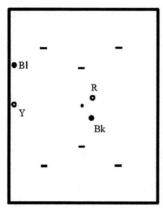

Imagine that you are the player of red and yellow in the diagrammed position, with your red clip on hoop 3 and yellow on hoop 4. (When this occurred in a recent game, blue was for hoop 1 and black was for hoop 5.) Which ball would you play?

Although the roquet is longer and therefore less certain, the only thing that makes sense is to shoot with yellow at blue. Unfortunately, like the player I was watching, many players find it difficult to bring themselves to play such a shot in a serious game, even when they know it is the correct thing to do. They instead take the shorter roquet by shooting with red at black, and say that they did not want to leave the red ball out in the lawn for black to use.

It should be obvious that there is a much better chance of setting up a break with yellow than with red, assuming that you roquet, by going to red and using it to load hoop 5 while getting a rush on black to hoop 4. Taking a 50% chance of making a break is much better, and more likely to win you the game, than taking even a 100% chance of keeping the innings but making no progress. There is nothing safe about failing to take the risks necessary to set up breaks when the opportunity is there.

In this situation a player who plays red and roquets black should forget about trying to make hoop 3 in this turn (unless at international level), and simply play to leave an opponent ball at each of his hoops (3 and 4), with his red and yellow balls near the west border and a useful rush for either; but any player who would think of this and have the shots to do it safely would have played yellow rather than red in the first place. It is often not easy to convince yourself in such situations that the less certain roquet is in fact the safer one, because you are actually taking a bigger risk of losing the game if you 'chicken out' and opt for the shorter roquet.

DON'T SET UP TOO CLOSE TO THE BORDER
by John Riches

In the position shown on the diagram all clips are still on hoop 1. The player of red has rolled from near the peg with his yellow partner ball for hoop 1, but now finds that he will not be able to make the hoop. An almost automatic reaction is to use the one remaining shot to hit red out to border near the first corner, perhaps with the idea of getting it as far as possible from the black ball which the opponent will play in the next turn.

John Riches and Wayne Davies

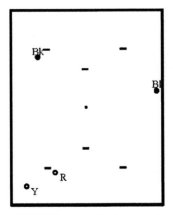

This gives your opponent a relatively safe shot with black at your balls in the 1ˢᵗ corner, since if he misses you will have difficulty making more than just the one hoop; and setting up a break will require several accurate and rather difficult shots.

It is far better to hit red gently about 2 yards due west to a position about 1 yard from hoop 1 toward the 1ˢᵗ corner. (Those who have read my booklets will recognise this as a "trap-line" set-up.) Then, if black shoots at red or yellow and misses, you should be able to set up an easy break by playing yellow, roqueting black, and using a stop-shot to send it back to hoop 2 before making hoop 1 from red.

Note that this is better than trying to hide red from black in front of hoop 1, since in your next turn you will want to make a break with yellow rather than just making hoop 1 with red, and will not want to roquet red away from the hoop. Also, you want to encourage the opponent to shoot at your balls rather than discourage him from doing so. If black shoots at his blue partner ball and misses, you can play yellow, make hoop 1 from red, then hopefully rush red in an easterly direction, to a position from which you can use it to load hoop 3 while going to the opponent's balls on the east border and rushing one of them to hoop 2, with a break set up.

A BREAK IS BETTER THAN A HOOP *by John Riches*

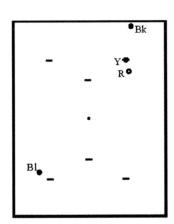

There is a strong tendency for people to over-emphasise the importance of technique (being able to roquet and run hoops well), and downplay the importance of two things which in fact play a larger part in determining the results of games: the ability to play split shots, and tactical choices.

In the diagrammed position the player of yellow had stuck in hoop 3 with the other three clips still on hoop 1, and his opponent had missed the shot with black from near hoop 4. Although he was one of our leading players, he now made the mistake of walking onto the lawn without stopping to think, and making hoop 3 with yellow, obtaining a cut-rush to hoop 4 with some chance of making it (in fact, he failed to do so), but with little chance of selling up a break.

A few seconds thought would have been enough to convince him that he would have had a much better chance of winning the game by playing red, rushing yellow to the border near black, then rushing black to either hoop 2 or the south border, and thus playing to make a break rather than just one or two hoops. If he had to play yellow, it would also have been better in making hoop 3 to run past red and then rush it back near to black, after which black could be rushed to the west border near blue and used to load hoop 5 with a stop-shot before rushing blue to hoop 4. This at least gives some chance of setting up a break, but with a lower percentage chance of succeeding than if he had played red.

For many players there is a psychological urge to make an easy hoop or take the shortest roquet, then think afterward about how they are going to continue.

Although it seems so obvious as to not need stating, we must emphasise once again that there is nothing safe about passing up opportunities to make breaks—and in fact that is how most games are won and lost.

THE RIGHT ROLL *by John Riches*

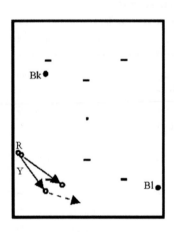

The first diagram shows a fairly common situation shortly after the start of a game, where the player of red has roqueted the 'tice' ball after pass-rolling the black ball to hoop 2 from the 2nd corner, and now is attempting to make hoop 1. Many players would again use a pass roll, placing their yellow partner ball 2-3 yards behind hoop 1 and hoping to get a forward rush after making the hoop.

This is good if you make the hoop, but if you find yourself unable to do so, it leaves you in a vulnerable position where you will have to allow the opponent a "free" shot at yellow with black, or else if you cover the south border to stop this, you allow him to shoot at blue with relative safety.

A better method is to roll yellow about a yard past hoop 1 as shown by the unbroken arrows, and then if you cannot make the hoop you can more safely cover the border (see the unbroken arrow) and any shot your opponent takes will now be much riskier for him.

If you succeed in making hoop 1, you can rush yellow to the south border as shown by the unbroken arrows in the second diagram, then send it to hoop 3 while going to blue on the east border (see broken arrows), and from there take off to black with the advantage that blue will now be off the yardline and easier to bring into the break.

WATCH WHERE YOU LEAVE PARTNER *by John Riches*

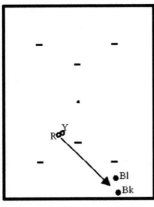

A common tactical mistake is to leave the partner ball near the middle of the lawn when there is only a small chance of getting a break set up. (It is also a common mistake not to bring your partner ball into the lawn when you do have a good chance of setting up a break; but that will have to be the subject of another article.)

In the first diagram red has made hoop 1 and roqueted yellow toward the peg. The ideal continuation would be to send yellow to hoop 3 while going to the opponent's balls, but here it is not possible. Many players would take off from yellow to the opponent's balls, roquet black, and then rush blue to hoop 2; but if they do not succeed in making the hoop they will have left themselves in a very vulnerable situation, either with both balls in the middle of the lawn, or with their balls widely separated.

The correct play is shown in the 2nd diagram: Yellow should be rolled to within 2-3 yards of the east border as illustrated by the arrows. If the yellow clip is still on hoop 1 a reasonable alternative would be to send yellow toward the 1st corner, but it is better to put yellow where you may be able to use it to continue your break. In this situation getting your partner ball out of the middle is not "negative" play; it costs nothing, is sound common sense, and shows that you are thinking ahead.

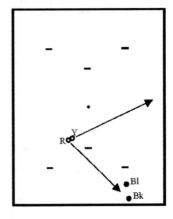

TAKE THOSE BREAKS *by John Riches*

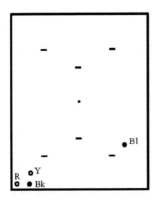

This is yet another article on what is probably my most commonly recurring theme: Do not pass up opportunities to make breaks. Sometimes this involves looking past what is immediately obvious and recognising other possibilities which may give you less certainty of making your next hoop, but a much better chance of setting up a break.

The situation shown in the 1st diagram occurred in a recent game where yellow was for hoop 4 and the other three clips were still on hoop 1. Black had just shot at yellow from near hoop 2 and missed. Now the player of red roqueted black, then rushed yellow to hoop 1 and made it with little difficulty—but also with only a small chance of continuing the break.

The correct play is to use yellow instead of red, roquet red, then rush black to the east border as shown by the arrow in the 2nd diagram. From there black can be sent accurately to hoop 5 while coming in behind blue for a rush to hoop 4, after which it should be easy enough to also bring red into the break (provided you had not left it right in the 1st corner). Note that rushing black to the east border is preferable to rushing

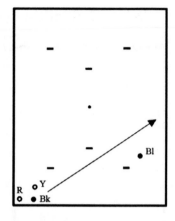

it to hoop 5 and then taking off to blue. If you doubt this, try it several times both ways to convince yourself.

MAKE USE OF YOUR PARTNER *by John Riches*

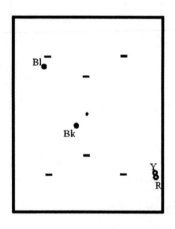

Many players have been told over the years that it is wise to leave your partner ball near the border so that if something goes wrong you will have somewhere safe to come home to.

While this advice may be reasonable in some situations, it can often involve passing up valuable opportunities to set up breaks.

The first diagram shows a position in which the red clip is on hoop 2 and red has roqueted yellow on the east border. Many players as red would take off from yellow to black and hope to set up a break by loading hoop 3 with black before making hoop 2

from blue. A more experienced player will split yellow immediately to hoop 3 while going to black, with a 4-ball break fully set up. With the blue ball waiting at hoop 2 you should have no doubts about making that hoop, so putting yellow at hoop 3 involves very little risk and makes it much easier for you to continue the break. It also gives you a second chance of loading the hoop accurately with black if the first loading attempt with yellow goes astray. In the 2nd diagram red is for hoop 4, and sending yellow to hoop 5 while

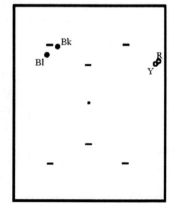

John Riches and Wayne Davies

going to the opponent's balls at hoop 2 before rushing one of them to hoop 4 is a bit riskier, but it is again a risk well worth taking for most players because it is the only good way to set up a break.

FINDING THE BEST PLACE *by John Riches*

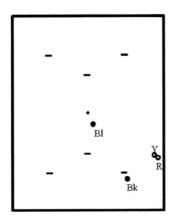

The two situations diagrammed here illustrate a tactic which is often overlooked by players because they have an aversion to puffing balls close together, since it will make it easy for the opponent if you happen to break down. Unfortunately they fail to realise that with balls close together you should be less likely to break down, so pulling them close to each other may actually be the safest thing to do.

In the first diagram red is for 3-back and after using blue has rushed yellow to the east border, instead of to the 4th corner as intended. He now cannot load 4-back with yellow as planned, so what should he do with it in the croquet stroke?

There will be no difficulty in making 3-back from black, so the best place for yellow is as close to the blue ball as you can get it.

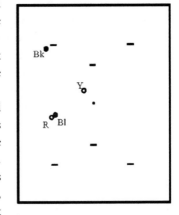

Then after making 3-back you can load penultimate with black while going to the two balls you have carefully placed near the peg, and use one of them to get an easy rush on the other to 4-back.

In the 2nd diagram red is for 1-back and has used yellow but failed to get a useful rush on blue, so roqueted it about halfway between 1-back and 2-back. He cannot load 2-back, but should send blue as close to yellow as he can while going to make—back from black. This may seem rather obvious when it is pointed out to you, but would you have thought of it in a tense game situation?

A PIVOTAL CHOICE *by John Riches*

In the first diagram red has just shot from near hoop 3 and roqueted black which was in front of hoop 2. The player of red now used a stop-shot to send black to hoop 3 while going to blue, roqueted blue, and took off to yellow to make hoop 1, with the next two hoops 'loaded'.

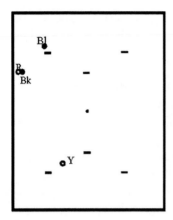

It seems like a good way to set up a break, but it would have been better to roll black in front of hoop 2 while going behind blue for a rush down the lawn to somewhere near or past hoop 5. Then the blue ball can be sent to an ideal "pivot" position between hoop 1 and the peg while getting an easy rush on yellow to hoop 1.

This will allow you to load hoops 2 and 3 more accurately, rush yellow closer to hoop 1, and avoid having to play a difficult shot (or else leave a ball behind) if you fail to get a forward rush on yellow after making hoop 1.

Similarly, in the 2nd diagram where red is for hoop 3, yellow should be rolled to hoop 4 and then blue rushed nearer black, preferably to the border near black, from where it can be sent in toward the peg while getting a good rush on black to hoop 3. It is not good enough to simply take-off from yellow to black, or take-off to blue and then from blue to black, or to send yellow into the middle of the lawn while going to blue, as although each of these options is quite playable, they involve having to play harder and less accurate shots than if you do it the recommended way.

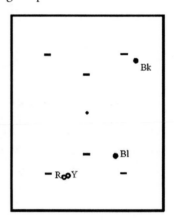

MARGIN FOR ERROR *by John Riches*

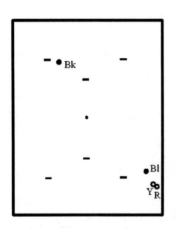

In the position shown on the first diagram the player of red has made hoop 1 from yellow and rushed it to the border near blue alongside hoop 4. He will now place yellow at hoop 4 and use blue to load hoop 3 before making hoop 2 from black.

The most common way of doing this is to rush blue to hoop 3 and take off to black, but it is better to play for a rush on blue not to hoop 3 but to the second corner, planning to load hoop 3 in the croquet stroke and also get a rush on black to bring it closer to hoop 2. The accurate loading of hoop 3 and rush into hoop 2 should be achieved easily enough if you can rush blue to anywhere in the large shaded area shown on the second diagram.

This allows a much greater margin for error than if you rush blue to hoop 3, as there is a much smaller area (also shaded) into which you would need to rush blue.

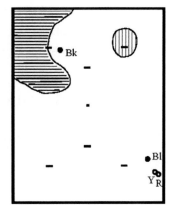

It is perhaps somewhat paradoxical that although top players can play shots more accurately than the average player, whenever possible they choose the option which does not require them to play accurate shots, whereas a less experienced player will more often choose the option which requires more accurate shot-making. If you try to picture in your mind the area into which you will need to rush the ball when deciding where to rush it (or earlier, where you want to get the rush to), you will be more likely to choose the best option.

AIMING HINTS—HAMPERED SHOTS (*by John Riches*)

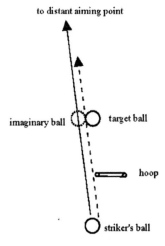

In my early days of playing croquet I was fascinated by the way some of the top players were able to roquet without fail a tiny fraction of a ball which was almost completely hidden behind a hoop as indicated by the dotted line on the diagram. I later discovered that there are some secrets you need to know, especially in selecting your line of aim.

Firstly, it is important when starting the swing not to look at either the hoop or the target ball Looking at either of these will make you almost certain to hit the hoop. Some players instead imagine a ball alongside the target ball, as illustrated by the dotted ball in the diagram, and try to roquet this imaginary ball almost dead centre.

An even better idea is to walk back a few yards and carefully select a point in the distance, off the far side of the court, so that if you hit your ball to that particular aiming point", it will miss the hoop leg and just hit the target ball.

Then stalk the aiming point to get your body and mallet face square to the desired line of swing (i.e. the unbroken line on the diagram). If the target ball is an opponent ball you should hit the shot firmly enough to reach the far border, and this will also keep your ball in the correct line, as gentle shots can tend to wobble off line, and seem to always wobble away from hoops which are often on slight mounds due to the frequent filling in of old hoop holes.

Using this method you will probably be surprised at the confidence with which you can play the stroke and hit an eighth of an inch (3 mm) or less of the target ball. Remember that during the swing you must concentrate on "roqueting' the aiming point, while ignoring completely the hoop and target ball.

AIMING HINTS—RUSHES (*by John Riches*)

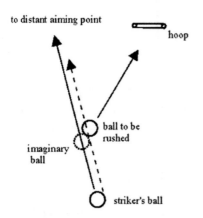

The ability to play cut-rushes accurately is an essential for all top players.

There are several important factors, one of which is the ability to select the correct line of aim and then swing the mallet straight in that direction with a square mallet face.

As for severely hampered roquets which we examined in the previous article, some players imagine a third ball in contact with the ball they are going to rush, and exactly on the opposite side from the direction of the desired rush. This is illustrated by the dotted ball in the diagram, and they aim so as to roquet this imaginary ball dead centre.

Most players will find it easier to select an aiming point in the distance behind the imaginary ball, or else forget about imagining a ball there and just choose a distant point so that your ball is "wired" from it by a particular amount of the ball you are intending to rush, as illustrated by the dotted line.

The less the rushed ball overlaps the dotted line, the finer will be the rush.

It is also important to remember, especially for a fine cut, that you must avoid causing your ball to jump, because even a slight jump may be sufficient to cause it to completely miss the ball you are rushing by jumping over its edge. For this reason you should try to use a swing with along, flat bottom, which will be easier if your mallet and grip (and arms) are longer rather than shorter. A further point worth remembering is that almost all cut-rushes which are cut at the desired angle are under-hit. In fact even straight rushes are far more often under-hit than over-hit, so it is a good idea to allow for this by hitting noticeably harder than may at first seem necessary. However, this must not be achieved by hurrying the mallet through with the bottom hand. Instead, take a longer backswing and let the mallet swing confidently forward under its own weight.

PLAY TO MAKE BREAKS, NOT JUST HOOPS *by John Riches*

In the diagram, the player of black, after taking off from blue in the 4th corner to the opponent's balls in the 2nd corner, has attempted to make hoop 2 from red, but failed.

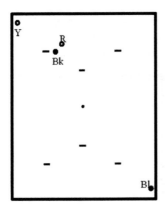

If you are the player of red and yellow, and red is also for hoop 2, what will you now do? It is safe to say that at least 9 players out of 10—probably 10 out of 10—would play red, roquet black and make hoop 2, probably trying to get a rush to hoop 3 after making hoop 2. Even if they succeed in getting the rush to hoop 3, the chance of being able to continue the break is not good. If you doubt this, set up the position and see how many times out of 10 you can get an immediate break established by playing red and making hoop 2 immediately.

The correct thing to do, for any player capable of making even limited breaks, is to shoot with red at yellow in the 2nd corner. If you hit the roquet you can send yellow to hoop 3 while going to black, with an immediate break set up; and you should be able to establish an immediate break this way more often than you can by roqueting black instead of yellow. Notice that if you miss the shot at yellow, black could attempt to roquet one of your balls; but if he succeeds he still will not have a break to follow, whereas if he misses you should have a good chance of creating a cannon with another easy chance to establish an immediate break.

Another method would be to roquet black, then take off to yellow and attempt a load-and-hold shot which sends yellow to hoop 3 while making position to run hoop 2. This, if successful, would also give you an immediate break, but it is riskier since you will have to make the hoop with the black ball present and it is also black's hoop. In any case, few players could succeed with the load-and-hold shot as often as they could roquet yellow, so the immediate shot at yellow is your best chance of establishing a break before the opponent does.

DON'T BE AFRAID OF TOGETHERNESS *by John Riches*

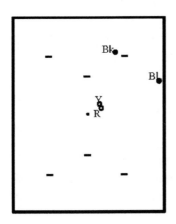

How should the player of red continue the break in the first diagram, where he is for hoop 3 and has roqueted yellow near the peg? He will take off to blue, and it would make things easy if he could rush blue to either the 3rd corner or to the 4th hoop; but more than likely he will have to be satisfied with roqueting blue more or less where it is.

What then? I hope that most readers will immediately see the best way of ensuring the continuance of the break: send yellow as close to blue as you can get it while going to make hoop

3 from black Then, after making hoop 3, you can send black to load hoop 5 while going to the two balls you have placed together near the border, and it should be a simple mailer to use one of them to get a rush on the other to hoop 4.

It is so easy when you think of it, but many players have been conditioned in their thinking to keep balls apart "in case you break down", instead of putting them together to ensure that you will not break down. Nothing other than placing the balls together gives as good a chance of continuing the break.

In the second diagram red is for 2-back, and had taken off from blue intending to use black to load 3-back, but has accidentally roqueted black in the take-off and now finds that he cannot get black to 3-back while going to make 2-back from yellow. He should simply take off from black, leaving the blue and black balls close together.

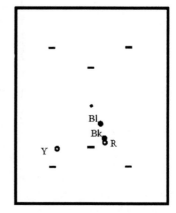

TUNNEL VISION? *by John Riches*

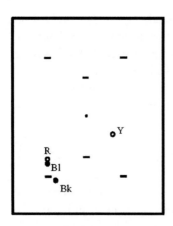

In the diagram all clips are still on hoop 1. Black had failed to make hoop 1, then red has just shot from hoop 2 and roqueted blue.

Most players, even when they fully appreciate the importance of loading the next hoop before making the current one, suffer from a sort of "tunnel" vision.

All they can see is an easy chance to make hoop 1 from black, so that is what they do—only to then discover that continuing the break will not be easy.

Can you see a way to load hoop 2 before making hoop 1? How many of the following ways did you consider?:

1. Stop-shot blue to hoop 2, then turn around and roquet black.
2. Leave blue where it is, rush black to A-baulk, and use a stop-shot to send it to hoop 2 while making position to run hoop 1.
3. Split blue to hoop 2 going to yellow, then take off back to black.
4. Roll both red and blue near to yellow, then roquet yellow and play a split shot which sends yellow to hoop 2 while going to make hoop 1 from black.

5. Take off to the right side of yellow, rush it to hoop 2, then take off to black.
6. Take off to the left side of yellow, rush it to A-baulk, and then send it to hoop 2 in a croquet stroke while going to black to make hoop 1.

In the diagrammed position option 3 would be the best for most players, followed by option 6; but if the yellow ball is in a different place one of the other options could be preferable. The important thing is to consider them all and select the one that best suits the position and your own skills. For example, if yellow is in the 4th corner, then options 2 and 4 (starting with a take-off rather than a roll) are likely to be the most attractive ways to load hoop 2 before making hoop 1; and if yellow is at hoop 3 then it is OK to immediately make hoop 1 without hoop 2 loaded—can you see why?

DOUBLE LOADING *by John Riches*

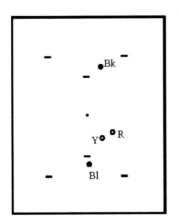

The first diagram shows a situation where red has made hoop 4 and attempted to load hoop 6 with black while going to yellow. However, the black ball did not go where it was intended, and is a rather poor "load" for hoop 6.

Instead of being satisfied with this, red should now rush yellow somewhere near hoop 1 and then not leave it there, but use an angled stop-shop to place it in front of hoop 6 while going to black to make hoop 5.

If you want to play tight breaks and reduce your chance of breaking down, the principle to follow is "If at first you don't succeed . . ."; or in other words, be prepared to double-load hoops when the first attempt has not been as accurate as you would have wanted.

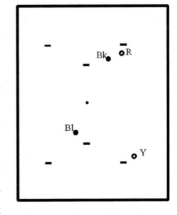

One often sees players playing "messy" breaks with hoops poorly loaded, hoping that they will somehow manage to keep going. Often they will—perhaps often enough for them to think that what they are doing is OK so they keep on doing it—without realising the importance of making sure they can easily continue the break by double-loading any inaccurately loaded hoop. In the second diagram red has just made hoop 3. He should not rush black to hoop 6 and leave it there, but should use it to load hoop 5 while going to blue, so that if the first loading attempt is inaccurate, he can try again with blue.

A DIFFICULT JUDGEMENT *by John Riches*

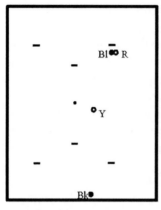

A difficult decision in selling up breaks is at what stage to bring your partner ball into the break. If you have an excellent chance of succeeding in getting the break established you should not hesitate to bring your partner ball out into the lawn; but until then it may be wiser to keep the option of a sound leave if you should fail to establish an immediate break. In the first diagram red is still for hoop 1. He will use blue to load hoop 2 while going to his yellow partner ball, but instead of trying for a rush on yellow to hoop 1, he should prefer to rush it near black on the south border, and then rush black to hoop 1. This not only gives a slightly better chance of establishing the break; more importantly, if you cannot make hoop it allows you to return to yellow with a good leave so that your opponent gets only one chance at a long roquet, and if he misses you will have a break set up for your next turn. Many players miss such opportunities because they have the misguided idea that it is "safer" to make hoops from their partner ball than from the opponent's balls.

In the second diagram red is for hoop 5, and has roqueted blue near hoop 2.

He should now use blue to load hoop 6 while trying for a rush on yellow not to hoop 5, but to the black ball which he will then rush to hoop 5. Until you have the break established, bring your opponent's balls out into the lawn, rather than your own balls.

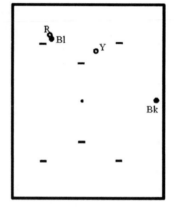

IT IS SAFER TO ATTACK *by John Riches*

In the position shown on the first diagram, black is for hoop 3 and blue is for hoop 2. What would now do if you were playing red? A missed shot at yellow would allow blue to rush black to hoop 3 and take off to your balls to easily set up a break, so the only sensible thing to do is to shoot at blue. Some players would avoid this because they would not want to "give the opponent an extra ball", particularly when he does not already have a rush to either of his hoops. However a missed shot at blue would not make it all that easy for black to establish a break, although he should at least make hoop 3. The important question to ask yourself is not would amiss

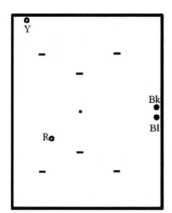

allow my opponent to make his hoop?, but "would it allow him to load the next hoop before making his current hoop?", because that is the only way he will have a good chance of setting up a break.

Hitting red into a corner or returning wide of your partner in such situations is not only "negative" play; it reduces your winning chances by passing up a reasonably safe chance to roquet

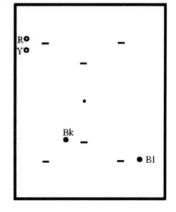

and gain the innings. The same applies in the second diagram where black is for 2-back and blue is for hoop 3. Rather than shooting at yellow, which would give blue an excellent chance of establishing a break if the shot is missed, red should shoot at blue, and for the chance of roqueting be willing to concede black one hoop.

WHEN FURTHER AWAY IS BETTER *by John Riches*

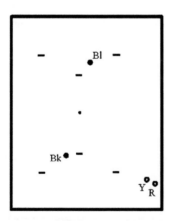

You have roqueted with your yellow ball which is for 4-back, so instead of making hoops with yellow you want to set up for red, which is for hoop 4.

Where would you leave the four balls? It is surprising to me as a coach that many players, even at state level, have never worked out the best leaves for each hoop that their partner ball's clip may be on, so they tend to make a 'leave' such as the one shown in the first

diagram. This is not too bad, but if black shoots at blue and misses, you will have to play some accurate shots with red before you have a break fully set up. A better 'leave' is the one shown in the second diagram where your balls are set in the opposite corner of the lawn from hoop 4. If blue shoots at black and misses, you can rush yellow to blue, then blue to black and black to hoop 4. Only the 3rd rush, which is not such a long one, requires some degree of accuracy. If blue does not shoot, and instead retires into the 3rd corner, you can rush yellow near black and put yellow near hoop 5 while getting a rush on black to hoop 4. There is also a reasonable chance that your opponent's balls will be wired with two hoops between them. You should be able to establish a break more easily and more often from this leave than from the one in the first diagram. The rule for good leaves is: Don't set up near your hoop—it is better to put an opponent ball there.

SHORTENING THE RUSH TO YOUR HOOP *by John Riches*

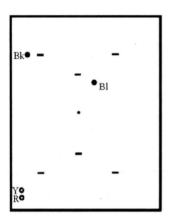

In the first diagram the player of yellow has set up for red to make hoop 6.

Notice that the rush is set to the black ball, not to hoop 6. There are two good reasons for this:

1. it can discourage blue from shooting at black if the opponent's balls turn out not to be wired; and

2. wherever blue goes (provided it does not roquet), you are threatening to rush yellow to black, load—back with yellow and rush black to hoop 6. This will mean that the final rush to hoop 6 is much shorter than if you were rushing yellow from the 1st corner, so you can expect to get closer to the hoop and make it more easily. This idea of rushing to a ball rather than directly to your hoop, so that the rush to the hoop will be a shorter one which you can control more accurately, is an important one that players often overlook. Later they will probably blame a poor hoop approach to hoop 6 from 3 yards out for the loss of the game, when the real fault was their failure to set the correct rush.

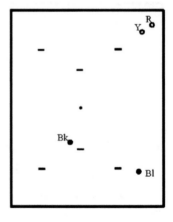

In the second diagram red is for hoop 4, and again the rush has been correctly set to the black ball, whereas many would set it to hoop 4.

However in this case you must first check that black can be rushed past hoop 5 to hoop 4 without undue difficulty. There is also the advantage that blue is less likely to want to shoot at your balls when you do not have a rush set directly to your hoop.

AN OLD THEME *by John Riches*

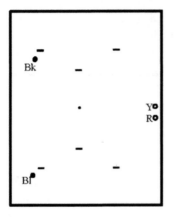

In the first diagram all clips are still on hoop. The player of red and yellow has set up on the east border. What should black and blue do?

Shooting at his balls, if you miss, will give him an easy break by enabling him to use your ball get a rush to hoop. Shooting with blue at black is the best option available, even though if you miss (as shown in the second diagram) he may be able to take off to blue on the north border, roll it in to hoop 2, and rush black to hoop 1 to set up a break.

The only reasonable alternative to shooting would be to hit the blue ball into the 1st corner (since if you hit it into the 3rd or 4th corner he will have a rush to it), but this is a poor and negative thing to do because he can still take off to it, play a roll approach to hoop 1, and if he cannot make the hoop he can return to his partner and start all over again In fact he would probably be more likely to set up a break this way than if you had shot at black and missed; and you would have denied yourself a possible chance to roquet and obtain the innings. The moral is a theme I have returned to many times: There are very few situations where hitting away into a corner gives you a better chance of winning the game than shooting at a ball. If you

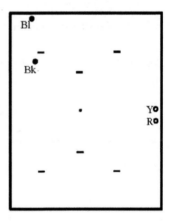

do it more than three or four times a year you are doing it too often and you are almost certainly losing games you could have won.

JOINING UP IS DANGEROUS *by John Riches*

In the first diagram blue has set to make hoop 1. As red, many players would now shoot at (or "join up with") their yellow partner ball on the east border.

However, if your opponent is capable of playing a break, then this is likely to make things far too easy for him, as unless you hit the roquet he will be able to set up a break by making hoop 1 with a rush to anywhere up the court or anywhere on the east border, and send the black ball to hoop 3 while going to your two balls on the

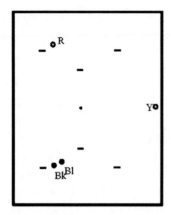

east border and rushing one of them to hoop 2. A much better option is to shoot at blue, even if you suspect that if you miss he may turn around and roquet your red ball on the south border. In fact, if he had set his rush back on the south border as shown in the second diagram the correct thing for red to do would still be to shoot at the opponent's balls, as it is far more difficult for him to set up a break with three balls together on the south border than if you had joined up with yellow on the east border. Joining up in the hope that he will fail to make the hoop, of course, is nothing more than wishful thinking against an opponent who is anything other than a beginner; and if he cannot make hoop 1 you may still be just as well off with your red ball on the south border sitting over him anyway.

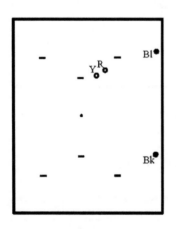

The moral is: Always think ahead before joining up.

POSTPONING THE EVIL DAY *by John Riches*

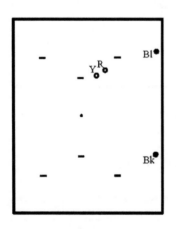

In the first diagrammed position red is for hoop 6 and yellow is for 4-back. The most common continuation would be to rush yellow to hoop 6 and make it, hoping then to make 1-back, and if you are lucky 2-back as well. That is, you play a 2-ball break with your partner ball, make as many hoops as you can, and then reluctantly allow your opponent a chance to roquet. The trouble with this is that you are unlikely to have a break set up if he misses the roquet, so you will probably have to do the same sort of thing again, and allow the opponent another chance to roquet.

Unless you are playing at international level, it would be better to make hoop 6 with a rush to somewhere on the east border and then set up as shown in the second diagram. This allows the opponent one chance to hit a long roquet, but gives you an excellent chance of a break if he misses it. Note that if you had made 1-back you would have been unable to set as good a leave because you would then be for 2-back and you could not afford to leave a ball near that hoop, while any ball you leave near the 3-back hoop is not likely to remain there, so you would face a difficult task to get a break going.

Instead of trying to "postpone the evil day" by making another hoop or two before you give the opponent a chance to roquet, it is often better to ensure that he will get only the one chance, rather than two or more.

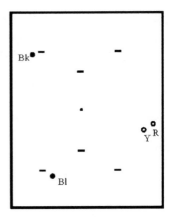

TAKE A BREAK, MATE! *by John Riches*

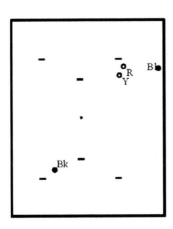

A mistake, which one sees far too often, is the failure to take a break when one is on offer. The first diagram shows a position which occurred in a recent game. Yellow is for hoop 3 and red is for hoop 1. The player easily made hoop 3 with yellow, but then found that continuing the break would require having to play some accurate and rather low-percentage shots—e.g. take-off to blue on the border trying to get a rush on it to hoop 4, with hoop 5 not properly loaded. He apparently did not consider the better alternative of playing red, rushing yellow down to the south border, and using a stop-shot to send it to hoop 2 before making hoop 1 from black with a break setup.

A similar situation is shown in the second diagram, where yellow is for 2-back and red is for hoop 6. Again, instead of making 2-back with yellow (the player ran through the hoop and roqueted black, but did not manage to make any more hoops), the correct procedure is to play red, rush yellow to blue (better than cuffing it to hoop 6), and then rush blue to hoop 6.

After losing games, players can tend to say the opponent did not give them many chances, when

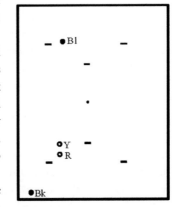

in fact they did not take the chances they were given, because they were too intent on making one easy hoop instead of 'taking a break'. It is often worth taking a small risk to make a break rather than one certain hoop.

SETTING UP IN THE MIDDLE *by John Riches*

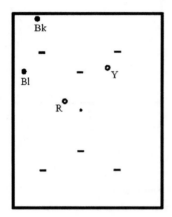

In the diagrammed position red and blue were both for hoop 2 while black was for hoop 3 and yellow for 4-back. The player of red shot at yellow, but only hard enough to go 2-3 yards past it, instead of going right through to border near the 3rd corner.

Then the opponent shot with blue at yellow and roqueted. After the game the player of red was criticised by observers for leaving both of his balls out in the court and thus giving blue a relatively safe shot at them. He was taking a risk, but was his play incorrect?

Usually one would not want to leave both balls out in the court, but in this case it caused blue to take a longer shot than the one he would probably have taken at black if red had gone through to border, since shooting with blue at black is rather risky when red and yellow are within easy roqueting distance and red is for hoop 2.

In this case it did not work, but if he had gone to border and blue had missed black, he would have faced the problem of what to do with yellow, as shooting at red would risk leaving two balls near black's hoop.

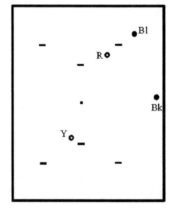

In fact leaving both balls out in the court in this sort of situation would be a good percentage tactic for players at most levels.

In the second diagram red is for hoop 3 and wired from blue. Once again it is a good idea to stay near yellow instead of going to border.

A TEST OF NERVE *by John Riches*

In a recent doubles tournament game I was playing the red ball and reached the unfortunate position shown on the first diagram. Black was for the peg, and yellow was for rover, while red and blue were both for 2-back. I had just played a poor approach shot for 2-back, with my red ball finishing where it had no chance of making the hoop.

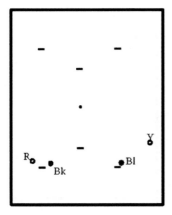

What could I do now? I had used both blue and yellow, had given a lift, and a 'saving' shot on black was only likely to make things worse. I could envisage the opponents picking up blue (which had no backswing for a shot at yellow), taking it to A-baulk, roqueting black and going to the peg to end the game.

After some thought I decided on a gamble designed to test the nerve of the opponents, and hit red gently in front of the 2-back hoop open to black which was only about a yard away. When I returned to my seat my partner politely asked if I had taken leave of my senses, and asked why I had not hit my ball into, say, the second corner.

However I had assessed the psychology of the opponents correctly. After some rather agonised discussion they decided that it would be too dangerous to pick up blue, since if it missed the 6-yard roquet I was likely to finish the game (they apparently had more confidence in my ability than I had myself!), so black took the turn and roqueted red. This gave me another chance at a roquet before blue could get in. Thankfully I hit it, and we won the game. I cannot claim that what I did was objectively correct, but it did serve to put the opponents under pressure, presenting them with a severe test of their nerve. It is this sort of tactical possibility that makes croquet such a fascinating game, even though by doing it I could well lose more games than I win. If you would never have considered such an idea, perhaps you could give it a thought in future—depending on how much of a gambler you are.

TIDYING UP *by John Riches*

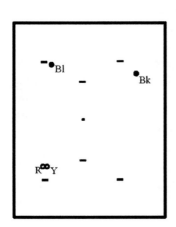

In the position shown on the first diagram red has just made hoop 1 and roqueted yellow. Blue is well placed at hoop 2, and black is about 3 yards from hoop 3 as shown. It is very common to see players in such positions take off to blue to make hoop 2, when their first thought should be that hoop 3 is not well enough loaded, and they should be looking for an easy way to improve the load.

This can be done by using a split shot to send yellow right to hoop 3 as you go to blue at hoop 2 (this is called "double loading"), or if you are not confident about playing this big split shot, then you should at least take off to black rather than blue, with the idea of using the roquet and take-off shots to get black closer to hoop 3 before making hoop 2 from blue.

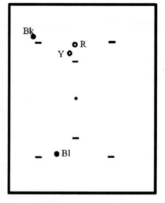

The second diagram shows a similar situation where red has just made hoop 6 and instead of just roqueting yellow a few yards forward as many would do, the player of red should rush yellow to hoop 1 or just past it, in order to improve the load of 2-back before rushing blue back up the court for use as a pivot ball. Note that this "tidying up" costs you nothing. It involves no noticeable risk and you will be no worse off even if you do not manage to improve the loading of your next-but-one hoop. It is interesting to see people who insist on everything being kept tidy around the clubhouse, and no doubt also at home, yet who show no interest at all in keeping their breaks tidy.

WATCH THOSE HANDS *by John Riches*

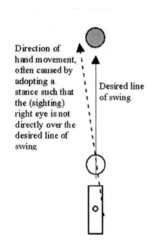

Direction of hand movement, often caused by adopting a stance such that the (sighting) right eye is not directly over the desired line of swing

Desired line of swing

Players are often told of the importance of watching the ball, or watching to see that the backswing is straight but coaches often fail to stress the importance of watching to see that during the swing the hands move back and forth exactly in the desired line of swing.

The player may start with his hands noticeably to one side of the line, and swing around a slight curve which attempts to bring the mallet head into line as it approaches the ball. That can work, but it is better to start with everything inline, so that all you have to do is keep it all in line as you swing—which is quite hard enough!

The suggested method is to line up the mallet with the mallet face square as best you can while standing over it then see to it that you move your hands back and forth exactly in the desired line of swing. If you do that, and allow the mallet to hang vertically below your hands (i.e. do not tighten your grip suddenly as the mallet approaches the ball), there is little chance for the mallet to get off line; but if you think about it you will realise that it will be almost impossible to swing the mallet in line if your hands are moving m a different line, and the only way you can hit your roquets that way would be to turn the mallet face so as

John Riches and Wayne Davies

to correct for the fact that the hands and mallet are moving in the wrong direction. There are players who manage to swing across the line and still roquet well, but it must be easier to achieve real consistency if you try to ensure that your hands, and therefore also your mallet are always in line through the entire swing—during the follow-through as well as the backswing.

You may have other things to think about during a game, but when practising you can give at least some thought to your hand movement.

TOO MANY OPTIONS *by John Riches*

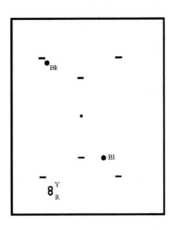

The diagram shows a situation where the player of red is about to make hoop 1. He is faced with a choice between several reasonable options after he makes the hoop, e.g.

(1) Try to get a forward rush on yellow to the border alongside hoop 2, then send yellow to load hoop 3 while going to make hoop 2 from black.

(2) Make hoop 1 with the aim of sending yellow to hoop 3 while going to blue, hoping to be able to rush blue past the peg and use it as a 'pivot' ball.

(3) After making hoop 1, rush or roll yellow to hoop 4 while getting a rush up the lawn on blue, then rush blue to hoop 3 and take-off to black to make hoop 2.

There are other possibilities, and the choice will depend on the shots you are comfortable about playing. Most players would say there is not much to choose between the options, but if an option provides only a slightly better percentage chance of success, that is reason to adopt it.

Here the preferred option is number (2), as it will make the continuation of your break easiest and allows you a second chance to load hoop 3 accurately if your first attempt goes somewhat astray. Option (1) leaves the 'pivot' ball rather misplaced, which is not usually a big problem, but why not take the chance to position it m the best possible place to facilitate the continuance of the break? Option (3) involves loading two hoops ahead which is seldom advisable. Note that in order to continue your break easily, both option (1) and option (3) require you to get a useful rush after making hoop 2, but option (2) does not depend on getting a rush and allows you to concentrate on simply making the hoop. **The moral is: choose the option which will make things easiest in future.**

USING A DISTRACTOR *by John Riches*

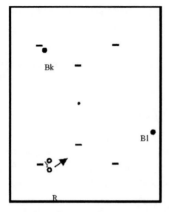

Imagine that you are playing red, and have just approached hoop 1 with your yellow partner ball, but failed to get position to run the hoop, as shown in the diagram. You have one stroke left. Where will you place the red ball?

Most players would consider that yellow is a bit too far in-lawn to allow 'covering the border' against a shot by black to be a useful tactic, so they would hit the red ball in front of the hoop so that it will be wired from black and can easily make the hoop in the next turn.

It has been suggested that it is better to give red a rush to hoop 1 by placing it about one yard from yellow as shown by the arrow. The idea is that black would be more likely to roquet if he has only one ball to shoot at. If there are two balls, and they are too far apart to provide a useful double target, then the second ball can act as a 'distractor', inducing the black ball to go between the two balls. I cannot claim to have any evidence that this idea will in fact lessen the likelihood of black roqueting, but it does at least give red a better chance to organise a rush in any desired direction after making hoop 1, and also allows you the option of playing yellow with what may turn out to be a useful rush on red.

However, sitting red in front of the hoop may be the best option if black is for hoop 2 or hoop 6, or maybe even hoop 3, and it could deny him the chance of rushing red to his hoop if he should happen to roquet yellow. It may not seem like a big deal as to which option you choose, but over the course of a game there can be a number of such choices, and the player who thinks through the options carefully, rather than unthinkingly doing the obvious thing that first comes into his head, will give himself a distinct advantage and increase his chance of winning the game.

NO 'FREE' SHOTS *by John Riches*

You are playing red, which is for hoop 5, and have started your turn by roqueting yellow on the border as shown. How do you proceed? Many players would see nothing better than rolling out to hoop 5 with yellow. The problem with this is that the chance of making hoop 5 with such a roll from the border is not good and you are likely to leave the opponent a 'free' shot at your balls with either black or blue. [A 'free' shot is one which has little risk because if he misses you will still not have a break set up.] Even if you make the hoop you will have no easy way of continuing the turn.

A far better approach is to forget about making your hoop in this turn, and instead set up the lawn so that any shot your opponent takes and misses will allow

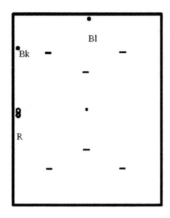
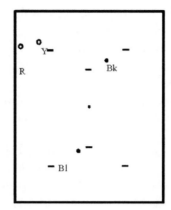

you a good chance of establishing a break. To achieve this, roll both red and yellow near to black, and put black into the lawn past hoop 6 while going to blue. Then send blue between hoop 5 and hoop 1 while returning to yellow, setting a rush to the north border as shown in the second diagram. Now you have an excellent chance of establishing a break in your next turn.

TAKE OFF THE BLINKERS *by John Riches*

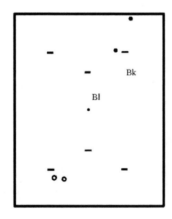
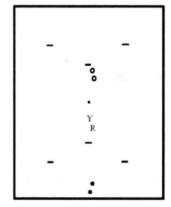

In the first diagram, red was for hoop 1 and yellow for hoop 3. The player walked onto the lawn, played red, made hoop 1, roqueted yellow, and then saw that he faced a long take-off to the opponent's balls with the peg and a hoop in the way, and only a slight chance of making hoop 2.

It would obviously (but not to him) have been far better to play yellow, rush red to hoop 4, and take off to black with a 4-ball break easily set up. When I ask people why they did such things, they usually say either that they did not stop to consider playing the yellow ball, or that they did not want to have to play the long take-off from hoop 4 to black, with the possibility of falling short or going out. This, of course, overlooks the fact that after making hoop 1 they may well have to play an even longer and more difficult take-off People who use such a 'blinkered' approach and fail to consider all the tactical possibilities will be losing games they could have won.

As red and yellow, which ball would you play in the second diagram, where red is for hoop 6 and yellow is for hoop 4?

DEFEATING THE "YIPS" *by John Riches*

Most croquet players will have experienced the yips. It is a sudden involuntary jerking and jabbing action which causes you to miss a short roquet or fail to run a hoop that you should easily have made. Most realise that it is caused by nervousness which results in a tightening of the muscles, but many have no idea of even one way to combat and overcome it. There are many different things you can do when afflicted by this "illness". What works for one player may not work for anyone else. Here is one possible "cure" which often proves to be effective:

First make sure that you have a well-balanced and stable stance. Address the ball with your hands about one foot out in front of your body so that your hands (not just the mallet head pivoting from the wrists) can move backward dining the backswing. During the swing try to avoid moving any part of the body apart from the arms which should swing comfortably from the shoulders. Slow down the swing, and once the mallet head has started to move forward, study the milling on the ball m the area where the mallet will contact it.

Forget everything else and take a genuine interest in the milling. Don't just look at it **study** it. The idea of this is that when you start to think "I must hit this roquet" or "I cannot afford to slick in this hoop", your mind senses a danger situation and triggers an involuntary defence mechanism which causes a sudden flow of adrenalin and a consequent tensing of the muscles. This is designed to help you avoid the danger, but in croquet it is counterproductive. Studying the milling serves to remove from your mind any thought that you are performing an action winch the brain connects with danger. Since there will be no danger associated with studying the milling, there should be no involuntary jerking or jabbing reaction. There are many other ways of overcoming nervousness, and a number of them are aimed at either relaxing the muscles or modifying the psychological reactions which occur in the mind and cause the muscles to lighten.

Some other ideas from a long list winch may be worth trying are:

1. As you start the forward swing, smile (to yourself).
2. Relax your foot muscles to flatten the soles onto the ground.

3. Try to convince yourself (and anyone else who will listen) that it is only a game, the results do not matter, and that you are simply here to enjoy yourself.

TIMING THE SWING *by John Riches*

Many people fail to appreciate the importance of correct liming. This is the ability to swing the mallet so that when it contacts the ball the mallet is in an exactly vertical position. This does not apply to all croquet shots, of course, but it is highly desirable for most roquets and rushes. Some players have naturally good timing, but many of us are not so fortunate. We tend to either hurry the forward movement of the hands or use the wrists to give added force to the forward movement of the mallet, and in most cases this will cause the mallet face to be tilted slightly forward when it contacts the ball as illustrated by the dotted lines in the diagram.

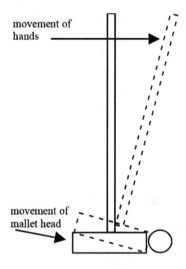

For most players wanting to improve their timing the first thing to do is eliminate all movement of the knees, trunk, elbows and wrists. The more moving parts you have to control, the harder it is to co-ordinate them all consistently and successfully so as to achieve the well-timed result that is desired. A few gifted players are able to play well with such body movement, and from a coaching viewpoint they should not be criticised if they can cope with it all successfully, as there can also be advantages; but for most of us the unnecessary additional moving parts will often result in strokes being mis-timed.

This will mean that some of the energy from the mallet does not go into moving the ball, and can cause the ball to jump when we do not want it to, which will often completely nun a rush stroke, or will require us to use more effort in playing the stroke than we should be using. The best way to develop correct timing is to practise short roquets using only the top hand on the mallet; or if you want to also use the bottom hand, then you should make sure that its grip on the mallet shaft is very light and does not lighten during the swing. [Dining a game use both hands of course, but by to achieve the same liming.] Getting the timing right will not automatically mean that you are contacting the ball when the mallet is in the desired vertical position, but once you are timing the swing more consistently you will have a better chance of correcting your stance and body position (if necessary) in order to achieve the desired result.

HANDICAP PLAY *by John Riches*

This is the first of a series of articles on handicap play. There are some important ideas which can easily be overlooked:

(1) Bisques should be used aggressively rather than defensively. Only use a bisque when you can see that it will enable you to set up and play a break. Do not use a bisque to prevent your opponent from playing a break unless it will also give you a break. If you believe that your opponent will peg out if you do not take the bisque, then take it but unless it enables you to establish a break your chance of winning—other than perhaps on time—will be very small. Bisques are given to enable you to make hoops. Using them merely to stop your opponent from making hoops can make the game last longer, but makes the loss more certain.

(2) Plan to use your bisques early. Do not start the game as if it were a level game and only think about using the bisques later on when you start to get into trouble—as you inevitably will. Look for the first opportunity to set up a break by taking a bisque.

(3) Know the rules relating to handicap play: e.g. when you can take a bisque; when you can peg out a ball; when you can change your mind about taking a bisque; the difference between a half-bisque and a full bisque; and also the rules governing the replacement of balls after a fault playing a wrong ball in the first stroke of a bisque turn, the restoration of bisques following a fault or interference, and so on.

(4) If you win the toss at the start of a handicap game, always elect to play second. This applies whether you are receiving bisques or giving them. By ensuring that you play the 4th turn you can give yours elf either one additional chance to start using your bisques with all four balls in play before your opponent gets a chance to roquet; or the chance to roquet and play a break before your opponent can start using his bisques. It would seldom pay to start using bisques before all four balls are in play, as it would be too difficult to set up and continue a break.

(5) In handicap doubles play it may be better for the stronger of two partners to use some or all of the bisques, as he is likely to make more out of them. He should be able to make some hoops for himself and also set up for his partner in the next turn.

(6) The giver of bisques should not hesitate to go right to the peg in a break if he gets the chance. Conversely, it is usually unwise for the receiver of bisques to peg out his opponent's ball, as the opponent is a stronger player

John Riches and Wayne Davies

and more likely to win a 3-ball game; whereas the receiver of bisques will need all four balls in his breaks.

Some further points on handicap play:

(1) Some players believe that is it a good idea to hang on to at least one bisque for as long as possible, as it will mean that your opponent cannot set up for himself by leaving balls near your hoops, and has to keep on modif3ring his tactics to allow for the possibility that you may take the final bisque. I have found it quite difficult to convince them that this is a rather pointless strategy unless your opponent is very naive.

Suppose you have a good chance to set up a break, or keep one going, by using the last bisque, but you refuse to take it. Your opponent will notice this and from then on he will be able to trade on the fact that no matter where he leaves the balls you will be wanting to hang on to the bisque. You may never again get as good a chance to use the bisque and set up an easy break for yourself; which is all you are going to be able to do with it whenever you use it. You will usually do better to use it, make the break, get ahead and put more pressure on the opponent.

(2) When giving a number of bisques, some players try to 'bleed" the bisques out of the opponent. Instead of trying to make a break themselves they do this by setting up in a way that encourages or forces the opponent to use a bisque. This sort of policy can easily backfire, so needs to be carefully considered in the light of the number of hoops already made and the amount of time remaining. A better strategy is usually to take every opportunity to make breaks yourself and try to finish the game before the opponent has had much of a chance to use his bisques.

(3) When you have a considerable number of bisques, take the first reasonable chance to start using them to take your first ball around, and plan to use at least half of them to take it as far as possible before you come off the lawn. If you break down and still have the break set up ahead, take another bisque and continue the break. Do not let the opponent have a turn in the hope that he will miss, because even if he does he will have moved the ball most likely to be of use to you in your next turn, and your chance of continuing the break will have been substantially reduced.

(4) Do not keep a half-bisque until the end of the game. Remember that you cannot use it to peg your bails out, as no point can be scored for any ball in a half-bisque turn. Also do not use the half-bisque to get out of trouble by separating the opponent's balls. Instead, use the half-bisque early in the game to set up a break for your next turn.

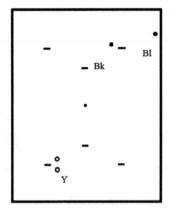
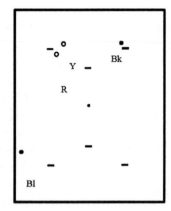

Many players make two serious mistakes in handicap play: (1) they use bisques to get out of trouble, instead of to set up breaks; and (2) they fail to get Ml value from the bisques when they do take them.

In the first diagram all clips are on hoop 1. The player of red had approached hoop 1 but was unable to make it. He decided that he could not allow the opponent the chance to roquet with two balls at hoop 1, so he used his continuation stroke to hit red gently in front of the hoop and then took a bisque. He wasted the bisque in making only the one hoop with it. A bisque allows you to use all of the balls again before you make a hoop, so even if he had already used the opponent's balls he could have used the continuation shot to shoot at blue, then take a bisque and send blue to load hoop 2 while going to black, and then take off back to yellow with a break set up. In the second diagram red is in a similar situation at hoop 2, where he has approached the hoop and cannot make it. He should use his last stroke to shoot at blue, then take a bisque and rush blue up the lawn to set up a 4-ball break.

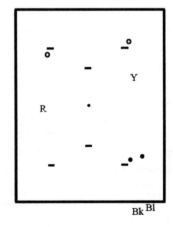
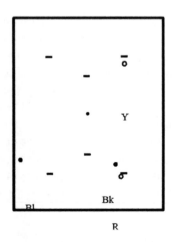

John Riches and Wayne Davies

In the first diagram you are playing red and yellow and have several bisques. The opponent has left the balls as shown, with one of your balls at each of his hoops [Bl is for H2 and Bk is for H3; while R is for H 1 and Y is for H5]. There are various ways of using a bisque here, and it would not be easy to decide between taking one, and waiting for an opportunity where you will be more certain to be able to set up a break. If you do decide to use a bisque, then the best way is to shoot at yellow just hard enough to go about one yard past it if you miss it Then take the bisque, rush yellow back toward hoop 2, take off to the opponent's balls and rush one of them to hoop 1.

In the second diagram Black is for hoop 3. Red has failed to nm 3-back and has one bisque left. Red cannot roquet black, but black can roquet red. This is an example of where NOT to take a bisque, as all you would be doing is stopping the opponent from making hoops, without having much chance of making any yourself in the bisque turn. You would have a better chance of winning if you do not take the bisque at this stage.

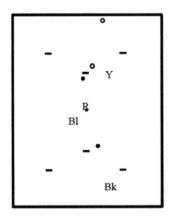
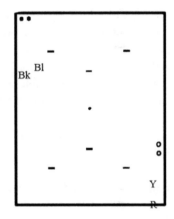

In the first diagram the player of black and blue had one and a half bisques left. Blue was on the peg and black was for 4-back. He saw a chance to finish the game immediately and shot with black at yellow, then took the bisque. This was a mistake as he should have taken the half-bisque and sent yellow to rover while going to red or blue. Then he could roquet one of those balls, rush or roll the other to 4-back, and set up right in front of the hoop, after which he could take the whole bisque, make the last three hoops and peg out. There was little point in retaining the half-bisque, as if he broke down he would not be able to use it to continue his break anyway. He should have used it to reduce the chance of breaking down.

In the second diagram all clips are still on hoop 1 and the player of red is receiving bisques. He should rush yellow near to hoop 3, take off to the opponent's balls, roquet blue, stop-shot it out to hoop 2, then roquet black, send it to hoop 1, hit his red ball also to hoop 1, and take a bisque with a break setup. This is better than rushing one opponent ball to hoop 1 without first having loaded hoop 2.

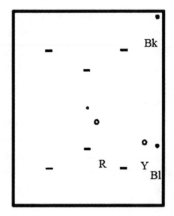 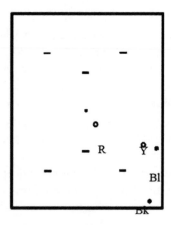

In a recent handicap game the player of black and blue won the toss and wisely chose to hit in second. His opponent, who had three bisques, started by hitting the red ball in near the peg. This involved a hopeful attempt to create a situation where he could use just one bisque to set up a 4-ball break as soon as the four balls were all in play, without allowing the bisque-giver any further chance to roquet. The blue ball was played to the east border about level with the rover hoop, whereupon yellow followed it, being careful not to allow a double target from either baulk. Then black can either shoot from A-baulk at red, or from B-baulk at yellow (or blue), and if it misses the results will be as shown in the two diagrams above. Now the bisque-receiver can play yellow, roquet blue, send it to hoop 2 going to red, roquet red, take-off to black, send black to hoop 1, and hit yellow back near red. Then he can take a bisque with a 4-ball break filly setup. This is an excellent strategy: **plan to use a bisque to set up a 4-ball break at the first reasonable opportunity**. Many players would have sent blue to hoop 2 and tried to rush or roll red to hoop 1 in the hope of saving the bisque, but it is more likely that they will have to give the opponent further chances to roquet before they succeed in getting the break set up with all 4 balls in play.

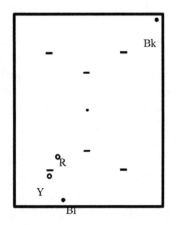 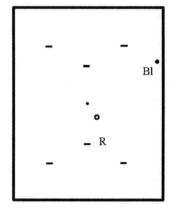

John Riches and Wayne Davies

In fact the likely result in shown m the third diagram, where yellow has failed to make position to run hoop 1 and has had to set up in front of the hoop, after which blue has missed the shot at red (a shot he should not have been allowed). Note that yellow could have taken a bisque after sitting in front of the hoop, but he would still have work to do in getting the black ball out of the 3rd corner. The fact that he is receiving bisques suggests that it is likely he will not have a very good chance of being able to play a 3-ball break and bring the 4th ball into the break without breaking down at some stage.

In the third diagram yellow can again try to save the bisque by shooting at blue, but even if he succeeds he will again have only a 3-ball break. A player giving bisques will usually be delighted to see his opponent trying to save bisques by allowing additional chances to roquet, or by taking risky shots which even if successful do not a filly set up a break. One further point: How should the bisque-giving second player have answered the unusual tactic of hitting the first ball near the peg? Answer: He should have set a lice from B-baulk as shown in the fourth diagram. The only reason the second player does not always set his lice from B-baulk is that in a standard opening it would allow his opponent to shoot at the tice and finish near partner ball if he misses; but it is a good reply anytime the first ball does not go near the 4th corner.

John Riches

John started to play croquet in 1978 at the age of forty, and when he moved to Adelaide in 1987 he began to take it more seriously. With John's background in teaching, he began to take an interest in the laws of the game and coaching it. As a born teacher, this soon became more important to him than playing the game.

John went on to further accreditation as Australia's first Level 3 coach, and coached both state and national teams, including the 2000 MacRobertson Shield team. As a player he worked on improving his own game, and has won many major South Australian events. In 1995 John was a member of the winning South Australian team in the Interstate Cup, winning all his singles games, and in the Australian Championships succeeded in eliminating the then World Champion Robert Fulford. He was officially ranked #2 player in Australia at that time.

With a strong motivation to help players and coaches improve, John started writing and publishing his own booklets in the early nineties, and has continued to write booklets and magazine articles for the past 17 years. He has also helped with the writing of Coach-Training Courses for the ACA and in 2007 was appointed as National Coaching Director, and is currently (2008) involved in the huge task of re-writing and up-dating the courses. He is constantly seeking to discover better methods of coaching, especially in the area of tactics, and document them for the benefit of other coaches and players.

This book sets out to collate all of John's most important ideas, and to this end it is a must read for both the novice and serious player.

Wayne Davies

In 2005, Wayne became Head Tennis Professional at the "The Westmoor Club" in Nantucket. He also found out that he had the task of being the croquet coach!

Despite never having played before, Wayne jumped into the task head first and has never looked back! Hungry for knowledge about the sport, Wayne searched out fellow Aussie John Riches. He began what has become an exhaustive correspondence with John (which Wayne insists is far more to his benefit than the other way around!).

Along with Wayne's athletic prowess, and help from John, Wayne has progressed to play and coach Croquet at the highest levels.

Wayne was Australia's first Real Tennis World Champion (1987-1994) and achieved major successes in Squash and Rackets as well.

In the year 2000, Australia awarded him the Australian Sport's Medal.

Lightning Source UK Ltd.
Milton Keynes UK
29 November 2010

163615UK00010B/185/P